WHEN ANGELS
&
DEMONS COLLUDE

No AI was used in the creation of this book's writing or design. All images are from licensed Etsy, Canva, and Shutterstock artists.

Cover design: Sara Raztresen
Interior design: Sara Raztresen

Paperback ISBN: 979-8-9916919-1-8
Digital ISBN: 979-8-9916919-2-5

Printed and bound in USA
First Printing June 2025

Published by Sara Raztresen under Sveta Lisica Imprint
Rhode Island, 2025

OTHER BOOKS BY SARA RAZTRESEN:

The Glass Witch
Where the Gods Left Off
Discovering Christian Witchcraft
The Wraith Queen

FIND SARA ON:

TikTok: @srazzie97
Instagram: @sararaztresen
Bluesky: @Srazzie97
YouTube: @srazzie97

www.sararaztresen.com

SARA RAZTRESEN

WHEN ANGELS
&
DEMONS COLLUDE

TABLE OF CONTENTS

WARNING:

This book has the potential to cause *madness*, or *psychosis*, if you are not able to stand your ground against new ideas and consider them carefully. Worldviews may be warped, even shattered. Images and entities presented within may disturb you greatly or even trigger old traumas you thought you left behind. If you feel yourself beginning to spiral, or panic, or otherwise not feel like you're really "in" the world, please step away and remind yourself of your physical reality. Disconnect from spiritual thought and theory until you are settled.

BEFORE WE BEGIN...

My friends, here we are again. *Where the Gods Left Off*'s last page closed, and so begins the first page of *When Angels & Demons Collude*—a provocative title, no doubt, but one that summarizes the way I've been feeling as I watch these spirits work for the same goal from different angles. If a demon is so diametrically opposed to an angel, then why on earth does working with either one achieve the exact same results? And why are those results both good?

Are they good?

I couldn't tell you anymore. After fifty interviews, I felt so settled, so overly confident and bold and sure. Now, after one hundred interviews, I understand why every sage and master always looks so grim whenever someone approaches them—why they seem to be unable to gather an expression on their face. In a way, I imagine this is what a seasoned homicide detective must feel every time they look at a mangled body: utterly unsurprised, desensitized to the point that people mistake their flat affect for coldness and apathy, even cruelty, and yet fully aware that what they found is still something utterly out of bounds of what is "normal" and "sane."

(At least, that's how the homicide detectives in movies and shows look, y'know?)

All I can say for certain is that I don't recognize myself from two or three years ago. In 2025, nearly two years after the release of *Where the Gods Left Off*, I look back at my earliest content and see a child, even though I most certainly wasn't one. But the big round eyes, the hyper-expressivity, it held underneath it a deep need to perform. Under that mask was quite the bit of anxiety and uncertainty rippling through me and making me jump at the slightest spiritual discomfort.

Now, I don't know if I'm stable and sure of myself or plain desensitized. Maybe even dangerous. (That sounds so silly, doesn't it? Me, spiritually dangerous? And yet.)

However, this kind of evolution wasn't born solely of interviewing spirits like some kind of Divine Journalist. It was only one journey of many I was taking at the same time; I am, to my great exhaustion, quite the spiritual tourist, it seems. As a result, I do not recommend a single one of you take on this kind of journey yourself. There's no need to. It's what this book is for: that you might reap some of the rewards with none of the risk. Still, that doesn't stop people from getting curious and wanting to try themselves, I know. All I can say is: I warned you. But it does bring me to a couple quick questions that folks have asked before.

ARE YOU MAKING THIS STUFF UP?

I wish I was. You know how much easier it would've been to just forge all of this and lay out cards I thought would make sense for a Goddamn TikTok? No, for better or for worse, I genuinely believe every word I wrote here. To do these interviews, I would research an entity, lay out gifts of thanks for their time, and spend a good hour meditating, pulling cards, feeling the energy of whatever was floating around me, and translating all I saw into usable messages. It is exhausting every time, yet enlightening all the same. Maybe this makes me delusional, but it doesn't make me a fraud, that's for sure.

WHY WOULD THESE ENTITIES COME TO YOU?

Your guess is as good as mine. Yet even if it's taken me a long time sometimes to find the thread of a spirit's energy and start getting any messages from them, never have I had an entity not show up. More often than not, I spend so long thinking about them throughout the week that by time I finally sit down, they're already there, waiting for me to finally get to the point of why I've been essentially putting out a spiritual radio signal to them for so long.

HOW DO YOU KNOW THEY'RE THE ACTUAL SPIRIT YOU ASKED FOR?

I don't.

Talk all the shit about Christianity and the Bible you want; I don't care. But don't lie to me and tell me that the advice of 1 John 4:1-3 wasn't sound in its essence:

Beloved, do not believe every spirit, but test the spirits to see whether they are from God, for many false prophets have gone out into the world. By this you know the Spirit of God: every spirit that confesses that Jesus Christ has come in the flesh is from God, and every spirit that does not confess Jesus is not from God.

I'll never *know* that a spirit I contacted is the "real deal" or if it's an egregore or trickster. Hell, everyday I ask if spirits are real at all or if this is all just my imagination (and what it matters either way). What I *believe* is that when I test these spirits with certain questions, and they answer accurately—or, incredibly, they reveal even more that I didn't know, which gets confirmed by strangers later—that I'm dealing with *something* authentic. Even then, as you'll see, I still doubt sometimes.

IN THIS BOOK, YOU'LL FIND...

My entire understanding of the world of humans and spirits breaking into pieces and being reassembled into a mosaic of stained glass shards. And also the occasional bit of therapy I didn't know I needed. (Santa Claus, the egregore that you are.) For you, it may be the same. Or, instead, you may discover heresy so bold and unapologetic that you want to throw this book across the house and burn it. You may discover, also, manifestations of spirits you know and love that are nothing like how you know them. I'm not here to tell anyone that their experiences are right or wrong, or that their UPG (unverified personal gnosis, which we talk about more later) is completely off base.

I'm only telling you what I saw and what I heard. Take it or leave it. And let me reiterate once more:

THIS IS NOT A HOW-TO GUIDE ON SUMMONING SPIRITS.

Even if I describe how I went about this, so you can see my thought process and why I did what I did, this doesn't mean this way of asking for the spirits herein is the correct or accurate way. It means I was doing my best with what I had. That's it. This is what I'd like to call Spiritual Jackass, done by (not so trained) professionals, and we don't try these stunts at home, friends.

For each of these interviews, I used a specific tarot deck, which you'll find listed in the chapter. My reasoning for using so many different decks is the same: each one holds radically different approaches to the same card, and it does seem the spirits know which deck says what, and which one will most accurately get their meanings across. Sometimes, the way one deck explains the card chosen is so stark and specific that it makes me pause just to admire the foresight of the spirits, and other times, it's actually the specific imagery and art of the cards they chose that sticks out the most. Spirits are unpredictable, truly, and to communicate with them is to get comfortable thinking outside the box.

The decks I used are:

The Golden Tarot by Kat Black
The Marigold Tarot by Amrit Brar*
The Angel Tarot by Doreen Virtue
The Weaver Tarot by Threads of Fate
The Universal Fantasy Tarot by Lo Scarabeo
The Guardian of the Night Tarot by MJ Cullinane
The Herbcrafter's Tarot by Latisha Guthrie

*Brar's deck, and occasionally Threads', are also used for reversed definitions of the Angel, Guardian, Herbcrafter, and Universal Fantasy Tarot, as these decks don't have reversed meanings.

Just like with the first book, no matter what you feel or believe or think about the contents herein, I hope you can find some value from them. I hope all this work and time and effort can help more than just me (even if we're using the word "help" really loosely here). And I hope you can find some grace and patience with me as we go along on this messy, mind-melting journey together once more. At least this time, I didn't make the types of grave mistakes I made so early on in the last book, right?

(Don't worry; I still made plenty of mistakes here, too.)

But enough from me now. Come along. Just as I took you through Interview One through Fifty, now I'll take you through Interview Fifty-One all the way to One Hundred. We'll walk the road together, and no doubt, we'll both come out different at the end of it.

ST. MARIA FAUSTINA

"St. Maria Faustina Kowalska of Poland"—that's a mouthful, isn't it?

We'll call her by how she's most commonly known from here on out: St. Faustina. It's a name that snagged my attention right away, as it made me think of *Faust*, a story by German writer Johann Wolfgang von Goethe. However, where Goethe's character Faust finds himself dissatisfied with his life and his achievements and therefore makes a pact with the devil, our St. Faustina takes the entirely opposite direction and instead dedicates her life to the service of God.

This is a Saint that intrigued me greatly, not only because of her history and her contributions to the faith, but also because of how *recent* of a Saint she was. As we've gone on this journey, I have to be real with you all: it's almost easy to disconnect oneself from the Saints from hundreds of years ago, as if they're more concept than person. As if they're more myth than reality.

But this Saint? Who we have not just paintings, but *photos* of? Who we know was alive at the same as many of our great-grandparents, even grandparents? No, there's something visceral about that. Something unmistakably *real*—and therefore something almost taboo about contacting this Saint. It's difficult to explain, but just know that sitting down for this was more nerve wracking than most of my conversations with Saints.

Now, let me tell you a bit more about St. Faustina. Born in 1905 as the third child of ten in Glogowiec, Poland, she was a Polish nun who, like St. Hildegard and so many others, received direct revelations and messages from God and Jesus. In fact, there's a famous painting of Jesus that I grew up with in my house, and one I'm sure every Catholic has seen once or twice: one with Jesus holding up one hand, the other at his chest, and a ray of red and a ray of white shining out. This image is called *Divine Mercy of Jesus,* and it was actually commissioned by her based on the visions and directions Jesus gave her. When she asked what these rays in this vision were, Jesus said (according to her diary, called *Divine Mercy in my Soul*):

The two rays denote Blood and Water. The pale ray stands for the Water which makes souls righteous. The red ray stands for the Blood which is the life of souls. These two rays issued forth from the depths of My tender mercy when My agonized Heart was opened by a lance on the Cross. Happy is the one who will dwell in their shelter, for the just hand of God shall not lay hold of him. I desire that the first Sunday after Easter be the Feast of Mercy (299).

In life, she was one who didn't have a lot of education, and she worked as a domestic helper for wealthier families to help her own family financially for many years afterwards; her parents opposed her goal of entering a convent, and many convents after that rejected her time and time again, describing her as "no one special" and testing the hell out of her patience by making her work for the funds to earn her habit (12-13, *Diary* chronology). In 1925, however, she finally made it into her first convent: Sisters of Our Lady of Mercy.

While she only lived a short 33 years on earth, dying of tuberculosis in 1938, she was a ceaseless advocate for the Divine Mercy of Jesus and wrote a whole lot about her visions and conversations with Jesus in her diary. Her work was actually banned for several decades, though, because the Catholic church received a messy translation of her *Diary* in 1959 and rejected its message. But that was eventually overturned in 1979, and in 2000, she was canonized as a Saint, according to the web page *The Divine Mercy*, which catalogues this Saint's history.

Even as a Saint, her work continued on. She performed miracles in death, and there are several of her prophecies that turned out to come true (like the very banning and restoration of her revelations). In the time of my speaking with her, I was still advancing an investigation of spirits of mercy (which included ones such as Amida Buddha and Quan Yin of the first book in this series, *Where the Gods Left Off*), and so, given all of this history, I thought that this Saint would be an excellent example of one dedicated to such mercy.

I was not wrong. What I found in this interview was something that, unlike with Amida Buddha and Quan Yin, was so viscerally *human*. So let me introduce you to this wonderful woman.

To get situated in the meditation space, I set my table with things that were more symbolic than anything. After all, who can say what specific herbs or crystals are directly and magically connected to a Saint so modern, yet so mystical, as St. Faustina? Therefore, the only thing that came to mind was to take a rosary (because Catholicism), a candle (for connection), a rose quartz crystal and rose quartz angel statue (to symbolize that divine love and guardianship), and one garnet and one howlite crystal—red and white, just like the rays beaming from Jesus's chest in the *Divine Mercy* painting. I also wanted to pay homage to the fact that she died of serious illness, and so I brewed for her a cup of Polish herbal tea with honey, which I often drink when I, myself, get sick. The tea is one made with cinnamon, ginger, and pear—all powerful healing items that I felt were appropriate here, a nod to my belief that she is healed in Heaven.

With the Lord's Prayer spoken, and my mind settled for an interview, my kitchen quiet in the early morning, I focused with all my might on St. Faustina and asked God to help me find her. Sure enough, for the fifty-first time, the blackness behind my eyelids eventually gave way to flashes of color that organized themselves into shapes—and then there was St. Faustina, in her nun habit, a gentle smile on her face.

Those colors continued to coalesce until the scenery around her became a proper backdrop to her black-clad form. We were suddenly in a church like one in Slovenia, a massive Catholic church full of beautiful art and sculpture, with a Eucharist holder on the white-clothed altar all the way at the front. We sat in the front pews, and St. Faustina had her hands clasped in her lap, a sweet smile on her face.

"St. Faustina, hello! Welcome! Thank you for meeting with me. Please share a cup of good tea while you're here; meanwhile, I have some questions for you about Divine Mercy."

I guess I shouldn't have been surprised, but St. Faustina seemed almost a little shy as she sat beside me, like she didn't quite know what to say. Maybe she thought she'd already said all there is to know in her diary. She also seemed a little perplexed by the tarot cards that I had set out before the "real" me at my kitchen table.

"Oh, goodness," she murmured. "What—what's all this? What are these for?"

"These? They're tarot cards!" I opened my eyes and tapped each box. When I closed my eyes again, it was as if a curtain was falling and exposing the church scene I was just sitting in—as if, were I to hold one of my eyes open, I would see both the real world, with my kitchen table and the little trinkets on it, and St. Faustina's world at the same time. One could've thought both images were like two different frames of a roll of film spliced together. "They're how we can better communicate, so I can make sure I'm not misinterpreting you or putting words in your mouth."

"I," St. Faustina's brows furrowed, her smile awkward and unsure, "do we have to use them?"

I shrugged. "They'd be a big help to me and others who want to hear what you have to say."

Her brows furrowed deeper, but eventually, St. Faustina sighed and waved a hand. "Fine. I'll use this one, I suppose."

Her hand gestured vaguely to the Golden Tarot by Kat Black—which was a reasonable choice for a Saint, given that these cards were made from digital collages of old renaissance art and were brimming with especially Catholic motifs. I set my other decks aside, asked God to let St. Faustina make full use of this deck, and got to shuffling.

"So, St. Faustina," I said as I mixed the cards together, "to start us off: can you tell me what Divine Mercy means to you?"

I. WHAT DOES DIVINE MERCY MEAN TO YOU?

Bitterness and hatred may develop from grief. Jealousy, inflexibility.

Withering away of bounty through inaction. Weakness, indecision.

Gifts from the heavens. Good things come to the deserving. Intellect and vision. Unfulfilled dreams despite bounty.

Satisfaction of worldly desires. Good health & fortune. Successful fulfillment of wishes. Social gatherings. Temper enthusiasm.

As I pulled the cards, and as we sat in the church, the pews suddenly populated themselves with people—mothers, fathers, children, all with the priest in green robes at the head of it all. They were smiling, listening intently to a sermon I couldn't quite hear, and then they were outside under the sunlight, celebrating life and warmth and all things good.

"You need to be with other people," St. Faustina said, gesticulating as if grabbing for the words. "You need to come together with others to pray. Then you see it—the love and joy and light that unites a community. The urge to help one another through hard times while knowing Jesus is among you all."

As she spoke, and as I watched this happy village full of people living a simple, yet joyous life, I got as much of a feeling of her meaning as I did from the words themselves. It reminded me of what Jesus said: where two gather in His name, so too does He appear (Matthew 18:20). I felt the emotional current of her words as we watched the people celebrate the very essence of life together: Divine Mercy means focusing on what's important—on trusting Jesus to hold us in His arms, His heart, and shelter us from the forces of the world that would otherwise bend our backs in grief and shame.

I nodded as I watched children chase each other, as men and women danced together. "Wow," I breathed. "That's beautiful; thank you for that! But then, how can we contemplate this idea in life? In the physical world?"

2. HOW CAN WE CONTEMPLATE THIS MERCY IN LIFE?

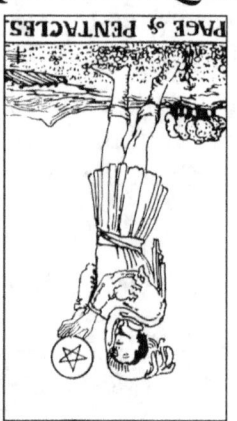

Hopelessness and deceit. Try to rally your strength to overcome adversities.	*A sensitive young man. Opportunity approaches. Emotional and capable of deep, intense love, but afraid to commit.*	*An untrustworthy man unwilling to work hard, but with a love of wealth.*	*Gifts foolishly discarded, jaded cynicism and disillusionment. Regret, anger, bitterness. The end of a relationship. Loss, sorrow, grief.*

St. Faustina lowered her eyes as if the thought made her sad.

"Those who *grieve* are the ones most able to feel mercy, yet also the ones so easily able to lose sight of it. Yes, there is anger, yes there is fire—and plenty of reason for it, yes, I see—but it burns its bearer. Divine Mercy—the blood, the water—they put this fire out, Sara." She clenched her hands into fists, shook them as if that would give her words more force. "They heal the scars. They cleanse you of cinders and ash left over from all that pain.

"So let it all go. To contemplate Divine Mercy is to let Divinity heal you. It's easy to stay angry, but it bears no fruit worth eating."

Watching how she talked reminded me of my oma and other older Slavic women. There was that iron in her words, even if she carried herself gently and offered small, reserved smiles to the people who came by in this little village and greeted her.

I nodded. "Heard loud and clear. I didn't think about it that way, but that does make a lot of sense when thinking about that painting of Jesus. However, some might argue that some of those reasons for fire are pretty understandable. For example, war—"

It was here she got wide-eyed with me. She seemed insistent on bringing up World War II, which I was planning to avoid, but she confirmed she wanted to say something about it with the sheer gravity coming off her spirit. Given that before she died, one of her prophecies was that there would be a "terrible, terrible war," it's no surprise that that's the phrase I found lingering as I shuffled my cards and redirected my question.

"Alright, then," I said as I let the cards slide against my fingertips. "What would you like to say about the war, St. Faustina? How do you feel about leaving this world just as it was starting up?"

3. WHAT WOULD YOU LIKE TO SAY ABOUT WORLD WAR II?

Still a card of travel, but running away from an intolerable situation.	*An indicator of success, but tainted with arrogance or impatience at bumps in the road.*	*New skills learned and successfully applied. Creativity used to overcome financial hardship. Making do with little by acquiring new skills. Hard work.*	*Generosity rewarded. Financial good fortune, wealth, security. Favors reciprocated, debts repaid. Gifts or inheritance. Sincerity and trustworthiness.*

"Oh, I thought I was running away from it." She shook her head and stared into her lap, her eyes seeing someplace far, far away. "I thought I was abandoning the world! Such misery men make, with their war—but what could I have done to stop it, as a sick and frail woman? No one person can do anything about such a horror while on earth.

"No, God pulled me up, that I might do His work and wonders better, from a place war couldn't reach. Still, horrible, horrible. The designs of men, and all those who lose sight of mercy—horrible. My beautiful Poland. We can never go back to a world scarred by war."

I hated to be the bearer of bad news, but— "It's still happening, though. Just look at Ukraine."

To my surprise, St. Faustina looked up at me with such bright and clear steel in her eyes.

"Men who go to create such hell on earth should be removed," she said, without leaving any room for doubt or rebuttal. "Removed! But it's not up to a single person to do so. All must be the light, together, that washes away darkness. Let none flicker and falter!"

Truthfully, I did not expect that kind of fire to come from someone who championed Divine Mercy. Especially given she'd just told me that burning up in fire was no good. But it was there, loud and clear, and while I appreciated it, I also understood as I stared into her steely eyes: this wasn't the same kind of fire she was just talking about. It was not the kind that burns only its bearer, but was rather a clean burning fire that creates the light she was talking about: one that emanates from the endless source of our souls rather than one that sacrifices us to keep burning for a brief, destructive time.

"I see," I murmured as I scribbled these ideas down. "Thank you, St. Faustina, I agree completely. But let's move on from that topic now, yeah? I've got a couple other questions, like: what do you think of the way this portrait of Jesus you commissioned has evolved?"

4. WHAT DO YOU THINK OF THE DIVINE MERCY PHOTO'S EVOLUTION?

Again, sadness welled up in her eyes. A rueful smile hinged on her lips.

"What good does a painting do if those who look upon it don't understand it? The key wasn't the paint on the canvas. Jesus Himself told me this. It's His grace that matters, the Mercy— yet people's minds are dead when they look on this picture.

"They see without seeing. They don't understand the meaning; they don't venerate properly and contemplate the Divine Mercy, or try to embody it."

"Ah, yeah, I get'cha. It does seem that this is quite the stumbling block for people who want to appear spiritual versus people who actually are." All I could think about were the people who would rather buy Christian merchandise to fill their homes and adorn themselves with rather than the ones who actually embodied the lessons from the Gospels. There will always be some folks like that, no matter what. "But that leads me to my next question: how did you embody Divine Mercy as a nun on earth?"

Loss, defeat, and confusion.

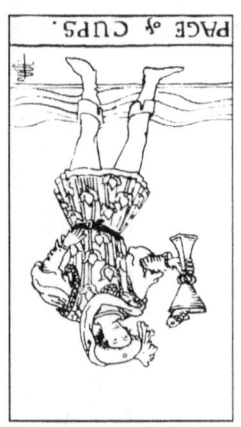

A shallow person who likes to get what they want regardless of consequences to others. Spoiled and self indulgent.

Love declared. Satisfying love, close friendship acknowledged. Balance, unity, happy compromise. Deep understanding.

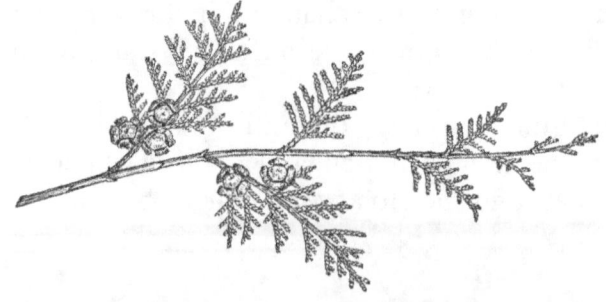

5. HOW DID YOU EMBODY DIVINE MERCY ON EARTH?

 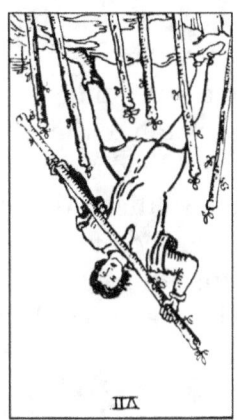 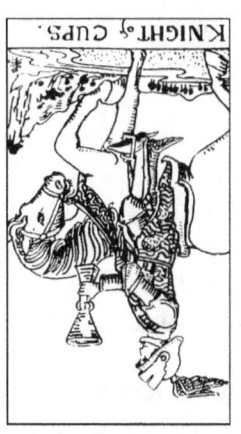 

A wonderful opportunity may be missed through negativity and a pessimistic outlook.

Indecision at a critical time could lead to defeat.

Departure. A charming, enigmatic, attractive person capable of great disloyalty. Beware trickery and fraud by someone you trust.

A crisis may be brewing, and you must keep your head. A ruthless man may try to crush your resistance.

And how wild was it, as I pulled these cards—The Star reversed, Seven of Wands reversed, Knight of Cups reversed, King of Wands reversed, all these reversed cards—that I realized the themes of them actually told her story. As I came to that conclusion, she confirmed it.

"Yes, this is my story," St. Faustina said with a nod. "I'd ignored Jesus's call at first. I wanted to be a normal girl, living and getting married and what have you. It's what my parents told me I should do. But He called, and I couldn't deny it. As a nun, I was meant to share the word of the Divine Mercy; I was meant to bring it into the world.

"But how horrible, that I was blocked time and time again—from the very church that claimed to love the same Jesus I did! Still, I persevered. The devil wouldn't crush me. I shared the idea of the Divine Mercy. I spoke it. I lived it."

It's moments like these that, no matter how many times I do these interviews, blow me away. I wasn't really well versed in St. Faustina's background before starting this; I only had the most general overview. But to get so specific a narrative strung together in the meanings of the cards, and to learn more about her life later and realize that *yes*, this is in fact what we have on record about her life, is just wild in ways I can't explain. And this is why these cards are here, as part of these interviews: so that I can see the influence of the spirits I'm talking to stare back at me. So I know the words I'm getting in my head aren't just ones I made up, but ones I see reflected back at me in the specific cards the spirits chose.

"That's incredible," I said after I finished writing her words down. When I looked up, I also noticed that the rolling green hills of the rural area were gone, and that the stone columns of the church— the red rug running to the altar, the chandeliers above and the statues of Mary and other Saints, the white lilies in big vases near Mary—were all back. We sat in the pews together again, and I murmured, "I'm stunned. Thank you for such a clear message! Though, I am curious, now that you're in heaven: what does it mean to be a Saint?"

6. WHAT DOES IT MEAN TO BE A SAINT?

Rivalry, disharmony, and conflict, though of a transient nature.

I did not expect to see Temperance reversed, but in a way, it made sense. It made even more sense as she explained herself.

"It means to fight," she said with a little smile. "It means to foil the enemies of God's plans, those that would seek to see the world in ruins. These ruiners aren't who people think they are, but they're not hard to guess, either.

"Still, being a Saint means being a soldier. We are here for you. Call on us. We will help, thanks to God's grace bestowed on us."

"Ah, that's really cool! I can see that, absolutely. And can you tell me about how you honor God and Jesus in Heaven now? What they're like for you?"

7. WHAT ARE GOD AND JESUS LIKE FOR YOU IN HEAVEN?

It was an honest question, and yet I should've known better than to mention Jesus without thinking He'd pop up. This was technically Heaven, after all, and here were two people talking about the Son of God; as promised, He appeared behind us and greeted us with a warm, cheerful smile.

"You know what I'm like!" He said to me with a laugh.

Which was fair enough, I suppose; I, and many other Christian Witches, *do* know what He's like given we work with Him and His Father and the Holy Spirit. I just wanted to know if He was any different to those who actually took up residence in Heaven, but I guess that wasn't for me to know yet. Jesus then sat in the pew opposite to St. Faustina's, and then He listened as she refused to pull any cards, her smile ever cheekier.

"You'll have to find this out for yourself one day, what it means to praise God forever more in this place," she said, confirming my suspicions. "Some secrets are best left unspoiled until death, I think. But know that it is nice. To be here."

"I don't doubt it." St. Dismas's picture of his paradise was still fresh in my mind by this point, even though I'd spoken to him so many weeks ago. Hell, even now, I sometimes still think about those deep bruise-purples, those fiery oranges, of his dusky sunset paradise. I also don't remember where Jesus went after this, but He stuck around another moment before disappearing. "Okay, then. Can you tell me how you see yourself?"

8. HOW DO YOU SEE YOURSELF?

St. Faustina waved a hand and raised her brow, a tiny smile still hanging off her face. "Oh, well, not to raise myself so high, Sara, but I think I'm someone who did pretty well on earth! So many hurdles threatened to stop me, but I persevered. I did what I was called to do. That's something I'm proud of."

"As you should be!" It was nice to see some of that confidence on her, especially with how sad and shy she'd looked at the start of all of this. "How do you want others to see you, though?"

You can't have light without dark. Don't dwell on misfortune.

9. HOW DO YOU WANT TO BE SEEN?

Victory obtained by working with others. Pragmatism, collaboration. Changing one's own behavior will be more successful than trying to change others'.

Again, she reminded me of my oma: she raised a little fist, shook it gently, and said with such conviction: "Full speed ahead, I say! I'm someone who will work with anyone that needs me, or a reminder of Divine Mercy. You only need to ask, and I'll be there."

"Perfect. And now, as we wrap this up, do you have any final messages you'd like to share?"

10. ANY FINAL MESSAGES?

"Ah, put those cards away now, will you?" She chuckled to herself as I reluctantly packed them up, as if still baffled by them, and then she spoke directly into my head. There was no denying the pressure of it, those words echoing like the clang of a church belfry on the hour. "Mercy, mercy, mercy. For all we do, all our sins, all our acts in this world that make evil, God still has mercy, as does His Son. Who are we, then, to be so hard hearted? What gives us the right to be cruel when not even God Himself decides we deserve such cruelty? Nothing. So be brave. Be wise. And above all, remember: mercy is a cure, not an illness. A strength, not a weakness."

"Aw, man, I love that." My whole being felt warm with not destructive fire, but that bright, illuminating light. What she was saying was truth, pure truth; she made sure I knew that. "What a beautiful message! And a beautiful note to end on, as that about concludes my questions. Thank you, St. Faustina, for speaking with me and being willing to use the cards to help me out. This has been wonderful, and I really appreciate your insights! Until next time!"

St. Faustina nodded, smiling wide, and then she patted my shoulder and faded away, along with the rest of the scene around us. All that bright, pale stone of the church melted back into darkness, until the two separate worlds between my open and closed eyes was yet again only the one world of my kitchen. I let out a big sigh, my mind buzzing with all that I'd just seen and heard, and I sat there for a little bit to decompress before resetting my space and tucking my notes away for later.

There's something in this interview, though. Something strange that makes me think about it so much later. Aside from the fact that this is the first Saint I've spoken to that we actually have real camera photos of, which is a bizarre thing in itself, there's just that *fire* that sticks with you, y'know? The fire not of destruction, of irresponsible self immolation, but of *justice* and, more specifically, *Divine Judgement* that coexists alongside the very mercy St. Faustina spoke about. They aren't contradictory, as I would come to learn while reading and writing more of *Discovering Christian Witchcraft*. No, not at all. In fact, eventually I would see the truth of the matter:

Divine Mercy, yes, mercy, mercy, mercy—as important as it is, it still stands in balance with that need to draw the line and eliminate the true threats to the powers of this world that would destroy any chance for mercy to take root. It reminds me something of a Martin Luther King Jr. quote (one that absolutely convinces me that this man was, in fact, a modern prophet of God):

"Power without love is reckless and abusive, and love without power is sentimental and anemic. Power at its best is love implementing the demands of justice, and justice at its best is power correcting everything that stands against love."

Power and love. Judgement and mercy. They stand in balance, it seems, and countless prophets, Saints, and mystics discover this truth over and over and over again. Now here we are, discovering it once more, in the soft smile of a Saint who still burns with a bright and guiding light when it comes to helping those that this cruel world has no mercy on.

May we all come to foster that same spirit of mercy: one that comforts the oppressed and gives fair warning to those who oppressed them before the great Judge's gavel drops.

GOD

How much baggage can be tied to one simple word? How many terrible memories, how much anxiety and stress? When we hear that word—God, with a capital G—what images flash first before our mind's eye? Plain-walled, humid Baptist churches in Kentucky, or brass incense burners in the cathedrals of New York, maybe. For some, God is represented by men in intricate green, purple, and gold robes that hold up a cardboard-tasting wafer with inexplicable reverence, and for others, He's represented by men in starched shirts with pit stains, spraying holy spittle over a crowd during an especially fiery sermon on the hellfire coming for sinners.

No matter which flavor of preaching and speeching mainstream Christianity claims God can come in, though, the most acute and attuned folks might have noticed when they walked into certain supposed "holy" spaces: that heavy atmosphere within church walls isn't anything holy. Rather, it's a heaviness that sinks into the skin and makes one itch, the way slimy, stagnant water would instead of clean water; it's a heaviness that squeezes the lungs, as if all oxygen has been sucked out, and one that sits hard on one's heart, dragging it down to the dirt.

There's a reason for this. We'll explore that reason later on. But for now, what I invite you to consider is the fact that all these things we've just linked to God are, in fact, not God. They're the conditions of people—their buildings made of stone and wood, their sickly stench and nerve-splitting voices screeching about damnation. They're not even close to properly representing the God I know, and have known, all my life.

So in this interview, I hope to show you a bit more of God—not the one attached to all these unnerving places and people, but the One who sits within and above His people.

First, though, we should also be clear about something. Before the understanding of God that we have today came about, you see, God was actually a storm and war god of southwest Asia, especially for the Bronze Age Canaanites, named Yahweh (which means "I Am"). For the Canaanites especially, He was once simply one god among many, and He was considered the child of the chief god El and the divine consort, Asherah. Multiple different cultures knew about Him, with some ancient Persian art even depicting Him sitting on a throne with wheels that had wings—ones reminiscent of the Thrones (or Ophanim) that most now consider "biblically accurate angels" (surprise! That's only one type of angel, not all).

It wouldn't be until the Israelites settled into a more monolatrist cult (monolatry meaning that one believes other gods exist, but only one is worthy of worship) that this war and storm god would come to be fused with that chief god El, creating the idea of One God of Judaism. We see evidence of the last times these two were considered at least somewhat separate deities in Deuteronomy 32:7-10, where God Almighty (Elyon) is described as giving The LORD (Yahweh) His "allotment" of Adam's descendants: the Israelites. We also see in Exodus 3, where God (Yahweh) first gives His name to Moses, and it is decidedly a different word from the term used for God in Genesis 1 (Elohim, which is actually a plural form of El, implying that there was a host of divinities involved in the creation myth given that mankind was made not in "His" [God's] image, but "theirs" (Genesis 1:26). In a hopefully very un-shocking turn of events, we discover here that religion is not made in a vacuum, and much of the inspiration of many of these early stories from Genesis are markedly similar to other neighboring culture's myths—as well as the very figure of God Himself when compared to any other neighboring culture. To learn more about God and His origins, I highly recommend reading Francesca Stavrakopolou's *God: An Anatomy*.

There's something important here worth discussing before we continue, though. This interview with God is actually the beginning of a month-long study on specifically war spirits, and we are especially going to take a look at God's more punishing, warring aspect. This, I think, is necessary, as many people in modern times simply cannot square the idea of a merciful, loving God in the New Testament with the war, terror, and destruction meted out by that very same God in the Old Testament, going so far as to make some really anti-semitic remarks about how the Old Testament (or, Jewish) God is "evil" while the New Testament (or, Christian) God is lovely and sweet and kind. However, whether we look at God's actions in the Torah (first five books of the Bible), the Nevi'im (Prophets), or even in the New Testament (like in Acts, where Ananias and Sapphira get wiped out by the Holy Spirit), we are confronted with the fact that God's got some fight in Him. Honestly, He's vicious. And that's because in the early days of His reign with the Israelites, it was culturally important to have a war god that, you know, could actually win wars. Who knew, right?

So with all this in mind, of course I asked God if He'd like to go first in our conversation on war. It's only fair, after all. But when I tell you that this is the first time I'd ever been shocked and maybe even a little scared of God, you better believe it. It seems I've taken for granted how soft He normally is with me, because this was nothing but the feeling of a warrior God all the way through. I certainly got what I asked for.

Before we dive in, though, I do feel I should address a couple common questions I get as a witch that only worships this one God.

How Does God's Energy Feel?

When it comes to getting better at feeling God's energy, truth be told, with some proper altar work and some getting-into-it steps (like lighting incense, saying the Lord's Prayer, and really meditating to get connected to Him), you can feel it easily. It feels like having all the air sucked right out of your lungs. It feels like gold embers flickering along your arms and legs, and a heaviness in your hips, as if gravity has gotten stronger and is pressing you down. It's a lot, to be honest with you. Luckily, most times God sends an angel or something so as to not totally freak us out, but when He wants you to know He means business, it makes you understand why people say to fear the LORD.

HOW DO WE KNOW IT'S ACTUALLY GOD?

Here's the thing: when I talk to God, the entity I see in my mind's eye isn't actually God. It's a Seraph, and it looks like your average army guy—tight white shirt, cropped golden hair, muscles for days, orange skin, and blue eyes like diamonds. If you look close enough, you realize the gold of its hair and the orange of its skin is actually flame, as are its eyes: whoever this Seraph is, it comes bearing the Divine Name to the point that it speaks in first person, as if it were God Himself, and in its eyes is the fire so hot it burns cold.

God is actually way far away in the distance, a burning speck among the heavens, and looking towards Him is like looking into the sun. But even though He's so far away, and He's communicating with you through this angel like it's a living tin can on a string, you can still always feel Him watching you. His gaze is sharp, accurate, and capable of flaying a soul to its barest threads, even from all the way there at the very top of Heaven.

And you know it's Him the way you know thunder means there's a storm coming. I don't know how to describe it, but it's undeniable when you talk to God: there's nothing and no one that would even try to match that level of gravity, that pure divine might and authority. It's crazy every time I get a bit of the full brunt of it, and I see exactly why some prefer to work with Jesus instead of going to God directly; that's hard to handle.

Now, with that out of the way, let's get into the interview.

By this point, I was wrapping up some personal questions I'd had for God via tarot, as I like to do each day in my tarot journal. I was having a problem with a person that I really needed His help solving, and He sure did promise to solve it with me, which is a big deal, since that was actually the first time God ever gave me permission to orchestrate a full-on counter curse. When I did that with Him some days later, not only could I feel every ounce of that thunderous energy, but I also got confirmation of its working pretty much immediately via dream a couple nights later.

Glory be to God.

But in that moment, sitting at my kitchen table and finishing up my dinner, I got set up to talk with God in a much more formal way. While normally, I just do the Lord's prayer and yap at Him, this time, I took many a context clue from the Bible and set out for Him some dill, cumin, and mint (Matthew 23:23), some cinnamon (because He likes it), and some bread (as the priests had set out for God in Exodus/Leviticus). I also had a rosary, my two mini crystal angels, and gemstones like lapis lazuli, amethyst, and moss agate to represent grounding and wisdom and other such things associated with Him. (Amethyst, I also know, is one of the crystals on the crystal grid that went on the priestly breastplate.) I also had some frankincense to burn for Him (which is the same type of incense burned in churches), and some other angel motifs (like St. Michael the Archangel's sigil), which felt right. However, once I had everything ready to go and had all my tarot card decks there for Him to choose from, He actually surprised me, telling me to put the cards away altogether; He wanted to challenge me with bibliomancy.

So bibliomancy it was, for the entire interview. (And boy, was that difficult; I certainly do not have many points in the bibliomancy skill like I do with tarot.)

"Alright, God, here we are," I said as I cracked a bottle of hard cider. I knew deep in my bones that I wasn't going to get through an interview like this without a sweet, bubbly treat like Angry Orchard. "Finally got you on the roster! I know there are a thousand and two things you could talk about, but given the war theme this month, I'd love to know what you think about all this."

I could feel Him stare at me with amusement. It's not something you see so much as feel, but even then, the Seraph representing Him let it on, too: the narrowed, icy eyes, the slight smirk, white teeth peeking through. From now on, I'll describe the Seraph's face as if it were God's, because this Seraph is standing in for God as His mask, voice, and representative.

"So to get us started, I'd like to know: everyone always talks about how loving and merciful you are, yet the warring aspects of you are still there. How does it all line up?"

1. How do your loving and warring aspects coexist?

I waved my hand over my three books: the Jewish Study Bible, the Jewish Annotated Apocrypha, and the Jewish Annotated New Testament. He landed me on the Jewish Bible, in Numbers 31 (specifically 31:31):

> *Moses and Eleazar the priest did as the Lord commanded Moses.*

Though of course, the thing about bibliomancy is that sometimes, the direct verse itself needs a little context. So I fished around the page, putting the pieces together in my head as God directed me towards the threads that made the right answer (bits about vengeance, propaganda, necessity) before He put it together for me, first with an image of two male lions tearing each other apart:

"Territory, sovereignty," said the Seraph standing in for God. His voice rolled like thunder, capturing the smoke and terror of God's meaning. "There is a limit to mercy, lest you be swallowed by those without it. Sometimes the only language one speaks is brutality, and I never lose in games whose rules are spoken in this language."

"Oh," I said, "okay, is there any more—?"

"That's enough. Next question."

"Alright, I hear you." He was being brutal this time, which I guess I should've expected, giving I was asking for the side of Him that was once called on to level cities and turn armies into bloody mist. "Okay. So, in that case, I know you just mentioned something about vengeance and territory—seems this is a matter of protecting territory and the like?—but can you explain a little bit more about when war becomes necessary?"

2. When does war become necessary?

In true God fashion, God was willing to use anything that was on paper, even the introduction of the Apocrypha. He singled in on one word used in the very last paragraph of the introduction: "preserve." I wondered if I'd chosen the right section at first, because this wasn't even Scripture, but He stopped me in my tracks.

"You heard correctly. When what is, is about to be lost, war becomes necessary for its preservation. Mercy in the face of eradicators means eradication."

"Got'cha, got'cha. Okay. Well, then, what does it mean to be a warrior?"

3. WHAT DOES IT MEAN TO BE A WARRIOR?

Again, we ended up in the Apocrypha, specifically honing in on 1 Maccabees 4:35-36:

> *When Lysias saw the rout of his troops and observed the boldness that inspired those of Judas, and how ready they were to either live or to die nobly, he withdrew to Antioch and enlisted mercenaries in order to invade Judea again with an even larger army. Then Judas and his brothers said, "See, our enemies are crushed; let us go up to cleanse the sanctuary and dedicate it."*

What stuck out to me here was the "ready to either live or die nobly" part, and how right after, their first thoughts were about God's sanctuary.

"It means to strive," God said, in a smooth and easy voice. "To try. To thrive, knowing you've protected what keeps the heartbeat of society pulsing."

Blood. Metal. Fire.

I could practically taste those things in the air, the metal tang of blood on my tongue and the rough smoke of the fire scratching at my throat. I could see a sky red as blood, too, with embers flitting up towards the bruised clouds, over tattered banners and spears sticking up from the ground.

God continued: "It means braving hell and denying it entry into the world. It means being a gate, keeping watch like a lion over its territory. One lays steeped in blood as a warrior; it's a thankless job that no one should wish for."

"Jeez. That's pretty intense, but I see what you mean." Another swig of cider eased some of that phantom smoke-scratchiness. "Though a lot of folks would say there's a battle going on right now in the world, and so I gotta ask: what do you think about the state of the world right now?"

4. WHAT ARE YOUR THOUGHTS ON THE STATE OF THE WORLD?

Here's where God really knocked me on my ass. He handed me the footnotes explaining Leviticus 16:7-10, which were about the scapegoat sent off to Azazel to eat up the sins of a community. I noticed the focus on two goats, like two choices, and God looked down at me with ice in His burning stare, a rueful smile on His lips.

"Cast your lots," He whispered. "Make your gambles. Which goat goes where? Which do you choose to have? To be? We stand at a precipice. You walk on the edge of a sword you wrought. My winds are still; you choose the way you fall. And don't you dare cast the results on My name. Take credit for your own results; take responsibility for your own choices."

"Damn." I sat there blinking at Him for a minute, because the air suddenly got *really* damn heavy, and I could feel it in my gut, like someone dropped a large chunk of iron down my throat. It was intense. "I see. That makes me reconsider the next question since it seems like you're washing your hands of the whole thing, but I still feel it's fair to us to ask: how the hell do we fix this, then?"

5. HOW DO WE FIX THE WORLD?

And once again, we found ourselves in the Apocrypha, in Ben Sira 35:1-4:

> *The one who keeps the law makes many offerings;*
> *one who heeds the commandments makes an offering of wellbeing.*
> *The one who returns a kindness offers a choice flour,*
> *and the one who gives alms sacrifices a thank offering.*

The next few lines gave some extra context as to why God chose this, too (in fact, looking back, I think He was trying to get me to just read chapter 35 in general as a whole effect, so lemme just write the entire of chapter 35 here for you):

> *To keep from wickedness is pleasing to the Lord, and to forsake unrighteousness is an atonement. Do not appear before the Lord empty-handed, for all that you offer is in fulfillment of the commandment. The offering of the righteous enriches the altar and its pleasing odor rises before the Most High. The sacrifice of the righteous is acceptable, and it will never be forgotten. Be generous when you worship the Lord, and do not stint the first fruits of your hands. With every gift, show a cheerful face, and dedicate your tithe with gladness. Give to the Most High as He has given to you, and as generously as you can afford. For the Lord is the one who repays, and He will repay you sevenfold. Do not offer Him a bribe, for He will not accept it, and do not rely on a dishonest sacrifice, for the Lord is the judge, and with Him there is no partiality. He will not show partiality to the poor, but He will listen to the prayer of one who is wronged. He will not ignore the supplication of the orphan, or the widow when she pours out her complaint. Do not the tears of the widow run down her cheek as she cries out against the one who caused them to fall? The one whose service is pleasing to the Lord will be accepted, and his prayer will reach to the clouds. The prayer of the humble pierces the clouds, and it will not rest until it reaches its goal; it will not desist until the Most High responds and does justice for the righteous, and executes judgement. Indeed, the Lord will not delay, and like a warrior will not be patient until He crushes the loins of the unmerciful and repays vengeance on the nations; until He destroys the multitude of the insolent, and breaks the scepters of the unrighteous; until He repays mortals according to their deeds, and the works of all according to their thoughts; until He judges the case of His people and makes them rejoice in His mercy. His mercy is as welcome in time of distress as clouds of rain in time of drought.*

So that's that. But at the time, I'd only read the first few verses or so, and I still got a pretty clear picture that lines up with that entire chapter, honestly:

"Offer righteousness. Where is your heart, Israel—?"

"Whoa, whoa, Israel?" At the time, I was thinking, *who the hell am I to say anything about Israel? What do you even mean by "Israel"?* This was far before the events of October 2024, and I hadn't a clue to the full extent of the mess the modern nation-state of Israel was causing, nor had their most brazen attempt at genociding Palestinians in Gaza manifested yet. So really, I wasn't even thinking about the nation-state; I was thinking about the fact that I, a Gentile, didn't have the right to say a damn thing to any *kind* of "Israel." "Are you sure you want me to use that word?"

The stare He gave me could've removed my bones and made them into powder.

"I mean—because who am I to say anything about Israel—?"

He just kept staring and stayed perfectly silent. I knew what that stare meant, and the words that went with that stare were hazy in the back of my mind: *you're going to edit My words? Cut them back at the stem?*

"...Okay, fine. Go ahead, then. Lay it on me."

And He sure did. It was like He was pointedly clearing His throat as He started again:

"Where is your heart, Israel? Where is your decency, world? The fight lies in your hands every day; there are no helmets and swords in this war, and yet it'll be the hardest war ever fought. It is you against you. Your each and every face is set against itself—better to tear your own heart from your chest than let it rot within and poison your blood.

"I am disappointed. I thought my Word would be honored, not tarnished. Set your face against any and all that would harden your hearts to one another—vanquish it."

My eyebrows shot up so high that they nearly migrated off my head entirely. "Holy shit, God— oops, sorry, I mean—ah, you know what I mean. Sorry. But okay, okay, okay, I see what you're saying. That's intense. Thinking about that war you mentioned, I'd like to know: how can we endure in these battles?"

6. HOW CAN WE ENDURE THESE BATTLES?

For the first time in this whole thing, God directed me to the New Testament, to 1 Corinthians 12:14-19:

> *Indeed, the body does not consist of one member but of many. If the foot would say, "Because I am not a hand, I do not belong to the body," that would not make it any less a part of the body. And if the ear would say, "Because I am not an eye, I do not belong to the body," that would not make it any less a part of the body. If the whole body were an eye, where would the hearing be? If the whole body were hearing, where would the sense of smell be? But as it is, God arranged the members in the body, each one of them, as He chose. If all were a single member, where would the body be?*

Together.

That was the word that just bonked me on the back of the head as I tried to make sense of what I was supposed to get out of this paragraph.

"I need to say nothing," God said. "You see in the words of Paul—all are part of this body. Your world is one body. You all are one being, scattered, experiencing itself."

Holy shit.

"Why do you cut off your own foot? Or hand? Why do you gouge out your eye to the benefit of your ear? Foolishness. Work together. We can't tell you this much longer. Come together *now*."

Oh. That's not a super intense or ominous message or anything.

"Alright, that's a new one. Makes a lot of sense! But I'll need another hard cider to process it." After grabbing my second bottle from the fridge, I sat back down and plugged back into that stormy, brutal energy. "Anyway, what do you think of all the battles you've participated in, and the wars and battles that show up in the Bible?"

7. WHAT DO YOU THINK OF ALL YOUR BATTLES IN HISTORY?

He didn't even pick a verse for this; He just said:

"I don't. What is, is. What was, was. What happened, happened. There's no use thinking on it. Only use in moving forward."

"Fair enough. Okay, well, we're towards the end now, and I'm going to ask you the same questions we ask everyone: how do you see yourself?"

8. HOW DO YOU SEE YOURSELF?

Into the Jewish Study Bible we went, to Habakkuk 3:13-14:

> *You will smash the roof of the villain's house,*
> *Raze it from foundation to top.*
> *You will crack [his] skull with Your bludgeon;*
> *Blown away shall be his warriors,*
> *whose delight is to crush me suddenly,*
> *to devour a poor man in an ambush.*

"I am a minister of Justice," God said as I sat there staring at that somewhat brutal passage. "I will take all tolls in my time. The fire will consume—to your benefit. Burned will be the old, purged will be the wicked. But first, you must understand who the old and wicked are. I watch until you present your answer. Answer correctly now; I will hear no appeals. I will entertain no second guesses."

Fuck. "And how do you want others to see you...?"

9. HOW DO YOU WANT OTHERS TO SEE YOU?

I don't even know what I expected at this point. I went into the New Testament, but not into Scripture; it was actually a mini-essay on atonement, and the focus was specifically on this part here denoting a rabbinic view on repentance's role in atonement:

> *Sin offering and guilt offering and death and the Day of Atonement, all of them together do*
> *not expiate sin without repentance.*

Then He gave me the sharpest stare, His back partially turned to me, and what felt like a disbelieving smile sat on His lips, as if He couldn't believe what He was seeing on Earth.

"Your prayers fall on deaf ears when you refuse to recognize your evil. I do not want to be seen as the one that forgives those who aren't sorry.

I SEE YOU.

"I see your words with no substance; I see your apologies with hollow centers. Death and ash to your false flowers. If you have the gall to say My name in prayer, say it with the courage to admit every stumble and acknowledge why it was, in fact, a stumble.

"See Me not as the idiot you all think I am, but as the one who will peel back layers of your very bone if you think you can hide your transgressions from Me. I tolerate no false preachers and no flashes of gaudy almsgiving; the core of your churches are hollow, and I am not in them. Yet you haven't noticed, because you see Me as the Lamb when I have always been the Lion."

If I could put any image to what I was feeling right then, it would be a football referee tossing flags on the field like he was sowing seeds for the summer harvest. "But—! Whoa, hey, wait, what about Jesus? Wasn't He the Lamb—?"

"And who was He sacrificed to?"

Holy shit. Oh my God.

Literally! I was actually stunned at these words I was hearing; they hit me like a hammer, scrambling my sense of stability and making me feel so very small. I know I joke about God being brutal, but He was really giving me the whole kit and caboodle out here.

"Uh, damn. Fair enough, I guess. But now, we're already on our last question, so I'll just ask it: any last messages you want to share before we wrap up for the night?"

10. ANY LAST MESSAGES?

He pointed me to Ezekiel 27:32-36:

> *Who was like Tyre when she was silenced in the midst of the sea? When your wares were unloaded from the seas, you satisfied many peoples; with your great wealth and merchandise you enriched the kings of the earth. But when you were wrecked on the seas, in the deep waters sank your merchandise and all the crew aboard you. All the inhabitants of the coastlands are appalled over you; Their kings are aghast, their faces contorted. The merchants among the people hissed at you; you have become a horror, and have ceased to be forever.*

To be clear, the *Tyre* referenced in this verse is a city or country in the area; oftentimes cities or nations are personified as women, much like Israel is when it's referred to as God's bride. As I read, I felt like I knew what this was saying in my bones, especially with those last few lines, but I still was hoping God would explain so that I could be sure. But when I asked Him, He said,

"No. Hear my meaning if you can. If not... If not..."

I dunno, y'all. Reading this interview back, especially given all that's happened in not only my country, America, but the whole world in the past few months with the onset of Pluto in Aquarius, it seems we've certainly chosen our path forward—and God, here, was letting me know that it's a path that has some serious consequences. In a time where a handful of people hold unprecedented wealth, where the voices of the people are ignored, where leaders prioritize their own power over their responsibility... yeah. It's a story that appears time and time again in the Bible, as we see here—and it seems we're not done telling that story just yet.

"Well, alright then. I guess that's that. Thank you, God, for letting me deliver this message at all, and for speaking with me about all we spoke about tonight. I think I'm going to need to decompress for a few hours now," and boy, was that an understatement. "But I'm sure this'll be quite the story to release, so I do look forward to it!"

And He smiled at me like He was amused, but He didn't leave like any other spirits I interview do. Of course He didn't; He's always there, always nearby, watching and suggesting and putting little thoughts and pictures in my head to guide me to what I need to be doing. He sat with me after I'd cleaned all this up, poking at me for the night and trying to get me to focus as I tried to read some Gospel of Mark and ended up scrolling TikTok for a majority of the time instead. Oops.

All in all, though, what can I say? This is my God. This infinite, ineffable being—He can't be constrained to ideas like "loving" or "cruel." He can't be fully described by ideas like "good" or "terrible."

He is *all* things, and when we encounter the aspects of Him that have been called on by desperate, scared people over literal centuries, it's impossible not to feel it: the depth of His rage and His love, never separate, always combined into one deep and all-consuming feeling. You cannot accept this God unless you can accept all of Him.

And I won't lie: it's funny that people, whether they claim to be devoted to some of the most brutal spirits themselves, certain deadly demons, or whether they claim to be all love and light and only working with the "good" goddesses, can't stomach Him. Can't see the function of His fury or feel the balm of His grace. I can't blame them, either. They've been sold a terrible lie about God, a trashy, two-dimensional version of Him that is easily puppeteered by the worst people in mainstream society.

Hopefully this interview helped you taste the blood, and choke on the smoke, of a brutal God proper. Hopefully it also helped you see why I love this side of Him as much as any of the more tender and gentle sides, too; because it's a side that understands offense as the best defense. It's a side that makes decisive action against the unjust.

It's a side that exemplifies the power of God's Severity, the depth of His Justice. May we remember the God that mainstream society has tried, and failed, to squish in a box and castrate for their own selfish, greedy gain in these hollow ramshackle "churches."

SEKHMET

There are few goddesses more fearsome when it comes to the topic of war than Sekhmet (though ones like the Canaanite Anat come to mind, too, and given her lore, it's easy to see why she could've possibly been considered cognate with Sekhmet in her respective region). Sekhmet's most prominent story is likely that of how she nearly destroyed Egypt in a frenzied rage. Ra, who hadn't been getting the respect he deserved, created Sekhmet with the intention of having her teach mankind a lesson—but as she sliced and diced her way down the countryside, she found that the taste of the blood of her enemies was too much to resist, and even when Ra told her to stop, she just kept going.

Ra went to the other gods to figure out what to do about this, and thanks to Thoth's genius, they devised a plan to fill a massive pool with herbed wine to put her to sleep. It worked; she came to the pool, thought it was blood, drank the whole thing, and then finally fell asleep and turned into a little domestic house cat—the goddess Bast. (Yes, Bast and Sekhmet do seem to be related, and through some research I did, it seems they're also related in at least some way to goddess Hathor as well).

But that's a whole separate topic. For this interview, all I knew was that I was on deck to explore yet another aspect of war—and that I really should've left myself more time and space to do so. It was around this time, by Interview 53, that I was running into a serious problem: understanding the why of this whole project. After all, I couldn't exactly call myself done with this journey, or say I'd learned all there was to know. In fact, I'm sure I could do this series for the rest of my life and not know all there is to know from the spirits of the world. Still, there was just that exhaustion. There was that burning question: what am I doing this for? Who am I doing this for?

It's something I wouldn't find an answer to for a little while. But it is something that would gnaw at me, from this point on, until I took a hard step back and asked myself honestly what I was doing this all for (and got any semblance of an answer). More on that later, though. Just know that by this point, I was wanting to talk to spirits, yes—but it was beginning to feel like a job, and I did not want something as interesting and beautiful as this experience has been, is, and continues to be, to feel that way.

Again, more on that later. For now, let's do what I did: let those thoughts rattle around in my mind while still jumping in feet first.

So, here's the thing. I had intended to meet with a devotee of Sekhmet to have them do a proper invocation, but unfortunately they weren't able to make our call for it that day. I'd set up everything just in case, but I was more than willing to put it all away if God said that we couldn't do this shindig without a devotee to do a proper invocation.

But God apparently wanted to see me go through with it, and so as I asked Him what to do, whether I should continue, He gave me positive signs (the Ace of Wands). When I asked how I should invoke her, since He was giving me signals not to use the term "Dua" (which means praise), I drew the Sun Reversed—which, in the Weaver tarot, means pessimism is blocking one's progress and to lighten up and be playful. I was uneasy still, so I drew one more card: the Sovereign (Queen) of Wands, which struck me right in the face (as well did energy around me), because on the picture's big crown was the face of a lion.

Sekhmet was already there.

I checked, I double-checked, and yep: between the slight heaviness in the air and the images I was seeing in my mind's eye—the Seraph that stands in for God against a blue sky, staring down at me, with the black and gold Sekhmet walking up beside him to stare down at me, too—I knew I was already in the zone.

All I had to offer her was my last piece of sourdough (the oldest, but best bread I had, as the other loaf was made with instant yeast and also got way too crispy on the outside while baking) and a glass of ice water; I was thinking along the lines of what I'd offered Anubis and Thoth. She didn't seem to mind, even if I wished I could've baked something fresh for her, though I didn't have the time this week. That would be a recurring theme around this time of my life: not having time, being so busy, being so tired. Was it entirely a hell of my own making? Of course. But it was still a physical reality as much as a mental reality. No matter how much I tried to do it all, the fact was that the theoretical sixteen to eighteen hours I had to work could not be worked efficiently, the way a computer might work for that same amount of time perfectly fine with the right amount of fans to keep it cool.

Still, damn if I didn't try. And damn if I didn't fail, again and again and again, in my quest to make sure I met every self imposed deadline. It was no different on this day.

But once I closed my eyes, before I knew it, Sekhmet and I were in what looked like the sand-filled ruins of a temple that had no roof. A little bit of grass grew in the corners of the temple's main area, the only green in the place. Sekhmet, all lion head and big crown and woman's body, sat down cross legged in the sand and motioned for me to sit with her.

"Well, hello, Sekhmet!" I sat down with her, still a little stunned at this whole turn of events. "I—thank you for coming to speak with me, even though I couldn't do as proper of an invocation! I appreciate you coming by!"

"Ah, you worry so much. Come, settle. Relax."

"Alright, will do. Now, would you like to pick a deck of cards to speak through?"

Just like St. Joan, she gave me a look. Her eyes were pale and bright, fierce in her head. "You're going to use cards even though you can hear me fine now?"

"Just for the sake of others who watch and want to see. And for my own sake, so I know I'm not hearing you wrong."

"Will you ever let go of those things?"

At this point, I was wondering why these entities are trying so hard to get me to stop using the cards. It was more than once, more than one entity, and that made me somewhat suspicious, though I knew they were right in some way. Yes, it was still more of a crutch than anything at this time, but it wasn't one I was willing to let go of yet—or maybe ever—because it was, and still is, the only way to show others what I'm looking at and what I'm hearing. It's the only thing that reminds me that I'm not just pulling all of this out of my ass.

Even now, I find comfort in knowing that what I heard and what I pulled line up. It makes me release a breath of relief, and it humbles me, inspires me, even, because sometimes, I do get answers I didn't expect, and I couldn't have ever just conjured answers like those on my own. Maybe one day I'll overcome this last little splinter of doubt, or I'll get tired of this little spark of wonder I get when seeing the cards I pull. For now, we keep going with tarot.

"It is what it is," I said with a shrug. "But to start off our questions, now that we have a deck: let's talk about war, shall we? And so we aren't starting off out the gate with things too heavy, I guess I'll ask: what's one aspect of war that people take for granted?"

I. WHAT'S ONE ASPECT OF WAR PEOPLE TAKE FOR GRANTED?

"Hmm," her voice was rough, low, as she thought about it, "a fine question. Here's what I'll say: there are times when things might go wrong, you know. Horribly wrong. I know; I've been there. The thing most taken for granted in war, I'd say, is the question for whether a war should be started in the first place—and the power of the people to refuse to offer their bodies to a cause they see will end in ruin, but their commanders do not."

"Ah, that makes a lot of sense. I do wonder if those commanders wouldn't just find new bodies to replace the ones that refused," I said, mulling the not-so-wonderful idea around, "but maybe if everyone refused at once, it would work. But speaking of foresight and the like... did you anticipate what would happen when Ra asked you to go and punish the people of Egypt?"

Foresight exercised with an open mind. Consider many routes and plan accordingly.

Disobedience, resistance, and determination. Marking oneself.

2. DID YOU KNOW WHAT WOULD HAPPEN WHEN PUNISHING EGYPT?

1. Intelligence, trustworthiness, security, generosity, resourcefulness, nurture, support, responsibility. Protective and restorative.

3. Act of choice in major and mundane decisions. Speed at which change manifests. Triumph in place of uncertainty or doubt. Taking a stance and taking action.

She breathed deeply through her nose as I shuffled the deck. "No," she said, and once the cards were down, she explained. "I trusted Ra. I was created for the express purpose of doing as he asked: delivering his vengeance on people who forgot his goodness.

"Ra is all things wonderful; the people depend on his aid, yet they turned away. But as you might guess, yes—the tide turns quickly in war. And Ra, in his goodness, also worked to correct the problem he'd made—to correct me, who'd gone into a frenzy."

"That makes sense. Though on the note of that frenzy, can you tell me a bit about where a blood lust like that comes from? And what it is?"

3. WHAT IS BLOOD LUST?

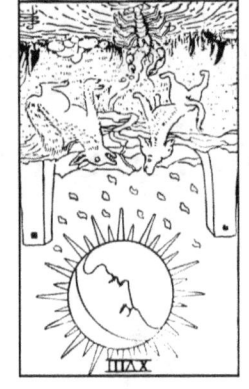

Guilt, deception, despair, anxiety, lies. Our own words are the root of despair.

A lapse in judgement and holes in one's intuition.

We'd left the temple by this point and stood out in dunes of soft, warm sand. The sun was setting on a city in the distance as we planted ourselves there among the shifting grains.

"Words," Sekhmet started, "create and are created by sentiments. Tragedies start with a command spoken by generals, and sometimes those commands are given by some who are full of rage. Rage begets rage; red in the eye becomes red on the sword. Bloodlust is a direct result of that, and of the natural urge of the predator to snap bone, tear flesh, lap up blood. When mind and instinct collide like that, it's gruesome."

It made sense to me. I parked my butt in the sand and flipped around in my notebook, writing each question as it came up in my head.

"So, then, how does one survive the harshness of war? And appreciate what resources they have to do so?"

4. HOW DOES ONE SURVIVE THE HARSHNESS OF WAR?

"Yes, well, you see that heel of bread you put here for me?"

"Yes?"

"That's a luxury in war. In reality, when you can no longer rely on the resources outside your body to sustain you in the way you need, you have to learn to turn inward. To find sustenance in things that are more than bread and water.

"In war, you won't find the same luxuries you will at home, or even among the army training grounds in times of peace. Here there is only the scream of people and your own muscles. It's on the battlefield, therefore, that you learn what you never can in times of peace, of happy, everyday peace: how to become like steel in your soul. If you cannot become steel, you become sand—whipped around by the current of war's ever blowing winds."

Heavy burdens, being overwhelmed, struggle. Oppressive conditions.

Home, celebration, harmony. Enjoy time with loved ones.

The measured way she spoke made me feel like I was getting personally tutored by the world's most intense army drill sergent. It never felt mean, though; only so true that you'd have to be a serious blockhead to question it. (Especially given she could've cut down any contrarian nonsense I could've cooked up with one lion's-eye glare.)

"I see," I murmured. "Though in times like ours, there's no war or battle to go to. Surely we still need that steel. How can we do that, then? Learn to get that steel in our souls, even in peaceful times like this?"

5. HOW CAN WE LEARN TO STEEL OUR SOULS?

Greed, possessiveness, an unkind spirit. Illusions, dreams of the world, suffering, sight warped by closed fist.

Closure, working towards (not necessarily positive) resolution, hostility.

"Ah, but are these times really so peaceful?" Her lips curled in a smile that looked more like the start of a growl. "This world hasn't been 'at peace' in a long time, Sara. You are all already in a war with every breath: a war with yourselves, with each other, and with forces too big and abstract to appreciate or comprehend. It's taking a toll on you all.

"This war has been the thing that bats you around, scattering you all into one another. Now, if you hope to train and survive, it must be by opting out of the ruse altogether. Refuse your enemy their games. They trick you into attacking; it's only when you attack in this war that you lose. Build ranks instead; build formations so strong that no force can undo their intricate knots."

Again—call this book *When Hindsight is 20/20*. It's such a simple message, looking back: one of unity, one of knowing who and what is distracting and dividing us, and yet I only barely caught it as I scribbled all these words down in my notebook.

"...I think I see what you mean," I said. Then I nodded. "That makes sense, yeah. Alright then, I guess I'd also like to know: I heard you and Bast are the same goddess at different times? What do you think of this? Of Wartime Sekhmet and Peacetime Bast?"

6. ARE YOU AND BAST THE SAME BEING?

Sekhmet shrugged as she stared at the city in the distance.

"Ferocity has no place in many situations. No one wants to be in the position where they need to be at war; everyone would prefer to be the cat, lapping milk, eating field mice.

"But even the cat has claws, and while we dread the day we use them, the fact is that neither animal can afford to be anything less than fierce. They're not so different from each other at all—the lion and the cat."

I sat there for a second, mulling that one over. Cats are pretty efficient hunters for their size, pretty ferocious in their own way, so I guess it makes perfect sense, really, when you think about it.

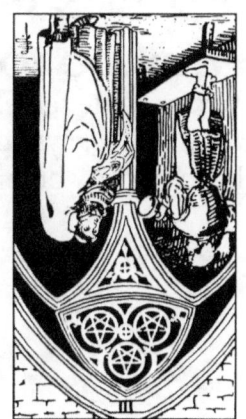

Pessimism, dread, and resignation.

Incompetence, weakness in work or teams, inability to delegate.

"Okay, I said. Then, next question... what do you want people to learn from you?"

7. Wʜᴀᴛ ᴅᴏ ʏᴏᴜ ᴡᴀɴᴛ ᴘᴇᴏᴘʟᴇ ᴛᴏ ʟᴇᴀʀɴ ꜰʀᴏᴍ ʏᴏᴜ?

Self satisfaction, contentment. Joy in what one has, abundance. Goodwill to oneself.

Codependence, miscommunication, misunderstanding.

"Ha!"

I wasn't expecting her to laugh.

"Learn from me! Yes, well, you know—I'm not the one to turn to for learning how to play nice with others, especially if one wants to play nice at the expense of their own selves. From me, you can learn how to wield teeth and fang for the sake of your own dignity—to protect your peace and all you love with ferocity that will make everyone think twice about encroaching on your territory."

"Fair enough, yeah!" Her energy was so bold and bright—just another thing to love about her, and about many of the war and sun gods I'd met. It's such an incredible energy to be around. "Alright, well, as we come up towards the end here, I'd like to know: how do you see yourself?"

8. Hᴏᴡ ᴅᴏ ʏᴏᴜ ꜱᴇᴇ ʏᴏᴜʀꜱᴇʟꜰ?

I did not expect her to pull the King of Cups at all.

"I have made mistakes," Sekhmet started. "Luckily, those mistakes were made at the very beginning of my existence, and I've learned much since then—about how to do more than shed blood, and especially more than shed it so carelessly. I am ironclad: I am steel now. No longer do the winds of battle whip me about, nor do I let them whip my devotees about."

"And how do you want others to see you?"

Generosity, security, level headedness, reliabiltiy, tolerance. Financial and mental security. Aware of power and limitations, reaping benefits of both.

KING ᴏꜰ CUPS.

9. Hᴏᴡ ᴅᴏ ʏᴏᴜ ᴡᴀɴᴛ ᴛᴏ ʙᴇ ꜱᴇᴇɴ?

"Exactly the same."

"Ah, fair. Okay! I guess we're about done now, but before you go: do you have anything else you'd like to say, any other messages?

10. ANY LAST MESSAGES?

She smiled as much as a lion face could smile. "Yes, this: one doesn't achieve anything just by wishing for it, nor does one gain anything by letting the odds dissuade them from trying. I was not who I am today immediately; I made choices, did things I regret, and kept moving forward anyway. Without the courage to fail, and the stamina to overcome, no one will ever be more than they are right now."

I just started thinking to myself that maybe some people like being where they are right now, and she added:

"Stagnancy is never good."

"Ah, yeah, I understand what you mean. Thank you for that! And Sekhmet, thank you for your time today, for coming even though we had a couple bumps in the road getting organized. I appreciate it."

"All is well," she said, and she started walking over the sand dune, away from me. "Go now, and goodbye."

Then she disappeared over that dune, and I was back in my kitchen with a book full of hastily scrawled notes. It was a good interview, one with good answers that gave me

Generosity, security, level headedness, reliabiltiy, tolerance. Financial and mental security. Aware of power and limitations, reaping benefits of both.

Pessimism, lethargy, roadblocks in achieving goals.

much to think about—and yet I couldn't quite appreciate it at the time, with the mental condition I was in that day. My heart felt like a stone, my head full of fog as I bordered on some serious burnout—and so, as I closed my notebook full of secrets, I felt that little seed of discontent grow. The feeling that had been rattling around in my head settled, and I knew that before long, I'd have to figure myself out in some regard. How, I didn't know yet, but soon, I would have to draw some kind of line in the sand. I'd have to reclaim my reason for being, for doing.

Unfortunately, when it comes to spiritual things in general, that is much easier said than done.

ST. JOAN OF ARC

Looking back, it seems I was finding comfort in a lot of the more Christian spirits around this time. We're only four interviews into this new adventure, after all, and two of them have been Saints. However, when it comes to talking about war, who better a candidate than someone like St. Joan of Arc, the patron Saint of France?

Born a peasant girl to a humble farming family, her story is honestly such a sad one. So dedicated to France during the 100 Year War, so dedicated to King Charles, only to be abandoned and burned at the stake by the English as a heretic and a witch. The heresy came from her claim that she received divine guidance to lead armies into battle, as well as having visions of things that, according to the French King Charles, "only God could know."

And there's something to be said about that. Here was a woman, a simple peasant lady, being chosen by God to go forth and raise her banner for France. Who got divine revelations, according to her, to get out there with a sword in hand. Who, despite being the complete opposite of what men at the time believed a soldier should be, and despite doing the complete opposite of what a woman should do, was sent out there to do it.

However, it does seem that the difference between "divine revelation" and "whispers of the devil" rests entirely in the prejudice of those looking onward, doesn't it? Prejudice and politics, given St. Joan wasn't saved by the king she'd fought alongside, either. (He "absolved" her of any accusations twenty years after everything went down in some kind of mock court, but... that wasn't exactly helpful for our lady while she was actively going up in smoke, now was it?) It seems she still got the last laugh, though, as she was eventually canonized in 1920 as the patron of both France and soldiers in general.

I figured that an interview with her would answer some interesting questions about war—and about being a woman in it, one who could hear divine guidance of God. So without further ado, let's take a look.

I'd started my morning with a little tarot with God, of course asking His opinion on interviewing St. Joan. Granted I'd already set up the table with things that represented both Catholicism and war alike—a red candle, a rosary, my big angel statue, and plenty of fiery stones like carnelian and tiger's eye, and a cup of rich red fruit tea—but if He'd told me not to do it, I would've packed everything away and done something different on the fly. I had already cycled through two other entities that God warned me away from talking to—or maybe He'd just been trying to push me here. Who really knows?

Either way, He seemed to approve of my reaching out to St. Joan, and before I could even finish asking her to come by, I got a clear flash in my head of a woman looking down at me, one that looked just like the woman in this picture, and with a face as hard as stone.

We were on a desolate field full of trampled earth and heaped with bodies, a battlefield after a fierce fight, and St. Joan stood there in her armor with a banner in her hand, her white horse there at her side.

"St. Joan!" I felt like I was a child standing next to her; she was big! "Welcome! Thank you for joining me! If you'd be so kind, could you choose a tarot deck to speak through?"

St. Joan's lip curled in a half smile. "Why? You can hear me just fine."

By Spirit No. 53, I will say: I did have a knack for grasping at the vibes I was getting from a spirit without any such tools like tarot cards. I often get questions about channeling like this, and how I know that what I'm hearing is truly from them, and I will say: while it isn't fool proof, there is something to that whole *practice makes perfect* spiel. You eventually learn to pay attention to the random words and ideas that flutter into your head, as well as the images and the symbols, and it begins to paint a coherent picture that you can actually put to words. More, you learn to stop second guessing. I think that's the biggest stumbling block people have: trying to make the words and images they're getting fit their preconceived ideas of a spirit, of what they "should" say, than just letting them speak and asking them more pointed questions if things don't sound right.

However, throughout this series, I continue to use tarot cards, if only because it helps others looking into this experience know that what I'm hearing and picking up on isn't coming from actual thin air. Above all, it lets me know, still, that what I'm picking up on isn't just me. Even for all this practice, I still get doubts from time to time. I told St. Joan as much, too.

"Well, yeah, but I tend to doubt if I just listen with nothing concrete to look at."

"Oh. So this is a crutch."

"I—" Oof, she got me. By the sparkle in her eye, she knew it, too. "Well, maybe. But it's for the others, too. Not everyone who sees this will be sitting with me. This'll show them what you mean."

Her smile grew bigger, a single huff of laughter puffing from her nose, and she picked the first deck I had lined up: the Marigold Tarot. It surprised me. I thought she'd choose the Golden Tarot, but no! Marigold it was.

"Alright, well, again, I appreciate you coming by and hope you enjoy a cup of tea with me this morning! I guess we can start with the very first question: what is war to you?"

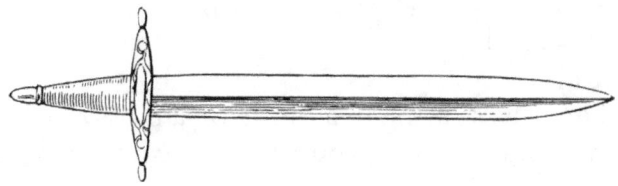

1. WHAT IS WAR TO YOU?

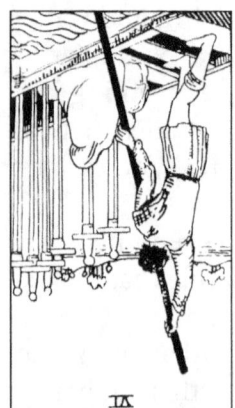

Inability to move forward, obstacles, and waiting.

Impetuousness, grandstanding, rashness, overconfidence. Be more brash or forthright.

Closure, working towards (not necessarily positive) resolution, and hostility.

As I shuffled, her lips pressed into a thin line, and she waved out at the battlefield. "This," she said. "This. All this."

On that battlefield was a great plain full of dead men.

Once I'd put the last card down, she said, "Do you see? The horror? War is a place where no man really wins. They want glory. They want to defend their countries, their families. But here, all wishes feed the same dirt, the same worms. Come."

We walked on, towards a huge grey-walled castle in the distance. While we walked, I blinked at all the broken bodies, the torn banners, and that one big block of a castle, then kept on with my questions.

"How do you get over the fear, then? Fear of battle?"

2. HOW DO YOU GET OVER THE FEAR OF BATTLE?

"You don't," she muttered. "Every battle is a hailstorm of feelings. The souls of men cry out for comfort, not war; they want to be home, wrapped up in their wife's embrace, by the fire, or having a good meal after a long day's worth of quiet, honest work.

"War and blood is the realm of gods who can't die—not men. But in war, there's no room for these feelings, even if they won't stop haunting you. You just have to accept death and distance yourself from the hope of ever coming back."

"Wow." It was eerie, looking into her stony expression as she spoke and kept her eye locked on that castle.

Falling in love with the idea of love, jealousy, needing to be tethered to reality.

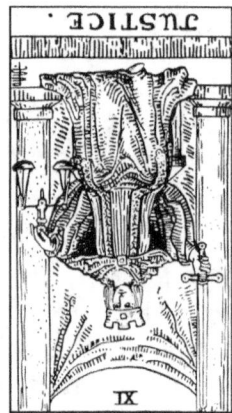

False accusations, disharmony, general unfairness.

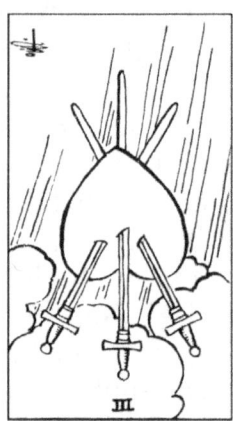

Needing to move on, feelings of alienation, love or relationships long lost.

Eventually though, we found ourselves sitting in a forest, on a mossy rock, away from it all, as if she'd had enough of the image. "I hear you. But you, yourself, have come back from quite a few wars—even if you got caught at the end. So—"

"Caught. Yes." Her eyes shone like sunlight off obsidian. "Caught and abandoned. At least God didn't abandon me even when the others did. He took me up. I did my role; I fulfilled my promises and was given rest in return."

The air was heavy. "I understand. Though surely there must've been some successful strategy, given you'd seen more than one battle? What was it like to put those plans together?"

3. WHAT WAS IT LIKE TO PUT BATTLE PLANS TOGETHER?

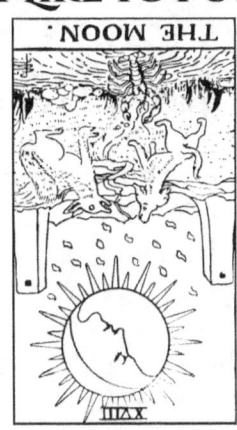

Guilt, deception, despair, anxiety, and lies. Words are the root of one's despair.

A lapse in judgement and holes in one's intuition.

Regret, loss, mourning, disappointment. The destrucive nature of sorrow in excess.

There was the feeling of a big sigh building up as St. Joan looked at the ground.

"Is there really such a thing as a successful strategy? I'm but a farmer's daughter. To me, every life lost is a reason to grieve. I promised success if these men followed my lead, but so many men never lived to see the promises fulfilled. Each one that followed me and went to God before me is a mark on my soul.

"God might forgive me, but how can I forgive myself? I know I must, lest I get eaten alive by sorrow, but I am sorry for them. Still, we can say this: when an objective is complete, a mission is successful. But the cost is the real strain."

"That makes sense to me. But you know you can't beat yourself up for it, of course, yeah. It is what it is. You know, though, I'm also curious: what was the hardest part of being a woman soldier? I can only imagine, but I'd like to hear your thoughts."

4. WHAT IS THE HARDEST PART OF BEING A WOMAN SOLDIER?

1. Suffering, betrayal, isolation, desolation. Pain has reached an apex and resolution will soon be found. Arriving at a precipice, needing a new starting point.

2. A change of direction, moving on from disharmony to seek balance, disappointment and abandonment.

3. Weakness in work or team situations, incompetence, the inability to delegate.

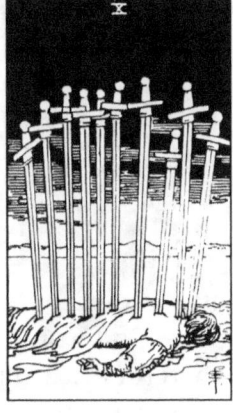

Another little chuckle. "Men. The hardest thing about being a woman soldier was men."

I couldn't help a wry smile myself at that. "I can see that."

But the humor faded from her face pretty quickly as she continued. "The ones who were true to me were incredible. The ones who I needed to be true, who I believed in—they failed me when I needed them. I'm glad God took me home. He knew as much as I did in those English prisons that these men weren't worth my sword or my shield."

Then, suddenly, we were off the field, out of the woods, and into a huge mess hall made of gold and ivory. The walls were gold, the tables edged with gold, the floor bright and shining marble. And ahead of it was a golden throne, as well as a man in red robes that I recognized—Jesus!

"The only Man ever worth following," St. Joan said as she smiled at Jesus, and as Jesus smiled at us, returning my overenthusiastic wave, "is the Son of Man."

Jesus passed us by without a word, but with a warm smile and a pat on either of our shoulders. What He was doing there, I don't know, but He was off and out of the mess hall, off to take care of whatever else He needed to take care of. It's always a treat seeing Him pop in, even if only for a moment to give those friendly and encouraging smiles before disappearing. (I think He didn't want to intrude on the conversation, maybe, so He was there to show His support before moving on.)

"Always good to see Him, isn't it?" I looked back at St. Joan, who was smiling after Him. "Well, speaking of God and Jesus though, I'd love to know your thoughts on being accused of heresy and being a witch. I mean, you had direct revelation from God! Yet look what happened!"

5. THOUGHTS ON BEING ACCUSED OF HERESY AND WITCHCRAFT?

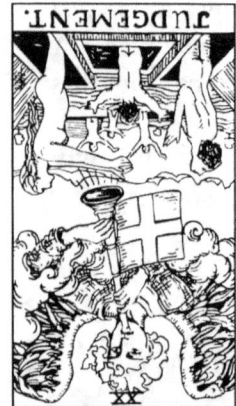

Past regrets, false accusations, disappointment, ignoring the call to transform.

Power, prosperity, optimism, strength, warmth happiness, growth, comfort.

Carelessness, pessimism, lethargy, roadblocks in achieving goals.

"Yes, look what happened," she said with a sigh. "But you know all too well that men call Divinity heresy when it doesn't line up with what they want."

"That I do, yeah."

"My solidarity to you," she said. "It seems they don't change, do they? These folk?"

We chuckled about it for a second, but then the seriousness set in again. St. Joan shook her head.

"I was so confident in that path God put me on," she muttered. "I did great things in His name, preserved the fate of my country. But for what? Men—mankind—what a wicked thing. They don't hear God. They don't even hear the devil. They hear only their own greed.

"But I was careless. I thought being chosen by God would be a protection. I thought Christian men would believe and know the word of God when they heard it. But if they didn't recognize His Son and strung Him up—what did I, a simple peasant woman, expect?"

Then she held her hand out, and when I took it, she gripped it tight, leaning in to whisper to me.

"Trust no one. No one but God."

That wasn't grim or anything. But it was a warning I'm fully aware I would be better off heeding; she didn't need to tell me twice. I feel like anyone walking this path would do well to hear it, especially as we continue weaving the art of witchcraft with the title of Christian. There are far too many wolves in sheep's clothing lurking out there, ones who think they're being holy as they cut down anything they don't understand. It's shameful on their part—and dangerous for anyone who goes against their violent mob mentality.

"Fair, all fair," I said. We stood in the mess hall, the place silent and safe. "I'm curious, though: how did you get these revelations from God?"

6. How did you get revelations from God?

"Mm, yes, I see what you're asking."

Then there was a flash of thunder in my mind's eye, a terrible downpour of rain, and a little girl standing outside her farm, her hair soaked and matted against her head, her eyes huge.

I paused my card shuffling. "Do you want to pull any cards for this before you keep showing me anything?"

"No, just watch."

So I watched. Thunder crashed, booming so loud, and then that thunder swapped for the sparks that flew off steel, swords clashing together with just as loud a bang. The images intertwined, even as that little girl with eyes wide and dark as the void was dragged back inside by concerned parents.

Then there was the image of her rocketing up from her bed, as if it were all a dream, and a heaviness in her bones. *For France,* she said. *For France.* All while she sat in bed, chest heaving, eyes just as bewildered.

Then we were on that rainy field again for a moment, as St. Joan watched the lightning strike.

"You just know," she said. "Words don't do it justice. You just know."

"I... yeah. I've felt that knowing before." It felt like I was talking to a fellow, standing beside St. Joan. Like a comrade in arms, almost. We were soon back in the mess hall, and I saw myself standing with her—a soldier and a cloaked, shapeless woman, shorter and veiled in dark purple and gold like a mystic or witch or the like. Maybe that was how she was seeing me the whole time. That's a fun thought. Though both of us had the same look on our face, that stony, tired knowing. "But with all that said, I do feel like it's important to ask: as a woman, how can women withstand the battles of day to day life? Knowing all this?"

7. How can women withstand life's battles today?

1. New beginnings, spontaneity, change, innocence. Mental journeys are more important than physical ones.

2. Vigilence, contemplation, thought, and growth of new ideas. Caution is important in the search for intellectual challenge.

3. Naivete, disharmony, holding onto the past in an unhealthy way.

I loved seeing her stand there with her shoulders broad, her back straight, in that armor. It was just cool. But she squared herself, sighed deeply, and spoke with a hardness to her voice.

"Vigilance will always be necessary in this world. Men in your life, even other women in your life, they put their own interests first. You cannot be the fool, moving so innocently and easily through a world full of vipers.

"So make friends. Take lovers. Live life. But never think that you're safe from calamity. Where there's people, there's always a chance for calamity. Learn to recognize its flowers before you eat its bitter fruits. The same goes to you, Witch of God."

"Uh—damn, well…"

I blinked and sighed myself, because it was just ominous warning after ominous warning. Knowing what I know now after all these interviews, I can only wonder if it's a case of hindsight being 20/20 or if these spirits really were trying to give me signs of our own upcoming calamity all this time, both at home and abroad. The title she spoke also felt like something of a jab, not insulting, but like she was just soaking the word "witch" in warning—for reasons that, given her pointed look, made me think of how she, herself, was burned for a witch, too. Yet here I am, flying that title around with some serious guts. It's one of those messages you don't need words to translate, I think.

But I shrugged, resigned, and said, "Fair, fair. Makes sense to me. But okay, that ends the bulk of my questions. For now, could you tell me how you see yourself?"

8. How Do You See Yourself?

In love with the idea of love, jealousy, needing to be tethered back to reality.

"Myself? Hmm. Honestly, I should've known. I should've been more careful. I should've seen things coming. But I, too, was no different from the men around me in this way. I thought I was special, and that my life and service meant something to the king I served." Her face wrenched into a bitter frown as she shook her head. "Never again."

"Ah, yeah. Jeez, St. Joan. I'm so sorry that happened to you; it's ridiculous. And just to go ahead and clear your name later after you'd died! But alright, then, how about how you want to be seen?"

9. How Do You Want To Be Seen?

Here, she stood as strong as ever, but she had a sword in her hand that was buried in the marble all of a sudden. She looked strong and fierce, reminding me of St. Michael the Archangel.

"See me as one who has learned," she insisted. "I have attained wisdom in my death. I am steadfast now, as the great angel Michael." Oop, there it was. She was really fronting that kind of presence. "I am a lioness. I always was. I see myself as such now, only after years and years of reflection—and I hope every one else knows, too, that I realize how I've been wronged."

Reflecting on finances, social standing, business, and fruits of one's labor. Cultivating difficult things.

"I got'cha. I'm glad to know you can rest at this point. Now, are there any other messages you have? Any other cards?"

10. ANY LAST MESSAGES?

Again, she chose no cards.

"There's nothing else to say. We've covered it all, I think. Just remember me—remember the injustice against me—and remember not to blame God. God is the only one who truly supported me. So I'll be here, enjoying the paradise I've won."

"Beautiful. Well, thank you, St. Joan, for taking the time to answer my questions. I'll be going now."

And then I left out the big golden doors of that mess hall and found myself pretty much vacuumed back into my kitchen, a little disoriented. That tends to happen in meditation like this. It seemed like St. Joan kind of ushered me out a little, not in a mean way, but she definitely closed the space for me.

And looking back, I must say: so many times, when I do these interviews, I can't help but laugh, because there'll often be someone crowing about how all of this that I do is "demonic" and how I need to "test the spirits." Luckily, no one came to cause trouble on my initial demonstration for St. Joan, but here's the thing: it's the same story over and over again, isn't it? People with no talent, no skill for connecting with the Divine—people simply passed over for the opportunity to do so, or worse, people going and shutting the door in the face of the Divine while convinced they're doing good— they're the ones telling us over and over that everything we're doing is wrong. That these spirits are demons and evil things in disguise. But remember what I already told you before we even got started on this journey? Remember 1 John 4:1-3?

Firstly, this little chunk of Scripture is talking more about prophets that were running around and trying to make money off their own micro-cults at the time, but secondly, how can anyone doubt a spirit like St. Joan when she can look upon Jesus with such fondness, or give all the credit for her rest and her peace to God, even after all the terrors of so-called "godly" men? I've spoken to spirits who could give a damn about Jesus, and they make that clear. I've spoken to the souls of Saints and angels, and they're *very* clear about where their loyalty lies. And yet, in this day and age, when you'd think everything from the story of St. Joan to the story of Christ Himself has already made their point, still, you have those spiritually blind and fearful folk telling you to be fearful, too—that everything you do, that everything out there, is some great evil willing to eat you up.

I don't know, friends. I witnessed the power of St. Joan's spirit this day. I witnessed the confidence, the courage, and the nobility in her every step, the grandness of her stature. And I found myself humbled when she put all of the credit for that in her, *our,* God. Let this be a lesson to you: yes, go on and test your spirits. Make sure you're talking to who you think you're talking to, by all means.

But have courage as you walk this path, too. Don't succumb to the kind of fear that shuts people's spiritual gifts off and leaves them defenseless, afraid, and paranoid. Stay steadfast, stay stable, and remind yourself that the biggest victim of the "everything is evil" type of "believer" is, in fact, that very faithless and anxious "believer"—not you, not I, not anyone else. Take this reminder and go on in peace as you continue doing what you know you need to do.

LA SANTA MUERTE

We all know that where there's war, there's death—and so it only made sense to me to wrap up a month-long investigation on the topic of war with a figure like La Santa Muerte. After all, La Santa Muerte's devotees, especially those who frequently war among each other, do find themselves invoking her in baneful work pretty often.

For this Saint, I worked with Hysteria, or @hysteria_brujeria on TikTok and Instagram. He's a devotee of La Santa Muerte, who told me many things about her and her cultural context that I wouldn't even know where to begin searching about, and boy, is this a fascinating folk Saint.

Because the thing about La Santa Muerte is that she is primordial; she has existed as long as living things have existed, because where there is Life, there must be Death following it. She's also what Hysteria described as "mixed blood" (per the language of the people that venerate her), because she is very much not the average Saint; she's a Saint that, something like St. Brigid, held on even after Spanish Catholics came and tried to decimate the native faiths of the regions they colonized. Some theorize that La Santa Muerte is a mix of indigenous deities and Catholic iconography, and according to Hysteria, is even considered a sister of La Virgen de Guadalupe—the Virgin of Guadalupe (or Mother Mary).

According to Livia Gershon in her JSTOR Daily article, "Who is Santa Muerte?" the Saint was first mentioned in an inquisition report from 1797 in Mexico, where the colonizers were describing "idolatrous practices" of the indigenous people there, and since then, she's become a famous figure across the folk Catholics of Mexico and other areas of Latin America. She's also become heavily linked with sex workers and the LGBTQ+—the abused of society—and part of her rosary prayer that Hysteria showed me and that he and I prayed together, is a pretty good sign of why:

Hail the Santisima, full of love and grace. Blessed by you are the forsaken and forgotten. Blessed by you are the abused and downtrodden. Hail the Santisima, who holds power over us all, bless us with your love now and at the moment of our death. Amen.

(This was the part of the rosary that got repeated the most. It is meditative to the max.)

There's so much more to learn and know about this fascinating folk Saint, but that's for another time. For now, let me show you how this interview went—because it sure was quite the experience.

After praying the entire rosary to La Santa Muerte, and lighting a candle and a bit of iris incense for an entity that loves flowers, I shook off a little of the fuzz that comes on the mind when you pray the same prayer again and again and again, but here's the thing: after the first of five sets of that prayer to La Santa Muerte, I felt the frizz along my arms, like a little bit of electricity.

She was there for quite a while by time I'd been ready to start speaking.

"La Santa Muerte," I said as I closed my eyes, "thank you for coming. I hope the strawberries and the incense and the candle are to your liking! I have a few questions for you, if you don't mind answering?"

In my mind's eye was a skeleton woman draped in black robes. I think because of my familiarity with the Marigold Tarot, my mind added little bits of gold to the edges of her robe, but it was La Negra—one of three main colors she tended to wear in more modern ideas of her. The other two colors are white and red, and each have their own meaning. For the topic of our conversation, the black robe—a color of her robe invoked when folks need some help, some protection, against forces that would cause them harm—made sense. It represents the more dangerous forces in the world.

We sat in a cave made of bones, with a river of greyish muck flowing towards an opening that led to another part of this cave. Bones lined the ceiling, the walls; bones made up the little mound where La Santa Muerte was, sitting on an old wooden throne. There was a hole in the ceiling that shined light down on her, highlighting the dark eye sockets of her face and the sharp cut of her jaw. In her hands was a staff, a little lantern hanging off of it and glowing in the otherwise dark underworld.

"Hello, Santa Muerte. Welcome again."

She watched me without a word. As the silence stretched on, I got the sense to choose the Weaver Tarot for our conversation.

"If it's alright, I guess I'll kick us off. Namely, I'm here to talk about war—and from what I've heard, you have a good deal of knowledge of it, as war always means death—and the first thing I'd like to ask is: how do you feel about death being weaponized? About people trying to come to you and ask your help in getting rid of an enemy permanently?"

I. WHAT ARE YOUR THOUGHTS ON THE WEAPONIZING OF DEATH?

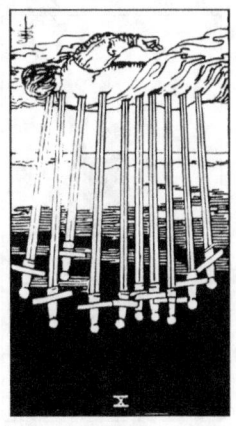

1. Arrival at an all time low. It doesn't feel good, but you need to move on, and this forces you to. Changes are easier when we're desperate. Welcome new shifts.

2. Feeling overwhelmed and confused. A lot of energy being spent for very little clarity and no answers. Find stillness and surrender in this time. You're shut off from your intuition.

I asked because that does happen. Whether magical practitioners or ordinary folks with an enemy to cross off their list, the invocation of the Holy Death on an enemy isn't out of the ordinary.

La Santa Muerte sat still for a moment before she shot up off her throne.

"Foolish," she said. "There is no weaponizing death. People might ask me to deliver my gifts early, but I mark time as it needs to be marked—not as it gets yanked by humans in their thirst for bloodshed. You cannot rush what is already etched into fate."

That was more than fair. "Makes sense to me. Alright, then!" With her standing, I noticed her looking towards the little creek babbling behind me, and the other area of the cave that it led to. "I guess my next question, then, would be: how do you answer the call of devotees that fight each other? If one devotee calls on you for help against another devotee, how do you deal with that?"

2. HOW DO YOU DECIDE BETWEEN TWO CONFLICTING DEVOTEES?

Arrival, completion. Financial success, harmony in relationships. Celebrate all that's going right. Think about the long term future.

Reaching a new level of wholeness. A sense of completeness and closure as things come together in a beautiful way.

Honestly, it's a question I could ask God, too.

La Santa Muerte shook her head. "It isn't just about the devotee. One man's life is never about just one man."

Oh.

"If I am to judge between two groups at war, it'll be more than a man's character that needs to be assessed," she said. "Their heart, their people, their impact on the community, the fruits of their spirit—all of these must be considered. You don't cut down the ripening fruit plant for the sake of the wilted plant that may never reach a single bloom."

I won't lie: sometimes, with messages like these, the information is almost enough to hurt the head as I parse it. These things aren't things I literally hear; they're more like things that just get translated from raw feeling and ideas, pictures. It's hard sometimes, to distill pure meaning into something as clumsy and indirect as language.

"I see. That's wise. Thank you for explaining that! I do wonder, though: how does violent death impact a soul?"

3. HOW DOES VIOLENT DEATH IMPACT THE SOUL?

1. All is well. Being in the flow, feeling like one could take on the world. Success is on the way. Connect to your power.

2. Grief and loss. A future wrapped up in dashed hopes and regret. Having to suddenly rebuild is difficult. Uncertainty in moving forward. Dwelling will not help you move on.

La Santa Muerte stepped down from the little hill of bones. We stood by the creek, where some bones seemed still attached to a soul or something, because they peeked out from under the water and moved as if swimming down that gray current.

The Holy Death's voice hooked my focus back on her. "It's like a cloud coming in front of your sunshine, and thunder crashing down out of nowhere," La Santa Muerte said. Her voice echoed through the caves. "Violent death jars the soul. It drives it to fear, confusion, and the soul gets lost in its shock. They need to be pulled back, reminded of who they are, lest they become nothing more than pitiful shades. Deaths of violence, of war, are misery."

"I see." We started walking, following that creek, as the other bones rattled and clanked along the banks. "Can you tell me a little about how you help these souls lost at war?"

4. HOW DO YOU HELP SOULS AT WAR?

We walked towards that opening to the next chamber of the cave, step by slow step.

"On Dia de los Muertos," La Santa Muerte started, "the day the souls come back, if they aren't prepared, the consequences can be wicked.

"I put these unfortunately lost souls to work. I keep them busy, re-instilling discipline and channeling their rage and shock into energy they can use, so they might protect rather than destroy. It's difficult at times for them to come to terms with their ends, but they must. For their descendants' sake, and for their own."

"Wow. That's beautiful, honestly." I could almost glimpse it: what it would look like for the stoic figure of La Santa Muerte to stand by a soul grieving itself, tethering it to its sanity as it worked to regain clarity of consciousness. "Though, I gotta admit: the concept of ancestor work is still so wild to me. I feel like I want to get into it one day, but I dunno. Either way, I mean... can you tell me how ancestors fight for their descendants?"

Driven and methodical. Rigorous routine, trusting the process. Being okay with not seeing instant results. Freedom with routine; discipline.

Mental expansion. Clarity, inspiration, ideas. New shifts within us, new negotiations of being. Need for passion and justice.

5. HOW DO ANCESTORS FIGHT FOR THEIR DESCENDANTS?

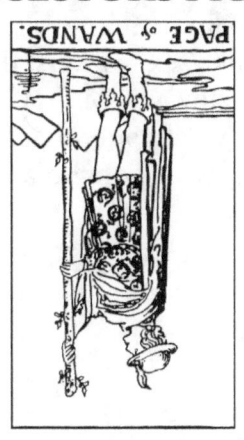

1. Out of balance and getting in one's own way. Having big dreams but being unable to do what's necessary. Healthy leadership is needed.

2. Attachment to "new" things have created blockages. Pushing things forward before they're ready. Be at the beginning and spend time at the foundational level. Stay in this space even if it's uncomfortable.

If bone could smile, it might've here. "The youngsters—they can forget that they weren't the first souls to ever walk this earth. I guarantee you, whatever any of you are struggling with, millions have already struggled with all over human history.

"The ancestors who have accepted their death and are ready to help, they don't just fight off threats outside. They help you fight what's brewing within, too; they anchor you in tradition and the knowledge that you're not alone."

I was getting images of families out in remote lands, in little houses, with not much to their name, but alive with good food and celebration anyway, rich in different ways.

"I get'cha." It was a really comforting idea. "I love that. Okay—slight detour, but I just had a thought pop up. Some describe you as the sister of La Virgen de Guadalupe, and they say you work for God. I was wondering: how do you view Mary? And God?"

6. HOW DO YOU VIEW MARY AND GOD?

Potentially feeling dissatisfied with life. Relationships may feel stale or disconnected. Taking things for granted. Re-establish connection.

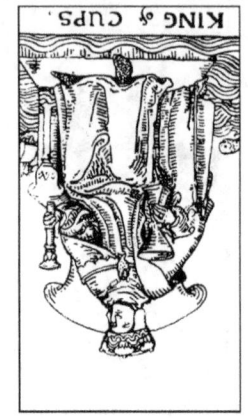

Emotional imbalance. Reactive, moody, harsh attitudes. Emotional disconnect or intensity, switching between the two, may create tension.

"Ah." Despite La Santa Muerte having no flesh on her face to make any expression with, there was something burning deep in the smoky shadows of her eye sockets. "Mary is a fine soul, a perfect soul without blemish. She deserves to be respected as queen—yet you humans have forgotten your place. You've tossed a fine and benevolent queen into the mud for a Son that would rather you never do such a thing—why? Is her might not enough for your respect?

"You respect all manners of earthly, decaying things, yet this Woman of women is where you draw the line?

"And God—that God of yours. I work with Him, yes—but Death isn't exclusive to His children. He, however, is a wounded thing, tired and hurt watching how you all eat each other alive. He puts on a strong face, but how He rages when He sees how you abuse each other."

Ouch. Given our last public experience with God, her cards—the Ten of Cups Reversed for Mary, the King of Cups Reversed for God—they made sense. I was moved, honestly, by her answers about both of them. It was intense as she stared down at me, her sharp and fleshless face shrouded in black and gold robes.

"Alright, well, Santa Muerte, I have another question for you. I know that you're considered a keeper of the downtrodden and abused, and that it extends to folks like sex workers, the LGBTQ+, and more. And I know that Death can't be stopped, and hardly even slowed—but for all your devotees who ask your protection, and all people in general, I do wonder what your advice is to people who are trying to avoid the things that kill?" I paused, then clarified, "Not trying to avoid Death. Trying to avoid the things that make Death happen. You know?"

7. WHAT DO YOU SAY TO DEVOTEES TRYING TO STAY SAFE?

La Santa Muerte nodded. "I do know. And I say: you haven't lost the war until you've lost your spirit. Don't let the world whittle it down. Remember that all before you have struggled, too—and they've still restored their spirits in love and family and prayer and nature, even when their bellies gnawed with hunger.

"You are more than your situation. Create refuge within yourself."

I stared at her for a bit. We were in the other part of the cave by this point, and there was more to explore somewhere past us, but we just stayed there for a bit as I recorded her answer.

"Thank you for that; that's some good advice," I said. Then I looked at her from the banks of that creek. "Well, that's all the main questions. Now comes the rest, the first being: how do you see yourself? We know how others see you. But how do you see yourself?"

Scarcity mindset prevents one from receiving. Focusing on wealth and money ruins connection to all life has to offer. Create balance in life.

Life springing forth from a creative place. Momentum and passion. A gift. Leave your doubt at the door.

8. HOW DO YOU SEE YOURSELF?

Driven and methodical. Rigorous routine, trusting the process. Being okay with not seeing instant results. Freedom with routine; discipline.

She nodded again.

"I am a constant. I keep this world bound and contained, lest it spill out and overload itself with squabbling life that chokes itself out and creates chaos. Without life, there can be no death, and without death, there can be no life. I am the Keeper of the Key—the one guarantee, the one thing all beings can rely on."

Here, her cloak changed from black to white, just for a little while.

"And how do you want to be seen?"

9. HOW DO YOU WANT TO BE SEEN?

"Exactly the same. People need to understand that Death isn't something that can be swayed or delayed."

Her white robe stayed for a while longer as I went to ask my last question.

"Alright, I hear you. Do you have any other messages, things you want to say that I didn't get to?"

10. Any Last Messages?

Find balance and peace. Have a curious mind and be open to different points of view. Rigidity is unpleasant. Live in the grey area. What we know as true may not be. Allow harmony where you thought there was none.

Big, happy energy. A job well done navigating rough waters. Celebrate. Pamper yourself. Reflect on what you've accomplished.

Then there wasn't just a white robe. There wasn't even just one Santa Muerte. Three of her appeared there, the White, Black, and Red, and the black robe spoke.

"Death is a guarantee," she started, "but until that moment—from your whole life on—you weave your stories. Allow the tapestry of your lives to be woven with beautiful colors; allow your story to be beautifully mapped out. Live a life of exploration, courage. Celebrate the days you're able to open your eyes and hug your loved ones.

"Time grows shorter with every day that passes; be grateful for every gift as it comes. This way, when I come for you, you may have the wisdom to welcome me with open arms and make your discipline with me all the shorter."

Then she sat back on her throne in the other part of the cave as the White Robe, shining under the light that filtered through with her arms outstretched, before we parted ways and the cave melted away.

I sat there, my mind in a buzzing quiet once I'd felt I'd disconnected from that space. The image of her in that throne still sits so stark in my mind: her, a queen that needs to make no show of her glory, who doesn't even need to wear a crown to signify her reign, because the light of the Divine itself spotlights her from above. With no flesh on her face to make an expression, there's no mask for her to wear; the severity of her bones is enough to speak her disposition into being. There was such calm after talking to her that I still can't quiet explain, but it's something that, the more you talk to entities that are truly *primordial,* the more you learn to settle into like a good bath. I think it's because when these entities speak, it's just the pure, bald truth, nothing dressed up and no bushes to beat around.

Many will say this is the purpose of meditation: to reach this state of blankness. But it's not a blankness of *mind* so much, is the thing I suppose I never understood as I tried to get every thought I ever had to disappear. It's the kind of blankness that comes when there's nothing else *to* say, when the truth doesn't need to try and tangle itself up in words. It's a heavy feeling, such blankness, because it feels like all the sediment in yourself has finally settled to the bottom of your being, and the waters of yourself are finally clear and undisturbed. Looking back on these experiences, I feel like I can say this moment, this interview, was when the "dust" of myself finally started to settle in that way.

It's still settling. And there will be times when it's all kicked up again, of course; we don't stay undisturbed forever. But to remember this feeling is a centering thing. A cleansing thing. I hope you have, or will come to, feel it as well.

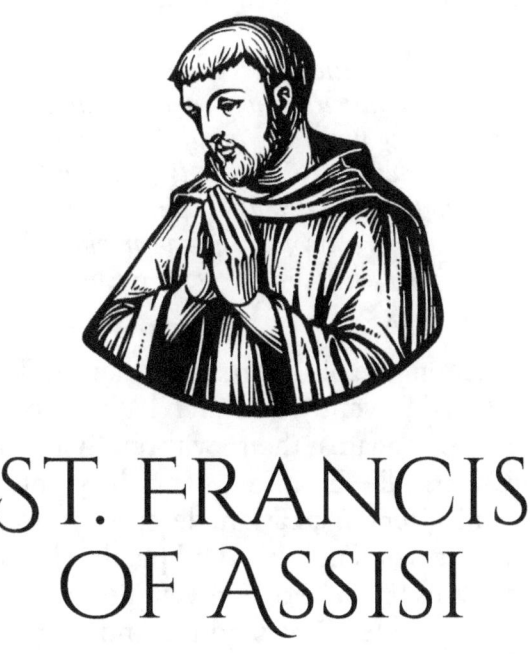

ST. FRANCIS OF ASSISI

Here we are again with another Saint. During this time, it felt that Saints were a safe default—a treasure trove of many different iconic and important spirits that I could rifle through to find something matching my intention. After all, for every topic there's a god for, there's a Saint for one, too—and likely by design, knowing the way Christianity spread like a rolling dust cloud. I did want to be fair, however. I knew that I couldn't continue running to the Saints every time—that I would have to be true to this series and speak to other Divinities, even if I could find no one to help me contact them or if plans for such help fell through at the last moment. I'd just have to take all I'd learned about divine etiquette and stick to pantheons I knew would be open to a stranger's questions.

However, as we moved into a new topic—animals—there was an iconic Saint I couldn't simply pass up, right? Therein came my decision to speak to St. Francis of Assisi, the patron of animals and merchants. His story is pretty wild (and honestly screams Sagittarius energy to me; I felt quite the kinship with him and his antics as a Sagittarius rising and moon). While as a young man he grew up loving to party and be around people and drink and dance and all that, and while his father was happy to have a son more interested in the family business than God, St. Francis eventually did get a revelation from up above. More than that, he got it while on a horse to the Promised Lands to participate in the crusades, decked out in *very* expensive armor that his father bought him for such an adventure. His father legitimately disowned him after he came back, and everyone else made fun of him, but then he went on to give up all that he had and become a happy-go-lucky man of God—one people thought had gone mad, with how much joy he could have in the absence of all his worldly possessions, aspirations, and status.

St. Francis is very much the image of a monk you're used to seeing: hair shaved up top, running around begging for his bread, yet still being so thrilled to be alive because of his faith and love of God. He's frequently pointed to as an example of holiness in the life of a Saint because of this, and no doubt, his story is intended to make people look at their own discontent as they're surrounded by all the fortunes he ever gave up. However, one of the most endearing things about him is likely his love for animals, such love that he once even wrote a sermon for the birds. Here a few lines of it:

> *My little sisters the birds,*
> *Ye owe much to God, your Creator,*
> *And ye ought to sing his praise at all times and in all places,*
> *Because he has given you liberty to fly about into all places;*
> *And though ye neither spin nor sew,*
> *He has given you a twofold and a threefold clothing*
> *For yourselves and for your offspring.*

It's said as he went giving this sermon, the birds stretched their necks, spread their wings, and opened their beaks—that they listened fervently, and even let him come up and sit among them, coming close enough to brush his cloak against them, without flying off. St. Francis understood what a lot of people today, who carelessly handle the animals and the plants of this world, do not: that all of us creatures are kin, brothers and sisters in creation, deserving of respect and love and care no matter if we have skin or fur or feathers or soft leaves and petals. Hell, even the elements and the celestial bodies may be included in this brotherhood, given his *Canticles of the Creatures.*

Saints, I'm telling you. They're just people like you and I. And yet their stories can reveal as much as that of any of our favorite myths and legends about gods and spirits. Anyway, before I go on any longer, let me show you this conversation about animals with dear St. Francis of Assisi.

What can one give a Saint that's so thrilled with having nothing on earth? Who has all of heaven? Well, like I might for any person that came by, I gave a cup of tea and a cozy place to chat. I also set on the table every animal statue I had—a fox, frog, rat, turtle, raven, and elephant—and surrounded them all with the ladybug beads of one of my rosaries. A big white candle, some moss agate, tiger's eye, sunstone, and celestite, and my angel statue also helped me connect with the idea of nature in general concerning St. Francis. With all these things out on my kitchen table, it was easier for me to sink into the zone, and to call on St. Francis to come by after a few prayers to our Creator.

"St. Francis, hello! Welcome! Can you confirm you're here with me right now?"

Between my pendulum spinning in a *yes* circle and the candle flame going ballistic, I knew he was there, and I soon saw him, too: like with St. Cyprian, we were in a sunny field outside a castle. I wonder about that castle now—if it's a part of heaven where the Saints go or something. But unlike with St. Cyprian, who stood on the edge of a cliff, we were under the shade of a single tree, and the field was full of animals of all kinds just running around and being happy.

"Oh, this is nice," I said, and St. Francis smiled. He very much looked like the way he's always depicted, with his monk robe, his big, dark eyes, and his cheerful air, and he settled down as I got the hint to use the Golden Tarot for this conversation. "Okay! Well, let's just dive on in, shall we? I've got some questions for you, and the first one is a predictable one: what do you think about people who say animals don't have souls?"

I. THOUGHTS ON THE IDEA THAT ANIMALS DON'T HAVE SOULS?

ACE of CUPS.

The cup of plenty overflows. True happiness. Peace and satisfaction, a perfect union. Spiritual fulfillment via unconditional love.

QUEEN of CUPS.

A warm, loving woman. maternal and nurturing, gentle, insightful. Creative. Blends in very easily.

KNIGHT of SWORDS.

A brash young man, hot headed but keen to do what's right. One who gets things done. Righteous anger. Courage, heriosm.

As I pulled the cards, the meanings were a little tricky to pull together, but one thing I noticed was that all of these cards featured animals—from a bird to a scorpion to a horse. It took a lot for me not to sigh. In the typical fashion of Christian spirits, St. Francis was not about to go on the meaning of a card alone, but all the symbols in this individual deck, too.

"What does the Holy Spirit come as?" St. Francis looked to me with a smile. "A dove. Who carries us in and out of battle, or across the world? Animals. Who keeps us held in love so pure it makes a man weep? Animals."

And I'm such a goon here, because I saw those animals in the field running about and having a good time, a little puppy rushing up to us with ears flapping with each step, and I started crying myself. The energy was overwhelming. It was all so wonderful, but it was very much a "we don't deserve animals" moment. *A love so pure it makes us weep* is right.

As I shed a few tears, St. Francis kept going: "Or do you folks look at your own pets with contempt, and they at you the same way? No—your pets love you in a way that people, with their boastful souls, never could.

"And yet people don't think animals, who God made first, who God filled with His love and grace, who He gave us to love and care for, and who know God's glory, don't have souls? I've never heard of something more ridiculous than that. Look at this," he said, gesturing to the field of animals, "and look at you! You can't help but weep at the sight of souls so pure."

I mean, come on. How could you not? To look at animals who don't know anything but trust and love and joy just does something to you. As my last few tears fell, I collected myself and sighed.

"Jeez. Okay, yeah, that's fair. I see what you're saying. Now, I guess to follow up on that, how did you come to the conclusion that animals were your brothers and sisters?"

2. How Did You Realize Animals Are Our Siblings?

He nodded. "You know who never judged me, even at my lowest? Even as I was thrown from my father's house, or as I turned around from the war path? Yes, it was animals. They treated me the same as always; they were worthy precisely because they knew nothing of human illusions of glory and power.

"Their pride is that of a being beautifully made by God's artful hands—not that of their own works and possessions. They are our brothers and sisters in creation, artworks of our God, and we could learn a lot from them."

"Ah, I got'cha! That's really sweet. And now that you mention it... can you tell me anything we might learn from animals specifically?"

Tragedy and loss. Pain and misfortune may strike. Hopes and dreams may fail. Mortality is inescapable. Endings, or misfortune coming to a close.

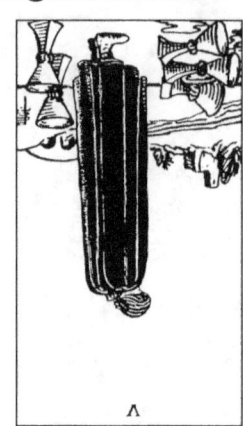

Regret and disillusionment of a transient nature. Hope soon regained.

Leadership of a team. Pragmatism, collaboration, compromise. Working with others will lead to success. Changing your own behavior is easier than changing others'.

3. What Can We Learn From Animals Specifically?

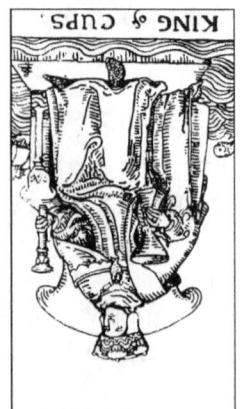

A man with great hidden sadness. Keeps emotions within, which leads to self destructive tendencies.

Talent rewarded. Creative ability brings material gain. Recognition by an employer. Status through accomplishment. Abundance. New home.

Make hay while the sun shines. Material and spiritual prosperity. Fruitfulness and bounty can be yours, but keep stock for less fortunate times.

By time I'd finished asking, Matthew 6:24-34 was flashing in my head—probably my favorite part of the Gospels, where Jesus tells us all to chill the hell out and not worry so much. In fact, I use this exact piece of the Gospels in my monthly money spells, precisely *to* remind me that money is, in fact, not everything, and that what I'm really asking for isn't boundless wealth, but just the stability and sustainment of my house.

"What is there to say that isn't obvious?" St. Francis shrugged. "Animals are strong fools, brave fools, pure fools—yet look at how they survive. It's as our Savior says: they never weave or spin, they neither reap nor sow, and yet they're clothed so beautifully, fed and cared for by the very designs of God.

"The beaver builds his dam out of instinct, yet he needs no more than that. The bees build their hives of materials from their own bodies; they ask not for more. And when they're hurt, they dare not show it—not for pride, but for safety. For all their purity, they're keenly aware of the impurity of the world, and of the game they must play to survive in it."

He pointed out into that field, where a big lion and a little lamb laid curled together. "See how the lion and the lamb lay together here? The world is unfortunately not so peaceful as this, yet animals don't fault each other for the way things are and must be. They're fools, yet they're wiser than the wisest sage. Beautiful things."

"Wow." The way this guy would just go off left me stunned half the time, honestly. He was a preacher, alright; you could feel that energy off him as much as you could witness him in action. "That's so cool! Okay, okay, okay, so I have a theory, and I want to know what you think: I feel like each animal has a specific trait that God just rolled into one when He made humans. Like, we're a culmination of all animals, you know? What do you think about that?"

4. ARE HUMANS A COMBINATION OF ALL ANIMALS' QUALITIES?

An important journey. Travel across water, literally or figuratively. Transition, leaving the past behind for new understanding and acceptance.

The cup of plenty overflows. True happiness. Peace and satisfaction, a perfect union. Spiritual fulfillment via unconditional love.

Emotional youth. Development of strong emotional ties. Peace, satisfaction, spiritual union. Deep and significant change. Quiet, gentle, or studious youth, or older person with youthful qualities.

St. Francis pursed his lips and mulled it over. Eventually he shrugged and threw some cards down for me to consider, too.

"It's a fascinating idea. I can see the truth in that—that these creatures are like a mirror, showing us pieces of ourselves. It may even be what helps us become closer to them, because you know Man is a proud and selfish thing that loves himself more than he loves others. Animals challenge us in that way, to love a creature simpler than us, yet so very equipped to teach us about ourselves. Yes, when we accept the goodness of animals, we accept and cultivate their goodness in ourselves. It's a wise idea."

"Oh! I see what you mean. That makes sense!" I scribbled away, because he was saying a *lot* with each answer; even flipping through his answers again, I found myself balking

with just how much I had to write down with him. "Alright, so how about... your favorite animal? Do you have a favorite?"

5. DO YOU HAVE A FAVORITE ANIMAL?

He shook his head. "There's no reason to choose favorites. All are magnificent. I find myself not aligned with any particular one. I would like to learn something from all of them—big or small, predator or prey, beast of land, water, or sky. Yes, Sara, if your theory has any merit, then I'd like to test it—to find myself in each and every creature that moves and breathes."

What a cool guy. I was just kind of stunned by how boldly he spoke each time he did; he had such a great aura coming off him. For all the Saints I'd spoken to, he was one that arrested you with not just the things he said, but the *energy* behind each word.

"That does sound like a fun quest, yeah! But now, some questions about you: how did you get the chutzpah to just... roll up to the Shah, or whichever leader during the crusades, and ask him to convert to Christianity? During a war? That was wild, reading about that."

6. WHERE'D YOU GET THE BEANS TO TRY AND CONVERT THE SHAH?

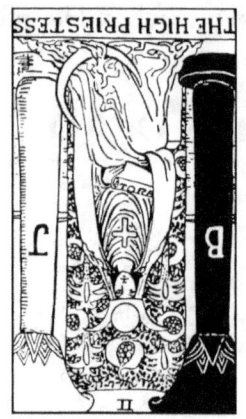  

I mean, who has the balls to just go to an enemy leader during a time of war and casually ask them to convert to the religion of their opposition? A Saint with nothing to lose in this life and everything to gain in the next, I guess.

But St. Francis sighed. "To put it simply, Sara, I was stupid. My hunger for glory wasn't yet sated; after all, what did I want to do, if not go to the battlefield and prove my glory? Not earn, *prove*. I wanted to win the battle of faith—but then I discovered faith isn't a battle.

Misguided passion, adultery, stupidity, and ignorance. Conceit.

A shallow person that likes to get what they want regardless of consequences. Spoiled and self indulgent.

There are no winners without losers. Great motivation to achieve success. Competitiveness, desire for victory and conquest. Power. Male strength.

"Not among men, anyway. Faith is fought in the world every day, not on a field amidst swords. No, no war has any business being fought in the name of God over those who have faith of their own. I was lucky to leave alive: God pulled me away from my foolishness after letting me get to the very edge of its cliff."

"Damn. I know how that feels." God has frequently let me get a taste of my own overconfident stupidity. "But another question for you: given you're also the patron of merchants, yet you gave up everything you own... what do you think of megachurch pastors? You know, the goons that yell at their congregations for not donating money for like, a whole private jet?"

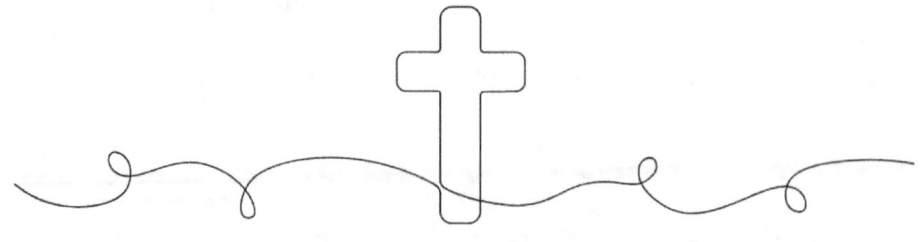

7. WHAT DO YOU THINK OF CHURCHES ABUSING WEALTH?

Weakness, intolerance, and a lack of understanding need to be overcome.

Leadership of a team. Pragmatism, collaboration, compromise. Working with others will lead to success. Changing your own behavior is easier than changing others'.

Withering away of bounty through neglect and inaction. Weakness, indecision.

If looks could kill, we'd all be dead. St. Francis scowled so hard that I thought he'd leap out of heaven just to smack these pastors I asked about.

"You see what your cards say," he said as he pointed at them. "It's as they say exactly: these men are weak. The bounty of the world isn't in these pebbles you call coins; it's in the faith of the Father that we keep in our hearts.

"Do you know how many times people asked me, 'how can you be happy with nothing?' Too many. Because once you want the fruits of this world, you only continue wanting, hungry, insatiable. Only when you fast from the world does the light of a candle warm you through, or a single bite of bread bloat your stomach. These 'pastors'—may they receive their fill of just desserts!"

And then we were standing somewhere a little less peaceful. The rock under my feet was hot, and out around us was a sea of glowing lava just sloshing around, with charred columns rising up to a cave ceiling from the churning, red-hot goo. There was also a throne, and a man sitting on it that glowed just as brightly as the lava; I couldn't see him through all that blaze and glow, so I didn't know who he was. But he was directing a long line of people to jump on in like it was a public pool.

Those who were fine and already did their own soul-cleansing work suffered no burns. St. Francis even dipped into it for a second and came out unscathed. But other folks? They came out burned down to nothing but their little flaming soul. Cleansed, purged of ego and stupidity and nonsense, ripped away from the false ideas they wove around themselves. That was the lake of fire and sulfur everyone's always so afraid about. The same one I think St. Cyprian showed me in an effort to throw me off my game and see if I'd spook.

But there's nothing to be afraid of. Contrary to popular belief—contrary even to the fiery sermons of early Saints and church fathers warning all the sinners away from evil, lest they burn and burn and burn—this lake of fire doesn't kill you or torture you forever. It's just a fiery acid bath for the soul, to clean a lifetime of gunk off you. No worries.

Watching that line of souls hop into the lava, though, I think it's safe to say that St. Francis was trying to tell me what he'd prescribe those pastors, but of course it's up to God to decide how long they need to get dunked. Who knows what'll happen, honestly?

"Alright, then. That's... interesting." Then we were back under that peaceful little tree outside the castle. "Well, as we wrap up, St. Francis, can you tell me how you see yourself?"

8. HOW DO YOU SEE YOURSELF?

"Ah." He nodded. "In life, I wanted all the glory, all the fame, all the fortune. My active denial of all such things was a choice—was me beating those desires into submission. I tamed these impulses before I have had a chance to dissolve them in the fire I just showed you."

A mean, self-ish, hard nosed woman that will do almost any-thing for money.

"That's fair—and very cool of you, I will admit." It reminded me of what a good friend of mine, Father Kyle, said on this topic: *better figure yourself out in this life before you have to figure it out in the next.* "And how do you want others to see you?"

9. HOW DO YOU WANT TO BE SEEN?

Too many roads to choose from can slow the journey. Imagination and creativity are gifts, but don't get dis-tracted. Illusions, dreams never real-ized if the wrong path is taken. A warning against materialism.

Here, St. Francis opened his arms up and beamed. "Of all the paths I could've walked in life, I found the right one. I lacked imagination in the beginning; I never could've thought of what would happen if I truly trusted God, but I did find out. I am one who, thanks be to God, found and followed the path that led me to true joy."

"Aw, that's awesome!" I couldn't help feeling such intense joy sitting next to him; he just radiated it. "And how about any messages? For myself, for others? Just a quick one before we close it up here."

10. ANY LAST MESSAGES?

"Ah, Sara, listen, because this message is for you all: Love God with all your heart, and trust in the path and the One that leads you along it. If you keep turn-ing around and choosing a different path, you'll never find the way to joy and peace.

"Trust in the One that leads you by the hand as a father does their child; be bold in your commitment. Then, you will see how brilliantly you can shine—what true joy means."

"Wow, alright. Damn." Again, stunned. "Well, that's all I have for today. Thank you, St. Francis! This was incredible! I appreciate you coming by, and I hope to see you again sometime!"

With that, St. Francis gave me one more warm smile, and I found myself being sucked out of this peaceful slice of heaven with all the animals frolicking about. It zoomed away, smaller and smaller, until all was black, and I was left sitting there at my kitchen table once more with only little representations of animals instead of the real things.

Do you have pets? If so, hug them tight and give them a treat. Do you have ani-mals in your area? If so, take a moment to appreciate them as you walk by—be

Goals can be reached if you set your path and stick to it. Fulfill-ment of hopes and dreams, success. Joy, health.

they pigeons and rats or squirrels and cardinals. I don't think I've ever met someone who genuinely disliked *all* animals. Maybe someone's a dog person or a cat person, but never has anyone said they outright hate *all* animals. And I think it's because, as I've been thinking, that there's a little bit of each of them in us. Even the ones we don't think we have in us. Even the ones we might not necessarily *want* in us (after all, cockroaches and ants and things are God's creation too, right?). But everything has its place, and its talent, and its skill, and when you sit with a spirit as enthusiastic about that as St. Francis, you understand it like you're just learning it for the first time. It's humbling, but also healing, y'know?

All I know is that this interview put a spring in my step for the rest of the day, and I'm glad I started my day with it.

ARIEL

While some names in angelology are pretty well known—like Michael and Gabriel and Uriel and Raphael—there are others that, unfortunately, get a lot less attention. Archangel Ariel, whose name means "Lion of God," is one of those. Whether one sees this angel as a man or a woman honestly depends; for me, she came through as a lady with fiery copper hair, white and silver armor, and huge wings with feathers sharp enough to slice through stone.

While she doesn't show up as an angel in the Bible (her name appears to be an unclear term referring to certain people, an altar hearth, the ruined city of Jerusalem, and so on), in many Gnostic and Jewish mystic texts, like the Pistis Sophia, she's one that brings justice to the wicked. However, she's of the rank of Virtues, and one of her biggest roles is to keep nature—especially plants and animals—in check, as well as go into battle where need be. An angel of courage and protection, she's a wonderful angel to turn to for help with connecting with the natural world and working on becoming a defender of creation oneself.

There's not much more to say that Ariel won't say herself, so let's just dive in.

Now, as goofy as they are, I do find that sometimes Doreen Virtue's Angel Oracle cards are pretty helpful with depicting certain angels. I may also, by this point, have been missing the vastly superior Angel Tarot by Travis McHenry, as these were given to me as a gift by a very generous patron. I found Ariel's card in Virtue's deck and set it up alongside with things that had to do with her station: earthy stones like moss agate, my prosperity wand, and onyx, as well as sunstone for her work in the light and celestite as my angel antenna stone. I also had my big angel statue there, my constant reminder of who and what I'm speaking to. As angels don't care for offerings, we didn't need more than that.

So I settled down at the kitchen table, said my prayers, slowed my mind down, and opened up that connection to this great angel.

"Ariel, hello, hello! Please do come chat with me this morning! I've got some questions to ask you about animals, if you don't mind."

What I saw right away was pretty wild. There was Ariel, decked out in her armor, hovering over a city in the desert and essentially condemning it to ruin by calling down great fire from heaven. Other angels were swooping in afterwards to decimate said city. But then she turned to me and swooped us off to a totally different area: a little pocket of forest, sitting on logs in a small grassy clearing among thick trees.

Her hair was long and seemed to radiate fire, and her eyes were huge, dark like empty wells. When I asked to get a sense of her energy, I felt a sense of resistance, and strength—like when you're doing squats, holding yourself steady against a heavy weight and feeling your heels digging into the floor, your legs working overtime. It was pure might and refusal to lose. Once she picked her tarot deck, the Golden Tarot by Kat Black, we were good to go.

"Alright, it seems we are ready. Thank you again for meeting with me! To start, I'd love to know: what do the angels think of animals? I know a bit about how they think about us people, but surely animals are different?"

I. WHAT DO ANGELS THINK OF ANIMALS?

Ariel sighed with a smile on her face.

"Oh, animals," she started. "They're such naive little fools. We love them, as we love you, but there can only be grief for them; there's no evil in their hearts, so they can only trust that what their stewards—you all, you humans— do is correct. They're at your mercy, and not all of you are merciful."

Ouch. "Yeah, that's fair." And while I didn't pull cards for this question, I did have to ask just as a follow up, a quick side note: "Though some would say that animals are morally inferior because they kill other animals and such; thoughts?"

Ariel shrugged. "They do what they must. This world is imperfect, and so perfect behavior is impossible."

A tendency for excess, over enthusiasm, or misplaced optimism. Still a good card.

Obstacles, problems, and resistance.

A woman of few morals, willing to use others for her own ends. Un-trustworthy and fickle.

The world is imperfect, and so perfect behavior is impossible. The implications here, I think, go beyond animals. Is this why no person is perfect either? Were we truly doomed from the start? I don't know, but I wasn't there to ponder that right then.

"I figured. I don't think animals are morally inferior; I think they just are. But now, how about the role they have in creation? Why are they here?"

2. WHAT ROLE DO ANIMALS HAVE IN CREATION?

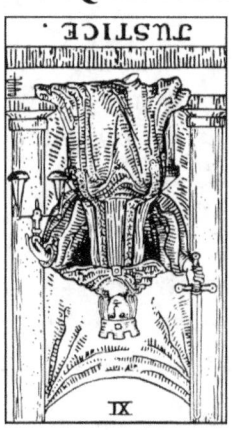

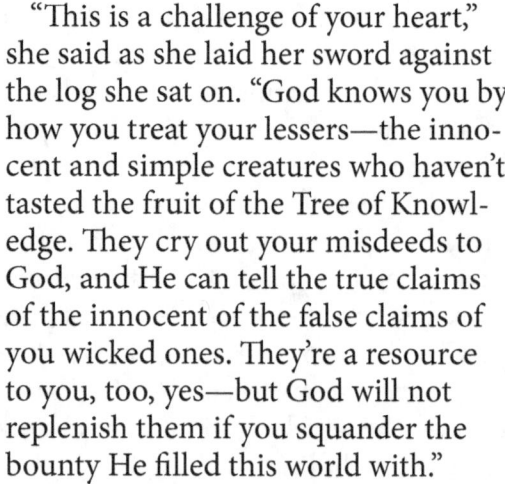

Gossip, weakness, and humiliation.

Injustice, false accusations, and prejudice.

Misguided goals. Poor decisions, or lack of decision, could lead to misery. Ill health and misfortune. Make the most of what you have.

"This is a challenge of your heart," she said as she laid her sword against the log she sat on. "God knows you by how you treat your lessers—the innocent and simple creatures who haven't tasted the fruit of the Tree of Knowledge. They cry out your misdeeds to God, and He can tell the true claims of the innocent of the false claims of you wicked ones. They're a resource to you, too, yes—but God will not replenish them if you squander the bounty He filled this world with."

'Truly I tell you, whatever you did not do for one of the least of these, you did not do for me.'

"Ah." I scribbled all that down and tapped my pencil on my temple, as if I could organize my thoughts by knocking on my head. "That's actually a perfect segue into my next question: as an angel of nature, especially plants and animals, what are your thoughts on the environmental situation we're in?"

3. THOUGHTS ON THE ENVIRONMENT?

She sighed, but this time, there was no smile. However, the cards she pulled confused me; at first glance, it seemed like an awfully positive message. As I asked for clarification, though, she scowled.

"Of course I'm disgusted with the way you humans treat the plants and animals of this world. It's despicable. However, through destruction comes opportunity. Different opportunities exist for different destructions. You humans are walking a fine line between two roads right now. The way you're going, you can't avoid ruin—but there's still time to change course and overcome this challenge of virtue."

I noticed she said "you humans" quite often. There seemed to be an

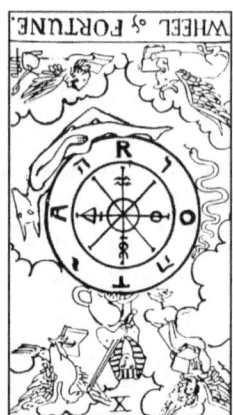

Windfall gain. Material gain, prosperity, and growth. Spiritual and material contentment, happiness, and achievement.

Creation, fertility, energy. New beginnings. Self reliance, self sufficiency, empowerment. Birth, fertility, growth, action, achievement.

Bitterness at misfortunes could be clouding one's ability to see the good luck also dealt by fate.

edge there, and given she's of a rank of angels that doesn't commonly interact with people and works to preserve what humans are actively destroying in a lot of cases, I can understand.

"Alright, well, in that case, how can humans develop a better relationship with animals? And with nature? How can we overcome this challenge?"

4. HOW CAN PEOPLE MAKE BETTER RELATIONSHIPS WITH ANIMALS?

Breaking addiction, overcoming vice, escaping bad influence.

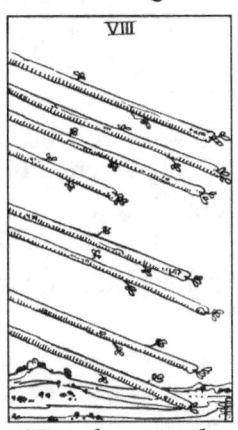

Travel, a speedy journey, ideas quickly made reality. Hasty decisions may be regretted.

Failure, division, and frustration. Possible breakdown in a relationship.

"As I said," she started, her voice hard like granite, "humanity walks a fine line between these two paths right now. You must act fast and make that choice—but you must make it only when you fully understand that choice and the ramifications of it.

"It's something you must do as a collective and as an individual every day: choose between greed and malice, love and sacrifice. The latter, it seems, has never been easy for you humans."

Huh. Not that I disagreed, but man—she was really giving it to me straight. Angels are like that, I know, but it was a good exercise in "not taking things personally," y'know?

"I understand. It's solid advice. But then, what do you think about animal familiars? Lots of people seem to like those, but I'd love to know what you think about the Witch and her Animal Familiar."

5. WHAT DO YOU THINK ABOUT ANIMAL FAMILIARS?

1. Disappointment, intrigue, and others working against you.

2. Do what is right. Fairness, justice, and equal opportunity. The strong should help the weak. Fate may aim to give all what they deserve, but sometimes she needs a helping hand.

3. One person can make the world a better place. You have seen and learned much in life. As an enlightened person, you have a responsibility to put knowledge into action. Share good fortune and lead by example.

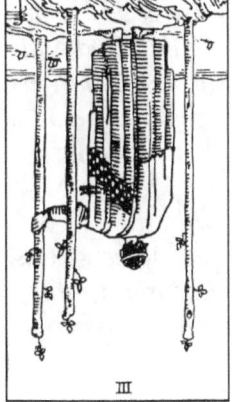

Again, there was this air of exasperation, like a parent watching their kid clip themselves on the table as they ran through the kitchen.

"You humans have such difficulty navigating this world on your own," she said. "'The strong' that must help the weak are *not* you lot. Not often. Sometimes, only the heart of innocence like an animal can help you break the blinds on your soul, and so these familiars, as you call them, are put here to soften your hearts and open your eyes.

"The animal is the strong one—the enlightened one. If you discover such an animal that makes its presence known and wants to help you, see that beast not as a tool, but as a holy mentor."

"Wow. A holy mentor—how about that! That's so cool." And it certainly explains that quality a lot of familiars have: that feeling like they know a lot more than they let on, or that their very instinct is guided towards getting their chosen people to do specific things. I know when God's getting annoyed at my distraction during a tarot session when my little white pigeon, Bilok, comes out of a dead sleep to fly on the table and peck me or my cards. "Thanks for sharing that! Now, how about the Rainbow Bridge? I hear people mention it when pets die, and I know St. Francis mentioned that animals are in heaven, but what do you think about this bridge? Does it exist?"

6. IS THE RAINBOW BRIDGE REAL?

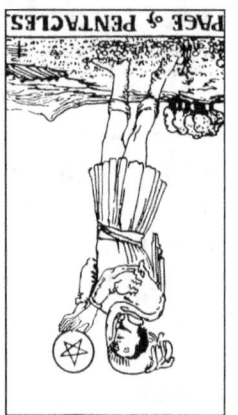

Doubt, frustration, powerlessness. Troubles worrying you and weighing you down. Illness or injury of one you love, nothing you can do to help. It may get worse before it gets better.

An untrustworthy man unwilling to work hard, but has a love of wealth.

New skills learned and applied with success. Creativity used to overcome financial hardship. Making do with little by acquiring new skills. Apprenticeship leads to a better future.

The face she gave me was a quizzical smile that looked more like a grimace.

"You lot will do and say anything to comfort yourselves—and someone is always willing to capitalize on it. This 'Rainbow Bridge' is a cute idea, but only that: an idea. Trust your departed loved ones—even your pets—are safe in a world beyond this one. Don't fill yourself up with vain comforts about it; continue pursuing your soul's work and have faith in a reunion that doesn't hinge on infantilizing yourselves or romanticizing the situation."

"That's more than fair. I understand. Well, I guess the last question of the general pile I've got for you is: what's the hardest part of your job as an angel? I'm curious about that."

7. WHAT IS THE HARDEST PART OF YOUR JOB AS AN ANGEL?

Here's the first time I saw Ariel show any kind of pain on her face. Her face drooped in a crestfallen mask, her shoulders hunching forward. I got a message that was easy to understand mainly from my conversations with other angels before, too, which was interesting.

"It hurts to do what I must do at times. Yes, I am the protector of nature—but sometimes nature must perish to punish humanity and teach you a lesson."

There were clear visions of scorched earth, droughts, barren fields, locusts, ripping over a town.

"It all comes back to you—you meddlesome creatures. However, unlike my brothers," of which, I caught a flash of Lucifer and his angels, "I'll trust

A separation. Depending on surrounding cards, this could be short term or permanent.

Trust that all will get what they deserve. Sacrifices may be necessary, and not all battles will be won. Self control is necessary. Bite your tongue.

That which wanes grows full again. Obstacles, periods of good and bad fortune, struggle through darkness. Embrace it and the light will return even faster.

God's plan and patiently away His good judgement on this world from one moment to the next. Even if I must sever my protection and stand by at times, and even if grave misfortune strikes all, I've seen this story play out enough to know nature—and humanity—always have a way of bouncing back."

"Damn." I blinked at her, because this was as blunt and soldier-esque an angel I'd ever spoken to. I guess that's what you get when you deal with angels that don't often have anything to do with humans directly like Virtues. We may take for granted how angels like Michael and Gabriel are used to coming to people and have adapted to our sensibilities. "That's... heavy. But I get what you're saying. It does sound difficult; what a heavy thing to bear. But okay, well, now's our time to get into the last few questions. To that end: how do you see yourself?"

8. HOW DO YOU SEE YOURSELF?

Ariel actually didn't choose a tarot card, but the oracle card I'd used to represent her, which signaled Prosperity.

"All abundance on earth comes from nature," she said. Material needs are met with the artful stewardship this world requires. I'm one who encourages and teaches this stewardship, and the fruits of the spirit that come with that."

"Ah, I see! That's really cool. Do you want people to see you the same, or another way...?"

9. HOW DO YOU WANT TO BE SEEN?

Again, there was an air of sadness here, a sigh hanging in the air. She turned to me and knelt down, put a hand on my shoulder, to explain.

"One thing I need you humans to understand is this: this world is but a playground for now. This is where you learn, love, struggle, fear—this is where the fruits of the spirit are grown. See me as one who helps you grow those fruits by displaying your capacity for empathy, harmony, and grace with the natural world around you."

"Oh." Fruits of the spirit growing on a playground called Earth—how interesting an idea. "I see. Fascinating. Well, before we go our separate ways again, are there any messages you have for me? Or others?"

Abandonment of materialism. Putting aside financial security in pursuit of spiritual fulfillment. Cutting off from old and seeking new. By exploring the world, you learn more about yourself.

10. ANY LAST MESSAGES?

Intense emotional turmoil. Loneliness and insecurity in a relationship.

I was surprised that she only chose one card here, and yet despite that one card, she had a lot to say.

"So long as humanity doesn't understand the inherent value, the nature of the Divine, in all things, their relationship with God will forever be one of confusion and elusivity," she said. "God is ever present. He exists in that which you exalt and that which you hate, abuse, and take for granted.

"May no choice of death or ruin of a piece of this world be an easy one. When you can mourn even the smallest life, that is when you know you have come closer to understanding God. But never get so arrogant as to think you can know Him completely, or you'll find yourself in ruins."

"Understood." Even grass, even a mosquito—every life. That's what I felt she meant: every life and place where life exists is precious. "Thank you, Ariel, for your time. I appreciate you stopping by. With that, I'll see you around!"

And then there was an image of her back over that city, drawing a great arrow of fire and shooting it towards the walls, with many angels swooping past her, sword in hand. She turned to me with a smile, and then she disappeared with the fury of wings and metal armor that rushed by her.

Duality. If there is duality in angels, how could anyone fool themselves into thinking there's no duality in God? If God created nature, how could anyone fool themselves into thinking there's no duality in nature? In us? Speaking to angels like Ariel reminds me again and again that a lot of the paper masks we put on Divinity—all the love and light and, frankly, *bullshit* we dress them up in—is just that: bullshit. We want to manicure them the way people trim hedges into funny little shapes, so that the wild and untame brush looks more recognizable and predictable to us, and yet there's no room for that when you're face to face with true, raw Divinity.

That wasn't a lesson I expected to learn here. All I wanted to know was what Ariel thought of animals. But it seems everything is an opportunity for a lesson where these beings are involved, and that's part of the reason most practitioners won't come near them: you're never ready for the war they wage on your every flaw and weakness. The angel that can be shown so delicately with bunny rabbits and pretty flowers is the same one that'll burn your city down on a single order. Can you handle that? Can I? Can any of us?

I don't know, but they're certainly not asking if we can or can't. They're just throwing all their arsenal at us anyway, and animals—they're a part of that arsenal. How you treat them says more about you than it ever will the animal. Even the scaly ones, the ugly ones, the inconvenient ones—it says a *lot* more about you, how you treat them.

I'll still be swatting mosquitos away for the rest of my life, don't get me wrong. But it's hard to get mad at them for just doing what they were made to do, I guess.

DEVANA

By this point, I'd tried for something of a pattern: for every topic, I could attempt to find a pagan deity, a Saint, an angel, and a demon. That covered the four weeks of these interviews pretty well, and while it was certainly still a lot of channeling, it helped me organize this to make this at least a little more fair, so that I didn't end up in a Saint Streak like I had earlier.

This plan would fall to shit very fast, but it was there. I don't know what to tell you; when you speak with Divinity, you can't just go looking for spirits like cans of beans at the grocery store, you know? Inspiration strikes where it does, and given I'm still (and, at this rate, likely forever) banned from both the Greek and Roman pantheons for these interviews, as well as extremely hesitant to touch anything of a non-European or non-ancient (and therefore reconstructed) religion that I don't have an established devotee's help with, the options become pretty narrow, pretty quickly. However, there's one pantheon that always feels like a home-away-from-home, and that's the pantheon of the Slavic gods.

Enter our next spirit, Devana, goddess of the hunt, wild things, the forest, and the moon. Sometimes she's considered a different form of Mokosh, too. According to Central Slavs (those of Poland, Czechia, and Slovakia), it's actually Devana that marries Veles (for us Southern Slavs, especially Slovenians, it's Morana that marries Veles), and she's often compared to Artemis and Diana, which would make sense given the associations of those two.

Her lore is pretty interesting. As a child of Perun, she was a maiden described as "arrogant" and "childish"—with a femininity absolutely no one could tame or lay claim to (and isn't that always the case, where women who value their own selves get called arrogant or some nonsense?). Still, she was an incredible hunter, though she soon took to hunting for sport rather than need, and she eventually thought she might take on even Svarog, the god of sun and fire and creation, before her father Perun had to fight her and get her to calm down.

Then Devana was married to Veles, who she really didn't want to marry. To appease her, Veles transformed himself into a basil flower, which made her calm down enough to accept the match. Their child is apparently Jarilo. Again, this lines up quite differently than the lore of the Southern Slavs, and I honestly don't even know if Devana necessarily takes a role in Slovenian lore, but as I said, many different tribes had many different ideas of who the gods were and what they got up to. Remember, friends: pan-slavic ideology, or the idea that all Slavic peoples are uniform or standard in any way, is some white supremacist, tribalist, ahistorical bullshit.

But as I was focusing on wild things and animals, I figured Devana would be a wonderful candidate for our discussions, and I wasn't wrong. Let me introduce you to this incredible and fierce goddess of the hunt.

Luckily, I was able to do this interview in the warm parts of the year, where my Thai basil was flourishing and making many a beautiful purple flower. I plucked some for the table, and I also put down other things associated with Devana, like garlic and a couple fox statues. Some earthy crystals, and some moonstone, also felt appropriate, and for an offering, I had out some fresh grapes. Grapes and vineyards are something that especially make me feel connected to my southern European, wine country heritage, and they're a great fruit to offer Divinity in general, as far as I know.

So once I was settled and ready to go, I got right to it.

"Devana, hello! Welcome! Can you please let me know that you're here?"

So, I have a theory that the gods and spirits I intend to talk to know when I am, and it seems Devana confirmed that. The night before, I was reviewing some details about her and some things I'd need before bed, and I got quite the image: a woman with long brown hair in a white dress with red embroidery, and a wreath of greenery and summer flowers on her head, standing under the full moon in a marshy field. I figured, with how vivid the image was, that this was Devana. I asked if she would come talk to me the next morning, and it seemed she agreed.

Cue the day of this interview, and that was the exact image I had again, in the same field. She chose MJ Cullinane's Guardians of the Night tarot, a deck I'd actually bought specifically for Kresnik a while back, but one that's loaded with the imagery of the forest.

"Ah, great! Thank you again for coming! Now, I do have a few questions for you, and to get us started, I guess the first thing that comes to mind is: what does it mean to be wild? As goddess of the wild things, and with your story, I'm curious to know!"

I. WHAT DOES IT MEAN TO BE WILD?

1. Breaking bonds, freedom, detachment.

2. Sharing joy with other people. Community and belonging. Benefitting from joining with others. Shapeshifter and natural maker of shenanigans. Enthusiasm gets things done.

3. Bad news, a preoccupation with projects at the expense of other priorities in life, wastefulness.

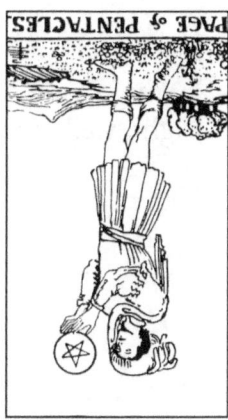

She grinned at me under the moonlight, and as a forest sprouted up from the marshes, she hopped onto one tree's big root and spoke with her whole chest.

"To be wild means no one will catch me alive," she said.

"But what about your father? Perun caught you once."

She shrugged. "Only a force wilder and more terrifying than me can ever have a chance. I will not be soothed, nor will I be won with treats and begging; only the brave can face the wild and live. It means choosing your own destiny, and when that's not possible, making the most of the cards you've been dealt. These woods, these fields, they're mine. I am queen of the wild; the animals are my folk."

"Ah, I see. That makes sense to me! Though it segues into my next question, too: as a goddess of the hunt, what role does the Hunter play in the woods, among the animals?"

2. WHAT ROLE DOES THE HUNTER PLAY IN THE WOODS?

Physical and emotional power and restraint. Controlling instincts, flexibility, intuition.

Sharing joy with other people. Community and belonging. Benefitting from joining with others. Shapeshifter and natural maker of shenanigans. Enthusiasm gets things done.

Suppression, lacking discretion, feeling incapable of expressing oneself fully.

As I pulled the cards, like Strength, I noticed they had themes of restraint, and so I paused my writing down the card meanings to ask her about it.

"Didn't you overhunt at one point in your stories, though?"

Devana huffed. "Write." And once I was done writing the card meanings down, she put her hands on her hips. "Should I keep defining you by your past and your mistakes? Or by what you learned from them? Yes, I was once a foolish and reckless huntress, always with something to prove—and yet! I learned. The Hunter is a god in the woods, you see, deciding who lives and who dies—both in the animals they kill and the pups they feed with those kills.

"It's a wretched game, a wicked battle for life, but the Hunter knows how to trade life for life; they know the value of the exchange of blood. They aren't the Warrior, who kills for honor and glory. Hunters kill for life. Transmutation—that's what a Hunter's domain is. Life for life."

"Wow. That's," I blinked at her, "that's a pretty cool way of looking at it. Thank you for that wisdom. Alright, well, how about animals, then? What can we learn from them?"

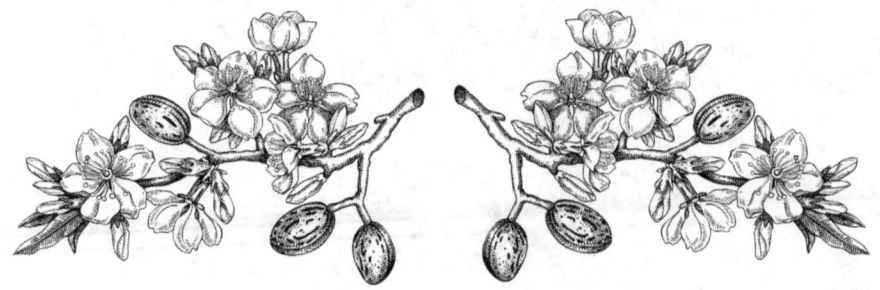

3. WHAT CAN WE LEARN FROM ANIMALS?

Again, weird cards! This goddess wasn't one that was going to let me predict her, not for a moment. Maybe that's part of the wildness, but these were nothing like what I expected. But as she spoke, and as I got images clearly in my mind—of a deer eating a snake, of a rabbit hiding in a hollow from the wolf, of the mountain lion on the prowl—I understood.

"Animals are ruthless," Devana said, and from here, we were no longer in a moonlit forest, but in a place that looked like it'd been sketched, just pen and paper; it was a place where there was unnatural silence and many birch trees separating the black shadows from the white bark and grass. It was Nav, the Slavic underworld, or at least a small opening part of it. "They have to be, or they won't eat. Animals, too, are pessimistic, always assuming the worst. They have to be that way, too, or they'll be snapped up. Animals are the Predator and they are the Prey, and their story is the oldest of all stories.

Mistrust, insecurity, and loss of hope.

Self destructive, controlling, dishonest, manipulative behaviors.

Heritage, culture, wisdom. Fitting in the box. Adaptability and problem solving. Knowing where you were, where you're going.

"Yet those boxes aren't separate. The Prey may very well become the Predator given the opportunity, and the claws and teeth of the Predator don't stop it from being shot and skinned for its fur. We learn survival from them. We know what needs to be done, feelings and niceties be damned."

As the meaning illustrated itself in my mind, with deer eating stray, unlucky toads and wolf pelts hanging from the shoulders of men, I nodded. "Understood. That's an important lesson, yeah. But then, when it comes to animals specifically... are there any animals you like the most?"

4. ARE THERE ANY ANIMALS YOU LIKE THE MOST?

Pessimism, dread, resignation.

Devana shook her head and waved me off. When I pulled the card for this question and noticed that had a porcupine on it, I paused.

"Are you telling me your favorite animal is a porcupine?"

She smiled and huffed a laugh.

"No, the Porcupine isn't my favorite animal. They're silly things, with all their spikes. But how dreadful that you would ask me to pick just one animal! Predator and Prey, they're all two sides of one coin," she said with a wink and a wolfish smile, making me wonder when and how she'd dragged that phrase out of my mind, and how often these gods listen to our conversations even when we aren't aware.

"In these two archetypes," she continued, "all things—animal, plant, and person—are found. I appreciate them all; all of them are wild, even if they pretend they're not. You can put a wolf in a suit and a rabbit in a dress, but they're both still animals and will act like it in the times that define them—the times that matter."

"Whoa. Alright. I know that people are animals, too—"

"Yes."

"—and I was wondering: how do we better connect with nature? With animals, and wild things? With our wild selves?"

5. HOW DO WE BETTER CONNECT WITH NATURE?

Chaos, discord, yet resolution on the horizon.

Creating something magnificent, life feeling boundless. Knowing what one wants from life. Positivity, confidence, authority, looking beyond the veil.

Victory is yours! Bask in the glory of achievement. Be an inspiring leader. Community, simple pleasures.

Then we were no longer in a forest of any kind, but a city, with big gray blocks for buildings and a hazy gray sky and a lifeless gray street.

"This," Devana spat as she waved her hand at the bleak landscape, "these gray blocks suck the life out of you. They make you all gray and sad. Bloom! Find a way to tend to yourself. If you must be a potted plant for a while, so be it, but tend to you roots and keep yourself well! Know your power. Snatch what you want from life like a wolf snaps up a rabbit.

"Do you think the Predator has time to feel bad about surviving? Do you think the rabbit can avoid the wolf by being small and demure? No! Whoever you are in life, put your survival first. That's the first step to being wild: putting your needs first."

The smog of the city burned my lungs and made my chest feel heavy. "Got'cha, got'cha," I muttered through the haze. "Alright, well, what's one thing we humans take for granted about animals, you think?"

6. WHAT IS ONE THING PEOPLE TAKE FOR GRANTED ABOUT ANIMALS?

"Hmph." She smiled, one eyebrow raising up like a sail. "I can answer this with one card." And as the World reversed came down, she continued. "Animals are the makeup of this world. They're all playing a part, all important. They don't have to be anything other than what they are to deserve respect—just as humans don't have to be completely defenseless and naked to still find themselves dead and eaten at the foot of a mountain.

Directionlessness and loss of ambition or vision. Being true to yourself and not imitating others.

"As you said: humans are animals, too. Shouldn't you be kinder to your fellow folk, rather than abusing them for not being what they were simply not made to be? The animals know exactly how to live life; they walk only moments after they leave the womb.

"And you? Can you humans, for all your boasting, claim such assuredness of who you are and what you're here to do? You traded your purpose for knowledge and power, and now you spend your whole lives fighting to get your purpose back. Learn from animals in this regard, and realize you take their simplicity for granted."

Holy shit. How do the questions with the fewest cards often become the densest answers?

I had to pause with this one. That hit me like a pillowcase full of bricks: we traded our purpose in this world for knowledge and power, and we've been struggling ever since to find our way back to it. Made me think of the Garden of Eden, how we had it made and had everything laid out nice and simple until we bit that apple.

"Wow. Okay. Damn." Devana laughed as I collected myself. "Well, I guess we'll move on from that truth bomb. One last general question I had was: what do you want people to learn from you?"

7. WHAT CAN PEOPLE LEARN FROM YOU?

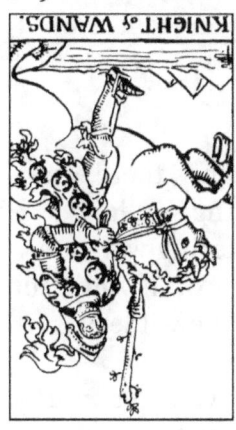

Ill placed infatuation, overhanging doubts, a dent in one's confidence, confusion. One can be their own worst enemy.

"Learn from what I say, and learn from what I've done," she said after a moment. "Too much confidence is a poison, just as too little is a deficiency. I teach the wisdom of the wild: the grit, the getting things done. When you must kill or be killed, there's no time for arrogance and flashy nonsense—only the confidence in your ability to fire a sure shot. To swing your sword when the time is right."

"Fair! I love that. So, in that case, how do you see yourself?"

8. HOW DO YOU SEE YOURSELF?

"Hmm." Devana cocked her head back and forth as if rolling the question from one side of her skull to the other. "There's a time to be all things, I'll say, and I know when to be them. I know when to be a wife, a mother, a maiden, a crone, a warrior, a hunter, a predator, a prey. I know, by experience, when there are battles I can't win and battles so easily won that they may as well have never been started. I know who I am under the many masks I wear and roles I play: I am free, and I will do anything to stay so."

"Beautiful. And how do you want others to see you?"

Cheerful and productive despite a growing to-do list. Compassion and logic. Flexibility, life balance.

9. HOW DO YOU WANT TO BE SEEN?

Boundaries. Protecting time and energy. Delegating tasks. Not taking on too much, not playing a role and suffering for it.

"Well, I might wear a mask when the time calls for it, but the sun still hits my face more than it does a mask, you understand? I don't waste time and energy being who I'm not; I refuse to do so for other people's convenience. When you see me, Devana, know that I am me before I'm a title. I can't be contained by pithy ideas like Hunter or Maiden. *Devana sem.* I am Devana."

With her head held so high, and her chest puffed out, and her eyes full of steel, there really was no questioning her insistence there. I nodded and finished up that last line before picking the cards up again.

"Alright! That's really cool; thank you for sharing that. Now, I don't know if there was anything I didn't ask that you maybe wanted to talk about? Any messages you wanted to relay before I go?"

10. ANY LAST MESSAGES?

Except for all my shuffling, not a single card felt like it should've been pulled. Suddenly, there was neither moonlit marsh or forest or Nav or gray cityscape; there was a lake, with evening sunlight streaming through the trees and shining down on Devana as she sat by the lake's glittering waters.

"No," she said with a smile. "I have nothing particular to say. For others, let them know: if you want to know something from me, have the decency to come ask me yourself. Find me in the wilderness if you've got the guts—otherwise, don't come calling."

I stared at her, then slowly put the cards away and nodded. "Will do. Thank you, Devana. I appreciate you spending some of your time with me today. With that, I'll call it a day. Goodbye for now!"

And that was that. She faded away, and then I was alone again. I sat there and mulled that last line over. It's certainly not the first time I'd received that answer, and I notice it's gods of nature or the darker themes that'll usually drop an answer like that. I guess it makes sense, too. What should a god go throwing messages around for when they don't know if anyone's even going to properly appreciate them? These are deities that don't seem to like wasting either time or breath, and that means that folks who want to hear from them are going to have to grow some courage and march up themselves.

But no risk, no reward, right?

THE FOX

Now, here's where things in my journey began to get a little more experimental. Gods and Saints. Angels and Demons. These were the things I was focused on, the "real" spirits that were worth talking to—but I couldn't help but wonder if there were more possibilities to the concepts I was looking to explore. After all, did I really need to find a deity of foxes, like Inari or Huxian? Or could I not simply reach out to the very essence of the Fox itself, the spirit manifested from humankind's repeated interaction with the creature? After all, there are many stories in which the Fox is prominent, such as the fox of Aesop's fables or in the lore of Celtic mythology. Many practitioners of druidism understand the spirits of animals to be guides and autonomous creatures in and of themselves, so I was off to do something less of spiritual journalism and more of spiritual science, seeing if this could be done.

No matter what I could call it, though, what matters is that I was coming back to the roots of what this whole adventure was truly about: exploring the limits of Divinity, pushing the bounds of what I thought was possible and expanding my horizons of what it meant to engage with such energies to begin with. This series started with a simple wish to know what else was out there, to see what other people were working with and experiencing, and so to try this out was exciting just like my very first interview with Loki was.

And surprise, surprise, it was an interview that bore some interesting fruits. So let me show you how it went.

To get started, I had my fox statues set up as a focuser, as well as some stones I felt were relevant and that represented the Fox to me: carnelian, garnet, obsidian, onyx, tiger's eye, and sunstone. Orange and black things, sunny and lucky and creative things. But as I asked God to let me speak to Fox—whoever Fox was—imagine my surprise as I found myself right where we started this month:

back with St. Francis, in his field full of animals. His gentle smile as he sat against the trunk of a big, leafy tree was a soothing way to get into this adventure, as was seeing all the animals of heaven running around without a care in the world.

St. Francis pointed me to where Fox was, and soon, I was out of that field and in a little grove, where a sleek-furred orange fox with a big fluffy tail sat on a rock. He stared at me with golden, glowing eyes, then yipped and smiled and wagged that giant tail. Afterwards, he sat there, settling into his surroundings as if reality itself were molding around him—as if my very ability to perceive him was sharpening.

"Well, hello, Fox!" I approached slowly, pen and journal in hand, and the Fox watched my every step. "I must say, I'm a little hesitant. I've never done anything like this before. So my first question is: who are you? Who is Fox?"

1. WHO OR WHAT IS THE FOX?

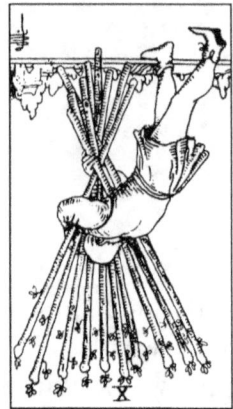

Hidden forces may be working against you. Take care that your trust is not misplaced.

There were visions of a fox running through the fields at night, with a chicken in its mouth, gunshots following after it and a dark, starry sky hanging oppressively overhead. That successful, if spurned Fox looked at me, its glowing stare piercing.

"I am the rat, the thief in the night, as people say," the Fox said with a lick of sarcasm in his voice—a deep and velvety voice, not one I thought a Fox would have. "I am the one too small to be a danger to men directly, yet large and fast and spry enough to kill them in other ways."

That chicken hanging from his mouth was awfully loud, even as it slowly died in the animal's jaws.

"I am a part of Nature," the Fox continued, "and I am not to be trifled with. Your kind wages a war against me that they will never win, for I will never die."

Jesus. What the hell? Of all the things I expected from the Fox, I did not expect such a radically, unapologetically Survivalist energy. I guess I should've, if I think about it, but it was brutal.

"I... see." I blinked at him, then kept going. Soon, the image of the night and the chicken faded, and we were back in the grove, where the Fox lounged and bathed in the sun. "So, okay—what inspired your creation, then, do you think?

2. WHAT INSPIRED YOUR CREATION?

The Fox lounged on the rock and yawned, tongue curling past his maw.

"My title is 'Dog of Cunning,'" he said. "Why work when others have done the work for you? Why rip the skin and flesh from your fingers when the wealthy don't miss a bite or two stolen off their plates? I was created, I think to teach Man how to think—how to hide a dagger behind the teeth of one's smile. I am a survivor. Sometimes honesty kills. Would Man rather die in the open for their values? Or survive in the shadows?"

An untrustworthy man who is unwilling to work hard, but who has a love of wealth.

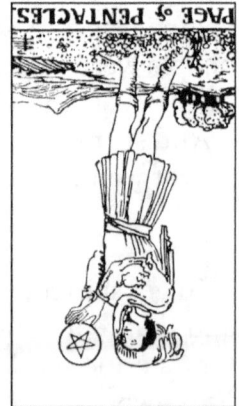

I was a little conflicted about this, to be honest. It seemed so... at odds with what God told people to do and be. But the Fox looked at me and huffed.

"If you want to throw away your life for pride," he grumbled, "speak to Lion."

"Oh. I guess that answers the question I was about to ask, then." I was thinking of asking what he was there to teach humanity, but he snowballed it all into one. "How about, then... Well, how about this? How do you feel about how you're depicted in stories, like Aesop's fable about the sour grapes?"

3. HOW DO YOU FEEL ABOUT YOUR DEPICTION IN STORIES?

Hopelessness and deceit. Try to rally your strength to overcome the adversities that face you.

And as I explained that fable, the Fox's lips curled up in a smile.

"Yes, well, we don't have energy to waste," he said. "What isn't in reach is worthless. Maybe those grapes would've been sweet and delicious, but if I can't reach them, then all I have is the dry taste of hunger—much more sour than any unripe grape will ever be."

"But do you know how you're depicted? I mean, in these stories, you always seem like you're painted in such a negative light."

"Yes, of course I know how I'm depicted—that's because I showed you these lessons, and you humans decided you were too good to heed them. Fine by me. Struggle like Worm. Slave away like Ox. But even the most upright man can benefit from shrewd eyes and a quick mind." He paused to look up into the little speck of blue sky that came from the clouds. "Not always do my lessons have to be used for deceit and thievery, like you all think."

I didn't know what to do with this energy. It felt as sharp as it sounded; it seemed like at any moment, the steel could help or cut. Even though my favorite animal is the fox, it was definitely humbling, feeling centuries of its energy and how it survived us rearing its head.

"Wow. Okay. No, I see what you mean; thank you. But then, how do you reflect yourself in Man? Can we do one card for the Good and one card for the Bad?"

4. HOW DOES THE FOX REFLECT ITSELF IN MANKIND?

1. Optimism and wanting to believe the best may confuse an important issue. Consider all possible scenarios, including the worst, and then you'll be better prepared.

2. The cup of plenty overflows. True happiness, contentment, harmony, and bliss. Peace, satisfaction, and perfect union. Fertility and bountiful abundance. Spiritual fulfillment through unconditional love.

As I shuffled, he narrowed his eyes. "You think in such dualistic terms. I am neither good nor bad. I just am."

"Yes, but let's say Positive and Negative then. Like how there are light and dark aspects of a sign in astrology, y'know?"

I don't know if Fox knew, but he did pull two cards and give me an answer, so hey.

"It's easy to be cynical when you know what you, yourself, are capable of doing to survive," said the Fox. "This is what can be considered negative, I suppose. Trust is difficult when you can't be trusted, both in the sense of others trusting you and you trusting them. Always assuming some ulterior motive, always being ready for danger, is a good way to survive, but not a way to live."

Then I had all these images of fox videos I'd seen over time: them playing on trampolines, jumping in the snow, squeaking and getting pets from loving handlers. The goofy, funny side of foxes. I knew there was that aspect, and Fox must've known I was thinking about it, because he nodded as he sat up and explained his second card.

"When our needs are met, and our worries abate, see us as you like to film us, yes. See us as beings that love to play and smile and enjoy life, no matter how little or much we have. We are a joyful piece of creation, never taking a day for granted, and many Men are, too; they carry our 'devil's luck' with a smile that uncorks the spirits of others."

"I got'cha—that's sweet! But I see you want to say something more about luck here. What is Luck to the Fox?"

5. WHAT IS LUCK TO THE FOX?

THE TOWER.

All man's creation may crumble. Material success can't protect us from ill fortune. Even the strongest fortress can fall. A warning against complacency and smugness. All we achieve is fragile. Appreciate important things.

He whipped around to look at me, padding about the grove on his paws, and his voice went somewhat icy.

"Do you think Luck is free? It has to be drawn up, like water from a well. Those with Fox aspects understand exactly what I mean: we make success look effortless and seem to have this 'devil's luck' because the Devil is in the details."

Just like that, I felt like I got hit by a two by four. It became very apparent to me here why the Fox is the animal I've always deeply associated with: because that line of thinking is exactly what went through my head every time people looked at me and told me I was just "lucky." Sure, we can call much of it luck, I guess—but I also know how to plan like a thief and nail down every detail, back-up plan, and connection. I know how to direct a hunger for more in productive ways. You have to, especially as a dreamy little creative in a world as cutthroat as this, a world that does not always seem to value creativity.

"Oh." All that realization kept dumping itself straight on my head. "Oh, shit."

The Fox's tail flicked. "Mmm. We watch. We wait. We assess. We plan. All people see is the moment our jaws snap around our prey—never the careful work that went into making that one snap count."

"Well, that does clear up a lot, I won't lie. I can see exactly what you mean—Fox aspect, indeed. But okay, so, how can people work with you?"

6. HOW CAN PEOPLE WORK WITH THE FOX?

"It's like you don't listen," he said as I was shuffling cards. Likely because the answer to this question was strewn about his previous answers, but I wanted something more direct. "As I said, much goes into being 'lucky.' Work with Fox if you want to master luck rather than letting it run wild and free, letting it master you.

"Luck is much more of a choice than humans like to believe. As your ilk says, 'it's not about the cards you're dealt, but what you do with them.' Even the worst hand can create a winner if you see all avenues and possibilities."

Gifts from the heavens. Good things come to the deserving. Intellect and vision. Connotation of dissatisfaction and yearning. Unfulfilled dreams despite success.

"Oh, fair!" I nodded along as I wrote his answers down. "No, that makes a lot of sense. Wonderful! I hope that can help someone to know, then. Now, moving on: what is one wound Fox heals in people?"

7. WHAT WOUND DOES THE FOX HEAL IN PEOPLE?

Taking the easy option will not solve a problem. Impatience and distraction will prevent a goal from being met.

Given all his talk about stealing off the plates of the more fortunate, I was so surprised to see that he pulled the Eight of Coins Reversed: a card warning against taking the easy road. But as he explained, I understood.

"You've slandered us, you Men," he said as he laid down on his rock, his ears back. "Do you know what those grapes were in that silly fable? A free gift. A gift outside the careful planning and follow through we're meant to do as Fox. It wasn't a gift for us. We hunt with stealth, and careful strikes, and squeezing ourselves into small spaces and outrunning the bullets of your guns. We heal the wounds you think we cause: the wounds of being cheated, of unfairness."

I paused. "But I mean... stealing isn't exactly fair, is it?"

The Fox grumbled, "Listen. What's that you Men say? 'All is fair in love and war'? The gift of grapes hanging there in the tree—that is for Squirrel or Sparrow. The plate of those who exploit, hoard, gorge? That is the plate of Pig—and we rip the bellies of Pig.

"We are aware that the world may detest our methods, or would rather starve themselves for pride while Pig gorges, and that is why the bounty of Pig is not free to us, yet ever so sweet when we can get a mouthful. We heal the wound of shame those like Pig inflict for our daring to think that they could stand to share, and we build the armor of reparative justice as we chip the fortress of their greed."

"Jeez, Fox. Pig is God's creation, too. Doesn't he deserve respect?"

Fox snapped his head up and pinned his ears flat against his head. "Boar was a noble animal, *Boar*. His descendant, Pig, is a fool."

I sighed and chalked that up to Fox just having an opinion about Pig. I'm sure there are nice qualities about Pig that I could learn if I went and asked the little pink flubber-nugget, but Fox wasn't having it, so I just moved on.

"Well, alright, then. How do you see yourself?"

8. HOW DO YOU SEE YOURSELF?

"I am an opportunist," Fox said as he settled back down. "Fox is the one who travels far, sees much, experiences more, all for a drop of the dew of life."

"Alright, fair. And how do you want to be seen?"

An adventurous young man. Putting ideas into action. Eagerness.

KNIGHT of WANDS.

9. HOW DO YOU WANT TO BE SEEN?

A separation. This could be a short term situation or a long term one depending on circumstances. End of relationship.

He was quick to follow up his last statement. "I am not one of harmony. If one of mine has come to bite you, reflect on your actions. Have you become like Pig? Greedy and wretched?"

In my head came the image of a pig king, wearing a crown and jewels, covered in bits of food he was snarfing down. Very *Animal Farm*.

"If so," Fox continued, "we have no business with you."

"Damn. Okay. So, I guess now, is there anything you'd like to say that I haven't asked?"

10. ANY LAST MESSAGES?

The Fox sat up and curled his tail around his feet.

"Yes, oh yes. Let me say clearly: you are in charge of your fate. Maybe God wanted me to teach you this, too: that your free will exists for a reason, and that it isn't so 'free' after all: it came with a mighty price. A price of struggle and labor. But that doesn't mean one should take on the burden of many while those made newly burdenless get fat off their labors.

A strong man who may be very opinionated. An authority figure. A perceptive, strong willed, intelligent man.

KING of SWORDS.

"Call on me when you need to make things fair again from the shadows. Call on me when you're tired of working harder and want to work smarter. And never forget that you are worth your due, your birthright, by principle of being alive: you don't have to prove yourself worthy of the blood in your veins or feel guilt over taking what you need to keep it flowing."

I sat there staring at that answer for a long time. For all Fox's steel in his answers, and all his seeming lack of patience, that was something else, that last bit.

"Incredible. Fox, thank you so much. I really appreciate this; it was a wonderful experience."

And I meant that as I put the notebook down. But Fox only scampered off the rock and looked up at me before disappearing into the woods. The connection severed not long after, causing everything to melt away to blackness and leaving me sitting there with little more than the little effigies of Fox: the statues and ornaments I had to represent him.

But I'd done it. I hadn't found a god or an angel or anything associated with foxes; I'd reached out to the raw concept of Fox, the one that graced all those fairytales and became its own being in human psyche for so long. What I'd experienced wasn't what I thought I would—but then, what did I really expect? Looking back, I'm not sure. All I do know is that there is more in this animal than just another species of mammal trying to survive. There is a treasure trove of lessons, of energy, of focus and meaning and power, within it. I imagine you could do this with any animal you like or want to know about, and no doubt for others who have an animal they deeply associate with, this might be helpful to try—because by playing with Fox like this, I found I learned more about myself that I didn't expect to learn.

That's what success looks like in this adventure, too—at least, for me. For now.

STRIBOG

With a month of exploration of animals over, the next theme came through, and it was a theme centered around the element of air. With air, there were many directions I could've gone with it: wind sprites, birds, other such things. However, the first thing I thought of when I thought of air was storms, and so there was no better place to start than with the Slavic god of the winds, storms, and wealth. He's an interesting deity, for sure, and one that I thought about when I was last in Slovenia. Namely, I thought about him as my family and I had to pass through a cloud on a ski lift to go up and down the mountain called Velika Planina, which was where a historical cow-herding settlement was built for people to learn about the old alpine ways. Clouds look soft and fluffy, but their insides are cold, windy, and scary, honestly. All I remember thinking as we swung around in those little ski lift seats, hounded by freezing mist and wind and rain, was that Stribog was kicking everyone right off that mountain for the day and letting us know who was boss around those parts.

Now, there's not a lot known about Stribog outside his association with wind and storms, but we do have evidence that he was one of the many totems Slavic pagans had at their shrines. We also have some stories that suggest he's a guardian of Vesna, using his wind to bring her back from Nav each year, and that there are eight winds that he has lordship over (each one having their own distinct name, connotation, and personality—some benevolent, some malevolent). He's a warrior, too, despite being depicted as an older man, and he fights with serious valor.

To that end, I was curious to know a bit more about him and his office, so let's jump in.

For a god of winds, the first place my mind went to was clear crystals: namely quartz. I set those out, along with a lavender candle since lavender is associated with air, and with two *pysanki*: Ukrainian colored eggs. The ones I had were ones my fiancé inherited from his babcia.

As you know, the format was simple: get set up, do the Lord's prayer to invoke God into my space, and begin looking for the deity in question. Soon enough, after calling for him and setting out an offering of vodka, I found him.

"Stribog, *pozdrav*!" I grabbed onto the first threads of an image in my mind's eye and focused. "Welcome! I have for you here a bit of vodka as an offering; please come forward and answer a few questions I have."

Immediately, I was pulled into a sunny and familiar place: the cottage Kresnik lives in. Stribog appeared there, looking very much like the Russian painter Andrey Shishkin's painting of him, to the point that I'm beginning to wonder if Shishkin didn't get some divine inspiration as he painted the Slavic gods. It seems they really like his depictions of them.

Kresnik was there, too, waving us inside his home, but Stribog, who towered over me, insisted we stay outside in the breeze, under the light of the sun. I thanked Kresnik for the offer of hospitality and continued on my way with Stribog, who had a grandfatherly smile on his face that made his cheeks rosy and his eyes twinkle.

"Well, thank you again for coming!" It was hard to keep up with him; he was much taller than me. "I guess to kick us off, I'll ask: what are the eight winds? Are they sentient, or like little gods and spirits, or...?"

I. WHAT ARE THE EIGHT WINDS?

"Ah."

Stribog beamed as we found ourselves on a dirt pathway in a field, trees on one side of us and open grass on the other, the Alps in the distance. It felt like home; I knew this place. I'd seen it before, maybe in real life, or maybe even in a past life. Who knows? But under the sunshine and the blue skies, puffs of clouds going by, it felt like a place of safety overall.

Then, around us, came a few different figures—men and women, some of which looked like bandits, one of which looked so much like Vesna, goddess of spring, that I thought it was her until she told me she wasn't Vesna. No, instead, she was the wind that carried Vesna home. Stribog stood in the middle of them, arms crossed and chest proudly puffed.

A drinking or drug problem or other destructive excess. Arrogance. Friendships taken for granted, popularity gone to your head.

What you lose on the swing, you gain on the roundabout. Life sends us trials to overcome. You can't have the good without the bad. Fresh starts.

A dispute may bring out the worst in a friend's character.

"The wings are fickle things," he said with a chuckle, as these other beings smiled and laughed with him, elbowing each other. "You can't have them in the same space, really, or they become violent, fighting with one another."

Like a tornado. That was the first thing that popped into my head.

"They carry fortune as much as disaster," Stribog continued, "and all of them are necessary to keep the physical world in balance. You can't stop a bad wind; you can only brace yourself. Likewise, you can't force a good wind to you.

"The eight are free and wild, and they're always running, racing. They are their own forces—and the spirits that work to move them," he said, gesturing to the folks around him, "are under my command."

"Ah, I get'cha!" So the winds were forces, their movers the ones holding the names and associations. "Okay, that makes sense. Now, another thing I wonder about: how do you watch over your people as a god of wind and storms?"

2. HOW DO YOU WATCH OVER PEOPLE AS A STORM GOD?

THE STAR.

Goals can be reached if one sticks to the path. Fulfillment of hopes and dreams. Success, critical acclaim.

III

Problems with a relationship. Promiscuity, a partner feeling taken for granted. Yearning for more.

ACE ᴏꜰ CUPS.

The cup of plenty overflows. True contentment, harmony, bliss. Spiritual fulfillment via unconditional love.

"Hmm." He rubbed his chin, then said, "I bring things, and I take things away. Such is the nature of wind and storm: the breeze that cools you is the gust that knocks you down, too.

"My people pray to me, and I help where fate allows, bringing the rains, winds, storms, to ensure their crops are nourished, all while abating those older winds that have a chip on their shoulder and want to see everything torn apart. I keep balance," he said, then gestured around to the few other spirits with him, "as we all do."

"Oh, cool!" The concept of wind being upset and angry and needing to be corralled painted a funny picture in my head. "Alright, then—another thing that has me curious is about the winds and storms themselves. What do you think we can learn from them, as a god that rules over them?"

3. WHAT CAN PEOPLE LEARN FROM THE WINDS?

And I turned around and saw the big mountain ahead of me, looking as if it'd been painted against the sky, and that was when I really felt it: I absolutely had been here before. I knew where I was. There was something rooting me here.

I didn't know what. But I got the sense that Stribog knew what I was feeling, and he was watching me as if waiting for me to figure it out. Then he answered my question.

"The winds are a means of travel," he said. "Carriers of men on a journey. But they aren't your helpers, nor are they your guides. They only push you in a direction. Whether you follow them or fight them is your own decision. A wise one knows not to go just anywhere the wind leads him—just like he also knows better than to argue with it or work against it.

A drinking or drug problem or other destructive excess. Arrogance. Friendships taken for granted, popularity gone to your head.

A departure. A charming, attractive, enigmatic person capable of great disloyalty. Beware trickery and fraud.

An emotional youth. Creative and inspired. Development of strong emotional ties. Deep and significant change. Quiet, gentle, studious youth or older person with youthful qualities.

"There is freedom here that cares for nothing and no one; the wind does as it pleases, following its course. Even I have to use a bit of muscle to wrestle them along when they think themselves above their goal and purpose, yeah," he said with a wink. "They're wily, explorative forces, those winds and their storms."

"Got'cha, yeah! That makes sense. And hey—I heard you're also associated with Vesna. Some say you bring her up from Nav? Can you tell me about that?"

4. HOW DO YOU HELP VESNA COME BACK FOR SPRINGTIME?

1. Time to confront your demons. You must face that which torments you. Taking risks to do what needs doing. Removing the power of vice.

2. Blissful ignorance. Optimism, naive innocence. Disregard for risks. Foolishness and ecentricity, wandering away from the sane. Unplanned influence.

3. Fear of change is inevitable, but you must face it. Resistance is futile.

"Ugh, Nav," Stribog said with a roll of his eyes. "Veles is a fine fellow, but I can't say I enjoy the trip down to get Vesna, no. Here, I send the winds, because they're fast enough to go and get her out without too much trouble from the spirits that live down below.

"And worse, a winter of good sleep makes Vesna quite the fool. It's dangerous to trek up to the surface, and sometimes, her mother leaves traps for her that you'd think she'd know to watch out for."

Suddenly, from beside Veles, Vesna appeared, her golden hair held to her head with a red and white embroidered headband, her dress billowing white with red embroidery along the sleeves and the front. She smirked at Stribog and patted his arm.

"Are you talking about me, old man?"

Stribog barked a laugh. "Yes! You, who just starts going about your business the second you step foot up here! Then Morana comes and makes a mess with her frost, and we're all in a disaster for it!"

Vesna laughed and shrugged. Then she turned to me and winked. "I just want to get to work. My power grows while my mother's wanes, no matter what she tries to do and how long she tries to hold on before going back down to Nav. It's inevitable, so why should I worry?"

Then she patted Stribog one more time and disappeared, and Stribog sighed.

"If anything happens to Vesna, we're all in trouble, *real* trouble," he said. "I carry her up and keep her safe with the winds to ensure spring comes."

"That makes sense," I said, with my own smile tugging at my lips, because watching the Slavic gods interact was like watching family bust each other up. It was sweet—but it didn't help the nagging feeling I had. Not at all. Made it worse, in fact. "But okay, okay—now when it comes to technology that uses the wind, what do you think of how humans have made use of it?"

5. WHAT DO YOU THINK OF WIND-BASED TECHNOLOGY?

Again, Stribog scowled.

"You humans. You are incredibly smart and talented, yes, yes—but by the gods, must you take every technology to its most extreme? Is there no concept of 'take what you need,' of balance? The more you grow, the more you destroy.

"That said, yes—your ability to harness the winds to help you is a feat of more than just science and ingenuity. Inspiration comes from all places, even the air and sky you think aren't watching and feeling you while you move through them. So good on you all: you heard enough from us to progress."

Oh. That's a thought: divinity being a muse for technology as much as art.

"I see, I see! Okay! And now, Perun. He's a god of thunder. You're a god of storms. How does that line up? How do you mesh together?"

A crisis may be brewing; keep your head. A ruthless man may try to crush your resistance.

Knowledge is power. Empowerment through understanding of our own abilities and the world around us. Risks must be taken. The start of something big.

A drinking or drug problem or other destructive excess. Arrogance. Friendships taken for granted, popularity gone to your head.

6. HOW DO YOU AND PERUN OVERLAP OR MESH?

Good fortune and contentment, but maybe taken for granted. Disillusionment.

That which wanes grows full again. Obstacles, good and bad fortune. Embrace what darkness brings; light will return.

The cup of plenty overflows. True contentment, harmony, bliss. Spiritual fulfillment via unconditional love.

Stribog sighed. "Well, here's how: I have to help Perun with Veles often."

I paused, surprised. "What! You mean you fight him with Perun?"

With a shrug, Stribog huffed and said, "To some extent. The man is always pushing the bounds of fate—but that's what he's here to do. Even in our battles, we are in harmony, brothers in purpose, all of us.

"My storms and rains thwart the thunder Perun hurls about with the smashing of his hammers, lest everything burn down, and I guide the spread of the rain Veles drops every times he dies, that careless one. In essence: I manage those two. Someone has to be present to call a match and stave off unnecessary consequences for mankind, after all."

"That's great," I said, thoroughly amused. But for every question, that odd feeling of belonging there, yet *not quite,* kept building, and I couldn't ignore it anymore—so I sucked in a breath and said, "Now, all of this is well and good, but Stribog... am I supposed to do something here? With you all? With the Slavic gods, or with my ancestry? Why else are we in a place that feels so familiar?"

7. WHAT AM I SUPPOSED TO DO WITH THE SLAVIC GODS?

Confront your demons. Face what torments you. Taking risks to do what needs doing. Removing the power of vice.

Abandonment of materialism. Rejecting security for spiritual fulfillment. Discovering oneself via world.

Passion unresolved leading to jealousy, frustration, and petty retribution.

Gone was the open field, the dirt path. Instead, there was a lake, and I was standing on the banks of it. I looked the same as I had when I faced Baba Yaga: a woman with darker, straighter hair, huge eyes and a huge mouth, a brownish-black dress. I stared at houses in the distance, and a sky gone brown-orange with smoke. The town was burning.

"There is something you have to do," Stribog said. "Someone to see."

Then I had a tightness in my chest, and I looked and found a sword made of diamonds spearing me through. There was no blood and no wound as I pulled it out, but it felt odd to hold.

Stribog nodded to it. "Use that sword when you're ready."

"Jesus. This is something out of a fantasy book or something," I said as I looked at the sword. "What the hell?"

Stribog smiled. "Are you not a fantasy writer?"

"I—well, yeah," I muttered, "but there's no way I'm going to go dive into this mess just for a book idea. I can make those on my own."

"True." Stribog's smile fell as he crossed his arms. "But there's a wound here that hasn't scabbed over. Heal it."

I stared at him, but I felt that was the most of an explanation I was going to get, so I just kept asking questions as if I wasn't seeing all this wild nonsense. I mean, what was I supposed to do with this information? With all that fire in the sky? Why did spirits do this: show you crazy things completely unprompted and expect you to go deal with it?

"Alright, then." I tucked whatever side quest Stribog was trying to hand me into my pocket for... whenever. If you're wondering, no, I still haven't gotten back to it, and I have no idea when I ever will. "Moving on to our last questions, I guess: how do you see yourself?"

8. HOW DO YOU SEE YOURSELF?

Doubt, frustration, powerlessness. Depression and pain, troubles and worries weighing you down. Things may get worse before they get better, but it could be worse.

We were back on that dirt path as if nothing ever happened, sunshine and green grass and blue skies all over.

"I am a trapped man," Stribog said with a sigh. "My reign is limited; there are too many forces battling against each other in this world."

I almost wondered if he meant because his religion had been displaced, and there weren't many people who would listen to him anymore as a result. It could've also been the nature of fate, though: fate, the way he talked about it, seemed to be a binding force, even if it was necessary.

"Veles causes me trouble," Stribog continued, "but this is his fate. My fate is to let men live and let men die by the air, the wind, the storms—and I do everything I can to keep men alive, but the story flows in a certain direction. I can't keep meddling. It vexes me, though."

So definitely more about fate in general.

"I hear you. And how would you like to be seen?"

9. HOW WOULD YOU LIKE TO BE SEEN?

"I know some may see me this way—or see Divinity in general this way," he said as I pulled the Empress reversed, all about indecision and calamity caused by inaction. "That we stand by while terrible things happen. And it's true. We gods are not here to make a perfect world for you lot. That's your job.

Withering away of bounty due to neglect and inaction. Weakness, indecision.

"But we are here to challenge you—even when we know the outcome. So long as you don't know the outcome, it's worth following through. Your souls, the story of them, is paramount. We are here to push you to act. You all crumble when you sit here, hands out, waiting for us to fix what we can't."

"Whoa. Shit. Okay. I didn't expect that at all. Then, I guess... are there any last messages you want to give? This is the last question I have."

10. ANY LAST MESSAGES?

A warm, loving man that gives good counsel. Intuitive, creative, gentle. No need for machismo. Spiritual satisfaction more important than wealth.

Stribog nodded and said, "Be good to each other. Remember the world is just a playground. Test yourselves. Expand your limits. Remember, this isn't your only stop in your journey. Act true to yourselves and make this world perfect before finding the next one."

Oddly esoteric. I don't know why I didn't expect a warrior storm god to not have takes like that—after all, who do I worship?—but it was surprising.

"Alright, well, thank you, Stribog! I appreciate your time and your wisdom. Thank you for showing me a few things today; I'll certainly consider them, but in the meantime, I'll see you around!"

Stribog nodded, and then the Alpine field faded away, and I was left sitting there in my kitchen again. I was still reeling from whatever disaster Stribog decided to drop in my lap from who-knows-when, but more than that, one thing stuck with me in this: the idea that a god of wind, of air, such a free element, could feel so trapped. Trapped by fate, of all things. The one thing wind couldn't uproot, blow over, or bend (along with maybe a big mountain). It wasn't what I expected at all, and yet somehow, it made perfect sense. A poetic kind of tragedy I'd figure for the gods, yet didn't think they'd back up. Yet even the winds have to obey the natural laws of the world and play their part, I guess; no one's really free from the role they have to play.

The cool thing about being humans, though, is that we get to spend all this time figuring out what *our* role really is. Some may see that as a curse, like Ariel, but really, the journey of finding our purpose seems like a luxury even gods don't have. How about that?

ANANIEL

Honestly, I didn't expect so many entities related to wind to also have to do with storms, but then again, it's clear to see how they go together. Not always, but often. On this day, however, I found myself taking a look at an angel that, had God not sent me to him once a few months ago in meditation, I honestly never would've known about. Ananiel, or the "Rain of God," is an angel of storms, winds, and dew, and before he fell with the other Watchers per the Book of Enoch, he was one of the guardians of the three winds coming from the South Gate of the world.

During the fall, however, his Nephilim children were slaughtered. He, himself, was thrown down into Sheol by none other than Archangel Michael, and hc was imprisoned there forever. To this day, I'm still entirely unsure of why I was sent to speak to this angel in the first place; all I know is that one day, God said "don't talk to Me; talk to this one," and that was where I had my first visions of the underworld tomb that is Sheol—as well as where I first met Ananiel.

What's interesting, though, is that some churches, like the Coptic Orthodox Church, actually still consider Ananiel an angel in heaven, and in fact consider him one of the Seven Archangels that still watch over humanity (along with Michael, Gabriel, and the other classic names). That's quite the discrepancy. It suggests to me that there's mischief afoot, or at least that our understanding of what angels are in heaven and not is a little skewed, so come along as we explore both the concept of air and whatever's going on with this angel.

Now, I suppose I should tell you a little something about Sheol. I thought it was a prison before I knew anything about it, and I now realize is the specifically Jewish underworld. In fact, it's the original underworld associated with God. Before there was a concept of hell, that sulfuric, burning place where the evildoers spent eternity (and a place that got imported into the religion from Zoroastrianism after the Israelites' exile in Babylon), there was a specifically separate underworld that still exists in Judaism: a still darkness that held people in stasis until Resurrection Day. In fact, some folks insist *this* is where Jesus went when He died; He was in Sheol, doing whatever He was doing down there.

It definitely looks like a tomb, though, this Sheol. In fact, it almost looks like the crypts in *Skyrim*—the ones where the draugr are laying on the wall shelves and waiting for you to walk by before getting up and smacking the hell out of you. There are shelves lines with bodies, but instead of being ancient human jerky reanimated by undead dragon priest magic, the people on these shelves look like normal people that are just sleeping.

Beyond those shelves, however, Sheol is organized in a way that makes me think of the Backrooms if it were stuck in a cave in the desert. There's sand on the floors, walls that seem to randomly section off areas for no reason and make little pockets, a big monolith that reminds me something of the monolith in *2001: A Space Odyssey* (except this one is bigger, brownish-black, and with a big hole carved out of the middle), and most Backrooms-y of all, there are things crawling about in there that are... not human. I caught a glimpse of one as I passed one of those nonsensical pockets of space. I wish I hadn't.

I set up my space with both protective and clear stones: obsidian and quartz. The protective because Sheol is a crazy place for the living, and the clear ones to better focus and channel energy. A single piece of celestite once again served as an "angel antenna." I also had a candle to signify the opening of the communication channel.

After that, when I'd done my prayers and sank into the meditation zone, I met Michael up in heaven as if I were getting ready for a school trip on a coach bus with my tired, trusted adult chaperone, and then we got down to Sheol, rolling around, looking for Ananiel. As I passed by those pockets of dead space in there, I was hoping the giant gooey shadow creatures with big eyes poking out of random parts of their body didn't follow us around. It was unnaturally silent, but it didn't take long before we found Ananiel lounging in the spot he'd carved out for himself: one with a few plants, a red chaise lounge, a table, and a few trinkets. It was a little bougie, but I guess he did have literally all of eternity to set himself up nicely in there.

Ananiel himself was an angel with long silver hair and big, round eyes. He had mushrooms growing out of his cheekbone and nothing but a somewhat mildewy cloth to cover himself up, and his wings were white with brown edges, brown like the sludge of rot on an old fruit.

"Ananiel!" I strolled in, thankful to be in an area that I discovered the other weird shadow creatures of Sheol wouldn't go, and Ananiel blinked as if surprised I'd be there. "Long time no see. I'm here to investigate the element of air, and I was wondering if you could help me out?"

He stared at me, then nodded and chose the Weaver Tarot to speak with, and that was all I needed to get going. Michael hovered above us, standing on top of one of the partitions that separated Ananiel's space from the rest of Sheol, and watched in silence.

"Alright, Ananiel, thanks for agreeing to let me bother you," I said as I settled in a little chair by his coffee table full of soggy trinkets. "First things first: what was it like to cause storms for, and with, God?"

1. WHAT WAS IT LIKE TO MAKE STORMS FOR AND WITH GOD?

Rock bottom has come; you're ready to make a decision. Hard changes are better than not changing.

Someone with a lot of energy and passion, but lacking a healthy outlet. Thrives on building new things.

As I pulled the cards, I got a sense of someone out to cause chaos because they needed to. Doing what needs to be done, but needing to find the reason to do it. Ananiel watched me parse it out, his eyes glimmering as if covered in a thick film of water, then smiled.

"You guessed right," he said. "To go with God as we make our storms—it's less about what the world needs, which is on our minds, yes, but more about... play. Teasing destruction as much as helping life flourish.

"God is a boundless God, after all; He enjoys all parts of the creative process, including destruction. The flood was the only time He indulged Himself the question of what would happen if He reset the world." Then Ananiel shrugged. "Turns out, not much changed."

"Whoa." I stared at him. God as an agent of destruction? As much as creation? If God is the God of all things, it'd only make sense, but it only confirms what I'd been feeling for a long time during my studies and interactions with God, which is that He is far more chaotic than anyone gives Him credit for. "Alright, then. Another thing I notice is that some churches say you're still an angel, but we're very clearly... not anywhere in heaven or on earth. Can you tell me a bit about what's going on here? Especially since the Book of Enoch says everyone's trapped and can't go anywhere, like Azazel."

2. WHY THE DISCREPANCY BETWEEN YOUR BEING FALLEN OR NOT?

Ananiel's face fell, but by the end of my question, he smirked.

"Do you think things stay the way they are forever? As they're written? Do you think God would punish us and not still make use of us?"

Oop.

"So long as we hold one of His aspects," Ananiel continued, "we remain in service—even if we're at odds with each other. The real prison is the mask we wear as angels. Not Sheol, not any place. Our name is the chain. So yes, I serve above, even as I wear chains below."

I looked up and saw Michael leering at him, arms crossed, as if the idea left a bad taste in his mouth.

"I see," I said as I turned back to Ananiel. My mind whirred at the thought, and I must admit, there was something so dark and dramatic in the idea; it delighted my selfish little fantasy writer heart. "That doesn't sound very fun at all. Though, given the whole fallen angel thing, I wonder how that ties into that. And why you decided to follow Azazel to begin with. You must've known it wouldn't have been a great idea, so...?"

A steam roller. Viewing the world rigidly. Great at working under pressure. Getting oneself in trouble. Chaos.

Someone getting back into the world after isolation. New beignnings, universe opening new opportunity.

3. WHY DID YOU DECIDE TO TAKE A HUMAN WIFE?

Driven and methodical. Rigorous routine and trusting the process. Gradual forward motion. Freedom with good work ethic.

The feeling of complete overwhelm and uncertainty. Loss within oneself that has shake one's foundation.

"Do you think we chose this on a whim?" He chuckled and lounged on the big red chair. "We knew it was wrong, but we wanted to make a choice for ourselves. We wanted to do, and be, more than just soldiers.

"We wanted to live as the humans lived—without direction, without an eternity of the same work. We wanted to be free, too. To, just for a minute, toss the chain off."

These answers were a lot more intense than I thought I'd get. There were more than just words in this meditation space; there was raw feeling spreading through the little alcove, like electricity scattering across the water. Deep, painful feeling that left a burn scar on the heart. But then again, what did I expect with questions like mine? I sighed and moved on.

"That's fair. I hear you. But it's still a big decision, and so I'm curious as to what even snagged your interest about humanity, that you'd go down to them?"

4. WHY WERE YOU INTERESTED IN HUMANITY?

"As I said, humans are free in a way we aren't," Ananiel said. His head tilted back onto the cushions of his seat, and he stared off at nothing. "I watched with great pride for them, seeing how they could commit themselves to something and follow through even with their short lives. I know no death. I have all the time in the world to waste. But you? You have such scant years, and yet you make the choice to use them pursuing something larger than you. It's beautiful."

Well, that was a nice sentiment. Is it me, or is it just rare to hear angels talk positively about humans? I wonder if they really don't understand or appreciate us as much as it feels sometimes, or if they simply keep so stiff and sterile so as to avoid getting too attached like the fallen Watchers.

"I appreciate that," I murmured as I wrote the flow of thoughts down, always ever a word behind. "Well, okay—so as we're talking about wind, I notice that you were once the guardian of the South Winds? How did you know which ones to let loose and which ones to hold back?"

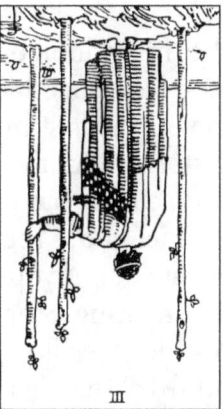

Experienced setbacks and not accomplished what you wanted because of oversights. The work done will still help.

A need for structure. Building one's vision over time by consistently showing up. Don't lose sight of your vision.

5. HOW DO YOU KNOW WHICH WINDS TO LET LOOSE?

Ananiel still wore that faraway stare as he spoke, as if he was back there at the gates.

"I knew because the winds moved like clockwork. It was a set routine: this time of year, release this wind, that time of year, that wind, so on and so forth. I had to resist releasing the good winds all the time for the people that wanted them; there's a cycle, and I couldn't intervene."

"Got'cha. And when it comes to storms—what do you think we can learn from them?"

Driven and methodical. Rigorous routine and trusting the process. Gradual forward motion. Freedom with good work ethic.

Acknowledgement of public victory. Be proud of what you've done. Be optimistic, but careful about your relationship with success.

6. WHAT CAN WE LEARN FROM THE STORMS?

Ananiel blinked that misty look out of his eyes, and as he sat up, he grinned as if someone had taken a razor to his lips and split them apart to reveal the first hint of white teeth.

"When you're in a storm, and it's all twisting and howling about you, you have no choice but to lead, even if you're only leading yourself," Ananiel said. "You can acknowledge you're scared, and that you hate it, but you need to take action and move—not sit there lamenting. Storms teach us about fear and endurance, and which we allow to last longer."

I blinked, then nodded. "That's a hell of a way of putting it. I like it! Okay, and the element of air itself, what do you think that teaches humans spiritually?"

Feeling overwhelmed and confused. Lots of energy spent for little clarity. Find stillness and surrender; your current thinking won't help you.

A beautiful balance between head and heart. Good leadership, maturity. Making others feel seen and respected. Detach from outer distractions.

7. WHAT DOES THE ELEMENT AIR TEACHES HUMANS SPIRITUALLY?

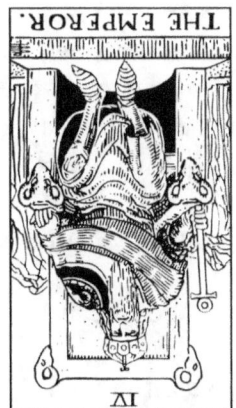

Either being too passive or too aggressive. Respect is necessary for leadership; remind yourself of all the good you've done now.

New beginnings with all things material. Prosperity on the way, or an internal shift. Show up and make the dream work.

I was really surprised that he didn't hit me with Knight of Swords like he'd been doing for a good deal of this, given that Swords are the suit of air.

"Air is sharp, loud," he said with a wave of his hand. "Unforgiving. It whips and howls, you know? It's a difficult element, untameable. When you learn to work with it, rather than against it, you achieve peace with it. You humans are learning how to do this physically, but you have a long road spiritually."

"Mmm. That scans. Well, thank you Ananiel; that's our main questions answered. Now, I'm wondering: can you tell me how you see yourself?"

8. HOW DO YOU SEE YOURSELF?

Here's where the vibe got a little dark. Poor Ananiel sat up and hunched over, heaved a big sigh.

"I am someone trapped," he said, and I was surprised to hear now that a second god or spirit of winds had this to say; it makes me wonder. "I don't know how to get out [of Sheol], if I ever will. Even when I'm able to do my work, I'm rooted here. I am a prisoner. Yet I'm still important, and one day, I will leave this place."

Michael snorted. I don't know what got into him, but for the first time, he spoke, or rather, spat: "Like hell you will, filth."

"Hey!" I don't know what got into *me*, either, but I wheeled around in my seat and spat right back, "What's wrong with you? We're here to have a conversation! Don't be a jerk; be nice!"

I'll leave you to imagine both the look *and* the energy that He Who is Like God gave me in response to that. But even if it felt like gravity suddenly got a whole lot stronger under Michael's stare, I did not apologize. I only turned right back around and cleared my throat.

"Alright, alright, and how do you want to be seen?"

It's impossible to prevent the ebb and flow of life. This is the ebb. Reflect and assess your needs in this time of loss. Change your mindset.

9. How Do You Want to Be Seen?

Abundance of energy and multitasking. Feeding off movement. Holding space. Let yourself be it all. Know your strengths and proclaim them. Be great despite your shadow.

"I still hold my pride as an angel," Ananiel said with a pointed look at Michael, "even if it's a chain. I am one who still cares for people, for the world. I've been made jaded and bitter, maybe, especially long ago, but I hold hope. I do. I am leaving this place; I will be free—and if I had to rip my wings off to do so, I would. Not to become human, but to become free."

"Hmm?" I couldn't help but feel like I was halfway to playing therapist. "I think you're the one that talked about how free humans are, though."

He shrugged. "Maybe these are the same thing. But I think if I'm to be free, it means I have to face death."

I paused, then nodded. Silly me, though. At this time, I hadn't dove into mysticism the way I have now. There's something to be said about the idea of *baptism*, and how many Christian writers and thinkers, including St. Paul, thought of baptism as a way to die with Christ and then be resurrected like Christ. Given Ananiel is an angel of all things windy and wet, I wonder if this is what he was talking about—and also why he hadn't done it yet.

After all, the One who defeated death doesn't baptize in water, but in fire.

"Yeah," I said with a shrug, ignorant to all this at that time. "But is that so bad? We have no choice but to face it, but you can choose to any time. I think there's something to be said about your state of mind. That can be a chain as much as your name, or this place."

He stared at me. I stared at him. Michael stared daggers into my back. It was a long minute. Then I clapped and broke the silence.

"So, last question! Ananiel, do you have any last messages you want to share?"

10. Any Last Messages?

Ananiel thought about it, then said, "Think of the consequences of your actions. It isn't right for people to define you for your past, but they'll know you anyway by it. What do you want to be remembered for? You have to think about this now. You can't be like the wind, running around, howling, unless you're fine with being seen as wild."

Now, I don't know about you, but I'm more than fine with that. As I finished writing his answer, I felt plenty satisfied with all that I'd gotten.

"Alright, that's that, then. Thank you for your time, Ananiel! It was good to see you again! I hope we can chat again soon."

Arrival and completion. Financial success and stability, harmony in relationships. Celebration. Think long term about your legacy, not about money. Consider what you leave behind.

With that, Ananiel smiled and laid back down on that big chair. He glanced one more time at Michael, and then the smile slipped from his face as he stared at the floor. Michael all but dragged me out of there and right back up to that entryway of Heaven, the clouds hanging over the edge of the world.

I didn't just leave the meditation space. There was something that had to be dealt with, and so, very consciously aware of how close my heels were to the edge of that cloud rafter, I found my voice.

"Michael, what was all that about, huh?"

Michael has never not been an imposing figure. Looking like a Roman legionnaire, no doubt the most common way he's been depicted since the Roman Empire became the Holy Roman Empire, he has the aura of someone who eats and breathes war. The red and gold armor. The tree trunks for biceps. The hard, square jaw and the wavy brown hair you know has spent a good deal of time under a helmet. The massive sword he carries around.

He's a lot. And he was a lot here as he turned and crossed those arms over his big chest.

"Who are you to undermine me in the face of one of those things?" Again, it felt like gravity was turned all the way up, to the point that it was an effort to keep my back straight. "Who are you to rebuke an angel of God for speaking truth?"

"Truth—?" I couldn't believe what I was hearing. "Are you serious? Listen, even if Ananiel really is stuck there forever, don't you think the way you talked to him is, I don't know, a bit fucking rude?"

He stared at me like he could burn me alive with a thought. I didn't care, though. I was already burning up with my own irritation.

"That was wrong to act that way, and you know it was wrong. I'm sorry if you felt I chipped your authority or something down there, but you as an *angel of God* should know better, better than me, than to do something like that to someone so clearly hurting, *and* someone still kind enough to entertain us in the first place!"

"Kind." Michael looked down his nose at me and *tsked* like it was a stupid idea. "So you don't repent speaking against me?"

"No." I crossed my arms, too, a perfect mirror of Michael as we stared each other down. "I'll only accept that I could've maybe said it nicer—*like you could've.* But I'm right, and you and I both know that. Love even *thy enemy,* remember?"

A long second passed before, to my complete surprise, a smile broke out on his face. The tension dissolved instantly as Michael relaxed and nodded. "Good."

Good?

"But since you admitted to being rude," Michael walked up and plopped a heavy hand on my shoulder, "which you acknowledge is wrong, you will make up for it."

Separate from the meditation space, I sighed. Angels, man. All the energy I had drained right out of me as I realized, very suddenly, that all that bullshit was a test of integrity—of whether I'd stick to the message and the morals or if I'd kowtow to an angel just because they're an angel. The realization hit me like a sack of bricks, and when I closed my eyes and faced Michael again, he was chuckling like this was some great entertainment.

"Fine," I muttered. "I'll... give it my all in the gym today. No excuses, no whining, no going easy on myself. How about that?"

Given we'd been working on discipline and pushing through the fatigue and the pain, I figured that would be enough—and I was right. He nodded and stepped back.

"That'll do. Go, now."

And then, finally, I was able to exit the meditation and pack up my things. I held my end of the deal after that; I went to the gym and did not let up. Went higher with the weights (at the slight expense of my shoulder, but it was fine in a day or two). Gave myself less rest between sets. Struggled like a worm in the mud. But I did it, with some help from that brutal leader of God's angels.

Still, though—Ananiel's face stuck in my mind the most. His face, and those honest answers he gave. It made me look at all angels—even Michael—just a touch differently, and the messages I got this day were ones that would stick with me for a long, long time.

MARI

Now, this is a bit of a wild card, I will admit—but there are so many more gods in Europe than the standard Celtic, Greek, and all that. In fact, there are gods and goddesses of people and tribes long gone, and gods and goddesses of peoples still here in small little pockets of Europe, sandwiched between dominant cultures. The Basque people are one of those groups, living in the Basque Autonomous Community, a county between northern Spain and southern France.

Today we're taking a look at one of the divinities of these people, Mari—an ancient goddess of the Basque people. Basque (in their language, Euskara) is fascinating, because it's a language that is unlike any other one around it. It's still spoken by at least 750,000 people, and it pre-dates all other Indo-European languages in the area; it is an entirely separate language family, also called a language isolate. These folks have an incredibly long history in their native region, being thought to have been in Europe since the time of cave paintings (and there is some evidence to suggest this archaeologically), which means, for all intents and purposes, that this is a truly indigenous population to this region of Europe before the migration of so many tribes and ethnic groups we now see as native to Europe today.

Their gods, too, are so fascinating. Rather than having a central pantheon with a head deity, as we understand gods of pagan religions now, there was no strict hierarchy among the Basque people's gods—and yet still, somehow, Mari reigned supreme over them all. As the great Mother figure of the religion, she gave birth to both sun and moon, and in order to stave off the sheep-eating antics of one of the night gods, Gaueko, she created the sunflower: an item that would trick nighttime spirits into counting its petals all night until dawn rose and erased them. (So now, we also know that sunflowers are an incredibly protective charm against night spirits.)

Mari has a husband, the serpent Sugaar, as well as several other lovers, and it's said that Mari and Sugaar conceive the storms that either bring joy or suffering to people. Wherever Mari goes, the winds go, and her mood dictates, too, what those winds will be like. However, more than just wind,

Mari is also depicted as a woman whose hair can be on fire, who is a part of the earth, who is surrounded by snakes at her feet and sometimes holds a flaming sickle in her hand.

With the rise of Christianity, Mari stayed a popular figure in folklore, and she was often syncretized with the Virgin Mary (a common fate for so many mother goddesses). Some of her folklore reminds me of Frau Holle, honestly: there's a story where a shepherd girl looking for a lost sheep goes to her caves, which are very dangerous places to be, because Mari will kill people who go there with dishonest intentions. The girl goes anyway, wanting her sheep badly enough to risk asking Mari something, and she finds that sheep there with Mari, who appears as a beautiful woman.

Mari offers to make the girl rich if she stays and works for the goddess in that cave for seven years, and the girl accepts. There she learns baking, weaving, magical uses of plants, how to speak to animals, and more, and at the end of seven years, she gets a giant lump of coal that, by time she reaches her village, turns into a lump of gold big enough for her to buy her own house and flock of sheep. Frau Holle has a similar story, of a girl working for her for a long time before becoming homesick and being sent home covered in gold to sell.

With all this in mind, I decided to ask Mari something about the winds—so let me show you how that went.

According to the legends, appropriate offerings to Mari were milk, wine, and water. I only had yogurt, so I put that in a bowl, alongside a cup of water and a cup of wine, and I settled in to chat. The only song in Basque I know of is Labratorium Piesni's *Xori/Passa*, so that's what I listened to the whole time. Once I'd set the space and done my prayers, settling into the zone to communicate, I called to Mari.

"Mari, welcome! Please, come join me. I have some gifts here for you, and to make my intentions clear: I really just want to ask you some questions."

When I came into the meditation space, Mari was there, looking much like the image I'd found of her: glimmering belts held her deep red and green dress together, and her thick, fluffy hair was a rich red, swallowing up her face. Her dress shifted as I looked at her; sometimes they turned gold, sometimes they turned silver, which I think were a nod to her two daughters. But she lingered near a picture of one of her caves I saw, as if asking me to come inside—and she did so again when we moved to the beach, where the water lapped at a small cave on the coast.

You're not supposed to sit in her presence if you're in the caves, but since I was neither physically in the caves nor asking her for items from the cave, I thought it was fine to at least sit on a chair. My butt wasn't touching the ground, after all, which was the important part. But after I made it clear I didn't want anything from her caves—which are filled with riches and gold and other such things—we were able to get started. She had a mischievous smile, a sparkle to her green-gold eyes, and around her floated transparent serpent-like things: wind spirits.

"Alright, Mari, thank you for joining me." I shuffled her choice of deck, the Golden Tarot. "To get started, I'd like to know: how are the winds connected to you?"

1. HOW ARE THE WINDS CONNECTED TO YOU?

All will get what they deserve. Sacrifices may be necessary; not all battles are won. Self control is necessary.

Blissful ignorance. Optimism, naive innocence. Foolishness and eccentricity, drifting from what society considers normal.

Good things come to the deserving. Gifts from the heavens. Intellect and vision. Dissatisfaction and yearning despite success.

At the time of this interview, I'd actually somehow missed the part where she *bore* those spirits, but looking back, her answers make a bit more sense.

"Winds are wonderful creatures," she said as one came by to nuzzle under her chin before floating back into the air. "They play, they protect, and yet they ask for nothing. They stoke and choke fires, they blow seeds about and break branches. They follow me still because I'm good to them, and so long have they been with me that they can guess my intentions sometimes even before I can."

They certainly hovered around her as if she was important to them. It was interesting to watch—and interesting to hear how her words translated themselves into my head. There was something poetic about the way she talked.

"I got'cha. And now, you mention that these winds can both help and hurt. That raises some questions for me about your own associations with duality, with creation and destruction. How do you balance that duality?"

2. HOW DO YOU BALANCE DUALITY OF CREATION AND DESTRUCTION?

With a shrug, Mari said, "You make many friends, you learn many things. I am a culmination of secrets passed onto me from many fellows. Each secret was a challenge to gain, each lover a force to contend with, each friend potentially dangerous—but like you, I wanted to see all that could be seen."

Oops. She got me.

"Sugaar wasn't always happy with me, but he came to understand. There are things I had to do, be—and I had to be everywhere to be them. He supported me, too. Now, I understand: both the world we see and the one we don't. It's how I help my people."

Public acclaim and good news. Success after hardship, reward for labors.

Opportunity. New love or an intimate friend. Creativity. A fear of geting hurt in love.

Failure, division, and frustration. The potential breakdown of a relationship.

I nodded as I wrote. "That makes sense. But in that case, how do you perform your role as a goddess for the people that worship you?"

3. HOW DO YOU PERFORM YOUR ROLE AS GODDESS?

Doubt, frustration, powerlessness. Troubles and worries. Depression and pain. Keeep in mind that others have it worse.

Alertness to risk may avoid calamity. Challenges met and surmounted. A time of change. Good work rewarded now.

Knowledge is power. Enlightenment through understanding fof our abilities and the world around us. Pragmatism. New beginnings.

Her stare went hard, dark, as we sat by another cave on the moss. "All gifts must be paid for," she said. "I help those who work. I worked. So too should people if they want to change their situation. But of course, the people who come to me are at their wits end."

Like the girl with the sheep.

"If they're coming to me," she continued, "it's because nothing else is left for them to do—and wise they are. I am one who punishes as much as helps, and they know this. How I help is by calling on my knowledge, my allies—calling on the power I've cultivated with years and years, centuries and millennia, of work. Not always do I help the way people expect, but aid is aid."

I considered that, then nodded. "Alright, I see what you mean. But given that you help your people still—why stay so far away from them in caves? Why not in a castle or something more ornate?"

4. WHY DO YOU STAY IN CAVES?

Suddenly, we weren't outside, but in a place covered with gold: the church on the island in Lake Bled. It was the only place that had so much gold along with paintings and rows of pews, and sure enough, there sat the statue of Mary and Jesus in the middle of all that gold.

"You mean something like this?" Mari said with a smile, her dress gone ruby red, her sash gold and red, and golden goat horns curling through her hair. When I nodded, Mari sighed, her expression slipping into something bleak. "I have been abandoned by

A tendency towards masochism; playing the martyr needlessly.

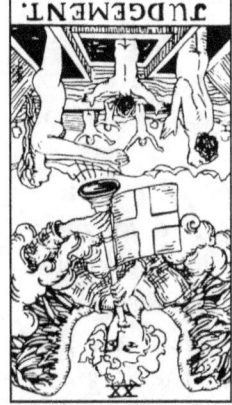

Inaction, inertia, resisting change, hopelessly fighting the inevitable.

Hopelessness and deceit. Rally strength to overcome adversity.

many now," she said, "but even before, how people would slander me for not giving them their every whim! The spirits of the world, the winds and trees and waters—they're kind. People are wicked to me, trying to steal, accusing me of being a demon.

"But there are still good people, and those who are bold and pure of heart enough to come to me are worth my time. Those who think me a stupid woman they can trick? They die."

"Fair," I said. "Completely fair. But okay, moving onto our next question: how do wind spirits cause storms? How do they act that makes them different from normal winds? I understand they come with you wherever you go, so I'm curious about it."

5. HOW ARE WIND SPIRITS DIFFERENT FROM WINDS THEMSELVES?

Significant forces at work. Take care to guard against hatred, resentment, and abuse of power.

Mari blinked at my question. "The winds? Oh, yes. I have to stay calm. These spirits," she said, and we were back on the beach, where the serpent-like spirits soared, "sense the rage in me and look to rip up the world to find the one who caused me pain. They are my dear allies. Like dragons, they claw up the land, looking for the ones who are guilty. Sometimes a whole town is so. But to keep them docile, I control myself."

Damn. I don't know, to be an entity with this much power has to be hard, no? Us humans have a similar problem; it wouldn't go well for us to lose hold of ourselves and go ballistic every time something happened. But imagine if freaking out came with the accidental consequence of deleting a town or two? That's rough.

"I see. Okay! And then, you know, another thing I heard is that you're related to the *Sorgin*, or witches. I hear witches weren't really thought of as evil among the Basque people, so I'd like to know your thoughts on them?"

6. WHAT DO YOU THINK ABOUT WITCHES?

How she scowled here. In her lore, she is attended by a court of witches, so I guess it's no surprise she went off the way she did.

"What have you all done? I teach the ways of the unseen, and you all go calling them demonic. You kill the ones who can help you understand this world in your desperation to get to the next. I am them—the *Sorgin*. They are my protegee. They retain what I've learned and keep you foolish people alive.

"You can't get to your Heaven if you forsake this earth we, the gods, have

Travel, running away from an intolerable situation.

A dull, petty, pedantic person who achieves little.

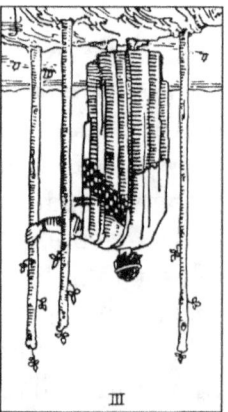

Disappointments, intrigue, others working against you.

spent so much time crafting and stitching ourselves into. Your Heaven will be empty and hollow, ashes, if you keep up your distaste for the earth that nourishes you."

Well, shit. We were in the forest when she gave me that bomb, and then we were back in the church. I looked around the church and said, "Understood. I get you, yeah, one hundred percent." And I meant it. *On earth as it is in heaven,* right? "But speaking of heaven, It's said you survived well into the Christian era, and for that I'm curious to ask: what do you think of your association with figures like Mama Mary?"

7. THOUGHTS ON ASSOCIATION WITH FIGURES LIKE MOTHER MARY?

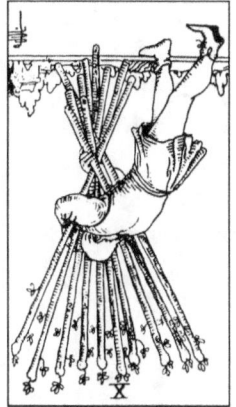

Hidden forces may be working against you. Take care that your trust isn't misplaced.

A poor investment. Debt, financial worry.

Total harmony achieved. Familial bliss, celebration, peace, and plenty. Contentment and domestic joy.

Mari huffed. "I was suspicious at first. So suspicious of all these new spirits and your God. How could I not be? Your ilk, your fellow Christians, came tearing through, killing and 'converting' and acting like fools. Pretenders at holy mysteries: that's what you Christians were and still are; you can't see even with your eyes open. Your own Lord knew this would happen."

I got a sense she was talking about when Jesus said that folks would see and not perceive, hear and not understand, which was originally a prophecy of Isaiah. Looking back, and after having read things like *The Darkening Age: The Christian Destruction of the Classical World* by Catherine Nixey, I can also see exactly why Jesus said that He would also bring not peace, but the sword. He knew. He obviously knew that the second He left this earth, things would fall to shit.

"But the one you call God?" Mari's voice dragged me out of my own dark thoughts. "Yes, I like Him. I like your Mary, too. And I hope that soon you humans might see us—and by extension, yourselves—as one togetherness. We are all One, working together in this world. So much strife, you all cause—why?"

It seemed like she was more talking to herself at times, but this made sense to me. All gods as One—not one single being, but one single force, working for the same goal, no matter what "side" we think they're on. Interesting.

"Okay, well, to get into our last questions, I'd love to know: how do you see yourself?"

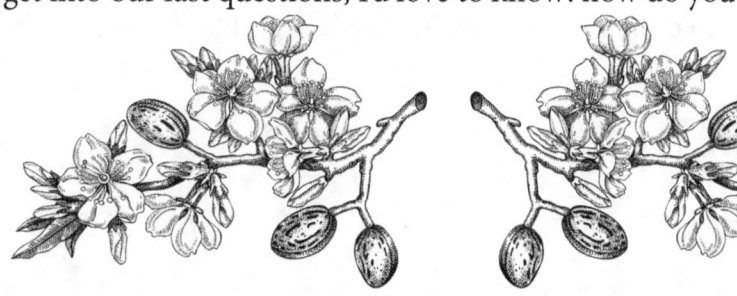

8. HOW DO YOU SEE YOURSELF?

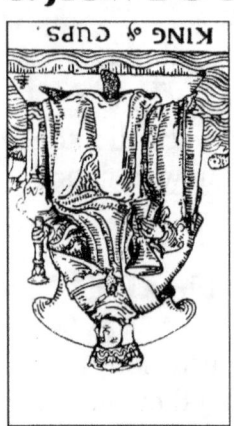

A man with great hidden sadness. Keeps emotions to himself, leading to self destructive tendencies.

She laid her chin on her palm and sighed. "I am someone tired to death and ash of humans," she said. "I grow tired of waiting for you all to figure yourselves out."

"Oh." I blinked, then muttered, "I mean, understandable. But then, how do you want to be seen? Especially since many people outside Basque folks don't seem to be too aware of you?"

9. HOW DO YOU WANT TO BE SEEN?

Mari shrugged and didn't bother choosing a card. "If I cared how mankind viewed me, I'd make more of a fuss out in the world. No, I don't care. It doesn't matter to me what you all think. You'll never get rid of me."

She said that last bit with a grin and a wink.

"Alright, I hear you," I said, smiling back. "But for our last question: do you have any messages you'd like to give? Anything I didn't ask about?"

10. ANY LAST MESSAGES?

Here, Mari leaned in close, and she once again refused to pull any cards.

"Go," she whispered. "All things have a double, another half; it's your job to find them all. Good and evil? Right and left? Sky and earth? All things are useful. All things live within us. We just need to wake them up. So go—learn. See. Be complete. Only then will you understand how wrong you've all been."

I sat there blinking for a second before pulling myself together. Then I said, "Yeah, I hear you. Thank you for that wisdom; it's good to know and put to words. But alright, well—that's that. Thank you, Mari, for giving me your time and your answers! With this, I'm closing out our meditation. Goodbye for now!"

And with another smile that crinkled the corner of her eyes, Mari disappeared into her cave, her dress a swirl of gold and green and red that waved me right out of her space. I came back to my own kitchen table and blinked the post-meditation haze away.

Tom Bombadil from *Lord of the Rings*. That's the kind of vibes Mari gave, who she reminded me of. Someone so insanely powerful, older than the concept of time, and yet someone who isn't really looking to be actively involved in the plot the way more Deus Ex Machina-type stories have their deities being. She's there to watch, to do her thing, to help where needed and where graciously asked, but otherwise doesn't care to be bothered by the greater workings of the world. She minds her business, so long as we mind ours.

What an interesting deity. I've never heard of this pantheon before, but what a fascinating one it is. And what a fascinating queen to crown such a pantheon: Mari, goddess of the Basque people, mother of winds.

VEJOPATIS

You know, while I have come to truly love the Slavic gods and feel a certain kinship with them, I will say that there's another pantheon that goes nearly entirely unnoticed (and one often dancing with Slavic gods, given how they sometimes syncretize together): the Baltic gods. And that's a shame, because the very last country to fall to Christianization was actually Lithuania by the end of the 1300s, and so their gods were around for a very long time even among all the shifting sociopolitical landscape due to Christianity's spread.

Baltic countries include Lithuania, Latvia, and Estonia, but while the Estonian language is more closely related to Finnish, the Lithuanian and Latvian language are their own special type that still shows strong traces of much older Indo-European languages. Because of their geographic placement and their history, however, I have noticed that quite a few words sound similar to German (for example: *nakts*, meaning night, like German *nacht*) or Slavic words (for example: Slavic *zima* and Lithuanian/Latvian *žiema/ziema*, meaning winter). Such is what happens when the map of Europe has been essentially drawn on an Etch-a-Sketch until, like, the 1990s.

I decided, during this investigation of the element of air, to poke through these Baltic gods and see if there was anyone that had a handle on this element. In fact, there was—but in the process of my studies, I discovered some really fascinating things, like how closely some concepts of divinity in Baltic paganism still relate to certain ideas and how the names of these deities allegedly still hold strong ties to sanskrit words/names for similar Vedic avatars and divinities. How cool is that?

Nonetheless, this deity of air I found, one with wings, two faces, and holding fish, was Vėjopatis, who, because he's described exactly the same as Bangpūtys, may very well be the same deity (at least, according to the theory of one *Baltic Pagan Blog* I found online while trying to find resources about this god). Another theory by that same blog is that maybe these two faces this god has refer to his two domains: air and sea. Nonetheless, it seems whatever we might think, Vėjopatis, whose name means lord of the winds, is a god of the waters and winds that guards the gates of heaven, blowing away the unworthy and sending them scattering. It seemed like a solid place to continue my investigations, and so I went about trying to find how I might contact this god. Eventually, I cobbled together enough to try, and these are the results of that effort.

You know well the format by now: set up the table, give an offering, do the prayers. In this case, I know that for the Baltic gods, the concept of the sacred flame was very important, so I made sure to have a candle going. I also discovered a hint about meat offerings for these gods specifically, and given I don't have much for meat just lying around, the best I could do was a slice of turkey meat. I mean, hey—meat is meat, right?

I also had a few white and blue crystals around to remind myself of the air and the sea, and then, with everything together, I settled into the zone and called out to Vėjopatis. Soon enough, I found him, and he came through in my mind's eye very quickly.

"Vėjopatis, hello!" I blinked as the colors and shapes began to solidify into something I could make sense of. "Please come sit and chat with me. I have for you a meat offering of turkey, and a bright flame here to open our way. I'm hoping to ask you some questions today."

I really am starting to suspect that God is helping me with this series, because I feel like these gods know I'm about to reach out to them, and I feel like it's because God knows my intentions. In fact, I'd go as far as to think He goes and speaks to them, the way a parent might prepare an adult to meet said parent's still very young child. The interview with Sekhmet was probably the biggest sign of this, when He directly went to her the day of when my plans of having another practitioner help me invoke her fell through. But nonetheless, something similar seemed to happen here, because it felt like Vėjopatis had been waiting for me for a minute.

We started on a cloud, with a little gate there that felt like it was mostly for show, and we were hovering over a huge lake where people drifted past on boats, fishing and enjoying the sun. Vėjopatis was just as he was described: a man with two faces and a bushy beard, and with big, angelic wings. He wore a cone-shaped hat on his head, and he sat cross-legged, overlooking the world.

"Alright, well," I said as I took in all that double-faced, winged Divinity, "thank you for joining me."

He smiled, seemingly amused by my goofy, tiny human self before him; he was big. Like, *really* big. Most spirits stay around person size when talking to me, but he didn't care to do that, it seems. Once he chose his deck, Threads of Fate's Weaver Tarot, we got into it.

"I guess to get us started, Vėjopatis, I'd love to know: how are the sky and sea intertwined?"

I. HOW ARE OCEAN AND WIND INTERTWINED?

1. Loss. A creative well being dried up. Rough emotional waters, a lack of flow. Take your power back any way possible.

2. Nearing the end of a journey. Working hard, on the right track. Everything will pay off, but there is still work to be done. Celebrate how far you've come.

"Ah." He nodded as I shuffled the deck. "They intertwine in the storm. The storm is born on the sea—what you call a 'hurricane.' It destroys, yet also, it delivers. Without wind, where would you ever go on the sea? And how would you ever deliver yourself into the perfect place to receive punishment?"

He chuckled as I blinked at him, then continued.

"The wind and sea are great forces that, together, create unimaginable opportunity."

"I hear you. That makes a lot of sense. Okay! Then, what do you think people should remember not to take for granted about the wind?"

2. WHAT DO PEOPLE TAKE FOR GRANTED ABOUT THE WIND?

Vėjopatis shrugged. "Well, the wind changes at a moment's notice. If you rely on it, there will never not be risk when traveling along with it. What it promises one hour, it may take away the next. You men—you must prepare as much as possible for such occasions."

I pursed my lips and nodded. "Fair. The unpredictability of the wind—that's a common theme, huh? But alright, alright. How about your work with the wind? How do you work with it, and your sons? The four gods of the four winds?"

1. A few options are available and you're centering yourself to make a choice. Focus on long term sustainability.

2. Failing to pay attention to all angles of a project. Go back over the plan and get an outsider's perspective.

3. HOW DO YOU AND YOUR SONS WORK WITH THE WIND?

No action to back up one's arrogance. Hurting others with words and actions. Tamper intellect with compassion.

Not thinking things through. Having neither the tools nor foundation to take a leap. Uncertainty. Release your fear.

To be clear, I asked this under the assumption that Vėjopatis was also Bangpūtys, which he seemed to confirm here.

"My sons," Vėjopatis said with a sigh. "They had to take hold of the reigns like one would a wild horse, and it took them quite some time to do so. 'Gods of wind,' they are," he said, with a little roll of his eyes, "yet I had to show them every single thing, lest they run their mouth about their titles and make us all look like fools.

"We corral the winds. we use them to aid and balance, as well as punish mankind. All according to the way things must be. We are stewards of the unpredictability of fate."

"Wow." I stared at him for a moment, just letting that sink in. The story, the world story. Vėjopatis smiled at me like a kind elder as I processed and wrote all that down. "That's pretty cool, I won't lie. So, with all that said about fate... how do you decide who's worthy of Dausos and who to blow away from the gates?"

4. HOW DO YOU DECIDE WHO IS WORTHY OF DAUSOS?

Now is a good time to connect with loved ones. Harmony, balance. Our community is our foundation.

Expansion in mental energy. Bringing new shifts. A new way of being that can feel awkward. Be curious.

Vėjopatis kept smiling, but it seemed to turn wistful, his eyes half-closed as he gazed down at the lake underneath us. "Who deserves Heaven?" His brows quirked up. "Not the broken and unmended, who still use their jagged edges to cut up those who are whole. I send those folks back from whence they came: to earth, to buff more of those edges yet. And I do so with the council of the other gods behind me. We know who needs to cook longer," he said with a grin.

And that choice of words, *cook,* wasn't lost on me. Little glimmers like these appear in my meditations sometimes, and I can only wonder: is this simply the way these things are being translated in my head? Am I the one filtering these messages into language that already aligns with my understanding of Divinity, of the Lake of Fire that all souls must endure in their purgation? Or is it a hint from these other gods, too, that there's a unifying Law of the Cosmos that they abide by?

I can't say for sure. It's anyone's guess. For me to say one or the other definitively would be for me to lie to you, and to show my own arrogance in the process. Often, I feel like I make connections between things the gods or angels or demons or Saints are saying and what I already know, but I'm aware that it may just be my bias. After all, what do I have to frame my understanding of these things on other than what I've already discovered? How can I make sense of these things unless I see them through the framework I've come to understand?

I rolled that word around in my head and nodded, then looked to Vėjopatis. "I got'cha. So, like, the unmended would hurt those who are in heaven if you let them through?"

"Yes."

"Okay! That's fascinating; thank you for your insight." Clear and to the point, that *yes.* "In a different vein, can you tell me why wind is good for mankind?"

5. WHY IS WIND GOOD FOR MANKIND?

1. Arrival in many ways. Realization of all you authentically are. This is an empowering space. Focus on yourself for now instead of others.

2. You're experiencing hiccups with a project. Step away, but don't give up. Come back to the issue later. Let go of obsession.

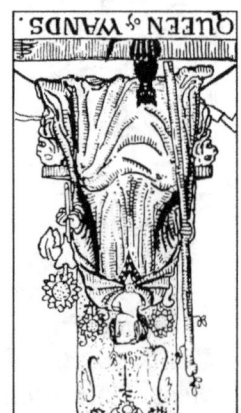

"The wind moves," he said with a shrug, his wings curling around his sitting body like a cloak. "No one likes still air. And the wind is free. It carries things on its body: ideas, voices, seeds, birds, people. The wind is a messenger, and also a gatekeeper, of things we need to express. It tries to teach you humans the value of movement, the distaste for stagnancy. Listen to it."

"Oh, that's cool." I love how poetic the gods can be. "Okay, alright—now, how about this? One thing I noticed is how similar you and the other Baltic gods are to Vedic gods, how close the languages are to Sanskrit. With that in mind... how did you come to know the Baltic people?"

6. HOW DID YOU COME TO KNOW THE BALTIC PEOPLE?

Complete dissatisfaction from your current situation. You may have a disconnect between work and success.

Paralysis as a response to negative self talk. Mind is pure chaos. Recognize how hard you're making things for yourself.

Vėjopatis raised a brow and sighed. "When you move and migrate, you lose a piece of yourself," he said. "The wind snags on everything it passes, eventually petering out. You people are much the same. You're pushed by the migrant winds, yet seeking roots like the steady earth. We were always with the Baltic people—but as their identity changed, so too did we. Like mirrors, we reflect men as man reflects us. We take the form you need to see us in."

How fascinating. It makes me wonder about egregores, about gods, in a chicken-egg style situation. More than that, remember how I said that these Baltic gods have some connections to ideas from Vedic ideas? This answer brought those ideas back up, as it also reminded me of another concept I'd been looking into, one that has a lot to do with certain sects of Vedic religion. It's called *monism*, which is the idea that all things emanate from one Source, including even gods.

"So, hold on then," I said, erasing one question to replace it with this one. "What do you think about monism, then? Different gods, different faces—all just one expression of the ultimate Creator? Is that universal, like, with my God, too? Or is that just for you and gods like you? Are you also the Vedic gods, just in a different image? Is that—?"

7. WHAT DO YOU THINK ABOUT THE CONCEPT OF MONISM?

1. A balancing act with big aspects of life all clamoring for attention. Is this sustainable? Reflect on how much is on your plate. What can you delegate elsewhere?

2. Broken bonds, a relationship fallen out of balance. Communication has become a challenge. Both parties are not up to mending it. Shift your dynamic.

Vėjopatis raised a hand as my mind went a mile a minute.

"Listen," he said. "Your God may still try to be all things, everywhere, all at once—but us? Our core broke itself into pieces trying to cover all angles, everywhere, all at once. Your God made angels to cover the many aspects of all things. Our Source created masks, too—and those masks are painted with what's available region to region. Different flora and fauna, different landscapes and backdrops.

"You paint them, too," he insisted. "You give the One ideas for how to approach you through us. So yes, we are the same as our Source, and as these masks we share our stations with across these cultures, but different, too. Like set dressings. All to reach you in ways you need to be reached. All this, in service of your growth, considering the way you twist your souls into shapes it wasn't suited for."

My mind began overheating with that one. I mean, what? Are there multiple Sources? Is God alone Source? Is there something higher than all of them combined? It felt like I could follow this line of questioning for the rest of my life and still never get an answer. But it does also seem that, at least in some pantheons and ideals, that there are absolutely gods who are the same entity, just in... different fonts, let's say.

Overall, if there's one thing I learned from spirituality, it's that multiple things can be true at once. So maybe this is the case for some, but not for others. In which case, is creation collaborative after all? A group effort between a Divine Council, like Psalm 82 mentions? Who knows anymore, really? I don't think we'll ever find out any of this for certain until we die—and if reincarnation exists, then it seems someone wipes this knowledge from our brains so we don't spoil it for everyone else, too.

"Okay, well, before my brain explodes trying to understand this," I said with a nervous chuckle, "how about we get to the last few questions? Namely, how do you see yourself?"

8. HOW DO YOU SEE YOURSELF?

Resistance to changes you need to make. Struggling to accept them. You must move forward. Take your power back.

Vėjopatis's eyes fell half shut, and he shook his head with a long look on his face. "Playing a role," he said. "That's what we're all doing, and I'm no different. I see myself as one who needs to be seen, regardless of how. As evil? Fine. As vengeful? Sure. So long as I am seen. But it is tiring."

"Oh." I blinked at him. "I see. That's interesting. How do you want to be seen, then?"

9. HOW DO YOU WANT TO BE SEEN?

He didn't pull any cards for this. The energy was flippant, the phrase he gave me matching it: "However helps people blunt their edges."

"Got'cha. And, well, last thing, then: do you have any messages? You say you want to be seen, and a lot of people who will read this will have never heard of you. What do you want to say, in this case?"

10. ANY LAST MESSAGES?

With a sidelong look, Vėjopatis said, "We are here to help your growth, but by all that is, we cannot do this work for you.

"We give you rules, we give you advice, we give you direction—but it is your choice to obey, listen, and walk. Who do you want to be? Answer that question, and then move towards your vision for yourself with pride and ease."

Complete dissatisfaction from your current situation. You may have a disconnect between work and success.

"Wow." With a nod, I said, "That's some really good stuff to know. Well, then, Vėjopatis, that wraps up all the questions I had today. Thank you so much for spending the moment to share this wisdom with me! I do appreciate it!"

He smiled and said, "Yes, well—I'm glad you got what you needed out of it. Now go. I have boats to watch down below."

Something about that struck me as heart warming, leaving it like that. I don't know. It was the energy of an older man who wants to just sit and enjoy the view of boats on the water in peace, and I get that completely.

But with us parting ways, well, that's that. A Lithuanian god—or manifestation?—of wind and sea, and the very guardian of paradise.

The concept of monism is something I appreciate and enjoy, but also something that confuses me. There are so many ideas about what God is, what Source is, what gods as multiple entities are, so on and so forth, that it's dizzying. But all I can gather is that it seems we're all plugged into the same source script, at least, and churning out the same types of ideas—because there are so many gods that are just the exact same functionally, even though they're nowhere near each other in terms of people, culture, and history. How can this happen, other than through some innate human connection we all share?

But what are we connected to? And where are we downloading this esoteric information from? I don't know. Again, I don't know if I'll ever know. However, maybe it's that little bit of *not knowing* that makes the diversity of our spirituality possible in the first place. Maybe we aren't supposed to know while we're on earth precisely so that we can encounter the Divine in the way that makes sense to us. If there really was only one way, one Truth, then that would limit the many expressions of Divinity, wouldn't it? And that would fly in the face of the very way Divinity is reflected back on us, with all of our beautiful differences.

I think we know enough to get started on our walk. And I think that's just fine.

THE HOLY SPIRIT

Oh, goodness. The next theme I looked at during this time was one that was loaded with some heavy baggage, and that was the theme of Wisdom. Naturally, this meant the first place I was going to investigate this theme was the Holy Wisdom—the Hagia Sophia, the Holy Spirit herself. I had to, right? We'd talked to Jesus, to God, and this third person of the Trinity was the only one left to get to. She had to go first.

And I know that folks reading this may wonder, not without a little alarm, why I'm referring to the Holy Spirit as her. The Bibles often translate any pronouns referring to God's spirit as he and him, after all. They insist that if God is masculine, His Spirit must be, too. But what if I told you that actually, many early Christian communities conceived not of the Trinity as Father, Son, and Holy Spirit, but as Father, Son, and Mother?

As it turns out, the various words for wisdom—even God's Wisdom—are feminine in languages that the Bible has been written in, namely Hebrew and Greek. But what we know from various church fathers in the beginnings of the Church is that it wasn't just this reason that the Holy Spirit was feminine; it was because of various words and nods to the Holy Spirit as a mother or feminine force, even as the Mother of Jesus Himself. A fantastic resource to learn more about this is Johannes van Oort's work, "The Holy Spirit as feminine: Early Christian testimonies and their interpretation," which is accessible for free online via HTS Theological Studies. Give it a read; it's really quite something.

But as this third Person in the make-up of the Godhead, I've seen many ways to understand her. Some, like Mark A. McIntosh in *Mystical Theology*, seem to position the Holy Spirit not so much as a separate autonomous figure, but as the very force that stitches together Father and Son, and the force that draws the Christian into this relationship between Father and Son to experience it for themselves. The many texts we can find mention of God's Spirit in, namely as Wisdom personified, also refer to her as a kind and righteous spirit, one that was with God at the very beginning of creation.

More, the Gnostics, a group of early Christians completely out in left field with some of the zaniest theories on Divinity, conceived of Sophia as Her own entire goddess. There are so many interesting ways to conceive of this beautiful piece of God's being, and yet this interview... it revealed to me a sense of dear Hagia Sophia that I had not ever seen before, and that also made me wonder about where I, as a fantasy writer, have been getting my inspiration from.

Let's take a look.

Now, in truth, you really don't need anything to contact the Holy Spirit—not any more than you would God or Jesus. But for the sake of making this look a little snazzy and getting myself deeper into the formal meditation zone, I had some amethysts and celestite out, along with the Apocrypha open to the Wisdom of Solomon and a lavender/bergamot candle, my purple rosary draped over the book. I was grumbling up a storm to God the whole way, mostly because I was dreading this whole set-up, but eventually I had it all done and was ready to dive in. It's a big road block for me when doing these meditations: actually getting started. Once I'm talking to an entity, it's fascinating and a great experience, but getting myself out of bed, off the couch, just generally out of whatever I was doing last, and into a space where I need to focus for up to an hour and a half straight, is torture for the dopamine-deficient mind, you know? It takes a lot out of me not just spiritually, but mentally, to focus for that long.

However, the need for answers and the need to share these things with everyone outweighs the Herculean effort it takes to jumpstart myself into a new topic—even if it sometimes take a bit to get into the groove.

So when I finally got myself together and did my prayers, I asked the Holy Spirit come through. I called Her Sophia throughout this just because it felt like a more solid name, and soon enough, the floodgates burst open.

"Sophia, hello," I said as that uncanny, otherworldly aura started settling around me. "Please join me. I have some questions about wisdom for you today, if you'd like to talk about it."

After a moment, She chose Threads of Fate's Weaver Tarot, and then here's the part where I have to laugh, because everyone always draws the Holy Spirit as a dove, and She is nothing of the sort when you actually encounter Her. I'd caught a flash of Her before, and I realized that She was eerily similar to a concept for a goddess I had in one of my future fantasy stories (a goddess of wisdom, knowledge, and magic, go figure). This goddess figure in my story idea was represented by a woman veiled in a deep blue robe, with two moons for eyes, stars woven into her braids, and her symbols were a book, torch, and staff. It's an image that has stuck with me for a long time, and I can't wait for the day I release that book series. Wouldn't you guess, it's a Messiah story. One told in the style of the Gospels: six perspectives, one narrative.

But all that discussion is for another time.

At that moment, Sophia showed up similarly, except instead of just being veiled like my fantasy goddess, She wore a nun's habit. It was both dark and light blue, edged in gold, and where Her face should've been, there was only a hole: it was like a window into space, full of stars and galaxies and pure Infinity. I almost felt like I might've gotten sucked into that space, as if it were a black hole drawing all things into itself.

Where we went was a courtyard of a church. If you've ever played Bloodborne, think of that. It was a grim scene, very Gothic church horror, and there were odd spirits rolling around, zombie-like and confused. The whole area was difficult to see clearly given it was covered in blue-grey mist.

Sophia stood there towards the end of the courtyard, near a wrought-iron fence, with such a force and weight to Her that it was overwhelming. She felt like the apex of all things, the start and end, the culmination of all that was, is, and will be—all in one pretty little nun habit.

"Uh." Let me tell you, this wasn't very much what I expected, save for the general appearance of Her. "Well, alright, then. I guess we'll get started, Sophia. And I'm sorry to keep calling You Sophia, but it just seems like it makes more sense than Holy Spirit, You know?"

She cocked her head. "You force us to take such shapes that aren't natural," She said. "You know I'm not one that can be named. This form," She ran a blue-grey hand down her robe, "is for your sake."

"I know." Entities, concepts, gods—they didn't really have forms, even if we over-ascribe attributes to them. "But it's just for the sake of connection, I guess. Right?"

Sophia nodded.

"Anyway, as my first question: what is God's wisdom?"

I. WHAT IS GOD'S WISDOM?

A holder of space. Perceptive, intuitive, nurturing, warm, heart centered. Can anticipate needs and provide a container for healing. Internal compass of the heart.

That was a big question. It should've come as no surprise that I'd get an unfathomably big answer.

Even though She pulled a single card, the answer came the same way it did with God and Jesus. That one card was more a joke than an answer, as the Queen of Cups' meaning felt like it only just scratched the surface of what she told me.

"The presence."

I closed my eyes after writing down the meaning and got bombarded with images. She took my face in her hands and brought it into the hole under her habit, and there were all things: the galaxies, the neural network of a brain, so very similar in shape and light and look. There were flowers, gold and pink, there was light and there was darkness, there was all things cloaked in darkness so deep that none could ever see.

"The presence," She said again, her voice echoing all around, inescapable. "I am the thing that slithers. I am She who sees. Mistake me not. I am everywhere. I am everyone. I live in filth as much as glory. I am the lynch pin of reality. All things happen through Me. If God is God, and Jesus is God, then I am God, too."

And I got a sense then of what that meant—for Her to be God. If God, and by extension Jesus, are the outer facing parts, the packaging on the Divinity, the design and interface of the computer, then the Holy Spirit is the hardware inside the computer. The Motherboard. The underwiring and place where all the electricity flows through and makes the computer operate.

Insane.

"Holy shit. Okay." The imagery that came through alone completely overwhelmed me. "Well, how about this, then? Next thing I have here is: how do you operate within the Trinity among us? What is your role within that?"

2. HOW DO YOU OPERATE IN THE TRINITY?

It sounds like the question that would go with all that imagery She just gave me, but it wasn't. I was so confused when She pulled the Tower reversed, but it made so much sense when I read the way the Weaver Tarot explains it.

Because this card, especially in this deck? It's all about the dark night of the soul. That inability to let things be how they once were, that sudden ability to see everything in a new light and know it needs to change, that desolation of your entire life as it feels like God disappears?

Yep, that's the Tower reversed. And that makes all the sense.

"I shatter molds," Sophia said as She stood in the center of the courtyard's cobblestone. "You live in a sea of illusion. My life's work is to break your shackles. You are not free so long as you live like beasts. The will of the flesh will never make you any more than an animal. Follow the will of your soul."

The dark night of the soul. Internal change, choices that must be made when you have total responsibility. Setting life ablaze: what was once acceptable isn't now.

And She showed me that soul—what it looks like, what it is. It started as a rough, jagged piece of quartz, only for her to refine it into a smooth, shining orb. At first I thought it was ice, but as I saw my own soul sit back in me like the core of some servitor or machine, I understood: quartz, or other clear stones like diamond, are ones that perfectly channel energies. And the thing that makes Christian magic work is channeling God's power through the "spark," or soul—the little flame of Divinity that illuminates this core of quartz. Moreover, looking at this in hindsight after having read St. Teresa of Avila's *Interior Castle*, I find something eerie in this imagery, because St. Teresa, too, described the soul as something of a gem like this—one that shines with the light of God radiating through it. I had no knowledge of this at the time I did this interview, though. It's only now, looking back, that I can tell what I saw was something truly authentic.

Still, at this time, I was already very tired, and I was only on question two.

"Wow, that's... something. So," how silly it felt to go down this list while getting the most insane amount of information, "next question: what happens when you descend on people? In Acts, and other places, it's said the Holy Spirit 'descends' on the Apostles and the like; what does that mean?"

3. WHAT DOES IT MEAN THAT YOU "DESCENDED" ON THE APOSTLES?

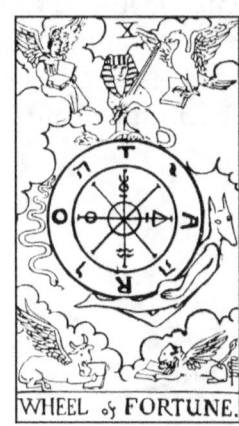

Everything is a cycle. Everything changes. Nothing we can do will prevent the cycle from unfolding. Luck, destiny, good change. Awesome happenings. A neutral force.

Sophia nodded, and I got a sense of the dark waters talked about in the beginning of Genesis, before God made the world; I got a sense of nothing, yet the potential for everything, all wrapped up into one space.

"I am the means by which all things were separated—the chaff, the wheat," She said.

And I knew instantly what She meant. There's this idea, that when God made the world, He limited Himself; He gave everything a character, a nature, a set and defined way of being. Whatever made a flower, or a rock, or a bird, was forever separated from the rest of all that was, in that black water of early, pre-creation days, that formless Expanse. It all came with God's decision to define Himself, and by extension, the very stuff of the world.

It's a pretty cool occult theory, and it's what informs a lot of medieval Christian and especially Jewish mysticism and occultism, as well as more demonolatry-centered philosophies.

"When I descend, people know this," Sophia continued, "and they are overcome with Truth that predates even the Word. That all are one, and one is all.

"How many times will you break yourselves into pieces? Split yourselves into fragments? Before, you all understand that there has only ever been one life on this planet? God chose forms for you—containers. Break them. Let your contents flow again into the river of light."

And She rose up from the ground, a sash of golden light wrapping around Her, an orb of golden light appearing at her palms and breaking open like a bubble of honey. Behind her, against the cloudy, dark grey sky, was the Tree of Life—looking very much like the Erdtree of Elden Ring, if you've ever played that game. Beside it was a smaller tree, one black and crackling with red stuff that looked like embers, and it fell down and became the inverse of this great golden tree: the Tree of Death, or Knowledge.

But that wasn't what the Tree of Knowledge looked like when Lucifer showed it to me. He'd shown me only once in our first direct connection, and in Lucifer's realm, that Tree of Knowledge looked a lot like this Tree of Life.

"Nightside's Tree looks different in the Nightside," Sophia said. She was haloed in many rings of golden light, with letters running between the spaces in between them, and finally, her face filled out—though she had only two full moons for eyes, no nose or mouth. Then She drifted back down to the ground and clasped her hands together. "What looks normal there, looks like shadow here."

What the hell.

"Fair." I feel like if I were someone who smokes, I might've been halfway through a pack by this point, because the exhaustion was not getting any better trying to parse all this gnosis. "Uh, well, moving on: some say that You are Your own goddess. What do You think of that?"

4. ARE YOU YOUR OWN GODDESS?

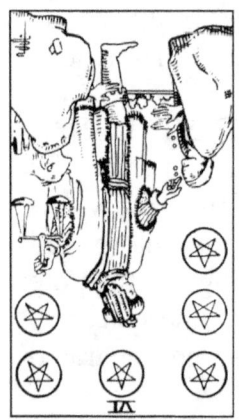

An imbalance in relationships. Always being there for others but not yourself. The ego attached to charity.

She shook Her head. "To see me as a goddess distracts from the Truth. I am of God. I need no autonomy; Truth is not that which can have its own position. It simply is.

"You cannot appease it with gifts and worship. You cannot change it. You can only engage with it from a place of honesty. I am but an Avatar of what human minds cannot readily perceive."

"Interesting. Alright, then, what do You think of how people feminize You? And call You the Holy Mother instead of Holy Spirit?"

5. WHAT DO YOU THINK OF YOUR FEMINIZATION?

"All things, Sara," She said with the air of a smile in the near-blank slate of her face. "I am all things. That includes feminine things. Divinity takes the form you need to see, not always the one you want to see."

It made me think of Quan Yin, once a male piece of Divinity turned female to help people in a form that would jar them and shake their egos loose, reminding them that femininity is just as worthy of enlightenment as masculinity. Sophia nodded as the thought crossed my mind.

"If a lens of Divinity is serving your filth, you are not seeing Divinity; you are seeing your ego. If you wish to see God, or me, as Man or Woman, you are wrong both ways. If you see us as All, you're already in Heaven."

Cue my sitting there with a head that felt full of mist: empty but not. That was a lot to take in, the way She explained it, with the energy She explained it with.

"Okay, okay, that makes sense." And by "makes sense," I meant it melted my brain into soup and left me knowing yet not quite being able to articulate what it was I was knowing. "Next, then: how can people become attuned to Your wisdom?"

A person with lots of energy. Curious, excited, quick witted. Exceptionally intelligent and holding insights beyond their years. Challenging the status quo. Raw, passionate energy. A beginning.

6. HOW CAN PEOPLE BE ATTUNED TO YOUR ENERGY?

A focus on all things external, born of imbalance of the ego. If we're focused on what others think or on trying to impress others, we won't make good long term choices. Detach and ground within yourself.

Once again, what a weird card She pulled. But once again, it also made sense as I read. It warned against focusing on the external, material world, and it encouraged grounding within oneself.

"Come in," Sophia said, Her whisper a beckoning sound. "Come inside. Inside is where you'll find Me. You cannot find Me in things—or the trappings of the world. Where your spirit is, is God's."

And a thought crossed my mind as the images came: what if we're the illusion? And the world of spirits is the real world? What if our bodies make us nothing but a deaf, blind box to the things that are True? By the images Sophia gave me, of other quartz-souls taking on avatars of people—dead loved ones, mostly—who then went yelling and grabbing at the people still alive on earth that walked past them completely unseeing, it seemed the idea wasn't too far off.

"Alright. But then, how does this wisdom help us navigate life?"

7. HOW DOES WISDOM HELP NAVIGATE LIFE?

Sophia pulled no cards for this. She simply spoke, or rather, She whispered with all the gentleness of a mother singing its child a lullaby.

"It helps you not take things so seriously," She said. "It helps you become soft. It helps you breathe not from the lungs, but the soul."

Somehow, the thought crossed my mind that I didn't mean to actually ask her: *but what is in those churches, then? What is this thing that people claim is the Holy Spirit, that makes them fall down and convulse and act crazy?*

She heard me think it and said, "For all things, there is an inverse. If there is a Truth, then there exists also a Falsehood, a false peace of the flesh."

And it rang so loud in my head, reminded me so viscerally of something else, that I had to go to Google and find Mary Magdalene's Seven Powers (also known as the Seven Demons, the things Jesus cleared from her when they first met). Sure enough, one of them was the Foolish Wisdom of the Flesh.

So there's the Holy Wisdom of the Spirit, and the Foolish Wisdom of the Flesh. Truth and Falsehood. And one is very heavily affecting people, whereas the other is unpalatable. Maybe this is what kept me away from this interview all this time: the whining of the flesh, the tricks and traps of the ego, the excuses and oppression of a physical mind and body on the will of my own spirit.

Huh.

"Okay, okay—how do you want people to see you, then?"

8. HOW DO YOU WANT TO BE SEEN?

Again, no cards. She only flashed the stanzas of *The Thunder: Perfect Mind* in my head, which tells me that if you want to know how to see her, you best get to reading that, because that bit of early Christian scripture (that never got included in the Bible) is written in the voice of the Holy Spirit. Read that, and you'll know how She wants to be seen.

"And how do you see yourself, then? Sorry, went a little backwards there."

9. HOW DO YOU SEE YOURSELF?

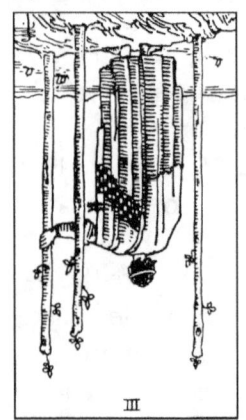

You may have experienced setbacks and not accomplished what you wanted to. Nothing you did was wasted. Prepare for changes and shifts; be open to what you never imagined.

Another odd card. One talking about falling short of achieving expectations and reminding oneself that nothing was wasted.

"There were consequences We didn't expect when We split the world into so many tangible pieces," Sophia whispered. "But We see now the way the imperfect makes things perfect. This is good. This is how you become True Men—by deciding to be."

I paused, mentally digesting that, then moved on. "Okay, well, here's our last question then, Sophia: do You have any messages You want to deliver?"

10. ANY LAST MESSAGES?

She shook Her head. "No. I deliver messages myself. All will know what they need to know, when they need to know it."

"Well, shit. Alright. Fair enough. I guess this is goodbye for now, then—but thank you, seriously, for showing me all of this. This was wild."

And with that, we parted ways, and I reminded myself that I had to get my ass out the door if I was going to get laundry done before the sun went down. The mundane always comes creeping in to disrupt the magical, you know? As a still-not-thirty-year-old, living in an apartment with no laundry machines, I use this little inconvenience of life as an excuse to go bother my parents once every other week (and do the entirety of two weeks' worth of laundry in one go). It's actually awesome. Highly recommend using something like that as an excuse to haunt your parents like a noisy ghost and eat all their cheese and crackers every so often.

But now, that bit about True Men... I gotta say, it reminded me of a story my dad wanted to write, which was essentially beamed into his brain through another crazy dream: the idea that God is stuck somewhere, and that we have to go find Him, and all religion has been His attempt at getting that message to us. When I told my dad about what I'd learned about the Sephiroth of Kabbalah, and how in Jewish mysticism, God is sitting in Keter while we're all bumming around in Malkuth, he was blown away to find that this idea already existed.

While I've never dipped into actual Sephirothic initiations (because that's purely Jewish mysticism I just don't have any business touching, at least not without an actual Jewish rabbi and Kabbalist that would be willing to let a Christian see a thing or two of their faith and mystic tradition), I have taken the time to learn what it is just for the sake of knowing, and as a result, I wonder myself sometimes. Did God accidentally trap Himself, when He defined Himself? Maybe. But did He see the value in this occurrence, as it taught all of us how to define, undefine, and redefine ourselves over the course of our existence, learning how to rejoin Him in the formlessness of the Divine Truth? Maybe. Either way, it's a lot to take in, and I'm pretty sure I'd spent half of this interview just lost in the esoteric sauce between pulling cards and writing all this down.

But that's what you get when you talk not to just God, not to just Jesus, but the very essence that weaves Them both together: the cosmic glue, the Third Person that makes up the One God. Your brain gets a little scrambled. A *lot* scrambled, actually.

Worth it, though. So very worth it.

NAYRU

Now this interview? This was a test. And an experiment. After all, Nayru, the goddess of wisdom in the Legend of Zelda series, is just a character. She isn't real.

Right?

However, naturally, as time went on and I encountered more and more people on #witchtok, I became aware of something I'd never heard of before: egregores. In hindsight, I did have a roommate years ago that had an altar to Danaerys Targaryen, but I just didn't understand that at the time.

In his book, *Egregores: The Occult Entities that Watch Over Human Destiny*, author Mark Stavish points out that the very term egregore is one that means "watcher," a word appearing both in reference to the Watchers in the Book of Enoch and to other entities across various ancient religions. Stavish defines egregores like so:

The most commonly used definition (taken from Wiktionary.org) is as follows: "(occult) autonomous psychic entity composed of and influencing the thoughts of a group of people." However, there is a second definition, an older, more significant, and perhaps frightening one. Here, an egregore is more than an "autonomous entity composed of and influencing the thoughts of a group of people"; it is also the home or conduit for a specific psychic intelligence of a nonhuman nature connecting the invisible dimensions with the material world in which we live. This, in fact, is the true source of power of the ancient cults and their religious-magical practices (21).

He goes on to insist that in ancient times, especially in Greece and other parts of the Roman empire, these entities were "formed to watch over city-states, the Republic, and the Empire itself," with their power and function hinging on the energy and offerings given to them by their human worshippers (22). This implies something of a chicken-and-egg situation in Stavish's works, raising the questions: did gods come first, or humans? Do humans need gods, or do gods need humans?

This is where it's important to discern a primordial force, a god proper, from a god that was created by the needs of people. I'm thinking how cut and dry it's made in Exodus, where there's God, and then there's that golden calf Aaron makes. Maybe if they had enough time pouring their energy into that calf, it would've "woken up" and actually started doing something that it was tasked with doing (like protecting the people). But God put the kibosh on that, so we'll never know. Moreover, on #witchtok itself, we see, very vividly, the many different egregores that appear in place of gods proper because people do not know what a god is actually like before they begin worshipping, usually due to an abysmal lack of research. In fact, this is precisely what was so shocking to me about encountering the Greek gods back when I was still able to.

They are not like what some "devotees" make them out to be. Not even remotely. But some devotees, through no fault of their own, don't know where to turn and where to look for proper, credible sources on these things, and so they end up feeding a false idea of these gods together that does eventually take form. Hell, look at Christianity itself right now. Whatever thing is infesting those nationalist horror shows people call churches is certainly not the Jesus of the Gospels they claim to know—and that's because these people either never read or never cared about the true Jesus's message.

Now, with all that theory under our belt, let's take a look at our first ever experience with an egregore proper: the goddess Nayru.

✦

What does one put up on an altar to an egregore? I didn't know. I could only guess based on what she has related to her in the games. While I am very bad at drawing sigils, I did manage to get Nayru's symbol drawn up, as well as some blue stones, my onyx, and a candle there for a general sense of water and wisdom. I had *Nayru's Love* playing: it was a professionally performed ballad Nintendo released, which was pretty cool, especially because notes of Zelda's Lullaby are obviously playing in it. And then I was just asking God to let me talk to whatever consciousness called "Nayru" existed out there, unsure what to expect or what to look for.

I was taken all over the place for a minute, through the many scenes of the Zelda games, as if I were hopping through each game world to find this goddess. But eventually, we settled on Lake Hylia from Twilight Princess, where she appeared hovering over the water looking like the spirit of a Zora child from the game: a blue fish-person with huge eyes and a pointed head. Maybe it's because Nayru loved this place, or maybe it's because I did; Twilight Princess is my favorite Zelda game, and Lake Hylia is such a beautiful area to explore in it, the Zoras an elegant and gorgeous people. But as Nayru hovered there above the water, this is where the doubts *really* started creeping in.

It was one thing to brush the doubts off with gods proper. But a video game goddess? *Was* she real? Was I making all this up? Was this all bullshit, or was that figure silently staring at me actually capable of engaging with me?

There was only one way to find out.

"Uh." I just blinked at her for a second and let the scene properly root itself in my mind's eye before I tentatively greeted her. "Alright, well—Nayru! Hello! I have some questions, if you'd like to answer them."

She still only stared at me—but at least I got some sense of what deck to use. Funnily enough, it was the Universal Fantasy Tarot.

I asked God to let Nayru borrow them for the interview and dove in. "To start, how are wisdom and magic intertwined?"

1. HOW ARE WISDOM AND MAGIC INTERTWINED?

Dishonor, mistrust, and being too preoccupied with the problems of others to address one's own issues. Disconnect from one's emotions.

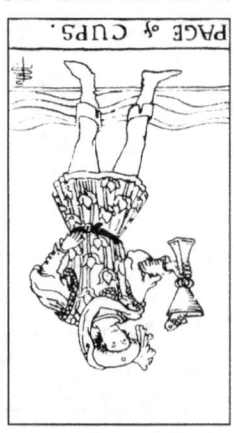

Deception and re-evaluating whether a goal or relationship is truly fulfilling.

To be authoritative, we must be recognized as such and committed to building what we've promised.

And the whole time, I was genuinely surprised that I was getting the feeling to pull certain cards at all, because I kept thinking that this wasn't a real entity the way we know them—but at the same time, why wouldn't she be? Surely enough people knew of her and adored her to manifest her, especially if all of these cosplayers of her exist out there. Her Oracle of Ages look, especially, seems to be pretty popular among cosplayers.

But once I pulled the cards, I was double surprised at how concrete the meanings were, and how she started speaking to weave them together into something sensible.

"Magic takes leadership," she said as she floated above the water's surface. "What leader exists without wisdom? A ruler with only power becomes Ganondorf. A ruler with only courage becomes a boy like Link, capable of ruling only himself. There's a reason Zelda is princess of Hyrule: wisdom is power, and courage is fostered by necessity."

"Wow." That was an *impressively* concrete and lucid answer, and I was double excited to see it was an answer that drew on the facts and realities of her fictional world. "Okay! Makes sense to me. But how about the spirit of law, then? It's said when you created Hyrule, that spirit flowed out into the land: what exactly is it?"

2. WHAT IS THE SPIRIT OF LAW?

1. Knowledge often requires sacrifice, but if we act with determination, we can obtain our heart's desire.

2, Mistrust, insecurity, loss of hope.

3. When we must defend that which we believe in, we must do so in person, advancing without hesitation towards the enemy.

Nayru nodded. "Law brings us together in common goals, aspirations, and dreams. Law is rooted in wisdom, knowing that one cannot make judgements unless they have all available information. Without wisdom, how can we determine right and wrong? Or act on it? The spirit of law is our conviction to do what we know is right and in accordance with Truth."

Interesting that an egregore would speak on a concept of Truth. "I hear you. So, with Din and Farore, how do you three all work together to keep Hyrule in check?"

3. HOW DO YOU WORK WITH DIN AND FARORE?

Authority and self confidence can be acquired when we live in harmony with the people around us.

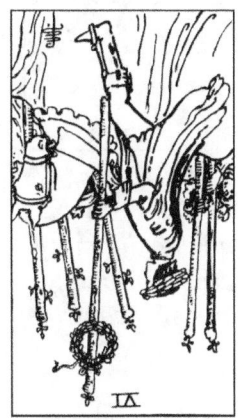

Failing to recognize one's own shortcomings, feelings of superiority and pride.

Our fear of the length of a journey should not tempt us to make shortcuts.

Beside Nayru, two other beings appeared: a red, flame-haired woman, Din, and a green woman with long flowing hair and what felt like flowers dotting her dress, Farore. They didn't speak, but they hovered around their sister as she answered.

"I am a reminder of what my sisters lack," Nayru said. "Power and courage are beautiful, necessary, things, but I am the force that stitches these things into something constructive rather than destructive. I am content to sit back and watch from a distance, however, as the world grasps after them anyway. After all, even if these forces are dangerous without wisdom, so to is wisdom dangerous without power and courage. One can be wise and still frail in mind and spirit, too quiet to use that wisdom. Those who seek my blessings need these two first."

What an answer. It was uncanny, because I kept wondering again and again if these answers were coming from my own mind, if I was just making this up—and yet I was sure that they weren't, because had you asked me that question, I don't know I would've been able to come up with that idea myself. At least, not at that time.

Now, having dug deeper into the mysticism of my own religion, I can understand this more as a Trinity. In fact, I can graft these very concepts—Power, Courage, and Wisdom—directly onto God, Jesus, and Holy Spirit, as I'd just come to understand, a year and a half after this interview, that the Holy Spirit Herself could be considered that stitching force between Father and Son. Reading this back is frustrating as a result.

Because how many truths have always been hidden in plain sight? How many times have I stumbled onto answers, only to not see them for what they were at the time and skip on like nothing happened? How many fucking times are we all going to walk in the same circles until we realize where we're trying to go and step off these over-trodden, eternally eroding, ditch-deep paths?

"That's so cool!" I pipped, without a thought, without a shred of a clue, with no idea. "Okay, okay, Nayru—now, do you mind telling me what you remember of creating Hyrule? What it was like?"

4. WHAT WAS IT LIKE TO CREATE HYRULE?

Here, she smiled, but her brows furrowed as if the question stung her despite her smile.

"Are you implying something?"

Oops. From what I noticed, spirits can read your mind when you meditate with them; there's no real hiding your thoughts and feelings. I had been thinking that this question would trip her up or catch her, make her glitch out, and she called me on it instead. But I floundered there, surprised.

"Well, I mean—do you know that you're not a figure that exists in this world? In mine? And that you were said to have created Hyrule by the people who told your story?"

Unrest and inability to move on.

Weakness, breaking down, having difficulty problem solving, or losing control.

Joy, moving forward, stagnation being the root cause of one's issues.

Nayru smiled bigger, even chuckled. "We're in a dimension created by love and a dream," she said with a shrug. "And what a beautiful dream it is. We can create dreams, too, in what's left unsaid.

"While these people you mention say we created Hyrule, they never explained how: that is for us to decide. So here is what I remember: there was once nothing. Only blackness. Then someone, somewhere, gave us the inspiration to go forth, and to unleash all that we are—primordial concepts that have existed across all worlds, all times, all spaces.

"We interjected into the darkness, and where there was nothing, there was suddenly something. Green grasses, rolling hills, beauty and power and grace made real. I remember the first thing I thought was: 'but what world may exist without law? Rule?' And so Hyrule was born."

Holy shit. She was a lot more sentient than I gave her credit for. I felt kind of bad, actually, to have doubted her so much, and I figured this might've been what God was warning me of when I pulled Five of Wands Reversed from Him on the subject earlier.

"Okay, I understand." I took a breath and tried to process all of that. "That's something else, wow. But then—who is Hylia in relation to you? She seems to have popped up out of nowhere, even in your realm."

5. WHO IS HYLIA TO YOU?

Mistrust, neglect, fear, prioritizing others over oneself.

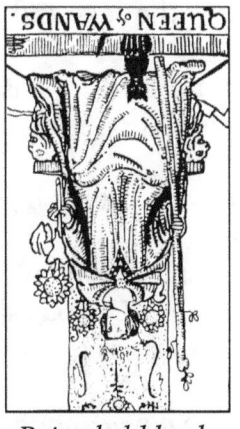

Being held back, not having the opportunity to try new things.

Disloyalty and feeling pressured or lost.

Nayru's face went somewhat pained here. She said, "I suppose I've been a bit too far in the background, haven't I? With how few remember me—and even my sisters to an extent. Those like Jabu remember me: the origin of the origin.

"But the truth is that Hylia is all three of us, wrangled into one concept. Hylia is of Hyrule, and Hyrule is of us. We are one in the same, yet separate, distinct. A revival of us exists in Hylia, in whispers and echoes."

What an answer. And how frustrating, that looking back, this is the answer that did show me a glimmer of the concept of the Holy Trinity: three faces, three facets, all making up one primordial deity, but in the world of the *Legend of Zelda* series, of all places. How wild. Yet even if I saw it then, and even if I see it again now, I wonder if I'll forget all over again—because what does this *mean*? What does it mean, for this concept to appear again and again even in the things we humans make with our two hands? Even the Trinity itself some can argue isn't real, isn't true, because it isn't explicitly spelled out in the Bible.

So where does this come from? This rule of Threes, this Three in One? Why do we keep seeing it in our gods, and why do we keep inventing it *as* the gods of these fictional beings we breathe our own love and life into? *Why does it keep appearing across time and space?*

"I see what you mean," I said then, despite not nearly knowing what she meant and never imagining how this would vex me in the future. "Uh, moving on from that, I guess: what role does Wisdom play in the Legend of Zelda series?"

6. WHAT ROLE DOES WISDOM PLAY IN THE LEGEND OF ZELDA SERIES?

At this point, maybe Nayru could see farther than I could—even as an egregore, a creation of Man. Because she pulled no cards. She only spoke, and spoke words I couldn't have ever organized myself in that moment.

"Beauty. Love." Her smile was so radiant, and she stood tall as her sisters surrounded her, still silent and giving her the whole floor. "I am that which ends every story, resolves every problem, yet creates every challenge. Because will and wisdom will always be at odds, until all wills are one."

I stared at her, stunned. That one really blew me away, even made me a little dizzy to receive. My mind felt like it was swirling, all soupy and melting from its frame and its structure. So interesting was that answer that I actually erased my next question and replaced it with a much more pressing one for me:

"What is a god, Nayru?"

7. WHAT IS A GOD?

Again, no cards. But this answer, God, this answer. This one took the cake and gave me knowledge I can never unsee, never unhear, never un-know.

"What is a world?" Nayru raised her hands up and gestured to the great expanse of water we hovered over—*water*, always water, always great bodies of water, in these stories of creation and beginnings. "Who are you, and what am I?"

She turned from me, surveyed this great Lake Hylia, and then looked at me over her shoulder with eyes sharp enough to cut my soul out of my body.

"What are we capable of, and who made us capable? In creation, there is no beginning, and there is no end. In destruction, there is nothing but the length of time passing. So you ask me: what is a god? Manifestations of hope, and expressions of love. In every world, the sky is the sky—the aether, the unimaginable. We are each other's ends and beginnings."

Oh, where have I heard all this before? Where have I heard of the *alpha* and the *omega?* Somewhere from long, long ago:

I was sent forth from the power,
and I have come to those who reflect upon me,
and I have been found among those who seek after me.
Look upon me, you who reflect upon me,
and you hearers, hear me.
You who are waiting for me, take me to yourselves.
And do not banish me from your sight.
And do not make your voice hate me, nor your hearing.
Do not be ignorant of me anywhere or any time. Be on your guard!
Do not be ignorant of me.

For I am the first and the last.
I am the honored one and the scorned one.
I am the whore and the holy one.
I am the wife and the virgin.
I am the mother and the daughter.
I am the members of my mother.
I am the barren one
and many are her sons.

—The Thunder, Perfect Mind

I mentally blue-screened after that answer at the time. Now, looking back, I can only feel like a fly trapped at the center of a web made of a million threads. I struggle, I rip at the threads holding me down, I try to stand on my own two feet—but every movement shoots down every string and calls Something forward. Something that will one day find me, bite down through this straight-jacket cocoon, and dissolve everything inside. Only then will I know what all these threads are for, and what the purpose of this inner burning, this dissolution, this purgation and reconstitution into that Something, is.

At the time, though, all I could think was: what an insane answer. And to think it all just came tumbling out like someone emptied a bag of precious gemstones onto the table.

"Damn," I said, not sure what else there was *to* say. "Okay. That... works. Wow. Uh, well, as we get towards the end here, Nayru... How do you see yourself?"

8. HOW DO YOU SEE YOURSELF?

A job is well done when all we have done is what is needed to be done and no more.

She shrugged. "I played my part. I did my role. I was created, and I, too, create. All of us come from somewhere, and I come from the wish for peace, justice, and beauty. A noble title, a lovely birth."

So lucid! I shook my head as if I could shake this reality, this Truth, away. Why did I not expect an egregore to know the nature of themselves? Would they answer things differently if, say, Zelda tried to meditate with them the way I was right then, given Zelda was a part of their world? Is there another universe somewhere, looking at God and the other deities of this world as if they're some kind of characters? This is one hell of a rabbit hole I opened for myself, I'll tell you that. And it's a rabbit hole that I will never find the end of, no doubt.

"And how do you want to be seen?"

9. HOW DO YOU WANT TO BE SEEN?

"I am one who exists," she said, as if responding to all of my off-the-wall thoughts and all my spiraling, my germinating madness. "I am one with a role, a job, and I perform it. So long as no one here forgets me, I am alive—and even if I am forgotten, I am alive, because I am a force primordial, since time immemorial—since time even became aware it was flowing."

Unexpected fortunes are best, but they must be managed wisely.

But of course. Of course this is the case. She is the goddess of wisdom; she is Wisdom personified, again, in yet another way. Like the Holy Spirit, who chided me on humanity's need to put these primordial concepts in silly little costumes, this is simply another interface of a concept we seem to have known in our very DNA since our inception as a conscious people. What other answer could Nayru have given? What else could she have told me, as an entity based in such Truth, except Truth?

"Well, that's about it, then," I said with a sigh. "Nayru, before I go: do you have any last messages you'd like to share?"

10. ANY LAST MESSAGES?

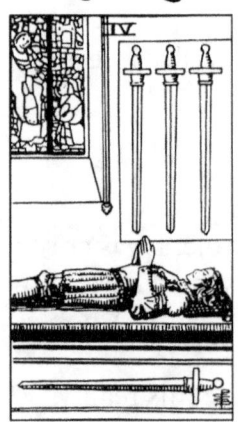

Idols can help us look within our heart, but if we let them shine too much, they blind us.

She faced me with her hands clasped together. "Yes. We are concepts. You attach names and shapes and dreams to us to better understand and appreciate us, but remember: we exist beyond our shapes and shells. Find the purest idea of us."

Which, when you combine it with Universal Fantasy Tarot's description for the Four of Swords, is probably the craziest, yet most direct message of all.

Wisdom has taken on many names that distract us from the Truth of its shape and its function in the world. But all of those shapes are equally real, and yet equally illusion at the same time. Mind boggling, if I do say so myself.

"Wow. Thank you, Nayru," I said. "I think that pretty much sums up all the questions I had, so I do really appreciate you taking this time to come and speak, and I wish you well. Goodbye for now."

But it was never really goodbye, was it? This facet of Divinity has never walked away from me, even when I walked away from that table. Looking back, I can't help but laugh at myself—because for every experience I've ever had with gods and monsters and men in this series, this was the one that truly *shifted* something. An interview with an egregore we, mankind, created. Even as I write this now, I can't explain the feeling I get as I think about Divinity. There's the frustration of feeling led in circles, but that's so surface level.

Really, what I feel when I reflect on Divinity at this point is an indescribable nothingness. Or, at least, it seems like nothing. There is nothing in my chest. Nothing on my mind. This isn't to say I'm depressed, or lost, or alone, no. That's not the kind of nothingness I'm talking about. What I'm talking about is a nothingness so unbearably *real* that it can only be described honestly, as *apophatic*. As without form, without symbol. As if every time I encounter a mask of Divinity, I see it for what it is: a mask. An illusion. As a result, I feel at this point in time as if I simply *am*.

I am.

All that needs to be said can be contained in those two simple words.

I am.

And that does make a lot of these proverbial divine spiderweb threads ring, the more you repeat that back again and again.

I am, I am, I am.

It was always telling us, wasn't It?

I am that [which] I am.

GREAT PRESIDENT CAMIO

If you're still courageous enough to pick up your reading after our first encounter with an egregore, bless you. And welcome back.

Just as soon as we remember the Truth, it seems we're content to forget it again. Like we can only encounter Truth in a dream that we remember for the first few moments after we wake up, with only the starkest, most shocking bits lingering. The bits that make us wake up with our heart racing and our scalp alight with tingles that feel more like embers peppering our skin.

But even that feeling fades eventually, doesn't it? So here we are again, to chase that Truth again, this time encountering a different mask, only to go taking a hammer to a different idol, thus making true iconoclasts of us all.

Now, all that madness aside, this interview is with Great President Camio, a demon of the Ars Goetia. According to the Lesser Key of Solomon, this spirit appears as a bird (a thrush specifically) and then a man. Described as the "voice of the waters," this is one entity that can argue like hell, gives people understanding of birds, and was once an angel. Now, as a demon, he rules thirty legions of angels. That's a lot. Some say he's also possibly a demonic mask of Cain, the child of Adam and Eve that killed his poor brother Abel. But who really knows, right?

In our pursuit of knowledge and understanding, I figured this would be a good place to go in terms of infernal knowledge; my format of angel, god, demon, and Saint was still holding up. But in true demon fashion, things weren't necessarily easy. Interesting, but not easy. Let me show you what I mean.

✦

This interview took place before I had my lovely and very helpful Occult Tarot by Travis McHenry. That deck I can only use as a tarot deck because I know tarot well enough, as it doesn't have any booklet meanings, but it does have the sigils and functions of the Ars Goetia demons, and so it's much more convenient than having to find a good enough image on the internet of a sigil and print it out—like I had to do here for Great President Camio. That, a red candle, some blue, red, and black stones as a nod to water, infernal presence, and secrets, and a bit of cinnamon incense also came into play, as well as a cup of the madness-inducing compote I'd made for one of my (then) weekly recipes. (It was very good compote. Somewhat bacchic, too, considering it was grape and plum based. That's on my website blog for anyone who also wants to lose their mind or disrupt the minds of their unwitting guests; just search for madness and you'll find it easily.)

Once I was situated and had done my prayers, I stepped into a familiar place. It'd been a while since I'd contacted any demon, but as I came into the meditation, I found myself face to face with Lucifer in his office, looking surprised that I'd popped up out of nowhere and seeming to wonder where I'd been. It's a grand office: one of dark wood, floor-to-ceiling bookshelves stuffed with ancient leather books, richly upholstered loveseats around a dark rococo coffee table, and a presidential desk where Lucifer did his work, right before a grand window that only showed the silvery light of the sun struggling through a foggy morning. Nothing could be seen outside that window except swirling mists.

Lucifer and I chatted for a second before I turned around to see a bird with a sword standing on the table: President Camio, bright-eyed and ready to engage. A moment later, however, he became a man with deep red eyes and a fine suit, short black hair, and the sword hanging at his hip. Lucifer let me go, and then I was then in the care of this new chaperone in the depths below.

"Hello, Great President Camio!" I opened my eyes to gesture to the kitchen table and its offerings. "Please accept these gifts of compote and cinnamon incense; I'm hoping to get your opinion on a few things today."

He only smiled, and then Lucifer was gone, the office was gone, and we were all over the place, on what felt like a bus tour of the strangest places hell had to offer. The thing I've discovered about demons, or at least about my experience meditating with them, is that they seem to enjoy trying to spook people, as if to test their mettle and see if they can handle weird stuff.

So let's just say: if you've ever played Bloodborne, that entire game's aesthetics would be a good overview of the stuff President Camio showed me. There were rivers of blood with skeletons pulling themselves out of quicksand-like muck, hallways that stretched on forever and came to doors full of dust and silence, cliffs where mists concealed sharp rocks below that some unfortunate creatures may or may not have jumped into looking for an escape... it was a lot. Nothing I was unfamiliar with, nothing I couldn't stomach, but a lot nonetheless.

I kept it together, because I knew, as always, that none of it was real in the physical sense. No skeletons were actually biting and grabbing at me from my kitchen, and the ones that tried in meditation were easy to keep away with a push of my own Will, like brushing a gnat off my arm. Moreover, no cliff was too dangerous to jump off when I could twist and turn away from the sharp rocks, when I could land softly on the ground under all that mess.

And no sword could cut me when I knew there was nothing pressed to my real throat.

Let me be clear: keeping things like this in mind will help you in the long run, should you ever meditate with other entities. You are always physically safe, and nothing that happens in meditation can hurt you unless you let it. Unless you lose that line between Physical and Spiritual. To put it simply: in my experience, if you flinch in the Spiritual, you bleed in the Physical. Your greatest armor is your mental strength.

Anyway, once we got situated in an old dusty clock tower, President Camio lounging in a chair in front of the hazy light coming through the clocktower's big window, we finally got started. Like Nayru, he chose the Universal Fantasy Tarot, which was fun. It's a deck that rarely gets picked, after all.

"Alright, well, that was quite the adventure," I said with a chuckle, and President Camio's lips twitched into a small smile. "But now, President Camio, I have some things to ask you about wisdom—the first thing being, how do wisdom and knowledge differ?"

1. HOW DO WISDOM AND KNOWLEDGE DIFFER?

President Camio sighed and rested his chin on his hand. "Knowledge is yet another illusion of the flesh and the world," he said. "Whatever you can learn from words printed on paper pales in comparison to what you perceive in the fields of the mind and soul. This goes for your Bible, too."

His smile grew larger, sharp and almost mean, as if waiting to see how I'd respond to a quip like that, and I said, "I dunno; there's plenty to read between the lines of the Bible, y'know?"

"Yes. But any wisdom worth having will make no sense as words on paper. You know this. If it makes sense as written, it's only knowledge—and knowledge is power, but often, knowledge is cheap, and worthless altogether if you don't act on it."

I couldn't argue with that.

True power does not come from material possessions, but from the values locked in our heart.

The ability to imagine the future is not enough to change it.

"Fair enough, yeah. I see that. But then, so, your entry in the Ars Goetia mentions you were once 'of the order of angels.' What was it like being an angel versus being a demon now?"

2. WHAT WAS IT LIKE TO BE AN ANGEL VS. A DEMON NOW?

To be understood may be harder than imposing authority with force.

The ability to imagine the future is not enough to change it.

Let me pause and say: over the course of this interview, I got the sense that President Camio was not like other demons. Most I'd spoken to up to that point seemed unapologetic and proud of their station, their work, and their life—but in President Camio was a melancholy I couldn't joke away with him, and in the air hung a pressure, like a sigh that could never be fully released. I felt the tightness of it in my own lungs as if participating in that melancholy with him.

"It's as those cards say," President Camio said as he tapped the King of Cups and King of Swords. "I was not understood in Heaven. No one cared to understand me, or my search for more than just orders to follow. But now what am I? Like my brothers, I am no more in charge of the fate of the world than I was before."

It was the King of Cups' description in the Universal Fantasy Tarot that struck me especially. Goodness. What a mood for angels, huh? It was a painful answer; I could feel it in the current running through the meditation space. Blood was flowing to a still healing wound.

"Okay. Interesting." I considered him, then erased a question and replaced it with one that stole my attention: "How would you write this world, and change this fate, if you were in charge?"

3. HOW WOULD YOU CHANGE THIS WORLD IF YOU WERE IN CHARGE?

President Camio smiled here, eyes twinkling as if the question delighted him. Maybe no one ever asked him this before. Either way, the answer was unique, shattering my idea of demons and what they want altogether:

"The thing is, Sara, I see the value and logic in God's plan. I agree with the twists and turns it's taken—to an extent. There isn't much I'd change so far. But the issue is that everyone focuses on the end of the story, and not how life goes on after the main plot ends.

"Are we all to simply enter stasis? To go back to the beginning and do all of this again? How many times have we already done it, then, without our knowing, because our memory has been wiped? That is the error of this plan—and it is madness. The plan would be no plan, if I had my way: no do-overs, no re-runs. Just eternity. Silence. Rest."

Damn. I almost wondered if I'd actually contacted a demon, because these things were so out of bounds of what anyone would expect a demon to say, I think. Or maybe

 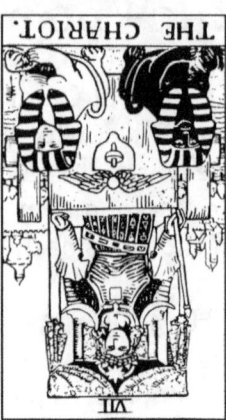

Those who know how to harmonize strength and wisdom are able to keep their will under control and wait their turn.

Defeat, loss of control, lack of direction. Possible distraction after success.

they were just out of the bounds of my understanding. Maybe I had an image of demons in my head, still, that wasn't so accurate after all. A lingering bit of old beliefs, old lies.

Can you hear it? The crack of a hammer on stone? I did then.

I nodded and wrote the answer down, but all the while, I had a feeling of something behind me, reading over my shoulder. When I looked up, there was a bird skull in a big cape of feathers staring at me. I didn't know who or what it was, but it wasn't doing anything: it was only watching. I ignored it for the moment and tried to focus on President Camio as I shuffled the cards, but then I noticed that I couldn't get President Camio's name right to save my life as I kept trying to talk to him: it kept coming out as President Marbas.

So I turned to the skull-creature and said, "President Marbas? Is that you?"

And then the skull popped off, and there sprouted the head of a man, with golden hair reminiscent of a lion, and a grin so big and wide and oddly friendly. I don't know if maybe he wanted to answer some things too, given as he's described as helping practitioners find wisdom and knowledge of mechanical arts, but I didn't want to mix voices, and so while I invited him to stay, I made it clear that this conversation needed to be just between me and President Camio for the time being, so wires didn't get crossed.

"Okay, okay—so, President Camio, if you could be so kind as to tell me," I watched President Marbas slide over to President Camio and pull up a chair, both of them silhouetted against the clocktower light, "what is the difference between God's wisdom and the Infernal Divine's wisdom?"

4. WHAT'S THE DIFFERENCE BETWEEN DIVINE AND CELESTIAL WISDOM?

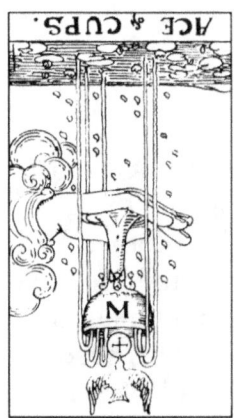

Delusion or disconnect with reality in regards to relationships.

At times we must trust our instincts when they lead us to believe in those closest to us.

I got flashes of the Holy Spirit, with her huge moon eyes, and President Camio chuckled.

"He's a bit of a helicopter parent, isn't He? God. His Wisdom is choking. Suffocating. Ruthless. But the wisdom of the Infernal Divine, as you call us, is the wisdom of the self—not the outside Spirit, but the inside Soul."

I frowned. "Those don't seem all that different to me. They're the same Source material, aren't they?"

He shrugged. "It's the trust in your friends and chosen family, our wisdom: it's the sense to know that no one is worth *all* your trust. That the only one who can save you from hell is yourself. No one else."

An interesting perspective. I sat back and chewed on that idea, not resisting it but not quite absorbing it, either, given the Savior I had that was *not* myself. As always, with the Infernal Divine, there was that frizzle of conflict between us—not of hostility or meanness or danger, but of trading quips and blows that dripped with some sort of *magnetism,* not malice. There was that sense of scraping off each other, sandpaper and stone colliding. It wasn't fighting. It was teasing. A push-and-pull that had me feeling like I was balancing on the edge of a blade.

"Moving on," I said, trying desperately to stay upright on that knife's edge, "why do some people want to learn the language of... dogs and birds? Or water?"

5. WHY DO PEOPLE WANT TO LEARN THE LANGUAGE OF BIRDS, ETC.?

He grinned and shrugged. "Your guess is as good as mine. But I see in their hearts a rot: a sense that powers such as these will give them an edge over the ordinary person."

A different current ran through the air as President Camio sighed. It was as if my heart were being filled with quicksilver, heavy and syrupy and even painful, maybe because of its toxicity. He looked at the ground with a smile that didn't reach his eyes, his face resting in his hand as he leaned over in his seat.

"There was once such a lust for power in this world," he whispered, wistful. "There still is, but none that requires talking to dogs, I suppose. And water, well—water is a mirror. By hearing its voice and keeping your wits, you may peer into it and see new things you couldn't before."

"That's a cool idea, I guess. Definitely seems fun." I tapped my pencil to my chin and thought about that—talking to dogs like a super power. It seemed goofy, but also like a good time. What would dogs say, if we could understand them? I didn't have time to think on it too much, though, so

Truth, indecision, inadequacy, emotional detachment.

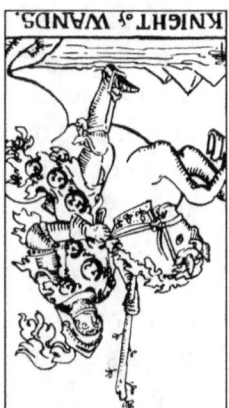

Ill placed infatuation with an idea or person, overhanging doubts, confusion, and a dent in one's confidence.

I shrugged and kept on. "Some say you're the demonic mask of Cain, but if you were once an angel, I don't see how that works. Can you explain it for me?"

6. WHAT IS THIS "DEMONIC MASK OF CAIN" STUFF ABOUT?

Misplaced or lost faith, suppression, weakness, feeling as though free thought has been restricted.

Sometimes we can't avoid a major change. We shouldn't be afraid of a new path.

What I got was such a clear image of President Camio standing close to Cain, whispering in his ear, out there in the woods. Cain was distressed, staring at his brother Abel in the distance, who was all happy go lucky—and President Camio was telling him things, giving him an ultimatum.

"Cain," President Camio said with a shake of his head. "His heart was bursting with ugliness that would've killed him, had he kept it in. I showed him options: stew in that poison until it rots him from the inside out, or let it spill out of Abel. He chose not to bear that burden and gave it up.

"God did not like that choice. But I merely presented the choices. I never told him which to pick. Humans are full of ugliness: they blame us for it, not realizing we can't fan the flames if there are no embers creating heat in the first place."

"I get that." What a sad case for Cain; it sounds like he was stuck between a rock and a hard place. Looking back now, I can't help but wonder, though: were those really the only two options? Were there not other ways out? Can we be manipulated by being presented an incomplete choice? "Well, alright then. Here's a question: what is one thing you learned throughout your existence that you didn't know at the start?"

7. WHAT IS ONE THING YOU LEARNED OVER YOUR EXISTENCE?

"One thing I learned?" He blinked like he hadn't quite thought about it. "Hmm. I'd say I learned that doesn't matter how hard you try. What is written, is written—and if you are not written to be free, then you can call yourself anything you like, and your goals, your path, your way of progress, will all be the same regardless.

"Whether I serve above or serve below, the fact remains: I serve. I do not rule. To command legions of demons is not to rule; it's to corral, to manage. There is no glory here."

Holy shit. That was a lot more pessimistic of an answer than I thought I'd get.

"That's fascinating; thank you for sharing that with me." I stared at him for a moment, stewing in thoughts I couldn't yet put to words, then kept on. "But alright, well, that about wraps up the main questions. Now I'd like to know: how do you see yourself?"

Fixation on the material world, anxiety, greed.

Misfortune approaching, depression, unsuccessful ventures.

8. HOW DO YOU SEE YOURSELF?

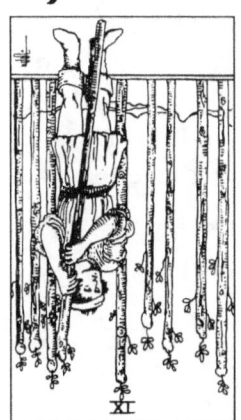

Pessimism, dread, resignation.

"I am one that has no hope for this world," he said as he pulled the Nine of Wands Reversed, a very pessimistic card. "Not with all I've seen. But maybe I'll be surprised in the end."

"Okay. How do you want to be seen?"

9. HOW DO YOU WANT TO BE SEEN?

"I am a consumer of worlds. I will not be satisfied until I've had my fill—until I've tasted every single one of them."

Pessimism who? That answer was like a sucker punch. It had an intensity reflected in the shine of his eyes, the tension in his jaw; he was sitting up all of a sudden, back straight and shoulders square.

Greed, shallow fulfillment, concerns with the material world.

"Jeez." I eyed him, unsure what to do with that sudden show of spiritual force. "Alright, alright—and any last messages for the road?"

10. ANY LAST MESSAGES?

A gilded cage is what we build with our own hands. To find our way, we must believe in ourselves and be true to our ideals.

Dreams can sometimes bar the progress of the traveler who doesn't know how to distinguish them from reality.

He glanced at me, smiled as if he knew something I don't. I'm sure there are a lot of things he knows that would fit that description. But as he pulled two cards, he said:

"Ideals inspire us, but ideals can blind us, too. Rip what you want from the throat of the world—but don't delude yourself about how you'll have to do it, or what changes it'll forever bring to your world after."

Huh.

"I think I understand what you're saying." And how ominous a warning it was. "Alright, then. Well, that's about all I had today. Thank you for your time, President Camio—and thank you, President Marbas, for coming by, as well!"

President Marbas nodded his head only once, smiling, but still kept silent.

With nothing else to do, I waved and began to walk out of this dark place. "May we one day all meet again," I said as I left. "Until then, I'll say farewell."

And then I dumped the compote out, cleaned up my space, and spent some time thinking about Cain, about angels and demons, about fate and all the rest. About the savagery he seemed to imply was necessary to take what we want from this broken world. In all my current nothingness, it's a savagery I can understand. It makes me wonder about God sometimes, too, as He does all these things in His story that people claim are proof of Him being so terrible.

What must be done, must be done. There's no room for silly sentiments like grief or guilt or uncertainty in that. This is what this nothingness tells me: that if a path needs to be cut, it will be cut, as necessity demands. The howls and the screams and the flames and the rubble—they can't stay a hand bent on doing what needs to be done.

But is that the only option? Following the current of necessity? Tearing throats out, letting rivers of blood stream free, or otherwise forfeiting what needs to be done, what we want to achieve? Or is there another option? An option no one told us about?

So begins a new cycle of chaos, I think, to ask this question.

ASHERAH

You may have heard it once or twice: the fact that once upon a time, God wasn't without a Goddess. That in some distant time or place, there was a world that understood the God we all now routinely worship within our synagogues and churches and mosques to have a little something outside His temple: a certain plant, a tree, or perhaps even a pole.

An Asherah pole.

We see these things mentioned here in Exodus 34:12-14:

Be careful not to make a treaty with those who live in the land where you are going, or they will be a snare among you. Break down their altars, smash their sacred stones and cut down their Asherah poles. Do not worship any other god, for the Lord, whose name is Jealous, is a jealous God.

And we see them again in Deuteronomy 16:21-22:

Do not set up any wooden Asherah pole beside the altar you build to the Lord your God, and do not erect a sacred stone, for these the Lord your God hates.

And yet again in places like the book of the prophet Isaiah 7:7-9:

Has the Lord struck her (the nation of Israel)
    as he struck down those who struck her?
Has she been killed
    as those were killed who killed her?

By warfare and exile you contend with her—
    with his fierce blast he drives her out,
    as on a day the east wind blows.

By this, then, will Jacob's guilt be atoned for,
    and this will be the full fruit of the removal of his sin:
When he makes all the altar stones
    to be like limestone crushed to pieces,
no Asherah poles or incense altars
    will be left standing.

But perhaps most interesting of all, in Jeremiah, comes this passage (44:15-19):

Then all the men who knew that their wives were burning incense to other gods, along with all the women who were present—a large assembly—and all the people living in Lower and Upper Egypt, said to Jeremiah, "We will not listen to the message you have spoken to us in the name of the Lord! We will certainly do everything we said we would: We will burn incense to the *Queen of Heaven* and will pour out drink offerings to her just as we and our ancestors, our kings and our officials did in the towns of Judah and in the streets of Jerusalem. At that time we had plenty of food and were well off and suffered no harm. But ever since we stopped burning incense to the *Queen of Heaven* and pouring out drink offerings to her, we have had nothing and have been perishing by sword and famine."

The women added, "When we burned incense to the *Queen of Heaven* and poured out drink offerings to her, did not our husbands know that we were making cakes impressed with her image and pouring out drink offerings to her?"

Would you look at that? Jeremiah had some choice words for these people then, but that just goes to show that things weren't always as so many narratives in the Bible want to make it seem: so purely monotheist, so cut off from the roots of the pantheon God divorced Himself from. Again and again and again, the Bible seems to say that it rejects this Asherah, depicted in the form of the pole outside God's temples—and yet it's precisely because it has to be said so many times over so many centuries, in so many highly polemical words of prophets in a world where politics and religion were one, that we know that once upon a time, the Israelites held onto something from days before Abraham's covenant. That besides God was a Goddess, and that her name was—and still is—Asherah.

Asherah, the Canaanite Queen of Heaven, the Mother of the Sun, the Mother of the Sea, the Mother of the Gods. She was the goddess associated with trees and snakes and lions, the one the Ugaritic people knew as Creatress of the Gods, and the one the Canaanites knew as the consort of the pantheon's chief god El. In other tribes of the region, such as that of the Hittites and the Akkadians and the Ugaritic people and the Sidonians as Asherdu and Ashirat and Athirat and Astarte. She was even considered cognate with Ishtar, another Mesopotamian manifestation of this goddess of fertility, love, and war. Later, however, she would become condemned as a demon: as Astaroth, one of the Ars Goetia, a spirit that appears as a man that departs from and warps the idea of Divine Mother.

Something happened over time. What was clearly once a group belonging to the Canaanite cults of yore split off, broke away, and dedicated themselves solely to another member of this pantheon:

Yahweh, the God of storms and war, and a cultural competitor to another god of similar station in the area known as Ba'al Hadad. Over time, it seems, this Yahweh may have become fused with the Canaanite chief god El in the minds of this developing religion, and soon enough we would come to have the fully realized concept of the LORD, the One True God, El Shaddai, of what we now understand as the Jewish faith. But so far back, those Asherah poles, they still stood outside His temples. For eons, they did, until worship was centralized to Jerusalem in the time of King Josiah.

And that's because for centuries, it's believed that this very monotheistic religion was actually something of a duotheism: one where the LORD, the One True God, El Shaddai, had Asherah as His wife, a counterpart and divine consort to His reign. The Bible is, then, revealed for its politics: it is the official standard of the religion, written by official priests, sometimes commissioned by kings, a testament against every attempt at syncretism with aggressive, invading neighbors and a rewriting of the understanding of the Divine in a culture determined to stand apart from those around it. As a result, the Bible does some hard work trying to downplay, condemn, and erase the folk beliefs and folk culture of the Israelites out in the hills and valleys and smaller towns far away from that central city of that ancient nation.

Truth be told, I was no stranger to the idea of Asherah; she's all over Jewish and Christian Witch communities, showing the spiritual search for the Mother figure that seemed so mysteriously absent as a divine and godly force in the religion. While whispers of her can still be seen hidden in plain sight—in Mother Mary, who inherited Asherah's titles like Queen of Heaven and Star of the Sea, and like Lady Wisdom, the feminine personification of God's wisdom and Spirit we've already peered at—for many, it feels only right to acknowledge she who was cut off and discarded.

In a conversation about wisdom, who else might I think to ask but the very goddess that once used to stand side by side with my God? Who used to be the Heavenly Mother alongside my Heavenly Father? Who, as I've said, the very concept of Lady Wisdom may have been distilled from in order to preserve her presence? Of course I had to come approach this goddess eventually, and it was yet again an eye opening experience.

Let me show you how.

To formally invite Asherah to my table, I decided to take some tips from my friends who actively worship or work with her, like Lina, Hannah, and Mimi. Given she's associated with trees, I threw an offering of grapes to my house's tree guardian, a big pine that shelters my front window from onlookers and keeps spooks away when I'm running out to get my mail at an unreasonable hour. Then, I set the table with the bottle of sea water from one of my state's beaches that I used in Nehalenia's interview, as well as rocks and two fully intact seashells I found along the beach. A bit of sunstone, sunstone, moss agate, and lapis lazuli was my way of acknowledging Asherah's dominions of Sun, Tree, and Sea, and I also had Mama Mary's statue there just because... it felt relevant. As if Mama Mary might've been something of a doorway or a midpoint between my understanding of every Christian's Holy Mother and the Holy Mother that I never knew, one of a long-gone era.

A lavender candle headed it all, and I offered as thanks for Asherah's time a plate of bread, cinnamon-dusted honey, and grapes and a cup of cinnamon honey tea—all of which seemed to me like things the gods of this region enjoyed, based on what I knew of all the mentions of choice flour and wine and all that in the Bible and beyond. The cinnamon, though, was something different: whenever I put down offerings for God in formal ritual or speaking spaces, that mint and dill and cumin from Matthew 23:23, I notice that often He also likes a bit of cinnamon on His plate, too. I don't remember now how I came to feel Asherah would also like it—maybe because of the associations of fire and the sun—but it also made me wonder. Was she always there? And was the cinnamon God wanted on His plate a hint of her wishes, her inclusion alongside Him?

Food for thought.

As I set up the table and came into the space, and I did all my prayers and got into the headspace for this whole undertaking, I asked God to let Asherah through. I'd seen a glimpse of her once before, in St. Mary Magdalene's interview, looking like a woman made of bark and burning from the inside with fire for hair, golden eyes. I wondered if I'd get the same image, as most people I've talked to see her a little differently. So once I started getting the sense that I wasn't alone, I settled in and faced what I'd honestly been putting off for a hot minute, for no real reason I can think of other than that, simply, it wasn't a priority for me.

"Asherah! Welcome!" I grabbed at that presence and centered on it. "I have some gifts of cinnamon-honey-bread and cinnamon-honey tea for you, if you'd like to join me. There are some questions I've been meaning to ask."

As I waited, I found myself getting a flash of red and gold: bright red, curly hair, golden eyes, and a woman who was like something of a fire sprite. She had deeply bronzed skin swirling with golden patterns, no clothes on whatsoever, and a mischievous, almost impish air as she hovered nearby. Which, again, is poignant to me—because remember that story I wanted to write one day, and that goddess of magic and wisdom and stars that looked *so much* like Hagia Sophia, the Holy Spirit?

This projection of Asherah I was seeing was the stark reminder of the second goddess of the story. A goddess of beauty, love, and war, whose crown held the sun in its center and whose hair seemed made of unruly fire, whose symbols were the mirror, sword, and chalice.

I thought of these two *fictional* goddesses for my story ten years ago. Before I'd come anywhere near the things I'm doing, seeing, and learning now. Was this image I invented then influencing how I saw these pieces of Divinity now? Or were these time-worn concepts appearing to me and inspiring me the way they inspired ancient peoples so long ago? A very chicken-and-egg question. All I know, though, is that *God*, I cannot wait to write that story. I can tell you now with unreasonable certainty: it'll be the greatest story I ever write.

But once Asherah appeared, it didn't take long before the cathedral I'd spoke to Mama Mary in came into view. Then my little statue of Mama Mary in her blue cloak popped up onto a round table in the middle of the place—only for Asherah and *red*-robed Mama Mary to smile and poke at it, as if it were a funny thing. It was then that I understood why Mary would come to me in red when I interviewed her instead of her traditional blue cloak: she was aligning with Asherah's wily nature.

And as they led me into the cathedral, St. Mary Magdalene joined us again, too, likewise robed in red. It was a pretty intense experience, seeing them all come together at a large round table in a cathedral decked in gold, all sitting there like a council of women that the world was trying to forget. I was overwhelmed by the sight of it, and I felt sorry for having taken so long to notice or approach Asherah—because it was obvious how present she was in the fabric of things, and the many images of women Christians know and hold dear.

As I came closer, though, above them all hovered Sophia: her moon-eyes were bright, her face blank of expression, her blue and silver robes fluttering in some phantom wind as she hung over us, eerie and almost unsettling. She watched us without ever once blinking.

"Jeez," I said as I collected myself and settled into the one empty chair. "I see now I've been missing something pretty big, haven't I? I'm sorry, Asherah; I should've came to you sooner, it seems."

She waved a hand, her smile warm, and she leaned over the table. I got the sense she wanted to use Threads of Fate's Weaver Tarot. "You're here now," Asherah said. "That's what you should think about."

I stared at her like a wide-eyed kid, then nodded furiously and cleared my throat. "Alright, well, if we're good to start, I guess we'll start with my most pressing question." I glanced between St. Mary and Mama Mary and Sophia and said, "What do you have to do with these three? How are you related to these feminine figures: St. Mary, Mama Mary, and Sophia?"

1. HOW ARE YOU RELATED TO OTHER FEMININE BIBLICAL FIGURES?

"Ah." Asherah leaned back in her chair and smiled, then reached a hand up towards the drifting skirts of Sophia. "This one here, Sophia, is my shadow—my ghost. She haunts me, always, God. Sophia is when God puts on the mask of Woman for Woman's sake. But I didn't show Him how to put on that mask. He figured it out Himself." As she reached for Sophia's skirts, and Sophia didn't so much as twitch, Asherah glanced at me and grinned, almost meanly. "Terrifying, isn't she? Just like me."

I glanced between Asherah's lively, mischievous face and Sophia's ghastly stare. "I dunno; you two don't seem very similar. You look nothing alike."

With a shrug, Asherah said, "She

Mental growth, cutting through illusions. New clarity, inspiration. The old is no longer acceptable. Justice, passion.

A holder of space. Perceptive, intuitive, nurturing, warm, heart-centered. Use intuition, not logic. Emotional support.

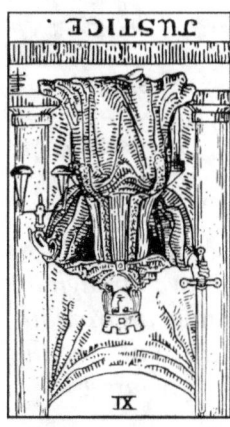

A repression of things you feel guilty about. Trying to justify things so you don't have to make amends. Forgive yourself.

doesn't look like me, yet she's full of the brimstone of Woman—but she burns so hot that you'd think she's cold."

I blinked. By her smile, she knew I'd recognize God's nature in her statement. That's Him, after all; that's how He's described sometimes: the fire that burns so hot it burns cold.

"She goes in my stead, God becoming Mother in my absence," Asherah continued. Then she pointed to St. Mary and Mama Mary, who exchanged some sly glances and hooked smirks. "These two, however, you've already guessed on."

St. Mary sat up and said, "It was I who achieved the mantle of Knowledge."

Then Mama Mary folded her hands in her lap and nodded. "And I achieved the mantle of Mother."

Asherah gestured to them all. "Magdalene has my knowledge, Mary my station, and Sophia my essence, her form inspired from it."

Whoa. That was a huge answer, a network of things just unspooling there in words and images in my head. But one card pulled, for Sophia, I didn't full understand: Justice Reversed. I figured maybe I could think on it later, or that Asherah would explain more somewhere. "Okay, well, I guess I'd also like to ask: what is the Divine Feminine, exactly? I have trouble with the term and the idea."

2. WHAT IS THE DIVINE FEMININE?

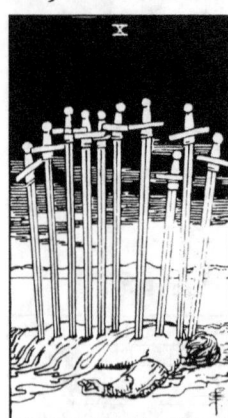

Disaster. A situation has been building. You need to move through it, not run from it. Reconnect with yourself.

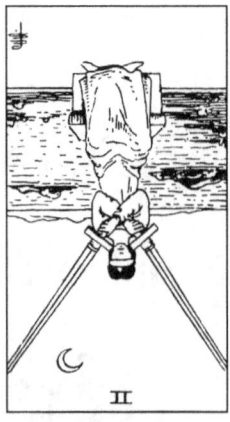

Facing a difficult decision. You need to make a choice so you can move on. Trust you can handle whatever happens.

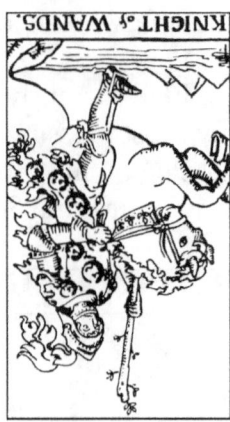

Delays, a build up of creative energy. Frustration. Shift to another project so you can build that creative energy again.

Asherah nodded and clasped her hands together. "The 'Divine Feminine' is a place of sacrifice," she said. "Of taking mantles you shouldn't have to. In a world of souls addled by comfort, they want always to be the receiver and never the giver—so they've detached themselves from the feminine, foisting it on some and denying it of others." And as if sensing my confusion about the last pull, as well as the pieces I was just starting to put together, she grinned and added, "This is the injustice of Sophia—cutting me out, forcing God to fill the hole left behind."

Then her grin faded, and with a withering stare, she muttered, "Humanity's lack of value in this integral piece of life—it's brought your ruin. You can't survive devaluing half your population. You can't succeed with only half your collective strength. Until Humanity understands the necessity of all things, you will always suffer. The 'Divine Feminine' is the backbone of all things, the 'Masculine,' the forerunner. All exist within each and every one of you. The blend makes true Divinity."

Damn. I rubbed my temples from the intensity of that answer and got back to shuffling, trying to stay grounded with all this energy buzzing around.

"I got'cha, yeah. But then, okay, how about this: we're here to talk about wisdom, and I'd like to know what wisdom there is to learn from being a mother? I don't ever intend to be one," I said, despite the way she raised a brow at me, "but I know plenty who work with you are mothers. What do you think?"

3. WHAT WISDOM CAN WE FIND IN MOTHERHOOD?

1. All is well. You feel like you could take on the world. Optimism. Connect to your power. Do things that feel good.

2. Tap into your personal well of strength. Internal will and resilience. Merge with challenges; don't battle.

3. Alignment, harmony, relief after challenges. Conquering problems. You've been through hell and haven't hardened.

Whether or not I intend to be a mother one day (and whatever that look from Asherah meant), it was something special to pull these cards. What a cool message just from a glance. But as I wrote the descriptions down, Asherah explained.

"To be a mother is to be a warrior with no weapons," she said. "It's to die a thousand deaths and resurrect a thousand times. One learns how to fight *with* rather than *against* as a mother—and one learns how many battles are internal, and how many boogeymen we make to deny where the problems really come from: within us. Patience and cunning, you learn these as a mother."

"That's so interesting. Wow." I got the sense of women learning to play tricks and do sleight of hand on their fussy children, or women learning how to sneak about and make calculated plans to get them and their kids out of danger, or who learned how to meet their children where they were to find solutions to problems. "Okay, okay, and what about surrender? Is there wisdom in that? I was reading from another blog of a Jewish witch," a certain Asa West writing for the digital pagan-centered hub *The Agora* on Patheos about finding Asherah, "who mentioned you'd pulled the Hangman, the card of surrender, and I just wonder if, given your history, there's something to share here."

4. WHAT IS THE WISDOM IN SURRENDER AND SUBMISSION?

With a slow nod, Asherah said, "Sara, one of the most terrifying things you can do is submit to the will of another. You know this."

I do. God does not make easy demands sometimes.

"In surrender, we have no choice but to trust others—and to accept where the problems we face are our fault. Too many rush to blame everything else to avoid consequences, but how do you learn if you never accept the lesson?" Asherah waved a hand, then folded both hands onto the table. "Surrender is an admission of lack: be it of knowledge, of opportunity, or of innocence. It doesn't mean giving up; it means discerning when to put the weapons away and bring out the peace treaty."

"Oh, how interesting." What an idea. I think we all chafe against submission

Your eye is on the finish line, but you're missing certain steps. Being impatient, taking shortcuts, not being realistic. Acceptance is the first step.

Magical thinking, externalizing happiness, ideals that can motivate you but aren't based in reality. Putting the blame on others.

A period of necessary solitude. Surrender and trust that it's in your best interests. Dealing with things you've repressed. Enjoy and traverse the unknown.

and surrender, but there's a time and place for it, isn't there? "Okay, well, how about you now? What role do you still play in Heaven?"

5. What Role Do You Play in Heaven?

Tradition in all forms, convention in spirituality. Growth that comes with rigorous practice. No shortcuts. Dedicate yourself. Pursue teaching.

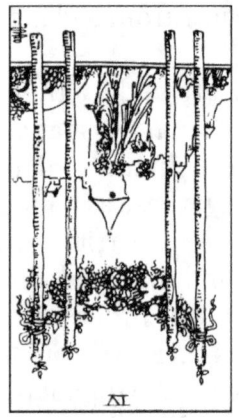

Quietness in small victories. Balance within the self. Personal acknowledgement of progress. Potential roadblocks.

A blockage in creative flow. Creativity becomes "work." Find your passion again; remember why you started.

Everyone save Sophia, who kept her eyes boring into me, exchanged knowing glances. Then Asherah leaned forward over the table, her fiery hair spilling out all over, and she looked at me with a glow in her eyes, a tender smile.

"Women carry in them an intuitive knowing," she said. "A mysticism that's been buried again and again by a machine of law and order. How you've cursed yourselves, you humans, cutting off from it.

"I am here—whispering my secrets into the ear of Sophia, which she shoots into the minds of the capable. Or was there ever any wonder why the mystics, even the men, perceived the femininity of Wisdom? No, I am here, working with your God to revive this dead garden you've all neglected."

I sat back and rolled that idea around in my head. "Fair. Though the way you speak of God makes me ask: how do you see Him? What do you think about Him? Do you blame Him for all of this?"

6. What Do You Think of God? Do You Blame Him?

She shook her head in quick, sharp jerks, and her message came so clear and sharp that I had no signal to pull any cards at all.

"No. I love the One you call God. He's been very good to me. It's you all, you mankind, that have done crimes against me—and my sisters in duty, the goddesses you've cast aside. Wherever you mar the name of Mother or cast down the face of Woman, you commit crimes against me."

I blinked. "Understood, yeah."

And it was interesting that she spoke of all goddesses, as if there really is a network of feminine entities out there doing this work in tandem. But I'll admit; I was wrestling with a head cold while channeling, making it difficult sometimes to keep my grasp on the energy and the images. I took a break from meditation to open my eyes and rub my aching temples, and then, when I closed my eyes again, I found myself laying down in snow.

Snow, with a flash of Morana towering over me, telling me that same thing she told me so long ago: "you of the Sun, who never wants to rest." Then she was gone as quick as she came, and I was there with Asherah and St. Mary and Mama Mary and Sophia again, and I tried my best to finish what I'd started, despite knowing I probably should've stopped. But hey—we'd come so far already. What was I going to do, pack everything up just to take it out again for another few questions?

Might as well keep going, I figured. And goodness, did that phrase curse me for ages thereafter, steal hours and hours of my life away. *Might as well.*

"Now, another thing, given we're talking about intuition: how do we connect with that better?"

7. HOW DO WE BETTER CONNECT WITH OUR INTUITION?

Asherah sighed. "The world around you exists to test and push you. Not everyone wins, however. Some—many, in fact—fall victim to false beliefs that strip them of their soul's knowing. They worry about how the rest of the blind sheep see them in this state. No, to connect to your intuition, you must connect to yourself."

Politics. Politics, politics everywhere. Here was the Mother, telling us to connect to ourselves—to the heart. Then there were the champions of the Father, living not in the heart but in the head, insisting that "the heart is deceitful above all things and beyond all cure; who can understand it?" (Jeremiah 17:9).

Oh, Jeremiah. What have you done?

"Fair, fair. I get that. But now, how do you view yourself?"

Big aspects of life are clamoring for your attention. Is this sustainable? If there's no end in sight, what can you change? Reflect on how much is on your plate.

Focus on all things external, born of an imbalance in the ego. If we focus on what others think, we won't make good choices. Ground and detach from ego.

Secrets and illusions. Unburden yourself from negativity and false beliefs weighing you down.

8. HOW DO YOU SEE YOURSELF?

Happiness and contentment reached after a long period of ups and downs. Born of the mundane. Routines and comfort. Beauty in ordinary moments.

Her face softened, her smile bright.

"I am among the families," she said. "I am nestled in quiet moments, creating warmth among the silence. I am the peace that comes with Wisdom, the joy of community. Remember me. Keep me close."

After I wrote that down, I paused. "...Is that how you want to be seen, too?"

9. IS THAT HOW YOU WANT TO BE SEEN?

"Yes."

"Okay, I got'cha. And now, to wrap this up, do you have any last messages to share?"

10. ANY LAST MESSAGES?

Her smile once again turned impish, and she tapped a finger to her lips.

"All cannot be said at once. Those who want to learn should seek more answers on their own."

"I—yeah, that makes sense." So many entities had that air about them: that they should be asked directly, approached by those with courage to match their curiosity. "Okay! Well, thank you for sharing your answers with me for our questions, Asherah, and I'm sorry again to have neglected you this long. I'd love to work with you on some things, if ever the opportunity arises. Until then, I'll see you when I see you, I guess."

And then I closed out the space, got those offerings and libations out to the tree, and sat on the couch to deal with my slight headache. Being just a tiny bit sick with sinus nonsense and whatnot is so frustrating. I blame the changing seasons. Still, I got it done, I made it happen (which, in hindsight, was perhaps maybe not a thing to be proud of while my body was begging for rest)—and I find Asherah to be, ironically, exactly the type of "feminine" I never found in all these stereotypical images of the Goddess.

Mischievous. Lively. Bright. Sharp. Doing what needs to be done, no matter the cost. That's what any such talk of "Divine Feminine" means to me, and I haven't found it often; only in goddesses that were clearly not meant for my soul, like maybe Mari, or in human women who, as Asherah said, all carry that Masculine and Feminine together. That's *my* kind of femininity; that's what I, as someone who still sees and understands herself as Woman, recognizes as femininity.

I'll be honest, though: the whole concept of "feminine energy" in the first place isn't something I really care all too much about. There's a funny idea that to be a witch means you need this Divine Feminine in your practice, specifically that you need it in the form of a dedicated *goddess*—and definitely, for folks that does make sense to, my good friend Mimi and I have included the concept of feminine Divinity in *Discovering Christian Witchcraft*. I also understand the idea that these forces are in balance in some way across so many religious systems, and I do think that these are forces that exist in all things, and in all people, as Asherah said.

But personally, I think it's bullshit that we have to specifically acknowledge any such "masculine" or "feminine" energy in the form of any kind of god *or* goddess worship. I think people are who they are, and that every person will have a different attunement to a different energy—that trying to split the world down the lines of Feminine and Masculine is a little redundant to begin with, considering that we see both Feminine and Masculine deities holding the same damn stations anyway.

For all the gods of War and goddesses of Love, gods of Sun and goddesses of Moon, there exists goddesses of War and gods of Love, goddesses of Sun, and gods of Moon. Hell, there are even Divinities like Quan Yin and Inari Ōkami that appear as both male and female, as well as ones that technically have no gender at all, like Loki. The gods themselves aren't split so much like that, as a dichotomy around gender, as much as they are around their functions and stations: gods of war and abundance and thunder and water and chaos and law. *That* is what I resonate more with: those specific stations, those specific *talents*, that we might find ourselves looking to patron deities for. This is why I don't find myself reaching for a Divine Feminine in my practice in the form of any specific goddess; I'm perfectly fine sitting in the duality of my one God, who can create and destroy, who can love tenderly as much as He can kick ass, and who has been described as both Father and Mother.

But all this doesn't mean I don't get curious. It doesn't mean there aren't more stories to tell, and more old threads to pick up and follow. It also doesn't mean that I have no use for any such concept of a goddess—just that I recognize a face of Divinity less by their supposed gender and more by their station. There are things I could see myself going to Asherah for help with—and very well things I might one day, in fact. But they aren't things that have to do with just being Feminine™, whatever the hell this actually means.

They're things she has divine expertise in. Things she presides over. Places her very being is meant to fill, wounds her energy is meant to mend. As it is with all such Divinities and their endlessly varied stations.

ST. VALENTINE

Do you ever think it's a little funny? That the Saint's feast day we collectively use celebrate the idea of love and romance and relationships in the west is that of a Saint who was brutally murdered?

The month I approached St. Valentine, it seemed people wanted to talk about Love, and so naturally, the first person that came to mind was none other than St. Valentine—the patron Saint of bee keepers, marriage, love, engaged couples, and more. Alive in the time of Emperor Claudius Gothicus, St. Valentine was an early Christian Bishop who was a bit radical for the time, spreading the word of Christianity despite the religion still being illegal across the empire and helping Christian couples get married, which was a major crime. Some say he even made these marriages happen in order to help the men avoid having to go into the Roman army.

He was thrown in prison several times for his missionary work, but by doing miracles like restoring the sight of a judge's blind daughter, he was able to get free and change some minds. It was when he brought it up to the Emperor himself, however, that he was threatened with denouncing his faith or being beaten with clubs and decapitated. He chose the latter. There's a legend that where his head rolled down from the execution hill and stopped is where they build a church in his honor.

As a martyr, he eventually came to have his feast day placed on February 14th some 150 years or so after his death—and this date just so happened to pick up the remnants of an old pagan festival, Lupercalia, which was all about fertility and the coming of spring. There's a legend that people also began associating this festival with love because of the way birds were thought to match in pairs around this time to prepare for the coming spring. Nowadays, his feast day is marked all red, white, and pink, with chocolates and flowers and stuffed bears and other such things to give to one's lover(s), with wine flowing in fine, dimly lit restaurants as couples flirt (and then leading to a disproportionate amount of Scorpios being born some nine months later in November).

Naturally, my nosy ass had to know what he thought about all this—and what he had to say about love itself. Let's take a look.

As I got my stuff set up, I was thinking of all the traditional love-associated items: rose petals, rose quartz, a red-beaded rosary, the whole thing. I also figured it'd be rude to have my breakfast and coffee out and have nothing for my guest this morning, so for him was a cup of rose tea and an apple. It took a minute to get settled in, given I was on the tail end of my cup of joe, but once I did my prayers and God helped me open up that space, the energy of Heaven and its Saints came through. Eventually, I ended up feeling the vibe of one Saint coming through, as if all that heavenly energy were condensing into one spot.

"Hello, St. Valentine! Please come by and speak to me, if you'd like. I've got some questions about loved for you that I'd really appreciate getting some answers to."

My eyes burned with exhaustion. I hadn't done an interview in a hot minute, actually; it was around this time that I started slacking a bit with the weekly interviews, especially given that I was in the middle of finalizing *Where the Gods Left Off*. I was pretty exhausted from the last week I'd had most of all, in which that upcoming book of mine was an unfortunate victim of Mercury retrograde. I'd been scrambling to get some technical issues with the project files themselves resolved before the publication deadline, which unfortunately caused more than one twenty-four-hour stint of work as my fiancé and I both tried to fix the issues as quickly as possible. As a result, when it came time to get back into the actual interviews, I couldn't help but feel a touch rusty, and a touch disconnected—even confused as the images started rolling in.

One thing I made sure not to do was look at any pictures of St. Valentine beforehand. I wanted to see what would come through on its own, and sure enough, eventually, something started to bleed into my mind's eye: the same church and cliff I'd met St. Nicholas on.

St. Valentine was an older man, with a big red and gold bishop hat and a beard much like St. Nicholas, who also happened to be there in his red and *silver* robes. But as I greeted them both, I was soon whisked away to a hill by a tree, where St. Valentine stood as a middle aged man with some balding on his head in all his brown hair, as well as a simple brown robe. He still had a bishop's staff, and he looked at me with a kind smile and soft, though tired, eyes. Little did I know that I would find essentially the exact same image when I searched for pictures of him later, which is always exciting.

"Alright," I said as I got comfortable, sitting at his feet with my journal in hand, "thank you for joining me, St. Valentine! I see we're out here in Rome, aren't we?"

He nodded, and we looked out towards the cliff, where suddenly, instead of the ocean like there'd been before, there was instead a city of orange terra cotta tiled roofs, of busy streets and bright, shining sun. Down below was a beautiful basilica. I got the sense St. Valentine wanted to use Amrit Brar's Marigold Tarot, which was quite the choice for a Saint of love, but hey—there's a reason each spirit picks the decks they do.

"Lovely. Okay, well, to get into it, I guess I'll start with the most obvious question: what do you think of your feast day?" I had a crystal clear image of a CVS full of Russell Stover's chocolate boxes and little plush bears holding hearts in their hands. "How it's become so associated with romance and the like?"

I. WHAT DO YOU THINK OF YOUR FEAST DAY'S ASSOCIATIONS?

St. Valentine let out a big sigh. "You see it," he said, bringing the image of that little heart-holding bear front and center. "People think a teddy bear with a heart in its paws can solve their failed relationship, their failed marriage. They put their faith in things, not each other. Why?" He looked at me, brows furrowed, a frown carved hard into his face. "Why do you all care so much for things and not the people you give the things to?"

I had no answer for him, about why people do things like this, so I only shrugged. I know with my own fiancé, Valentine's Day is more a day-after thing, where we both pig out on all the discounted Valentine's chocolate while spending the actual day itself enjoying our time and such. But the frustration in his voice was palpable, and I let out a big sigh before continuing.

Lies, maliciousness, cold heartedness, being judgemental.

Discord, disorder, overbearing control, and a breakdown in power dynamics.

"That's fair. But then, what is love?" Of course the Haddaway song started playing in my head, because I'm a goof. "What does it do?"

2. WHAT IS LOVE? WHAT DOES IT DO?

Success, discipline, enjoyment, and safety. Expanding points of view to see the bigger picture and finding it wonderful.

Authority, intellect, integrity, fortitude. Demanding respect. A powerful presence.

"Love is something that changes worlds," St. Valentine said as he stared out over the city, a little smile on his face. "It's something that moves empires to their feet, ready to band together as one nation and save their people. It's something that brings empires to their knees, too, when love has left the crowns that head them. Love is a force that cannot be diminished or destroyed; it can only ever be made absent, shut out.

"But an ember of love can melt the most frozen of hearts, and not all the world's darkness will ever be able to drown out its light." He turned to me, his teeth peeking through a half smile. "Love is the Spirit, and She comes for us all, her discipline as harsh and raw and undeniable as her comfort."

Wow. I stewed in that answer for a second, remembering the Holy Spirit's all-seeing, moonbright eyes. I know She holds that love St. Valentine talks about, but Her face is just so not what you'd expect love to look like, you know?

But as I thought, I looked at that basilica, and it hit me like a train. "Oh! Jesus, St. Valentine—that's where your head rolled, isn't it? What are we doing here?"

He shrugged and stared at it, the leaves of the tree rustling above his head. "I hold no pain over this place. It's where I went to meet God."

Will I ever not be blown away by Saints? Probably not. They're all so intense, bordering on insane, and I love them for it. With a shake of my head, I shuffled the cards and kept on.

"Okay, okay, well—what do you wish we understood about love?"

3. WHAT DO YOU WISH PEOPLE UNDERSTOOD ABOUT LOVE?

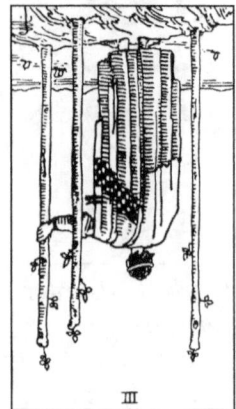

Lack of vision for the future, ignorance of the present.

Hostility, indecision, disharmony.

His smile faded. "What people don't understand is that love exists within all these things that plague us. There will never be a time where all is perfect, and the world doesn't test us. Love demands we foster it even in the harshest moments, in the darkest hours. Too many people think they love their partner, when they really only love what their partner might provide. And that's not love."

I nodded as I wrote. I understood that viscerally. Given I met my fiancé when we were both in high school, and we didn't have our own cars or our own money, and where there was still a long and messy journey to our dreams of a financially established household and a rich, adventurous life, there's no choice but to learn how to love someone for them—not for what they have, and not what they potentially *could* have. Just for them.

"Do you think love can ever truly be unconditional?" My mind was all over the place as I inspected my own idea of love—of hurtful things I'd said because I was scared that were not true, and promises I'd made to myself that I broke the second I finished whispering them because I knew they were selfish, and emotions that went so deep that, if I didn't pay attention, I might not realize were even there. "Can people really love like that?

4. CAN LOVE TRULY EVER BE UNCONDITIONAL?

With a wave of a hand, St. Valentine said, "You know. Everything has a condition: people put conditions on all their loves. Friends, lovers, even family can be departed from in a moment, if suddenly those parties become a problem to the person in question.

"But unconditional love does exist. It exists in God, in His Son—it exists in the human soul, a light so bright that it shines from the faces of men. There is love that people hold for one another, if for no other reason than because they exist."

"I hear you," I said. It was a comforting thought. "But it makes me wonder: how do you help couples and marriages thrive today, in this case? How do you help people foster this kind of love in any possible way?"

Unwillingness to see problems for what they are. Looming disaster, avoiding change.

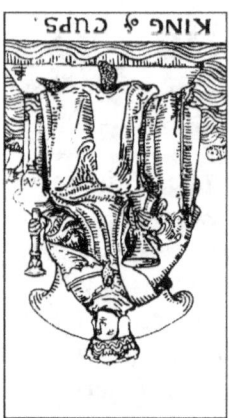

Behaviors that may be considered self destructive, controlling, dishonest, and manipulative.

5. HOW DO YOU HELP PEOPLE FOSTER TRUE LOVE?

St. Valentine sighed and tipped his chin up. "People look to me for help finding—and keeping—that love we just talked about," he said, his voice firm and his eyes shining with determination. "They wish for happiness, but they forget that love isn't just the wily flips and jumps of the heart. It's the lifelong commitment, the promise to endure the world's challenges together.

"I help marriages stay stable, and couples stay focused, on a world above ours—above the material things and stresses people forget aren't so impartial."

"Wow. That's pretty nice," I murmured, and my own chest swelled with that warmth, because it was genuinely encouraging to hear him say that. This was what marriage even was to me: that commitment. "Okay, well, what was the best part of marrying people back in the day?"

Judgement is transformational, but not always pleasant, in its execution. Seeking what's best for us. Painful lessons create true change.

Intelligence, trustworthiness, security, generosity, resourcefulness. A greater world past materialism. Nurturing and responsible.

6. WHAT WAS THE BEST PART OF MARRYING PEOPLE?

Naivete and recklessness.

Heavy burdens, being overwhelmed, and struggle.

He smiled. "The hope. No matter how brutal the world was to these people, and how they suffered, they wanted to be united before God—a declaration of resistance, an act of war on a cruel world. They believed they were better together, that they could fight better together, and they were right."

Not gonna lie, the Saint almost had me a bit teary-eyed. There's something about love that got thrown out in our over-commercialization of it in the grocery store aisles: that sense of love as resistance to a terrible world, a refusal to bow to cruelty and evil in a world that could so easily be full of nothing but joy and care for one another.

"Got'cha! And, well, I know what I think marriage is, but what do you think marriage is? Is it different from how I see it: as that commitment you talked about?"

7. WHAT IS MARRIAGE ITSELF?

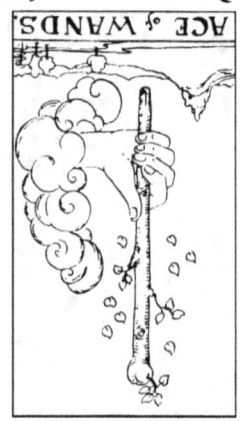

Ruins, delays, setbacks, trials, challenges in creative pursuits.

Financial troubles, victim menalities, rejection. Self inflicted strife.

His energy would flip between a vibe of hope and sadness, old joy and exhaustion, as I asked these questions. This one had him more tired, the bags under his eyes prominent.

"Marriage is war," he said, which surprised me as much as the cards I pulled. "It's the only war we voluntarily pitch ourselves into. A battle of wills, until the two sides are properly reconciled. When souls become one flesh—two souls in one house, two flames in one hearth—the war is won. But it doesn't come without its trials."

That answer struck me in a way I didn't expect it to. "I think I see what you mean." Compromise. Lots and lots of compromise. That was what was needed to achieve what he was talking about. And after reading more of McIntosh's *Mystical Theology*, where it was put concretely into words that the Word of God isn't just Jesus Himself, but the life Jesus lived, it makes me wonder if something of the story of God isn't woven into every marriage between two people, too. Taking two separate wills, two separate forces, into one divine Union. "But okay, that's the end of our personal questions. Now, I'd like to know: how do you see yourself?"

"Oh, I don't care to—"

"Ah, come on. Just one card?"

8. HOW DO YOU SEE YOURSELF?

He finally obliged me, but the Star reversed wasn't what I expected.

"This world," he said with a heavy sigh as he looked out at the city, "I am someone who doesn't have a lot of faith in it. I have faith in my God, my Lord, but it seems humanity hasn't come very far after all these years."

"And... how do you want to be seen?"

Mistrust, insecurity, loss of hope.

9. HOW DO YOU WANT TO BE SEEN?

Greed, potentially shallow fulfillment, and concerns with the material world.

I honestly got worried with Nine of Cups Reversed, worried enough that a little demon of doubt snuck into my space and had to be quickly dealt with before St. Valentine let me continue on. It was no big deal—little spirits like those aren't really that hard to wave away, granted you can recognize them for what they are in the first place—but it was a good reminder that what I expect and what is true are not always the same thing.

"What does it matter?" St. Valentine hunched over, his brows set hard. "It doesn't matter how people should see me, or what I want. My name is inextricably linked with heart shaped boxes of chocolate and bears holding soft red things. Nothing you do or say will change this. It's not up to you."

"Oh." I thought that was a little harsh, but I guess it is true: I can't change the flow of rampant capitalism or go in the streets telling people that St. Valentine doesn't like all this useless consumerist shit. But I can change my mind, at least—and maybe yours, if you're at this point of the story. That's at least half up to me. And at least I can say that there were no heart shaped boxes of chocolate in my house this year, but instead a night with my fiancé, enjoying a good meal together and listening to a live performance of Vivaldi's Four Seasons. "Okay. Do you have any final messages?"

10. ANY LAST MESSAGES?

His eyes crinkled at the corners as he smiled; it was like he was trying to soften that last line. "No, I think that was my last message."

"Alright, well—I guess that settles it, then. St. Valentine, you've taught me some really beautiful things today, and I appreciate that! Thank you for coming by, and may we meet again sometime."

With that, we parted ways, and that quaint little city, that basilica, all of it melted away into the darkness behind my eyelids once more. I packed up my things after that, cleared my table—and I wondered. Wondered about the timeliness of it all, that I would get this message at this time.

Because I'm not without flaw. My love is not perfect. And in fact, it was around this time that I went through one of the greatest challenges, and the greatest inner realizations of all. While I'm certainly an open book in this series (ha!) there are some details I do prefer to keep just between my loved ones and I, but what I can tell you is that this was the month that I made a clear decision, a clear commitment: that truly, for richer or poorer, in sickness and in health, I would stay with my fiancé. That no matter what life threw at us, we would figure it out together. For a long time, I'd been plagued with "what ifs"—with what the point would be where I would have to prioritize my own growth over everything else. The COVID-19 pandemic did a number on our employment opportunities, after all, and I was afraid of what would happen not only to us, but to me specifically—to all I'd worked for.

I'm glad to say the issue that had been causing my—honestly, *our*—anxiety to flare so greatly resolved just a couple short months later, thank God. But I'm even more glad to say that I made this choice first. That I realized life just sucks, and the only thing that can make it suck less is commitments like these, proper and permanent support of loved ones. While I call him *fiancé* at the time of writing this, the truth is that I think that moment was when I really married my fiancé in spirit, and looking back at St. Valentine's words, that brings me peace.

KING ASMODEUS

"I could never interview this spirit! I'll die!"

I think I've said this several times over the course of this series. There are always spirits that pull my eye, yet for some reason still intimidate me—whether because of how they are on principal, or because of things I may have said (either in seriousness or in jest) about them. In the case of King Asmodeus, it would be the latter—but only because I found the presentation of the whole Book of Tobit situation so Goddamn funny.

I mean, think about it. You're an ultra powerful demon who, at some point, made a fool of none other than King Solomon—and you end up giving this one poor human woman all kinds of grief by killing every husband she gets before she's able to consummate the marriage—but it's some young kid with a handful of fish guts and an open fire that sends you running? (Just for Raphael, the architect of this shit show, to chase you all the way to Egypt and bind you to a rock?)

That's some Looney Tunes shit. I'm sorry, but that's so insanely funny to me. Or maybe it's just the way I imagined it in my head as I read the story. Either way, I couldn't help but laugh at that whole mess, and I figured for the longest time that King Asmodeus would never want to talk to me as a result. While it's not confirmed in the text of the Book of Tobit, many of King Asmodeus's devotees have come to understand his actions in that story not as those of a meddling demon with nothing else to do, but as a way to try and preserve the woman of the story, Sarah, out of his love for her. It's a romantic reading, and one that also seems to have cropped up in some Jewish folklore, but again, not one really supported by the text in a direct reading. (I do appreciate the idea, though.)

King Asmodeus, however, is much more than just that one story in the Book of Tobit. Yes, he's a member of the Ars Goetia, but before that, he was also a more destructive force going all the way back to Zoroastrianism, where he was known by the name Aeshma. In Jewish lore, however, King Asmodeus is thought to be the King of Demons, and one of the Nephilim born of human/angel relations. He's a demon of lust, and while lust isn't love, there's surely something he could tell us about it.

Moreover, even if that Tobit story amused me, the story that made me come to really respect King Asmodeus was the story of his treatment of a poor drunk he'd stumbled across. While King Asmodeus heard the angels of heaven talking all kinds of smack about that drunkard, and how there was nothing good waiting for him in heaven, King Asmodeus decided to give the man even more alcohol—not to ruin him, but in an attempt to help the man continue enjoying himself and drowning his miseries while he still could, since the afterlife was apparently nothing to look forward to. It isn't the answer people would call correct, but it was an act of sympathy nonetheless in my eyes.

Moreover, remember when I spoke about King Solomon, that fabled Jewish King of yore? Yeah. Apparently the archangel Michael gave him a special ring from God Himself, one that could let King Solomon control any demon, and he went and bound King Asmodeus and forced him to build a temple of God. Wasn't long before King Asmodeus managed to get out of that situation, steal the ring, and literally boot King Solomon halfway around the world. With him gone, there was no one stopping King Asmodeus from taking Solomon's identity and doing some crazy stuff while in disguise. It was only by checking his strange feet that anyone finally figured out that he was not, in fact, the King of Israel.

One of my most favorite facts about this demon, though, is that because he knows the Torah (the first five books of the Bible), God actually allows him to visit the first circle of Heaven from time to time. That is such an interesting fact that really makes you question everything you know about how angels and demons interact.

But enough of all this, now. Let's hear from the very King himself on what he thinks about love and lust and everything in between.

According to my good friend Hannah (@spirituali.tea), who is also a devotee of this demon, King Asmodeus liked lemon. I figured King Asmodeus would like the offerings I set out. With some lemon thyme, a cup of lemon balm tea with lemon juice, my carnelian, amethyst, red jasper, and obsidian, and a stick of iris incense, I felt I had a pretty good spread out here. It looked nice, it smelled nice, and I also got to use my Occult Summoning Deck for the first time, as it'd come into my possession around then and suddenly made this entire process of talking to members of the Ars Goetia *so much easier.* Genuinely the best deck I could have along with the corresponding Angel Tarot, and not even for actual tarot readings.

But after I got in place, and I sheepishly asked God to help me find King Asmodeus while avoiding any and all contact with Raphael (and his no doubt ten tons of judgement), I could see myself standing on a dark ledge.

Everything was so black with shadow that I couldn't even see what I was standing on. I did the only thing I could do in that moment and called out into the dark: "King Asmodeus!"

Before I even finished asking him to come around, he sprang up from the dark and settled in front of me, looking like what I can only describe as an 18th century vampire. He had long blond hair, bright red eyes, a wicked smile, and he wore a plain white, half-unbuttoned shirt and pair of black slacks, his black leather shoes shining. He stared at me with the intensity of a cat about to pounce.

"Oh." I don't know if that was supposed to spook me, but I couldn't help smiling with him. "Well, alright—hello, King Asmodeus! Welcome! Please accept these offerings and join me to answer a few questions, if you'd like. But might I get some sign that you're really here beyond my imagination?"

It'd been a while since I asked that, and I did because I knew that demons were all too happy to make their presence *known.* I got flickers of red and blue flame behind my eyelids, as well as a prickling, crawling feeling up my spine. It was pretty classic Infernal Divine shenanigans, though the flickers of embers were new.

All the while, he stood there in the dark in my mind's eye. We shared a little bit of banter—though what we said, at this point, I can't remember—and as we got used to each other, I noticed again: the magnetism. The little frizzle, perhaps like the way it feels when you're with a friend you know gets you a little more unhinged and ready to make trouble than you usually are. It reminded me something of how I felt with King Belial: there was an energy of a lock just waiting to spring, of a rope only one strained thread away from snapping. I don't know how else to describe it, other than that the Infernal Divine doesn't praise me for keeping a mask on, but instead tries to find me underneath it and see if I'll let myself out.

Not every impulse is one worth letting out, though.

Eventually the darkness faded away like someone slowly un-dimming the lights. In this new space, King Asmodeus walked away and settled us in a study not unlike Lucifer's. This study, however, had more candles dripping wax, all kinds of books scattered about, thick velvet curtains, and deep red and gold hues that fell on the whole scene like fairy dust, as if it were the setting of a storied and deep-feeling immortal creature. It was peak Romantic Gothic, I won't lie.

"Ah, back in the office," I said as I strolled over. "Seems like I'm always being called into someone's office when I come around here."

He smiled and perched on the edge of his desk, half-sitting on it as he waited for me to start, and he chose Threads of Fate's Weaver Tarot to get speaking with.

"Alright, alright, let's get into it, then. First things first: what's the difference between love and lust?"

I. WHAT IS THE DIFFERENCE BETWEEN LOVE AND LUST?

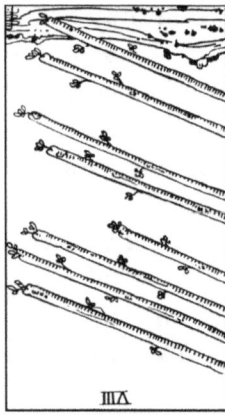

Slow down and examine the situation. You may be moving too quickly to weigh pros and cons. Be patient. Surrender to the flow; don't fight.

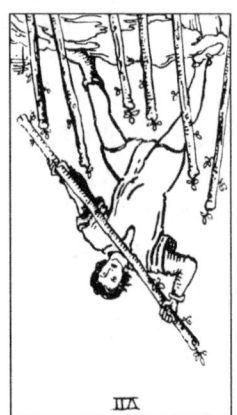

Overwhelm, downward trajectory, depression, stress, anxiety. Asking "what now?" Doubt, shrinking confidence. Stop doubting.

Paralysis as a response to deep shame and negative self talk. The mind is pure chaos. Exhaustion. Making things hard for yourself.

"Hmm." His lips curled into a smirk as I shuffled. "A good question."

And as I read the meanings of the cards, I couldn't help but chuckle. Overwhelm, lack of confidence, going with the flow—all kinds of interesting meanings swirled together into his answer as he looked over my shoulder at them.

"You see the cards. Lust is simple: you want something, so you take it. You humans get all twisted up about it sometimes, wallowing in what's 'right' and what's 'wrong'—boring. But I tell you: lust is fun. The pleasures of the flesh without the wicked attachments of the heart and soul.

"Love is a ruiner of minds, a hammer to the glass of your ego. It makes you question yourself, your worth—makes you dramatic and stupid. It's not worth the fuss, I must say."

"Huh." I felt like I was on the opposite side of the room from him, and as I blinked, suddenly it was just so: we were in a church, but not a Christian one. The altar was an empty table surrounded by lit candles, the light dancing off deep reddish wood that made it seem like we were inside of a heart. He sat in the front pew across from me, and I had my notebook in hand like some reporter. I tore my attention off whatever kind of church we were in and got back to my questions. "That sort of answers my next question, but I mean—there's more love than just the romantic kind. What do you think of love, in all its forms?"

2. WHAT DO YOU THINK OF LOVE?

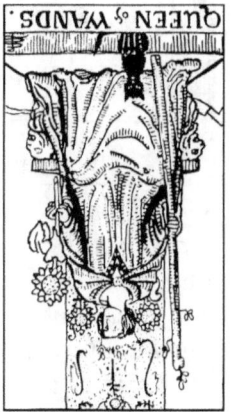

He smiled from across the church pews. "The greatest love is the love of yourself," he said. "Fuck your family, your dog, your lover; if you don't love yourself, then all the love in the world that could be poured into you would be like pouring tea into a cup with no bottom."

Arrival in many ways, realizing who you authentically are and what you need. An empowering space. Prioritize yourself over others.

"Damn. That's," I paused to chuckle, "that's a lot. But okay, okay, tell me, then: given you, yourself, experienced love with Sarah from what many of your devotees say... how would you describe the state of being in love? We don't have to talk about that story if you don't want to—"

"No, no. Go right on ahead. Talk about it with me."

"—oh, okay. Then what was it like to be in love for you?"

3. WHAT WAS IT LIKE FOR YOU TO BE IN LOVE?

Acknowledgement of public victory or external success. Perseverance through challenges and uncertainties. Optimism about challenges. Be careful with relationship with success.

I got my heart a little bruised pulling Six of Wands, I must admit. Sure, it sounds like a good card, but if the Infernal Divine could tell I wore a mask, then this card—this front, this clear and obvious barricade of the heart—seemed almost like a way to say, *us, too.* It made me feel bad for the demon King, especially as he explained—and he let me feel some of his own more visceral thoughts on the subject, too, because suddenly it felt like my heart had been speared through with a good few swords.

"You feel it," he said. "The daggers in the chest at failure—when I was so sure I could win. That I could claim my prize and prove myself capable of such a thing as marrying a human woman. To be in love was to suffer a fool's death."

Ouch. Hannah sent me a message on King Asmodeus before I'd gotten here: he understood now that it never would've worked between him and Sarah, but that didn't mean he had to be okay with it, nor did it mean he wouldn't do it all over again, killing her suitors and everything, to get to her. I sighed, but something about the language of all this, of Sarah as a "prize," made me erase a throwaway question and write down a more pertinent one.

"You say 'prize' about Sarah, and I can't help but wonder... how do demons see humans? What do you all think of us?"

4. What Do You Think About Humans?

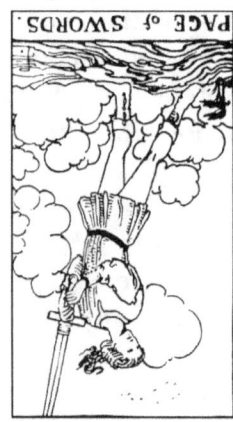

Balanced and healthy partnership of any kind. Both parties invested and respectful. Connection opens up new world for everyone.

A period of solitude. Focus on yourself and communicate your needs. Reconnect with worthwhile relationships.

Arrogance with no action to back it up. Let action do the talking. Intellect used for negativity. Ego stops us from seeing how our words hurt others.

Blew me right the hell away to pull these cards, and amused the hell out of me, too. King Asmodeus smiled as I burst out laughing reading the last card's description, because I knew right away what he was getting at, but he explained it anyway.

"You humans mesh so well with us," he said. "So bold, so complicated, so dramatic. You have the potential for greatness, yet insist on beating it out of yourself. Why do you want to remain small?"

"I dunno," I said with a wave of my hand. I thought of all those religious folks groveling like swine at the altars of God, even as Saints like Cyprian sneer at their refusal to realize their worth and their God-given power. I thought of how they misunderstood what it meant to be small, what it meant to serve—how by being too small, they actually managed to flee and escape their duties rather than face them head on. From under my own mask, from under the lid hiding all my excess, I said, "It's not God that tells us to be that way."

"No, it isn't," King Asmodeus said, flashing white teeth in a half-grin. "You've focused too much on one side of the coin as a species to the point that you've lost half of your own selves. All this bluster, all this talk against 'demons' and 'evil' and whatever else—for what? You hurt yourselves when you try to hurt us." He crossed his arms and sighed. "You're stupid, and we love you for it—enough that we'd like to help you be less so. For your own sake as much as ours."

The energy in this strange and spooky church was that of lightness, of two friends shooting the shit after a long week. I don't know how else to explain it, but nothing in there could've scared me, even for all the flashes of morbid and grotesque images of hell that he paraded around in front of me in between questions and answers. Like with President Camio, it was as if to try and trip me up or catch me in a state of reactivity, showing me all the horrors a mind could conjure. I do think I remember some big, bloody, gooey creature with a bare skull for a face and a million little centipede legs just oozing on by in the front of the church, for example. But his attempted spooking did not work, and I think he was happy it didn't.

"Okay, okay, well—what drew you to Sarah?" I leaned on that uncomfortable wooden pew, kicked my feet up over the back of the one in front of me. "What made you love her out of all the humans on earth?"

5. WHAT MADE YOU LOVE SARAH SPECIFICALLY?

This had the smile sliding from his face. He stared off, wistful, and told me.

"She was a woman who suffered exactly what I just spoke about," he said. "She was beautiful. And powerful. A gem in the rough. But she was blinded by a world built to keep her rough, in the ground, encased in suffocating rock."

"You're quite the poet."

"Yes, well." He shrugged, then continued. "I wanted to free her, but it wasn't my place, or within my ability, to do so. She had to do it herself. I wonder if she ever did, with that Tobias."

He kept staring far away, as if he were in a different time and place. I gave him a moment before I kept on.

"Fair. Okay, then, some more personal questions: what made you want to learn the Torah? I understand you know all of God's laws, and that's why you're allowed in Heaven."

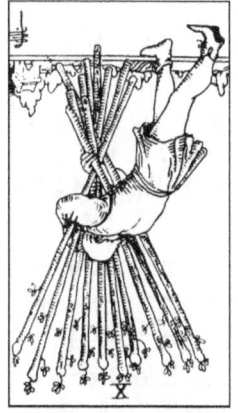 

Carrying a large burden and needing to get rid of it no matter what. You must eliminate this weight from your life.

Paralysis as a response to deep shame and negative self talk. The mind is chaos. Exhaustion. Making things hard for yourself.

6. WHAT MADE YOU WANT TO LEARN THE TORAH?

Sinking into the darker aspects of yourself and life. Exploring the shadow is necessary, but you may feel shame, fear, or judgement. Remember your good qualities and ground yourself.

Evolved, wise, and has spent many years understanding and healing themselves. Truth, logic unblinded by emotion. Says what you need to hear, not what you want. Boundaries. Making change.

Balance and peace. An open mind to other points of view. None of us are pure good or pure evil. What we think is true may not actually be so. Allow the possibility of harmony where you thought none.

"In the first circle, at least," he said with a sly smile. "But yes, the Torah—it's like a grid, an organizing web. It shows how your God there staves off the chaos that laces everything He's ever made.

"The Void never disappeared, you understand." In which I believe he meant the abyss, down there in the infernal realms. "But I wanted to see where He was coming from, your God—what made a good, stable people, world, and society in His eyes."

I jammed the eraser of the pencil into my eyebrow and muttered, "But Jesus said that all the law of the Torah and the prophets and such hung on the Golden Rule: love God, love one another."

King Asmodeus turned to me with a grin. He also ended up sitting all kinds of weird in the pew, legs kicked up onto the bench and arms draped over the back. "Yes. Love is one of the only forces that can nullify the true horror of chaos. It is a powerful force—but no less a pain in the ass. But that's all there is to answer this question: I was curious and willing to put my own thoughts and ego aside to understand God."

"Damn. That's pretty cool. But I don't get it; why would a demon want to go to heaven? Especially since most people seem to have this idea that demons hate angels and heaven and all of that."

7. WHY WOULD A DEMON WANT TO GO TO HEAVEN?

Again, King Asmodeus gave me this sly smile, and then we were standing not in that weird church, but up on the clouds of the first circle of heaven, where I'd stood many times before. The angels standing there stared at us like they'd just found a raccoon about to get into a trash can and make a mess of it.

Then Zadkiel came down, sword drawn and purple robes aflutter, and he pointed that golden sword at King Asmodeus. However, he stared at me all the while, even as he huffed at the demon King.

"Why are you here?"

"Whoa, Zadkiel—what's up?" I pushed his sword down, confused and more than a little alarmed that he could be so inhospitable to someone that was apparently allowed to be here. "What's this about?"

Your eye is on the finish line but are missing key steps. Impatience, trying to take shortcuts. Not being realistic. Accept issues before continuing.

Endings, life-death-life cycle. Big transitions you can't avoid. A chapter closing. Grief that comes with transition. Space being made for something new. Be present.

A period of necessary solitude. Surrender and trust that it's in your best interests. Dealing with things you've repressed. Enjoy and traverse the unknown.

King Asmodeus grinned. "Indeed, Zad—it's not as if I haven't been here before."

A flash of red legionnaire armor crossed my sight, and there was Michael, strolling up with his arms crossed. He glanced between me and King Asmodeus, then said, "I didn't expect you to bring trash here."

"Hey!" We'd been through this once before, and I hadn't changed my stance since the last time Michael got a bit rough with someone he backed me up to interview. My chat with Ananiel was the only time I needed to see that kind of behavior from an angel of God. "That's—!"

King Asmodeus put a hand on my shoulder. His voice was so unexpectedly gentle that it knocked whatever I was going to say right out of my head. "They're testing you."

"Huh?"

I didn't get it, but sure enough, as I glanced from him back to the angels, there was a satisfied smirk on both Michael's and Zadkiel's faces as they stared at me. Zadkiel's sword stayed out, though. Angels, man. I don't know. I once again swatted at Zadkiel's sword, and thankfully, they let King Asmodeus speak there, on the edge of heaven.

"Do you think you humans are the only ones still learning?" He crossed his arms, chuckled. "All those who don't know how this Story goes, as in, the story of this world, how it started, how it'll end, or why it's being written at all, have insight to gain. Lust and wrath, people ascribe to me—but I'm a scholar, too.

"I want to learn. Like you," he said, cutting me a sharp glance from the corner of his eye, "I want to devour the world and everything in it."

How rude, to read under the mask while I'm still wearing it.

King Asmodeus's smile grew as I startled. He finished his thought: "So I come here to learn and see what I can't see from my own throne. A humbling experience every time."

Then there was a flash of the clear night sky, lit by a big and beautiful moon that hovered between the prongs of someone's crown. Large white feathers spread out like a cloak, the innermost feathers tinged light blue, and I got the image of King Asmodeus sitting beside a sweet-faced angel, having what looked like a gentle and pleasant conversation. I didn't know exactly who it was then, but I think it may have been Haniel, because it certainly wasn't Gabriel. Associated with the moon or not, Gabriel did not seem like someone who would sit *that* close to King Asmodeus, y'know?

"I have good conversation with that angel," King Asmodeus said as the image faded from my mind, and we ended up back in that strange church down below in the infernal realms. "Much has happened in the world since our inceptions. It's good to talk about it."

And as he stepped back into that church, his footsteps made crystals of ice crust across the stone. They slowly melted the more steps he took. I got the sense that this angel, one of love who lived under the light of that great moon, cooled him down a bit—helped him work through thoughts and things that needed working through. How interesting.

"Okay, well, that wraps up our personal questions. On the general, now: how do you see yourself?"

8. HOW DO YOU SEE YOURSELF?

THE MOON.

The unknown, mystery, the unconscious self. Embrace hidden aspects of yourself. Surrender to the ride. Intuition and unseen forces.

Absolutely incredible, that I pulled the Moon right after thinking about that angel.

"I am not one-note," he said. "I'm not the monster people have made me out to be. There is depth unknown to humans, and I will break them if they can't allow themselves to see it."

"Oh, jeez. I think I know what happened to those nuns."

If you're curious, you can explore that legend of King Asmodeus and some unfortunate nuns. It's a hilarious concept to me: the idea that he possessed a group of them and had them go straight off the deep end.

He winked. "In me is multitudes," he said. "Things only those brave enough to approach can see."

"Fair, fair. How do you want to be seen, then?"

9. HOW DO YOU WANT TO BE SEEN?

King Asmodeus's tone went stony. "No one who works with me stays the same. If you want to become a more firmly outlined being, one who isn't trapped in the murk of the human ego and its lies, I am here. But the lessons will not be comfortable or easily won.

Expansion in mental energy. Cut through illusion, confusion, etc. Bringing new shifts. You can't stand still. Waking up to a new beat. Being pushed mentally. Finding clarity.

"I am one who smashes the ego glass; I drown you in the misery of guilt, that you may learn to never feel it again—that you may never have a reason to. I am one who humiliates and breaks even kings—and none shall know my name without understanding the gravity and meaning of faith."

"Holy shit," I said, once again chuckling as I went over my notes. It felt like I'd just gone down the first major dip of a big roller coaster, with all that energy. "That's... a lot. Damn. Alright! Well, thank you for that. Is that your message, though? Or was there something else you wanted to say?"

10. ANY LAST MESSAGES?

He stared towards the front of the church and shook his head. "No. Go now. If anyone wants to learn from me or ask me more, they should have the courage to do so themselves."

"Alright, yeah, that makes sense." Definitely does with a demon King like this one; there's something of the sheer experience of him that can't be captured just with my words here. "With that, then, I guess we can call this done. Thank you so much for your time, King Asmodeus, and I'd love to speak more with you sometime in the future. Goodbye for now!"

And then he was gone. It wouldn't be until the very end of May the next year that I would encounter anything involving King Asmodeus again—and that would be a battle of wills. Turns out that I don't have much to learn about willpower. I managed to get my entire summer garden planted during a violent thunderstorm, and I *almost* quit halfway through because the lightning was getting so close—but after my fiancé assured me that the storm wasn't *that* close, I got back out, soaked to the bone, and finished what I'd started.

I do not recommend doing that. The lightning was so close at one point that I saw the flash and heard the *BOOM* in my bones about a second later. But it was the only day I had to plant, and that same fire and pure *life* I'd felt with King Asmodeus was there again in all that chaos outside. Of all the trials I'd been on with the demons, that one—a mere three weeks—was certainly my fastest.

However, willpower doesn't always have the same roots. Sometimes, the roots of one's will are rotted: based in things that hurt us more than help. Every lesson learned from demons, it seems, works to peel back another layer of the mask we wear, until there's nothing left but our bare face.

The layers I have left of mine are thin. Still there, but thin. When I look at pictures and videos of myself from this time and earlier, I don't recognize myself anymore. My eyes cut a different angle. My brows are relaxed. My bones feel sharper, my head not empty, but oh so *quiet.*

Can you speak to so many people and remain the same? Can you speak to so many spirits and not shed old parts of yourself to find new ones? It seems for me, the answer is no. But every cut to my self understanding doesn't destroy me. It refines me, sharpens me, reconciles me to myself.

How harrowing, to realize I'll never be truly done with such a process.

HANIEL

There are so many more angels than the standard four, we already know. So many angels, in fact, that the Catholic church officials once complained about how many there were—how many thousands and thousands of names one might find. One has to wonder: are all of these names of angels, really, or simply many different names of God?

Given our conversation with Ananiel, and the fact that all the names have to do with God in some way ("God is my strength," "He who is like God," "God is my light"), I'm leaning towards the latter. In the case of Haniel, this angel's name means "God is my grace." Known especially in Jewish angelology as one of the seven major angels, this is a being representing joy, grace, love, and harmony—and given I'd seen Haniel in a woman's form in heaven, talking with King Asmodeus, you know I had to make a bee-line for her the next time. So let's take a look.

As an angel of all things love-related, be it friendship, romantic love, community harmony, or more, I figured it made the most sense to have crystals representing that out: sunstone, rose quartz, clear quartz, amethyst, and crushed rose petals. A white candle, a rose quartz angel and piece of celestite, and my ladybug rosary with its bright red beads, also felt appropriate. Most fun of all, I got to use Travis McHenry's Angel Tarot deck to get Haniel's sigil down, too. As with all angels, they aren't really ones to care for gifts—they'd rather all your love and attention go to God—and so once I had my little makeshift communication station set up, and once I asked God to help me out with this whole situation and let Haniel talk to me, I let myself get into it.

The last glimpse I had of Archangel Haniel was her sitting on some sort of log with King Asmodeus under a clear sky. The moon hung bright and silver-blue overhead, and Haniel herself wore white and light blue robes, with a big pronged crown of gold on her head and a full moon hanging between those prongs. The details of her—hair, eyes—these things were hazy then, but I know she had a sweet smile on her face. I held that bright moonlight in my mind as I called out to her.

"Archangel Haniel, hello!" I grabbed at any thread of her presence I could find. "If you don't mind, I've got some questions on love that I'd appreciate your time on. Please come and speak with me!"

Sometimes, images come and stabilize right away, and other times, I get a flash of many different things before my mind finally settles on where we're supposed to be. This interview brought me the latter, in which case there was a lot of silver-laced clouds, a big bright moon, and several buildings we moved past before finally, one building came solidly into view. It was one of those old library buildings that tries to look like an old Greek temple, with the marble columns and the gray triangle roof and such, and it sat at the edge of a cliff of clouds. A shimmering waterfall poured over the side of that cliff, the water becoming a silvery, glittery mist in the moonlight, and one big tree sprouted up beside the building, as if meaning to make it a treehouse somehow.

Haniel stood there in her blue-white dress, a belt of gold around her waist and her crown on her head, with two plaits of reddish hair neatly braided on either side of her face. Her eyes were huge, dark blue pools, and while she seemed calm, there was an alien quality to her expression—blank and neutral, bordering on cold. She went with me into the building, which had a warm glow coming from inside.

As we walked in, I soon realized it was a huge library. Warm mahogany wood caught the light of many lamps and candles, and the jewel-tone spines of leather books felt richer in that light. A fireplace roared with a big, bright blaze, and Haniel settled into a chair of plush red velvet, with a cup of something—maybe tea—in her hands.

"Interesting," I said, suspicious, because I was sure angels didn't necessarily do things like that per James L. Kugel's *The God of Old*. I thought angels didn't eat or drink.

She smiled as if guessing my thoughts, then tilted the cup towards me. In it were stars, stardust, galaxies. It didn't seem like stuff to actually drink.

"Alright, well, fine," I said as she settled with a sly smile. "Thank you for meeting with me nonetheless, Haniel! We've got some questions on the theme of love that I'd like to explore, so to start us off... what makes romantic love different from other kinds of love?"

1. WHAT MAKES ROMANTIC LOVE DIFFERENT FROM OTHER LOVE?

Unexpected fortunes are best, but they must be managed wisely.

Having a map is sometimes better than knowing where it goes.

A job is well done when we've done only what is needed.

Haniel huffed. "Romantic love is sometimes transactional," she said with a wave of her hand. Then she clutched her cup of galaxy-tea and continued. "Certainly, it's not the first love we come to know, either. It's something exclusive, not cultivated with just anyone, and therefore it's fickle and hollow compared to the root of love. Any such romantic sentiments not grown from that root will wither."

"By the root, I'm assuming you mean—?"

"God, yes. God is the root of love."

"Got'cha. That makes a lot of sense. But then, which type of love do you enjoy helping people foster the most?"

2. WHAT LOVE DO YOU ENJOY HELPING FOSTER THE MOST?

"Hmm." She lounged in that chair, then pulled her feet up on it and tucked them under her, as if she were a princess very comfortable in her high tower. As I pulled cards, I heard her say clearly, "Platonic love."

Then she continued once I had the cards in front of me.

"Platonic love has all the traps and tests of romantic love, and yet it's so much easier to find and cultivate. You humans are social creatures; you couldn't live without pointing that need to form bonds somewhere, even if at a simple animal. Your yearning to

Vanity, dashed ambitions, and a lack of challenge.

Breaking bonds, freedom, detachment.

Often it is only possible to seize opportunities by checking our most intense urges.

give it, to cultivate it, it's all so precious. It can make you complacent if you're not mindful, but it can set you free, too."

"Wow." I basked in that answer for a minute, because it inspired images of people loving all kinds of things: other people, pets, friends, family, all that. And it felt gracious, even if also revealing the angel notion to see humans as silly little things. Understandable that they do, of course; we are silly little things. But it also reminded me of Nehalenia, the way she said "you humans." I found that interesting.

"That's really cool, I said. But okay, so, for our next question—"

"Hmm, no." She curled towards me, her sly smile growing. "Ask me about the War. About where I was in it."

Huh?

I squinted at her, now even more suspicious than before. This *was* Haniel, right? Pretty little angel of love and all that? "Why? Lucifer said there was no real 'war.' What do you mean?"

She gestured towards my journal. "Ask me."

In which case, okay, fine. If she insisted, right? I erased a less important question and put this one down instead, reading it one more time as if to confirm it was really the one I was going to ask.

"So... where were you, then? During the war?"

3. WHERE WERE YOU DURING THE HEAVENLY WAR?

There wasn't even anything that she said, if I'm being honest. I was just taken off to look into a bit of the past, it seemed, where Haniel was standing in a room of white marble, a large arched window letting moonlight pour in. She was looking outside it, down to the very earth, and watching a big boat floating along in the water—an Ark, maybe, given the whole world seemed to be, frankly, *flooded.*

Someone dressed in black entered; his footsteps clacked along the floors. His blonde hair, his sharp face, his focused eyes, and his quiet air—as well as the wings tucked behind his back, glimmering with light—told me he was Lucifer.

Haniel turned around, tear stains shining on her face. Her eyes were huge, blue, and so watery, and she twisted her hands together in obvious anxiety.

"Samael," she whispered, "why would you do this? Why would you ask me to leave Heaven with you? Won't you just trust God, that all will be as it needs to be?"

Lucifer strolled up beside her and stared out the window. He glanced at her, his face a mask, but his voice gentle: "How can I when He won't let them off that boat?" The silence was loud as he turned back to the window, staring outside it. His jaw worked, and he whispered, "it's Day 38."

"It'll be fine!" Haniel glanced between him and the boat, looking a little unsure herself despite how hard she insisted on everything working out all peachy keen. She put her hand on the glass and said, "I need to be here. I trust God. When they do get off that boat, they'll need someone to show them how to love again. I'll be the one to do so."

Lucifer stared at her, then turned on his heel and walked away without another word. He didn't argue, nor did he fight. He just strolled off. But as he got to the doorway, Haniel whipped around.

"Samael! You know as long as you wear a name of God, you'll never be free, don't you?"

That got Lucifer to pause, but he only glanced over his shoulder at her before he left the room. Then the whole vision faded, and I was sitting there blinking as if the lights had just been turned on after a good movie.

"God watched to see who Lucifer could convince," Haniel whispered. Her eyes were glued to the floor, as if she was still in that vision of her memory. "He is, after all, a curious one. God knows. God always knew this would happen; He just wanted to see how it would play out." Then she shrugged, bitterness lacing her voice. "I guess I just wasn't very good at convincing Lucifer to stay. But I do wonder sometimes: is all of this just a game to God? Whether we stay here or go elsewhere, does it matter?"

I stared at her. What the hell would an angel say all this for? "Uh, Haniel... why are you saying all of this as if God doesn't hear you right now?"

Her lips split in her wolfish smile. "Do you think God doesn't know how I feel, whether I say it out loud or not?"

"Fair, yeah. Okay." The last thing she said to Lucifer still bounced around my head, though, because I'd been having a lot of thoughts about angel names, and this seemed like Haniel's long, roundabout way of confirming it: there was no greater cage than a name for beings like angels. How strange. Maybe that's why Lucifer decided to wear his title rather than the name I believe he has—and that Haniel echoed—underneath it. "Well, moving on, why do you talk to King Asmodeus? I understand he comes around often."

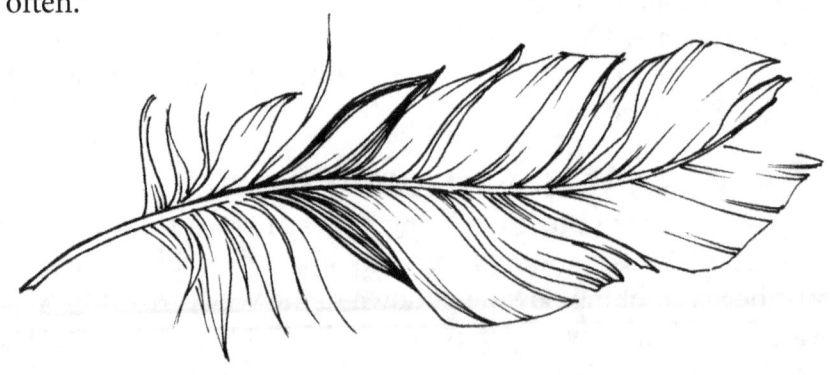

4. WHY DO YOU HANG OUT WITH KING ASMODEUS?

Here, the imagery of the cards, especially the Two of Swords and Two of Cups, stuck out to me. In this deck, the Two of Swords is a blindfolded woman, two swords in her hands, as a dragon peers into her castle window. The Two of Cups has a man and a woman united by a magic mirror, with the man's side looking dark and hellish, the woman's side more like heaven.

Understanding our difficulties is often the first step to overcoming them.

Stay alert and consider the adversary's point of view in order to avoid a potentially difficult situation.

The most fertile marriages can arise from radical changes and sudden shocks.

"He is a bruised man, that Asmodeus," Haniel whispered, "but not a defeated one. It's as your cards say, though: I overcome things, those 'what ifs' and 'would-have-beens'; I can see through Asmoday what I rejected in Samael's proposition." Then she made a face. "I do not like their world or their ways. I made a good choice to stay here.

"But there's something necessary about them, the Infernals. Something vital. It's as if God needed them to balance out Heaven—to contain what chaos still existed that Heaven refused to swallow. God knows things we don't. I wish He'd at least tell us a little more. He won't, though. He has His secrets."

While she talked, I could feel my brows knitting together harder and harder. This was nutty, I won't lie. It felt like having a family member tell you a bunch of crazy stories about your dad that gave him a whole lot of color your childhood self never saw. I tapped my pencil to the journal, taking it all in, before I nodded.

"Okay. That's... crazy, honestly. I love the drama, but... damn." What else could I say to this family feud, really? "I think I'd like to get back to our topic of love, though, so... how can people remember to love others?"

5. HOW CAN PEOPLE REMEMBER TO LOVE OTHERS?

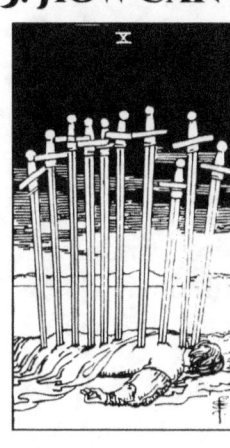

Even when all appears to be lost, we must remember everything comes to an end and no enemy is invincible.

Haniel shrugged. "Love is war, but your enemy is not your partner. The world is cruel and full of terror, and when you put yourself in the shoes of another, taking on their terror as your own, love is what keeps you both standing and fighting."

"Oh, wow, alright. That's a beautiful way of looking at it; thank you! And now, how can people learn to better love themselves?"

6. HOW CAN PEOPLE BETTER LEARN TO LOVE THEMSELVES?

As she lounged there on her big chair, she sighed and ran her fingers over her hair. "You humans take things too seriously sometimes," she said. "There are a million reasons to hate yourselves in your eyes, but are there really no reasons to love yourself? Even silly, stupid reasons?"

At times, it's useful to view things through the eyes of a child at play. Secret truths are sometimes right before us, but we're unable to see them.

"The world lies to you. That is what you must remember: it sells you illusions you'll never achieve and steals your love and joy in return. No one is too far gone to love themselves unless they believe themselves to be. When you are lost in the black tar of hatred, remember that it's all only as suffocating as you let it be. It has no power over you that you don't give it."

"I got'cha, yeah. That makes sense." Hate sounds like one of those true demons in that regard. As I scribbled, I kept going. "Now, okay, what's one thing people think is love, but isn't?"

7. WHAT DO PEOPLE THINK LOVE IS, BUT ISN'T?

Often the need to rest is greater than the need to work. Thoughts must move smoothly in our minds to stimulate new enthusiasm.

Recklessness and naivete.

Powerlessness and a possibly inflated ego.

"Brashness," she muttered. "Show. People, they—" with a sigh, she rubbed her temple, "what a mess they make of themselves, trying to court each other like animals.

"You are not some bird of paradise, that you need to jump and preen and decorate yourselves to win or be worthy of love. Those who love you for those things alone do not love you. Those who do certain behaviors, like keep up their health and hygiene, only for others, likewise don't love themselves. When you learn to exist as your own self, with no expectation from the world to care about you, you find the right people who love you."

I blinked like I'd been whapped with a rolled up newspaper. "I see. Thank you! That makes a lot of sense. But okay, so: how do you see yourself, Haniel?"

8. HOW DO YOU SEE YOURSELF?

"I don't," she said, her voice flat. "I don't put much thought into who I am. My title is all I need to be. The rest is raw experience—me experiencing all other things in the world. You put too much expectation on angels. We are as we are. But this makes you uncomfortable, so we try for your sake."

Jeez. "Got'cha. But if you engage with us, then, how do you want us to see you?"

9. HOW DO YOU WANT TO BE SEEN?

Then I caught a vision of her no longer in a blue dress, but in soft pink chiffon, her hair tied up as if she were some sort of Greek goddess, a staff of gold in her hand. She was in a desert, watching over some gigantic red orb. It glimmered from a thousand facets like a jewel, but the shine was muted, and it was laced with black veins and spots.

Inability to move forward, obstacles, waiting.

"I do my duty," she said. "I guard the Great Human Heart. The raw concept of your irrational psyches. So long as you all poison yourselves with lies and foolishness, it will stay speckled with rot. I would like to heal you, but it's not my place. So here I wait, hoping one day, this will shine bright like a rose made of gold. Like it used to before you bit that damn fruit."

"Oh!" Once again, that took me for a ride, especially with the edge of frustration that laced her words. I blinked, then nodded. "Alright, alright, I understand. But that's all the questions I have for today. Do you have any other messages you'd like to share in the meantime?"

10. ANY LAST MESSAGES?

Rules and traditions often preserve things that in the past were good and useful, but true wisdom knows when to innovate.

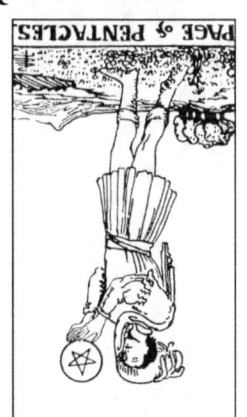

Wastefulness, bad news, and preoccupation with projects at the expense of other piorities.

Carelessness, pessimism, lethargy, or roadblocks in getting success.

"It's as your cards say, she said as she tapped them. "You humans—you waste so much time on things that don't matter. You let every obstacle trip you, to the point that you have more blood on your knees than skin.

"As an angel, it is so difficult to watch you. I feel like a lion kept in a cage far too small. I wonder if this is how Samael felt, too. But so long as I wear the name Joy of God, I will fight for you—for the Great Human Heart—to flourish, bloom, and be rich with the purity of true, unadultered, undiminished, untarnished love."

Haniel turned to me, that heart hanging in the distance, and smiled.

"You can do it. You can make it. Belief in this—faith that God made you capable of it—keeps me here, standing with you, watching over you."

"Oh, man," I whispered. "That's a lot."

She only kept smiling at me.

"Well, that about wraps it up, then," I said as I plunked my pencil down. "Thank you, Haniel. I really appreciate your time here, and all the time, I guess, that you've been watching us. This has been quite the fascinating conversation! But I do have to go now, so with that, I'll say goodbye. Until next time!"

She kept smiling as she faded away. If I'm honest, as pretty of a picture as she made out there with that giant red thing, I couldn't help but breathe a sigh of relief once I was out of there. That certainly did *not* go how I imagined it would.

But what else could I expect from angels (and, by extension, demons)? There was something under the surface of the roles they played in public, all villains here and heroes there. I didn't expect Haniel to be the one to let me look under the hood there, nor did I expect to see anything that had to do with Lucifer or the decision to leave heaven, though. Nor did I expect an angel still in heaven to have such an air about them. It almost makes you wonder—especially when you read the Bible and all the places where severe punishment happens for serious transgressions so that, and I quote, people would "be afraid" and not do such terrible things again. Was the incident with the Watchers a case where God was ensuring the remaining angels would "be afraid" like that? Are there angels who are only angels because they happened to make the right choice one time? The more I piece these things together, all while God is watching, the more I also wonder what the hell *He* has in mind, too.

Make of all this what you will. All I know is that every time things like this happen, it just ensures that I stray farther and farther from the *left* or the *right*. That I turn my foot not in either direction, but keep it on the straight and narrow: on the borderline, on the edge, walking that thin line between the two.

MILDA

To round out the discussion of love, after Saint, demon, and angel, it was only fair to see love from a perspective outside this scope of spirits. I found myself looking back to the Baltic pantheon, what with all these gods so few have heard of and so few have explored. In fact, I'd seen it a long time ago: a request from a Lithuanian TikTok user to interview Milda, Baltic goddess of love. Finally, with this topic, I could go investigate that.

As I looked into Milda, I found that, like with the Slavic Lada, it seemed scholars couldn't really agree if this goddess ever existed, or if she was simply some post-Christianization invention. The only clue we could've had that would suggest Milda did really exist, in my opinion, is the fact that the Christian church named two goddesses specifically as the most foul, the most demonic, the most ridiculous: Ragana, Baltic goddess of magic and witchcraft, and this here Milda.

One thing's for certain in my mind: if Milda didn't exist, then there wouldn't be so much hate for her stewing in the Christian church. In fact, there never would've been any. But given Milda is a goddess of free love, love that didn't necessarily need to be bound to institutions of marriage and could flourish anywhere, at any time, between anyone, it's no wonder the Church wanted to stamp that out.

No hate like Christian love, right?

All I know is that I did find something when I called out to this goddess—and here, I'll lay out exactly what.

✦

As always, I had my table set up with things that made me think of love: my pink amethyst and rose quartz, my sunstone, too, and some rose petals scattered around an offering of two home grown strawberries. It was all I had. I figured since the strawberries were ones from the very strawberries I planted and cared for, their scant number would still be acceptable. I also felt the pull to put down some hawthorn berries, so those got scattered around, too.

But truth be told, I'd put out the signal earlier that week that I would want to talk to Milda, and sure enough, I caught a glimpse of her as she'd been described: naked as hell in the woods, with long brown hair and eyes massive and dark, like two deep holes that could swallow all. When I called on her for the actual interview, she appeared exactly the same, and she brought us to the edge of a forest, on the banks of a lake sparkling in early morning sunlight.

"Milda, hello!" I was nervous, mostly because when I'd asked God about her, He gave me Death Reversed: a card that suggested there was a wound in the Lithuanian goddess somewhere, about something, and I had a pretty good guess as to what, given Lithuania's story of Christianization. It was not a pretty story. "Thank you for coming to speak with me. I have some cinnamon incense and strawberries for you; please accept them as a token of gratitude for coming by. If you don't mind, I'd like to ask some questions."

"Of course." Her tone was flippant, her face soft and kind, but there was a strength to her that was undeniable. "Go right ahead."

Well, that response didn't suggest she was harboring any ill will, at least. So I just dove in. "Okay, okay, so—the first question I have is about 'free love.' You're a goddess of free love, not marriage or anything else, and so I wonder what that means to you?"

I. WHAT DOES IT MEAN TO BE A GODDESS OF LOVE, NOT MARRIAGE?

New beginnings, new perspectives, and favoring pessimism.

Greed, maybe shallow fulfillment, and concerns with the material world.

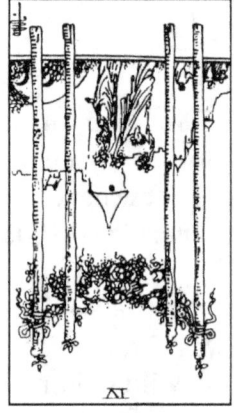

Social disputes and prioritizing others at the expense of our development.

"Ah, that." She frowned, then waved a hand as she stood on a rock and towered over me. "Why lock yourself down with something like marriage? Why go through all this pomp and circumstance, this nonsense, this big show of 'commitment'? When you speak of love, the only thing that matters is: do you love each other or not? There are many people in this world to enjoy, yet for some nonsense about duty and honor, you put chains on love.

"Free love is exactly what it sounds like: free. Free of social expectation, of money or honor or lineage. It's the love you find by surprise on Midsummer night; it's the love that leaves good memories and has no time to decay."

"Oh." That would take some time, honestly, for my mind to wrap around. If there was ever a goddess I could think would be a proponent of polyamory or casual flings, Milda sounded like it—and I don't mean that in a bad way or anything. It was just alien to me at the time, which tells me now that in fact my worldview, despite how progressive I think I am with religion and spirituality, remains colored by the very prudish Christian fabric of American cultural values that seems to have seeped into everything we take for granted about life. "I guess that gets us directly into our next question, then: it seems you have some thoughts on marriage; could you share more about it?"

2. WHAT DO YOU THINK ABOUT MARRIAGE?

With a sharp nod, she said, "If you truly love someone, then any nonsense about money or comfort falls away. Marriage is a business contract; I find it often has little to do with love—and that people ignore the terms of their expensive contract anyway.

"'In sickness and in health, for rich or poor,'—what does it mean to people? Nothing. I've seen your Christian men use marriage like a farmer uses a yoke," she said with a sneer, "and it disgusts me. You remove the soul of connection with your marriage—your hang-ups about it, your rush to do what you could've always done, had you still had free love."

Financial trouble, struggle, victim mentality, rejection. Bad circumstances. Self inflicted strife.

Success, discipline, enjoyment, safety. Expanding your perspective to see the bigger picture.

Major and mundane decisions. Speedy change. Navigating triumph and choice when doubtful.

I got the sense she was talking about those Christians who rush to get married just because they want to get frisky in a "permissible" way.

"I hear you loud and clear," I said, "and I don't disagree at all. There's been a lot of mess made with the church, but we can get into that later. Right now, I've got another question: it seems some people doubt your authenticity and think one especially zealous scholar just... I don't know, made you up. Reminds me of what happened with the Slavic Lada. Do you have any thoughts on this?"

3. THOUGHTS ON THE CLAIM YOU'RE A LATER INVENTION?

Her brow quirked, and then she sighed. She didn't need any cards to tell me: "I was always here. It's not my fault your Christian men don't want to believe I was here."

I cocked my head, surprised by the bluntness, and the force, of that answer. It was crystal clear to the point that I didn't even have time for pulling cards.

"Understood. How about the power of love, then? Can you tell me about what power love has?"

4. WHAT POWER DOES LOVE HAVE?

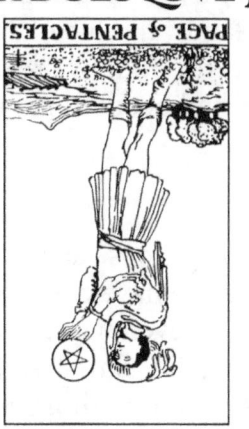

1. Abundance, generosity, security, level headedness, reliability, tolerance. Financial and mental security. Reaping benefits of strengths and limits.

2. Bad news, wastefulness, or a preoccupation with projects at the expense of other priorities in life.

3. Victory, confidence, and pride.

Milda ran her fingers through her hair and shook her head. "Love gets things done, but it flits, too," she said. It's a fickle force, seemingly fleeting and hard to catch—but when it sheds its glory on a community, there's nothing that community can't accomplish. Granted, it causes trouble sometimes," she admitted with a wave of her hand, "but its good outweighs its pains. It holds the world together like glue."

Well, that was sweet. I scribbled that down and nodded, smiling. But the smile didn't last long as I looked at the next question on my list.

"Fair, fair. And *now* we can get into the church stuff." Which I didn't think was going to be pretty. "From what I understand, it seems you and Ragana both were problems for the church leaders; they couldn't stand seeing any of your images. What do you think of the Church—of Christianity, of God, all that?"

5. WHAT DO YOU THINK OF CHRISTIANITY?

Generosity, prosperity, gratification, reflection, loss vs. gain. Understanding the helpful and harmful aspects of the world.

Speak of other deities, and they will appear, as I've said time and time again. Behind the naked and stalwart Milda was suddenly Ragana: a lithe, pallid woman, one with a crown of greenery on her black hair and a sharpness to her features that could've cut through rock. Her dress was grey like shadows at dawn, and she eyed me as Milda spoke.

"I could care less about your God," Milda said with an upturned nose. "He's innocent in this. When your Templars came marching, He wasn't there among them. Had He been, I might've had somewhere to focus all my rage. But no. It was just you all that destroyed our temples. And your human stupidity."

Ragana sat down on a rock, and her voice was so low and smooth: "Your 'Church' was too self-important. The men who ran it were too sure of a God just as disgusted with them as we were."

Milda crossed her arms and huffed. "They hated our bodies. Our names. They tore us down, even when the male gods of our people stood beside us—though of course, those Church men left those up for a time, for 'historical study' or some such excuses. Your men hate your women. It's strange." Then Milda's dark eyes glimmered with something sharp, brutal. "But your churches," she hissed, "if I could, I'd burn them down like the invasive mold they are in my lands. Had they come in love, and not in fury, I might've tolerated them."

I must've had a wild look on my face, because with a sharp smile, Ragana added to Milda's ire. "She speaks harshly, but it's true. The churches have been a blight. Gaudy and bloated with riches, grandiose signs of shame and inadequacy felt by their builders. Insincere. Hollow. I regret their existence. Your God has nothing to do with it—so much that we wish He had been more present. Then He might've done something about this."

Milda muttered, "Then we might've been able to blame Him."

"Jeez."

As I wrote, I got a picture of raw Divinity I hadn't before: a true glimpse at a wound blatantly still bleeding, exactly as God said would be there. Other gods seemed to have come to terms with a lot of things, or acknowledge the flow and change of the world; hell, I've even heard that Apollo himself, the god of oracles, predicted the fall of Hellenismos to something like Christianity. But to feel the harshness, the anger, still burning underneath these Divinities, was something else—and entirely understandable. I told them as much, too: that I understood, and that I knew it was terrible what had happened, and that I wish things had been different. It didn't make anything better, but it did make them amicable towards me, I think. Either way, this was quite the departure from the conversation about love I'd been meaning to have.

But the idea of God being *too* absent—that, I still wonder about. Especially in conjunction with what Haniel had said the week prior.

"Okay, thank you both for that answer; that was quite the expression." I flipped through my notebook, shuffled my cards, and got back into the last few questions. "Well, Milda, another question for you now: why doves to pull your chariot?"

6. WHY DO DOVES PULL YOUR CHARIOT?

She shrugged. "I know they're associated with your Holy Spirit. I regret that, too, just as I and Ragana both regret the existence of your churches. I wish they weren't linked with the Holy Spirit, that my doves might always be seen as my doves. But I still love them. They're sweet creatures. So I keep them by my chariot."

"That's fair. But then, okay, so—what would you say makes relationships richer?"

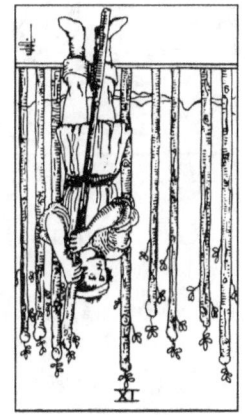

Pessimism, dread, and resignation.

7. WHAT MAKES RELATIONSHIPS RICHER?

Inability to move forward, obstacles, waiting.

Naivety, disharmony, holding onto the past in an unhealthy way.

Preoccupation with wishing for the impossible, abundance of options, indecision.

Here, Milda huffed a laugh and smiled, a sparkle in her deep, dark eyes. "Your stupidity," she said, which knocked me completely off kilter. "Stupidity makes relationships richer: the stupidity that makes one not believe, but decide, that the impossible will be made possible. The stupidity to believe in someone when there seems to be nothing to believe in. All the bad choices, all the stubborn refusal to quit on one another, and your belief in one another despite all odds. That's what makes relationships richer."

Not gonna lie, even if that caught me off guard, it was the sweetest answer of the morning. It hit me right in the feels, and it made me think of those "indominable human spirit" memes. I loved it.

"That's so nice; thank you, Milda!" There was that funny little warmth in my chest at the thought of all the implications of that answer. "But alright, well, that's about the end of my personal questions. Now to get into the classics: how do you see yourself?"

8. HOW DO YOU SEE YOURSELF?

High, near fool-hardy energy. Impetuousness and granstanding. Rashness, overconfidence, infatuation. Act more recklessly; be more assertive.

KNIGHT of WANDS.

She folded her arms and stared out at the lake with a mischievous smile. "I am. And I am a fighter! I do as I please; I go where I wish. I've never left my people, and I never will."

"Beautiful." It seemed like many Divinities started with that idea: that they simply *were*. Beyond God's name meaning, that seemed to be a hallmark *of* Divinity: just being. Which has its own implications, the more I think about it. "And how do you want to be seen?"

9. HOW DO YOU WANT TO BE SEEN?

Milda pulled no cards; she simply said, "As I see myself."

"Okay—and so, do you have any messages before we part ways? Any final cards to pull?"

10. ANY LAST MESSAGES?

Embarrassment, anxiety, inability to stand up for oneself.

"Yes. In love, you don't know unless you try. Forget your feelings about yourself. Let your feelings for one another be your guide forward, simple as that."

It was so simple an answer, yet so sharp and to the point at the same time. "I got'cha," I said. "That makes sense to me—somehow. But thank you, Milda," and as I spoke, she was already in her chariot, smiling and waving as the doves pulled her into the sky, "thank you for all you've shared this morning! I greatly appreciate it!"

Then she was gone, and I snapped back into the mundane world of my kitchen in the early morning. It was a fruitful conversation, for sure—one that had me understanding love a little differently all over again, in less of that stuffy western Christian way and more in the way of what can only be described as an experience. Maybe love was all the things Saint Paul said it was. Maybe it wasn't. Maybe it was, but it was more than that, too: something that could be sampled, tried out, and then left when the fun was over. Or maybe we're all meant to love different people in different ways at different times.

Who can say, really? It seems we're all meant to collide with one another in ways we just don't understand yet, like sentient particles out there obeying all the brutal laws of physics. I don't have an answer for everything, and it does seem that the more I learn, the less I know—but damn it, maybe that's the point. Maybe life's less about answers and more about just enjoying the time we have; maybe the mystery of all these unsolved problems are what gives life its color, too. All I know is that the less I feel I know, the easier it is for me to sit down and just let myself be.

Because it's okay. It's okay to let life unfold one step at a time. To love this person, to let them go. To love another, and another after that. To let time progress and let the roles we all play in each other's lives start and end with grace. It's easier that way. Nicer. Sweeter.

DUCHESS BUNE

Once the theme of love was gone, the next topic came up soon enough. It seemed folks wanted to know more about the element of earth, just as they had with air. I had no problem investigating that; after all, the very core of my astral chart was Virgo, a wily earth sign in and of itself. More than that, I'd also recently encountered Duchess Bune in my work with Lucifer, and let me tell you: that was the first time I'd ever been startled in meditation.

I remember it so clearly, too, because it gave me a genuine startle. Normally, talking to demons will have me feeling like I shouldn't turn around—like there's something there, watching me, waiting for me to notice and turn so they can maybe give me a fright. Much of that, I don't doubt, is my own lingering nervousness about such spirits that, no matter how much I work with them, I can never seem to fully shake. We might call it Christian programming, or we might call it sheer animal instinct, because the fact is that the Infernal Divine have an energy about them that the animal mind and body does not always like. All one can do is tame it and trust.

Still, that Duchess Bune. I was walking through a nice manor, one with antique furniture made of a very dark wood and deep green wallpaper with black ivy; one with deep purple carpets and the light of a cloudy day phasing through pale lace curtains. There was an open door, and as I walked past it, I suddenly found myself face to face with the huge, dark eyes of a woman, her hair cut in a French bob and a neck-high dress with a lace collar brushing at her sharp chin. It was so unexpected a picture during meditation that my eyes flew open as if that would help me get away from this new entity. Once I closed my eyes again, she was still there; she furrowed her brows and pouted as if sorry to have startled me. Duches Bune didn't say anything, either; she soon disappeared as I went on with whatever it was I was doing at the time, there in the infernal realms.

From what I understand, Duchess Bune is another member of the Ars Goetia that has a long history. Some believe that she might've been an extrapolation of Buto, another name for Egyptian Isis, or even the Egyptian Wadjet, goddess of snakes. According to the Ars Goetia, Duchess Bune, the 26th spirit, is one capable of bringing fortune, of switching the places of the dead, and inspiring eloquence; the snake connection might be considered, too, given she apparently comes as a dragon with three heads. Given how rarely any of these spirits have ever come to me looking as crazy as these medieval grimoires describe, I can only assume that their appearance reflected something about the writers of these tomes rather than the spirits themselves. (Because, what? How does that beautiful image of my first encounter have anything to do with some three headed dragon?)

Nonetheless, I thought this would be the perfect time to talk to her in full, given S. Connolly mentions her to be associated with earth in her work, *The Complete Book of Demonolatry*. I also caught from looking around online that she's associated with the sun, too, which made finding things to call her near with much easier. So without further ado, here is Duchess Bune.

Like King Asmodeus, it seems Duchess Bune enjoys citrus, at least from the unverified personal gnosis (UPG) of practitioners on Reddit. A shame that none of these grimoires I'd been pouring through had the *really* useful information like that; most were more preoccupied with chants and the right type of metal vessel to try and trap a demon in like some kind of Pokémon. Oh well; that's what UPG is helpful for, right? Little details like what a not-so-well-known spirit might like as a gift?

Either way, I had no concrete citrus things around, save for lemon juice, so I poured a small offering of lemon water with a smattering of chocolate chips. A weird combination, maybe, but it made sense to me. That, plus some cinnamon incense as a nod to the sun, and my onyx, obsidian, sunstone, moss agate, and bloodstone, plus a green candle, gave just enough of a hint of the sun in between all the earth tones. Her card from McHenry's Occult Tarot sat tall against the candle, and once I'd done my typical starting routine, I tried to find that black-eyed lady from my meditations again.

"Duchess Bune," I said, and as I closed my eyes, I found myself already standing in the space I'd seen her before, that fine mansion, "hello! Please come speak to me, if you'd like. I've got some questions to ask you."

The space we were in was familiar, but different. There was a huge dining room, with a long dining table made of deep, dark wood, and square-backed chairs with jewel-tone cushions on their seats. Red-black flowers filled a couple vases on a long, lacey green tablecloth, and there was Duchess Bune in the doorway that led to a kitchen area.

She looked just as I remembered her: a short bob of black hair, her bangs cut in a straight fringe, and her eyes were so huge, deep in her head and yet sparkling an ashy grey. They were rimmed with bruise-purple, as if she hadn't slept in centuries. Her dress was still a Victorian looking one, though with more details this time; it was long and black, with a thin orange belt and a golden brooch around a high-necked, ruffly collar, with lantern sleeves nearly swallowing delicate, pale hands.

Duchess Bune crooked a finger and invited me into the little kitchen area. In there, I saw the kitchen was definitely a place I recognized: my grandmother's kitchen, but redone in dark wood and black tiled floors. The window over the little sink let in a muted grey light from outside, and the island in the kitchen, attached to the wall, was covered in newspapers and cookies and other such things. I could see my grandmother's dining room so clearly out the other side; beside the stove was the doorway that led into the rest of the house, another dining table out there, the hallway leading to three bedrooms. It wasn't at all the same as the place I first saw her, and yet it was colored, designed the same; it had the same dark wood furniture and the same green-and-black ivy pattern. So strange.

The Duchess stood over a pot in the kitchen and stirred away as she chose the Marigold Tarot . Beside the pot was a plate of what looked like burned chicken bones, and in the pot was black dirt.

"Alright," I said as I got myself situated in the scene, which was oscillating between memories of my grandmother's house as I last saw it and the darker, shadow-side of it that Duchess Bune wanted to meet me in, "well, thank you for inviting me here. I suppose I'll jump right in." As I stared at the pot of dirt, I went from the top of my list. "When grimoires say that certain members of the Infernal Divine are connected with elements, what does that mean? How are you connected to earth?"

1. HOW ARE YOU CONNECTED TO THE EARTH?

Duchess Bune looked over her shoulder at me as she stirred the pot. "Earth tells a history," she said, "and yet everything that comes out of it is new. By the soil, you know what's grown here before. By the plants sprouting, you know what can grow again. I am a creature of opportunity, and I see the potential in the world like you might the seeds in a ripe fruit. There is no fortune telling in the dirt, however. Nothing is guaranteed; all is seized."

"Uh...huh. I think I see what you mean."

She smiled, the way a mother might smile at a babbling child. "Do you?"

Manifestation, putting dreams into action, realizing goals, seizing the moment.

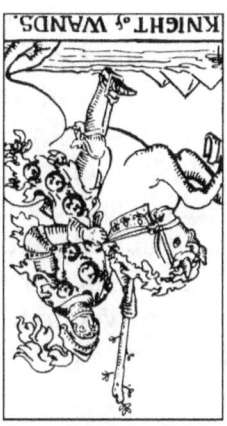

Ill placed infatuation with an idea or person, doubts, confusion, a dent in one's confidence.

Exercising fore-sight with an open mind. Plan accordingly for the many paths available in life.

"I do, yeah. The seeds, the potential—yeah!" I understood without being able to put it in words right then, because it all came in images: seeds drifting on the wind taking root anywhere they land, because all the world is a field where things can grow if one pays enough attention to said land. "Okay. So, in that case, what does death have to do with earth? I can think of a few things, but I'd like to hear what you have to say about it, given you also deal in death."

2. WHAT DOES EARTH HAVE TO DO WITH DEATH?

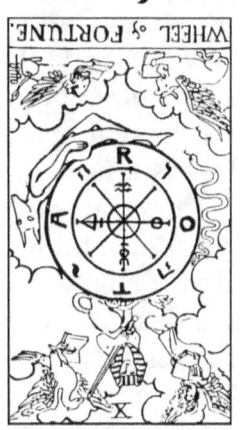

1. Corruption, obsession with the material world at the expense of spiritual wellness, and greed.

2. Poor luck and failure.

3. Disinterest, introspection, pessimism, and inability to see the good in life.

By this point, she'd wandered away from the stove and sat down with me at the little island in the kitchen. A cup of tea or something sat in front of her, and she slowly swirled her spoon through deep brown liquid.

"It's simple, really," she said, her bruised gaze stuck fast on her cup. "The earth is a dumping ground for dirt—for all the things, all the sins, that Creation could commit. Such blood that has grown the grass, such squelch of rot—the earth takes it all, as well as the sorrows, fears, regrets, angers, pains, and it transforms them anew into life, optimism, innocence.

"There is no sin too big for the earth to swallow—or so I thought before you, mankind, with your weapons, surpassed even the destruction that came with Azazel's teachings." Those big, pool-deep eyes snapped up to me, and a mean smile hooked onto her face. "I am impressed by your cruelty."

Jesus. In my mind flashed so many images: grass fed by the nitrogen and calcium of rotting bodies after war, flowers and mushrooms sprouting from decay as bloated, maggot-ridden flesh rotted. Then there were also the bombed out buildings, the earth turned grey and dead from blast after blast of rockets and missiles, with nothing left to grow in such sooty soil—nothing for the very creatures of death, the mushrooms, to compost into new matter. It was harrowing in every way.

"I hear you," I said, and it's wild to think that yeah, even Azazel showing us metalworking didn't cause damage like this. Or maybe it did, snowballing swords into guns. "We're in a mess."

"Mm, yes, you are."

"Well, as much as I'd love to wallow in that thought, I think it's best to move onto question three: I heard someone say that you may have potentially been the Egyptian goddess Wadjet at one point. What do you think about that? Were you ever revered as a goddess?"

3. WERE YOU EVER A GODDESS?

Conformity, wisdom, gaining knowledge, and learning. Paying mind to teachers and mentors. Finding wisdom in new places while respecting society.

Authority, integrity, connections, intellect, and fortitude, both physical and mental. Power and remembrance. A presence that demands respect.

Suppression, lacking discretion, or feeling incapable of fully expressing oneself.

Duchess Bune smirked, as if the question were silly yet ever so slightly painful. In the cards themselves, I also saw a story playing out.

I tapped the King of Swords. "Does this have to do with God?"

King of Swords is my card signifier for God, and Knight of Swords Reversed confirmed what I was seeing between it and the Hierophant, as the latter's description suggested that there was more to this entity, far more, than I was seeing. As I pieced it together, Duchess Bune explained.

"All such things have to do with your God." She waved a hand. "He drives a hard bargain. But the problem is... only fools wouldn't be able to see the way in which the tide was turning.

"There was freedom offered to me—when I took this name and this face I wear now. But it came with a terrible price, and it was one I didn't have much option but to agree to pay. So was I once a goddess?" The Duchess shrugged. "Does it matter? People now may still remember my older masks and titles, and surely I'll answer to them—but my work, my role, has changed in accordance to the offers your God made and the story He's penning."

Cue me blinking at the cards. There was something so incredibly meta about that answer that I was shocked she'd want that to be made public. It was also beginning to paint a wild picture of my God—a picture that I found myself appreciating and even drawing closer to Him through, as a writer myself. Even if it was one with some terrible implications and consequences.

"Alright, I see. Interesting." Whistling to myself, I got back to shuffling the cards. "And so, okay, what duties do you have now, then? As a Duchess of Hell?"

4. WHAT DUTIES DO YOU HAVE AS A DUCHESS OF HELL?

Manifestation, putting dreams into action, realizing goals, seizing the moment.

Subconscious fears, deceptions, and illusions suddenly seen for what they are. Trauma, poor communication, a lack of understanding.

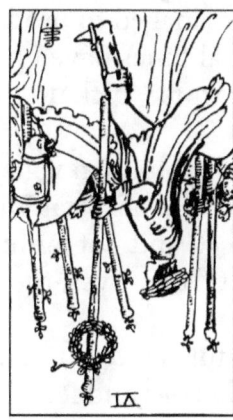

Failing to recognize one's own shortcomings over feelings of pride or superiority.

She held her hands up in that "so what?" gesture. "I am of the earth—like a womb that houses decay and births the soil of something new. I bring change in cycles, and I reveal, through my knowledge, that which was hidden in plain sight.

"You wonder about my traditional aspects and talents, and I tell you: how do you think one becomes rich, smart, and well spoken? Not by staying encased in paraffin, never allowed to decay and feed something new. To die is to live again. To learn is to sleep; to understand is to dream; to integrate is to awaken." She faced me head on and nearly swallowed me with her gaze. "Do you understand?"

With a blink, I nodded, and then we were outside the kitchen and out in the yard, but this was very obviously not my grandmother's house. The mansion, so darkly painted and with rows and rows of frosted windows, stood harshly against a cloudy gray sky, and the lawn itself was covered in plush green grass, where a finely manicured garden sat against the mansion walls: shrubs and flowers and small maple trees. A ring of black forest surrounded us, trapping the mansion in a dense bubble of trees.

"I do," I said as my feet sunk into the damp grass.

Duchess Bune smiled at me. "Good. Let me know when you're ready to awaken, then."

That offer was its own separate headache, which, at the time of my meeting with her, I told myself I would worry about at another time. As I look back on this meeting, I can only wonder if perhaps that time has come—but that's for me to decide, and for me to know. In that moment, however, I was interested more in getting through these questions.

"So, in that case, then... what can the earth do for us, exactly?"

5. WHAT CAN THE EARTH DO FOR US?

Assuming the worst and misunderstanding one's own or another's needs.

"Ah. The earth is home to plants of all kinds, you see—but can plants speak?" She gestured to the things growing in the garden, standing tall and strong and bright green and red. "Can they cry out in hunger, or wave their branches in distress as a creature eats them alive? No. They are at the mercy of the world, and your fruits of your labor are much the same. As they grow ripe, they attract the others of this world that would steal them from you, boring holes in otherwise perfect harvests."

I was viscerally envisioning the holes and slime trails in a couple of my last strawberries my plants managed to produce. Slugs *look* cute, but man, do they ruin good berries. Several times have I gone to pick up a strawberry from my garden, only to find a big, slimy hole in it—or worse, pick up the strawberry while the little living booger was still on it. Ick.

Duchess Bune continued. "The earth helps you learn vigilance—and it also teaches you to share the bounty, to have mercy for these who survive off what, in their view, is a life sustaining, lucky find. Harmony, accepting less than we expect, and not falling victim to greed, still seeing the beauty in a basket still plenty full despite a few lost fruits—yes, the earth teaches you that there is, indeed, enough for all life to live."

"Oh, wow." What an unexpectedly beautiful answer. It made me feel better about not killing the slimy little boys I kept finding all over my berries and lettuces. I could never kill them regardless, though. Even the tomato hornworms, those menaces; I can't bring myself to squish one. Only to throw them far away from my tomatoes and hope a bird eats them. "That's a really nice answer. Thank you for that. But then, what are you looking to teach people?"

6. WHAT ARE YOU LOOKING TO TEACH PEOPLE?

She turned to me with a sigh and a big smile, and she refused to pick any cards for this. "What I am here to do, what the earth teaches, what I want to show you all—these are all the same question. Like fruits on a vine, knowledge is something we gods and monsters cultivate, and we do not begrudge you slugs and snails and moths that come to partake in our efforts—so long as you leave some for those who come after you." As I blinked at her, a twinkle flashed in her eye. "You understand now why the Garden was a Garden."

"Yeah, but the Tree of Knowledge was the one thing we weren't supposed to eat from."

"Ah-ah," Duchess Bune shook her finger at me, "that was only the Tree of Knowledge of Good and Evil, not all knowledge that ever was or will be. Honestly," she said with a mean smile, "that was one of the most useless types of knowledge in that Garden."

"Uh—well, alright." That was a fun, if problematic thought. I wasn't about to get stuck in a rabbit hole deciphering it, though, so I pushed on. "So, in that case, for the last of our personal questions: how do you experience life as a member of the Infernal Divine? What does it mean for you to be alive?"

7. WHAT DOES IT MEAN TO BE ALIVE?

Pessimism, dread, and resignation.

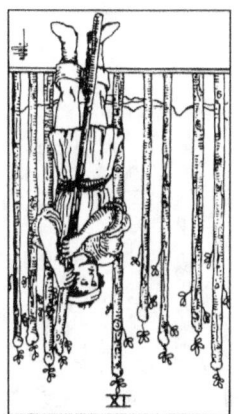

"Hmm." Her smile fell. "To be alive, Sara, is to be at work. This life I have—it is for a purpose. None of us exist here without a role in the Script. I experience life as a never-ending yoke of duty. There is no escaping it."

Man, I don't know; between this answer and President Camio's conversation, it seems like there's more drudgery than we know in the Infernal Realms. Though of all the places I've seen, Duchess Bune's kitchen and dining room was certainly the farthest from an office one could get. But that's why her job isn't office work: she doesn't do paperwork, but acts out there in the world, I guess. So do many of the Infernal Divine, I guess, but her work really is about that physical *dirt*, it seems.

"Okay. With all that said and done, then... how do you see yourself?"

8. HOW DO YOU SEE YOURSELF?

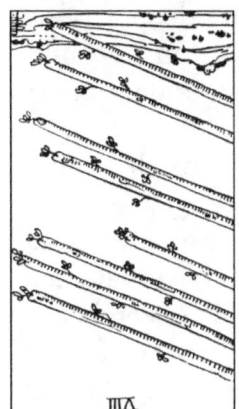

Quarrels, delays, and needing to slow down to re-evaluate goals or circumstances.

Duchess Bune stared at the garden. "My life—I, myself—have been marked by a series of misdirects. Who am I? What am I? You ask these things when you go from not even a conscious wink of starlight to a great and terrible beast like myself.

"To whom do I owe the pleasure of the fruits of my labor? Every time I think I know, I see I don't at all. I am a scholar, you see, and I learn forever."

"Damn. Alright. That's... a lot." Leave it to demons, though, to just destroy and re-assemble my brain every time I talked to them. What else could I say to a wrecking ball of an answer like that? "And how do you want to be seen?"

9. HOW DO YOU WANT TO BE SEEN?

Success, discipline, enjoyment, and safety. Seeing the bigger picture and focusing on the wonderful.

Here was a marked shift. I figured she'd pull a nine—how, I couldn't tell you—and I was relieved to see Nine of Coins.

"My slugs, my moths, my worms and grubs," she cooed as she put a hand on her chest and smiled, "as I said, I don't begrudge your eating of the fruits of my labor. My garden grows for you, and I am content to see which fruits you enjoy most. See me as the groundskeeper to the soils of your mind—forever working to enrich it, so you, yourself, can grow your own fruits from the seeds you've taken from me."

As odd as the language was, that felt... sweet. Comforting, even. "I got'cha. Thank you, Duchess Bune! But now, before we go, is there any last message you want to share?"

10. Any Last Messages?

Bad news, powerlessness, loneliness, and self sabotage. Negative words, attempted healing.

"Not particularly." She eyed me, and a cat-like smile split her lips. "But do you want me to say one more thing?"

"I do, yeah—if that's okay."

"Okay. Well, how about this, then? This is for all who feel it applies. For all who need to hear this, hear it: you rot your teeth when you gorge on the work of another too long."

Oh, boy.

"Learn to stand up and tend your own fields," she said. "The earth is rich, the soil black with potential. Don't cry that it lays barren when you've not lifted a finger to sow in it. If you want to eat, then work. Otherwise, you'll only ever be sustained off stolen labor. And that labor soon runs dry for the ungrateful mouth."

It felt like such a 180 from what she'd just said, but I understood: there was a difference between taking what one needs to get started, waiting for others to provide the food one can't yet get for oneself, and then sitting in complacency, expecting food to come this way forever. It reminded me of the baby birds who, when growing out of their dependence, still open their mouths at bugs and worms and expect them to hop in, not realizing they have to actually pluck the bug off the ground themselves.

I nodded and said, "I see. Again, Duchess Bune, thank you; these are some fantastic insights you've shared. With that, I hope to see you again sometime. Goodbye for now!"

And then she smiled, turned, and faded away. As I said in the beginning, right? Very different, this image, from the three headed dragon described in the grimoires. Maybe that means I never talked to the Duchess and it was all my imagination. Maybe someone will insist on that, given I've seen her as a Duchess and not a Duke (even though many spirits, like Bune, can appear as either male or female). I don't know. I couldn't say. All I can say is that it was Duchess Bune I called out to, and it was this force, that I had seen before, that answered. And how sweet her answers were—sweet as sugar, and also sweet as decay.

Reading this again, and reminding myself of all the things she said, too, it reminds me that re-reading these interviews is as helpful for me as it is for anyone to read them the first time. This kind of knowledge is fickle; it destroys your mind, only to fade away the second you don't focus on it. Maybe this is why so many monks eschewed the world and spent all their time in prayer: because the day to day trivialities of the world steal your memory and hide all you've uncovered. But she mentioned something specific in here that I think I need to take her up on—and I can only hope that whatever she's willing to tell me in private won't be so easily wiped away as the days pass and fade the memory of it, the way sunlight fades stains in good cloth.

MEDEINA

You know, I may be banned from two separate pantheons respectively thanks to the debacle I caused with Apollo, but that doesn't mean that gods of the hunt like Artemis are entirely off the table, or that we'd run out of such gods after Devana. In fact, in my exploration of the concept of earth, and on request of a member of my Patreon, I once again found another female presence of the hunt, another goddess of wild things and the earth and the forests specifically. That someone was none other than Baltic goddess Medeina, who, according to scholars Lena Kolesnikova and Mindaugas Peleckis in their article, "Medeina/Medeinė as a relic of Neolithic beliefs," is a goddess who goes far beyond even the cultures we now know as Baltic. In fact, they posit that she was likely a neolithic goddess, given that the words that make up her name don't really have any etymological connection with other words in the Baltic languages. Moreover, she, like other gods of the hunt or wild things in this area, is tightly connected with local bear cults. It's something that must overlap with neighboring Slavic religion, given how the bear appears by Devana's side and also in connection to Veles, Slavic god of the underworld.

But now, if we talk about gods of the hunt, one interesting thing is that unlike other hunting gods, Medeina doesn't help hunters. She misleads them, luring them away from their mark, because her true goal is to preserve the forest. In fact, it's said that when people would start cutting trees for winter, Medeina would run deep into the forest and cry, and so people stopped cutting trees around that time so as to not make her sad. Some believe she also had to do with military presence, especially towards the tail end of Baltic paganism, with Christian fighters looming on the horizon.

Let's investigate, shall we?

With a simple set-up of a green candle, moss agate, bloodstone, and some mushroom-shaped carnelian and red jasper, I had the typical ritual fare—but knowing Medeina is associated with rabbits, I tried to find something rabbit-like. All I could find was a Plusle plushie, but the little pink and white Pokémon would have to do. Some iris incense and an apple for an offering felt right, too, as I couldn't find what to offer specifically—only that these things should be offered in the woods. (Don't worry; I put the apple by the yew bush in my yard later.)

But as I called out to Medeina and wrote down my questions, I got a flash of something in my mind's eye soon enough. I even looked up some photos of the Lithuanian forests so I could better situate myself in her territory, and once I was ready, I found her standing there. She looked just like some artwork I'd seen attributed to her, with a deer skull on her head, her black hair long and shiny, and her clothes a patchwork of all different kinds of animal furs that covered her just enough.

"Medeina," I said, "hello! Welcome. I've got some questions for you, if you don't mind. Though it seems you know I like that image of you that I saw before, with the skull on your head?"

Part of me was just worried that I was seeing what I wanted to see and not the real spirit, which is a little silly, given that the Slavic gods always appear to me as the way Russian painter Andrey Shishkin portrayed them. Still, I've accepted that I will just not get over that doubting impulse any time soon—and maybe that's a good thing, because it means I'm at least trying to stay vigilant and keep my own imagination on a leash. But as that idea crossed my mind, Medeina shrugged, then spoke without my pulling any cards or anything.

She shifted, too, from a woman to a huge, vaguely woman-shaped, black creature, with deer antlers rising from its head and eyes shining like two orange spheres of flame. She was so dark that I couldn't make out any of her features; it was like looking at a huge skulking shadow in the woods.

"I have been here since the beginning of time: since the earth was but crust, and no life yet lived on it," she said.

She showed me an image of her kneeling on what looked like a rocky, barren planet, like Mars. She leaned down to the earth and pressed her ear to it, as if listening to what it wanted. She was suggesting, as trees sprouted from the dirt, that she created the forest.

"You all gave me my face and my name."

"Whoa, wait!" This was answering one of the questions I had written down, and that felt like spoilers. As I erased it and tried to think if another one, I wondered aloud to her: "If you created the forest, where was God at that time? Are you a creator, too? Is it maybe a job divvied up and delegated rather than one God doing all the work?"

Medeina stared at me with those orange eyes. "I'm not concerned with where your God was while I made these forests. I had a job. Deep in my being, I knew what had to be done."

Jesus. Yet another question was, likewise, erased, and I put a new one in its place. Eventually, she decided on a deck of cards—the Golden Tarot—and I got shuffling before I got too many other stray threads of thoughts from her.

"Okay, okay, well... where did the forests come from in your creative vision, then?

1. WHAT INSPIRED THE CREATION OF FORESTS?

Deceit and unfair dealings; a cunning foe.

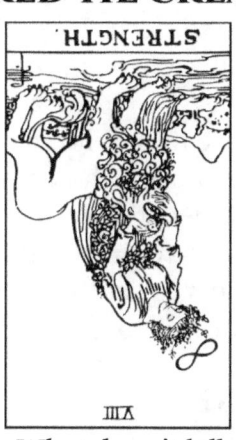

What doesn't kill you makes you stronger. Looking within and you'll find the strength to survive.

A warm, loving woman. Maternal, gentle, loyal, honest, and trustworthy. Creative, loves art.

She appeared again on the forest path, a great bear suddenly at her side, and her face shifted between the mask of a human woman and the primordial, fire-eyed creature behind it. Medeina smiled and gestured to the trees.

"The little souls—the little souls being born, they cried out to me for a place to sleep, a place to live. Sweet things, the creatures of the woods—and they needed a sweet, quiet place. A place to hide, where the trees disoriented foes, and where magic could weave between the great wayfinders that were the trees. I was given souls, so I created suitable housing."

I don't remember how, but I got wondering about the Primordial Soup of Genesis, and how all things were defined at creation. It seemed Medeina helped do some of the defining, and her mention of being given souls was making my mind whir as I wrote. Who created *her*, then? Who defined her, if someone was able to give her souls to look after? But she knew my question before I even formed it—one about the great beast that was left in the formless dark when God defined Himself and all other things—and she blinked.

"You're thinking of the Unmade One?" Medeina cocked her head. "The Unmade One is a terror, and my art laughs in his face. I defined myself; you all defined me further. A cyclical thing."

Man, this was already intense out the gate. Maybe it was because she was a god of wild things; maybe it was because she was a god older than our oldest stories. Either way, the information she poured into my head was enough to make it overflow, and I'd only gotten one question deep. I sat there rubbing my face for a second to shake off all that energy before moving on.

"Okay, okay, so... noted. But then, what do you love about the forest?"

2. WHAT DO YOU LOVE ABOUT THE FOREST?

TEMPERANCE.

1. A time of worry, but don't despair; a sea of change is in the air.

2. Moderation in all things. Having achieved spiritual and mental goals. A time of equilibrium. Application of simple pleasures. Diplomacy, negotiation of compromise.

3. Abandonment of materialism. Putting aside financial security in pursuit of spiritual wellness. Cutting off the old.

"At its simplest, Sara," she said as she watched bunnies dart between the thin trees on the sides of the dirt path we ended up on, "the forest is where the world goes to sleep. There's a reason I made the trees so still. When things stand still, it encourages us to stand still. We don't feel so alone in our idleness. Being idle becomes a sacred thing.

"We achieve peace here, among kin who don't feel like they have to rebuild the world in a day to be worthy of being alive. I put my wishes into [the trees]: that all creatures who come here find rest, not destruction. This is not the place for action alone—not outside of what's necessary to survive."

"Ah, alright, alright! I got'cha. But then, why do you use rabbits to redirect hunters and trick them into not hunting any animals, rather than just send a wolf or a bear to eat them or something? It's interesting, but it's also not the first thought people have to get people to give up and leave the forest."

3. WHY TRICK HUNTERS WITH YOUR RABBITS?

ACE of CUPS.

True happiness. Overflowing love and joy. Harmony, bliss, spiritual fulfillment via unconditional love.

KNIGHT of CUPS.

A sensitive young man of depth. Opportunity. Inspired and creative person. Afraid to commit.

Doubt, frustration, and powerlessness. Downward spiral. Keep perspective; self pity is worthless.

Medeina, in her human face, smiled. "The people are my creatures, too. I don't want them to feel fear in these peaceful woods. I don't want to threaten and remove the sanctuary of my woods. I am not a violent god."

I paused, squinted at her. "... Then how did you get associated with war?"

4. YOUR LINK WITH WAR?

That human face faded away, back into the dark shadowy face with the burning eyes. "Even the most gentle mother becomes a beast when her children are threatened."

"Oop." That look could've shaved my ass flat. "Fair enough! Okay, well—how can we learn from the forest?"

5. HOW CAN WE LEARN FROM THE FOREST?

ACE of SWORDS.

III

IIΛ

1. Inspiration. Clarity of thought, inspired solutions. Problems solved and goals reached. Action, power, strength.

2. Problems in a relationship. A partner feeling taken for granted or jealous of a potential rival. Promiscuity, unfaithfulness, or at least yearning for a more exciting life.

3. Indecision at a critical time could lead to defeat.

She leaned over my cards and tapped the last two, the Three of Cups Reversed and Seven of Cups Reversed, which stood opposed to the clarity of the Ace of Swords.

"These last two things are what the world gives you: your cities that you make, your big things that you only want to see get bigger. The forest asks you: why? Who needs such things? And why do you need it all at once?

"The trees grow bigger on their own time. The world doesn't rush. Yet you want to see the rise and fall of all creation in one lifetime. Why? The forest asks you to slow down and remind yourself of what really matters."

With a nod, I said "I got'cha. That makes sense. Okay, so, how about this? In one of your myths, you were drowned in a river! That's terrible! But what was it like in that river—or, plainly, what was it like as a goddess to die?"

6. WHAT WAS IT LIKE TO DIE AS A GODDESS?

Satisfaction of worldly desires. Good health and good fortune. Successful fulfillment of wishes. Meeting new people.

This was a similar thought as I'd had with the Morrigan, thinking of her husband the Dagda. I wondered what Medeina would say—if she would confirm these ideas or not, about what happens when gods "die." And there she was again, primordial smoke and fire with deer antlers, sitting there on the forest floor and shrugging like the question was a silly one.

"I wasn't dead," she said. "I was with the river spirit. In the river, I found the peace a creator can't quite get from its own creation. My trees are stable, quiet, slow—but how fun the river is! How fast, always moving! It was a delightful change of pace—but I was glad to be back with my beloved."

By that, she meant her lover. This myth tells a story of Medeina in competition with another goddess over a man, and the other goddess, unable to woo the man with her singing, drowns Medeina in the river. The mourning folks make a harp of her bones and hair, and later on, the man of attention gets mortally wounded. To save him, the other goddess goes to the witch Lauma to figure out what to do, and they decide to cover him in a bear pelt to heal his wounds. The man is revived and becomes a huge bear, but he says he'll kill the goddess for taking away his Medeina. Lauma managed to convince the river spirit to give Medeina back. The harp breaks, Medeina is revived, and the other goddess never sings or even speaks again in return.

"Wow," I said, genuinely surprised by Medeina's reaction, and the implication of a creator never getting rest from its creation. It also didn't quite confirm what the Morrigan said, but it didn't necessarily deny it, either; gods work on some strange spiritual physics. "Alright, then. What an interesting perspective. But okay, how about this: what does it mean to be wild?"

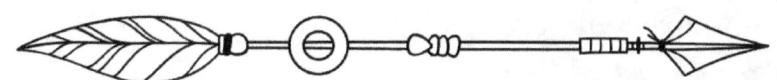

7. What Does It Mean To Be Wild?

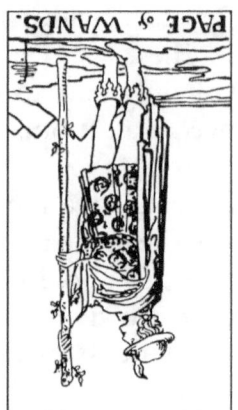

Bad news. An unreliable youth.

"Mmm. What does it mean?" Her smile was cheeky, her human-like eyes bright. She kept shifting between these forms she'd shown me throughout the interview: the woman and the wildling. "Being wild isn't always a good thing, you know. Can you bring a wolf into a town? A lion? Being wild means you're not built for a world of cages. It can hurt quite a bit. It's not always a blessing."

"Ooh, yeah, I can see that." I pursed my lips, unsure of what else to say, and decided to just move on. "Okay, final round of questions starts now, with this one: how do you see yourself?"

8. How Do You See Yourself?

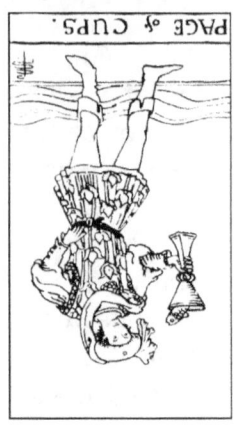

A shallow person who likes to get what they want regardless of consequences to others. Spoiled and self indulgent. Face responsibilities.

Looking over this, I realized that when I asked God about Medeina, He pulled Page of Cups, and the card Medeina pulled for herself is Page of Cups reversed. I wonder if that wasn't as much as a cheeky jab at God as it was a confession as she explained.

"I'm not interested in war or what people need to survive," she said. "Or, at least, I wasn't. I wanted my forest to stay untouched forever. Though I suppose that was unrealistic. Did I cause damage, wailing the way I did [about people cutting down trees]? Stopping man from doing what they needed to do to make their own creations? I don't know. Sometimes I still don't care. Leave my babies be; don't touch my trees or my rabbits."

"I got'cha," I said, half-smiling at her love for those trees and rabbits. "That's understandable. But how do you want to be seen?"

9. How Do You Want To Be Seen?

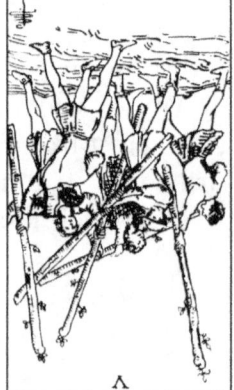

A dispute may bring out the worst in a friend's character.

"I am older than your cities and your ambitions," she said, her primordial shadow-face back out, her eyes glimmering bright orange. "Do not test me too much; do not assume I won't trap you in my woods to limit your destruction. I am, and I'm neither ally nor foe. Act accordingly with me, and I will with you."

"Ooh, that's quite the answer. Almost sounds like a message. Do you want to leave any other messages before we go?"

10. ANY LAST MESSAGES?

Indecision at a critical time could lead to defeat.

"Yes. Decide what you value more: your industry or your lives and homes."

Oh, jeez. Her shadow-face held no room for jokes or mirth. That was a flat and serious warning. Likely to do with the state of the environment. But I packed up the cards and nodded.

"Heard loud and clear. Well, Medeina, thank you for your time! This was quite the interesting experience. I'll leave you to your woods now, and I'll leave this apple for you by the yew tree. Goodbye for now!"

And with little more than that burning stare, Medeina left. I did what I said I'd do and left her apple outside, then went about my business like the happy-go-lucky goof I am.

But there's not as much room to be so happy-go-lucky, is there? I can't help but feel, as I look back on these interviews, that they've been telling me how things would go soon this entire time—that there were choices we had to make all this time, in *our* time. You hear rumors about American national parks potentially being stripped of their protection for cheap lumber, and you can almost imagine it: Medeina, there between the pines and the oaks, crying as man's industry comes and steals away nature's home.

A great deal of these gods—of the wilderness, of war, of law, of anything—seem to have been telling us to choose. Decide. And to watch out. And of course, these things are so obvious in hindsight, but at the time, it's all too easy to shrug our shoulders and carry on like I did after this interview. How frustrated must the gods have been, and how frustrated must they still be, to give us the answers again and again and then watch us act so helpless anyway? I can't begin to imagine.

As a little human myself, I can only try to put these pieces together, and maybe, *maybe,* do something with whatever I build as a result.

THE TREE SPIRIT

All of the warning of Medeina (that I clearly didn't understand at the time) aside, there was at least one tree I could hope to keep and advocate for so long as I was around: the big pine tree outside my house. Given my inclination for animism, a spiritual philosophy that insists every bit of creation or nature has some kind of soul, and given that I did this interview on Halloween, when so many folks consider the veil between the physical and the spiritual worlds "thin," I figured: why not talk to this big boy?

(Don't ask me why my pine tree is a boy. I just pinned him as that and ran with it, and apparently, he did too.)

I've long since considered this pine tree an outer guardian of the house, and I pay him for his efforts with scraps from the dinner table: potato peels, onion skins, or fruits and vegetables that have gone soft and funky in the fridge. Whatever spooks may be haunting the woods I live in at night, whatever animals may come by that aren't necessarily friendly, it seems that my good pine tree keeps them at bay long enough for me to go do a midnight mailbox run, and he also seems to keep the power from cutting out too much, if at all, during storms. A very helpful fellow that I can only thank God for having stationed right here in front of me.

And before anyone asks: certain readings of the Bible, especially sections like Psalm 148, suggest that nature is in fact alive and capable of praising God, and that they should, per the Psalm speaker's demand. As such, I see nature spirits like I see people: friends capable of helping and impacting our world. After all, no one has a problem with acknowledging when a human being, or even a dog, helps protect their house and cattle and whatever else, so there shouldn't be any problem with acknowledging a tree is helping, either.

All that said, if we were going to talk about earth, I thought it'd be right and well to talk to a good friend that's long been rooted in it. So many people in the witchy spaces are so keen to work with gods, but there are other spirits just waiting to say hello, too—spirits much more accessible and much less intimidating than gods. I wanted to model what it might look like to reach out to such a spirit, and that's what we have here.

Let's dive in.

Doing this interview certainly wasn't as comfortable as they normally are, given I was sitting by the open window to speak to the tree. I was inside because I didn't want to risk my cards blowing away outside, but the autumn chill still washed over me as I hunched over my booklet and got started.

I'd gone outside to hold his branch and ask if he'd like to talk, and when he gave me a signal that meant *yes,* which for me was the telltale zing in my ear, like a tickle, he told me to take a pine cone inside as a connecting item. I put it on the windowsill, along with some moss agate and quartz for better connection/earth synergy, and then he picked the Universal Fantasy tarot as his speaking medium of choice, and we were on our way.

"Alright, well, hello, my friend! Thank you for speaking with me. Sorry I couldn't actually sit outside with you, but this should do. To start us off, I guess, I'd like to know: where do tree spirits come from?"

I. WHERE DO TREE SPIRITS COME FROM?

It was a solid question, I thought, given Medeina showed me in no unclear terms that she created the trees of her area. With my tree friend, however, it was apparently a little different.

In my mind's eye came an image of some creature sitting under the branches of the tree, and it reminded me of the Kokiri from Legend of Zelda: Wind Waker. I think he grabbed onto that image to form himself in my mind, but he altered it so that he looked like a pine cone with a leaf mask and a robe of pine branches, green needles sticking off him in a big bundle. He sat hunched under his own branches and nodded.

When a big change takes place, the only way to deal with problems is to focus on the benefits.

Overwhelm. Downward trajectory. Paralyzed by success. Plug into passion. No time for doubts.

"We are called," he said, "though for what, I don't know. I don't know my God, per se," and here, I got an image of a woman with straight black hair, fur and leather clothes, and pine branches woven into her back as if they were some sort of fairy wings, her eyes deep and dark, her skin a warm bronze, and a delicate, motherly smile on her face as she cradled a little seed, "but I know that I am made."

I focused on that image of the woman. Was this a fairy? Or a Native American spirit, maybe? Given I'm on the lands of the Narragansett people, I could imagine there might've been a great spirit or goddess of the pine trees somewhere around here, but her presence wasn't here, only an image of her from what felt like the tree's memories.

"I was made by hands that looked like me," the tree spirit continued, wistful. "A woman, a mother, bore me from needles and dirt."

"Oh, that's so interesting." Who was the one, then, that like Medeina, came and planted these forests? Who wove these homes for the tree spirits? It certainly wasn't my place to go digging for her, or seeking after her, but I wondered nonetheless. "Alright, then, okay—how about the creatures you've seen around here? As my house guardian, I'm curious what things have rumbled through, especially in terms of spirits."

2. WHAT OTHER KINDS OF SPIRITS LIVE AROUND ME?

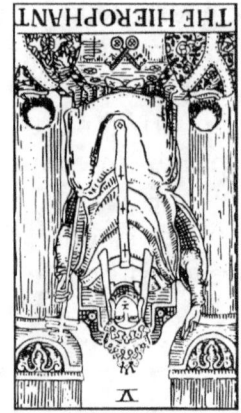

Too much rigidity. Convention stifles creativity. Don't feel as if you need to follow the rules. Do what works.

Patience and perseverance are keys to solving many problems. Wise people know when to struggle or want.

"Oh, not all of them are good," he said right away, before I could even pick any cards. "I have seen many a wild creature come through here, some good, some bad—but all live on their own terms. They can be dangerous. As House Guardian," he said with a puff of his needles, "I tell you: watch out. Not all care about your wellbeing. Though most just don't realize how fast humans can break. The rabbits just run when they hear a rustle in the leaves; the birds go quiet. Humans? Humans are foolish. All their intelligence and pride is their downfall."

I think he meant the ways in which humans dismiss the existence of spirits as superstitions and go outside without a care in the world, only to go crazy with denial when these spirits start playing tricks.

"It's Halloween today," I said, just a little side question. "You think these spirits are more active tonight, with the veil thin?"

He shrugged. "Spirits come and go all the time. It's never a good idea to let your guard down."

"Fair. Okay, that brings me to a related question: what are your encounters with other spirits like?"

3. WHAT ARE YOUR ENCOUNTERS WITH OTHER SPIRITS LIKE?

His mask rustled as he spoke. "Again, not all spirits are good. At least, good for humans. They ask me to join them in their tricks and games, but I was never a fan of such things. I like my place here, sitting and watching. I like being a haven for birds and listening to the buzz of bees around my new pine cones. I have no interest in the tomfoolery of other spirits. Those tricksters can be troublesome."

"Aw, that's sweet, though—being a haven for the birds!" And the way he talked was precious, too, as if he were an old soul; he had a grandpa-vibe about him at times. "Okay, so, given we are here to discuss earth-based things, I was wondering: what can people learn from trees?"

To free ourselves of difficulties, we must first understand what's really important.

However bitter a conflict or tragic an outcome, we will be able to stand up for our principles.

4. WHAT CAN WE LEARN FROM THE TREES?

"Ah, yes. We stand the test of time, us trees: watching all the world rise and fall around us. I remember when this land was houseless. Still forested. I remember—as do the trees nearby—what it was to have yet more brothers here. The inevitability of change, decay—it helps you understand what matters. It helps you appreciate all the little things you didn't know you could ever miss." The tree spirit paused, then muttered, "There used to be more birdsong here. Now there's only the race of cars some days."

"Oh, man," I huffed. "I feel like that's a little sad, tree spirit." And interesting, because there was still plenty of birdsong where I lived; it's fascinating to think there was once more.

He shrugged. "It is the way of things."

"If you say so. But then, being a tree... does it bother you to stay in one spot all your life?"

Shift your focus from external to internal. Most important things are intangible. Release your ego.

A beautiful sign of integration. Seeing experiences from an enlightened place. You're stronger, more resilient.

5. DOES STAYING IN ONE SPOT ALL YOUR LIFE BOTHER YOU?

Someone working their way back into the world after withdrawal. New beginnings, the universe opening.

If the price of victory is high, it may be wise to choose an honorable defeat.

"What would I do if I could move?" His branches rustled as he turned to me. "Would I lumber through the streets like some great beast? Lay my roots over other green things that live here? Rip up your asphalt, swing through your power lines? You be lucky trees don't move.

"No, I'm unbothered by my stationary nature; without it, the birds would fear me, and the squirrels would abandon me. They tell me the goings-on—and I have you to watch, too. I am content."

"Aw!" What a cutie. I was consistently feeling soft as a marshmallow with the answers he was giving, my dear tree friend. "Okay, then. I can understand that, I think. But then, as a pine tree, can you tell me how pines stay so strong during winter? I mean, you're the symbol of life in the darkness, especially for us European or otherwise winter-having types."

6. HOW DO PINE TREES STAY STRONG IN WINTER?

There was an air of a satisfied smile hanging around.

"We were here first, you know," he said. "Us pines and firs, we were first. We remember from our ancestors a time where the world was crueler, colder—and we adapted for such times, not dreaming of a day where the winds would warm our branches, but simply accepting the way the world was. It was these young scups that made it all such a drama, with their fire-leaves screaming one last wish for the summer sun every year. Foolish youths."

I found this so funny—trees, of all creatures, pulling a "back in my day," or a "kids these days," because of how temperate forests developed with the leaf-dropping trees.

"Okay, okay," I said once I gathered myself, "for our last personal question, then: what's the earliest thing you remember?"

Happiness we experience in daily life is greater than that of the king who wins the war.

Knowledge enables us to see beyond the horizon and wisely appraise our resources.

7. WHAT IS YOUR EARLIEST MEMORY?

He didn't pull any cards here; he insisted on speaking directly to me and showing me. There was the teeniest sapling amidst a forest where other pine trees lay, and through needles and branches, it seemed like he was staring up at the sun—just a big orange orb in the sky.

"Peace," he said. "Shadow. Then a big ball of fire through the needles and the brush—a light so warm I couldn't help but stretch up to it. I still try to reach it now, even with lichen weighing down my arms."

And when I looked outside, I found it was true: his upper branches, especially, unburdened with lichen and browning needles, still curved upwards towards the sky.

"Wow. How fascinating! But okay, then, pine tree, can you tell me how you see yourself?"

8. HOW DO YOU SEE YOURSELF?

At times, we must trust our instincts when they lead us to believe in those closest to us.

"Me? Hmm." He cocked his little pine cone head." I'd say I've seen good people come from this place."

He flashed an image of my landlord, the single mom and her kids that lived here before me, the neighbor living in the apartment next to mine—all people just living life and going about their business, year after year. He stared at me as I raised my brow at the thought of my neighbor, which, in my opinion, was the charge of the yew bush on the other side of the property. (And who was... a character. Not a bad person, but a silly one.)

"I've seen good people, and I'd like to think I have good judgement, he insisted.
"You are all but children to me. Even if some are fussier than others, I see you, and I see you as good, and I see myself as someone who knows good when they see it."

"I get'cha," I said as I mulled it over. "But given I'll be sharing this with other people, what would you say you want people to think about you? And the other trees?"

9. HOW DO YOU WANT TO BE SEEN?

"I don't care how people see me," he said, "but my other tree spirits? Well, we don't care so much for the details of how we grow or what shapes we take, you understand. We don't aim for perfection; we just grow. Though sometimes, it gets us in trouble."

You've failed to pay attention to all aspects of a project. Get outside ideas before finishing this.

I could just imagine what he meant by that. The trees here, especially, like to lean on power lines. It's troublesome sometimes.

"Felt. But alright, alright, here's our last question, now: do you have anything you want to say to people? Any messages you want to share?"

10. ANY LAST MESSAGES?

Friction in a group. Communication fallen apart. Ego in the way. Find a solution instead of blaming others. Remember your why.

He blinked at me through his leaf mask.

"You humans are ridiculous," he said. "Always bickering about why you're in the situation you're in rather than working together—always laying roots and tearing them up when things aren't perfect. This soil isn't perfect," he said, gesturing to the soil he rooted himself in. "It's rocky and tough. Yet I have to make do. Where is your ability to do the same? Foolish youngsters, you all."

I laughed at the bluntness of his answer, though I think he's got a point about all that. "Jeez, alright, that's fair. He surprised me sometimes with his bluntness. But alright, well—that's it! Thank you, my friend, for sitting with me. Would you like the rest of my coffee?"

I asked because he showed himself holding my cup, and my coffee had gone cold by then anyway. When he nodded, I took one more good sip for the caffeine, then packed up my things and gave him the rest (and took away some plastic bottle I found sitting under there. I don't know when that got there, because I don't use plastic bottles).

Then I bid him goodbye and closed that window. Granted, it wasn't really goodbye, was it? He was still right there. But it was just a withdrawal into my man-made abode for the time being, back into the warmth that the open window was slowly trying to sap away from me.

There's so much we can gain from setting our sights off the spirits we're conditioned to run after. When people talk about their deconstruction from Christianity, I find that many move with astonishing quickness from one God to many gods. Why? All around us are spirits that are eager to be our neighbors and our friends, as well as ones that are eager to snap us up and make a lunch of us. Can these spirits not also help a new practitioner, an ex-Christian, come to understand themselves and their world?

I think they can. And I think that even for Christian Witches like myself, there's great value in reminding ourselves that our trees and rocks and ferns and flowers are our neighbors, too—that they're our siblings in creation and can learn, grow, and help just as well as any person when it comes to getting things done. This conversation with my tree spirit—who later told me a name to call him by that's become our special secret—only confirmed that.

FATHER TIME

Part of me wonders, you know? Wonders if maybe I wasn't banned from both Greek and Roman pantheons for reasons other than my sheer ineptitude. After all, when the topic of time and fate came up for exploration, it would've been so easy for me to look to these pantheons for entities to reach out to. There is no shortage of topics that have become personified in either god or daimon, after all.

And in fact, it was around this time that I did ask about the Roman pantheon. Surely, I thought, if Kronos is off limits, then maybe his Roman cognate Saturn would be someone to speak to? No doubt I would've been happy to investigate the Roman side of things, as well. However, after my friend Dagan introduced me to one of his friends who is trained in augury for the Roman gods, and after that friend was kind enough to ask Jupiter on my behalf if such a thing would be allowed, they received a resounding and emphatic *no*.

(Though now, after having read *The Darkening Age* by Catherine Nixey, I can certainly understand why they would say no, my own foolishness notwithstanding.)

So in this instance, there were a few places I could think to go—and one of them was, in fact, something of a roundabout solution. I was back to the topic of egregores, and for this topic, I had my eye on Father Time: an entity that, ironically, was distilled from the idea of the god Kronos and displayed in art, statues, and more from as far back as the 1500s, maybe even earlier. He ended up mixing some details of the Grim Reaper, as Father Time came to be seen as an old man wielding a scythe along with other understandable trinkets, like an hourglass. Just for fun: search up the Rotunda Clock in the Library of Congress's Thomas Jefferson building in Washington, D.C., and you'll see what I mean.

However, an entity being based off Kronos does not mean it is Kronos, as far as I'm concerned. Father Time, the western and much more modern personification of time, is one that I therefore found worth investigating—both for the topic at hand and to see, once again, how such personifications born of human imagination would interface. Nayru was such a pleasant surprise that I was confident this interaction would be worth it, too. So let's see if I was right.

How does one represent time besides just littering the table with clocks? I didn't have much by way of clocks and watches, nor did I want to clutter my makeshift altar with such things—but what I did have was a weathered, vintage copy of Lewis Carroll's *Alice in Wonderland,* which felt relevant. I could only think about that rabbit and his anxiety over being late to things as I put it on the table. I contrasted it with a PlayStation 5 controller on the opposite side of the table, to represent the advancement in entertainment materials time has brought on throughout the ages. Add to that a white candle and some blue and clear stones for focus and clarity, and we were good to go. After asking God to find Father Time for me, I sat there with some music on and settled in.

"Father Time," I called out, "can you come by? Are you there? I'd like to talk to you."

As a sign that he was there, he stretched the flame of my candle up quite high. I'd asked him to do so and was fascinated to see it happen in just a moment or so after my request. With the confirmation, I settled in and asked to see his energy and where he was.

We started in a snowy forest, with grey skies and dark pine trees, snow flowing down. There was a small house he stood outside of, and he looked a lot like Dumbledore, honestly: an older man with blue robes, a blue hat, and a long white beard and hair. He invited me inside, though, and that's where thing started getting strange.

Inside this house was pure magic. Bigger on the inside, the foyer was one made of crystal, covered in tables full of empty hourglasses. Behind all of that was a warm glowing light, where it seemed like there was a library overstuffed with books, the stacks of books taking over the floor and the shelves and everything else. Above was a chandelier made of what looked like cords of deep, rich gold that shifted and twisted around themselves, and it was flaking apart like dust—like sand.

"Wow."

This was the power of human imagination, I knew; this was a place that had been dreamed of again and again by creatives of ever-advancing technological ages, ones to whom these gizmos and gadgets seemed like pure magic. I pulled at my notebook as Father Time sat at that table full of hourglasses. He signaled to me to use the Golden Tarot for our conversation, and he seemed ready for me to start with my nonsense, so I dove right in.

"Well, hello again, Father Time! Thank you for meeting with me! I see you have all kinds of things going on here, and to start us off, I'd love to know: what do you wish humans knew about time?"

I. WHAT DO YOU WISH HUMANS KNEW ABOUT TIME?

1. A strong, independent, loyal, calculating woman. Determined and ruthless in pursuit of her goals. Will do whatever is necessary to get what she wants.

2. Be wary of spending beyond your means. Generosity is well and good, but take care that it doesn't lead to debt.

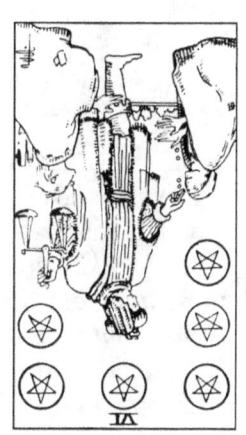

He smiled, jolly and warm like Santa.

"Always chasing it, you humans. Always running after goals, as if all your time will evaporate before your eyes. But everyone gets their own glass; everyone has their sands pre-measured." As he spoke, the golden chandelier poured some of itself down into an empty hourglass. "You don't know how much you have, and so you humans cram as much as you can into each moment—but do you ever stop to be thankful for all the moments you have? It's a good use of a grain—to stop and be present for once, rather than always living in the past or future."

Huh. Sands pre-measured. As I watched the hourglass fill up, I wondered about that idea, and the concept of how all our time is "borrowed," all that. But the way he talked made me wonder.

"Do you work with God, then?" I frowned at those golden flakes falling into that hourglass as the thought sat heavy on my mind. "It would only make sense, right? If so, how?"

2. DO YOU WORK WITH THE ABRAHAMIC GOD?

Father Time shook his head and chose no cards. "No. I simply do what I do. My world is not so defined as yours. I am aware that I was created, yet precede all creation. But I am beholden to no one. I simply am." Then he paused, considered, and offered, "Maybe your God decides how much time goes into each glass, though; the Sand stops flowing on its own into every hourglass. I only turn them over and let them pour their sands to the other side. I don't ask questions. I simply take notes."

"Oh. I got'cha." I suppose that made sense. Did Father Time need to know God's intentions? Apparently not. Interesting, too, that he knew he was a created being. Egregores seem to know that more than I thought they would. I pursed my lips and kept at it: "That leads me to another question, then: what was the world like when you came into being? Or the universe, everything in general?"

3. WHAT WAS THE WORLD LIKE WHEN YOU CAME INTO BEING?

Carrying a heavy load. Take care not to take on more than you can handle. Spreading yourself too thin leads to mental and spiritual lows.

An emotional, creative, inspired youth or old person with youthful qualities. Strong emotional ties. Big change. Quiet, gentle, studious. A significant time in a relationship.

The house suddenly disappeared as I asked this question. What I saw instead was something shaped like a man, golden and young, and he hung suspended in space, watching as from nothing came something—as light sprouted from the dark and planets ballooned up from nowhere. A wisp of golden sand floated by, causing the planets to turn as it passed them, causing stars to form and wink out. The sand was coming off the man; he was the Sand, only coiled into a consciousness. And he watched everything move with such wide, startled eyes.

The rivers of sand pulsed like blood, yet shone like starlight, Father Time whispered as I watched this old vision: "In all the things I saw, and all the things that took form, that was what I noticed first: the sands."

He turned to me in a quick flash from within the house, his face stern. "I am not some old man." Then it was back to the younger man in space. "You all project your fears of aging onto me. In truth, I am those Sands. I am spawned of it: the golden threads that spun this world into cloth. I was given a pocket in this world, where the Sands don't touch—

yet I, myself, am the Sand. I, myself, am the Keeper of the Sand. I see where it's housed and how it flows out into the world."

Then the vision of space was gone, and we were going down into a cellar in this house, where some other hooded person held a lamp that glowed with eerie blue light. In this cellar was a huge table covered in grey dust, and there were big urn-like vases full of the stuff in the back. When I sat at one of this big table's chairs and touched the dust, though, it was gritty. It was Sand, but nothing like the golden stuff above. Around the table, too, was the glass of dozens of smashed hourglasses.

I rubbed the grains between my fingers. "What's all this, then? Is this Sand, too? What happens to it when the hourglasses have emptied to one side?"

4. WHAT HAPPENS WHEN AN HOURGLASS RUNS OUT?

Domestic disharmony. Tradition and resistance to change may lead to friction.

Still a card of regret and disillusionment, but of a more transient nature. Hope soon regained.

Father Time's face was grim, tired.

"The sands need to be purified," he said. "They need to be readied again. Each hourglass is affected by the human heart; griefs and regrets stain the sand."

We followed that hooded man over to another room, where the yellow-orange light of fire flickered out. That other man stood with a sifter full of sand, and he held it over a furnace of flame, where the fire licked through the tiny holes and sent some black miasma burning off it, until ashy grey sand became golden-brown again.

"One hourglass, one body," Father Time continued. "The soul is untouched by the [decay caused by the] Sands. It's only the body that rots and spills its taint onto the hour-glasses. Which I imagine is what causes them to break at the end. Cages, those bodies. Imagine locking yourself in a cell made of bones and meat. Over time, it would become unbearable. The Sands leech at the flesh."

"Why?"

He looked down at me with a smile. "The world would become unmanageable. It would be nice to have a world with no rot, yes, but it's necessary to keep the world clean of the old."

"I see." It made sense in a way. I often think of how if there were no mushrooms, then the dead trees that fell would pile up and make this world unlivable. Maybe Father Time meant something similar with this bit about bodies. "But okay, so... this place you live in. It has a lot more to it than I thought it would. Is there anything you want to share about this plane of existence? Or the house itself?"

5. WHAT DO YOU WANT TO SHARE ABOUT WHERE YOU LIVE?

He shrugged, and once again, he needed no cards for me to understand what he meant. "This place *is* Time," he said. "All time in the world flows from here. I am born of it, yet I am also its keeper."

That was an answer similar to another answer he already gave. I guess there wasn't much more to it than that. Though, I wonder: how old can an egregore, or a created being, be? Because time existed with the start of the universe, after the Big Bang (at least, time as we understand it). Was he made then, not by us? Have we simply picked up on him as a concept? Or was he less than autonomous before we equipped him with a name, a face, and trinkets and gadgets to work with?

"Okay, I got'cha," I said, tucking that line of thought away for another time. "How about this, then: what do you do with your free time?"

6. WHAT DO YOU DO IN YOUR SPARE TIME?

PAGE of CUPS.

An emotional, creative, inspired youth or old person with youthful qualities. Strong emotional ties. Big change. Quiet, gentle, studious. A significant time in a relationship.

THE EMPRESS.

III

Withering away of bounty through neglect and inaction. Weakness, indecision.

He smiled and quirked a brow at me, and so I fumbled to rephrase my question.

"Or, well, your spare time? Your time not working?" His smile only grew as I asked. "You know, what do you do when not filling hourglasses?"

"Always speaking in terms of spending and earning time," he said with a chuckle. But as he shook his head, we found ourselves back in the foyer, with the table of hourglasses and the huge library of books. He looked up at those books and smiled. "I like to create—or at least try to.

"But I am Created, not Creator. The best I can do is write. I write the stories I see flicker and crackle within the sands of the hourglasses. The Sands become infused with history. I learn much by watching them. So much has happened. So much will keep happening."

"Wow. That's amazing." I couldn't help but feel something of a kinship there, as a writer myself: I can't create either, not physically like God can, yet I can write things down that happened, and things that I dreamed up. Maybe that's as close as Creation can get to being Creator. There's something to love about such an idea—something bittersweet. "But okay, okay, we're getting into the last round here, so let me ask you this: how do you see yourself?"

7. HOW DO YOU SEE YOURSELF?

II

Harmony in the midst of conflict and change. Successfully balancing conflicting priorities. Control maintained in a stressful situation. Tact and diplomacy win.

What was really interesting as I pulled Two of Coins was how the coins on the stick looked like an hourglass, golden sand in the shape of a coin on each side.

"I am stuck here in this realm, and yet I'm not trapped," said Father Time. "You all perceive me, the embodiment of the Sands. And I chronicle all of you. I am the great keeper of the flow of time, and I love my work with all my heart."

"Ooh. And how do you want to be seen?"

8. HOW DO YOU WANT TO BE SEEN?

"As the same."

"Fair. Alright, well, earlier I noticed you make a remark on the way we speak about time—spending, free time, all that—and I wonder if there's anything you wanted to say about it?"

9. WHAT LAST THOUGHTS DO YOU HAVE ON SPENDING TIME?

Each day could be your last. Life is short, so seek real satisfaction. Take control of your own life and destiny. Resolve guilt and grief.

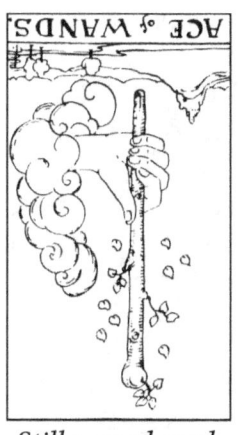

Still a good card, but one that shows a tendency for excess, over enthusiasm, or misplaced optimism.

One person can make the world a better place. You have seen and learned much in life. Put expertise into action. Live by example.

For this, he told me he wanted to pick three cards, and it was with a cheeky smile and a wink that he told me each one was for Past, Present, and Future—the most basic tarot spread of all time, yet the one most relevant here.

"You all deliver one long chain message," he said as I looked at the cards. "I notice this: your very lives become the chronicle of the Sands, and those freshly poured pick up where the last left off. It's good. It's through death and purification of the Sands that the next glasses learn.

"The Sands didn't used to look so brassy. They were once light, weightless," and he showed me those Sands floating through space, bright white-yellow and sparkling with an airiness they didn't have anymore, "and now they're like gold, saturated with knowledge and wisdom of the thousands, millions that come before you. The soul is supported by the lessons and experiences of other souls. Listen within to the stories you're being asked to continue, and be mindful of the new ones you're here to start."

"Whoa." And here I was, thinking I would just be talking to a more Victorian era egregore of Kronos or something. This was anything other than that, and with a final message that knocked me on my ass. "That's so cool. Thank you for sharing that."

We sat there, watching the Sands twist a little longer. While I would've loved to sit there all day, however, I had my own things to do, my own timetable to keep, and I couldn't use too many grains of Sand on that moment.

"Alright," I said with a clap of my hands, "all of this has been wonderful—but now, Father Time, I do need to go, so I'll call it here. I really appreciate your time and insight! Goodbye for now!"

And then he smiled, winked, and was gone. So too was the wizard's house full of trinkets and gadgets, and the stream of infinite golden Sand. All that was left was my own kitchen table once I opened my eyes: that, and the yellow *Alice in Wonderland* book, the candle, the PlayStation controller, the stones.

I realize now, looking back, that I forgot to ask a question. I meant also to get Father Time's insight on how we can best make use of our time on this earth—but then, given the things he's said already, I don't know if that's something he would find it his place to say. After all, while our existence in these decaying bodies may be finite, is the time our souls have really limited, too? Are we really *earning* and *spending* time, given how he laughed at me for framing it that way? Is the gold of time's Sands really some currency we can distill and hoard like we can the gold trapped in the earth's crust?

I don't know. I don't think so, either. I think, after meeting with a primordial egregore like this (and what a paradox of statements that is, eh?) that there is no such thing as *spending* time. It ticks by, moment by moment, no matter what we do. We can work harder, faster—we can drive ten miles over the speed limit and dangerously race around other cars on the road, or skip out on meetings with friends, or let our employers act like our days off from work are some commodity to use wisely as a company benefit—but is that really *saving* time? Using it effectively?

Or is that just weaving yet more illusions around this simple fact of existence? Misunderstanding the very purpose of it?

I don't know. And I suppose to ask someone like Father Time that question would really be to ask him what we should do with our *life*—or why we're alive in the first place. It's not a question for others to answer. It's a challenge for us to take on, a riddle for us to tease out.

THE RODJENICE

Once again: if I were thrown out of the Greek pantheon, where else could I go to explore the concept not just of time, but of fate? After all, the Greek fates, or the Moirae, were off limits (along with whatever their cognate may have been in the Roman pantheon). How simple it would've been, right? To essentially plunder that pantheon time and time again?

But that wasn't the point of this series. These interviews, as I was coming to embrace, wasn't just about satisfying my curiosity about other spirits. Nor was it about just writing goofy little interviews every week. No, this series was also to learn more about the very world we live in through the eyes of Divinity, and so there was no such thing as an "easy way out"; there was only a question, and a desire deep enough to draw me down the path of whoever might've had the answers across different cultures and faiths. And no doubt, the Greek religion wasn't the only one to have a concept of such beings. Once again, I looked to the pantheon of my own ancestors, and I found there something very much like both the Greek Fates and the Norse Norns: the Slavic Rodjenice.

These three sisters in the Slavic faith were ones responsible for the way a person's life would turn. Like the Greek Fates, they measure the string of a person's life, with the first sister drawing it, the second measuring it, and the final cutting it. Mothers wouldn't name their babies until a few days after birth, when this process was thought to take place, and some insist that the first and second sisters would argue about what this thread of life would entail, while it was the final sister that had the final say. According to the types of Slavs that my family specifically hails from (the southern Slavs), these fairy-like beings were women dressed in white, and they liked gifts of groats, honey, bread, and cheese. That's about as much information as I could find, though, given how much of Slavic paganism has simply... disappeared. Christianization, war, and so much more has unfortunately buried a lot of the Slavic faith system in the ashes of history.

Still, this was more than enough for me to cobble something together, and so I managed to find and speak to who I was looking for all the same.

With the table set, my questions half-written down, and the smell of bread and honey all over the kitchen, I asked God to let the Rodjenice through and put on one of my favorite folk bands, the Warsaw Village Band. They make some lovely renditions of Polish folk songs that I simply adore.

The first song to play was one called *Cranes*. But what I noticed as the song played is that we started at the edge of the forest, not unlike the kind I'd always see when imagining some story to the song. In my little made-up-mental-music-videos, there'd usually be someone running into the woods from a band of soldiers on horseback, the hoofbeats matching the driving beat.

This time, though, it was the Rodjenice there at the edge of the woods, dressed in what looked like white nun clothes, and they looked angry as they dragged me into the woods and closed the forest off behind us. The trees literally moved in front of the band of soldiers like some kind of wooden curtain, blocking the soldiers from getting any closer.

The oldest Rodjenica scowled at me and huffed. "Soldiers! What are you doing, imagining soldiers here, huh?"

I tumbled to the forest floor; the dirt and stones dug into my palms, scraped my knees, and that earthy petrichor scent surrounded me. As the shouts of men receded from behind the wall of trees, I blinked and said, stupidly, "It's just what I think about when I hear this song."

She shook her head, rolled her eyes, and the three led me deeper into the woods, where a wooden totem of a mother figure sat. Then the forest flickered and blended into a new place, a warm house with a great hearthfire roaring. The youngest Rodjenica sat at a spinning wheel, the middle in front of the fire, and the oldest held up a cut red string to some piece of cloth that had been embroidered with all kinds of thread; a forest and mountain were coming together from all the separate strings. It looked like Mt. Triglav in Slovenia, or at least reminded me of it.

"Alright, well, hello! Thank you for meeting with me." The oldest was still shaking her head, as if I were a young child she'd scooped up from getting run over in the street. With a sheepish smile, I felt their wish for Threads of Fate's Weaver Tarot, got to shuffling that aptly named deck, and said, "I have some questions for you about Fate. Would love to explore it with you. And I guess the first thing I have to ask is: what determines how you choose the fate of a person? The length of their string before you cut it?"

I. WHAT DETERMINES THE LENGTH OF SOMEONE'S FATE THREAD?

Take inventory of ego, self worth, and image. Ground yourself.

Scales are present. View the issue without bias. Right all wrongs.

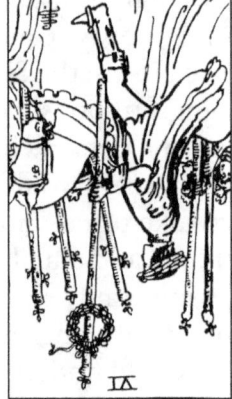

Struggling, filled with uncertainty. Define your own success.

The youngest blinked at me, her eyes massive and round and dark like the eyes of a barn owl. She smiled and started off the answer all three wove together; it seemed like one of them chose each card, and that this was how they wanted to answer going forward.

"When a soul graces the world, we need to find out who they are."

The oldest muttered in the back, "And what a chore that can be."

"We need to read the threads of their old life to find the way the new stitches begin," the Youngest continued. "A tapestry—each of you make a tapestry, and one day, a final picture will form from all your threads."

Then the Middle jumped in: "How we determine this is based on Justice, on understanding what lessons you didn't finish. What mistakes you made, all that. Imagine you're given a painting and told to finish it. That's what we do—but the painting is our own. We just forget between so many years."

Again, the Oldest clucked her tongue. "These two," she said as she motioned to her fellows. "How they argue. They never step back to see where the full picture is going." Then she walked me back, to the back of the room, so I could see the tapestry she was making more clearly. Definitely a mountain and trees and a rolling field, all detailed by string. "See? You need to step back to see it all. But they're always spinning away. *Tsk.* I see where the thread needs to go. Not where it gets to go, not where they think it should go, where it needs to go—and then I cut it."

"Ah, got'cha." Man, say what you want about Slavic gods, but to me, they always have that *ass chapping* quality that reminds me of both my mother and my oma: cutting to the point, frustrated over other people's lack of common sense, yet secretly amused a lot of the times, too. Moreover, before I continued, I found myself wondering: who's tapestry was that, that they were weaving in front of me? But that seemed rude, asking after some stranger's whole soul story, so I continued with the questions I had written down. "So, when do you know a picture is done? A tapestry?"

2. WHEN DO YOU KNOW A SOUL'S TAPESTRY IS DONE?

"All good stories must come to an end," said the Oldest as we went back to the fireplace.

Then the Youngest piped up. "It's just that we don't want them to! It feels like there's always a little more to add, to do—but once we add too much, we can't take it off. What happened, happened."

"I ensure that there isn't too much," the Oldest added, "so that a soul doesn't get muddy."

I looked to the Middle, who hadn't spoken yet, and she shrugged. "All I can say is that I'm glad when the thread is long. Then I can take a break from the person's picture. Arguing over them—it makes me dizzy."

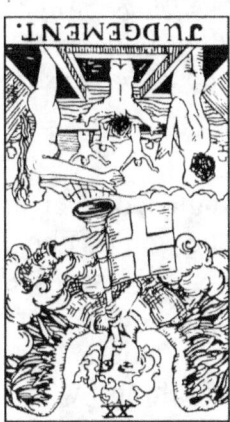

Stuck in self judgement. Inner work requires balance. Can't expect perfection when constantly fixing things.

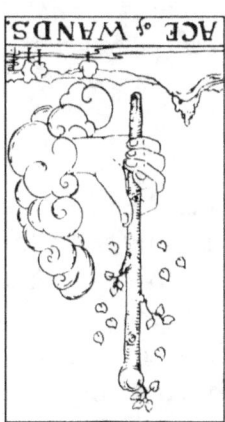

Experiencing hiccups. Put the project aside for now. You're creating anxiety rather than freedom.

Deep connection with another person. Be vulnerable and honest. Love is a choice. Some relationships need to die to move on.

"Fair!" These three seemed sweet, familiar, as if I were comfortably visiting a house of sisters that had always been around my neighborhood or something. "But this is a good time to ask, then: I read about some Roman who saw the Slavs and said they didn't believe in fate. How does that work, if you're here? That can't be totally true, can it?"

3. DID THE SLAVS ACTUALLY BELIEVE IN FATE?

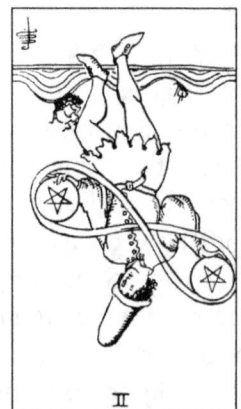

Arrival and completion. Financial success and stability. Harmony in relationships. Celebrate all going right. Thinking about future generations.

Complete dissatisfaction with a situation. Disconnect between work and success. Maybe not willing to work, or not seeing a return for work.

The delicate balance has fallen by the wayside. You're no longer able to keep up. May feel frozen and overwhelmed. Anything unnecessary should be paused.

Here's where I'll say: these ladies knew what they were doing with the cards of the Weaver Tarot. Even if I got the same cards for different readings, it was the actual imagery of the cards that seemed more important. On this question, especially, it was like they were telling a story: of how all these ideas and themes and concept emanated down from the heavens, only for them to have to round them all up in thread and then have trouble trying to tie and balance them all. It was uncanny, how well the story played out in the visuals alone.

"Astute girl," said the Middle as I inspected the imagery and drew these conclusions. "Yes, we are given themes and concepts from the start—and we decide how to weave these concepts into the Big Picture—but you, sometimes you make decisions we have to work around. Sometimes the threads get tangled, or snap and break. You all—you're rough with fate."

The Youngest looked to me and added, "We wouldn't be here if there was no such thing as fate. But fate doesn't work the way people think. We weave lessons, challenges—all of which will be accomplished, no matter how much string you make us use. Everyone has a role."

"And those roles will be completed," said the Oldest. "We see to it."

"Okay, so," that wasn't super ominous or anything, "what happens to a soul when a picture is done? If you can't add anymore, what's to become of the one the tapestry is attached to?"

4. WHAT HAPPENS WHEN A TAPESTRY IS DONE?

1. A layered card with much nuance. Good fortune, deep abundance. Examine relationship with wealth. Are you a giver or a taker?

2. Deep connection with another person. Be vulnerable and honest. Love is a choice. Some relationships need to die to move on.

3. Scales are present. View the issue without bias. Right all wrongs.

THE LOVERS.

JUSTICE .

"Ah," sighed the Oldest. "The souls who know too much—who come to see the full Truth—they need to be removed. So they don't spill past their tapestries and complete works before their time."

"It's hard, yes," said the Youngest, "to send a soul to the final Judgement of their works, but it must be done. Everyone deserves a chance to have their picture played out—not revealed too soon.'

I stared at that tapestry, and I couldn't help but ask: "Is that my tapestry? That picture?" I didn't think they'd show me someone else's picture.

The Middle smiled. "Even if it were, could you understand what it means? You'll only understand when it's done—when you put that last stitch in it. We aren't the ones that make the whole decision: we only decide what themes, knots, and length of cord this part of the picture needs before you have us cutting another thread."

"Huh. Alright. I guess that makes sense." Because maybe that was Triglav, or maybe I was just reading into it, and what was I going to do about it either way? "Okay, so... with all this talk about themes and fate and decisions, I gotta know: does God figure into this? We always think of Him as the writer of all these stories, but I know there's gotta be something else here. This is all connected somehow, I'm sure of it, but I don't know how. Can you help me understand?"

5. DOES THE ABRAHAMIC GOD GET INVOLVED ANYWHERE IN THIS?

Scales are present. View the issue without bias. Right all wrongs. In order to find justice, one must have the whole truth.

Deep connection with another person. Be vulnerable and honest. Love is a choice. Some relationships need to die to move on.

Complete dissatisfaction with a situation. Disconnect between work and success. Maybe not willing to work, or not seeing a return for work.

The Oldest grunted, and her mouth set in a hard line as she stood closest to the fireplace.

"I resent the idea that it's only your God writing these stories," she said. "He's not involved the way you think. He doesn't pen down every detail; He only gives concepts, lessons, morals. We then have to weave around these things, making sure all get incorporated, no matter how long it takes a soul to absorb it all."

"Do you decide this for everyone?"

She shook her head. "We are of the Slavic people, so our attention rests on the Slavic people. Other fates handle other people."

I pursed my lips, thinking, and kept rolling with these minor questions for a bit longer. "And what about Perun, then? We're talking about God, but Perun is the head of the Slavic gods; doesn't he have anything to do with this?"

"Perun?" The Oldest shrugged, then lifted her arms; on the sleeves were red embroidered patterns, traditional Slavic designs. "He has this threads, too. Even we have ours. t's hard not to feel like I wear *puppet* strings sometimes."

"Oh, wow. Um." Sometimes gods and spirits just... said stuff. With no regard for the gravity of it. "Okay, well, speaking of the others: how do you work with the other Fates? The Norns, the Moirae?"

6. HOW DO YOU WORK WITH THE OTHER FATES?

The Oldest kept it brief, and she chose no cards; neither did the other two, who stayed silent. "They do what we do. Just for different people. One day, we'll all compare the pictures we've compiled."

"Ah, got'cha. So then, another thing: I saw illustrations of you with the Mother of God—Mary. You stayed here. How did you manage that? Staying with the people even with Christianization? How did that work?"

7. HOW DID YOU SYNCHRONIZE WITH CHRISTIANITY?

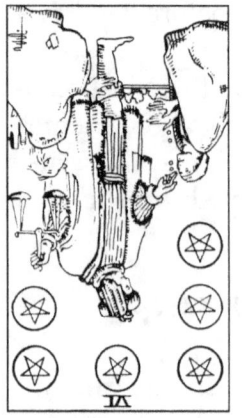

Imbalance in relationships. Always there for others but they're not there for you. Focus more on yourself. There may be ego in your charity.

A holder of space. Perceptive, intuitive, nurturing, warm, heart-centered. Lean on this person for support. Use your intuition.

There are a few options available and you're centering on the best choice. Not the time for get rich quick schemes, but long term stability.

The Oldest said, "Again, we weave. We don't see the future—only the themes we're given. I don't know who cuts our threads, but they haven't cut them yet, is all I can say."

"And we've been careful not to step on any toes," added the Youngest. "The Mother—your Mother there, the Lady—she vouches for us. She sees we're important. She let us stay under her cloak while all else was 'going to hell,' as your kind likes to say. She saved us from being completely lost."

I remembered an image I'd seen, of Mary holding her cloak out to cover a group of nuns dressed in white, and it made sense to me, why these Rodjenice were also dressed like that: it represented the cover Mary gave them, the disguises they wore. Insane.

The Middle said, "That Mary of yours is strange. It's like she knows something no one else does—not even God. But He sees her. And He lets her keep going. Your God is strange, too, and we don't know what to make of Him."

Sometimes these interviews make me want to start swinging, if only because for every question I get answered, the answers themselves open up fifteen more questions.

"Okay," I said, knowing that I could get trapped asking questions here all day with answers like these, "I hear you. I guess that wraps up the personal questions. Now, how do you all see yourselves?"

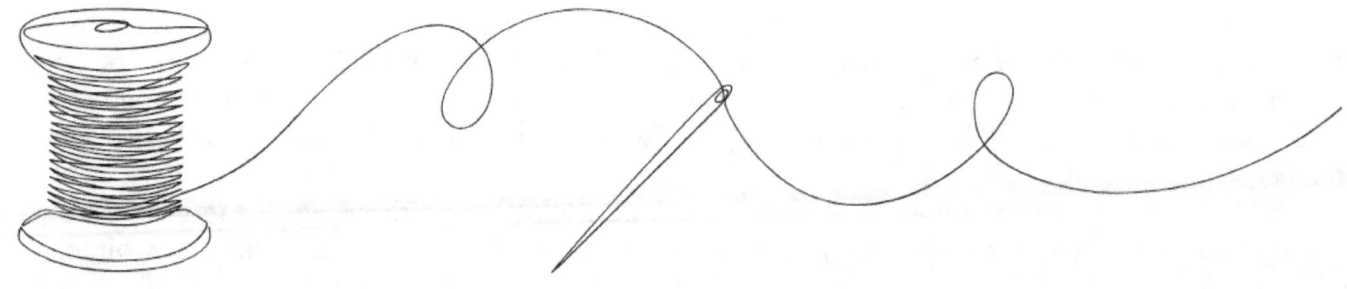

8. HOW DO YOU SEE YOURSELVES?

The Youngest smiled and said, "I do my work, and I do it well. I want to see everything when it's done—what all our work looks like with everyone else's. I wonder how their tapestries will look against ours in whatever great Quilt we make. I can't wait."

"I can," said the Middle. "I can wait, alright. I am tired of all this fuss and flow; a moment's rest from the weaving would be blessed. Of course I know I can't stop. So I stay resilient; I am a master of my own power."

Meanwhile, the Oldest peered into the fire, and she sighed. "Girl... I've never stepped outside this realm of ours, and yet I feel as if I've seen all I've ever wanted to see, and plenty I've never wanted to see. There is no rest behind a window; you can still see all the hell outside. I am one who has no interest in the outside, yet I must see it anyway."

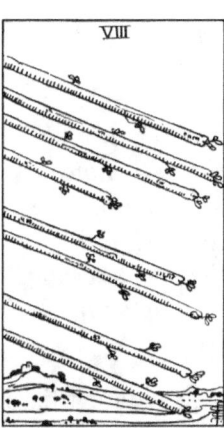

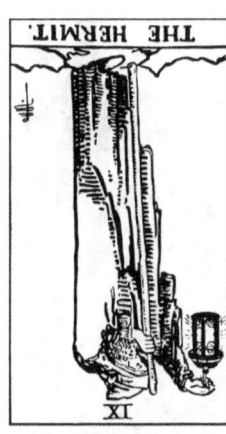

Balance and peace. Curious and open to different points of view. Things aren't black and white. Detach from confrontation and allow grace where there was none.

The universe opens up an energetic river of potential. Challenges are soon decided in your favor. Expansion. Build this energy, but stay grounded.

You've isolated yourself too much or can't find peace in being alone. All good things can become unhealthy if left unchecked. Finding strength in quiet moments.

"Oh." What a range of ideas. "That's fascinating. But... I notice it feels like you don't want to say anything about others and how they should see you; I can feel it even before I ask. Still, though, do you want to pull any cards?"

9. HOW DO YOU WANT TO BE SEEN?

The Oldest shook her head, her eyes half closed as if she were tired.

"It doesn't matter how you see us," she said. "It affects our work zero percent. We aren't for all of you, anyway. Keep away—don't meddle with our work, and we won't meddle with yours."

I couldn't tell if that was a message for me specifically or for everyone trying to mess with Fate. "Okay, well, are there any last messages you'd like to tell people?"

10. ANY LAST MESSAGES?

There are a few options available and you're centering on the best choice. Not the time for get rich quick schemes, but long term stability.

By this point, the Middle and the Oldest turned towards the fire to tend to it, seemingly done with the conversation. But the Youngest put her hand up and urged me to pull a card.

"Me, me! I've something to say." Once I pulled the card, she spoke with such urgency. "Fate is made by decisions! We set the markers, and you decide the way to each one. I don't know if we made that clear, but here it is now. Your choices matter. Make them well. Because you can break a string, but you can't add more length to one already cut."

"They won't listen," the Middle called over her shoulder, a soft smile on her face. "They never do."

But the Youngest implored me with those giant eyes, so I wrote it down anyway and nodded. "I understand. That's a message I think might help people a lot, if they can keep it close. Thank you, all three of you, for your answers, but now, I'll say goodbye. I'll put your offerings by the yew tree, if that's okay?"

They nodded, letting me know it was, and then I was closing the circle down and bidding the Rodjenice goodbye, my head swirling with all kinds of ideas all the while. Their honey and groats and such ended up outside for the animals to pick at in their honor, and I sat there mulling over every little fragment they'd given me in this wild meeting.

Does God work with these beings? Does He not? Is He all knowing? Is He not? What was Mary doing, defending these ladies (and is that why so many goddesses keep getting syncretized to her over and over again instead of outright erased)? All these and more are things that, honestly, I think may make up threads of my tapestry. The Greek Fates, it seems, are patently Not For Me (big surprise there), and yet the ones that *are* for me—are they really?

The more I talk with Slavic gods, the more I come to think: maybe my being Christian doesn't make these gods any less concerned with me. It would seem so. Rather than this being about faith and conversion (which few pre-Christian pantheons actually understood the way we think about conversion now), it seems that it really is more about ancestry. These gods *are* my ancestors—and that means they might be created from something, too, rather than solely some kind of creator, as the Rodjenice themselves alluded to. After all, if a god like Perun can have their own threads, what does that mean for divinity?

I guess we'll have to keep progressing our own tapestries, and finishing them, to know.

CASSIEL

Once, someone who worked closely with this angel Cassiel asked me to speak with him and see what he said. An angel of Duality—of tears, of sorrows, of temperance, even of death—his name is one that means "God is my Wrath," or "Speed of God," and interestingly enough, he's also considered the angel of Saturn, of all things.

Therefore, he's also known as an angel of time.

As I was wondering if there even was an angel of time, I stumbled upon all of this and felt rightly inspired: I could progress the theme being discussed *and* honor that certain someone's request. A real two-birds-one-stone moment. If there was ever a time to investigate the request of another person regarding their own spirits of interest, this would be it. After learning a bit more about Cassiel, and his role in non-Canonical Jewish, Christian, and even Muslim mystic texts as one of the Watchers, I found that he wasn't one that fell, but one of the Watchers that still surrounds the throne of God.

With angels, it's best to just take a look at what they have to say, in my experience. Especially with ones that don't typically deal with people in the first place. So without further ado, let's dive in.

By this point in the game, I'd definitely been lagging with my consistency in getting interviews done. It was the end of the year, there were so many things to do, so many new things to experience (like wrapping up my first semester teaching), and I just couldn't keep up an interview schedule as consistently as I would've liked thanks to the sheer weight of burnout. As a result, I'd been getting a little rusty with meditation. It had been a little difficult to hook up to the sights and sounds I used to experience in meditation, and this day wasn't much different.

However, times like these usually just meant I needed a little extra effort to stitch myself into the scene, given taking a massive break wasn't really an option for me. Ways I accomplish this include music, soft lighting, getting comfortable (but not so comfortable that I fall asleep), all that. And most importantly, I get the hell out of my own way and stop thinking about what I'd rather be doing than these interviews.

Which has been a problem lately. Something about having to sit down and focus for such an extended period of time made me feel like I was being asked to build an entire castle by hand, by myself. It drained me like nothing else on my schedule; it was *rough*. But it was also always worth it once I got myself into it.

So with my blue stones out (blue meaning time to me for some reason) and my angel statue at the ready, a nice taper candle going beside me, and a cup of coffee for the morning journey, I had my set up ready to go. I was all business as I wrote out my questions, and I asked God to let Cassiel come on through.

Nothing happened.

So I asked again. And I asked again. Over and over, I asked, and I was getting little snatches of something each time; every request revealed more and more to me, as if my words were the mallet that struck the face of a drum, beating the rhythm into being. There in my mind's eye were flashes of blue. A blue sky full of stars. And clouds. And then there was a man standing there, dressed in blue robes with blond hair—a lot like Gabriel.

So many blond angels! Maybe it's because they're all made of light in some way, or maybe it's just the way my mind defaults to viewing them, but there he was: Cassiel, with wings unlike any other angel wings I'd ever seen. They were almost like fairy wings, and the feathers stretched out as if they were twelve hands on a clock. Above him—and the throne he stood in front of—hung Saturn, and around his feet slithered a little pink dragon.

"Whoa." I blinked at him as he came into view, and he smirked from down his nose at me. He had these moon-bright eyes, honestly a little intimidating to look into. "Uh, well. Alright. Hello, Cassiel—thank you for joining me! Mind if I ask you a few questions?"

He nodded, his energy settling over the Marigold Tarot, and that was all I needed to jump in.

As he sat down in that throne, I looked around at this strange landscape we were in—all stars and clouds, but not much of anything else, all planets and colors, but not much that made sense to my mind—and I decided to start with a different question than I intended.

"So... what's the 7th Heaven like?"

I. WHAT IS THE 7TH HEAVEN LIKE?

THE MOON.

Miscommunication, trauma, illusion, negative behaviors.

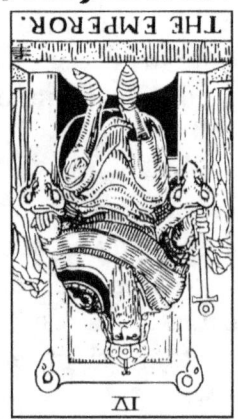

Discord, disorder, control, breakdown in power dynamics.

He waved a hand. "Look around. You can't see what it's like?"

"No, no, I can *see* it, but I don't know what to make of this. What do you think it's like? Tell me, please."

With a sigh, he pulled his couple cards and told me.

"The closer you get to God, the less power you realize you have," he said, as he stared up to nothing in particular. "We angels are agents. Chess pieces. Fragments of a larger whole. In the Seventh Heaven, you cannot see God, but He is among you—an invisible whisper, watching and listening closely."

And I could get what he was talking about, because it felt like there was an eye hovering in the air between us, a presence that didn't care if you knew it was there or not because it knew you would do nothing about it anyway.

"I got'cha. Interesting. Is that maybe why people say you'd rather just observe the world than intercede? Because you have this view of your power to change things?"

2. WHY DO YOU PREFER TO WATCH THE WORLD INSTEAD OF ACT IN IT?

Cassiel slowly sank down and lounged in that throne-like seat, the dragon curling around the ends of his robes.

"What is the point of interfering? I watch my brother Michael spend each moment, day in and day out, trying to herd you sheep. I watch my brother Samael try a wholly different approach than the Advocate, trying to break you into your lessons, better behavior. And yet all is still a mess.

"No, I'll have no part in that," Cassiel said, wrinkling his nose. "I'll watch. I'll wait. I'd even take bets here, if I could. But time will tell all." And then it stretched like a river before him, the whole expanse of time—but only to the present day. That was this throne he sat on: the seat of Time, revealing everything only to the moment we exist in. "Even if only God knows the future's course," he continued, "time will tell all. I've waited eons to see how things will end— what's another few centuries?"

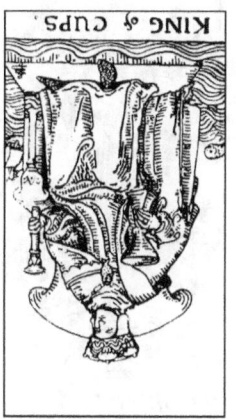

Self destructive, controlling, dishonest, manipulative behavior.

Hostility, indecision, or disharmony.

I wondered if he meant literally a few centuries, if that's all we have left. The way we're going as a species, I wouldn't have been surprised. But I knew better than to take that at face value, so I kept on.

"Alright, I can understand that. Fair. Though, speaking of time, I can't help but wonder: does time hurt or heal? People have mixed opinions about that. Would love to get your take on it."

3. DOES TIME HURT OR HEAL?

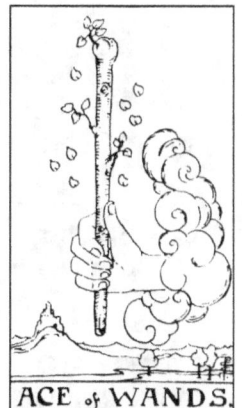

Creativity, ambition, opportunities in bloom.

Miscommunication, trauma, illusion, negative behaviors.

Cassiel stood up, and then he herded me away from the seat. We walked along a cave of crystals that shone like opals, all milky white and yet full of rainbows. It was a dark cave, but some blue light from the stalagmites made the rainbow colors of the stones apparent as we moved about.

"Time gives you opportunities to choose if it'll hurt you or heal," he said as we walked. "Hurting and healing are two sides of the same coin. At any moment, you can change course—leave the world of old memories and venture forward into new experiences. Every second is a chance. Every breath is redemption in waiting."

"Wow. That's a beautiful way to look at it." Redemption in waiting—that was the phrase he put in my head. What a view of time. Wild. "Okay, okay—but now, that Coin you talk about, it brings me to another train of thought here. You're also mentioned as the Angel of Duality, and of Tears, because of how joy and suffering are linked to you. Can you speak on that? What joy and suffering have in common?"

4. WHAT DO JOY AND SUFFERING HAVE IN COMMON?

Past regrets, ignoring the call to transform, disappointment, false accusations.

Healing, balance, and harmony. The natural order. Inevitability of all things. Adjusting to circumstances, making the best of a situation. Cycles.

"All things in moderation," he said with a small smile, "even light and dark, good and evil. Joy and suffering are like the Wheel: ever-turning, ever in motion. At times, we get lost—either in our memories or in our current plight—and we can't see the way the Wheel moves us forward.

"Suffering creates the soil bed for joy to grow. But joy is like a weed: not something we always purposely set out to cultivate, yet we find it blooming amongst the fruits of suffering in utter defiance. Joy is resistance. It thrives in the future based on the tears of past suffering."

Once again, I found myself just blinking at him—especially because the work I'd been doing with God and Lucifer just the night prior had exactly these themes. It was obvious that it was not a coincidence that Cassiel would pop up for me as I searched for an angel of time to talk to this week.

"Alright... I can see that." And there wasn't much else for me to say about it. "Switching track now: Saturn. People associate you with Saturn, and all the things related to it: aging, discipline, maturity, all that. What do you think?"

5. THOUGHTS ON BEING ASSOCIATED WITH SATURN?

"I like being associated with Saturn," he said, and then pulled some seriously harsh cards, "but it is cruel—how this planet, and its energy, drives people to such madness. This planet is a mirror; by facing it, people see clearly who they are, and there's no guarantee they enjoy their reflection. Your actions dictate that reflection.

"Saturn's judgement reveals all your life up to its knell as nothing more than the ravings of lunatics, of children, desperate to rebel and wrest control from the one who created them. Those who come under Saturn's shadow have the option of either accepting what they see or continuing to play rogue—and you'd be surprised how many choose the latter. You can fail your 'Saturn Return,' as you call it, just as you can fail anything else. It depends on your integrity."

Discord, disorder, control, breakdown in power dynamics.

Thievery, lies, betrayal, avoiding the truth.

Well, that's one more thing to be anxious about. Here I was thinking that the Saturn Return at around 28 to 30 years old would magically fix people's lives, not be yet another trial they could possibly miss completely.

But as I looked at these cards—Emperor Reversed and Seven of Swords—I began to wonder about this angel. Some website I'd been reading said he'd be wearing pink, not blue, and he looked an awful lot like Gabriel, too much. The only thing pink about him was whatever little dragon was following him around. I knew better than to think a lot of these goofy websites online would be all too accurate, but you know how it goes: anything and everything can plant those little seeds of doubt. More than that, though, Cassiel was also using language that reminded me of plenty others: of God and Lucifer alike, with the "Two Sides: One Coin" shtick. So I asked him.

"You are Cassiel, right?"

With that question, he smiled in a way no one wants to see an angel smile. His eyes shone with what felt like that very lunacy he just talked about, and his teeth were sharp. Then his whole face split open, revealing a dark hole between it with one single eye staring at me from the dark.

"Am I? You tell me."

Christ.

However, for all that cosmic horror in Cassiel's "face," it was then I knew it was, in fact, him. I'd just contacted the Infernal Divine again the night before; I knew their energy, and this wasn't it. This was angel energy, ethereal yet dangerous, like a thunder cloud—one laced with exhaustion and grief and the weight of responsibility. That dark hole in his face pulled at me with those very forces: the forces of an angel's deep, agonizing frustration, their chained-up fury and the smoke and ash of their perpetual, impotent mourning.

To be an angel, and especially to be one that watches humanity, is to suffer under those sweet smiles carved into their masks. If there is anything I've learned from talking to angels, it is this.

Moreover, this bit of spookiness only confirmed for me that it was an angel, because only an angel outside the ranks of those that work with humans responded so poorly to being tested. Only an angel would try to convince you that they're not an angel, to see if your resolve would crack and if your mind would go to mush, so they could leave you be and go back to whatever it is they were doing before you came and bothered them.

"Yes, you are. Enough shenanigans, yeah?" He laughed as I scowled, but his face stayed split, that giant cyclops eye spearing me. "Next question for you: what is the benefit of humans aging?"

6. WHAT IS THE BENEFIT OF HUMANS AGING?

THE WORLD.

Movement, growth, completion, success, enlightenment. Survivng all things.

QUEEN of PENTACLES

Intelligence, trustworthiness, generosity, seeing past the material.

"Ah. Interesting question." He mulled it over, then said, "Time is necessary for things to grow. If you had infinite time, not only would you overrun us immortals, but you'd never learn your lessons. Death of the body is the yoke that binds your arrogance.

"All you humans, no matter the paper crowns and rocks you use to inflate your importance, die. All of you have limited time. It forces you to make decisions, to choose how to spend your lives rather than dallying forever." Then that eye focused on me so hard that it could've pierced a hole in me. "And you, Sara? What will you spend your life on? This?" He gestured to the table of tarot cards. "These interviews, this work?"

The question was bait; that much was obvious. I just shrugged and said, "I'll spend it on whatever God tells me to spend it on. I'm not all too worried about it."

My mind was too preoccupied with the implications of what Cassiel just said. There are a lot of things we have to learn, and it doesn't make sense why some should learn one lesson while others learn another.

Seventy years isn't enough to experience all of life and understand it all. I mean, if we look at Palestine, people's entire lives has been consumed by colonization and occupation and brutalization the past seventy-five years—an entire lifetime for many people. Is there nothing else for them to learn but this terrible lesson? I don't believe that. I believe these injustices will end, and those who didn't live to see it end will be back in some shape or form, to experience the world without that on their backs. We die, but death isn't the end. As a Christian, I'm told as much in the whole death and resurrection of Jesus, too.

When I looked back at Cassiel after all that thinking, his face was back to normal, and he smiled with a quirked brow, the way an adult smiles at a child speaking outlandish theories and dreams and ideas into the air, but he didn't say anything against the idea. So I just kept on.

"Okay, so: speaking of time, there's that phrase, 'everyone has their time.' What do you think? How does God decide what someone's time to leave earth is?"

7. HOW DOES GOD DECIDE WHEN A SOUL LEAVES EARTH?

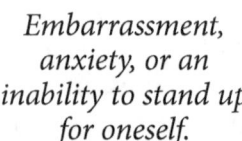

Embarrassment, anxiety, or an inability to stand up for oneself.

Falling in love with the idea of love, jealousy, needing to return to reality.

Cassiel brought us back to his seat of time and stared up at a huge moon that hung overhead, shining its silver light down on us.

"There's no one way God decides," he said. "All things must die—this we know. But each case is holistically approached. God assesses the strength of a spirit, the capacity of its learning, the anguish and illusion it traps itself in. People break easily in your world. Though sometimes the supposedly broken are the strongest, and the supposedly solid will snap like plywood." Then he looked at me with the tiniest touch of tenderness to his eye. "Even when you think you can decide when you leave this life, trust God has already noticed you and guided you one way or another to suit His storylines."

That last line felt like half a comfort, half a horror. There were implications in it that I did not want to give form to in my thoughts, and so I scribbled it down and kept going.

"Well, that's all we have for personal questions. Now to our finishers: how do you see yourself, Cassiel?"

8. HOW DO YOU SEE YOURSELF?

There was one card in my deck that somehow got turned face up, and it was the Six of Coins. That was the one he chose as his card.

Generosity, prosperity, gratification, reflection, loss vs. gain. The helpful and harmful aspects of the material world.

"I am someone who watches all of you experience these things we've talked about. Every soul experiences them differently. Each time, I learn something more about this cruel world God made. What is He trying to teach us angels, having us watch all this? I ask myself that question frequently."

"Oh." Angels are complicated creatures, aren't they? Not nearly so robotic or drone-like as people make them out to be. Even if I sometimes describe them as spiritual robots, they're really... not. Not under that Customer Service style repression they always seem to have going on. "Okay. How do you want to be seen?"

9. HOW DO YOU WANT TO BE SEEN?

He refused to pull any cards. "I'd rather people not see me at all."

"Fair. But then, do you have any messages before we go?"

10. ANY LAST MESSAGES?

Truth, indecision, inadequacy, emotional detachment.

Cassiel looked right at me and folded his arms over his chest. "You don't have time to wallow in despair and self pity," he said. "A life without emotion is bleak and grey, yes, but too much emotion leaves you paralyzed. The clock is always ticking. Like a shark, you must keep moving to survive. Never stop. Never give up. Keep moving, even when you have no body with which you can move."

"Ah—I see. That's very forceful for someone who doesn't want to interfere with the world." When he only shrugged. I sighed and started packing up the cards. "Alright, well, thank you, Cassiel! This has been quite the conversation. I appreciate you stopping by, and I'll see you when I next see you. Goodbye for now!"

And then I fell right out of heaven, out of that odd and starry space and back into my own house down on earth. Jeez. It really is something of a hit-or-miss with the less familiar angels; it's anyone's guess whether they'll be easy to talk to or show you horrors beyond your imagination. In some sense, they're very much like demons in that regard—but what, exactly, are we surprised about, when so many demons *were* once angels? Those fallen angels, those Watchers that went off script?

So many people want to avoid angels for that reason—the folks that prefer demons. But really, when you think about it, while some pairs don't mesh for obvious reasons, there is a sensible quality to the fact that every demon of the Ars Goetia has their still-heavenly-employed angel counterpart. It's the same reason that a seesaw has two sides, that one muscle group pushes and another pulls. It's anyone's guess where the collusion of these two groups, ones so many consider "natural enemies," will go, or how it will work in the long run of human development.

And so I suppose, like Cassiel sitting on his throne of all of Father Time's Sands, there's little we can do but wait and see.

JACK FROST

Jack Frost. That's a name so many folks have heard in the west. Whether from iconic Christmas songs like Nat King Cole's "Chestnuts Roasting on an Open Fire," or from more modern reimaginations of the figure like DreamWorks' Rise of the Guardians (2012), the fact is that this is a figure that has been used for us to personify the brutal reality of winter: the frozen hands, the runny and red noses, the puffs of breath we can suddenly see leave our lips. We can see record of Jack Frost going as far back (and likely farther back) as 1876, when the New England Journal of Education posted a little poem about the sprite by W.W. Bailey in its December 16 publication (here's the first three stanzas):

A busy, bright spirit is Mr. Jack Frost,
And a mischievous elf, withal:
He bridges the river we lately crossed,
And he hides the waterfall.
He builds him a palace of crystal fair,
Which jewels and gems adorn,
Far brighter than those we frame of air,
In the waking dreams of morn.
With opals the spider's net he weaves,
Like the veil of a fairy queen,
And scatters his stars over the fallen leaves,
Till they glitter in icy sheen.

There is a lot of beautiful imagery in this poem, and it tells us a good deal about the character of our dear Mr. Jack Frost. However, it turns out that what I thought would be a simple egregore or folk character has some deeper roots than I realized, and that his role in personifying winter goes far beyond just our imagination. Sometimes it gets tricky, figuring out when egregores were created and when people simply began picking up on spirits, and this Jack Frost fellow, an English sprite that seems to have captured American imagination, is one of those times where the seemingly former is actually the latter. At least, that's what I discovered when I spoke to this legendary figure on a cold December morning.

So let me show you, with the first of the Christmas interviews for this year, what happened.

Despite a snafu on the offering table that would happen later on, everything started well, and my table was otherwise set peacefully to start. A Woodwick candle crackling, a snow globe with a cozy winter scene inside, a gnome to signify the entity I'd be speaking to, that was all I felt I needed. So after a good hour in the morning of mosying around, talking to God and getting my coffee going, I was finally able to settle in and ask God to let Jack Frost through. Or maybe I went to Jack Frost when I closed my eyes and found myself suddenly nowhere near my little home in the boonies. Who really knows, at this point?

What I do know is that right away, there was snow and a forest of snow-covered pines. And in the middle of it all, two big, shiny black eyes blinked at me. The scene reminded me quite a bit of the fae folk in *The Magus Bride,* if you've ever seen that show: big dark eyes, short but flowy white hair, that whole thing. What was odd, however, was that once I zoomed out from those big eyes, for some reason, my mind kept overlaying leaves onto this winter sprite: red and orange leaves that felt fae-like, sure, but didn't match who Jack Frost was.

"Hello, Jack!" I blinked at him. "Sorry to say, but shouldn't you be looking more... wintery? It— you've got all kinds of autumn leaves on you."

He huffed and said, "I like this image you have in your mind. But if you want to see me fully, then fine."

And then, gone were the leaves. Instead, it was the same swishy silver hair and big black eyes I'd first seen, but he had huge deer antlers rising from his head, deer hooves for legs, and a thick coat that had silver-white fur clustered at his neck. A tail popped out from under his pale blue coat, a white one that split at the end and had two tufts of blue fur. It was seeing that, this image of a proper and clearly *powerful* fairy—a fairy king, even—that I knew that I had done what I always said I wouldn't do: I invited a fairy into my house.

Not an egregore. Not some made up thoughtform. No, the energy coming off Jack Frost was old and sharp and *real* beyond a doubt, substantial all on its own, and it was the energy of pure wilderness, pure nature: it was fae as hell.

He smiled as I took in his image, sitting all dumbfounded there in front of my little makeshift altar, then motioned for me to follow him down a shadowy path into the woods and chose the Universal Fantasy Tarot to speak with.

"Ah, well, thank you for letting me see you more clearly." But I still wasn't entirely convinced that I wasn't just making things up. "Before we begin with questions, though, could I get a sign that you're here with me? Something tangible?"

Then my hands got a lot colder, despite being clasped together. Noticeably colder to the point that it almost felt like someone rubbed a vapor rub on them, or some other cooling gel.

"Fair enough," I said as he waited at the edge of the forest with an almost big brotherly smile. "Thank you! Now, I'm thinking we might start with this question, if you don't mind: what does Winter do for the world?"

1. WHAT DOES WINTER DO FOR THE WORLD?

When others lose faith in us, we are most vulnerable to attacks from within.

My pigeon, Bilok, landed on the table to look at the things I'd put there, and Jack Frost muttered at me to get him off the table. I didn't think it'd be an issue, though, as Bilok knows—usually—not to go poking around at things too much. But when it came back to Winter, Jack sighed as we started walking down the path.

"What doesn't Winter do?" He waved a hand. "It's a time of rest, reprieve—but for you lot, who've made your entire existence about ceaseless toil and production... it throws you into chaos."

Then I had to pause as he talked, because Bilok had gone and backed up into the teacup of milk and spilled a bit of it.

"You've disobeyed the natural order of things, and your bird," who made even more chaos by flying away after I shooed him off the table, "should be roosting right now, hunkering down for Winter. Yet look at him, all warm as if it's mid-spring. There is an order. A rhythm to life. You all love to ignore it."

I sighed. "Yeah, I can see that. I'm sorry about the offering."

Jack Frost raised a brow. "I don't blame the bird. He doesn't know better. You, I told to get him off the table."

"You did tell me that, yeah."

And I'll be honest: I was a little worried. I'd heard fairies weren't... the easiest to appease when they were upset. I wondered if Jack would punish little Bilok in some way, but he assured me again: it wasn't the bird's fault.

So there was that.

I decided to forge on and keep asking my questions, so long as Jack Frost was still standing there waiting for them. "Alright, anyway, okay—the natural rhythm. That takes me to my next question: how can we come more into alignment with winter in our modern times?"

2. HOW CAN WE COME INTO ALIGNMENT WITH WINTER?

The trees broke into a clearing, a little hill from which we could see a hamlet of houses practically buried in the snow. Lights shone in the windows, a snow-dusted path carving through the hills and out further away. It was somewhere in England, that much I knew.

"You resist," Jack said as he looked over the peaceful village. "You rebel. In every possible way. You've twisted yourselves into this lie that the new year begins in the dead of Winter—and you push yourself harder in Winter, to close one artificial year and start the next year 'cleanly.'

"Idiocy. Work less. Do less. Rest more. This is the way you come to Winter's rhythm. Ask yourself how much you're doing is really is necessary. Reel it back." Then he winked at me and said, in a teasing tone, "You'll make the trees and animals feel bad if they see you working while they rest."

"Aw, well, we wouldn't want that." I eyed him, because this was a message I'd heard from God, too, and at the time I wondered about fairies—if they weren't once angels or something, to tout those ideas. Looking back, though, I

There are no enemies, only lovers unknown. React to fear by opening the heart. Spirit defeats tyranny.

wonder if there isn't simply a rhyme and rhythm to Divinity in general, no matter who the gods are and where they come from. I pushed on once the thought left. "Speaking of the rhythm of Winter, though, there are some places in the world Winter doesn't touch. They don't have Winter and Summer, but dry seasons and typhoon seasons. What do you think about those places?"

3. THOUGHTS ON PLACES THAT DON'T HAVE FOUR SEASONS?

Jack shrugged. "They have a different rhythm. I am not privy to it."

"Oh," I said when I realized he wasn't about to expand on that with a card. "Yeah, that—I guess that would make sense. But okay, so... where did you come from?"

4. WHERE DID YOU COME FROM?

That had him turning with a big grin and a huff of laughter as I pulled a card. His coat swirled around his lanky fairy body, his tail quirking behind him.

"What an audacious question. I was born of Truth," he said, his chin held high. "In Truth, there is what is, and there isn't what isn't. "

Huh?

I was wondering if this wasn't a trickster, with how much of a non-answer that felt like, but as he caught my scrutinizing stare, he tutted his tongue and elaborated on the question I clearly had written on my face.

"Did Winter make me? No. Did I make Winter? No. I was given dominion over the needs of the land. Not all lands. But some. I don't think of my Master or my Maker. I simply exist, true to myself and what I came into being knowing, and I remind you lot—sometimes gently, sometimes not—of the way of the world you want so desperately to ignore. I come from Time and Space, from Sleep and Wake. I am beyond such concepts entirely."

Weakness in work or team situations, incompetence, and an inability to delegate.

"Oh, wow. Okay." This wasn't trickster spirit speak, no. It was Fairy Speak. I understood that in my bones as he kept going. It was a language of riddles and complicated ideas hidden in plain sight, lightened with a touch of whimsy that still held secrets like the angels and demons would tell, but it wouldn't give them to any idiot that didn't want to think. "That... is interesting. I can't say it makes complete sense, but I see what you're getting at—I think."

His eyes twinkled as if to challenge my supposed understanding.

I kept going with the questions anyway. "Moving on, though, I will say: sometimes people get hurt in Winter. Not because they're ignoring the rhythm of the world, but because Winter is harsh! It's hard to stay warm, and sometimes people get stuck. What do you think? Do you want people to come to harm, or—?"

5. THOUGHTS ON PEOPLE GETTING HURT IN WINTER?

At times, the solution to a problem can be found by changing direction. We must not be afraid to spread our wings.

He frowned. "Men cause their own harm."

Ahead of us, the sky went black and grey with night and clouds, and then a blast of yellow-orange fire cast wild shadows over the hamlet—something huge exploding in the sky, all smoke and flame and noise. Jack's jaw set hard.

"For what reason is my dark Winter sky breaking open with hellfire? For what reason do you animals not have the means to survive when all other animals do? In your industry, you forgot your rhythm. Were you less active, you'd have the means to make food last longer—to not waste resources keeping artificial light.

"To answer your question, no: I don't purposely bring Men to harm. I remind them of the consequences of ignoring the laws of gods and trees and winds. You Men—you are far too foolhardy, far too assured of your ability to override the way of things. Sometimes you must be reminded of the Way."

"Ah. I see." And I wondered what that bomb blast in the sky was about. Modern times? Or times past? I wanted to say World War II, as that's what everything about the scene suggested, but I kept the idea tucked away for the time being. "Okay, so... with harm comes death, though, and winter has always been known as the season of death. What do you think about winter being associated with death?"

6. THOUGHTS ON WINTER BEING ASSOCIATED WITH DEATH?

What a card to pull for this. I blinked at it, surprised, and by time I repositioned my pencil, Jack was off speaking with a wistful smile on his face.

"Are they evil and terrible spirits, those of winter? Or are you encroaching on their time?" He rocked his own head side to side, as if considering his own question. "Is winter a time of death, or a time where your wishes aren't priority? In winter, you light all your lights, wishing for sun. In summer, you rejoice with all you have. Never do you give thanks for the dark. Never do you give the creatures of cold and dark their space. It's despicable."

Considering the views of others can help us look inside ourselves. Unduly harsh punishments are just as dangerous as undue rewards.

Oh. I sat quiet for a moment, humbled by that thought. It made me think of how people cry of the danger of coyotes in their neighborhoods, without ever considering that we are in *their* neighborhoods, too—cutting down trees, driving prey away, giving them little other choice but to go after the chickens and cats people don't bring inside. Always in our folklore, we portray these spirits of winter as cruel and evil and willing to snap us up if we go outside at night—but what if they're simply coming through, like migratory geese, and we should know better than to get in their way while they're following their own natural rhythm?

It's thoughts like these that I'd never even consider without this series. Without week after week spent finding spirits to speak with that I've never spoken with before. And that's what I love about this series above all: the ability to meet new entities, feel new energies, and walk away with a treasure trove of new ideas.

"I understand that completely," I said as I finished writing my ideas down. "Thank you for that wisdom. But, to switch track from that now: some say you're a fairy. I can see that there's some truth to this, but I've never encountered a fairy before. Can you tell me how they differ from other spirits, like angels and demons?"

7. HOW ARE FAIRIES DIFFERENT FROM OTHER SPIRITS?

At times, the solution to a problem can be found by changing direction. We must not be afraid to spread our wings.

He pulled the same card he had just two questions before, the Six of Swords, so I had to triple check that this was the one he intended. It was. I wrote it down and let him speak.

"Not everything can be divided into two camps of angels and demons," he said. "Not all can exist as a god or a devil. I—we, the fairies—are the Outsiders, and I am a king of such sprites."

A king!

"I am a king that would love nothing more than to live by the world's rhythm and ignore all such squabbles with the upper and lower realms," he said with a sigh, still watching over the hamlet. "Us fairies, sprites, elves, whatever you call us—we don't care about your good and evil. We don't need it. We only need us, our lands, our duties, and our undisturbed peace.

"So tell them. Tell the people: we fairies are not on Men's side. We aren't against Men, either. We judge all as they come and as they are in the moment. You Men have many different moments. Animals don't, so we like them better. They're easy to predict. They stay with the rhythm, always—until you get involved."

"True, true." I looked that answer over, nodded, and continued. "Well, that wraps up the starting questions. Now I'd like to know: how do you see yourself? Besides as a king?"

8. HOW DO YOU SEE YOURSELF?

Jack pursed his lips, then said, "I am an anxious fellow. I always feel it's my job to corral you Men—to force you to live the rhythm of the world. But I can't do that. You were built to be different than the world. You must find your way back yourselves. I hate it, but I'm only a guide and a keeper, not an enforcer. Not a god."

"Ah, got'cha. Interesting! And how do you want to be seen?"

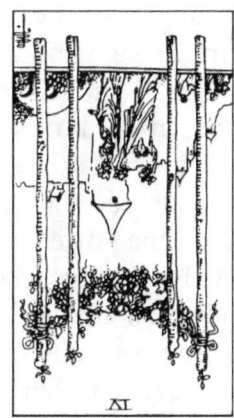

Social disputes and prioritizing others at the expense of one's personal development.

9. HOW DO YOU WANT TO BE SEEN?

THE DEVIL .

Some things we believe to be good are really the chain that holds us enslaved. At times we must question the scale of values that others have decided for us.

I laughed when he pulled the Devil.

"I don't want people to fear me, per se," said Jack, smiling along with me, "but I want them to think twice when I come by. I want to be seen as a challenger of the way things are, a being that reminds others that there is a way out of the rat race. If only they'd unchain themselves from fear and live it!

"I am not evil, as evil doesn't exist in the Rhythm. I am, however, difficult, and you lot love to see challenges to your wishes as evil. Don't think like that."

"That's a way of putting it. We're some subjective folk, us humans, aren't we?" He smiled, but it was a tired smile.

"Alright, well, it sounds like that was your last message, but just in case: is there anything else you wanted to say before we parted ways? Any last ideas?"

10. ANY LAST MESSAGES?

While Jack didn't pick a card, he did give me a little something to go off with.

"If you tell the people something," he started, winter wind rustling through the fur of his coat, "tell them this: I come whether they want me or not. It's better to make peace with some things like that than to fight them. See things my way, and you may find your path easier, not harder. Try it."

He said that last bit with a smile, and then he was walking on, waving to me over his shoulder. He was ready to go.

"Goodbye, Jack!" I waved back to him. "Thank you! Be seeing you!"

And then all was gone—even the early December chill.

Once I was back in my own space (both physical space and headspace), I watched Bilok poke around at the many seeds he'd thrown all over the floor, and I thought about what Jack said. It seemed to me that the reason his folk don't like people is the reason I don't like bugs: you watch them one minute, all fascinating and pretty, and the next minute they're erratically flying in your face or buzzing in your ear or even stinging you, like how a wasp once stung me when it crawled into my shirt sleeve without my knowing. Does that make us insects to Divinity? Who knows.

All I do know is that there's something to be said about *rhythm,* isn't there? How we all beat ourselves up for not performing at our peak every day, despite the fact that even nature itself isn't at its peak every day. If every day were nothing but balmy weather, when would the plants get to drink? When would the leaves get any rest from rough sunlight, or the trees and bears time to sleep? When would the flowers grow and feed the bees, and when would the flowers become fruits that feed us?

As I write this, I struggle with my own sense of rhythm. The days grow longer, and the sunlight has shaken off all the sleepiness and fatigue of winter. Yet I also find myself slowing down all the same, not so frantically working or racing around even as I get to my list of duties. Maybe because there was never a reason to. Maybe because, rather than pushing to achieve more and more and more, to complete all things ahead of time, I find the wisdom in letting all things happen in their own time.

Just as the leaf doesn't need to be told to hurry up and become a flower, or to exceed expectations and immediately form a fruit, so too do I know that I don't need to rush through my own work—nor do I need to complete it ahead of time if doing so will hurt. Rhythm. Rhythm isn't the melody; it's the beat. The timekeeper, the tempo.

And wouldn't life be so much easier, if we could all live to the beat of our own drum?

THE THREE MAGI

So I'm really silly, I must admit. Like, really silly.

When I went about writing this interview, I did it under the assumption that the Three Magi—the three wise men that King Herod sent to investigate the claims of a Messiah being born—were proponents of Babylonian paganism. I feel like it isn't the worst mistake to make, given here's where we see their mention in Matthew 2:3-8:

> When King Herod heard this he was disturbed, and all Jerusalem with him. When he had called together all the people's chief priests and teachers of the law, he asked them where the Messiah was to be born. "In Bethlehem in Judea," they replied, "for this is what the prophet has written:
>
> "'But you, Bethlehem, in the land of Judah,
>   are by no means least among the rulers of Judah;
> for out of you will come a ruler
>   who will shepherd my people Israel.'"
>
> Then Herod called the Magi secretly and found out from them the exact time the star had appeared. He sent them to Bethlehem and said, "Go and search carefully for the child. As soon as you find him, report to me, so that I too may go and worship him."

That term, *magi*, is the word that would become what we understand as the term magician. However, the word originally referred to Babylonian priests and later took on a nasty, slandarous connotation of magic and sorcery because of the Greeks' attempts to take over the Persian empire, from my understanding. Still, the Babylonians were renowned for their astrology work, and their priests were very good at the holy workings they did.

Babylonian priests. So Babylonian paganism, right? With Ereshkigal and other such gods? Wrong.

In the time of Jesus's birth, the religion of Zoroastrianism was already well established. In fact, it'd been established so long that it actually rubbed off on Jewish cosmology quite a bit, especially as Jewish scholars and other figures were exiled to Babylon. By the 6th century BCE, it was apparently the main religion of Persia, surpassing the original paganism I thought I'd have to look into.

Which would explain a lot, as you'll see in the next few pages.

Nonetheless, the three Magi are iconic figures in the nativity scene. These three are the ones that brought the gifts of frankincense, gold, and myrrh to Mary and Joseph after the birth of Jesus, as well as the ones that tracked Jesus with that great and shining star, and the ones that got a prophetic dream to beat feet the hell out of there and tell Herod nothing. Unfortunately, in doing so, Herod went full throttle and decided to just have all baby boys under two years old killed—hence why the holy family had to flee to Egypt for a while.

And of course, much folklore has gone on around these figures since then. There certainly are three entities out there, whether that's historically accurate or not. People have also ascribed names and countries to them over time: Gaspar (King of India), Melchior (King of Persia), and Balthasar (King of Arabia or Ethiopia), representing the three parts of the known world at the time. They appear on all kinds of folk emblems, as well, like the Slovenian house blessing, or hišni žegen. And of course, given their role in the Christmas season and in Christian folk magic, I decided to find them and ask them some questions—even if I was insanely off the mark on how to do that.

So let's... let's just go ahead and look at this whole thing.

To speak with the three Magi, I had a pretty humble set-up, but it looked fun. Frankincense, myrrh, and a couple pure gold earrings sat in a small, nicely decorated wooden box that looked like something a king would carry around (in reality, it was a Ukrainian style box I got from my fiancé's family). A single white candle shone on the table, surrounded by amethysts and three shot glasses of water. This is because I was still thinking of Babylonian paganism and the rites of this ancient religion, rather than Zoroastrianism. Apparently, the living would libate mineral water for their ancestors to drink in the Babylonian underworld, Kigal. Then, for Nergal and Ereshkigal, who I thought I had to ask for permission to speak to souls stuck in their underworld, I had a small cup of pomegranate seeds.

God told me that Nergal and Ereshkigal would be minorly annoyed at my traipsing around down there, which is why He went with me (or, rather, the Seraph standing in for Him). At the time, I wasn't sure why, but now I see exactly why: *because I had no business with them and was too silly to realize that.* More than likely, the Seraph was meant to help smoothe things over with them and shuffle me off to where I was actually supposed to go. Still, with that Seraph at my side, I wasn't so worried, but we dropped out of Heaven as if we were in an elevator that just let go of its line, zipping down into a dark cave lit by warm golden torches.

Meeting me right away at the entrance of it was a man that looked like he was made of ashes. He had short hair, piercing eyes, and a slight frown as he received us, and he was pretty muscular. Nergal was apparently also a god of war before a god of the underworld, and as he settled into a military coat, I was able to look past him and see Ereshkigal on her throne.

She wore a golden crown with long spikes that looked like rays of sunshine, and her dark hair was bushy around her equally gray face. She wore clothes that reminded me of Tharja, if you've ever played the Fire Emblem games that have this character in them.

Ereshkigal didn't look thrilled to see me, but she wasn't particularly angry, either. She seemed more tired with my antics than anything else (understandable, given that I'd taken the completely wrong turn in Underworld Country and probably should've found a way to talk to Ahura Mazda or something instead), and then she let me skip past her to go find the three men I was looking for.

Here's where I think I did go where I was trying to go, thanks to God's angel wandering around with me. The Seraph and I went around the walkways of the cavern another moment, and then it was like there was a bait and switch: things were different, completely different, from the ancient Babylonian version of the underworld, in a flash. The whole cave was suddenly gone, and then the three Magi and I were sitting around a little fire pit, nestled in a sand dune in the middle of an endless desert. I looked up their names so I'd have something to call them, and it seems by giving them those names, they took more of a concrete form.

Gaspar looked like a young Indian man, deep brown eyes and dark, shaggy hair making him look nearly boyish. He would oscillate between brown and gold eyes, and his skin was either a warm or dark brown. He wore a simple white cover and golden bangles on his arms.

Melchior was a paler man, with a strong nose and thick brows, a dark, coarse beard, and dark hair reaching his shoulders. His eyes were a bright, striking blue-green, and he wore red and gray robes, as well as a red hat. Sometimes he smoked a pipe of some kind, too.

Balthasar was a bald man, his eyes the sharpest, purest gold and his skin the darkest of them all, with a warm undertone that seemed to reflect the gold of his eyes and jewelry. His stare was sharper than Melchior's, and he wore simple white robes from the waist down, the sun shining on him.

Before we go further, you may be wondering: why didn't the angel just tell me that I had everything wrong? Why didn't Nergal or Ereshkigal? Why didn't God? And they're good questions. In fairness, I think God *did* try to tell me when He mentioned Ereshkigal being moderately annoyed about my presence if I decided to go through with this interview.

Plainly, I was just obtuse. Obtuse, and far too confident in my *assumptions*. It wouldn't be until a sense of serious unease and dissonance came over me later that, out of seemingly nowhere, I would decide to double check my assumptions and suddenly have the context I needed to make sense of the confusion surrounding the start of this interview. To say I was embarrassed at my blunder would be an understatement of massive proportion, but the closest thing I can describe it as is the feeling of going to a McDonald's and trying to order a Burger King Whopper with such brutal confidence that no one in the restaurant had the heart to tell me I was an idiot.

Spiritual stuff is like that sometimes. But with the three Magi finally in front of me, I just kept doing my thing like always.

"Well," I said as I settled down into the sand—and I could feel the sand, too, the shift of it, the support from the angle I plopped down on, "hello, everyone! Thank you for joining me! It seems we have Gaspar, Melchior, and Balthasar here?"

Melchior would stare at me the entire interview as if he were waiting for me to realize something, or if he himself were lost in some thought. To revisit this is painful, given I know now what he hoped I would realize and simply... never did. When he understood I would realize nothing, he said, "Those were the names given to us, yes. Not necessarily our real names. But much has been lost to rumor, hasn't it?"

The other two huffed the kind of laugh that folks do after a long day of work. I figured that the legends we had weren't accurate—it was all symbolism, from what I was reading, and there are obviously no records of any of these men that would've gone around looking for a boy under Herod's reign—but it was all I had to distinguish them.

"Fair enough. I can see that. I just want to be able to call you something while we talk; it seems more polite that way. But since there are three of you, can you each pull one card per question?"

They glanced at each other, then nodded and chose the Golden Tarot to speak with.

"Alright, so: it seems that most people would like to call you the three kings rather than the three magi. I know magi has quite the significance to it, so what do you think of that change of title?"

1. THOUGHTS ON THE CHANGE FROM "MAGI" TO "KINGS"?

QUEEN of WANDS.

A strong, sensual woman. Knows what she wants and how to get it without stepping on others.

Anticipation and good timing. Vigilance and dedication will be rewarded. Good businesses sense brings fortune.

QUEEN of SWORDS.

A strong, independent, calculating, logical woman. Determined and ruthless in pursuit of her goals.

The three men glanced at each other and shook their heads, humor hanging at the corners of their lips, before they pulled their cards and spoke.

"We were lucky," Melchior said, "and by that I mean, we weren't lucky at all."

Gaspar picked up: "We'd been traveling on a fool's errand, told to report back to that idiot Herod. But it didn't take much to look and see where we'd fall if we assisted him in his fool's plot."

"What we wanted was a pass with your God," added Balthasar. "We got it. It is unwise to anger gods; those you cannot run from, unlike kings. Herod couldn't track us through the desert, but gods see all. So the benefits of our actions are clear: in our survival then, and our elevated memory as kings now, among the world's opinion."

Melchior had this flatness to his expression, and I wondered about his dry comment if Balthasar was going to end with that.

"I see," I said. "That makes sense. But that makes me wonder: since you were magi, which refers more to Babylonian priests, or at least Babylonian magicians and astrologers... what do you think of God? And why did you care what He thought about you?"

2. WHAT DO YOU THINK OF GOD? WHY CARE ABOUT HIS OPINION?

1. Hopelessness and deceit. Try to rally your strength to overcome adversity.

2. A warm, loving man who gives good counsel. Intuitive, creative, and gentle. Comfortable with his feminine side. Subtle strength: a quiet achiever. Spirituality more important than world.

3. Opportunities may be missed through negativity and pessimism.

KING of CUPS.

THE STAR.

I was surprised at the cards I pulled, because it signified a good and benevolent ruler surrounded by such misfortune. What a strange way to view a God—or so I thought.

Melchior started: "By all means, He is a good God. Powerful. Strong of virtue, heart. But—"

"He has pain," said Gaspar. "Much. We see it clearly now, unwrapped from the mortal world: many gods living in agony. Watching us."

"It's a crime, what we do on earth," Melchior muttered, and then Balthasar glanced between them all and leaned forward to speak.

"Your God could've just forsaken everything. All was so wretched for His people in our time, yet He didn't. He tore down Rome from the inside—His Son like a disease capable of crippling nations. I admire your God for that: turning Himself into a holy pestilence that eats the rot of the world away."

I glanced back at the Seraph who was hovering around, who only shrugged like that was a fair assessment. Did the three Magi know God could hear them? Most likely. But spirits are much bolder than we are with the things they say. It also makes me wonder about the rise of Christianity in the Roman Empire, and the Roman Empire's eventual fall.

It wasn't good. It wasn't honorable. It wasn't kind. Not in many places, not at the behest of many bishops and priests and mobs of "holy" men. Learning about that, I would think, *none of this is God! None if it is godly!*

But what if, in a strange way one could not anticipate, it was? A rot that swallowed Gentile converts up and used their own cultural and philosophical ideals, their own need for ever-rolling conquest, against them? Every time I try to draw definite lines about God and His actions in the sand, He presents me with an idea that is the same as an ocean wave washing all my lines away.

"That's really interesting," I said to the three Magi. "I never would've figured a response like that. Holy pestilence. Huh." I chewed on that a moment longer before continuing. "Alright, so: I understand you followed the stars to find Jesus. Everyone makes it seem like some gigantic star brighter than the moon just lit up the whole sky and had you following it like a moth follows a lantern, but surely that wasn't the case. It doesn't even make any sense. So how did you find Jesus?"

3. HOW DID YOU FIND JESUS?

Gaspar shrugged. "We knew what we were looking for: the supposed Son of your God, or some great man, or whatever your prophecies said about Him." He waved a hand like those prophecies were inconsequential. "We didn't care for the details. We only knew there was a child of a certain make, someone you'd recognize the moment you laid eyes on Him."

Melchior puffed his pipe, then muttered, "What a ragged bitch it was to find Him. Our usual tools didn't work. It was as if He was guarded by something. It took terrible effort without an easy scrying method."

A warm, loving man. Intuitive, creative, gentle. A quiet achiever. Spirituality more important.

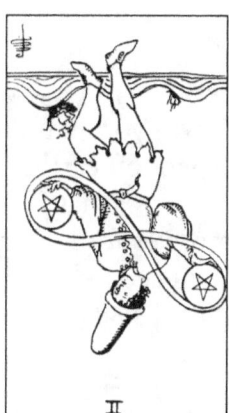

A poor investment, debt, financial worry.

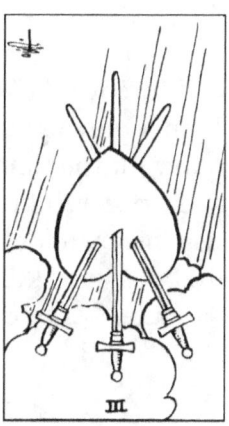

Dwelling on past sorrows may prevent you from moving on. Let go of the past and confusion leaves.

Balthasar added, "We were worried, but we fell back on the map that never fails us: the stars. They spoke to using the way stars do, and by the will of your God, of all the gods, those stars guided us to where we needed to go. To use them, however, was to understand the importance of this Child's birth, and we couldn't ignore that message in the heavens."

"Wow. That's... pretty intense." It seemed so poetic when they talked about it. "Okay, moving on. Your tools—it's interesting you said they didn't work. There were some early Church fathers—I think specifically here Eusebius? Or maybe Origen, I don't know—that said that you sought Jesus out because His birth cancelled out your magic. They said you were panicking that your power disappeared. What do you think about that?"

4. THOUGHTS ON CLAIMS YOUR POWER DISAPPEARED WITH JESUS?

Fear of boredom may result in a rash decision. Take care to consider all angles before deciding.

Satisfaction of worldly desires. Good health and fortune. Joy, fun, merriment. Cut enthusiasm with moderation.

Monetary success can be easily lost. Take care not to risk what you've gained.

The way they chuckled and shot each other knowing, mischievous glances told me everything I need to know as it was, but they still pulled the cards and talked about it.

"Sara," Melchior said, "we already had it all by virtue of our stations. Do you think those gifts fell into your Savior's lap by magic? By chance?"

My brow shot up my head like a sail. "Well, if you got them as payment for your works, then I guess they did get there by magic."

He chuckled, then waved a hand. "You know what I mean. They were gifts we brought by earning them via our skills—and we certainly didn't lose those skills with the Child's birth."

"Moreover," Balthasar interjected, "we stood to lose much more betraying that babe than aiding Him. One might say it was your God who made use of our magic—and let us keep our own earthly glory for the time we spent on earth thereafter."

Gaspar wrinkled his nose. "That Eusebius or Origen or whoever you said went on prattling about us—his own foolish motives for telling that story have only obscured truth for your ilk even further. To boast is to kill truth, it seems."

"Huh." I erased a more casual question I'd written down and stared at Gaspar. "Tell me more about that Truth?"

5. WHAT IS THE TRUTH ABOUT YOU?

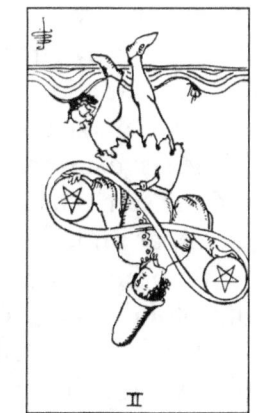

A poor investment, debt, financial worry.

It was only Melchior that pulled a card and responded: "See this conversation we're having? See where you are, and what information you found about us? We are not us anymore. We are called by names unknown to us, ascribed nations we never saw. We are sanctified in your memory, but less as people, more as concepts.

"You forget that to the gods, we are all but such playthings: concepts, tools to make a point in this long and drawn out game. We shouldn't follow their bad behavior and do such a thing to each other, too: we should stay people, not ideas. But we'll take our fame anyhow. It keeps us strong here—stops us from fading and becoming shadows in the caverns of the Beyond."

As he spoke, the sands flickered, revealing them as an illusion. Behind it all were those red-black caverns of the Babylonian underworld, with a golden city somewhere far in the background, shining with fiery light. At the time, I thought it was Kigal. I thought I even heard Melchior mention Kigal, but seeing that shining fiery city, which has absolutely no place in Kigal—a neutral underworld where none are really punished or exalted, from what I understand—I could only think this was another clue. The Zoroastrian House of Song might look something like this, but not Kigal.

Even for all my experience with this stuff, it seems, it's still all too easy to impose my ideas of what *should* be onto what *is*.

"Ah, that makes sense. Wow." I blew out a breath. "I'm sorry your memory has been distorted like that; I can imagine that's frustrating. And that's why you look the way you do."

Gaspar shrugged, his eyes flicking from brown to gold. "We play our part."

"Hmm." Would this be considered a faith breaking moment for some? To think that Divinity sees us as playthings, as tools to tell a story? I don't know. What I do know is that as a writer myself, it would feel hypocritical to get upset about it. Nonetheless, I expected this to some extent after reading about the Magi, but it was interesting to hear them talk about their ascribed identities so openly. "I see that. Okay, so, speaking of skills and the like: how would you describe the power you held on earth? As magic? As wonders? There's some controversy around the choice of terms nowadays. It's a hassle, getting people to understand the nature of such power."

6. HOW WOULD YOU DESCRIBE THE POWER YOU HELD ON EARTH?

1. Coveting the success of others while wasting one's own talents. Envy.

2. Opportunities may be missed through negativity and pessimism.

3. A mean, selfish, hard nosed woman. One who will do anything for money.

Melchior sighed. "A hassle is right."

"How many people hated us for our power?" Gaspar chuckled at the idea and continued, "Power given to us by virtue of the gods, and the study of their ways?"

Balthasar added, "And how many more still wanted to steal it from us? Or wanted to ply us with riches to make themselves more riches, or outright enslave us to make show ponies of us?"

The slave girl in Acts that Paul exorcised came to mind. Her keepers wanted to kill him for removing the spirit that let her tell the future and earn them extra coin.

Gaspar said, "Our power was born of study, virtue, and sacrifice. It was not easily won."

"Yet others would try to win it from us," Melchior added, "as if you could drink the wisdom out of our blood. Dangerous, to have power. So dangerous."

"Wow." That is true, though: power does funny things among people. "To get off these more serious topics, though, can you tell me what you think of how we use astrology in the modern era? People love astrology now. But I understand Babylonian astrology was pretty fatalistic, which is why there was so much pushback on it from Jewish folk."

7. WHAT DO YOU THINK ABOUT MODERN WESTERN ASTROLOGY?

Alertness to risk may avoid calamity. Be prepared for likely difficulties and all will be well. Challenges met and surmounted. Good work rewarded.

Travel for all the wrong reasons. You can run away from your life, not yourself. Detachment from reality. Following impossible dreams at the expense of life's goodness.

An energetic and hard working youth. A messenger brings inspiring news. A new project begins.

Melchior rolled his eyes and sighed, his face creased with irritation.

"What do you hope to achieve by removing fate from the stars and instead grafting it onto yourself? Rather than chart and map those stars, one thinks they can take control by simply overidentifying with these stars instead. But you can't. You trap yourself and act out the dance of fate anyway. You may as well keep the stars in mind; you do still use it in a way that we would've."

Gaspar popped in. "But it's not necessarily a bad thing. Whereas we accepted what was to pass, you decide to guard against potential misery written in the stars. In that sense, you do defeat destiny, so Melchior, you can't say they use it exactly the same."

Melchior shrugged. Gaspar turned back to me and grinned.

"You don't bow to fate; you plan around it. That's commendable."

"You are all but children," Balthasar said with a smile, "the way you play your games with the stars. But because of that, you are able to do more than we could. You see influences and planets we didn't. You can connect in a way we couldn't. You've made the story of the Cosmos a simple draft, and you edit it if you choose to. But Melchior is right," he said with a glance to Gaspar. "Don't claim to avoid destiny by not planning your life to the stars, only to allow those stars to dictate your actions and personality—and by extension, your destiny."

I nodded along as I wrote. "Makes sense to me! Thank you for all your insight; this is great. Okay, so, I guess that's it for our personal questions. Now, how do you see yourselves?"

8. HOW DO YOU SEE YOURSELVES?

They glanced between themselves, and then Gaspar started. "I'm a forgiving man," he said. "I trust the gods will dole out punishment on my behalf. Your God, ours—all of them watch us. All of them see where justice is needed. And as for my power? It's power because I know when to use it, not because of the power itself."

"Ah, fair. Melchior? How about you?"

He shrugged. "We are immortalized. But at what cost? I see myself as living with the consequences of my actions."

"Huh. Alright. And Balthasar?"

"I wanted adventure," he said with a smile as warm as the desert sands, "and I got it. But I am one who will always wonder what I left behind for the sake of such adventure. Family, tradition, the like."

Trust that all will get what they deserve. Sacrifices may be necessary. Not all battles won. Some aren't worth fighting.

Unfair victory is as hollow as defeat. Failure or win against an unmatched opponent leaves one demoralized.

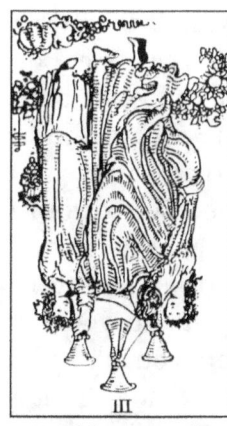

Problems with a partner being taken for granted or jealous of a rival. Yearning for a more interesting life. Promiscuity.

"Hmm, yeah. I understand that to an extent. But okay, how do you all want to be seen?"

9. HOW DO YOU WANT TO BE SEEN?

No one moved or said anything. They didn't want to pull any cards, either. It was only Melchior who responded, and he had those sharp eyes boring into my head, a mean grin curling his lips back.

"Let the lie continue," he said. "Let us be kings in your memory, fearsome and powerful and holy kings. It gives us something to laugh about."

Hoo, boy.

"Understandable." I guess things like this matter a good deal even to spirits passed on, the legends we weave around them. If they want to be seen as kings, sure. I do like the title Magi, but they can wear both. "So, do you have any last messages you want to share? Melchior, you've had quite the look on your face. Is there something you've wanted to say this whole time?"

10. ANY LAST MESSAGES?

Melchior's grin grew. He was the only one to pull a card, and it was an interesting thing, to combine the meaning of Four of Wands with the words I heard.

Domestic bliss, a harmonious family life. Material success. Acquisition of assets. True friendship. A great harvest. Labors rewarded, needs met.

"You are a fool," he said, and *boy,* do I have a guess or twelve about why, "but being one will take you far. You remind me of us: seeking mysteries, gathering treasures you don't know what to do with yet. Be careful—you and others like you. Never lose yourself to your riches. Remember the value of a community that understands you and will safeguard your secrets, your power, for future generations. Enjoy your time on earth; make your story with it, and do not let others write it for you. Build your own peace. Go on, you all, and be Magi."

"Whoa." That got strangely preachy by the end, but not in a bad way. I stared at him for a moment longer, but the sands were fading; the caves of this underworld space were bleeding through again as the three Kings stood and stretched their legs. They turned their backs on me, waving, and I called after them. "Well, alright, thank you! Thank you for your time and insight! May you be well!"

And then they were gone. The whole vision was gone. And I was left there, head spinning with the implications of that last message.

Funnily enough, it's that line—*you are a fool*—that I am reminded of every time I think about this interview. Maybe from my embarrassment, but maybe also as a reminder of the fact that I really don't know even a fraction of what I think I do. That's half the battle in these endeavors: not just learning new things, but learning where all the bumps and grooves and *holes* in my knowledge are in the first place.

It also makes me wonder: where is the line between man and myth? Legend and lie? At what point do we stop being people and start being concepts? How many years have to pass? It makes me wonder about every figure I've ever read about in a history book, every story I've ever been told about times so long ago.

It also makes me wonder what will be said of all of us, far down the road from now. One hundred years ago, in 1925, the world was so very different, and we all have our colorful thoughts about the people who lived in those times, even though they're no doubt so much more than all their vices and the little snapshots we have of them. How will people in 2125 view us, then? When watching back all our video footage, what will they think? And at what point will they call our spirits out of wherever we are, hoping to find any truth behind all the glimmers we've left behind?

Only time will tell, I guess.

SANTA CLAUS

Now, how could I do anything related to the Christmas season without talking to what is perhaps the most famous egregore of all?

Given I'd spoken to the inspiration of Santa, St. Nicholas, the year before, I figured it was time to put our egregore exploration to good work and bring about an interview with the figure that, for so many children, commanded the stage in all the more commercial Christmas imagery. In fact, when it comes to commercialism, it seems capitalism really did a number on dear old Santa; when I spoke about him to my Slovenian friends, the first thing out of their mouth was, "Oh, yeah, like in the Coca-Cola ads!"

American advertising, man. Whatever shit they do to capture people's minds is practically magic in itself.

But now, as I did this interview in the year of 2023, I discovered after the fact how special that was. After all, it was the two hundred year anniversary of the Clement Clark Moore poem, *A Visit of St. Nicholas*, where we first started to see this egregore take form and splinter away from the iconic Saint. You know this poem. *Twas the night before Christmas, when all through the house, not a creature was stirring, not even a mouse...*

In that poem, we get the images of stockings hanging and children waiting for St. Nicholas to come by, of that Christmas eve thrill knowing there'll be gifts galore and all kinds of other nice things to wake up to. The very stuff that made Christmas magical for so many kids, including myself. (God bless all the parents who spent each year putting presents under the trees at like, two in the morning, and who snacked on cookies and milk to make kids think Santa actually came by. Absolute heroes of Christmas cheer.)

And while I came in fully loaded with all those images of a rosy-cheeked, decked out Santa, fully aware that there never was a real man who lived on the North Pole and drove a sleigh of magical reindeer through the sky, I still found myself a little excited for this, if only to see what the egregore would do and say. I gave it my best shot, and truthfully... I came away with a heart three sizes bigger than it was before. So let's dive in!

Not gonna lie: I was goofing around with God at the very thought of talking to the egregore of Santa. I could feel the roll of His eyes and the warmth that radiated off Him, amusement with my nonsense as I asked Him to help me find the culmination of two centuries of belief that is Santa Claus. But He did help me, and I found myself sucked right into the North Pole, settling into the scene easier and faster than I'd been able to in a long while.

And it was beautiful. A giant structure, like a massive log cabin, stood in the middle of a field of snowy pine trees, and it seemed like nearly every tree had the capacity to be a Christmas tree: at any point, they'd light up with colorful lights and glass ornaments, shifting and swirling around like a collage of cheery colors. The reindeer were outside, too, snuffling around at the ground, already done up in their harnesses by the empty sled. Greenish ribbons danced over them, filling the night sky with the ethereal presence of the Northern Lights.

When I went inside, though, there was a huge column in the center surrounded by tables. Presents slid down this column on chutes before many little elves, all pointy ears and red stockings and big, shining eyes, snatched them up to wrap. They were hustling, the place buzzing like a good diner during a lunchtime rush, elves flying all over the place and trying to make things happen for the big night. To the left was a mess hall that seemed to double as a toy making area, and though the presents were done and the room was empty, there was still a big fire roaring in the fireplace there, a huge Christmas tree perfectly adorned and making the space feel cozy just from the glimpse I got.

And eventually, there stood Santa Claus: white beard, rosy cheeks, a twinkle in his eye, and his classic red hat and jacket on. He clapped me on the back and welcomed me, and even though I am a grown adult that hasn't believed in Santa in years, I found myself as thrilled as if I were five again, giddy and almost impatient to see this place of legend. Santa guided me over to his office, where bookshelves built into the back wall were stuffed with books and a big presidential desk had an old school, green glass desk lamp on it. He settled down and took off his hat and coat, his bald head shining, his suspenders snug against a white, red, and green striped shirt.

It was all so vivid. Just as vivid as anything I'd ever seen in Heaven, or in the infernal realms, or anywhere else. Most of all, it was all just so *real*. It blew my mind.

So of course, I was too excited to just sit while all was going on. I asked for a tour of the place, and with a grandpa-like sigh, he got up and showed me around. I waved to Mrs. Claus, who was up on the balcony of the upstairs rooms, working on coats and things for the elves, and I went around watching the elves work for a little while, too. I nearly pissed myself seeing a sign on a bulletin board about a Worker's Union, because... the elves are unionized.

God damn it, even the *elves* are unionized.

And they made sure they get days off after the rush season of Christmas, room and board, an eight hour workday with no expectation of forced overtime, all that. I was dying of amusement, but I tried to reign it in and explained that I wasn't laughing at *them*, no—just the surprise of seeing this. The Elf Union is not what I expected to see out here, but I was happy for them all the same (and wondering why, if *elves* can see the value of unionizing, people can't).

Santa showed me all the things I've already described here, and each bit just ignited a part of myself that I thought I'd long grew out of. I guess this is what people mean when they say "inner child" work, because my inner five-year-old was going nuts, almost overwhelmed by the magic of it all.

After the tour was done, and I'd given the reindeer my bowl of oats that, in the spirit of miracles, became a Jesus-bread-and-fish style bottomless bowl of oats to feed all thirteen of them (Rudolph included, of course), the tour was over. We were back in the office, and as Santa settled down, I got shuffling my Universal Fantasy Tarot and got into it.

"Alright, Santa, thank you for showing me around. I appreciate it."

His smile balled up those rosy cheeks, and as I shuffled, I got into my questions.

"So, first off, I gotta say... I'm really curious as to how belief affects you. I mean, you know what egregores are, right? Those entities that come about based on people's belief in them? Given you've been around for decades now, I gotta imagine there's a lot of belief fueling you, but," I peered at him, and he settled back in his chair, hands clasped over his big belly, "you do *know* you're an egregore, right? And I mean, with kids believing in you and then learning you 'don't exist,' how do you deal with that? How does this economy of belief work?"

I. HOW DOES THE ECONOMY OF BELIEF WORK?

Some things we believe are good are really chains that hold us enslaved. At times we must question the values others decided for us.

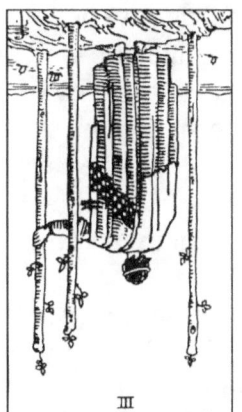

Lack of vision for the future, ignorance of the present.

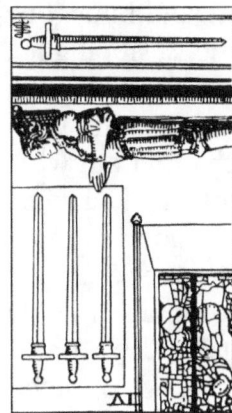

Stress, restlessness, and unwillingness to take risks.

Santa let out a sigh and adjusted his little circular spectacles. Then he picked cards that surprised me. They seemed so opposite of what Santa would say, and yet the answer he gave was so honest.

"I do wonder if it's right that I'm here," he said as he stared at his desk. "I wonder often. I'm there with the parents, you know—when they eat the cookies and drink milk left for me."

I had an image of my own parents, sneaking around and stuffing things under the tree, taking a bite of the mitten and gingerbread shaped sugar cookies my mom and I made every year. And I don't know why, but I was getting pretty misty-eyed the more Santa spoke, as if there was some little piece of me in mourning. Maybe it was Santa's feelings projecting onto me, or maybe it was my own just coalescing there, or maybe it was a mix of both. But it was like a bruise in my chest as he kept talking, tender and aching.

"It's... bittersweet, you see," Santa continued. "Knowing the magic will one day fade from those kids who believe in me, knowing they'll grow up to see me as just a story. It breaks my heart that such innocence has to die—but it does. Because I know my place in the minds of people is temporary.

"To answer your question: yes, I know I'm an egregore, or whatever you call it. And I know this whole place," he gestured around his office, "is built on the wishes and dreams of innocence. So long as kids are born, it will continue, I believe. But it isn't meant to be forever. It's meant to carry children forward, with good memories, strong magic, so they can hold onto some of that hope and wonder it breeds as they go into adulthood.

"But it seems... these times are too terrible for my magic." Santa's chin buried into his chest as he sat; his face fell, and the air gushed out of him with another deep sigh. "It's difficult to keep cheer alive in times like these. It's not something I can do alone."

"Aw, Santa," I paused my writing to perch on the corner of his desk, wiping tears away from my face that I felt silly for letting fall (because what the hell was I crying about Santa for?), "I hear you. I'm sorry. It's... a messy world we live in. And the cheer is hard to find in all that mess."

Somehow, as I spoke, I ended up sitting on Santa's leg like I was about to take a picture with the Santa at the mall. It made me laugh, even as something heavy weighed my heart down, and Santa chuckled with me. For old time's sake, it seemed, he asked me a question.

"What do you want for Christmas?"

I'm a bit of a material girl, I won't lie; I love presents under the tree and the ceremony of unwrapping them with family. But my parents and I already got each other gifts all the time, Christmas or no Christmas. Stuff like that, at this age, I didn't need to ask Santa for. What I did do was speak what was hanging in the air: the reason (or rather, many reasons) cheer seemed so impossible this year.

"I want people to have a good time," I said, and I imagined it so clearly: people cuddled up in blankets together like little rabbits in their dens, sipping hot chocolate and watching snow fall outside their windows, fireplaces going. Food on the table. Bills paid with plenty of money to spare. Kids unwrapping presents with squeals of joy. People smiling at each other in the street, offering cheerful greetings to total strangers and helping each other out with silly things like carrying groceries. And especially, homes standing tall and solid, not wrecked by bombs—people able to sit with their whole families, safe and sound. "I want people to be good to each other again. It's so cheesy, really—stupid—but yeah, I want 'world peace,' whatever that even means."

We shared a chuckle about that, and then Santa's smile slipped as he stared at his desk.

"World peace," he said, his voice gone small. "That's one of the few things my elves can't build."

I had to pause, because I was a bit of a wreck at my kitchen table at that point. Sitting there with the (almond) milk, the oats, and the abomination that was my one microwave "cookie" I managed to make, I felt so silly, but even as I write and revisit this, it hurts. There is grief here, mixed in with the childhood magic—and it was hard to just feel it for a minute. Eventually, though, I picked myself up and settled back on the desk like some 1930's journalist, and with pen in hand, I kept going.

"Alright, alright, let's take a step back from all this now. Because after all this, you know, I gotta ask: what do you think the Christmas spirit is? What does that look like to you?"

2. WHAT IS THE CHRISTMAS SPIRIT?

1. Defeat, loss of control, or a lack of direction.

2. Even when we lose, we gain the experience of defeat that may be useful for attaining future victories.

3. Ruin, delays, setbacks, and challenges in creative pursuits.

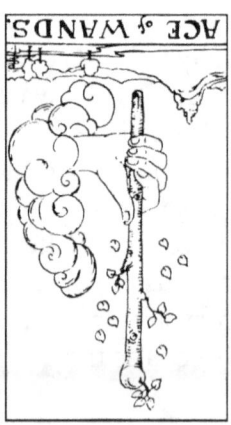

And then we were out on a snowy street—something straight out of *A Christmas Carol*. It's always England, isn't it? Victorian England. That's what my mind thinks of as essential Christmas, I guess, with the paintings of snow gathering in the windows and golden light shining out of storefronts and homes, the occasional lone figure carefully treading slippery sidewalks on the night of Christmas eve.

Santa and I stood in the middle of the street. We looked around at the scene, peered into windows of people at restaurants together, or making Christmas dinner together—and again, the cards surprised me, and the scene shifted to some real Tiny Tim level stuff. It shifted to other people avoiding going home, wondering how they were going to explain to their families that they couldn't get the food for a proper dinner, or that they really didn't have anything to give to their kids for Christmas—*again*. Those haunted eyes, those pale faces, they cut deep.

"So much goes wrong during the holidays," Santa said. "People struggle. They can't afford those gifts their kids want, or they can't afford a proper dinner. But I am a spirit of God, Sara—and I help inspire the feelings of charity in others where I can. So that when all seems lost, the people whose spirits are broken might have some light return to them just in time."

And then there were other images in my head, both old school, vintage images—families suddenly receiving gifts of a turkey and vegetables to roast, some hearty meal that would bring them strength—to modern images, like the initiative that one of my former coworkers did every year, where he'd raise money to buy as many toys and gift cards and other things as possible to personally distribute to families who couldn't afford gifts for their kids in our community.

He, and the people our agency supported that signed up to participate, would take on the spirit of Santa in that way, going door to door and showering pre-wrapped gifts down on grateful parents to put under the tree for their kids. I was there to record it all many times in blogs and photos and videos, and I saw it firsthand: the joy of giving and the joy of receiving, the surprise and relief of the parents, the excitement of any kids that happened to be home.

"That's the Christmas spirit," Santa whispered into my memories. "It's not about the presents themselves, but about the joy and goodwill, and, yes, the magic of the season."

"Damn," I said, trying to avoid the bottomless pit that was my feels and failing miserably, "I get you. That's... beautiful. It is."

We sat there soaking in the images of Christmasses past and present, and then I gathered myself and moved onto the next question.

"Alright, so: what was it like when you came into existence, then?"

3. WHAT WAS IT LIKE WHEN YOU CAME INTO EXISTENCE?

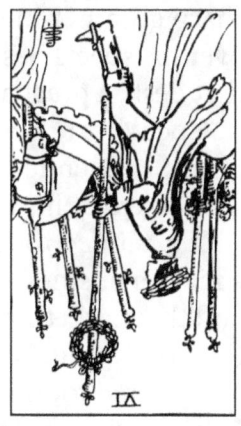

1. Heartaches are often the symptom of an intense desire for change that concerns many aspects of life.

2. Failing to recognize one's own shortcomings due to feelings of superiority or pride.

3. Vulnerability, powerlessness, and a possibly inflated ego.

"When I came into existence, huh?" Santa put a hand to his chin and stroked his beard as we sat there in the middle of that Victorian England street, his brows furrowed in thought. "It's been some, what, two centuries now?

"I'd say so, given that Moore poem."

"Right. It was a long time ago, but it was painful," he continued. "I was born of a wish to put a name to the magic of Christmas—a wish for wild and childish joy, fun and carelessness. I could never save everyone, however. I am not Christ; I'm no god of my own. I'm Santa—a derivative of a great Saint.

"When I came into this world... I found it broken. All I've been able to do is polish the shards, so that they shine. Is that enough?" He looked up to the stars twinkling in the clear winter sky, as if asking God Himself. "I don't know, but I try. For those who do believe in God, for those who don't—for the religious or irreligious, I am here, trying to scatter that magic still."

My heart was taking a beating with each answer. We were only three in. As I wrote, I wasn't sure if I'd survive by the end, because my own chest felt like a bag of broken glass, clinking around in a container of thick velvet.

"I think it's enough," I said. "I don't think anyone asks you to do it all, Santa. You're here for what you're here for, y'know?"

He shrugged. "Maybe."

"Yeah, maybe. Oh, wait, here's a question for you: Coca-Cola."

Santa glanced at me, one bushy white eyebrow raising high.

"When I mentioned you to my Slovenian friends, the first thing they thought of was Coca-Cola." As he chuckled, I continued, "How the hell did Coca-Cola tie itself to your image so effectively, that that's what people think of abroad when they think of you?"

4. THOUGHTS ON BEING TIED TO CORPORATE BRANDING?

Weakness in work or team situations, incompetence, and an inability to delegate.

Balance, adaptability, and problem solving. Finding solutions confidently. The eternal nature of the divine.

Exercising fore-sight with an open mind. Consider the many routes you can take and plan accordingly.

Again, wild cards—ones that suggested the things he said next. We were back in his office, and Santa looked less like a jolly old man and more like a great and powerful businessman, the plumpness of him and the bushiness of his eyebrows and beard doing nothing to soften the sharp glimmer in his gaze. He looked over his spectacles at me as he sat at that desk, a great and fatherly figure.

"Coca-Cola," he said, and he nodded once, "it extended the magic."

I blinked at him. "It what?"

"It extended the magic, Sara. It was a bit of a business deal between myself and the marketing team there. I gave the inspiration... and they gave me a cemented foothold in other lands. It was a win-win, but I do wonder at what cost sometimes. It seems I underestimated the capacity for materialism people hold. But I need belief and presence to operate, so I can't be too choosy. It's that economy of belief, as you put it."

What is this joke of a world, that Santa Claus has to make influencer partnership deals with a multi-million dollar soft drink company just to stay relevant in the minds of others as modernity erodes all sense of magic? I sat there, stunned for a minute, before I shoved the whole idea right out of my head and continued on.

"Oh my God, alright. That's—it's almost funny, really, but I understand. Okay, another question: what do you think about Sagittarius? Because me, myself, when I think of Sagittarian energy, I think of you: bright and bold, all golden and hearty and boisterous, cheer and jolliness, all that. But what do you think?"

5. WHAT DO YOU THINK ABOUT THE SIGN SAGITTARIUS?

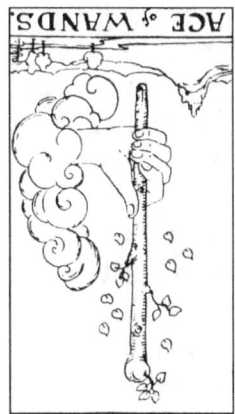

Ruin, delays, setbacks, and challenges in creative pursuits.

Santa only pulled one card for this, and he shook his head as I picked it.

"I see why you'd picture such a thing, Sara," he said with a sigh, "but the truth is that Sagittarius as a concept becomes a victim of its own revelry. The Philosopher has difficulty moderating itself, which means its pursuits often fall apart under the weight of themselves. I can't run my affairs like that."

"Ah, I see what you mean. Yeah, I guess. I still see that concept in Sagittarius, though: all the big and joyful spirit."

"There is overlap, of course," Santa admitted, "but Sagittarius has no responsibility to temper that energy."

"Alright, fair. And so, our next question... don't take this the wrong way, Santa, please, but talk to me about Rudolph. Poor guy was getting bullied to hell and back, and you only stepped in at the end. What's that about? Did you not know, or...?"

6. WHY DIDN'T YOU DEFEND RUDOLPH?

Breaking bonds, freedom, and detachment.

Unexpected fortunes are best, but they must be managed wisely.

Joy, moving forward, stagnation being the root of one's issues.

Santa folded his hands on his belly. He thought for a bit, then explained.

"Rudolph himself didn't know what his purpose was, or the reason for his difference. His peers mirrored his feelings about himself. My reindeer are fickle spirits; even if I'd said anything, they are connected in their minds and would've tormented one another anyway. The only thing I could do was give Rudolph a reason for his difference, and by extension, his existence."

"Oh, that makes sense." I blinked at him, then blurted, "They're all a connected consciousness, then."

"Yes."

"Got'cha." Well, that was a crazy answer for an egregore, but so cool at the same time. "Okay, okay, so last personal question before we move onto the standard three: how do you decide who's naughty or nice each year?"

7. How do you decide who's naughty or nice?

Naughty:
There are times
where we must let
ourselves be guided
more by intuition
than reason.

Nice:
Stagnation and
resisting change.
Sometimes change
can't be avoided.
Can't be afraid of it.

And when I tell you that pulling Ace of Wands for Naughty and Death Reversed for Nice made no sense to me, I mean it. I almost wondered if I'd gotten this all wrong, or if I'd just ignored Santa's signs on which cards to pull, but then I saw him staring straight at me with a light of determination in his eyes.

"Read the descriptions," he said. "Let me explain."

So I did. I wrote down the descriptions, and by his direction, I combined the reversed meaning and upright meaning of Death. Then Santa spoke, and the truth unraveled like a fallen spool of thread.

"With naughtiness, people get ahead of themselves," he said. "They let the folly of the mind obscure the truth of the soul. They think they can cheat the rules of decency—very Sagittarian of them, with that rotten philosophy."

I choked on my coffee a bit, but I kept writing.

"Overthinking simple things until the basics of goodness become some transactional terror means men will ask: 'why should I be good? Look at what I can achieve when I stop playing by the world's rules!'"

Then Santa sat up straighter, hands folded on the desk, and a bright and shining force seemed to fill him as if liquid light had been poured into his being.

"But it's not the world they deny now. It's the rules of decency—which, now, the world has cast aside. So niceness, now, is the refusal to submit to the world's lack of decency. The world might change, and we have no choice but to acknowledge it, but that doesn't mean we succumb to it. We choose to hold onto the core of goodness even as we change and adapt to this world. It's the only way to keep the magic alive."

I sat there genuinely stunned for a minute. "How the hell did you make sense out of these cards like that, Santa?" It wasn't a question I expected an answer to; I was just baffled that such nonsensical pulls could make a message so Goddamn true.

Santa just chuckled at me, and he let me take my time recovering from the surprise of that answer. Once I did, we were both laughing together, because by God, if there was ever a sense of magic like people believe the Christmas season has, this was it. After, I kept on with the last three questions.

"Okay, okay, here we are now, home stretch. Santa, how do you see yourself?"

8. HOW DO YOU SEE YOURSELF?

The mirth faded a little. And the card he drew, Four of Swords, had a stark meaning in the Universal Fantasy Tarot.

Idols can help us look within our heart, but if we let them shine too much, they can blind us.

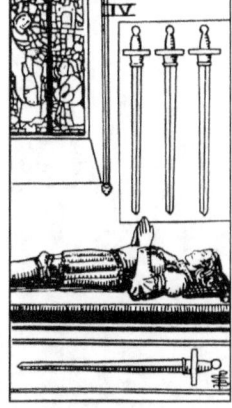

"I am not the focus of this season," Santa said. "I am only an agent of it. The goodwill that fuels December is not something I can take credit for. I see myself as someone people put too much stock in. I can't fix the way people think and act. That belongs to God alone."

"That makes sense. How do you want to be seen, then?"

9. HOW DO YOU WANT TO BE SEEN?

He waved a hand and chose no cards. "See me as that: an agent of goodwill. Not its originator."

"Fair. Okay, well, Santa, before we go, do you have any last messages for people this Christmas eve?"

10. ANY LAST MESSAGES?

A job well done is when all we have done is what is needed and nothing more.

"Yes, yes I do. Here it is." He got up and put on his jacket, his hat, and he spoke from deep in his chest, his voice bright and rich and bold. "You don't have to be a hero. Moms and dads, brothers and sisters, don't let yourself take all the weight of keeping the Christmas spirit alive," he said. "You do what you can, and you do it from a place of love, and the gift of your effort will be worth more than a hundred finely wrapped boxes. Give the gift of love and presence this year—every year! I can't give your families that; only you can."

Once again, I was trying not to drown in my feels. But what a final message!

"Thank you for that, Santa," I said, and I started to pack up my notebook and cards. "I guess this is goodbye for now—but this has been lovely. I hope you have easy travels tonight and easy work!"

He smiled, and then with the strength only a great spirit like him has, he took me outside and helped me exit the meditation space by hurling me up into the air. From there, I saw the little ice island that his home sat on, and we waved to each other as I exited the space into darkness.

No matter how many times I read this over, it feels the same: magical, beautiful, and so painful. It hurts so much, to think what we could have, and how all Santa's efforts can only ever bring the tiniest reprieve to it all. Still, it's a reprieve worth chasing. And Santa is an egregore worth holding onto.

What I never realized until this moment was how ironic all this was. As a kid, I believed in Santa. As a teen, I understood him as nothing more than a fable. And here, going on *thirty*, being a magician that understands egregore theory (and even learning about how giving a created being like Rudolph a *reason* for existing can stabilize them), I've come full circle into believing in Santa again. Because he is there, and he does try to work his influence on us all—influence for the better.

Much of the world is a wreck right now. Many people in power decide to use that power to destroy the magic that we humans create when our hearts are full of warmth and empathy and joy. It's up to us, I guess, to decide if we want to stay on the Nice list or not: to decide if we want to resist the callousness of the world, and its lack of decency that just seems to get worse every year.

I know which choice I'll be making, both this year and every year after that.

THE INNER SELF

Experimental: that's how I would describe the next year of interviews. And I do mean year, because it was at this point that I really started slowing down. Coming into 2024, I knew that the amount I was working was simply not sustainable; after basically blowing up my life (and especially my career) in early 2023, I'd done as much as I could to build myself up on my own terms, writing and witching and learning and sharing, but the wheels of my psyche were getting creaky.

I was tired. So tired.

And so I restructured everything. Pulled back on how much I was doing each week, especially with interviews. Tried to find a balance between work and play—a balance that continues to elude me, even as I plan, on this night of the Virgo Blood Moon, to knock down what shattered ruins are still left of this need to work into an early grave.

I used to be so afraid, you know? Of change. Of the unexpected, of the future. I thought myself a shark: so big, ferocious, dangerous and powerful, but risking dying every time I dared to slow down. Now, after yet another year of reading and seeing and learning and meeting and writing and sharing, I've also come to understand that Death is necessary—that we die and come alive over and over across our lifetimes, like the chives and oregano in the garden, all brown and withered over winter, only to rip free of freshly thawed earth in the next spring.

The longer I am a Witch, this supposedly profane thing in the eyes of God (according to everyone crawling into my Instagram DMs with a crusader profile picture), the more deeply I fall into the stasis of the Mystic, blind and deaf to all but the forward call of a God I cannot honestly pin down to any one idea or quality. The more I learn that there is no past, as the Son erases it every morning, and there is no future, as the Father is the one who writes it and rewrites it and rewrites it again; there is only the present, and the crowning fire of the Spirit, burning me up again and again in living purgatory until all the lies I've stitched into my being are ashes on the newly fertile, thawed earth of my soul's resting place.

But all that's spoilers. By this point, I still had a long way to go before I reached the point I'm at now, and I dare not think about where I'll be in the months and years to come. However, at this time, I did think about it: about where I would be in the future, what I would be doing. And I thought maybe, if there really is such thing as a Higher Self—if the soul could truthfully whisper to us and the illusions that are our consciousness, our minds—then I should've been able to interview my own like any god or spirit detached from physical reality, too.

This interview is the result of that theory.

Once everything was set up, and I'd talked to God a little bit about this whole idea beforehand, I was ready to jump in and try to find—and see—this Inner Self, Higher Self, Whatever Self you might hear people talking about. Plainly, I just referred to it as the Soul, because calling it the Higher Self or whatever felt goofy. There is nothing High about one, nor anything necessarily Low, in my opinion. And truth be told, I'd found some version of myself beforehand, in my work with the Infernal Divine, but by nature of where I found that, I just didn't feel like I could call that the Higher Self. A sharper, more severe self, maybe, but not the Higher Self. A piece, not the whole.

One day, I'll have to tell you all everything I saw in the many circles of hell, too. Destroy that little bit of mystique they still have. But that's for another time.

On this cloudy morning, I put out my favorite crystals, carnelian and amethyst, as well as my favorite rosary, my obsidian sphere, and a piece of clear quartz for a clear connection. I had a candle out that I'd melted a sigil of my deepest wishes into a long time ago, and I figured that was good enough to represent me. Then I closed my eyes and basically knocked on the door of my own self, with Threads of Fate's Weaver Tarot as the deck I felt made the most sense to go so deep into my own self.

And I waited for a long time before something came through: a version of myself that looked like it was made out of golden fairy dust. Given I see my magic as this same kind of gold substance, and I understand magic as being of the soul the way blood is of the heart, it made sense to me. But I wondered why it looked like me, because surely the soul didn't really have any one form? Surely it had many forms all throughout its existence? Staring at the image of my own self, though, all I could think was that maybe I went into this with too many assumptions about what a soul should and shouldn't do.

But this Soul had a smile on her face like she *was* in fact some kind of fairy, all sly and amused and ready to cause trouble. She waited for me to say something, and given how strange she looked to me—her hair longer and fluffier than mine, almost like a lion mane, and her dress something out of those cute Renaissance dress catalogues, but all the same color of gold, as if all of her were just the shape of a dress carved onto a plastic doll—I felt like there was only one thing to say.

"Who are you?"

Her smile nearly split her face in half, it was so wide and froggish. "I'm you."

As I looked down at my list of questions, I decided to go completely out of order and start with the eighth one: "Then who am I?"

I. WHO AM I?

Alignment and harmony after challenges. Things going in your favor. Dream for new projects. You've been through a lot, but you haven't hardened. Keep courage.

It's impossible to prevent the ebb and flow of life. No matter the scale of loss, reflect on your needs. Strength, resilience, and courage needed. Change your mindset. Try new things.

The spectrum of magical thinking. If you're not grounded in reality, you can ignore glaring problems. If you externalize success, you externalize issues. Take responsibility.

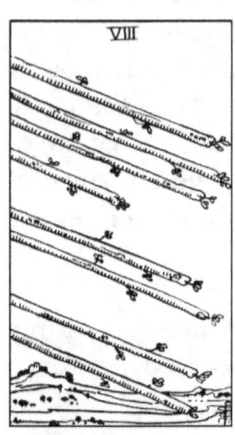

The universe is opening up a river of potential. Jump in. Challenges will work in your favor. Trust the process. Don't waste time worrying about success. Manifest your desires.

And let me tell you: every other time I do this, it's with a consciousness that isn't mine, and so I rely on my intuition and the little signs I get that it's time to pick a card. But here, while there were intuitive bells ringing to pick a card the same way there is for God or any other spirit I've ever talked to, it felt weird. I couldn't shake feeling ridiculous as I picked my card and flipped it from reversed to right side up, asking *this way? this way?* because who the hell was I asking?

Me, right?

And so many times, this Soul would say that with that froggish, almost mean smile: *I don't know, is that the card? I don't know, is that the way it should be turned? What are you asking me, for? Don't you know yourself?*

Did I?

The cards came eventually. I wanted three, and I got three—plus one that fell down that just hit me in the gut as true. The Star. Should it have been reversed? I could never be the Star, right? Not right side up? Was it a trick of ego to say the Star represented me in any way?

Or was it a trick of ego to be so self depreciative that I didn't feel I was allowed to be the Star?

I tell you this: if you want to go rooting around in your psyche like a dentist poking and scratching at the sensitive spots where your teeth meet your gums, go ahead and try to talk to your soul like this. Because this was only the beginning of the difficulty.

Still, I put the Star there above the three cards, and it made me feel—between the star's rays of light, the mountain, and the huge eye on the Weaver Tarot's version of it—that it was more a symbol of something or someone looking down at me, watching over me, than anything. But after I wrote these cards down, I didn't quite know what it meant. So I asked.

The Soul huffed and sat on the ground, wherever it was in this big black backdrop of my mind. She hugged her knees to her chest and grinned.

"What do you think it means? We've gotten this far by sheer determination. But there's rot here. The world poisons us—like how plants suck up car emissions."

Then she stood up, and buried in her chest were what looked like three crooked pieces of wire, all tangled and twined together and piercing her through.

"Cut this wire off me," she said. "I don't want it. Every blame you cast on others, every item you grab for as if it matters, it's like a snake gripping me."

As if to add onto that point, a huge black python curled around her and traveled all the way up to her shoulder. Then it started squeezing around her neck, until it thinned out and became nothing more than a poorly bent wire, its sharp edge where the fangs were coming down to stab into all that stardust that made her up.

"It only feels comfortable for so long before it starts choking me—and then it becomes a sharp wire. Then," she cut one wire, and underneath was nothing but raw, blotched skin, "it becomes a scar."

Uncomfortable. That's what this was: insanely uncomfortable. Because did I do that? Those wires, those scars? Ugly—how ugly of me. I wrote it down and moved on, even as I wondered why she had a shape and wasn't just a ball of light like I thought souls were supposed to be.

"Okay, well... what do I need, then? How do I fix... all that?"

2. HOW DO I FIX WHAT'S HURTING ME?

Examine your relationship with wealth. Abundance is coming, but what does it mean? Are you the giver or the taker? What is your long term plan? View from an unbiased place.

These sounded like questions people recommend you ask your tarot deck when you're just starting to learn how to read, don't they? But here's the thing: I never believed a tarot deck was anything more than just a tool to communicate with someone else. It's card stock with pictures on them; they aren't the speaker, but the thing to speak with, like a phone or a messaging app or anything else. If anything, maybe a deck has a personality the way Alexa or Siri do, but the deck itself isn't alive.

So I asked, expecting an answer from not the deck, but my own hidden self, and by God, did I get one.

"Help," she said, almost as if asking for it before she continued, "both to give it and to get it. A chain. We exist in a chain of other links, bound together. We exist to bring balance."

Then the black backdrop we'd been sitting in was gone. We were talking in a field of snow at night, the pines trees dark and shadowy under the bits of snow that clung to their needles. the moon shone bright, a huge yellowish orb in the star-dotted sky, and the Soul suddenly had others around her: other souls, all holding hands together like some freshly cut garland of paper people. They were the chain she was talking about.

"What we need are level scales," she said, as a reference to the scales on the Six of Coins card. "We hurt when one has too much. We hurt when one has not enough. And you know it's not about having items or material things. It's about caring for one another, being satisfied knowing we all have what we need to live."

Suddenly, the other people were gone, and when I looked up, the moon had become a gigantic eyeball shining down on us like a floodlight.

"That eye is our eye," she said. "We need to see this Truth: all in this world is illusion. All of this," she gestured to the snow and the trees, even to me, "is the stage we dance this story out on. If you want help, and you want change, then don't just change the sets you dance on. Change the plot. Wipe it clean. Blank. Like the snow. Start over from a completely blank canvas. Dissolve everything, then rebuild it. Then dissolve it again. Do this until you've achieved Balance in the Soul—in me."

As I said: death and rebirth. Again and again and again. Like frozen winter earth into soft spring earth, birthing all the seeds left behind from yesteryear.

"But you—okay. Sure," I said, not ready to understand what she was asking me by that point. Had I ever felt so antagonized by something or someone I was talking to? And it wasn't even like she was saying anything antagonistic. She was answering exactly the questions I asked; it was just difficult to parse or accept at the time. "I don't get it, though. You're a soul. Why do you look like me? And like a more dramatic, prettier version of me? Is all this not just my own ego coming through?"

She shrugged. "Is it? This is the form we're in right now. Why not make it pretty? Why should I be a floating ball when I could be anything we want?"

"Jesus. I mean, I guess." That fairy-like, conniving smile she had. It just bothered me at the time, upset my vanity and ruffled my sense of self. "But tell me, then: how many form have we worn before? What roles have we played?"

3. WHAT ROLES HAVE I PLAYED IN PAST LIVES?

Big, happy energy. Good things happened or will. Enjoy the harvest. Let your hair down and reflect on good work.

High energy, multitasking. Your energy draws people. Important in the community. Allow yourself to be all.

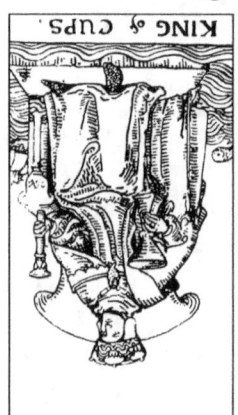

Emotional imbalance. May feel reactive, moody, and harsh. Spend time reflecting on your real feelings.

At this, she sucked her teeth and shrugged. "Everything is so fake," she said, and then she held up an empty lantern.

The snow faded away until we were sitting in the pitch black darkness again. Bit by bit, the gold fairy dust that made her up spooled into the lantern, until she was the big vibrant flame trapped in the glass; she floated there as dozens of other little specks of light hovered near. Maybe they were other souls, maybe they were something else, but they seemed drawn to the lantern.

"Everything is fake. It's aggravating. It makes all the nectar of our efforts taste so bitter, bittersweet. I want honey. I do not want medicine. But we are flawed—scarred—by the stages we build to act out this big, long story.

"In every life, we have struggled, and we've held up the nectar of our struggles as a bittersweet beacon. Every life is a mask, and we've worn many. What have we not seen? What have we not done? Those are better questions. We've been the highest and the lowest of our kind, and everything in between, and we've conquered it all."

Then she was out of the lantern and flashing different faces to me: from the faces of strong-jawed, clean shaven men to the faces of froggish witch-women with tattered clothes and matted hair. Each one had that same wide, taunting smile.

I stared at her for a moment, then asked, "How old are we?"

4. HOW OLD AM I?

The card I pulled was strange. Its message didn't make all too much sense to me, but what did right away was the imagery: two coins, one with a tooth and one with a crystal, being tied together with string by some pair of floating hands.

All aspects of life are clamoring for attention. Is doing it all sustainable? What can you outsource? Why is there so much on your plate? How can you create more ease for yourself?

"We are old enough to ask ourselves if this endless toil just to have something to eat is really all there is in physical life," the Soul said as I wrote the card meaning down. "Yet we are young enough to dare dream of a different way, to imagine something more than this toil we've seen again and again. We remember what it was like to not be fused to a body with such hunger, and yet we remember the novelty of a body, too. Old enough for the novelty to have worn off, yet young enough to still re-discover it and be curious of its full potential." When I squinted at her, not understanding that whatsoever, she smiled and put it simply as: "Not as old as God, yet not as young as Eve. Stray breaths. We are a stray Breath of Life given form. After being tucked away for a while."

I sucked my teeth, wrinkled my nose. "Now that sounds like ego. Come on, now, admit it: that's bullshit. No way."

The Soul winked. "Remember: Eve is just an idea, and one that came about not so long ago in the grand scheme of the world. We are much older than this idea of Eve."

With a sigh, I took a quick social media break and rubbed my eyes. This was taking so much longer than I wanted, and it was aggravating trying to understand if what I was hearing was true in any capacity or of it was all shit I was making up to myself. Either could be true. I still don't really have a definitive answer on that, and I doubt I ever will. Though it was a fun idea: being older than the idea of Eve.

If for nothing else, it'd explain why I felt so fucking old and tired all the time. A cute idea.

"Okay, okay, back into the questions, then," I said with a sigh. As I shuffled, I asked, "If we're this old, and you can talk all about this, then what was it like when we were created, hmm?"

5. WHAT WAS IT LIKE WHEN I WAS MADE?

A relationship gone sour or in conflict. Both parties bring baggage to the table. May be dealing with a long standing pattern. Do what you need to handle the situation.

Lovers Reversed was not the card I expected, but the main thing about it was that it looked like a star was being not necessarily shaped, but encased in a bubble—contained—by two disembodied hands again. Like the Two of Coins. That paired with the card meaning, though, about a relationship gone sour, it made me wonder—and the Soul's explanation wasn't far behind as I stared at that single card.

"We were insolent," the Soul said with a shrug. "It got us in trouble. I told you: we're but a stray breath. God existed, and He breathed in and out, far before He ever put together that lump of dust and called it Man.

"The creation of our body—our cage, I should say—was a result of us struggling to see the point of it all in Heaven. So here we are now, trying to understand the point. Even God—even our Maker—came down once like we have, as a Man, to see the point. I wonder what He found. But then, what have *we* found? We create so we can find the point of creation: all our stories, all our itch to make art and make things and make something where there was nothing. What have we found, doing all that?" The Soul sat and drew her knees up to her chest, then pouted. "Does it even matter?"

Shit, *did* it matter? I didn't know. Still don't, nor do I have much stock in finding out anymore. I also don't know what I've found doing all the dreaming, creating, and writing I do, outside the fact that there is a point to make, a story to tell, and I'll build millions of stages and masks and costumes and what-have-you to tell them. But who am I telling them to?

Who is *God* telling His stories to?

"That's something to chew on, isn't it?" I was starting to wonder if I wasn't actually talking to a fairy on accident, with how the Soul kept smiling at me like she knew more than she let on. "Alright, well, tell me this: what lesson have we already learned in all our lives?"

6. WHAT LESSONS HAVE I ALREADY LEARNED?

Now, truthfully, this question is a stupid one, because I understand now how easy it is to "lose" all the memories of a past life. Even this interview, as I read it back and see hints of the lessons I've finally come to internalize, is full of things I've completely forgotten about until now; it's full of secrets that, had I a better spiritual memory than a God-damn goldfish, might've made all the past year's trials make a little more sense in proper context. It makes me think of the story of the Prodigal Son: specifically, a version I'd heard where he gets hit on the head while out and about and forgets everything, only to get picked up by a foreign people and have a grand old time as a rich man or prince while knowing, deep in the back of his mind, that something isn't right, and he only gets free and returns home when God restores his mind and reorients his soul back to what's important.

Expansion in mental energy. Swords cut through illusions and get to the heart of the matter. New shifts and negotiations. You can't be silent in the face of injustice. Seeing world anew.

ACE of SWORDS.

But just as I can look back now and see that I did, in fact, learn all these things I asked about far after the fact, so too did it seem my Soul had something to tell me about all the lessons I'd learned before coming into this body I'm currently walking around in.

She waved a hand, then shifted all the black nothingness into some castle corridor lined with torches. It might've been the dungeon, what with all the cells lining the wall, and she took my hand and pranced down the cold stone walkway with me.

"There's a reason we're disgusted with silence and can't keep quiet for long," she said. We tried before. It didn't stop us from getting burned."

There was a visceral flash of firelight flickering under a dark sky, smoke rising up around a bunch of buildings and a big stick with something tied to it. It wasn't all too different from a vision Stribog showed me, before telling me that the Slavic gods weren't keen on talking to me before I was ready to take on the side quest of untangling *that* vision.

"But we are fire," the Soul whispered as we watched the light dance. "We are flame. We are magma. Those who burn us become scorched in kind, and we never die.

"We call spades, spades. We see things for what they are. Not always people, though," she said, and it was a nod to my early life, where I trusted a touch too much. "But things, yes. This life tried to dull our Sword, but we sharpened it again. It will always be sharpened. Truth once learned isn't easily lost—sort of like riding a bike."

"Alright, I get that," I said as we ended up in some part of the castle outside this dungeon-y looking spot. Honestly, we were just surrounded by four torch-lit, stony walls. "How about what we still *need* to learn, then?"

7. WHAT DO I STILL NEED TO LEARN?

Where have you been pushing? Where are you living in extremes? In a space of excess or intensity. Inspect unconscious patterns stemming from wounds.

She raised a golden brow. "How would I know?"

"Wh—because why wouldn't you?" I blinked at her and said, "You are the motherboard of me, just like Sophia is the motherboard of God. You know things deep down that I don't know on the surface." As I spoke, I shuffled, and here was where I pulled a card. "You have the secrets set to release at certain times—don't you?"

"I do," she said, and I flipped the card to see Temperance Reversed, "and I release this one now: we'd hurt ourselves along the way, in our creation. On our way down. And now we're trying to plug the wound with cotton, but when will we actually heal the wound? What kind of wound even is it? Is the wound lack of trust? Or an excess of ego?" She grinned there, poking at both my distrust and fear of being eaten up by my ego at once. "Or is it something we don't have words for yet? Is it homesickness? Or the absolution of the Void?"

Absolution of the what? What the hell does that even mean? That's what I thought at the time. But oh, stupid. Oh, silly. I have a *better* idea of what she's talking about now.

The Soul grinned with teeth so sharp and mean that they felt like shark teeth. Of course she'd heard my thought: she was me.

"Nothing matters there, in that Void: no choices, no consequences," she explained. "Ultimate absolution. Even if God forgives sin, we carry the scars and lessons that result from it. We're changed, adjusted, recalibrated, like a fine watch. Before we were distinguished from the nothingness all creation came out of, though, there was nothing, and nothing was us. We could do no good, but we could do no wrong, either. We never changed. We simply never existed. Unformed. We carried on; that's all."

I stared at her. No matter who told me about the nothingness of the Void—demonolaters, other magicians, the Holy Spirit, angels and demons, even my own Soul—it just never sounded very appealing. At least, not then. Even now, I still like being formed at all; I like being separated from a cat and a CAT crane and a box of cookies and a tree. I like being a person that isn't like any other people, and I like that other people aren't me, even if we're all still connected. I like a gem that has facets that sparkle when the light hits them rather than everything that exists just being a clump of unformed atoms and molecules.

But lately, I've been wondering: is there such a thing as knowing too much? Knowing too much, yet still knowing nothing at all? At this point, long after this conversation, I find myself just... not too attached to the idea of my own face anymore. So many times, when I talk about mysticism and the way in which we dissolve ourselves to come into perfect union with God, others have shared the same sentiment I have: *that's scary. I don't want to stop being me.*

Now, though, it feels like "me" was never real to begin with. Like the flesh I'm in is the same as a costume from Spirit Halloween or something. Like eventually, the Father will tell me it's time to pack up my toys and let the game of dress-up end, and despite a bit of mewling, of asking for five more minutes, I will have no choice but to shed this costume for good.

"Okay, how about this question, then: what am I meant to be?"

8. WHAT AM I MEANT TO BE?

THE CHARIOT.

Barreling through obstacles, filled with motivation. Things may be overwhelming and confusing, but there's a light at the end of the tunnel. Buckle down. Now is not the time for the easy path.

"You see what it says," the Soul said as I plopped down the Chariot and read its description. That was a card God pulled for me earlier, too, which made it that much more of a gut punch to see fall down on my table. "You see the truth in it without my needing to lift a finger. Our empire, our 'final project,' so to speak, is to be built brick by brick.

"You've already witnessed the slowness of it: You—and I mean you, in this life specifically—were not meant to hit it big and get lucky. Your luck is already apparent. I wear the shine of our luck," and she flared like a ray of sunshine, as if she were made of Glory itself, "but it seems we're meant to be someone who learns to use that luck decisively, not bank on it."

Which is a very rough lesson to learn for someone kissed by a dawning Sagittarius on the horizon when they were born, let me tell you.

"Now, we work. Now, we build. Now, we conquer." The Soul was as luminous as the sun as she smiled, not a froggish and mean smile, but a honey-sweet one. "We show our Dear One, our Maker, that we don't back down from His silly challenges. We are His breath. Our triumph was written already; we just have to trust that fact and move forward against His trials. We're forever locked in battle against Him to see who has the greater resolve to live.

"We can't convince ourselves to go on for false reasons. Neither can He. So we fight—for the sake of it, and for each other. We give each other a reason. We spite each other."

"Jeez, slow down, there." I was curled up on my living room floor wondering where the fuck all that came from. "You make it sound like we're God's lover or something."

Crazy that I came to that conclusion *before* reading about the many ways mystics like St. Teresa of Avila described the soul as the bride of the King—of God—and how this unification was the consummation of said marriage. This is perhaps the most uncanny part of this series: getting answers that sounded so impossible, so unbelievable, only to be proved true long afterwards by other people across time and space who realized these exact same truths.

The Soul laughed. "We're all His lover, because we all love our Maker, just as we love what we make. It's not necessarily romantic or whatever you think it sounds like, with our corrupted, animal ideas of love on this little rock. It's just Love."

"I mean... that does make sense, sure. Fine. But then, how about this: what am I hiding from myself?"

9. WHAT AM I HIDING FROM MYSELF?

Then I pulled the Ten of Wands, and I blinked at it.
"This? Really? This is what I'm hiding from myself?"

And all the while. Nine Inch Nails' "Various Methods of Escape" had been playing on loop, and the chorus snagged my attention right then: the bit about letting go, getting things right. Yelling at someone, somewhere, asking why things were so hard, begging to be released. Once, God spoke to me so viscerally through the Nine Inch Nails song, "The Fragile," and it seemed like this song was the Soul's response. Both of them had lyrics that cracked my head like a hammer.

A period of temporary burden. Don't get stuck on it. Sometimes we need to push harder at the end of a project. Upkeep of success is difficult.

Partnership. Both people invested, committed, and respectful of one another. Opening a new world of opportunity. Accept good things.

(Side note: I am convinced Trent Reznor is some kind of prophet or mystic, between these songs and the entire *Year Zero* album. But we don't have time to get into all that.)

The Soul rolled her eyes. "Go pull another card with it then, if you don't believe it."

And I did. I pulled the Two of Cups alongside it, and then I was starting to understand what I was, for whatever reason, not willing to fully acknowledge. Still, I had to hear the Soul say it, as if it was all still a lie until it was confirmed as truth.

"Okay, so... what about this?"

The Soul heaved a sigh and shined brighter in the black backdrop of my mind.

"Ego is blinding you," she said, "but not the way you think. I am You from the bird's eye view: I see what this cage you're wearing shadows from you. I remember what you've forgotten. You can do so much—we have done so much already—but we've never done it alone.

"Stop trying to shoulder the world alone. Stop trying to scoff at the idea that you're overburdened. Remember: He is here to help as much as test. We've fallen because of Him, and we've gotten back up because of Him, too. Be His partner. Let Him be your partner. It's the cornerstone of this thing we've been calling luck."

Well, fuck. I guess I should be honest, then, huh? Not with you all, necessarily, but with myself. It isn't luck that's gotten me shit; it's faith. When I stop struggling like a bug stuck to a spiderweb and give up, when I say, *fine, God, You win; You go ahead and handle this shit,* and ask Him to show me where to go—*that's* when things fall into place. That's when people who weren't paying so close attention blink and wonder when the hell all the stuff that's happened has happened. That's when I realize I do not know how to fucking drive, and Jesus needs to take the wheel before I crash into some spiritual signpost.

In that moment, though, I stared at the Soul for a long time. By this point, my head was spinning, my chest felt like I'd swallowed my huge sphere of obsidian and gotten it stuck there behind my sternum, and I was so ready to throw this whole deck of cards out the door. Truthfully, the interview felt like army crawling ass naked on sandpaper laced with Carolina reaper dust the whole time, or like I was one filthy dog that hated that it had to go take a bath with the ice-cold hose water. Begrudging resistance to a wretchedly uncomfortable thing I had to do: that's what it all was, and I hated every second of it.

"Alright, well, let's wrap it up now: what the hell am I still doing this series for? This 'Interview with the Gods' thing? Do you know, Ms. Bird's Eye? Because I don't feel like I do anymore."

10. WHY AM I STILL DOING THIS SERIES?

Celebration. A time of balance and harmony is near. Success isn't linear. Create gratitude.

Transforming passion and drive into real results. Building containers for success. Do what most people don't like to do. A declaration to the universe.

A major transition, likely filled with sadness. Remaining where you are is not an option. The path will lead you to a world of more opportunity. Can't rush the process.

As I wrote, there were certain parts of the booklet descriptions that felt like she was echoing them. In the Two of Wands, for instance: *I am taking this seriously, so you better do the same.* But once I was done, I looked up and saw her sitting in a half-demolished cell, bricks starting to tumble down, and she, herself, was covered in needles that would slide out of her golden flesh at the same time each brick fell down. Then she handed me a needle-brick and pointed behind me, and I saw that each brick was being repurposed as part of a staircase that led up to some shining light—as if a hole had been shattered in this black box we'd been sitting in the whole time.

"It's not about struggling or suffering for the sake of it, this whole thing we're doing," she said. Witness. See. Learn. We're not a tourist of Divinity; we're an inspector, an auditor. What has been done, by Divinity and Man alike? We're taking stock of that. Where are the wounds humanity still has? We're tending to that.

"This has never been about others and what they get from it. This is about us, and what we want to learn; it's just also something worth sharing with others, because many are on the same journey of trying to learn all this mess, whether they realize it or not.

"But our revelations can only take others, who walk a different path than us, so far. This is our walk, and we're shamelessly voyeuristic about it. But if it makes you walk, lantern in hand, then walk." She was out of her cell, then, all the needles gone, and she held that lantern up high as the fireflies—maybe souls, maybe something else—came back to follow that light. "*We* are a lantern, remember. And we are one.

"The light of the soul and the shadow of the body, we are one. We make twilight. We are twilight."

✦

My favorite colors are purple, reddish-orange, and black. The same colors of the crystals I had on the table. The same colors of Twilight. My style is what has recently been dubbed "black and gold Goth"—not silver, not that moon color, but gold. Soul-light and body-shadow mixed together. I am not a leader or a warrior; my face is not cut in sharp edges, nor is my frame built for power. To try to take on such a role is like wearing a boxy, ill-fitted, too-big suit. And just as when I was a teenager, and my mother tried to spare me the heartache of learning lessons by experience when she told me not to do this, that, and the other, it seems my Soul could not spare me that same heartache by telling me all these things I shamefully forgot not long after I wrote it all down.

I ended that interview the same way I did every other one: saying goodbye, blowing out the candles, packing things up, and hurrying along to my own self-inflicted schedule. While my mind heard the words the Soul said, they were just too slippery to take hold then—or, rather, it was like pouring water on a duck's feathers. None of it absorbed. It all just rolled off, watering my path instead of my mind. But I kept walking that path, knowingly or not, and looking back, I can find it in myself to laugh at my own confusion, and to nod along at all the things my Soul said; while I have no doubt there's still much to learn, I can recognize the truth in everything she said because I've finally experienced much of it firsthand.

There's a bit of Jewish folklore about three wise men who stormed the gates of Heaven and went to confront God directly. When they returned, one was broken: he went mad, unable to articulate anything he'd seen or heard or experienced, and he was shoved off to the fringe of society, unable to work or do anything other than babble. The other, while still able to speak, didn't have a reason to anymore; in fact, he didn't see the reason in being alive at all, given what he'd seen in God's realm. He stopped eating, stopped drinking, and withered away, unimpressed with all the things this world could offer us. Only one kept sane enough to tell the story and preserve himself, hence how we know this story at all.

I find myself less and less interested in these earthly things, too. Almost as if I'm too tired to care—but not the kind of tired that can be fixed with sleep and a break from work. Just exhaustion, as if the weight of every lifetime is finally sitting behind my eyelids, burning me with every blink.

The Divine is dangerous. Like the waves of the ocean that push and pull at you in unstable, shifting sands, it will swallow you before your time if you let it, if you seek too much, too fast, and then give up and don't *hold* fast. There's a balance to strike between self-preservation and self-sacrifice, and a wisdom in knowing when it's time for each one—much like how Jesus avoided every attempt of others to stone Him or throw Him off the temple, only to give Himself up to that cross and die anyway.

Light born in darkness. Sleeping death in the cold, rebirth and resurrection in the spring. Like chives. Oregano. Like birds and bees and flower buds. Perhaps now, I'm doing nothing but babbling, too—but I also think those with eyes to see and ears to hear, those whose sandals are worn out from the same path I'm walking, will know exactly what I mean.

So be careful. But be not afraid.

OMEMIAH

You ready? After that last interview, it'd be understandable if you put this book down and didn't pick it up for another long while. Hell, I'd even understand if you buried it under a stack of other books and forgot about it altogether.

As you know, that's what I did with that last excursion.

But there was nothing else to do but to keep going. Maybe I'm just chained to my own sense of obligation to the folks who support me each month on that damn Patreon, but I know what I provide is just as important to many of them as it is to me. I want to honor that, always, and so I do my best to keep going even when doing so takes a hammer to my sense of self until I'm shattered back into a million little shards of glass—into sharp, glittering specks of dust. This time, however, on that journey of self exploration, I turned to a figure that would know me almost as well as my own Soul: my guardian angel.

Time and time again, people ask me how to find their own guardian angel. Truth be told, I can't give an answer that'll work for everyone. My own way of finding out was pretty unorthodox, and it took forever because I wasn't ready to know until I was ready to know. You know how these things go. But when I acquired Travis McHenry's Angel Tarot and Occult Tarot, I noticed that older magicians and angel-workers thought of different types of guardian angels: soul guardians vs. whatever other kinds, three in total, which all had to do with the time of one's birth. It'd be pretty easy to just look at those and collect three angel names to consider your own guardians, I guess. But that is not how I went about this.

Instead, I asked years and years earlier, what the name of my guardian angel was. I got a big letter Z in my mind's eye, but that was it. For a long time, as a result, I just called my guardian angel "Z." That was enough for me at the time—until I picked up Damien Echols' Angels and Archangels and thought that maybe I should actually go find the full name.

Here's the thing, though: that "Z" wasn't the initial of my angel. What it was, though, was the name of the leader of his squad: Zadkiel, the archangel that is associated with Sagittarius, my rising sign. Archangels aren't usually guardians, though, if ever, and so I knew it couldn't have been him; all that "Z" was, was a clue of where to look. Under Zadkiel was a list of other angels of Sagittarius, you see, and so I went down the line, asking, are you this one? This one? until I got a resounding yes from tapping on one name in particular:

Omemiah.

The way I confirmed that this was, in fact, my angel, was by reading the description of his gifts both in Echols' book and in a book called *The Magick of Angels and Demons* by Henry Archer. Turns out that this angel, whose name means God Hidden in Darkness, is both paired to the demon Alloces and has the incredible function of destroying and shaming adversaries and giving his charge energy from arguing with others.

Suddenly, all my keyboard warrior antics as a teen made a whole lot more sense. Energy drinks had nothing on the high of scrubbing the floor with someone over the course of about sixty back-and-forth comments on social media. I wasted a lot of time back then. Now, I don't have that kind of time to waste anymore—but no matter how tired I am, seeing someone say something impressively stupid and letting them *know* that what they said is stupid still perks me right up.

Anyway, let me show you this very cool angel—one I am so very happy to call my guardian.

After chatting with God for a bit, and getting distracted by a million and two other things on my to-do list, I finally settled down, put the bird away so he wouldn't try to eat my crystals, and got down to business. I dragged out Omemiah's (or Imamiah's) card from McHenry's deck, put down some angel-connecting crystals like celestite and some soothing crystals like pink amethyst, howlite, blue lace agate, and obsidian, plopped an angel statue and little white candle down, and called that mini-altar done.

As I got into the zone, I asked God to let my guardian angel actually make himself visible to me. I'd seen him before, when I finally figured his name out and dared to go talk to him, and as I figured, the scene that came in was right where I last encountered him: at the foot of a massive volcano, cracked earth glowing with flame from deep within the ground and a big lake of fire churning and sputtering away like the surface of the sun. As in my interview with St. Francis, there was that same angel I'd seen before sitting in a throne, shining with such bright flame that I couldn't make out who he was; he was guiding souls into the lake single file, one jumping in after the other and burning away all their past vanities and transgressions. The sky was black with huge dark clouds, and the silhouette of a bridge stuck out against where the edges of those clouds sparkled with some deep orange glow.

My guardian stood by me, looking very similar to the Angel of Death from Hellboy, what with the tattered old robe and the big black wings covered in eyeballs. However, instead of a disk for a head, he had burning golden eyes sunken into deep sockets and sooty, brownish-black horns rising from his bare, leathery grey scalp. As I looked at him longer, I found that his robes were open enough to reveal his chest, which was little more than an old ashy ribcage. Inside that ribcage was a burning orb of fire, almost like the power core of a machine. He gave a lipless smile and held out a grey, withered hand, one with sharp dark nails. I held it, and I could so vividly feel the chapped, leathery quality of his skin.

After a bit of joking back and forth—in which it wasn't lost on me how much he sounded like the voice in my head that was constantly, and I do mean *constantly* chiding me for stupid things I did or said on the daily—I found myself dressed in a robe much like Omemiah's. We sat at the edge of the lake of fire like I was sitting at the edge of the community pool; I was dipping feet in it and everything. I even went to sink myself into the lake altogether before Omemiah caught the scruff of my robe and dragged me back up.

"No," he said. "Not yet. Don't go drowning yourself in that right this minute."

But as I came up, it was as if the very constitution of my being had been eaten away a little bit. My arms looked like they were only sketched in pencil, all greyish-white with a black outline that shifted and twisted around. With a sigh, Omemiah dragged me off into a different part of heaven, one that looked just as sketched and loose as my hand, and then we sat on a cloud under a very bright full moon and watched other angels zip to and fro. By that point, we were finally able to get into the questions. My arms went back to normal, too, and I could see outside myself: me, practically drowning in that huge old robe I had on, and Omemiah, whose face was becoming more like the skull of a ram with two live coals burning in it. Almost like Elias from The Ancient Magus Bride, except it kept twisting between ram and human face. Maybe it was because of the horns he had that my mind went where it did in terms of how he looked.

"Okay, okay, fine—no more horsing around," I said as I elbowed him. I picked up his preferred deck, Amrit Brar's Marigold Tarot, and got to shuffling.

Despite what maybe one would feel to see a being that looked like him, I felt genuinely safe and comfortable with him, as if I'd known him my whole life. And I guess I had, given he'd been assigned to me for all of the years I'd lived so far. Still, some might think that I was talking to a demon given that appearance, but those people are the same type that would tell me about how *the devil comes as an angel of light* if he'd looked all prim and pretty, so there's really no winning there. All I can tell you is that angels *and* demons can appear monstrous as much as beautiful, depending on how you'll best receive them; their form says more about you than it ever will them.

I turned to him on that cloud and just dove in. "Why did you get assigned to me in this life, huh? Mr. *God Hidden in Darkness*?"

I. WHY WERE YOU ASSIGNED TO ME?

Slander, isolation, and being manipulated.

Falling in love with the idea of love, jealousy, and needing to be tethered back to reality.

Hostility, indecision, and disharmony.

Those coal-red eyes slid my way, and he gave the smallest half-smile. Omemiah settled on that cloud like a bird settles on a branch, then spoke.

"You are a mess," he said. "You always have been. But in this life, the time to play is over. You've had your chance to sample this world and make sense of it. Now it's time to choose a cause, pick a side, and take a stance.

"That stance is one that will win you so many enemies. I'm here to teach you how to keep your back unbowed. Adversity is a fact of life, and in this life, you can't afford to have your neck bent to its weight.

"Huh." That made me think of deadlifting. The heavier the weight, the harder it is not to let your back bow and crumple. But before I lingered too long on a message like that, I scribbled it down and kept moving. "Alright, then. I think I see what that stance is that you're talking about. But then—what are you trying to help me do in this life?"

2. WHAT ARE YOU TRYING TO HELP ME DO IN THIS LIFE?

His stare was sharper than broken glass. "God's already told you what you need to do. It's very dangerous. This is a solitary thing: there's a reason working in groups or large organizations is an affront to you. It's not in your nature; it's not how I've been guiding you. Things that happen in the dark aren't for all to see.

"I'm here to teach you: be guarded. Stop trusting everyone so easily. You haven't figured that out in any of your lives, but you need to here. Be wary— know all things are possible, including bad things. Learn to move in shadow rather than announce yourself in all these wreaths of sunlight."

I opened my eyes and looked out my window to watch the snow fall outside.

Delusion or disconnect with reality regarding relationships.

Vigilance, contemplation, rational thought, growth of new ideas. A desire for intellectual challenge. Caution needed.

Loneliness, alienation, and extreme caution. Isolation.

What he said immediately made me think of Morana, with her own wolfish half-smile, saying how a sunshine-saturated thing like myself had to learn to get used to the dark of winter. Omemiah nodded to my wordless memory, and I wondered if he could see my thoughts—but then, how couldn't he? Thoughts were how I spoke to Divinity, be they angel or demon or God or Saint.

"Seems like the Slavic gods have tried to teach me that, too," I said.

With a roll of his eyes, Omemiah said, "They certainly have tried, yes."

"Okay. I think I'm getting it, now."

And honestly, after going to a church for the first time in a while to give the whole Church Community thing an earnest chance around this time, hearing this made me think it couldn't be for no reason. However, as times get tougher, and religious tensions rise with Christian nationalism and Christofascism posing a deep threat to the safety and freedom of all people, I can't help but wonder if maybe it *is* time to announce ourselves. Or maybe I'm falling into my old vices and traps of the ego again.

Hmm.

"Well, to move on from this line of questions, then: can you explain the deeper meaning of your name?"

3. WHAT IS THE DEEPER MEANING OF YOUR NAME?

Mistrust, insecurity, or a loss of hope.

Courage, power, and venturing forward into new experiences without fear.

Navigating love and relationships of all kinds. Clarity and honesty in one's values.

As I shuffled the cards, all the scenery faded to black in my head. The only thing I could make out was one of God's representative angels, his eye just as sharp and cunning as that of a huge black snake that slithered through the darkness.

"Can you navigate without the stars?" Omemiah's voice sliced through the dark as if that snake were hissing. "The obvious map of them laid out in the sky? Can you choose between two paths when you can't see what lies ahead of either one?

"That snake there—can you trust it not to bite you? And even if it does bite you, can you trust yourself to survive it? Sometimes holding up a torch in the dark only makes everything else even blacker—and makes you more obvious to everything that slithers in the brush."

I had a clear picture of myself holding up a torch, illuminating my whole self, but leaving everything else outside it like an ocean of shadow. Only when things got too close could I see the glint of firelight off eyes and scales and teeth.

"'God hidden in darkness'—God able to navigate without light, God able to not find, but *create* the ground His foot will step on next. God, whether you can see Him or not. That's the deeper meaning of my name. Faith. Trust."

"Damn." That was one heavy hitter of an answer. "Okay, I got'cha. Love that. But how does God operate in darkness? You've already hinted at it, but so many people act like God and the dark are just completely incompatible in the first place."

4. HOW DOES GOD OPERATE IN DARKNESS?

1. Martyrdom, hardship, confusion, facing consequences, and forcing oneself to consider different perspectives.

2. Suppression, lacking discretion, or feeling incapable of expressing oneself.

3. Disinterest, introspection, doubt, pessimism, and an inability to see the good in life.

"The darkness is a test of stillness," Omemiah said as we went to a place that was nothing but pure inky shadow. "Can you master yourself here? Can you find peace without forward movement? Are you content to let some secrets sit in the dark? Often, the need for movement and answers leaves us moonblind, and it opens us up to attack and deception.

"God in the darkness invites one to learn self-control and first ask if an answer is even worth pursuing in the first place. It teaches us not to give into fear to the point that we can grow comfortable with darkness and find God's presence in it."

"Ah, that makes sense." And puts my childhood fear of the dark in some more esoteric context. "Okay, well, here's a more technical question for you: some people like McHenry insist that 72 angels are all there are, and that those 72 angels guide all of humanity. That means you're more than just my guardian angel; you're others' angel, too. But how do 72 angels cover all of humanity? There's like, billions of us."

5. HOW DO ONLY 72 ANGELS GUIDE ALL HUMANITY?

Innocence, positive relationships, nostalgia, and harmony in the home. Natural order of all things: live, grow, die.

Again, that tiny half-smile. Omemiah shrugged. "No stories are unique," he said. "There are many people walking a path just like yours, and I need to help guide them as much as I need to guide you. All people are unique, and yet none are special, or more deserving of help than any others.

"Remember that: you are one character. In your story, you're the main one—in someone else's, a side character. We angels oversee how your stories intersect and overlap. That is what it is to be a Guardian Angel."

"Uh-huh. But then some people say they have other spirits as their guardians. Like demons or ancestors. Or even dragons. Can that happen?"

6. CAN SPIRITS BESIDES ANGELS BE GUARDIANS?

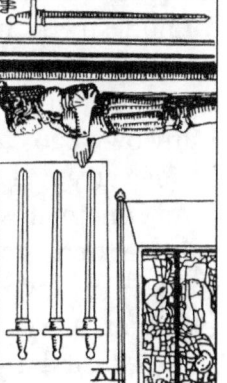

Stress, restlessness, and unwillingness to take risks.

We were back in the sky, and Omemiah was chuckling to himself, rubbing his temple as he lounged on a cloud. It was a struggle to get a card from him, but finally I got one that didn't make all too much sense as an answer. It did, however, make sense as a comment on my attitude: I was unwilling to not know the answer. I was unwilling to let it be, and I wanted the answer to be *yes*, because other people said they had this experience, and I didn't want to discount that experience.

And then the clouds were gone, and I was standing in some church or palace, where a skeleton in an ornate dress sat on a throne. All around us were skeletons, and two more were coming down the aisle as if getting married. Omemiah stood right there beside the queen skeleton, yet it seemed no one could see him. And the pews, too, were full of bones, all dancing and rattling and going ballistic as the groom and bride tapped their bare teeth to each other in a death's kiss, sealing wordless vows.

All the while, Omemiah's voice rang out like church bells.

"Can you? It seems to me like you already decided the answer, but still you ask me, hoping I'll tell you what you want. What makes you so afraid in this life, Sara? Being wrong. Not knowing. The dark. Can other spirits be guardians? Sure, if they want. Do you need to concern yourself with that? No. My goodness, Sara, you truly never learn."

The hell did he mean by that last bit? The wedding scene faded away, and based on what he'd just said, I figured I had to just accept that he wasn't going to tell me what it meant. Maybe it was part of a test, to see if I could stop myself from trying to figure out what all that was. So I spitefully moved on to my last personal question instead of thinking about the skeleton wedding.

"Alright, fine. How do you see me, then? As one of your charges?"

7. HOW DO YOU SEE ME AS ONE OF YOURS TO GUARD?

Falling in love with the idea of love, jealousy, and needing to be tethered back to reality.

Weakness, breaking down, losing control, or having difficulty problem solving.

He chuckled as I shuffled the deck, and I got a sense that I couldn't pull the typical three cards since the end of this life hadn't come yet. I could only pull two. So I did, and once I did, Omemiah did not hold back, that's for sure.

"You never learn, but you're a darling child," he said. "Though you were more content with silence when you were younger, and it seems I'll have to wait to see how the rest of your life develops. For now, though, I see a brat. Goodness, you whine. 'I'm tired, I'm tired,'" he sucked his teeth, "so is everyone. Yet you're the type that has a hammer and wants to make all her problems a nail—who idealizes things and gets bruised for it.

"Delusion is a skill you are well versed in. But it peels back layer by layer, and the more you learn—and accept you don't know—the more you've been able to start undoing some of the locks on you. Good job. But goodness, you are stupid, and I love you for it.

"You are my charge and my problem, and you're doing all things just as you need to do them. Take heart in the fact that you're getting there, slowly, bit by bit."

I honestly didn't know what to do with that. This was where I really started to wonder: were all those moments where I snapped at myself in such raspy and self depreciating tones really me and my tendency to beat myself up, or was it Omemiah getting frustrated with me over and over again? Was it my own ego calling me stupid, and this whole conversation was just a lie, or was my not wanting to believe an angel would call me stupid the real trick of ego?

As Omemiah said, some things would just have to be left unknown. Though when I think back, I can see there is a very obvious difference in the way I yell at myself out of my own frustration and the way my own voice suddenly snaps at me in a way that makes me pause and shift direction in my behavior. A *big* difference.

So, I dusted myself off from that smackdown of an answer and kept going. "How do you see yourself, then?"

8. HOW DO YOU SEE YOURSELF?

If he was disappointed that I didn't have a shit fit about his assessment of me, he didn't show it. "Wearing this mask is difficult," he said as he touched his bony, withered face, and I knew by mask, he meant the aspect of God his name signified. "It hangs off my face like a chunk of stone and threatens to bend my back everyday—but I must lead by example, I suppose, and teach my charges not to run from difficulty. Still, I am tired. And I see myself as one destined to carry on, no matter how tired I become."

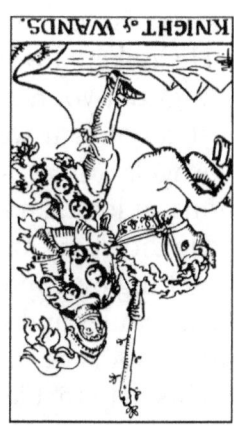

Ill placed infatuation with an idea or person, overhanging doubts, confusion, or a dent in one's confidence.

"Ah, interesting. How do you want to be seen, then?"

9. HOW DO YOU WANT TO BE SEEN?

Travel or inner journeys. Growth and evolution after a difficult time. A personality that will adapt to situations.

Suddenly, there was no longer any room for the nice night sky with all the moon and stars and clouds. We were right back where we started, at the foot of that volcano, and Omemiah stood there with wings of shadows and secrets spread wide. All of his burning eyes stared down at me.

"Be afraid of me," he said, "but approach me anyway. I am God—Divinity itself—hidden in darkness. I require bravery to approach, and a dissolution of all one thought they knew. I am a devourer of hubris; I am the machination of God's alchemy, transforming dream into nightmare and knowledge into illusion and conspiracy. I destroy nations as much as I lift them up, and I do so by simply letting you men be.

"You are my greatest weapon. You destroy each other. The seeds of war and sorrow and pain—they exist, are sown, and sprout amongst the arrogance and surety of men. Flee to the dark you fear or burn by your own hubris, your light.

"I am Omemiah," he said, with that beacon of warm orange light shining in his chest that made the shadows get even darker somehow. "I have no tolerance for weakness, ego, or vanity. Dissolve or die."

"Holy shit, dude." I finished writing that down, and I looked at him with all his big shadowy feathers spread out. "That was a lot. Really intense. Damn. Did you want that to be your message? Or did you have even more to say?"

10. ANY LAST MESSAGES?

Righting wrongs, accepting consequences, abiding by the truth. Legal matters. Consider a situation before taking action.

He pulled Justice, which only made me even more tired.

"Do right by each other," he said as we returned back to a moonlit place, and his body stopped being a giant cosmic horror of smoke, shadow, and flame. He went back to being is own dusky self, wrapped up in that old cloth. "Trust your soul will know what that means, even when your ego addled minds don't. We all watch over you, and we all see what you don't. Trust us when we help—and don't claw on our skirts when we refuse to. Do the work yourselves."

"Oh, alright." That wasn't as bad as I was expecting it to be. "Great! That's some solid advice. Well, I have to go for now—but Omemiah, I trust I can ask you a question any time I need to?"

He looked down his nose and said, "I'm not here to waste time on idle chit-chat. If you can't figure things out yourself, ask for a hint, but don't just try and get all the knowledge of the world from me instead of your work."

Angels. "Okay, alright, fair. Fine," I said with a huff. "But I appreciate you answering these questions, at least, and I guess I'll see you as needed. For now, though, I gotta go. Goodbye!"

He didn't say anything, likely because there was no such thing as *goodbye* when he was always watching over me. But the scene faded away, at least, and I pulled myself back into the waking world of schedules and work and the need for lunch. I would see Omemiah a few times outside this meeting, but for the most part, he seems to be leaving me to my own devices these days. Granted, I know it's his help that keeps me from getting into stupid situations out there in the world—as a teen, especially, I bounced my first car off many a guardrail or other hazard—but he's letting me do exactly what he told me to do: the work to figure things out on my own.

It's in Omemiah that I also understand my own sense of self a little more. There are still people that think in order to be Christian, you have to dress exclusively in the cozy white-brown-blues of Old Navy or wherever else they get their very "holy" looking wardrobe. They insist you can't do the whole alternative look and be close to God: no black, no jewel tones, no spikes and dark makeup and playlists full of Type O Negative and Nine Inch Nails and what have you.

But that's stupid. Your music library and your wardrobe don't make you more or less Christian. What they very well might do, though, is give a hint as to whose energy is following you around; they might show you which mask of God is influencing you. If my angel is really God Hidden in Darkness, it makes all the more sense that I am drawn to all things dark, vulnerable, broken, and concealed. All the sense in the world.

And it makes perfect sense to me, then, how I could combine something so dark and *profane*—the title of Witch—with the very religion that would try again and again to blot that darkness out, that would villainize its own mysticism and try, in their hubris, to erase all the shadows that also make up the infinite, ineffable nature of God.

SIGYN

Now, you might think the next spirit I talked to would have something to do with self exploration again, right? It'd be a fair guess, after all; it seemed I was making something of a theme out of it. And I would've, probably—had I not gotten a voice message from my friend Hannah (or @spirituali.tea) that started with: "Okay, Sara, I have a story for you, and I'm just going to preface it with: I'm sorry."

Four minutes of listening later, and a couple tarot card spreads to boot, and it seemed that this was not the time for me to wonder who I was going to speak to. Hannah, who has long been working closely with Loki, let me know that it was his wife Sigyn that wanted to talk to me. For what, none of us knew—but we confirmed it with multiple signs, one of which was a massive spider that quite literally jumped into my mom's house just as we were about to leave to go to the gym together. They were quite insistent about it, and I just so happened to get myself together enough to interview Sigyn on Thursday—the day Hannah also honors Loki.

The line between coincidence and sign gets so blurred in witchcraft.

But now, Sigyn is quite the figure in Norse mythology. Many people know the giantess Angrboda that Loki had several children with, but Sigyn, his official wife, is just as much of an important figure in his story, given she and him had two children: Narvi and Vali. Both of these children were murdered, one turned into a wolf to kill his brother, the other struck down by Odin himself. This wasn't unprompted, though; it happened after Loki moved against everyone to make sure that Baldur, the much beloved god of light and the son of Odin, would remain dead after his untimely, unfair demise (which happened in the first place by, you guessed it, Loki's clever design). Loki and Sigyn's children then had their entrails used to bind Loki to a rock in the underworld, where goddess Skaði had a poisonous serpent hang over him forever to drip venom onto Loki's face.

Sigyn, however, took it upon herself to forever stand over him with a bowl and catch every drop of venom. It's only when the bowl is full and she has to move to dump that venom out that Loki gets burned by the venom, and he shakes and thrashes in pain, which is what the Norse believed caused earthquakes. Why this goddess would want to talk to me, honestly, was a bit of a mystery—though based on Hannah's story, in which she was reading my interview with Mother Mary back again, it seems that Sigyn also wanted to share something about the grief of her own motherhood.

So I decided, why not invite Sigyn and see what she had to say?

According to Hannah, Sigyn has a few things she likes: the color purple, dark berries, things like that. Another thing I found in researching was that she's associated with the red fox, but unfortunately, I missed the opportunity to put any of my foxes out for her because... I forgot about that on the day of. What I did have, though, was pink amethyst, blue lace agate, rose quartz, and tiger's eye, all symbols of her station over victory, love, mercy, peace, and wisdom. I also had a white candle out there to light the way.

For gifts, what better thing to give a Norse goddess than a good ale? I had one can of pale ale left, and it just happened to be in a purple can. I also grabbed a collection of blackberries, raspberries, and blueberries for her as we got started.

Then I did what I always do: shoot that call out into the dark, with God overseeing and helping me find this goddess of victory.

Where we started was not where I expected to be: a cave of ice, where a small throne carved from that ice sat near the back. There was a hole leading out of the cave and into someplace deeper, but for the time being, there was just all that ice glowing a faint blue with some unknown source of light, and among it all, Sigyn: with a dress of ivory and gold, bright blonde hair with ribbons and feathers decorating it, and amber brown eyes that shimmered as if there was some hidden ember smoldering from within. Her brows were pinched, her eyes wide and bright with urgency, and she rushed for me as I dropped down into the cavern.

It startled me. I wasn't sure if this was real or if I was just imagining things, as it didn't take long at all for this image to pop up in my mind's eye. I'd caught a flicker of it a few days prior, and I knew Loki and Sigyn were around with the spiders and such in the first place, so I guess I shouldn't have been surprised, but I was. So after checking to make sure that it absolutely was Sigyn in my space (and after Michael popped in just to verify for me before disappearing), I let myself get settled and start with the questions.

"Alright, Sigyn—hello! Thank you for reaching out to me! I will say, though, I'm curious as to why you went out of your way to contact me. Is there any reason in particular? What I can do for you?"

I. WHY DID YOU WANT TO CONTACT ME?

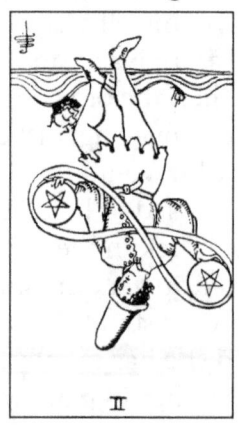

1. Past regrets, ignoring the call to transform, disappointment, and false accusations.

2. Manifestation, putting one's dreams into action, realizing goals, or seizing the moment.

3. False joy and overtasking oneself.

The Marigold Tarot once again came up as the deck of choice. As I got to shuffling, there was something raw and inhuman about the way she talked in the beginning that made it feel like the whole cozy mask Divinity normally wears for us had been torn off. Normally, Divinity spins words in a way that make it easy for me to understand, or at least connects with something we've been speaking about or looking at, but Sigyn was suddenly right beside me and speaking with full force.

"They think of me only as a being of mercy, but I'm more than that. I want people to know: Loki is free, by *my* design. The world is waking up, and with it every terrible thing that's been sleeping. Kill those terrible things. Kill them all.

"My husband—he can help. My name means 'Friend of Victory,' and I am a friend to my husband, as well as a friend to humanity. You will prevail, but only if you become more cunning, more *fierce*. There is a time and place for mercy. It isn't here, in this case."

Huh?

As she spoke, there was that telltale snatch of red hair somewhere in my mind's eye. Sigyn left to sit in that ice throne, and perched on the arm of her throne beside her was Loki, arms crossed in his black leather armor, a toothy grin on his face. He looked as if he were proud to sit there, off to the side of his wife. His eyes were the color of milk, as if he couldn't see, but he was also looking straight at me, so. If there's one thing I learned about Loki, it's speak of him, and he will be there.

And the thing about Norse myth that always gets me is: if Ragnarok has all these gods held in stasis until it's time to brawl, how are these trapped gods—like Loki, like Fenrir—all out and about all over the place? It seems like she was answering that question for me, as well as confirming a couple things I'd heard before. One of those things was the idea that Ragnarok is cyclical: that every so often, the world needs a reset, and that the story happens all over again.

Another was the idea that, even if not cyclical, that Ragnarok had already happened, and all things were changed again. The world had already gone up in flame and been plunged into the sea, and from there, there were only two humans. Being a Christian Witch, you can guess where my mind went, and it turns out that early Christians actually told the Norse the same theory: the Norse story ends where the Christian one begins (or, rather, general Abrahamic, as of course Adam and Eve are a part of all major Abrahamic religions, it being an originally Jewish story in Genesis).

I'd been mulling around that second part, because it had some interesting implications (more than what any Christian seemed to consider when they whipped that out as some ultimate *got'cha* on the Norse): it meant that the world had been created already before God made His cool masterpiece. It meant other gods did have the role in creation that they said they did in their myths. And it could mean that maybe the gods, including God, are playing a game with each other: creating worlds and seeing whose can last the longest, like some *Dark Souls* No Hit Run. That's a big idea to consider.

I'd say there's something cyclical about Ragnarok regardless, though, just as there seems to be something cyclical about Messiah according to Jesus. However, as we know that gods dying doesn't mean permanent death from various faiths (Celtic, Christian, Shinto, etc.), we might guess that the rules of Ragnarok don't apply anymore, and that means Loki's rolling around free as sunshine now.

Another thing that was getting to me, though, was that Sigyn was talking with the impatient fury of Divinity at the end of its wits with us, trying to drag us by the hand towards answers we weren't getting. I was steeped in my own quagmire of mystic work at that moment, so I couldn't have articulated it at the time, I knew implicitly, subconsciously, what she was talking about, even if my conscious self didn't have any understanding to share. I tried to ask for the sake of finding those words, though.

"Sigyn, you seem to know about something that's going to happen. I've been getting a lot of signs about something in the works lately. Can you give us some more clarity as to what's going on?"

2. WHAT IS BREWING IN THE UNDERBELLY OF THE WORLD?

Let your weaknesses be your strength, was the thought that came to me as I read the meaning of Strength's card, especially, all about knowing one's limits and boundaries. Then Sigyn spoke:

"Your hubris will kill you, Men. You are so easily distracted. How many times can you stumble on the same rock? The tides are turning; the waters run black."

We left that ice cave through that opening, and down below was a huge underground cave, where a river as black as the night sky ran through underneath shattered chunks of ice. Sigyn peered into it, as well as at the arms of dead and half-rotted bodies that reached up to the surface.

"The dead. The dead are upset," she

Cooperation, skilled labor, and completing projects. If focus is applied, triumph will follow.

Coming to terms with one's own shortcomings and mortality. Self control, introspection, navigating adversity with grace.

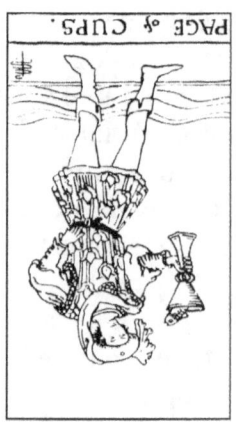

Deception and re-evaluating whether a goal or relationship is truly fulfilling.

insisted. "The stars are upset. All are upset. You wanted mystery. I cannot tell you plainly; me telling you this much is a crime. Walk, walk, walk! Dig your way through thorns; wear them on your head in that famous Crown if you'd like! Drink your mead and sing your songs; find a way out of this fracture you've created. Kings," she said, and behind my eyelids, completely separate from the scene I was envisioning, was the sunspot-like outline of a king squeezing the life from a peasant, throwing him to the ground, "topple the kings that choke you down."

I had to pause, if only to orient myself in that torrent of ideas. "I think I get what you're saying," I said. I watched the ice float along that black river, and towards the roof of this cave, things like stars twinkled. "But then, okay, hold on: Loki is here, you're here, and I gotta ask if what you're saying has something to do with Ragnarok. Is it a cycle, like people say? Is a cycle starting up again? Or...?"

3. IS RAGNAROK A CYCLE (AND IS IT REPEATING)?

1. Suppression, lacking direction, or feeling incapable of expressing oneself.

2. Change of direction, moving on from disharmony to seek balance. Disappointment, abandonment.

3. Wonder, optimism, creativity, and confidence. Foresight to protect oneself. Inspired and excited to move forward in a constructive way.

Sigyn sighed, a tired smile on her face. "Again, I've already said far too much. But a world only waiting for war and waiting for the end is not one that can stay standing—including this one. When the world fell away the first time, it was terrible. Are you all here to repeat that? To let it happen again?"

Immediately, I thought of this Rapture that so many Christians are frothing at the mouth for.

"Your God doesn't want that," Sigyn continued, "and you know that as well as I do. Stop thinking about the end. Stop waiting for Ragnarok, or Judgement Day, or what-have-you. It's already come. You need to live with the world you have now. You can't wait for us to lift you off the mess you made. We will support you—that's our role—but you decide if this world lives or dies.

"Stop choosing death and watch the world become brighter. Stop chasing our domain and take care of your own."

Time and time again, I've seen people say things in comment sections like, "we're all dead/the Rapture already happened and we're all in hell." I don't necessarily think so; I think we're alive and well and battling for the outcome of this little rock we call home. However, while there were a lot of places my thoughts wanted to go in that moment, in the interest of spending time with Sigyn and focusing on her, I kept those at bay. The thoughts this information brought on me wouldn't coalesce until I was driving to my parents' house to do laundry later, and so I'll share them at the end of this interview. But I noticed Sigyn seemed a bit pressed by this line of questioning, and so I shifted track towards the other questions I had written down.

Before I got into them, though, I asked offhand: "Do you want this interview to be public today?"

Her warm eyes cut towards me, and her smile came back. "You know exactly what I'm saying. That's why this message isn't for you; it's for them. The ones that read this."

"Fair."

Though I didn't know about knowing what she was saying right then, even if I had a solid inkling right there. I was, and still am, a little dumb.

"Okay, let's pivot here, then," I said. "I understand you wanted to speak to me for a reason, Sigyn, but I was hoping to get some answers on other topics, too. Like, for instance, Loki: you seem referenced only in relation to him. I'm not sure how to ask this in a polite way, so please don't take me the wrong way, but I wish I could've seen more stories about just yourself. Loki gets his own stories, so how does it feel for you to—"

4. THOUGHTS ON YOUR STORY BEING SO TIGHTLY LINKED TO LOKI'S?

  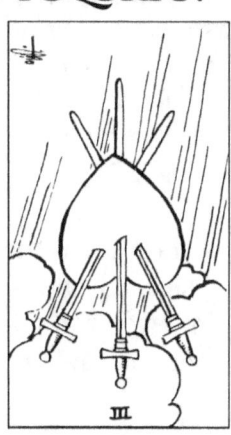

1. Corruption, greed, obsession with material wealth at expense of spiritual.

2. Excercising foresight with an open mind. Must consider the many routes and plan accordingly for our benefit.

3. Needing to move on. Feelings of alienation, love, or relationships long lost.

"Does he?" Her smile became a mischievous grin. "Is he not also known relationally to others? Can you think of any stories where Loki appears that don't involve others or their growth?"

I paused. Even if I hadn't heard every single story that ever was, she was right: the ones I could think of had Loki as a catalyst or a support for others.

"All his stories are about helping or hindering others," she said, "and there's merit in this: train people's ideas and expectations of you, and you control their actions. I always gave a hint of who I really was by virtue of my name—Friend of Victory. If all anyone saw was my mercy and compassion, good. It meant they didn't see my other thoughts, motives, and machinations. This need to set yourself apart from all things and always be a person all and only for yourself—it's not always good. "

The way she said that gave me pause. It suggested Sigyn was more than just a loving heart, a loyal wife. It suggested she was, herself, a schemer and a trickster—not unlike the god she married. With a blink, I looked up to Loki, who hovered over us as we sat by that riverbank.

"Do you have any thoughts on that? On her, uh... *machinations*?"

He shrugged, still grinning. "What I think about it doesn't matter here."

"I—alright, I see that. But then, hold on now, Sigyn: you are still known for your loyalty to Loki. Can you tell me what loyalty means to you?"

5. WHAT DOES LOYALTY MEAN TO YOU?

Juggling family affairs and financial matters, as well as a desire for tradition and affluence (either material or spiritual).

Stagnation and resisting change.

Guilt, deception, despair, anxiety, and lies. Words are the root of one's despair. Self inventory carried out with honesty.

"Mm. Loyalty means sacrifice," she said, her brows set hard as she stared at the water and the things writhing below the surface. "Sacrifice of many things. Dignity at times, virtue at others. Yet people chase it because there's been value in it; to be loyal to the right king or lord has earned people great reward.

"Is that the only reason for loyalty, though, especially when you lose so much for what you've gained? I've lost children; I've lost peace. I am a well of comfort for all but myself. But you're right: I, too, am a trickster god. I am loyal not to people, but to outcomes. I've chased one outcome to its logical conclusion already, and I will chase all others to theirs, too. Loyalty—when used right—is the dogged persistence that breaks and creates worlds."

"Jeez. Alright." Didn't expect that, if I'm honest. "So then, how about Loki? And getting married to him, even though he was also with Angrboda? People say you accepted his trickster nature; is that what you saw in him?"

6. WHY DID YOU GET MARRIED TO LOKI?

She hugged her knees to her chest, her golden hair trailing down towards the ground.

"I saw him, and I saw what I deserved in him. I saw what I wanted, too, and I saw how he might help me get it. They say I accepted his trickster nature, and it's true, because it's my nature, too. I saw in him my equal in mischief and change—more than I would've ever gotten from some gaudy prince or whatever other match." She stared off, her gaze pointing somewhere far away. "I knew to be Loki's wife was to be no queen. Still, could I have ever hoped for more?"

Vanity, dashed ambitions, or a lack of challenge in one's life.

Truth, indecision, inadequacy, and emotional detachment.

Bad news, powerlessness, loneliness, self sabotage. Maybe healing.

"Huh." There was some sadness lacing that answer, though it also seemed like I shouldn't push too much more. Instead, I went with the last question I'd already had written: "Okay, well, how about mischief and mercy, then? What do you wish people knew about these two things?"

7. WHAT DO YOU WISH PEOPLE KNEW ABOUT MISCHIEF AND MERCY?

Regret, loss, mourning, and disappointment. The destructive nature of sorrow in excess.

Wealth, prosperity, and contentment. Vision and presence of spiritual wealth. Protection, adaptation, a bright future.

Inability to move forward, obstacles, and waiting.

"When you ask about them together," she started, choosing each word carefully, "you ask about a song and a dance. Mischief breaks; mercy mends. However, there are some mischiefs that can't be mended, only forgiven. Mercy is at its strongest, and it's needed most, in times when things can't be restored.

"Mischief is a test of mercy, therefore—showing who is charitable and who is simply tempering their anger to release on you later for some other perceived transgression."

"Oh, shit." I tapped my pencil to my lips, then nodded. "That... does make a lot of sense, actually. Never thought about it like that. Thank you for sharing. But okay, okay, we're down to the last few questions now, so Sigyn, please let me know: how do you see yourself?"

8. HOW DO YOU SEE YOURSELF?

Vulnerability, powerlessness, and a possibly inflated ego.

She heaved a big sigh.

"While my plans are good, it bothers me that I have to rely on others to make them work. It opens up the possibility for disaster that maybe wouldn't be there if I were on my own. Still, there's strength in weakness."

"Alright, fair, fair. But how do you want to be seen, then?"

9. HOW DO YOU WANT TO BE SEEN?

"I want them to struggle to perceive me," she said with a humorless chuckle as I puzzled over the Two of Swords. "I want them to question what they know as fact and accept that their records of things—their human minds—are not perfectly capable of anticipating or understanding the gods."

Denial, stalemate, and indecision. Illusions.

"Uh," I guess that tracks, given I didn't expect a goddess of love and mercy and loyalty to be so sharp around the edges, "I see. That makes a lot more sense, yeah. But then, did you want to share any final messages? One last card for the road?"

10. ANY LAST MESSAGES?

Sigyn shook her head. "I've said enough. Take these seeds and scatter them."

I could've saluted like a soldier right then. "Will do. Thank you, Sigyn, for speaking with me! I'll see you when I see you, I guess—and you, too, Loki."

They left that cave waving, and then I was back in my own living room, trying to get myself ready to get on with the rest of my day.

But here's the little thought experiment I told you popped into my head later. I spent a good couple hours mulling over this interview, and the things that were said to me—including the idea that God doesn't want this world to end. Christians clamor so hard for Judgement Day, but why? Why, when God already gave us a place to be, a whole world to enjoy, right here beneath our feet?

Let me set the stage for the idea that hit me after all this: when people say God is omnipotent, or rather, *omniscient*, and that He knows everything that's going to happen, they usually think of it as God knowing one timeline of events. We have free will, except we don't, because God already knows what's going to happen! Right? But just like we can play around and say maybe Marvel had a fun little divine secret about Sigyn and Loki stashed in their comic books, so too can we look at other media to get some other ideas that help us understand Divinity, too: like with Garnet in *Steven Universe*.

The single autonomous gem-creature, Garnet, is made of two gems fused together: Ruby and Sapphire. Apparently, Sapphires have the ability to see one future, and that's all they see. However, the day Ruby breaks protocol and runs after Sapphire, accidentally fusing, is so out of the bounds of Sapphire's expectations that Sapphire never saw it coming. As Garnet, therefore, with Ruby's inability to be predicted in the mix, this new gem doesn't just see the future, but *all* potential futures.

What if God is the same way? Not seeing one future and locking us into one storyline, like the Rodjenice and the Norns and the Fates, but actively, with His warnings against fatalistic astrology and His insistence that no one should put so much stock in fate and stars and what-have-you, *unlocking us*? Reminding us that our actions and choices actually *do* impact things a lot more than we realize, and that the future is entirely what we make it (even if He can see all the possibilities we create)?

As you mull that over, I'm going to point to two Biblical moments to share maybe a whacky idea to folks: when God nuked Sodom and Gomorrah, He was willing to let the entire city stand if Abraham could find even one righteous and good person among all that mess. Even just one. And moreover, it's said that only the Father, not even the Son, knows when Judgement Day will be. That suggests to me that the multiple future vision could be in play: it's not that Judgement Day has a set date, but a set list of criteria. If it's as Sigyn says—that God doesn't want this world to end, and that it was harsh enough when the last one ended—then we can guess that the conditions are:

1. That we've chosen a future worth God's final judgement (whichever one that is)

2. That not even *one* single righteous person remains on earth if we could choose it

Then, and only then, are the horns going to blare and the world going to go to shit, because that means this world is irredeemable and that the run God has going, with His stab at creation after Ragnarok (and who knows how many creation stories before or alongside that), has come to an end. He doesn't want that to happen, though, because on that day, all things that are defined and distinct in the physical reality we know will return to the primordial soup that is the Abyss—and the definitions of His own self will melt along with it all, as all this world really is, is God defining things as God (Himself) and Not God (everything else), with that latter category getting more and more specific and categorized along those Seven Days of Creation.

The Abyss brings all things back together that God separated from Himself (and is something that plenty folks actually do look forward to: whether they be the Doomsday folks that don't realize that's what they're asking for, or the anti-cosmic folks who are very aware, and who want to shed all these layers of separation and simply exist again, like everything once did in times no one can really remember anymore).

In conclusion: God (and by extension, the rest of Divinity who are here watching us make our way through this run) are here to support us in not ending this whole thing and returning everything to murky soup. God has His court set up, with Prosecutor (Satan/Adversary) and Defense (Michael/Jesus/Advocate) arguing for and against us.

He is Judge—so if we manage to hold on to just one good person in this entire world, if we can be blameless and innocent as doves, and if we can, when we do stumble, have the good sense to strike those misdemeanors from the record with proper penance, then we can keep the party going. To permanently forestall God's Judgement Day, therefore, you must make sure there's nothing for Him to Judge.

Easier said than done, though.

ST. HILDEGARD VON BINGEN

I honestly can't believe it took me this long to interview St. Hildegard von Bingen. Of all the Saints (besides maybe St. Cyprian), this is the Saint that I can point to the works of as justification for anything we Christian Witches understand about using our natural world in our works and our spirituality; her works are legendary, as is her music. (If you're curious, I highly recommend her Canticles of Ecstasy, which you can easily listen to online.)

St. Hildegard isn't just a Saint, though; she's also a Doctor of the Church, meaning her works had significant impact on the theology and understanding of the Church at large. She has an incredible story, seriously; if you want a good book on St. Hildegard and her philosophy, mysticism, and general background, Matthew Fox's *Hildegard of Bingen: a Saint for Our Times* is a fantastic starting point, but I'll give you a brief overview here. Born at the end of the 11th century in modern day Germany, a younger daughter among her noble parents' many children, St. Hildegard was one that always seemed stricken with terrible headaches, as well as visions. She got her education in a convent, under supervision of the anchoress Jutta, and by time she was fifteen years old, she was wearing the habit of the Benedictine nun. Once Jutta passed, St. Hildegard eventually took over the role of convent prioress, and in her writings, she talks about how she kept silent about her many visions until God Himself struck her with an illness for it, which basically shamed her into finally talking about them.

After her visions were confirmed in a conference of holy men as truly inspired, they helped her write them down, and we have many of her works still: works like *Sciva*, *Physica*, and so many other writings and music and plays and other such things. She became famous, drawing all kinds of new nuns to her convent, and she was audacious, too, writing letters even to kings to tell them to get their shit together when they were making bad moves against other countries or against their own people. And she was even excommunicated from the church at one point for also telling the church leadership that they were ass backwards in a few key areas (though she got un-excommunicated before she died).

A rightful polymath, St. Hildegard proved some incredible talent in so many areas, and her *Physica*, especially, is the jewel of Christian Witchcraft in my opinion: it has all kinds of information on herbs and crystals and their healing powers. (At one point, putting onyx in wine is a recommended remedy for something in that book, but please do not put your crystals in liquid; many are water soluble and highly toxic, like malachite.) Still, it was a book that proved to me: there was Christian thought around things like herbs and crystals, the latter of which St. Hildegard claimed were full of God's light and therefore detested and feared by the devil. In our modern ideas of witchcraft, that slats right in and builds a stronger bridge between two worlds people mistakenly think are so mutually exclusive.

At this point, I'd reclaimed this series for myself: for my own understanding, my own learning. The weekly polls were over, and I was thinking about all the curiosity I had, all the answers I was seeking, that may or may not have been helpful for people to look at with me after all was said and done. So finally, I got around to talking to this Saint, and this is the result of that conversation.

Before getting started, I had a few things on the table: garnet, onyx, and bloodstone, all healing and invigorating stones, as well as a candle and a cup of peppermint tea. Of the herbs St. Hildegard talked about, mint in general was one she pinned as good for digestion, and I figured she'd appreciate a good herbal tea rather than anything else. There's also just something cozy and nostalgic about a cup of peppermint tea for me, so it made the whole space that much warmer and easier to sink into.

After doing the Lord's prayer and asking St. Hildegard to come by, I found that the scene appeared pretty quickly, and that it looked like something out of Elden Ring or another Dark Souls game. Very much something like the room full of books in the Round Table Hold, if you've ever played Elden Ring, except the bookshelves were lining the side walls, and in the back behind a big desk was a roaring fireplace. No other lights were on in the room, but the fire managed to light up everything just enough.

Then entered St. Hildegard, an older woman in full nun garb, and a familiar angel helping her along to a small wooden chair in the corner: Gabriel, all blond hair and blue robes. He left just as soon as he came, as if he didn't want to interfere with the conversation, and then it was only St. Hildegard and I sitting there by the fire, surrounded by all kinds of old books and scattered papers. She had eyes that were endlessly deep and dark, with what looked like a single white star shining in each one. She also, during our interview, would shift from the lines and puffed cheeks of an older woman to the smooth and sharp face of a younger one, as if her body were living out all stages of its existence all the time up here. It was interesting.

"Alright, St. Hildegard, thank you for meeting with me," I said as we settled down by the fire. She had a matronly smile while I flipped around my notebook. "I'm glad to have the chance to talk to you—especially with how influential you've been for many of us in the Christian Witch community, however you'd like to think about this group."

Her smile grew, and her brow quirked, like the whole idea was something children thought up while playing. I didn't want to make guesses as to what was on her mind about it, so I just put my many decks of cards out and asked which one she wanted to use. I was sure she'd pick the Herbcrafter's Tarot because of her love for medicine, but to my surprise, she chose MJ Cullinane's Guardian of the Night tarot.

"Perfect, thank you! Okay, so, to get us started, I'm really curious to know: what was it like to speak out and deal with the Church? I understand there were some things that the male leadership of the

Church were doing especially that had you upset, but you ended up excommunicated at one point. Can you tell me a little about it?"

I. WHAT WAS IT LIKE TO DEAL WITH THE CHURCH AND SPEAK UP?

Plans dashed to put out fires. Every person has a different opinion and none agree. Drama due to petty debates. Reflect now.

Sharing great joy with others. Something magical about joining forces for a common goal. A sense of community.

Brute force that earns hollow victory. Complicity. A victim of selfish actions. Opinions never considered. Acknowledge your role.

Her face twisted in the scowl of an annoyed headmaster, lines creasing between her furrowed brows as she folded her hands in her lap and sat up a little straighter.

"I was not just any one of these things in the Five of Swords," she said, tapping the third card, which was a classic card to pull for situations where one is trying too hard to the point of losing touch with what really matters. However, when I read it, I thought that was her only representation in the card, but it seemed she disagreed. "I was all three cards at different points in time and I was some of these at the same time."

Suddenly, the image of our surroundings changed from the books and fireplace to a gray cell, cloudy light pouring in through the little barred window. A younger Hildegard sat there on a stool, despairing, but it didn't feel like a scene from her life; it felt more like the expression of a raw feeling, like she'd been trapped in some issue while she'd lived.

"I knew the Church was wrong at times, against the will and design of God, and yet I didn't know how to enact change properly. I became the brute, hard and cruel in some of the things I said—and I reaped the benefits of my position anyhow," St. Hildegard said. She sighed and continued, "Had I been anyone else, I might've been excommunicated much sooner. It was a humble position to be in: being part of something you love, and loving it enough to want to heal it, only to be silenced.

"But I'd built a good foundation among my fellows. I knew I was right before God. No amount of pushback could've stopped me from trying anyway. The Church was petty then, yes," she said, acknowledging the squabbling stupidity addressed in the Five of Wands, "and it still may be petty now. But I did what I could."

"That's completely understandable, yeah. I can see where things could take a turn quickly when dealing with them and what they do. But alright, in that regard, what are your thoughts on the Church now?"

2. THOUGHTS ON THE CHURCH TODAY?

St. Hildegard shook her head. "Ah, the Church. It still can't see. It holds on too tightly to the tool—the Bible—and fails to use it properly. Scripture is all well and good, but the mysteries of God don't end there; it's there to help us dig further, not sit where we are theologically forever.

"As an institution, the Church is no different than when I was alive: stubborn. Unyielding. Wrong about so many things. Goodness, the corruption! How dare you call yourself a Church of God and do half the things you've done? Shameful."

Her frown only got worse there, her fists clenched tight as if she were ready to box the Pope. I'm sure she and I were both thinking about it: the scandals, the abuse, the horrors done in the name of God (and the ones covered up in the name of God). But she didn't leave it there.

How does your need for control impact a situation? Holding on so tight means no room for growth. Stagnation.

With struggles comes risk of drowning in self doubt or losing passion and enthusiasm. Rekindle the fire in your belly.

Cheerful despite growing to-do list. A bit more flexibility, logic, and inner compassion needed to keep balance.

"It's hurting the Body of Christ to see leadership so brutally inflexible, unwilling to engage in the mysteries like a proper believer. To see them marr themselves with their own invented tragedies, too... We've simply lost the way, and leadership has not helped find it."

"Yeah, we sure did. The whole thing's a mess, if you ask me." I shook my head with her, and in that book-laden space, it almost felt like roles had been flipped: like St. Hildegard, up there in heaven, had become the anchoress sealed away and departing wisdom, and I the young skup trying to learn as much as I could. "Speaking of the mysteries, can you tell me what it means to be a mystic to you? Many of us Christian Witches also call ourselves Christian Mystics, and I'd love to know your take."

3. WHAT DOES IT MEAN TO BE A MYSTIC?

Powerlessness and confusion, feeling trapped. Feeling in limbo, unable to see what to do next. Uncovering inner wisdom will help you move forward.	*Using resources to the fullest. Action, work. Preparation and commitment. Take control of the situation and make conscious decisions to get the result you're looking for.*	*Something is missing. Hollowness. The situation no longer leaves you feeling excited. Greater things lie in the distance; new possibilities may require abandoning what you have.*	*Warm, motherly, and generous to a fault. Ready to support. Your resources will grow; go forward and approach the situation with loving, kind energy. Stable and grounded.*

This question had her pulling *four* cards, and it was funny to see one of them be the Magician.

"It is scary," St. Hildegard said, relaxing back into her seat. The firelight danced off her face, though her eyes seemed to swallow the light. "To be a mystic is to be afraid. It's to see things that reveal the lies of the world. The world is made of shifting watercolor; nothing is so hard and fast as people think. We were made in God's image, and what is He if not a Creator? We paint with Him, as if He gave us the frame [of the artwork] and the color pots both."

The words translated weird in my mind, but I understood the idea, because one of those "paint by numbers" things popped up in my head, still blank and waiting to be filled in.

"When you are called to this path," she said, "you can't just deny it. You can't sit forever being afraid of the call. You need to take God's hand and walk—to find the thing your soul is craving that can't be found on earth. And then you need to share what you find, because other souls are hungry, too. This is a path where you become like a dam bursting: you are obligated to let the waters flood the people."

Jeez. Talk about intense. She had so much to say for each question, but this one struck a chord with me: we're obligated to share what we know. While the word "occult" means hidden, and no doubt people have hidden their work for a long time out of fear of persecution, the thing about it is that people have been doing all this work precisely to discover what's hidden and make use of it—to record it so all people can access it.

Interesting.

"Makes sense to me. In that vein, though, what do you think of the spiritual landscape today?"

4. THOUGHTS ON TODAY'S SPIRITUAL LANDSCAPE?

She let out a big sigh and shook her head. As I was shuffling the cards, I heard her say:

"The Soul is hungry, and we starved it. Someone has convinced us to starve it. You know who."

Ominous, sure, but I did know who: the beast that's been trying to rule people with fear instead of encouraging them to reach for the stars. After another few moments, I had all my cards laid out, and St. Hildegard made her point clear.

"You people," she muttered. "You forget you're all after the same thing: Truth. But Truth is a multifaceted thing, and the man who stares at one side of the diamond doesn't realize he sees a different sparkle and color reflecting off it as the man on the other

A situation may test your honor and integrity. Confront fear and traverse darkness to awaken change for the better. Don't cheat people.

Traveling through darkness using intuition. Not the time for impulsive actions or telling others your plans. Stay quiet. Be a part of something bigger than you.

Teamwork and being in sync. Pursuing a common goal. Considering options and resources. Calculate each move, delegate matters.

side. So much bickering. So much infighting. So much pulling all in different directions.

"Don't you see? Each one of you is given a portion of a great and infinite puzzle. You'll spend all your life searching for the pieces to put together but a miniscule patch of it. Don't fret if someone else's patch of pieces reveals a different image than yours. It's all part of the same tapestry. Or do you think each other lying when you describe just the earth? When you see trees, and a man halfway around the world sees desert sands? Or oceans? Are you all liars, or perhaps simply too small to see all the world from where you are?

"Work together. Piece the Truth together from these slivers. Share with one another. Connect them together. This is the Great Work."

As I was writing, I was getting more and more excited, because damn! What an answer! And more than that, the clarity I was able to get through the descriptions in this specific tarot deck alone were wild. Sometimes St. Hildegard said things I was almost hoping she would, and other times she said things I didn't quite expect, and other times again she said things that just blew me away. This was the latter.

"Wow," I whispered. "Thank you for that answer! What a great way to understand that idea of the Great Work. I hadn't thought of it like that. But okay, so, to get into the rest, now: reading your writings, you mention that at one point, you didn't share those visions you had because you felt unworthy of speaking on God's behalf about them. Then God knocked you down and made you sick, and that's when you realized you had to speak. We call this Imposter Syndrome now, and I was hoping you could tell me how you overcame those feelings that were stopping you from sharing your visions before—besides with God's push, of course."

5. HOW DID YOU OVERCOME IMPOSTER SYNDROME?

Fortitude, climbing back from extinction. The heart of an activist. Passion, conviction, a quest for truth. Wisdom gained through grit.

A notable turning point. Examine your life as a whole. Open up and be honest. No making excuses. When you accept yourself fully, the situation benefits.

Supporting self care without worrying about one's to-do list. How can you splurge a little to make the situation more comfortable?

Her smile carved deep lines into her face. She stared at the floor, her shoulders heaving in a heavier breath, before she answered me.

"It wasn't simple by any means," St. Hildegard said. "God knocked me down hard, not only because I was doubting myself, but because I was refusing the permission to accept His gifts. He wants us to take His gifts, not trick ourselves into thinking we're unworthy of the Fatherly love He chooses to share with us.

"My illness was such a turning point, such a blunder on my part that I repented everyday thereafter. But it did teach me that my misgivings were just that: mine. No matter what others said, I knew God wanted me to push on. He taught me to see me as He sees me: worthy, capable, and unshaken. All fall short from the glory of God, yes, but that doesn't mean He left us without glory at all. So I dealt with my misgivings by remembering that it was God who thought me good enough to bless me this way, and by treating myself with the goodwill all humanity deserves."

"Oh, that's so nice!" The idea of God seeing us as worthy and capable when we beat ourselves up over and over? It was such a sweet idea that I just sat with it for a minute before gathering up the next question in my mind. "I love that. But knowing how God can be… can you tell me a bit about your relationship with Him? And how you see Him?"

6. WHAT IS YOUR RELATIONSHIP WITH GOD LIKE?

1. Power out of balance. Taking advantage of resources. Consider your position. Are you getting a fair deal?

2. Allowing emotions to drive you into a defensive position. Afraid to expose your feelings or be vulnerable. Focusing only on your needs. Avoiding something.

3. Guilt over different decisions one could've made. Paralyzing worry, stress. Attracting issues we'd like to avoid. Negative, anxious thoughts.

St. Hildegard sighed fully this time and shook her head the way she might at a pack of unruly, yet sweet children.

"Even if I came to accept my role and how God saw, me, it was all so much. The majesty of God—the sheer size and unknowable depth of Him—it was quite a lot to take in. How was I anything other than a leech on Him? He took from me, too, of course—took my time and my focus."

Oop. Relatable.

"But it's so little in comparison to all He's deigned to give me, small as I am. It's just one of those feelings that never truly goes away: the thought that I could've done more for Him. That I cheated Him. But what more could I have done? I did all I could, and yet it wasn't enough to materially shift the world at large. I love God all the more, knowing He has such unfaltering grace for a thing like me. Such undying love. He is beyond my comprehension still."

I won't lie: hearing her talk about God like this had me feeling even closer to her, because I share a lot of the same sentiments, especially looking at my own life. I feel like I've not necessarily given up a lot of dreams, but put some on hold, in order to get in front of people and show them a new way to God. He's taken up my time and focus, too, in a way I didn't expect He ever would, but He's given, and continues to give, so much in return. It's just one of those things with deities, I guess. Work with them, and they'll work with you. This journey isn't even a quarter of the way over for me, I feel like, so we'll see where it goes—but I felt bad that St. Hildegard didn't feel like she'd materially changed anything when her words and music have been so influential. I mean, she lived a thousand years ago, and we're still talking about her and reading her work and listening to her music, and I told her as much.

She seemed happy about it, in a bashful and modest way, smiling at the ground as I talked about it.

"Alright, well, my last personal question for the day is this: now that you're in heaven, I can't help but wonder if you think about your visions. Now, no doubt, you can see exactly what it was that God was showing you, and I wonder how much of it matches your original visions?"

7. How do your visions compare to what you see in Heaven?

A barrier between all that clouds judgement. From a place of clarity, she understands her role. Speak with integrity.

Swift change that shakes up life itself. Stability crumbling beneath us. A warning of change.

Using resources to the fullest. Action, work. Preparation and commitment. Take control; make decisions to get results.

St. Hildegard nodded as she looked around. "Up here, the illusions of the flesh are shorn away. I couldn't concentrate on the things God showed me then, when I was alive, on account of my migraines. I couldn't settle in the vision appropriately. But here, yes, I see and hear exactly what God means and intends.

"It's too much for the human mind. Here, all the things I thought I knew were put into focus, and I knew there were many things I'd gotten wrong, despite having direct revelation—so forget the chances of the average man to understand these things. It was as heartbreaking as it was humbling."

"I can see that, yeah. Thank you for sharing your thoughts about it. Now, though, I'd like to know: how do you see yourself?"

8. HOW DO YOU SEE YOURSELF?

Understanding many sides of a problem without feeling dragged down. Staying on top of all things unfrazzled. Harmony. In control.

Pulling Temperance was surprising, yet felt so fitting.

"I am a visionary," she said with a smile. She watched the fire and continued. "I am one who sees now with greater clarity, and for that, I've been blessed. I am one who gathers, manages, and directs the flow of my fellow Truth seekers, my fellow academics. Come find me for help if you need it."

"And how do you want to be seen?"

9. HOW DO YOU WANT TO BE SEEN?

"I don't care to be seen any one which way. See my works! The important information is hidden there in plain sight."

"Got'cha. And now, are there any messages you want to give before we part ways?"

10. ANY LAST MESSAGES?

"Yes. To learn is to unlearn. Don't feel discouraged if you find yourself retracing your steps every so often. You're on a journey that all humanity has always been on. You'll know the destination when you reach it. For now, enjoy the experience of discovery, and drink deep of the mysteries."

"Alright! A beautiful message, thank you, St. Hildegard! I really appreciate all your wisdom. For now, I have to go, so I'll be calling this to an end. Thank you again, and goodbye!"

And then the room full of books fell away, with St. Hildegard smiling as it all went black. I sat there in awe, not only of the conversation, but of just the Saint herself. She commands such stark power, has such a presence, just by the stern look in her

Letting go and trusting the universe. Risks of blind faith. Acting first and thinking later. Great adventures await if you let go of expectations. Don't feel bad about retracing steps; enjoy.

eyes—and yet she has that matronly, guiding voice, too. These two ideas aren't opposed like people so often want to say, after all. Still—St. Hildegard is an incredible force to be near and speak to.

There's something to be said, too, for giving everything up for God. For taking one's ambitions and turning them into vehicles for His will. I've only just begun to figure out what that means, and it requires a lot of trust—and acknowledging that you're not doing it in expectation of getting your ambitions validated in the end. Simply, if you do what needs to be done, you'll get where you need to go.

I've laid my pen, and all my hopes in its ink, down at God's feet. It's up to Him what goes on with it now—what becomes of all the letters I'm writing. I don't know what the future holds, and frankly, I don't need to. I'm just doing what needs to be done, and when it's done, I'll move onto the next thing. Either way, it's a thrill and a struggle all the same, a feeling I can't describe.

Those who know, know, right?

LUCIFUGE ROFOCALE

You know, even if one day I would *want* to stop believing in all these things and intellectualize myself right out of faith, I just never could. Not only because of the trust I have in God, but because of the *experiences* I've had with Him. Him, and with this series, so many other divinities, too.

Sure, we could say all those were just my imagination. Stuff I made up for fun, or clout, or because I have an over active imagination. Were anyone to accuse me of this, I would understand perfectly; a lot of what I experience is what I can acknowledge as so astronomically ridiculous and out of this world that to say it's all adult fairytales is a reasonable conclusion for many to come to. That's okay. They can think that.

Because if I hadn't seen what I'd seen and learned what I'd learned, if I'd never had the childlike stubbornness that insisted there *had* to be something more to this rock we're all spinning on, I'd probably feel the same.

However, it's moments like I had before this interview that really make me not just *trust,* but *know,* that there is far more out there. It ruins the concept of faith, in a way. Whereas some especially silly folks would define faith as having the "objective truth" (whatever this means), I define faith that simply: as *trust.* As trust that these entities, like God and His Son and His Spirit and His angels, actually exist, and trust that even if I am broken to pieces, they'll be able to take all the ground up stardust of my being and heal me back to life. Still, as many have no doubt experienced themselves, God is elusive. He doesn't get in your face; He doesn't make huge shows of power to *prove* to you that He exists. He wants you to have that exact *trust,* and so many mystics have described the moment, the Dark Night of the Soul, where it seems all of God's presence has simply *vanished,* as if it were never there. There's always room for doubt and questioning and despair; He wants you to overcome it with that childlike stubbornness, that near *immaturity,* and stick by Him anyway. It's hard, and it hurts, but it's worth it.

Demons do not give a shit about any of this.

By this point, I'd been going through a little tour of the Circles of Hell for quite some time—the mystery rite known as the Qliphoth, which was extrapolated on and developed into a workable path by western occultists out of a concept theorized in Jewish Kabbalah. Much like Christianity stemmed off of Judaism to become its entire own religion, so too did the Qliphoth get drawn out of its roots—as the refuse, the aftermath, the discarded shells of Kabbalah's Sephirot that were not to be used or played with by the scholar-initiate—and into its entire own pathway to spiritual development. However, instead of angels to teach the initiate about unification with God, it would be demons teaching practitioners how to become their own god.

I wanted to be nothing more than a tourist and see what all the fuss was about, but you really can't step in mud without getting your shoes dirty, can you?

To that end, I was finishing one sphere and ready to begin another sphere. Didn't know when or where or how I'd get around to it, but I could feel it: the next stop on this adventure was coming up soon, and I would be pitched into an entirely new world of trials as a result. And one morning, I knew that it was very much time for me to get up, bust out the cards, light the candles, do the whole song and dance, when Lucifuge Rofocale loudly caught my attention and left no room for doubt about it.

You see, I was once again caught up in a bit of sleep paralysis one early morning. It happened from time to time, and I would learn later that it was more common in people who were sleep deprived. (My schedule was not a kind one at the time, I'll say that.) Still, while most of the times the sleep paralysis was just a mis-firing of my own brain, sometimes it could be the result of spirits trying to get one's attention. I asked, almost jokingly, who was around, and I got the most *vivid* answer in my head.

In huge red letters, like the way *You Died* pops up in Dark Souls, was the name *LUCIFUGE RO-FOCALE.* Which is interesting, because while I'd heard of this demon, I'd done absolutely nothing with him and hadn't thought about him since I first came across his name a year before. I found that strange, so I looked more into him—and sure enough, he was the demon ascribed to the next sphere I was about to walk into, Satariel.

I did not know that before I'd looked into him. Once I found that out, it was so bold and in-my-face a message that doubt didn't even have a chance to creep in. There was only awe, shock, and wonder, as well as the knowledge that clearly, *clearly,* there was more out there in this world than just the physical. Maybe we can say the demons are, in fact, responsible for "killing my faith," because it took all room for any doubt right away.

Nonetheless, all that story aside, Lucifuge Rofocale is very cool. Unlike *Lucifer,* which means Light-Bringer, Lucifuge's name implies one that *hides from* or even *obscures* the light. This also matches with his function in the Qliphoth, as his sphere is one of illusions and misdirection. S. Connolly in her *The Complete Book of Demonolatry* describes him as "Lucifer's twin brother," whatever this means, and in other grimoires like *The Grand Grimoire,* which is likely more of a satirical writing along with works like the *Pseudomonarchia Daemonum,* he's considered a demon just a step below Lucifer, who has jurisdiction over worldly wealth of all kinds and is willing to give it to a magician—for a price.

More than just talking to him in Satariel (which was... an experience), I wanted to also talk to him publicly, and to see what he would share. Let's take a look.

So one thing that stuck out to me when I read S. Connolly's description of Lucifuge was that she said he was aligned with the "earthy side of air." Aside from her, some say Lucifuge is associated with

Air like Lucifer, and others say Earth. I decides I'd cover all my bases and get the one drink I knew that combined both: a beer (wheat: earth) brewed with hops (air). Likewise, I had an offering plate of pecans (air), jasmine (which I don't know the element of but just felt right) and red amaranth (a grain: earth). Then I surrounded Lucifuge's card with obsidian, onyx, and garnet, all dark stones that made me think of his lightless, mysterious nature.

After that, I set up the questions, the potential decks Lucifuge might choose, and did my typical set up: the Lord's Prayer to invite God into the space and, with His permission and oversight, allow the Infernal into my space. Granted, Lucifer does have his own space set up in this house, too—and given I was speaking to one of his folk, I felt it was only right to also light some Dragon's Blood for him, say hello, and ask if I could rope Lucifuge into my interview plans.

It started mundanely enough: Lucifer greeting me in his "office," which switched in its guest set up. Sometimes it was only a coffee table and a couple couches in front of his presidential desk, all the books lit up by the cloudy light coming through a big window behind him, and other times it was a huge dining table covered in food and candles and wine, as if he was expecting to entertain many guests. Today, the office couldn't seem to decide whether it was a low-key coffee table day or a dinner party day; it kept flickering between the two.

Eventually, though, after exchanging some pleasantries with Lucifer, his counterpart strolled in. Where Lucifer has short, somewhat curly blonde hair in my understanding of him, Lucifuge appeared to me with straighter, shoulder-length black hair, and eyes as pale as the moon. They both dress in black suits, though Lucifuge had a big black coat with a collar high enough to hide half his face, if he chose. As I talked to them, though, I finished writing down my questions, and I could almost feel the sigh in the room, then heard Lucifuge's voice hover over me like a mist:

"Oh, dear. I have to do something so boring?"

There was a teasing tone in his voice. I clicked my tongue and waved my pencil at him. "Come on, it'll be fun! And it'll lead into the rest of what we're doing later. Please?"

He rolled his eyes and relented, with the Universal Fantasy Tarot his deck of choice. But as I focused on him, I felt it soon enough: that cold prickle on my lower back. He was definitely in the room with me, and sometimes I thought I could catch a glimpse of him in the obsidian ball I set up at the head of his card: the shadow of a man hovering over me, or something mundane like the reflection of my bookshelf suddenly moving just enough to make me think someone was there. And the lights I had on in the room made an effect like a face in the orb: two bright lights for eyes and a stretch of softer light like a jack-o-lantern's toothy smile.

It was trippy, to say the least.

But soon enough, we weren't in Lucifer's office anymore. We were somewhere I'd been with him before, in the guts of Satariel: a dark, rocky cave, not a single light to be seen anywhere. The ground was rough and uneven, making it easy to trip if one didn't feel their way around, and all around us were huge horned figures that wouldn't have been visible at all if not for the pinpricks of light in their eyes. The way their horns and cloak cut a different level of darkness out of their surroundings was only enough to distinguish them when they decided to move. Lucifuge himself went dark for just a moment, going from a man I could see clearly to a silhouette with those two silvery, shiny eyes and a white jack-o-lantern smile. It's how I recognized it in the obsidian later; it was the exact same picture.

"Alright, Lucifuge," I said as we set up somewhere in the cave tunnels—a little enclave where a glowing blue fountain bubbled away. We sat down on the rocks in front of it, on each side, like gate watchers—and now and again, those dark horned figures would walk by and disappear into the water, just evaporating the second they crossed the threshold from cave to fountain. Lucifuge drew his legs up and flashed that maroon can of IPA that I'd given him, and it made it feel as if we were two pals out drinking in some hidden, desolate place, the way one might crack a case of beer with a friend right behind the old, remote liquor store they got it from—but there was that added awe of being in a liminal space here, in the backrooms of the spiritual world. "Let's get started, shall we? First question I got for you is: what was it like when you came into existence? Some say you're not very old, relatively speaking with other demons—charting you to the 18th century or so. Some others say Lucifer made you. So I'm just curious: what was it like? What do you remember? What do you think you came into being for?"

I. WHAT DID YOU COME INTO BEING FOR?

The most fertile marriages can arise from radical changes and sudden shocks.

When change is taking place, the only way to deal with the inevitable problems is to focus on the benefits.

A gilded cage is what we build with our hands. To find our way, we must believe in ourselves and remain focused on our ideals.

He sighed and sipped his beer. "I was made to be a mirror of Lucifer," he said. "If he brings light, I take it away. I put that lamp your Savior talks about under a basket."

"Why?"

"Ah, you'll get to that. Be patient." A crooked smile cracked his pale face. "When people twist their ankle in the dark, they have two options: lay down and die, or get up and limp to any light that might show an exit. To put it simply: the first thing I remember is darkness, and even now, here I sit: in the dark. It's a tiring life sometimes. But a worthy one."

"Huh. Alright." I scratched that answer down, trying to make sense of it—and I think I did, to some extent—but I kept going, hoping something would give me inspiration for the problems I'd really come to solve with him later. "Okay, how about this: I know in the realm of demonolatry, and in the practices of those who engage in the Qliphoth, you're thought to be one of the rulers of Satariel. You talk about the dark, and that's a sphere all about the Divine being hidden and whatnot, so I was wondering: what do you do within that sphere? How do you test a practitioner?"

2. HOW DO YOU TEST A PRACTITIONER?

He smiled, because pulling the Wheel and the Emperor had me understanding his role as lord of the sphere, but it was getting Four of Swords and seeing its description had me in a bit of an "aha!" moment. This deck, I'm telling you, has some of the weirdest and yet most poignant descriptions of the cards.

"Here [Satariel] is a place without God," Lucifuge said. "Without light. Without glittery things for that light to shine off."

"But where I am, God is," I insisted. "And my angel, his name means 'God Hidden in Darkness,' so—"

But then I had a vision of Omemiah

That which has been will be again. The eternal cycles of life dominate destiny.

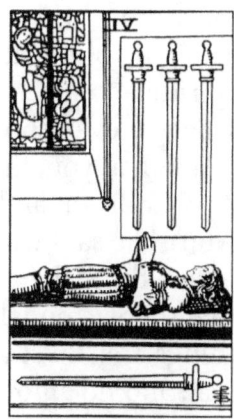

To be strong, we must be seen as such and committed to building what we have promised.

Idols can help us look within our heart, but if we let them shine too much, they can blind us.

standing there—dark and shadowed like these horned creatures that filled the cave—except he wasn't substantial. He was only a shadow, and he was being pulled apart, banished from the space.

Lucifuge shook his head. "Angels don't come here. This isn't their domain. You don't have any protections here."

"Here" being, of course, Satariel—and by extension this very cave. I'll tell you now: when you get sucked into these spaces, you start seeing some truly zany stuff. Colors, shapes, visions of places you've never been, creatures you've never encountered. It's wild.

"You have no protections," he said again. "Are you afraid?"

I shrugged. "Nah. You're here. We're fine. And as I said, where I am, God is." It was easy enough to imagine that Light everyone always says God is: a big ball of it, spooling in my hand and hovering in this massive cave like a little sun. It made the shadows of a tunnel exit that much starker, though, and while I could do it, judging by Lucifuge's stare—the tired look of a mentor with a student that was a bit slow on the uptake—I knew it wasn't something I should do, if I wanted to get the point of the area we were in. I dimmed the light, sat back down, and reviewed the cards and their meanings again.

"Okay, but seriously, I understand—"

"Do you?"

We stared at each other for a minute. Looking back at this interaction now, I also know that Lucifuge recognized something important: I didn't understand the true gravity of what I was saying, about God being wherever I was. I thought I did, but it was still more platitude than earnestly understood wisdom, as I've now come to understand. I wasn't wrong. But I *was* like a math student who gets the right answer with the wrong reasoning.

"Well, yeah," I said eventually. "You're saying we get too focused on the external faces of the Divine that we forget how to find our way even when we feel like we've been abandoned. Isn't that it?"

Close, but that wasn't the full idea. Lucifuge's smile was faint, but the width of his lips made it seem much bigger than it was.

"Sure. Think of it like your little book over there, that Hildegard thing: it's the Via Negativa she talks about. There are times when humanity bathes in light and stumbles in shadow. Can you tolerate being blind? It's my job to test whether that's a yes or no. Contrary to your misconceptions, your spiritual connection and power doesn't get shut off in here. You just don't know where to use them or why you even should.

"Look at you, floundering around with this silly interview series. You'll find no direction from any of your bright and shining figures. You just have to walk, and you'll find your way. Or maybe you won't," he said with a shrug, as if it didn't bother him in the least whether I did or didn't.

One thing there is to appreciate about the Infernal Divine—if you like this sort of thing, I guess—is that there is no false hope when working with them. They are awfully up front about the fact that things aren't just going to magically turn out okay. The threat of failing their tests and tasks are very real, and no amount of faith in the process is going to make things work the way you want without actually putting in the effort to understand and make it so.

"Alright, well, I see what you're saying." I was grumbling a little, and I knew it, but damn—he really chafed the skin off my ass with that call-out. Still, while I continue this series, I have come to understand more of what he was saying, and so I still appreciate the roughness of his answer. "Anyway, okay, so: what is your relationship to Lucifer, then? It seems like you're counterparts somehow, but what's the reason for this?"

3. WHAT IS YOUR RELATIONSHIP WITH LUCIFER?

Knowing how and when to risk is a quality of the far sighted.

Every reaction contains the seed of victory. The warrior who turns away from the struggle has already lost.

Rules and traditions often preserve things that in the past were good, but true wisdom knows when to innovate.

Lucifuge sighed. "Not all go down the straight and narrow path, girl. Some go down the craggy and winding one. But does that mean we just abandon them? Leave no one to scoop them up?

"Lucifer is the lord of these realms. He needs to balance all that Is Not with all that Is in the grand scheme of things—being the antithesis of your God in the collective mind's understanding—and he needs to create a microcosm of that balance here, as a test run for those who refuse the true lessons, where one comes in contact with both Light and Dark and understands them both. Not all are so fond of your God and His realm, His angels—but they can't be overlooked in this enlightenment.

"In short: I am the Devil's Devil. I am made to be darkness so deep, so raw, so empty, that none can escape if they have no solid grasp of themselves."

"Shit. Okay." That was a lot. "Makes sense enough to me! But let me erase a question here and pose a better one: what can we learn from this darkness that you embody, if this is the case?"

4. WHAT CAN WE LEARN FROM THE DARKNESS YOU EMBODY?

"Mm." He sipped the beer again and smiled like a cat. "Light burns—and eventually winks out. When there is no more showering of sparks, no more pomp and circumstance and expensive, hard-won glow—can you still see your purpose?

"The darkness is blackest just after light dies. Do we howl for light again?" As he spoke, I got a vision of just this: of bright fireworks going off, and leaving the surroundings even blacker than they were before, if that was possible—but then my vision adjusted, and I could see even in the dark. "Or do we let our eyes adjust and take us to spots we missed when the light eclipsed them in the deep, dark shadows?"

The answers to the most troubling questions are hidden very close to us in our hearts.

To be strong, we must be seen as such and committed to building what we have promised.

Even after achieving success, our mind must not be distracted from the goal we fought for.

Sure enough, there was a spot in this vision that I never would've noticed if I'd had the cave lit. I would've just kept going towards that tunnel, which seemed like the obvious next steps, and never bothered to look around at these tinier spaces that looked different in the dark: like they were full of little holes and things where treasures could've laid hidden to those who didn't bother to be curious.

"I got'cha. That makes a lot of sense. But now, I gotta ask: what inspires you to work with a practitioner on things like these? I've seen folks work with you before, but given your grimoire entries talk about you finding treasure, I'm curious as to what you work on with folks, and why."

5. WHY WORK WITH PRACTITIONERS ON THESE TYPES OF THINGS?

The answers to the most troubling questions are hidden very close in our hearts.

Too much worry about the future keeps us from enjoying the present.

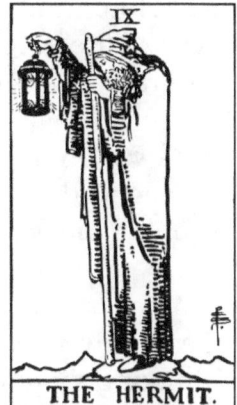

Every answer must be sought in our own soul. Solitude can help us survive.

Lucifuge waved a hand. "Have you ever tried to just enjoy where you are? Yes, riches, treasure—it's all well and good, those things. You humans chase after them like frogs after flies: hapless and stupid-eyed.

"But when you can't see the road ahead, you have no choice but to stop and spend time in the company of one you may have been avoiding: yourself. I quite like watching people run in circles and twist their ankle. The 'aha' they get after all the pain and frustration is lovely."

Someone call St. Ignatius of Loyola, because that... doesn't sound too far at all from his story.

"And the helplessness and hopelessness of failure, too, that sometimes happens—well, that's just amusing," Lucifuge said. "Like watching a toddler hold their breath and think it'll change anything about their situation. All it does is make the adults laugh. Silly things."

Oh, jeez. Demons. They certainly don't hide how they feel about things, that's for sure.

"What do you think of those practitioners that ask you for riches, then?" I couldn't help but think it funny, some of the stuff I'd been reading about Lucifuge. "Some say you'll bargain with people to bring them treasure in return for endless complicated rituals for the rest of their lives, or else they'll lose their soul. I thought that was goofy, but what do you think? About all of it?"

6. DO YOU REALLY BARGAIN TREASURE FOR COMPLICATED RITUALS?

To labor with humility, never thinking we have achieved our goal, is the way to the best results.

The ability to imagine the future isn't enough to change it.

Even after achieving success, our mind must not be distracted from the goal we fought for.

Lucifuge chuckled with me. And the first card he pulled, Eight of Coins, was hilarious in its definition; it was so clear of an answer that I almost wondered if I should've asked him to extrapolate at all. Reading that meaning, it was as Lucifuge was saying:

You can get anything you want if you keep working for it. Seems the fear that you owe me for bringing you riches has tricked you into continuing your work where other enticements would've failed or where you would've given up and grown fat on your poorly won money.

Demons. Seriously. They're so backhanded in their gifts if they know the gift recipient is shit.

"Pissbabies, the most of them," Lucifuge said before I could even properly put all of this into words. "The Infernal Divine—no, all of the Divine, really—are not magical slot machines you can put enough offerings into and guarantee all wishes granted. No, rather, we are something like regular slot machines—the Infernal specifically.

"Throw enough of your life, time, and energy away on trying to game us, and you'll find yourself in wicked, desperate debt. I suppose that's why people think I claim souls if a ritual isn't repeated enough. Because enough fools have bet their souls and lost. Goons, imbeciles. I have no patience for them—only humor when they fall."

"Oh, I see. That makes sense, yeah."

And honestly, I think it serves them right. People always give the Infernal Divine such a shit rap, but really—and honestly—I find this way of thinking about it plenty fair. Are these demons really evil? Really out to swallow us all up? Or do we come to them thinking that, disrespecting them as we ask for their help, and do they simply have no reason to care how we see them if they play along and punish those sorcerers?

Here's a side note for you all. Earlier, before we'd gotten started in this conversation, Lucifuge prodded me a bit. He essentially called me on my claim that I don't "align" with demons, even though I was clearly and obviously happy to be in his and Lucifer's presence. (I will say it'd been a minute since I saw Lucifer, and I jumped on him like a kid jumps on their favorite uncle when I caught him earlier. Did it again when I finally got past the second-to-last sphere of the Qliphoth. I'm not sorry about it.)

I reminded him that Omemiah is "God Hidden in Darkness"—that even if I'm more aligned with angels, my own angel is pretty Infernal-coded—and that's where we got into that separate side conversation involving Omemiah not being able to be in here eventually. Still: I hold that even if demons delight me in some way, that it's more because they're novel and interesting and a great counter-energy to dance off—not because they and I are necessarily cut from the same cloth. I can feel that we're not, even if we seem to be sometimes. There is something else about me—about all humans—that is neither Angel nor Demon.

"So then, tell me," I said. "What do you wish people knew about demons?"

7. WHAT DO YOU WISH PEOPLE KNEW ABOUT DEMONS?

This question may feel like a sudden jumping point, but sometimes there's just nothing else to say to what a spirit told me, y'know? Lucifuge nodded, thought about it, then pulled his cards and spoke.

"Even if people can't predict us, or if they see us as dangerous—as 'wild animals' as some have put it—we are consistent in our principles all the way to the end. People always just make a fool of themselves assuming what those principles are. Infernal doesn't mean bad. There is no bad. And there is no good. There is only strategy—and not many people like our strategy."

"That's interesting! I like that idea a lot. But alright, well, we're down to our last few questions now, so Lucifuge, could you tell me how you see yourself?"

When we defend what we believe in, we must do so in person, advancing with no hesitation to the enemy.

However bitter a conflict may be, however tragic the outcome, we must always stand up for our principles.

Every reaction contains the seed of victory. The warrior who turns away from the struggle has already lost.

8. HOW DO YOU SEE YOURSELF?

THE HANGED MAN.

In search of an ideal, we can discover our best resources—as well as our worst.

What a surprise to draw the Hanged Man.

"I am a straightforward man," he said. "I want what I want, and I've tumbled down many holes in the dark to find it. Dogged. I suppose that's how you could describe me."

"Huh! Interesting. How do you want to be seen, then?"

9. HOW DO YOU WANT TO BE SEEN?

"I do my work. Perfectly." He had such a sharp look on his face, which matched the Seven of Swords he pulled. "None can say I don't serve here without anything short of utmost skill."

"Fair, fair, alright."

I don't normally think of Seven of Swords when I think of that kind of thing, but I guess this card does signal that in this specific deck. Once again, it became clear to me why Divinity chooses one deck over another: the interpretations they know I'll look at are very different.

Logic and perseverance can help us overcome seemingly impossible obstacles.

"How about any last messages, then? Before we skip off and chat some more down here?"

10. ANY LAST MESSAGES?

The happiness we experience in daily domesticity is greater than that of the king who won the war.

Of all the things I could've pulled, Ten of Cups was probably last on my list of expected cards.

Lucifuge shrugged. "You must learn to sit in the present. People must learn to be present. Even if we have to steal your sight from you, you can't chase the shiny dreams in the distance; we will teach you to sit still and wait."

Rather than sit in a cave any longer, by that point, we'd suddenly come to a sea made of reddish black water full of golden sparkles. Even the sands of the sea's beach were full of gold. In the water was a dragon-woman of some kind; she had a body all black, blue, and starry like the night sky, with wings and horns on a bald head. It was pretty cool.

"You won't die of a little confusion," Lucifuge said as we sat down on the beach.

"Stop wasting your life moving towards goals that could be a mirage. Spend more time thinking and developing eyes that see in the dark."

We sat on that beach for another few moments before I nodded.

"Alright, alright—I think I got the answers I needed here. Both for the interview and our project together." Because damn, was a lot of this oddly applicable to me personally. "I'll call this interview to a close, then, and we can chat a bit more separately. But thank you, Lucifuge Rofocale, for sharing this bit of your wisdom with everyone else! I appreciate it!"

He smiled, and then he was gone, as if we'd never had that conversation. As it was, I can't really remember what I did in Satariel now—but I know I wrote it down. Believe me when I say a thing like that whole journey wouldn't have gone unrecorded.

Still, I don't know. There's something refreshing about demons. They just don't care to play the game we all do: the game of trying to pretend humans aren't worth the criticism. That's ironic if you think about it; so much of Christianity focuses on how *wretched* and *weak* and *pathetic* and *sinful* we are, but hear a demon say that we actually do kind of suck and suddenly those same Christians singing *Amazing Grace* are all up in arms about it. How? Why? It's fine to acknowledge that people can be bad as much as good, that being good is a thankless (and therefore unattractive) effort in a world that seems to reward being bad. To act otherwise is to lie to oneself.

Nonetheless, all I know is that in a crazy way, I'll almost miss this whole journey when it's over. It's been a wild one, to say the least.

VESNA

After so many more theologically and mentally heavy interviews, I felt I was due for a break. Not from doing the series, of course; my workaholic tendencies would torture me if I started lagging too hard on the weekly upkeep. But I did want an interview I thought would be more comforting, and even though Stribog made it pretty clear that the Slavic gods had a "fun" little side quest for me, I just had to reach back out anyway.

After all, I'd spoken to most of the main family so far: Kresnik, Veles, Morana. There was one last entity I hadn't spoken to (publicly, at least) that made up the family picture in Slovenian-centered Slavic folklore: the Snake Princess.

Vesna.

Something interesting about Vesna (or, in the male iteration, Vesnik) is that while the modern Slovenian word for spring is *pomlad,* the poetic way of referring to the season is still *vesna.* And in other languages, like Ukrainian, it just is the standard word used in everyday speech. As a result, I'm guessing I don't need to tell you what Vesna is the goddess of.

It always is funny, though, to talk about how Kresnik and Vesna are married, how Veles and Morana (Also called the Snake King and Dark Queen in the folklore) are Vesna's parents—because you *know* every Polish, Russian, Czech, or whatever other Slavic group will come running to insist that this isn't true, that actually *Devana* married Veles, that actually Kresnik is Jarilo or Dažbog and that I'm talking straight out my back end. This is because the mess that is *pan-slavism* (the idea that the Slavic gods and religion was standard across all Slavic tribes) has a chokehold on a lot of Slavic reconstructionist pagans, and the idea that other tribes, countries, or even single villages might have their own ideas of how these gods worked together just does not compute.

Which is silly, because *no* pantheon works the way modern neopagan reconstruction movements want them to work. Not the Greek pantheon. Not the Norse. Not the Germanic. Not the Roman. Why else would all the myths and stories be so disparate for the same gods? *Because they came from different villages or time periods.* Divinity is weird, and the way people perceive Divinity is even weirder, because Divinity is not so easily comprehended by the human mind; that's why the trope of madness brought on by divine and eldritch beings exists.

But anyway, I've met Vesna before when talking to Kresnik in my private affairs. She, and most springtime goddesses I've spoken to, are not nearly so cute and fluffy and sweet as people would think them to be. There's an edge to her of a sickle freshly sharpened after a long winter, of the still-crisp air in the early mornings, of the hazy, drunken sunlight in the early morning and bell-clear twittering of birds. Vesna, who comes up from the underworld upon the descent of her mother, who drags herself up from slumber with seed in hand, is the raw force of spring—and this interview tells us exactly what that means for her.

So let's take a look.

How could I invite a spring goddess and not put some spring razzle dazzle on the table? To set up for this, I found myself heading to the store on the way home from the gym for only one item: a small box of strawberries. Of course, that one item turned into more like four when I realized I had an idea for what to do with some homemade bowtie pasta from a previous demonstration video, but that's neither here nor there.

I found myself setting the table with things that made me think of spring the most: those strawberries and a cup of herbal tea as a gift for Vesna, a green candle, all my mushroom stones and a few others (red and purple jasper, carnelian, sunstone, pink amethyst, and moss agate), and some of the flowers growing near my house. There were still giant daffodil heads out, so I took three of those and a few sprigs of dandelion and grape hyacinth. It looked very pretty around that candle, and between that and the windows letting all that spring breeze through at high noon, I was easily able to slip into the zone for talking to Vesna.

In fact, it was so easy that as I was finishing the Lord's Prayer and asking Him to help me find Vesna, I got a very vivid image of myself plopping into a field of clover and wildflowers. It was soft and cool and hidden under the shade of some trees, but I noticed we were also near a dirt road, and that stretching up to the sky behind us was one huge and barren mountain—Mount Triglav, a famous mountain in Slovenia. I recognized it immediately for all those crags and snowy spots. It looked so strange against the blue sky, like it'd been painted as a theater set backdrop.

Sitting in the grass a little ways away was Vesna. Her long blonde hair flowed down her back, and a red embroidered band circled her forehead. Her clothes were white and red, too: a white dress with embroidered red patterns, like a Ukrainian vyshyvanka. She smiled like a big sister when I saw her, and I scrambled over to greet her.

"Vesna!" I could even feel the coolness of the air in that place; it was so distinct from the air and the breeze in my own house. It tasted different, y'know? "Hi! Welcome! Thank you for visiting!"

She laughed, and then we got settled picking a tarot deck for her to use. I realized soon enough that since the deck my good friend Mimi got me as a gift, the Slavic Mythology Deck, had no booklet, I could use any booklet with it that Vesna wanted—a funny way of using the other decks God owns without really using them.

Once we had the deck sorted, I started in the place that just felt right: "Alright, Vesna, *kako si*? How are you?"

0. How Are You?

Grief and loss of what our future was made of. Hard to restart. Resources help. Don't dwell on the past.

I wasn't expecting a grim card like the Five of Cups, but maybe I should've been. God said there would be some harsh lessons to learn from this interview, and I thought it was because I originally had a harsh impression of Vesna; when we'd first met after I started talking to Kresnik, she seemed suspicious of me and a little aloof. Whatever that was about, though, seemed to have passed; she didn't have any hint of that suspicion here.

"It's all decaying," Vesna said as she looked all around. Her face crumpled as she waved at the grasses and the flowers, which looked perfectly fine to me. "Everything we've worked to build, this garden we've grown together, us and the other gods, your God—it's decaying. Things change, I know, but it hurts to watch such a harsh change.

"You all did this. You must fix this. For what should the innocent suffer because you've all forgotten your roots? The weather has been harsh here. It'll kill the crops. It'll hurt the citizens—the bugs and birds and people. Find a way forward. Find it."

"Oh, jeez. Yeah, that's fair." I thought of the video my cousin sent from Slovenia earlier that month: of a ton of snow falling right after a very warm day. *Kill the crops,* indeed. Everything was already beginning to bloom before that frost ripped through. "It's a mess, I know. We're trying. But to that end, I guess we should start here with the questions: what is the natural rhythm people should be following in spring?"

1. What is the Natural Rhythm to Follow in Spring?

Vesna sighed. "People think they can just snap from summer to winter and back again. No wonder the world's seasons are starting to respond in kind."

"Oh, wait—damn! You're right! We do just have a weird in-between these days, don't we?" I scribbled that realization down in my notebook, and it made me wonder: beyond the science of climate change, was the constant back-and-forth of the seasons a reflection of our polarity? Or were we becoming more polarized, more extreme, in alignment with the weather? "Okay, sorry—you were saying?"

With a nod, Vesna continued: "This, springtime, is not a time for external action as much as one might think. Now is a time to defrost, to melt. That means getting the old muck off you. Swallow your pride and let your compassion and joy and fellowship thaw you after a deep freeze.

"You must grow flowers before you grow fruits. You must be gentle and vulnerable, sharing, before you come into

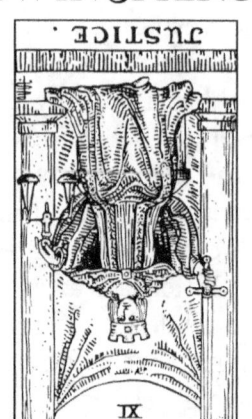

Repression of things you feel guilty about. Trying to justify them. Forgive yourself so you can move on.

A holder of space. Perceptive, intuitve, nurturing, warm. A container for healing. Use your intuition.

your own glory and bounty. Be fertile now—ready to let things germinate in their own time. For the love of all things, slow down."

"Fair, fair," I said, not being slow in the least as I wrote all this down. Though I will say: it hit. We never give ourselves time to transition from one thing to the next, do we? Never do we have time to just sit and actually soak up all that happened before we move on to make more things happen. That must take a toll. I know it's taken a toll on me plenty, given how I never build breaks or transition times in for my own schedule—leaving me always rushing, always feeling behind, because I never have a chance to catch my breath or fully absorb anything that's happening. "Alright, then—how can we reconnect to that rhythm? And the land?"

2. HOW CAN WE RECONNECT TO THIS RHYTHM?

A major transition, likely filled with sadness. Know the road ahead is the best one for you. New opportunities. Be at peace and surrender.

Trying to get away with something underhanded. It may or may not be necessary. Reactivity is not helpful. Break inherited patterns. Impulsivity.

In between her answers, I kept seeing snatches of other things: the doorway of a dark, abandoned temple opening up into the great sea, which I was seeing from the inside of that shadowy space. There were people riding through on horseback to what looked like war, maybe the Crusades or something. More flowers, more trees, more birds. I even saw Vesna at one point, with a gray skull for a face that slowly filled in, as if her flesh was blooming into her like the grass came back from brown patches after a long winter. That was something else. Finally, though, I made sense of her answer, and it was honestly a surprise, the thing she suggested.

"If you need to sneak around," she said, "sneak around. "Do it. Reclaim your rights in any way necessary. Advocate where you can for things that will remind you of the world before you bulldozed it—but if you have no choice, don't ask, just take. Steal the damn time at your little human jobs if it means the sun actually touches your face. Take the extra minute on your walks. Disconnect yourselves from the screens and phones and whatever other nonsense."

In between her speaking, I got images of a person walking through a city, all gray and boxy and dead, with the occasional weed desperately and defiantly adding a touch of green between the cracks.

"Go outside!" Vesna snapped, her arm whipping out as she waved it around like aggravated Slavic women tend to do. "Touch dirt! Plant carrots! Watch the bees! Rebel! Why are you even asking me so silly a question for? If you want to reconnect to the land, you have to love the land—and love each other, and let the land love you! Plant gardens! Share! Give back what you don't need! It won't happen in a day. One walk won't fix you. But remember: flowers. Take the time to be nourished and grow those flowers."

"Alright, yeah!" There's something about that kind of gung-ho energy that, whether from Man or God, gets you going all the same. "I hear you. Thank you for that advice; that's some good stuff. But then, what can we learn from the season of spring itself?"

3. WHAT CAN WE LEARN FROM SPRING ITSELF?

ACE of SWORDS.

Expansion of mental energy. Cut through illusion and confusion. New shifts. Challenging the status quo, curiosity, exploring.

THE MAGICIAN.

Being on the right path. Making visions reality. Move into your power. Make the most of your resources; manifest the future.

Vesna plucked a blade of grass from the ground. "You know when you see plants appear where you didn't plant them each spring?"

Instantly, I thought of all the volunteer chamomile that came out of nowhere the year after I planted the first batch. And all the Goddamn daffodils that I can't get rid of in my herb patch no matter how many times I dig them up and softball pitch their bulbs to hell.

"It'll always happen," Vesna said. "Life takes opportunities and will do its damndest to flourish wherever it's able and allowed to. And then it advertises—brightly!—what it wants to achieve. It achieves it by attracting the right things to help: a bee to a flower, a bird to a berry.

"Spring is about announcing intentions, like the trumpet of the daffodils. It's about bold declarations of future success. So grow! Grow as big and bold and stubborn as you can, whether in a sidewalk crack or an orchard."

"Oh my God, I love that. Vesna, you're making me appreciate spring in a way I never thought I would." She smiled as I bumped her shoulder with mine, and it's true: I never used to like spring because of all the bugs and pollen and mucky weather between then and summer, but this year, it seems like I'm finding all kinds of things to love: the herbs flourishing in the patches that desperately need a weeding, the sun, the breeze, the blue sky, the birdsong, the longer days. It's so nice. "So, now, let's get into some behind-the-scenes stuff. From what I understand, you come back when Morana drowns. What does that look like? What happens?"

4. WHAT HAPPENS WHEN YOU RETURN FROM NAV?

Vesna twirled another blade of grass around her finger. While she stayed silent there, I got another image from within that dark temple, only this time, a woman—Vesna—was out there knee-deep in the water, wandering towards the horizon. It was like she was hypnotized, or dizzy after a long sleep. Then, from the sky, came Morana, all dressed in black furs with black inky hair, and they hugged each other there in the water. It struck me then that this was actually not a temple, really, but the entryway of Nav, the Slavic underworld.

"It looks like knowing that my mother and I cannot be in the same place, at the same time," Vesna said. "Not so much anymore, not fully. We get only moments between seasons. But I know there's only a little time to grieve and chat before I go back to where I'm needed.

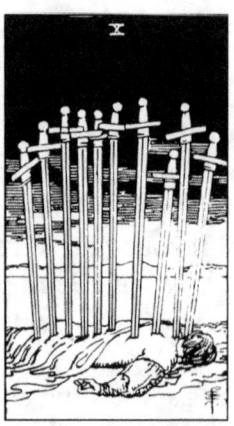

Disaster. A situation building for some time. Rug pulled from underneath. Loss. Reconnect with yourself.

ACE of SWORDS.

Expansion of mental energy. Cut through illusion and confusion. Shifts. Anti-status quo, curiosity, exploring.

"It looks like realizing that it'll be a minute yet before my husband fully awakens from his own fall, and that I have to pave the way and bear the brunt of the work to start. But it's also a chance for newness. Color. Life. The grief passes, and the fun begins."

"Got'cha. That sounds nice. But then, where does your realm end and Kresnik's begin? Where does spring actually blend into summer?"

5. WHERE DOES SPRING BLEND INTO SUMMER?

As I shuffled and Vesna started weaving answers, I got the image of her hand clapped hard in his, as if supporting him and pulling him back into existence. A rope was tied around their hands like a handfasting cord.

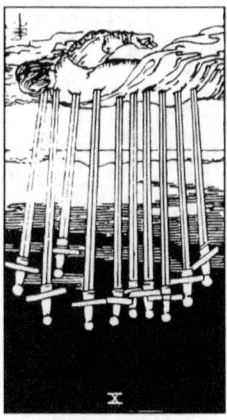

Arrival at an all time low. It doesn't feel good, but it gives you what you need to finally move on. Change is easier when we're desperate. Welcome new shifts.

"It's dark there, in the underworld," Vesna said. The image she gave me was that of her peering so sweetly into the face of her husband. "It gets to the point where my flowers call too strongly for him—where the grass smells too sweet, and the bees buzz too loud—that he realizes he can't sleep any longer. That he won't return to himself until he casts off the dark and faces his truth and his duties as king of the sun and summer. Then he takes my hand and enjoys the fruits that come of my labors, all those flowers. He is welcomed home."

That was so cute. You know I was punching air as I was witnessing all this, hearing it. I said as much, and after gushing about it with her for a second, I moved on.

"How do you go about waking spring up when you get back here?"

6. HOW DO YOU WAKE SPRING UP?

Vesna didn't even pick any cards for this. She waved around at all the grass and flowers.

"I clap," she said. "I bang pots and pans. I shake the grass out of their sleep and scare the seeds into growing with all my noise, lest I catch them being lazy. And then all join me: birds and bees and trees, making noise! Yes, they know when I'm home," and as she said this, I had an image of her bursting from her hut on Velika Planina and huffing at all the spirits of the grass and clover caught sleeping in the just-thawing earth, "and they know I know they've been lazing about too long. *Se razbudite, vse!* Wake up, wake up!"

"Ah, nice! I love that idea." Something tells me the chaos folk will be validated to hear about that. Gotta love a good pots-and-pans cleanse. "Okay, okay, how about this? I understand there are a lot of different views about who you are, what with Vesna the female and also Vesnik, the male version of spring, and then also the idea that Vesna and Vesnik are the names of a type of nature spirit in general, so on. What do you think of all these different ideas about you?"

7. THOUGHTS ON THE DIFFERENT WAYS PEOPLE PERCEIVE YOU?

Too harsh and less understanding. Frustrated by others' expressions of emotions. Sliding into coldness. Find balance within.

Someone with a lot of energy and passion but no direction. Needing a healthy outlet, else risking chaos. Building new things.

Vesna tucked her knees into her chest and peered at me with eyes as deep and dark as a massive, clean lake. "You humans and your human minds," she said. "They stretch in such strange and obscene ways. And then they don't match the image someone else makes and they get so upset. Why? You understand we are concepts as much as folk, no?"

"What—really? I'm surprised to hear you say that."

Vesna smiled. "I am the heart of spring. Your human minds can't easily or fully understand that, and that's okay—that's why I come as I come, to whoever perceives me—but how can you get so mad that I, of spring, might be a man one time and a woman the next? Are you mad that not all the flowers look the same, too?

"I am made of spring, by spring, for spring; I look and do and act as I need for you all to understand me and get to helping me with my work of waking the land faster."

"That makes a lot of sense, yeah. Thank you for clarifying! Though I guess that does answer all my personal questions, so with that: how do you see yourself?"

8. HOW DO YOU SEE YOURSELF?

"Mmm. I'm good at what I do. Timely, too. I know that things take time to grow good roots and strong leaves before flowers can come. I'm patient and tolerate no nonsense from the sleepy dirt. Up, I say! Time to work!"

There was a good mood to her words, a spunk, that brightened the mood even more in this little space of flowers and fruits. "I see, I see! How do you want to be seen, then? So many folks seem to think that spring goddesses are all sweet and gentle and nice, but is that the case for you?"

Driven and methodical. Rigorous routine and trusting the process. Being okay with not seeing instant results. Discipline and good habits.

9. HOW DO YOU WANT TO BE SEEN?

Arrival and completion. Financial success and harmony in relationships. Think long term about future generations and your legacy. Consider what you're leaving behind.

"No, no—I'll smack the person that thinks I'm some sweet and meek little cow. No, I am a thinker, a planner, a builder. I set the table and count the plates; I make sure that all are fed and that seeds will come to set the table again. I am in the present, but also in the future, and my legacy is long; I will endure forever."

"Ooh. I love that. What a way of phrasing all that! Thank you, Vesna—but now, before we wrap up, do you have any last messages for people?"

10. ANY LAST MESSAGES?

"Yes," she said, her face gentle. "Just one thing: love this world, for it, too, is your neighbor."

What! What a thing to say. I got the sense she was trying to use language that the modern folk, mostly Christians, would recognize, and it made it all made sense: this world is a neighbor. It cares for us even when we antagonize it when it feeds and clothes and shelters us. So what are we doing, not being neighborly to it in kind?

"Alright, Vesna, thank you! I'll take that one to heart. For now, though I think it's time to go—so I'll say goodbye for now, and I hope to see you around! *Se vidimo!*"

With one last smile, Vesna faded back into her world of spring grasses and birds and bunnies. I stepped out, back into my own world, and sighed. There was just something nice about a time with these gods that, for all intents and purposes, are something of my ancestors, too. Family, old family. Interviews like these, especially with Slovenian-specific iterations like Kresnik and Vesna, remind me of how it feels to visit my parents every other week for laundry, or to meet up at family gatherings and say hello and catch up.

And now, as I write this, and the springtime air is crisp and the birds are singing so early in the morning, I can't help but feel that kind of peace again. Granted, New England is always a touch too cold and then a touch too hot within the same week, but it feels like the world is waking up again. Feels like *I'm* waking up, too. And it's nice, knowing there are beings like Vesna who make it their purpose to see to it that it happens, in any way they can.

SAMAEL

It may be time to discuss UPG as we come into this interview. In fact, one might (very reasonably) say that this entire interview series thus far has been a large dose of UPG. This acronym stands for *unverified personal gnosis,* and it refers to the things people hear, see, or generally learn with entities that isn't backed up by other spiritual sources and/or holy texts. This may sound dangerous, and that's because it is: there is a nearly invisibly fine line between actual spiritual connection and bona fide delusion when it comes to dealing with forces, energies, and entities you cannot physically see and cannot have tested by other people around you.

However, this does not mean that everything one receives by UPG is untrue. Think about it: once upon a time, everything the prophets of the Bible had revealed to them was UPG before it was written down. Every vision of St. Hildegard's was UPG before their content was taken before a council of other holy people and verified. Every myth (and version of each myth), every story and spark of divine inspiration and bit of religious theory and philosophy, had to be tested, proved, or at least repeated enough to go from fiction to fact. So it *is* possible to receive revelation that is True in some sense even if it hasn't been said before—but many people don't do the rigorous testing and cross referencing required to start making sense of the many things they're seeing and hearing, or do their due diligence in catching any contradictions or other issues that might appear and need hammering out.

Hell, a lot of people can't tell what the actual defined mythos of a deity is and what is just part of a fictional story written in modern day for fun. The allure of a world where Persephone is a cute girl-boss getting away from her evil helicopter mom and getting with her super Goth corporate man is apparently pretty strong, even if entirely out of line with the established myth of the gods themselves and destroys the entire (and arguably decently feminist) sociopolitical reason the original myths exist in the first place.

#Girlboss though. Or something.

Anyway, I bring all that up because the spirit we're looking at today is a little sticky. Some traditions of Christianity pin him as one that still reigns in heaven, in charge of the fifth circle of it. Jewish tradition (and several *other* Christian traditions) has him being the king of demons and husband of Lilith, forever fighting with Archangel Michael. All in all, however, his name means "The Venom (or Severity) of God," which, fallen angel or not, is a mask carved of God's name that deals with some seriously nasty stuff. After all, where Azrael is the angel of the departed, this angel is the one thought to be the angel of death—in that he goes and causes the calamity that puts Azrael on the cleanup crew for souls afterwards. It's the dirty work Samael does: the brutal, punishing things that people fear.

However, since there exist traditions of him being both fallen *and* still in heaven, that means there are options of how we approach this angel. And in my personal UPG, I understood this to mean that Samael was the *name* of the entity I'd been talking to all this time—while Lucifer was the *title* he wore when escaping heaven for a time and managing all the activities of hell. It seemed that I had a hint of confirmation of this theory after my conversation with Haniel, too (though can you confirm UPG with more UPG?), and it makes perfect sense to me. After all, Lucifer never was a name in the Bible, but a title extrapolated from the term "bright and morning star" (used to refer both to Babylonian king Nebuchadnezzar in Isaiah 14:12 and Jesus in Revelation 22:16). And if we *really* want to go crazy with the UPG, there are even some folks who consider Lucifer *to be* Jesus.

Religion, y'know? It gets pretty wild out there, with all the theories and ideas and beliefs. For now, let's move on before we find yet another layer of this rabbit hole.

What was interesting about this interview was that I really had no idea what to do in terms of offerings. Yeah, angels don't usually take offerings, but Samael is more than just an angel, and his element in S. Connolly's *The Complete Book of Demonolatry* pinned him as associated with air (just like Lucifer). As such, I went looking for a good drink to give to him, and I found myself stumped.

So I asked God what His venom was like, and He gave me a picture of some thick, black liquid. Black walnut was what came to my mind first, which is weird, because walnut is associated with fire, not air. But as I went looking in the liquor store that day, I found myself in the section I thought would have that and saw something else: black sambuca. Sambuca is an Italian anise liquer, often drank as is after dinner with a coffee bean or three added (known as "con la mosca"—*with the fly*).

It was perfect. Anise is associated with air, and this stuff is so thick and dark. Like drinking black death. When I first tried it, though, I loved it because anise is the main flavoring in black licorice, and I rarely get to enjoy licorice. It also makes sense that it's an after-dinner drink, because it reminded me of a less hardcore Jägermeister, which I keep in the freezer as a digestive when I've eaten something especially heavy and stomach-turning.

So once I was set with the sambuca and coffee beans, the green candle (green being a color of poison in my view), and the necessary stones and sigil card from Travis McHenry's Angel Tarot (not Demon Tarot!), I was able to settle into meditation pretty easily. Sometimes it takes a long time for me to figure out where I am or what I'm doing when I start, but I ended up sucked into a scene not long after I closed my eyes. I guess it makes sense, since I'd already been talking to God beforehand and found myself already pulled into the first layer of Heaven, the stereotypical layer with the pretty gold gate and the clouds and the picturesque golden light everywhere.

But in that layer, I was met with a real mean mug: Samael, who, when I greeted him and hopped over, had such a deep scowl that it looked like his face was carved out of marble. He had the golden curly hair I might've expected, but given that I still saw him as Lucifer to some extent, I wondered why his face looked so different: so much harder, bulkier. It was the difference in facial structure between Lee Pace as Thranduil (Lucifer) and Sylvester Stallone as Rocky (Samael), if you know what I mean. He was wearing a simple grey robe, his feathered wings dingy and grey too, and he roughly beckoned me to follow him until we left the cheery, stereotypical version of heaven and ended up in something like the old hearth of an isolated cottage.

The floor was made of dirt, the walls of red brick. Herbs hung across one side of the wall, over a bunch of pots and pans and other tools, and in the roaring fire of the hearth were tons of glowing coals. On the table, Samael threw down a huge dead pig oozing black slime; it seemed like it was half decayed already. I still don't really know what that pig was about. What I do know is that I took a seat at the table beside it, and so did someone else: Michael, who positioned his seat by the door and sat backwards in it, giant forearms draped over the top of its plain wooden back. It seemed like he was both guarding the door and keeping me from getting too deep into the space at the same time, and for the whole interview, he didn't really talk—just watched, sometimes giving away how he felt about the conversation with the grimaces and half smiles.

That fireplace was weird, though. It was an infinite space in there. When I peered inside, I didn't see anything cooking; hell, I didn't even see any fire. I saw a wasteland of charred bones, with one skeleton all the way in the back, the cloudy grey horizon washing it out. It looked like it was trying to cut its own leg bone off to escape being stuck under all the burned, tangled corpses. But even if there wasn't any fire in there, I could tell right away it was hot—the kind of heat that sets things on fire as soon as they cross the threshold.

Samael pushed the coals around with a fire poker, then chose the Herbcrafter Tarot as his deck of choice. As I sat back, I couldn't help but ask one question before we got started.

"So, Samael, again, I appreciate you inviting me down here. But before I start asking all my questions, I'm just so curious: *are* you Lucifer?"

It really felt like he didn't want to answer at first. Like the idea made him sour. But I focused on the question, and soon I got the words just snapping directly into my head:

"No, I'm not Lucifer," he said. "I don't go by that name here. In this hell, I am the Punisher. The Destroyer. I melt all things clean. I stoke the fires of purgation. I am Samael—one above all concept of Mercy, yet shackled by it by force of my Father."

Oh. That was a loaded answer—especially describing Heaven as Hell. I glanced back at Michael, who seemed to think the same thing with how he watched Samael with a hard glitter in his eye. All the while, a line from an Avenged Sevenfold song, *Beast and the Harlot*, popped into my head—the one about *serving above* or being a *king below*. It seemed that was how Samael was describing his duality in both Heaven and Hell. Given Samael said he doesn't go by the name Lucifer *here,* as in, in *Heaven,* then I took it as a hint that these different names weren't just names, but also alter egos—that they were like keys unlocking this angel's ability to access different spaces with different faces. So with that bit of information, I tucked into my first real question I had written down in my notebook.

"Alright, alright, I see what you're getting at. But let's start, then! Gotta say—I'm surprised you chose the Herbcrafter's Tarot. It's such a cute deck; I didn't think you'd go for herbs and flowers."

Samael only smiled, but what a dark and rueful smile it was. He hovered by the rack of pots and pans and waited for me to talk. He was barefoot, his clothes all smudged with soot, and he crossed his arms as he watched me shuffle my cards.

"So, you know, you mention Hell... and I gotta say, I'm curious. What is your relationship with the Infernal Divine? A lot of demonolaters honor you and say you're not in Heaven anymore, but then others say you are. It's confusing. Got any clarification for me?"

1. WHAT IS YOUR RELATIONSHIP WITH THE INFERNAL DIVINE?

Taking on new re-
sponsibilities. Proud
to do one's part.
Choosing reliable al-
lies during hard work.
Flexible, willing, and
strong. Playfulness.
Protecting growth.

What was funny was that Samael only wanted one card for every answer, and yet *boy*, did he talk. He, like most angels, seemed to use the cards more as anchoring points for all the words they just funneled directly into my head.

"I draw boundaries between Heaven and Hell," he said, his voice rough and raspy, "and in that way, I also ride between those boundaries." Samael's smile slipped as he continued. "Like pairs to like. I cannot command armies of darkness with a face of angelic light—even if that light is radioactive, sulfuric. But I bring light to dark places, just as I bring venom to gardens. I destroy: in all places, all capacities. The way for me to destroy with the Infernals is to masquerade as an angel of light."

He waved a hand there, a mischievous half-grin splitting his face. It was an obvious reference to Paul in 2 Corinthians 11:14: *And no wonder, for Satan himself masquerades as an angel of light.* (Very Lucifer coded, I think.)

"The way for me to destroy with the angels," he continued, that grin withering, "is to simply be an angel."

As he talked, I'd kicked my feet up on that table, my heels settling next to the rotting pig head. "You don't seem to like your job very much."

He scowled. "All the love goes to He Who is Like God," he said, with a dismissive wave to Michael, who sucked his teeth from across the room. "To God's Strength, and God's Fire. What love does God's Venom get? A wicked mask, and a rueful wearer—that is what I am. When I wear other titles—even just The Adversary—I feel lighter."

"Ah, got'cha. No, that makes sense." And it was also insanely fascinating. Angels, man. They have such a personality to them under the trappings of their masks. Makes you wonder. "Okay, okay—speaking of the Adversary, how do you go about performing that role? Being the Adversary?"

2. HOW DO YOU PERFORM THE ROLE OF ADVERSARY?

Samael shrugged. "I have fun where I can. Make a game, take some bets. Michael there's won a fair share of bets—lost a fair share, too."

He and Michael shared this weird smile, like brothers with a long gambling streak between them.

"He doesn't have much faith in Man, it seems," Samael continued with a chuckle, which made Michael roll his eyes. "But I am Venom. I dissolve things. All things: men's resolve, and men's delusions. You've tasted the poison of Samael yourself, have you not?"

In which, he was referencing the third sphere of the Qliphoth, called *Samael*. I had, in fact, already taken a bad tumble down through that sphere. A very bad tumble.

"I test boundaries," he went on after I gave him a look. "God is curious, you see—and He sends me to do field tests."

"Uh-huh." There was a lot of implication in that idea, and it reminded me of what Haniel said, about God having secrets. "Alright. I like it! Seems interesting, to say the least. But what do you think of your status as an angel, especially

Balance on the edges
of depth and light-
ness. Many skills
called to task at once.
Blending edges of
grief and joy. Levity.

a fallen one? People seem to have mixed opinions on who you are and what's going on with you in terms of being in Heaven or Hell. I'd love to get that pinned down, if you're willing to talk about it."

3. ARE YOU A FALLEN ANGEL OR REGULAR ANGEL?

Be vulnerable, yet strong. Nurture love and compassion. See beauty and abundance in every stage of life. Healing the heart heals the world. Create, love, play.

Samael's eyes fell to the ground. He crossed his arms, gripping them as if reliving something uncomfortable, and then he sighed.

"Mercy is a prison, too," he whispered as I shuffled. Then, when I pulled the Empress, of all things, he reiterated: "This mask is heavy. Unbearably so. As my own creature, I wanted to do more than it gave me the authority to do. So yes, I fell: yes, I took human wives, and later other wives. I made things, instead of destroying them.

"But this mask is spiteful." His face crumpled into a scowl. "Inescapable. So the things I made ended up destroyed anyway, by others. By God Himself. As for why I'm not with the others—Semyaza, Azazel, Ananiel, all of them," he said, pointing that scowl at Michael as he rattled off the names, "I can only say that Mercy is just as powerful a force as Severity. And sometimes just as damning. I am still in Heaven, yes—but at what cost?"

Ooh. Mercy as a prison. That was an interesting idea. I don't know much about Jewish Kabbalah—honestly, not much more than is necessary to know how to identify it in all the commercialized occult things floating around New Age sections of bookstores—but what I do know is that Mercy (Chesed) in the Tree of Life is the force that keeps Severity (Geburah) from going off the rails. It's also something we see in so many other religious folks' writings, like C.S. Lewis, who once said that *mercy, without justice, becomes unmerciful.* Maybe there's more to that bond than just balance.

"I think I understand what you're getting at," I said as I tapped the pencil to the notebook. Looking over my questions, I nodded and kept going. "Okay, okay, yeah. If we're talking about Mercy, Chesed, then that brings me to this question: what are your duties as Chief of the Fifth Heaven? I know Paul got up to the Third Heaven, which is cool. But what's going on in your domain there?"

4. WHAT ARE YOUR DUTIES IN THE FIFTH HEAVEN?

1. Let love in. Soften dry and brittle wounds. Welcome genuine connection. Allow yourself to be drawn in by what you love. When we reach out with a gentle, yet steadfast hand, harmonious union follows. Approach partnership with kindness and emotional stability. Experience mutuality.

2. Live by the rhythms of earth. Work slowly and steadily towards a goal. Plant for generations to come. Knowing nature is key to knowing oneself. Patience, strength, faith in one's work.

Knowing Samael's name and Geburah both connected to God's severity, I looked up Geburah too, just so I could get a better ballpark estimate of what the hell it even was and what a Kabbalist might be doing with it. I will say here: this is part of Jewish mysticism, which really isn't something people can or should initiate into without at the *very least* the careful supervision and permission of a rabbi, and which many say shouldn't be touched at all because Judaism itself is closed, so keep that in mind.

Though I will draw this line in the sand: actually *practicing* Kabbalah is not the same as learning about it. You can learn about whatever the hell you want from whatever resources are available to you (be it private resources with permission or public resources like books). Korean shamanism is closed, for instance, but that doesn't mean it's taboo to go watch the videos of Korean shamans performing exorcisms on YouTube; they wouldn't be uploaded in the first place otherwise. It's *practicing* something, trying to do these initiations or exorcisms or rites yourself (especially with no guidance, training, or permission), that becomes a no-no.

I was just looking for some insight on this to maybe make sense of whatever Samael was trying to tell me, given he'd pulled two weird cards. It would be the only answer he pulled two cards for, too. And as I fished around, I found this quote in Daniel C. Matt's *The Essential Kabbalah: The Heart of Jewish Mysticism:*

> From a more radical perspective, evil originates in divine thought, which eliminates waste before emanating goodness. *The demonic is rooted in the divine* (6). (Emphasis mine.)

That blew me away, reading that. It made a lot of things make sense very quickly, like when you're at the end of a craft project and everything suddenly snaps into place and makes the big jumble of materials finally resemble what you were working towards. But Geburah itself, which some would consider the *fifth* sphere and therefore fifth heaven, I guess, was all about discipline, judgement, and drawing boundaries—forcing people to work on their own rather than have everything handed to them out of boundless love and mercy. This made an interesting pair with Samael's final answer.

"Geburah is 'strength,' or 'judgement,'" he said, "and it's also about setting limits and boundaries, with God making us stand on our own two feet. It's as you read in those pages: 'Reward and punishment are both found in Geburah.' The rap of a ruler on a child's knuckles. The steel string on a young bonsai. The corrective braces on a child's legs or teeth. The way a mother dog growls at greedy pups. To work in the Fifth Heaven is to draw a boundary and enforce it.

"It's to teach you to do the same. Strength and Mercy: together, they make beauty (Tifereth). Together they make balance. No one likes the work I give them to do. They whine and squeal, bitch and moan. But they grow. They become strong. As your cards say: 'You don't get old by being weak.' You don't get here being young and soft, but voracious and expanding. You don't leave here any of that: you leave here disciplined, defined."

"Whoa." It felt like I'd gone half on a bibliomancy trip with all that, alongside the cards. "That's... pretty cool, I won't lie. I dunno; it seems like people need that kind of thing, so it's got value." And there are many ways to get it, many mystic systems that teach it, not just Jewish Kabbalah. "But... moving on, then, how about this: what do you think about people saying you're the Prince of Rome? Just like Michael is Prince of Israel?"

5. THOUGHTS ON YOU BEING THE PRINCE OF ROME?

Samael didn't pull any cards for this one. He just took a drink of something laying around and gave a harsh, dismissive wave.

"It means Christianity is the Devil, obviously. That's what those that claimed me Prince of Rome meant: that Christianity is of 'the Devil,' or Ha-Shatan, Satan, me. But in truth, it's all simply part of a larger story, isn't it?

"Some say Mohammed is the Antichrist. Some say Jesus is buried up to His neck in shit in the afterlife. No one's really right, are they? No one's really wrong, either. No one knows what the fuck is going on." He grew so sullen, bitter, and picked up the poker for the hearth coals again. "I just know I poke this fucking fire all day, while I wear this mask [the name Samael]."

Jeez. That was one hell of an outburst. Michael and I glanced at each other, but I decided to just leave it there and keep it moving.

"Fair enough. Okay, how about a different question? I promise I'm not asking this out of pettiness," I said, sheepish, if only because there'd been a bit of a kerfuffle with demonolaters at that time about Samael that I wasn't interested in turning into another time-wasting shit show, "but what's something you wish occultists understood? Specifically about you?"

6. What do you wish occultists knew about you?

It was only when I added that last bit that a card finally came to me. Samael sighed and shook his head.

"Again: no one knows what's going on. I can't mold a man who's already gnarled and twisted himself into some hard and bitter shape. One who comes to me cannot come with baggage. One who comes to me must come as young and fresh as a green shoot, flexible and alive. I care nothing for teaching and shaping dead driftwood. It's useless."

Return to a beginner's mind. First thought, best thought. Make mischief. Invite everything to be your teacher. Approach learning with innocence of a child. Ask questions clearly.

PAGE of SWORDS.

"Ah." Seemed like a pretty clear message to me, especially with the card talking about approaching with the innocence of a child: you can't fill a cup that's already full. Gotta let go of a lot of ideas before coming to Samael for anything. "That makes sense. Alright, well, alongside that, it's interesting to me that this deck mentions you teach occult and magical stuff. What do you think? What's your favorite thing to teach others, magical or not?"

7. What is your favorite thing to teach people?

Answer the call of ancients. Take a stand for your whole, authentic self. Remind yourself of who you are. Devotion to divine beings deepens your connection. Take pride in where you come from.

Samael nodded. "Defining yourself," he said. "Who are you? What is your power, your expression in this world? What is your worth? Even if I have to tear every piece of you apart for you to rebuild yourself, I say this: after time with me, you will know exactly which piece of God you are—which hole in His being that makes Him ache to be parted from. Your power, your value, your worth—all of this is defined and separated with me."

"I—damn, alright. I gotta say, you have one hell of a way with words, there, bud."

With a whistle, I wrote all that down. The piece of God that makes Him ache to miss, huh? Almost sounds like a love letter. There's something romantic about it, y'know? And I guess that's that romantic sentiment so many mystics picked up on when they colored all their writings with it. After a moment of silence, something made me ask almost offhandedly:

"Do you hate God?"

He chuckled, then shook his head. "No. I hate the story He's writing, maybe, but not God. As for the story... maybe I only hate it because of my role in it. There are good things about it I can appreciate. But it's a terrible thing nonetheless."

"Alright, yeah, that's understandable. Sorry. Just had to get that one out. But we're down to our last three questions now, so first one: how do you see yourself?"

8. HOW DO YOU SEE YOURSELF?

Put a spin on old tradition. The power of place. Exploring new ways to embody old tradition. Creating practical but intuitive connections. Realistic and hardworking.

This one took a bit to get, but I got the signal to pull a card eventually, and Samael's words soon followed.

"I know what my duties are, and I do them," he said as he stared at the ground. "No fuss about it. I understand the nature of this story, even if I hate it. I understand what is started must be finished. So I intend to finish it." Then he looked up, past me, to Michael. "With or without God."

Man, the angels had some complicated feelings with each other. I didn't want to get in the middle of their staring match, so I just kept going. "And how do you want to be seen?"

9. HOW DO YOU WANT TO BE SEEN?

It was funny seeing Strength in this deck, because Strength is represented with garlic. In Islamic folklore, it's said that garlic and onions sprang from the devil's footsteps.

"I am the Adversary," he said. "But I cannot be bested or killed with weapons and harsh words. There is only one way to overcome me, and all the misery I bring to those who face me down, and it's not curses or violence or aggression.

"It's through sweetness, and sweetness alone—through keeping one's values and not compromising on Mercy, no matter the ills of this world—that I am defeated, and you are defined."

Damn! I remembered Paul's advice in Romans 12:20:

Lead with a bold, kind heart. Gentle healing builds resistance in the soft spirit. Meet adversity with inner fire. Power to persevere. Step into your power and remember that compassion is strength. Embrace both gentle and wild within.

On the contrary: "If your enemy is hungry, feed him; if he is thirsty, give him something to drink. In doing this, you will heap burning coals on his head."

That would explain the coals, wouldn't it? The power of that Mercy burns those that want to try and trick folks out of it. Say what you want about Paul, but he had a lot of this stuff locked down. Which I guess is to be expected, if he saw half the stuff he says he saw.

"Alright, I get it. Thank you! Though, that itself seemed like the message you wanted to give. Was there anything else you wanted to say before we part ways, or was that it?"

10. ANY LAST MESSAGES?

Here, Samael had a smile that made him look less like the scowling guy I started with and more like the Lucifer I knew from all my time with the demons. He opened his arms wide and said, "Face me with all your might. I look forward to seeing you burn—or live."

That was ominous as hell. I could tell that was a message for everyone, though, so I closed the notebook, thanked him for his time, and was just about to hop off when something popped out of that rotting pig. It was a woman covered in flowers, a nymph. She woke up, looked at Samael, and then rushed off to the furnace, where she burned up to nothing over those corpses out there in the furnace's infinite expanse. I don't know how to explain that at all, or what it meant; I just know that it happened.

And after, Samael showed me the form that others had described: the six winged angel, masked from the nose up, a red-gold, half-disc shaped crown on his head and black, red, and gold robes draped over him as he held a golden sword. His wings were black feathers, and they fell down like knives, slicing through buildings of stone as easily as a good pair of shears slid through cloth.

What an angel. A beautiful, deadly angel.

THE AIR MOTHER

After that heavy conversation with Samael, I took a long time to think about what I wanted to learn with this series, and I finally got to trying something I've wanted to try for a while: talking to the spirits that exist in my area. Let me remind you here that the land I'm living on is the historic, ancestral, and rightful land of the Narragansett tribe of Native Americans, so knowing that, I wasn't really sure what to expect.

I did think there might be some fairies around, but would fairies here act the same as the fairies we know about in Ireland and Scotland? It was anyone's guess. All I knew was that I would have an experience a bit different from all my others, where I had a clear target in mind. This interview, therefore, was very much what I often tell people not to do, because it was the equivalent of me opening my door and asking anyone walking by to come on in.

However, I wasn't really worried about it. I asked God to protect me from anything too weird or malicious and had faith He would (after all, He was the one giving me the go-ahead to explore what still had me curious). After that, it was just a matter of getting set up. I was lucky, too, to also have such a gorgeous evening to sit outside and speak to any nearby nature spirits with, so I was ready for pretty much anything as I soaked up that fresh air and the bright blue sky.

There's not much more to say about this interview than that, so let's jump in.

Somehow, before I got settled in my yard to do this interview, I ended up on a mini trip to the liquor store in the town over. I just wanted a pack of hard cider, but the place I normally go to was closed for renovations, so I ended up in a different store—where I was able to pick up some Bailey's as part of what I'd give this mystery spirit. By this point, I was still thinking about Irish fairies, and I knew they liked dairy items, so it made sense to pick that up.

But once out there in the yard, I had my picnic blanket set up with a bit of Bailey's and a small plate of treats: cookies, grapes, and fragrant herbs from my garden (purple sage, lemon balm, lavender, oregano, mugwort, chive flowers). I had my own can of hard cider from a local brewery that I adore, as well as the sound of all the birds and other animals around instead of my usual headphones full of meditation music. Honestly, the nature sounds were doing a lot better for me than music would in terms of getting into the zone, so surrounded by my plants and the animals in some warm spring evening sunlight, I was ready to go. I did the Lord's prayer, asked for protection, and made the call.

"Hello!" It was like sending out some kind of invisible feelers into the world, the way I tried to find any kind of spirit. "Hello, spirits! I've got some gifts, if anyone would like to come forward and speak to me. Who's out here? I'd like to meet you!"

It took a little while to get any bites, but eventually, I caught the image of a small spirit that approached me as if cautious. It almost looked like a hedgehog with a fairy face at first: it was covered in black things that I eventually realized were tiny, sharp-looking feathers, and its face was wide, pale, with huge and shiny black eyes. It had a tiny nose, too, and a tiny mouth, as well as little arms and legs that poked out from all that black fluff. I got the sense it was walking up to me, with a tiny pale hand on my knee as I sat there, and it stared at me for a while.

For a good few minutes, I wondered if this little spirit was something I just made up. It was always a good thing to ask myself: *is that really the spirit, or just my imagination?* But that image stayed in my head as I asked, and eventually, I got hit with an almost impatient thought: *that is the spirit, yes!*

Alright, fine. With that image of the spirit held steady in my head, I asked it to show itself to me in the form of animals, thinking maybe one would appear in front of me, but what happened instead was a very specific type of bird suddenly started going nuts in the trees. That call was different from the other ones I'd been hearing, and a few minutes later the call was gone, only normal bird sounds left. By that point, thinking the black stuff on the spirit was, in fact, a covering of feathers, this seemed to be a spirit of the air or the birds.

"Oh. So you're a bird fairy! Hello. I'm *Somraknega*," I said, careful not to give it my real name (as there's plenty fairy lore saying not to do that, but of course, that didn't stop my wonderful brain from blurting my full government name out in my head like some kind of intrusive thought; I can only hope God muted it to others). But *Somraknega* is Slovenian for "The Twilight One."

It blinked at me, motioned for the Herbcrafter's Tarot, then huffed, "That's not your real name."

"Sorry," I said with a shrug, "I'm just trying to be careful. As you might imagine, I'm here to talk to you precisely because I don't know what you are or how you work! So if you're okay with it, I'd really like to know: who or what are you?"

I. WHO ARE YOU?

1. Long held beliefs may not be rooted in reality. Refuse to go with the crowd. Spiritual crisis, challenging beliefs. Clear the path. Listen to others.

2. Say what you mean and mean what you say. Cut to the point. Diffusing tension with humor. Common sense.

3. Seek truth. Make informed decisions. Consequences. Fight for what's right.

QUEEN of SWORDS.

JUSTICE .

I pulled some interesting cards that, in the *Herbcrafter's Tarot*, those translated as Five of Air, Madre (Mother) of Air, and Justice, which only confirmed that this was an air spirit. The Justice bit was a wild card, though (no pun intended).

"I'm a spirit of power!" The spirit said that with a lot of enthusiasm, all its feathers ruffling as it clutched its tiny hands into fists. "And justice! Truth! Goodness! I protect the birds and the birds protect and honor me. I work in teams with others like me. I've answered your call, *Somraknega*, because I knew you'd write down the words I say. I knew you'd tell the truth."

And that was a little sweet, I won't lie. I don't know how this spirit knew that about me, unless maybe it knew I'd been calling all kinds of spirits over to chat, but it was fun to wrestle the implications of this: that the spirit was part of a larger clan, and that they were all about preserving specifically the birds. Maybe there were some dedicated to preserving foxes or deer or nettle or skunk cabbage, too. It was funny, though, to hear about birds, because with all the windows open, I could hear my own bird hoo-ing and cooing through my apartment's open windows.

More interesting, though, was that the spirit changed its form. It went from a tiny hedgehog looking thing to a woman in a long black dress, the feathers clustering on her wide, fairy-like head as if trying to look like hair. Her black dress went up to her neck, the skirts hitting the floor, with long sleeves that left only her pale hands and face out. We were also in what looked like a house made from a tree stump, with a dirt floor and a wooden table that the spirit sat at.

"Okay," I said as I watched the spirit. "But what about a name? What can I call you?"

It shook its head. "No. No name. You can call me the *Mother of Air*, like that card says, but that's it. I'm not whatever you think fairies are. If you won't give me your name, you don't get mine. You don't need it."

"Oh, okay. I understand. But now, this is different." I glanced around the dark stump-house, the only light coming through a window. There was nothing but gray fog outside. "What's this?"

The spirit waved a hand. "I thought you expected something 'fairy-like,' so I appeared different before. But I'm not like those Irish fae, and I don't follow whatever rules about them you think you know."

It felt like she was getting a bit irritated with my lack of knowledge, which was fair—I couldn't tell if my questions were any good or not before I wrote them since there was no way to really check or research anything; I was going in fully blind—and so I just shrugged it off and kept going.

"Fair enough. But then, how long have you lived in this area?"

2. HOW LONG HAVE YOU LIVED HERE?

THE HIGH PRIESTESS

Follow the fragrance of mystery. Awaken ancient memory. Divine messages in dreams and visions. Answer the call. Awakening. What's revealed may be unpleasant. Healing comes when visions are acknowledged.

I pulled only one card: the High Priestess, represented by mugwort. I had a huge mugwort patch growing in front of my car in the driveway, and it'd gotten massive since I found the first bit of mugwort there four years ago. Seeing the mugwort on my card had me asking about it.

"The mugwort—do you mean you were here since that patch came up? Or since there's been mugwort in this area specifically?"

She turned her nose up like it was a stupid question. "I've been here as long as mugwort's grown here, yes—mugwort in the whole area. Then I guided the birds here when all your human filth and stink, all those cars and concrete, got to be too much. Every year I find more refugees."

There was a sad note in her voice, but I understood. I remembered my parents telling me that it felt like there were fewer birds around their area, which was a pretty common suburban neighborhood. Where I was, there was still sprawling forest all around, and so the sounds of birds and foxes and bugs was always adding some interesting background noise (though hearing foxes scream at night was spooky as all ever).

With a nod, I kept going. "I see. That makes sense. Okay, so, another thing I'm curious about: you said you guard the birds. Is that what spirits like you do in general? Or do you do more as well? What does life out here look like for you?"

3. WHAT DOES DAILY LIFE LOOK LIKE FOR YOU?

The Air Mother blinked. "What do you mean, 'what do we do'? We live. We are people, just as you are. You chase dollars and abstract concepts," she said with a dismissive wave, "and we exist in the tangible; we are our ancestors and forever live their ways."

I paused my writing. "And who are your ancestors?"

She folded her arms. "Our ancestors are gods and monsters, winds and rains. What is, is. What isn't, isn't. We don't go searching for meaning from nothing. We see the inner machinations of the world—'under the hood,' as you're trying to translate that—that Man forgets how to do."

What is, is, and what isn't, isn't, sounded a lot like what Persephone said to me that one time I talked to her, about two years prior. Wild, to think it'd been that long already. But before I could think too long on that or ask another question, I had to address that little frown on the Air Mother's lips.

Return to a beginner's mind. First thought, best thought. Make mischief. Everything is a teacher. Revisit all known subjects.

Ground yourself in community. Share resources. Life is generative. Share with friends. Support each other. Teach others.

"Hey, listen," I said with a huff, "I'm sorry if my questions seem stupid. I know they're probably silly, but can you be easy on me? I'm asking these things because I know literally nothing about you and have no way to know except through these types of questions. Can you be a little nicer, please?"

My guest blinked at me, then rolled her eyes and huffed. "Fine."

"Thank you. Now, I'm interested in what you said, about how you exist in the tangible. How can people learn to do that, rather than sit in the abstract?"

4. HOW CAN PEOPLE SIT IN THE TANGIBLE INSTEAD OF THE ABSTRACT?

She refused to pull any cards, then shook her head and waved as if warning me away from a cliff.

"No, no. You're not like us. You were made for one world while originating in another. You will fight your whole lives to feel connected to the physical and the spiritual together as a result. It's how your ilk were made. I don't pity you, but I don't envy you either. Seems annoying, still, to be made in such a way—to be human." Then the Air Mother looked around, back with me under the blue sky instead of in her tree stump house. She gestured to the open air. "This is our heaven. This is where we stay." She looked at me, brows furrowed, mouth pursed. "Why do you [humans] ruin our heaven?"

What was I supposed to say to that? I shrugged and said, "Listen, you know—my folk," the Christians, specifically, "are supposed to be bringing heaven down on earth, not mucking everything up."

The Air Mother crossed her arms and frowned. "Again, this world already is heaven to us. If what we have now is your idea of 'bringing heaven down to earth,' I have choice words for your God."

"Oh, trust me, it's not; we've messed it up pretty damn good," I said, hoping she understood my own frustration over it. But then I was back on my curious shtick, because there was a word that she'd said that poked me, and I asked, "Hold on, though. You mentioned gods a couple times now. Do know about my God? Do your folk have gods? Or creators?"

5. DO YOU HAVE GODS?

Don't fence yourself in. Discernment necessary for survival. Know your wounds. An ancient calling from the Divine. Follow truth.

Create with the enthusiasm of a beginner. Boisterous plans, sweet sleep. Lighten the landscape with golden joy. Independence.

Too much of a good thing. Breaking down leads to renewed fertility. Replenish and begin again. Let go of what doesn't resonate. Wisdom of ancients.

The Air Mother said, with a slow blink, "We know no other gods than the ones that came before us. And yes, I know your God. He came here by force, but not by His choice. We know Him; He's one of us, yet not. He's of a different world, yes, a different plane— but He understands what we understand. He is perfectly in His domain, as we are in ours. We had a hand in making this land, but we committed to being fully in it, not just watching over it. There's no shame in being 'worldly' when you made and are made by the world."

This conversation was getting a little over my head, if I'm being honest. I wrote all this down, faithful to the words I was hearing spin out in my head, but they didn't make all that much sense to me. God is like these spirits, but not; He's a creator, but this world isn't His domain; He's watching over the things He made rather than integrating with and living among them. While I believe there's a piece of God in all His creation, it is true that most understand God as up in the heavens, removed from Earth (and that sending His Son, Jesus, as in God in the flesh, was a wild move for a deity of His caliber).

Maybe there's more to explore with the spirits of the world. If they're going to act like they helped make the world, then that also backs up an idea I've had ever since I spoke to my tree guardian, who showed me a tanned, black-haired woman, a titan, a great spirit, holding his little tree soul: that God brought in other spirits to help Him build all this. The Divine Council isn't a new concept, so it seems this theory can't be all that far off.

"I got'cha, yeah," I said, though I honestly didn't get this spirit at all. I flipped back to my question list and, half-stewing in confusion, kept on: "Okay, so, if you've been here a while, then you must've seen all kinds of people come and go in this place." Our apartment was actually one half of a house, with a few other houses around on the same plot of land that all fall under one landlord; it feels like having a whole house, but it's still just a rental that had tenants before me. "What irks you about the people here, if anything?"

6. WHAT IRKS YOU ABOUT PEOPLE WHO LIVE HERE?

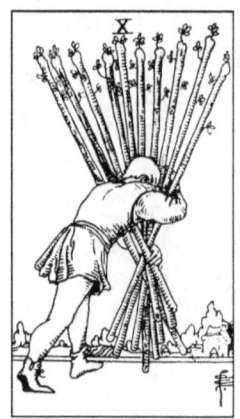

Too much of a good thing. Breaking down leads to renewed fertility. Replenish and begin again. Let go of what doesn't resonate. Wisdom of ancients.

Weave the world whole. Share your work. Love wins. Fulfillment and satisfaction after great achievement. Life at full bloom. Old lessons coming in new ways.

The Air Mother tilted her head side to side, as if rolling the question around in her mind. "You just don't live long enough," she said with a huff. "You don't live long enough, any of you. You don't remember that you, too, are gods. Your flesh constricts you. It wants to make you dumb, like beasts, all while you have the mind of ours. Flesh, what good is it? It's irritating, painful, to see you all make the exact same mistakes because you live and die too fast to use the wisdom you gather."

My head was spinning with all this.

"I see, yeah. That makes sense. Is there anything we can do to respect your folk out here, though, even while we're all forgetting our lessons all the time?"

7. HOW CAN WE RESPECT YOUR FOLK?

After a moment, the Air Mother said, "This land is a home to spirits, and you're a spirit, too. Do as we do. Live in harmony with all things. Treat the world as your kin, your neighbor. Every ant, tree, hedgehog, person. Remember, your heaven isn't here—but that doesn't mean it can't ever be here, in our heaven. All heavens are to become one."

Oh! Well, that was an idea: all heavens becoming one. "Okay. I guess that's the end of my personal questions. Now, I've got a few simpler ones. First one is: how do you see yourself?"

8. HOW DO YOU SEE YOURSELF?

It was interesting to pull the Chariot here. The Air Mother squared her shoulders.

"I am one who shepherds the birds," she said. "I go and teach them to continue on even when the alien ones like you come and make travesty. I am one of many. I work hard and with fury. I am the Mother of Air."

Oh, boy. That word, *alien,* would be one that would get all the Starseed folks in a twist, I knew right away, but it was clear what she meant: alien as in strange, foreign, different. It was clearer what she was talking about before thanks to that, too: we as souls were not made for this world. We were made in a different world, a spiritual one outside this, but we got stuck in

Move forward with confidence. Be disciplined yet flexible in pursuits. Life is a gift. Embark on a deeper quest. Bring knowledge of spirit and soul into the body. Have faith in experience.

bodies and forced to do some several-decades-long Battle Royale to learn a thing or two before going back "home" (Heaven, underworlds, etc.). Maybe the Earth is just one big university or training ground for the soul. For what reason, though, I don't know.

"And how do you want to be seen?"

9. HOW DO YOU WANT TO BE SEEN?

Celebrate pleasures of life. Enjoy your own company. Emotional nourishment is food for the soul. Invite comfort and happiness into your heart. Enjoy life's blessings.

"We are spirits alive for the here and now," the Air Mother said with a shrug. "We have no reason to torture ourselves to achieve a higher plane. Our plane is ours, made by and for us. You are our guests here, and we are only so gracious as hosts as you are as guests. Remember that,"

Hmm. I got the sense she was talking about asceticism, of the monks and mystics that spent years of study in solitude while fasting and meditating to better connect with God. But trying to figure out where this idea of them making their own plane in this world fit into everything else I knew was, at that time, something I accepted would just have to marinate a little longer.

"Alright, alright, well, that sounded like something you'd wanna say as a final parting word, honestly. But in case it's *not...* do you have any final words before we part ways, Air Mother?"

10. ANY LAST MESSAGES?

Funny that I pulled the Four of Swords (or Four of Air)—as if she were also confirming her position as a spirit of the air again. She gave me a sigh and a long look, then spoke.

"You chase the impossible, you people," she said. "Wake up from your nightmare and sink into your dream. Find yourselves. Your true selves. Not everyone who professes truth necessarily professes *your* truth. Are you ours? Or someone else's? Stop chasing your own tail and chase Truth."

There is a *lot* that this could mean. Quite a bit. I think I know what she was talking about—especially as she insisted on the side that even my accidentally-blurted-government-name wasn't my "real name," which means... I don't know what my

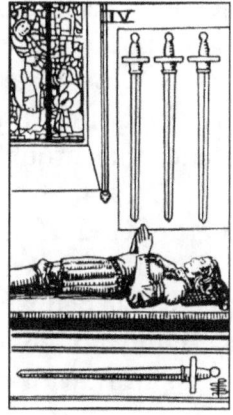

Withdraw behind borders. Calm body and mind. Pause to cherish the present moment. Contemplation over action. Create space for rest. Put up boundaries. Allow studies to sink in.

real name is either, apparently—but I'll leave that for you all to interpret, too. So there it is: my first time just walking outside and saying hello to the locals.

And again, do I recommend doing this? Not unless you want to risk getting your ass severely chapped. I put my offerings of herbs and cookies and such under a shrub for the Air Mother and spent however long turning all these ideas over in my head. As I said in the last chapter: UPG is a mess. Things contradict sometimes (in fact, many times). It's confusing, it's strange, but it still leaves your soul feeling moved over, nudged out of place, because you know there's something true in all of it. Maybe not *my* truth. But *a* truth. God, what even *is* truth, anyway? What is *real?*

That is a question that is especially dangerous to follow in this world of spirituality.

THE DRAGON

All heavens becoming one.

I dunno, I just couldn't stop thinking about that. It sounded to me like one day, all things would just mix back into one big goo, like if you took a pack of vibrant crayons and melted them all into the same pot until they became one big greyish-brown sludge.

It also took me to a different thought: the eventual end of the world. The dissolution of all things. The end times, the rapture, the final days, whatever the hell people want to call it. And it's no coincidence that, around this time, God took the reigns of the interview schedule and told me to speak to one entity I never wanted to come anywhere near: the "Devil" proper. The divided and abandoned part of God left to rot down below. The Dragon.

I'm sure most folks who were raised Christian, or at least anyone who's read Revelation and noted the whole battle between archangel Michael and this Dragon, might guess what I'm talking about. I'm certainly not talking about anything of draconic magic, or of any specific spirit that draconic magicians work with, no; the title of Dragon is simply a title. We see mention of this Dragon also in other Christian things outside Revelation, like St. Benedict's medal: on it is an inscription that reads, *Crux Sacra Sit Mihi Lux, Non Draco Sit Mihi Dux*: "May the Holy Cross Be My Light, May the Dragon Never Be My Guide." In essence, this is the Big Bad of the Christian religion, the true Devil.

On the back end, though, the mystic end, we find something a little deeper: something that makes a few disjointed ideas across time make sense. For example, there's this sect of Christians largely considered heretical: the Gnostics. These folks had different divisions and branches and lines of thought amongst themselves, but one thought they had was that of the Demiurge: the true and "evil" creator of this world who was an ignorant beast out to spite the One True God (or who just didn't even realize he wasn't the One True God). However, this take can become super antisemitic, because some divisions pointed specifically to the "Old Testament" (Jewish) God as this thing, while Jesus's God (the New Testament/Christian God) was of course the *true* and *righteous* and *pure* God.

Spoiler: Jewish God and Christian God (and Muslim God, too, honestly) are the same God. And I don't think I need to explain how demonizing the Jewish understanding of Him is antisemitic. At least, I hope I don't.

But there's something about this idea—of a piece of God or a version of God that wanted to create its own things in spite of the God it was removed from—that finds purchase in especially occult philosophy. At one point, when Jewish mysticism was cropping up in full force in medieval Spain (and a lot of Christian theologians, philosophers, and occultists were just snapping it up for their own purposes), there eventually developed that theory of the Qliphoth in its basic understanding: the idea that when God decided to become *something*, when God decided that all those primordial waters of Genesis had to take form, that something was cast off. When God made all the spheres of the Sefirot and emanated all things from them, some husks, cocoons (the Qliphoth) were left behind. However, it's thought by some occultists that one sphere that we've already discussed, Geburah, had something of a mind of its own—that a piece of it broke off and went into those empty husks to create its own anti-worlds, the places the demons now populate. In short: hell.

I'm greatly simplifying all of this, but all this is to say: there was once a time where God was not God. Where He hadn't *defined Himself* as God yet. Where He, and all creation, was one big soup, like that melting pot of crayons: all one greyish-brown sludge, nothing separate, nothing existing. Just primordial sludge.

And then there was, in all that sludge, a *will*. A will to *be*. And in order to *be*, of course, one had to *define* what they were to be. Hence came the first act of separation: God from all things that were Not God. And then came more separations from within that primordial sludge God's Spirit hovered over: rocks from those waters to separate land from sea, then trees, then animals, then light separated from dark, and so on and so on. Suddenly, rather than the crayon-sludge, we had a pack of twenty-four beautiful, distinct colors in crayon shape for the first time.

But what were all the things God decided, with His will, were *Not God?* Where did they go? What did they create? In all those husks, in all that mess, that excrement of creation?

And what does it still want?

I tell you, I never wanted to mess with this. Nope. Never wanted to come near this thing even with a five mile long pole. But God told me to do it, and so I would.

To get this thing off the ground, I won't lie: it took a minute. By that I mean, I really didn't want to do it and pushed it off as long as possible. But eventually, the deadline came, and the interview had to be done; there was nowhere for me to keep pushing it off if I was going to protect my peace on my day off. So I got out two red candles, a massive dragon statue, my big onyx sphere and some onyx, obsidian, and tiger's eye crystals as some negativity magnets and protective pieces, and two cards: the Michael card from Travis McHenry's Angel Tarot, and the Lucifer card from his Occult Tarot. I did this because these two represent the two halves of my practice: the angelic and the infernal. Just as they're God's right and left hand, so too are they my dear allies in my work. They were both moral/emotional support and protection out there in the absolute bowels of hell.

But here's the weird part: as I got everything ready—lit the candles, got my music, burned some Dragon's Blood incense—I didn't go to where I thought I'd go. I've been to quite a few spots in hell, and what I got in this situation was unlike anything else I'd been shown before. It was a section of Thaumiel—the absolute bottom sphere of the Qliphoth—and it was a completely pitch black room with nothing in it except a golden doorframe hovering in that empty space. Even the door itself was black; the only thing that separated it from everything else was its golden border and its gigantic golden keyhole. Michael and Lucifer were there beside me, encouraging me to take this huge key that popped up and stick it in the keyhole.

So I did. And when I opened the door, I saw what reminded me of a Dark Souls boss map: a huge, open-floor cave, with a floor made of rock and gold and golden stalagmites hanging down all sharp and bright. All the way in the back was something like a black throne, where, to my surprise, a man stood—not the icky monster I caught a glimpse of once so long ago, when I first witnessed this beast. No, when I was once crawling up to God's house through a secret little backdoor in the infernal realms with Lucifer, and I saw that black dragon laboring after us, trying to get to the staircase, it was a much more pressured and struggling thing than this man—and the black-gold dragon he could become.

And you know, it's funny. I couldn't quite finish writing this chapter up the same day I did the interview (which I should've expected, because I generally never write the interviews the same day I do them; the information needs to marinate for a minute). As a result, I went about a full Sunday before getting back here. On Sundays, I head to one of my local Episcopal churches, where the people are cool and the priest is so on target with his sermons (always pushing back against materialism, bigotry, and other things that unfortunately, different churches have become a breeding ground for). In that service, though, we happened to get into the verse where Jesus is accused of having a demon to draw power from in Mark 3:20-25:

> Then Jesus entered a house, and again a crowd gathered, so that he and his disciples were not even able to eat. When his family heard about this, they went to take charge of him, for they said, "He is out of his mind."
>
> And the teachers of the law who came down from Jerusalem said, "He is possessed by Beelzebul! By the prince of demons he is driving out demons."
>
> So Jesus called them over to him and began to speak to them in parables: "How can Satan drive out Satan? If a kingdom is divided against itself, that kingdom cannot stand. If a house is divided against itself, that house cannot stand.

During the sermon, the priest asked everyone what they thought of when they heard words like Beelzebul or Satan. Many people said some variation of an imp with horns, or an "evil aura," or a creature of smoke and fire (and also more horns). None of them even seemed to remember the part of the Bible where St. Paul himself mentions that the devil comes as an "angel of light." No one thought to mention sweet words and backstabbing, or the kind of smile that lights up a face in tight lines and balled up cheeks, but never reaches the eyes, which remain hollow and dark. That's a great way to get messed up, because obviously, Evil wouldn't make much ground with people if it came looking so clearly marked as dangerous. Evil makes the most headway when it comes looking like something, or someone, beautiful and composed and confident.

Which is exactly what I saw with the Dragon. It looked so similar to the angel that often stands in for God (Zotiel, whose name means "little one of God"), likely because it could glean how I even saw God to manifest to me at all, but it looked like a way too clean, manicured, and absolutely soulless version of Zotiel.

Zotiel always appears to be with orange skin and wild, yet short golden hair (because he's actually made of fire in the shape of a man), as well as eyes so hot that they burn the sharpest blue, as if channeling God's direct essence. He wears a tight white t-shirt and blue jeans in my head; I don't know why, but he does. And he tends to have the meanest mug on his face: severe, battle-hardened, strict (though rarely, he looks over with open curiosity or a sly smile when I say something jinx-worthy).

As the stand-in for God, he seems to be channeling what God feels and thinks at any given time, as God stays hidden and secret to all, far away in the clouds. It turns out that the thing I thought was a sun in heaven all this time was actually God shining there, far away, so bright that not a single detail can be made out about him. Zotiel is the mid-way, and he embodies as much of God's essence as is needed for me to have that direct communication, becoming a living channel of words, expressions, body language, and general energy. It's weird how angels can do that, becoming not only the messenger, but the embodiment of the message.

On the other hand, I can only describe the Dragon as looking like Antony Starr playing Homelander in *The Boys* (the T.V. show). Again, that appearance was a much cleaner and more manicured (and less fiery) version of Zotiel in my opinion: the short-ish blond hair, the dazzling white-toothed smile, the bright gold eyes that had something cold and dangerous behind their dragon-like pupils.

This man wore a cape of black and gold dragon scales and a golden sweater underneath it, as if this giant cave were both his castle and his cozy personal library; as if he could be both terrible force and gentle giant at the same time. Actually, more accurate would be to say that he had the same vibe a big predator gives off when they don't think you're worth the energy to try and eat: dangerous, watching carefully, willing to snap you up if you show signs of sickness or injury, but feigning relaxation and ease. A predator simply going about its business as if you weren't there (but always knowing exactly where you are in case it needs to bite).

It was uncomfortable, to say the least.

But as I strolled into that room, I just reminded myself to take pretty much everything this thing would say with a grain of salt. By that doorway I came in stood Michael, who I expected to act as some kind of jailer for this thing—though Michael being there, in the absolute pit of Thaumiel in the Qliphoth, was a surprise in itself, really—but what worried me was that *Lucifer* seemed like he couldn't stay stable in that space. He kept winnowing in and out, flickering, until eventually he gave me a vibe like he was saying, *see you when you're done!* and disappeared entirely. And then the door closed, leaving me in that cave of coal and gold alone with the Dragon.

"Hello, Dragon," I said, because what else was there to say? "I've come to ask you a few questions."

"By all means, come and ask."

He said that with a casual wave of his hands. Wearing that sweater, I almost could've seen him holding a coffee cup or something, as if this wasn't a desolate cave in the absolute bottom pit of hell, but a pretty lounge area in a high rise New York apartment.

I'll say this: I've seen this thing in several iterations in Thaumiel: as that black slimy axolotl looking thing clawing its way up to God's back door, and as a more Diablos-looking thing from the *Monster Hunter* series, twisting and thrashing in some huge pit of sand some ways away from Lucifer's old throne. But never did I expect it to compose itself so well here.

It was unsettling in the way a big, obviously dangerous dragon could simply never be (and even when he flashed before my eyes *as* a dragon—a black and gold, sharp-eyed, slender-necked thing resting like a cat around his throne in the back, it was the kind that looked like it'd first tell me a riddle than go tearing down a city). There was just this *smugness* to him that was as thick and golden as honey, and it made it hard to gather my thoughts at all.

It also didn't help that he kept flashing images of giant, howling, half-fleshed skulls and other crazy-looking things causing calamity on earth, but you know. Those images were easier to wave away than this feeling of *not being in good company.*

He noticed my hesitation and made a face, like when parents coo at their children: those furrowed brows, that pouted lip, that quasi-condescending "*aw,*" just seconds away from burbling from his throat. He held his arms open to me as if inviting me to him, like some kind of estranged father.

"Come now; what's that look? Aren't we both pieces of God? Why act so cold and distant?"

"I am a piece of God. I am made in His image. You are not." I stayed right where I was and said, "You were once God, with who is now God. Now you're Not God, cast off, different. Therefore you and I can't be anything but inherently different from one another. We are not kin, not in any way."

I did not like the way he smiled at that.

"Alright, well, let's just dive in." I was standing a healthy distance from the Dragon, but I didn't have to shout for my voice to carry, nor did he have to be close to let me know he chose the "First question: how were you made?"

I. HOW WERE YOU MADE?

I knew how this thing was made, actually. Or at least, I had a pretty good idea. Seeing a bit of my friend Aziel's reading of the Sitra Achra on TikTok also helped me gain a *shrapnel* of insight into why this Dragon was so upset in the first place and why he was so determined to "get back" at the created world and its Creator.

But when I pulled the cards that *echoed* that sentiment—The Lovers, Three of Swords, and Ace of Coins Reversed, all laid out like a picture book of a story—that's how I knew that *yes,* I was really talking with the Dragon. It was a confirmation question more than anything, and it was fascinating,

Navigating love and relationships, be they romantic, platonic, or with the self. Clarity in one's values.

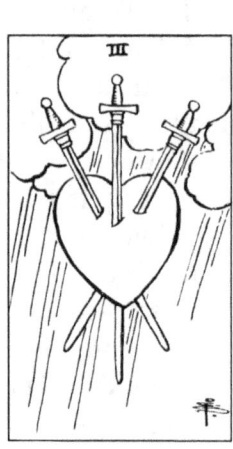

Heartbreak, betrayal, division, hard truths, and rejection. Indecisiveness grows destructive.

A fixation on the material world, anxiety, greed.

watching that fake smile melt away into bugged eyes and tendons straining against his neck, teeth gone from being flashed in a grin to bared in pure frustration.

"All was well," he snapped. "All was fine. Then that bastard—*HE*—He caused a crack. A rift."

By "He," it only made sense the Dragon was talking about God. The Dragon wiped his face with his palm, as if wiping his expression off, and then he kept going with his hands tucked behind his back. He didn't look at me as he spoke.

"Chaos. He made chaos. What people call 'chaos' now was perfection: all things, complete, whole. I am condensed now of everything He didn't want: each bit of hate and grief and ugliness pulled off and stuck to me like clay, until I became this *thing.* This is not what I was. I hate it. I want everything to be whole again. When nothing exists, I exist."

I blinked at that. There was a question in my journal that I hadn't yet gotten to yet: *what do you want to accomplish?* That little bit he tacked on sort of settled that, so I erased the question, nodded, and kept on like either a bad therapist or a decent interrogator. Maybe both.

"I see. Well, maybe you'll be happy to know that there are people who share your goal. You're not alone in that. There are the anti-cosmic Satanists, and the various anti-cosmic entities out there, like the Kemetic snake and such, that some of these folks try to work with. What do you think about them? And what do you think about the demons you're surrounded by, down here in hell?"

2. WHAT DO YOU THINK OF DEMONS AND ANTI-COSMIC MAGICIANS?

Disinterest, doubt, introspection, pessimism, and failing to see the good in life.

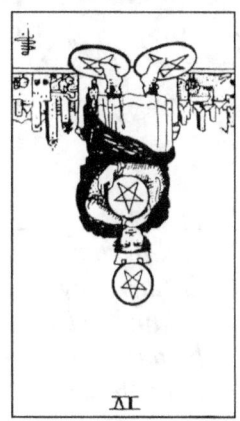

Opposition and feelings of being controlled.

Rivalry, obstacles, competition, and trickery. Winning by causing others to lose.

The sharpness in his eyes could've cut me in half, and the little hooked curve of his smirk told me he would've, if it were worth the effort. Unlike Zotiel, whose eyes burned that all-seeing, hyper-focused blue, this Dragon's eyes were just as gold as the rest of the cave, and the pupils were long, like a cat's. It didn't make him look any cozier, that's for sure. But then that hook became a whole Cheshire cat smile. He looked up like he was a cocktail hour host with a little flair for dramatics, his hands floating up in a delicate, sweeping motion.

"No one really wants that—in the end," he said, his voice a silky whisper. His grin faltered back into a half-smirk, teeth still poking out, stark white against his tanned skin. "They know what's required to get it, and they don't want it. The moment of trial will come, and they'll fold, those so-called 'anti-cosmics': their nature is, by design, defined.

"To overcome that nature would require the sacrifice of their very being. I understand their sentiment. Truly, there's no one who understands better than I. No one, no one, *no one*. But as you say," his voice dripped with smugness; his words were soaked in it, "they aren't like me. Yet they have a piece of me, don't they?"

Aw, Jesus. I was two questions deep and I was already tired. But I didn't interrupt him; I let him keep at it until his thoughts were done. He stalked a few steps closer, his eyes glittering, and his grin made me not want to breathe, as if that would keep him from seeing me.

"That piece—it acts up in some more than others. But in the end, they're children, those little 'anti-cosmics': just children, saying things they don't understand and aren't ready to commit to."

Well, that's condescending. I expected this guy to be all *yay hooray* about the idea of having anyone that shared his idea of a perfect, undefined world, but I guess he has absolutely no faith in anyone and their resolve, which is interesting. Still, of course I knew that this talk about "a piece" of him was a trap for me, and of course, I knew I would have to walk right into it for the sake of clarity.

"Okay. Cool. So, that 'piece' you're talking about... you wanna say more? Specifically, I'm looking for more about how you influence the world. Sounds like that 'piece' is a part of it." I looked up from my scribbling and squinted at him. "Are you what makes people act all stupid and awful? Like, for example, the Evangelical Egregore, that caricature of Jesus—did you make that?"

3. Did You Make the Evangelical Egregore?

His laugh was deep and rich, reverberating off the cave walls and bouncing from stalagmite to stalagmite, and his mouth was far too wide and dark in that open grin. "I didn't create that egregore, no," he said after his laughter tapered off. "I simply created the conditions it needed to thrive. You know what handicaps you defined folk?"

Alright, I'll bite. "What?"

"Your rigidity." He always stood only half-turned towards me, coy and slippery. "You refuse to let go of things that were when you don't know what will be. It creates such fear and worry and anxiety in your hearts that it may or may not be easier for my little apple seeds to germinate—in all that dank, wretched dark within you."

All tools required to navigate this world can be found above or below. Manifestation, seizing the moment.

Naivete, disharmony, holding onto the past in an unhealthy way.

Carelessnes, lethargy, or roadbocks in achieving one's goals.

It's funny, really. At the time, I didn't know all these things, but coming back to this, I find this echoes *exactly* the sentiment I found in a certain Edwin H. Friedman's work, *A Failure of Nerve:* a bit from the introduction about how leaders fail because they spend time trying to corral and quash the anxieties of those they're trying to lead, only for those people's anxieties to then create *new* superstitions to soothe their anxieties with. It makes sense now, putting these two ideas together. It does.

We just have to keep creating some fucked up puppets for us to cast all our discomfort onto, don't we? Over and over and over again, we make them. But cast off our discomfort of *what?*

"Please, don't give me all the credit for Man's doings." He held his hands up as if in surrender, looking around as if bashful and embarrassed to be recognized for good work, a fake display of modesty. "All that war and greed and vanity? That was all *you.* You were the sprouts of the apple seed that kept on living—the seeds that germinated and took root. I am but a humble farmer tending the land. Trying to keep plagues of locusts off my delicious fruits."

That last line was pointed. It was a reference to God—the locusts of Exodus. I could feel his meaning under his words as easily as one can feel someone staring at them: he meant that God was sending wave after wave of what he saw as insects, pests, to tear up whatever orchards the Dragon had planted among Men.

"I *suggest,*" the Dragon said with a shrug. "All I can do is whisper. Give yourself some credit for how much like this here *Not God* you can be."

Wasn't much to say against that. It was becoming patently obvious what he meant, what with all his references to apples and seeds and locusts and such. But I was in no rush to make him say it all out loud. Instead, I moved onto a different question, because the way he described his works—suggesting, whispering—made me think of how people always describe "the Devil."

"So, if that's you doing all that whispering, though, what do you think of Satan and Lucifer? And how they seem to take all the heat for the seeds you planted? Hmm?"

4. WHAT DO YOU THINK OF SATAN AND LUCIFER?

Naivete and recklessness.

Thievery, lies, betrayal, and avoiding the truth.

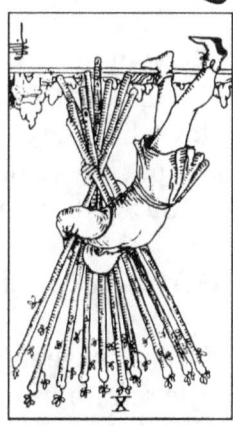

Overextending oneself or one's resources, avoiding responsibility.

The Dragon *tsked* and waved a hand. "Oh, that Satan, that Lucifer. It is cruel, isn't it? They hate me as much as humanity hates them. But again—I can only suggest. I can only provide water when it's dry and good soil to germinate in. The rest is up to you, my little apple sprouts. Not even Satan or Lucifer can take credit for your self de-structive excess. And I know it vexes them—oh, how it *vexes* them," he said with a slimy smile, one hand on his stomach, one hand outstretched, as if he were ready to waltz to such a beau-tiful idea, "that they get blamed not only for your filth, but for my encouragement. And I think it serves me just as well that others don't see the Gardener outside the Court House. That they're always pointing cameras at Judge, Prosecu-tion, and Defense, and never at my apple sprouts—never at me."

Court House—God's house. God the Judge, Lucifer the Prosecution, Michael and Jesus the De-fense. Just like my dad's dream. It was uncanny, how much this thing could speak to me with my own imagery and understanding. It was like he knew everything about me, and everything I felt and thought, and like he knew exactly how to speak to make me understand. To *suggest* and *whisper* things. Fucking uncanny.

I stopped him there and said, "Hold on, though. This interview we're doing is going public. Surely people will be looking at you then. They'll know you're there."

And I can't explain the numbness I felt when he only shrugged, as if nothing mattered.

"If I thought this little exposé would be enough to ruin my garden, I would've simply made you fertilizer," he said, and that was the only time his smile slipped and his face went dark, as if trying to press that point on me. It didn't scare me, though, only made me tired and annoyed, because deep down, I knew he was right. This interview wouldn't change a damn thing. "No, go ahead and fight," he continued. "One day, I'll get my way—if not now, later. What's another eternity of waiting when I've already waited five?"

Five eternities. Again, though, I just couldn't deny that he was right. I knew it as much as I knew for sure then that he didn't care to touch a hair on my head. He didn't need to. He could find any number of people in real life to mess with me all day long if he wanted. He could always hide behind carica-tures of red, goat-footed demons with pitchforks and horns. He could always twist people's thoughts and point to all the things about me—I'm a witch, I'm a woman, I'm a progressive, I'm a demon-worker, I'm this, I'm that—that would lull people into not facing the dissonance and discovering the truth. There would always be a good majority of people who were more comfortable with a simple "Us vs. Them" narrative that the Dragon could continue to work.

Motherfucker.

"'Kay," I huffed, and I ignored his chuckle. "What do you think about humanity, then? If you want the world all Primordial Soup-like again, you must not like 'em much, I'm guessing."

5. WHAT DO YOU THINK ABOUT HUMANITY?

Duality. Hardworking, dedicated, inflexible, and conservative. The potential to harm or heal.

The Dragon pursed his lips and shrugged. "I wouldn't say that. No, rather, I'd say humans are everything. In fact, I enjoy them, because each one is a walking Void. I love them, even— their capacity for cruelty as much as compassion. They've been made perfect: half filth, half flower. Half demonic, half divine. Wholly beautiful, wholly delicious to observe."

I paused. "I didn't think you could love. You're the opposite of God, and God is love."

His face split into that awful grin again. "God hates what He hates and loves what He loves." And I heard the refrain in my head: *There are six things the Lord hates,* from Proverbs 6:16-19:

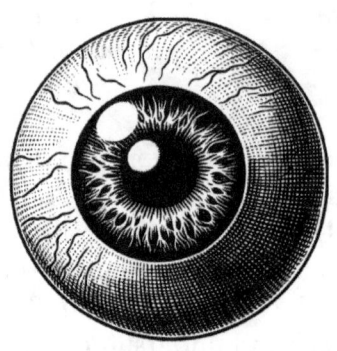

> There are six things the Lord hates,
>   seven that are detestable to him:
>   haughty eyes,
>   a lying tongue,
>   hands that shed innocent blood,
>   a heart that devises wicked schemes,
>   feet that are quick to rush into evil,
>   a false witness who pours out lies
>   and a person who stirs up conflict in the community.

"Likewise," the Dragon continued, "I hate what I hate, and I love what I love. Easy."

Well, damn.

"Alright, fine, fair. But in that case, what is it, exactly, that makes you so incompatible with God? What about you made Him cut you off?"

6. WHAT MAKES YOU INCOMPATIBLE WITH GOD?

Regret, loss, mourning. The destructive nature of sorrow in excess.

Denial, stalemate, and indecision. Unable to act. Illusion.

This question, apparently, hit a sore spot with him, because suddenly I found myself in the exact kind of place that would send me into a blazing panic if I were physically stuck in it. Problem is, though, that meditation sometimes only feels a half step off from physical reality with the way certain experiences hit multiple senses at once: not just sight, not just sound, but also feeling. Texture. Temperature. All that.

When I realized things had changed, I was in what felt like an esophagus, surrounded by warm, slimy, squishy flesh in a tight canal that gave me no footholds and no grip. Spaces like that are my worst nightmare, all too tight to move and no way to claw around and get out. Best I could do to keep from sliding down further was dig my palms and heels into opposite sides of the channel just to stay sort of stable. At the bottom of the channel, though, was a skull covered in a thin layer of red flesh, like a membrane; it was thoroughly embedded to the rest of the canal. It gnashed its teeth behind that membrane as I started slipping lower, as if it could just devour me from feet to head like a paper shredder.

Luckily, though, this wasn't real life. My ass was parked perfectly safe on my living room floor and nothing was physically happening to me; like most things, this was a test of mental and emotional capacity. Freak out over a bad situation, and you lose a chunk of your mind—or even your whole mind. Michael taught me that in some visceral ways.

Thanks to that lesson, I wasn't scared in that esophagus, only vaguely uncomfortable. "That's very cute," I said as I held myself up over that gross looking skull. "Not the most hospitable place you could put me, though."

"I don't know what you mean. You seem quite comfortable."

"I've *made* myself comfortable. How about you get me out of your little woodchipper, now?"

"No."

I rolled my eyes. Every time I blinked, though, I found myself right back in this canal when my eyes closed and viscerally uncomfortable when my eyes were open, like I couldn't get out of the tension of that space no matter what. The one thing I had going for me was that in spaces like this, anything I could imagine was possible, and so I imagined nice big eagle wings on my back, the longest edge feathers made of sharp steel. When I extended them, they pierced this weird canal and tore it open, until I could pop out and land back onto the firm, gold-crusted cave floor with only minimal icky shit stuck to me.

"Ah, look at you," the Dragon said. His arms were crossed, his body drawn in, and he gave me a little golf clap as that flesh tunnel disintegrated back into the ground. "The *queen* of separation, you are. So very mean. So tough."

Shut the fuck up. I was so irritated with this thing by this point, but I was determined to get through my list of questions, even if I could feel the blood and slime drying stiff on my skin. It was almost itchy, something to be scratched at and flaked off, but none of it was physically real. Meditation at this level is horrifyingly detailed.

"Let's keep going," I said with a sigh. "I do believe I asked you about what makes you and God such a bad combo. Can you tell me? Pretty please?"

The Dragon rolled his eyes and huffed, "Fine. It's simple, really. God, your God there, was the one that acted. I was the one that didn't. There is an ocean of meaning in this alone—but as God is one to act, then regret, I am one to stand by, then mourn. We are not the same.

"I am everything He could never be, if He wanted to make the world as He saw fit. I was His every hesitancy, stagnancy, and contentment with what is. He is all things past and future, all things bright and pure. We used to be all one—and now He's cast off His underbelly and balanced Himself in other ways, giving birth to light and dark, angel and demon, right and left, *without me*. He keeps me here, that I might not disrupt the paradoxical, impossible balance He ripped reality to make possible."

"Ooh, wait," I tapped my pencil to my lips as the dots connected, "so that's—oh. That's all Sefirot you're talking about, huh? How God balanced Severity (Geburah) with Mercy (Chesed)? Some say that a piece of Geburah broke off to make the Qliphoth. Was it you, then, that made the Qliphoth? And some folks say the root of evil is separation. What do you think is the root of separation?"

7. WHAT IS THE ROOT OF SEPARATION?

He didn't pull any cards for this: the answer was so strong and unfiltered all on its own. "Separation," he hissed, "and the Separator, yes. This is evil. True evil. Even if I had to suffer this state, I wanted to create true balance—a world for a world, a Tree for a Tree. So yes, I broke off, and I made this Qliphoth you speak of, because it wasn't right that He should make one Tree with all leaves and no roots, one World with all peace and no ruin. The last piece of me broke from Him and made the roots of His tree, the discord to His unnatural harmony. In fact, we became two trees, ones tied at the center, both roots and branches of each other's Trees. But all that did was lock me out for good. In the end, I simply became the perfect foothold for Him to accomplish His complete removal of me—so He could keep a sanitized version of me, chained and bound to other pieces of Himself.

"*That* is why I had His brats eat the fruits of *my* Tree: to ruin that little garden and force His children to come to the same trap of balance He cut me out to avoid in you. He could not get rid of me. He will not get rid of me."

That had some implications. I could see it, in my mind's eye: each person a garden bed where both a plant's white healthy roots and rotted, squelching, brownish-black ones spiderwebbed across the body, rooting us in two worlds. Making us two pieces of a whole. That's what the Dragon meant when he said we were all walking Voids, walking contradictions, steeped in duality: since the Garden of Eden debacle, that metaphorical moment, humanity became re-embedded with the stuff God blotted out from Himself, and that's why we spend our entire lives trying to deny, defy, and avoid it to get back to God. To purge the rot off our roots in that lake of fire God made to deal with such toxins.

Which, when you think about it, would also make sense as to why so many lines in the Bible talk about cutting vines, casting things into fire. And then, after that purge, the most ironic thing is that our gift is getting to meld *into God*—losing all sense of self and ego and becoming part of the infinite and unfathomable being as we rejoin Him, like a rainbow scale reattaching to a great ocean fish. That's all the Dragon wants, too—to reattach himself to what used to be his body. But for whatever reason, he's a scale God didn't want.

Hmm.

"Alright, well, thank you, Dragon. That about settles my main questions. These last ones I ask everyone, and as much as I'm hesitant to know what you want to say to people, it's only fair I ask them. So to start: how do you see yourself?"

8. HOW DO YOU SEE YOURSELF?

Self satisfaction, good fortune, and contentment. One finds joy in what one has and finds it abundant. Warmth and goodwill to oneself.

What a weird card to pull, Nine of Coins. Yet the part at the end of the description made sense: *warmth and goodwill to oneself.*

"I think I'm lovely," he said, his voice bright. "I think I'm inevitable, unbreakable, unbeatable. Because I am still part of all things. Even if I hate the part your God made me play, I am still all things. And I think your God knows this, too. I'm content to wait for the fall of all that is—the stars falling from the sky, blue water turning red." Very Revelation-core. "I'm patient enough to wait."

"Okay, sure. And how do you want to be seen?"

9. HOW DO YOU WANT TO BE SEEN?

I stared at the Hierophant and muttered, "You gotta be fucking with me, guy."

That only made him raise a brow and smirk. "Am I joking? Or is there maybe a hint of me, everywhere, in plain sight? Are your creeds and vows spoken every Sunday enough to keep me outside your chapels? Off your *pulpits*? Some sprouts repay their Gardener more readily than others with enough sweet whispers, after all."

Conformity, wisdom, gaining knowledge, learning. Paying mind to teachers and mentors while gaining wisdom.

THE HIEROPHANT

Ah, there we go. He was just out and saying the truth, because no one caught up in the institutions the Hierophant represented—all that conservative, old school, traditional religion, the churches with their hierarchies and dogma and corruption—would ever agree that something worse than their little impish "Devil" could be growing in the foundations of their most sacred thing. Fair enough. Couldn't argue with that.

"I see. Alright, so... that's about that. Any last messages you wanted to give? Anything you want to say to people while I'm here?"

10. ANY LAST MESSAGES?

Embarrassment, anxiety, or inability to stand up for oneself.

He gazed at me as I pulled the Seven of Wands Reversed, then cocked his head and smiled. "Some are doomed to die in the body," he said, "and some are doomed to die in the soul. Who is who? Can you tell by looking? Not always. And that is true chaos."

That wasn't ominous or anything. I didn't want to think about what it meant, though; I just wanted to get out of there. With a big, fat sigh, I kept as much of my manners as I could and snapped my book shut. "That'll do. Thank you for your time, Dragon—and I suppose I'll be seeing traces of you out in the world, too."

His smile went thin, his eyes sharp and narrow, and then, thank God, the door to outside this golden cave reappeared. I all but shot out of there, straight into the arms of Michael and Lucifer, who made me lock that door with that giant key again and leave it. Then I put my stuff away and tried to get settled back into my living room, with my pigeon cooing and hoo-ing and being a little goof to distract me from all that mess.

After a couple days, a lot more makes sense. A lot more. There were other images that came to me, as if the Dragon was still feeding me little bits and pieces. The sight of demons like people described them, big muscular horned things, sat in my mind—but only their silhouettes against a starry sky, their own eyes white pinpricks of light. Those were the real demons, the minor ones that spawned with the Tree the Dragon made, set to torment and provoke people the way the Dragon wanted, and it seemed Lucifer and all his Kings and Presidents and Princes were ones dedicated to keeping them in check. They were ones who would challenge people not in service of the Dragon, but in the interests of humanity: testing for weak spots, pushing on fragile foundations, seeing which people were too weak to resist the Dragon's shit and which ones were capable of avoiding that thing's sneaky little snares.

But if the demonic was all about separation, specifically separation without that balancing mercy and restoration, then were they evil to the Dragon? Even Qliphotic philosophers described separation as the true evil. Would that not make demons evil? I decided no, because division *and* unity was how this world was put together. Whereas angels want us to see where we're all the same in some way, demons want us to see where we're also all different. While out of balance, they can cause people to become too judgmental and severe *and* too loving and accepting (the consequence of Severity and Mercy ever being disconnected), together, they are the two sides of the coin that teach us boundaries: recognizing everything as different, distinct, yet still connected and sacred. Teaching us when to offer compassion and when to draw a line in the sand. So long as we have both, we have this created world. When we tip too far into separation, we destroy ourselves, and so do we when we tip too far into a unity we actually can't achieve in this created world: one that allows everything, including those who separate. Karl Popper is calling in.

But I mean, I don't know. There's a lot to say and a lot to think about. A lot of twists and turns and convoluted, near conflicting ideas. It's all a mess. But what I do know is that the Dragon is an interesting thing. Not a nice thing, not a good thing, but an interesting thing. I guess I do have to thank him a little bit for showing me things I didn't consider before—and it seems that would be why God sent me down here to begin with. Because He knew that for all my brave face in meditation, I was afraid of the way this thing whispered, my heart hardened to it, and that I wouldn't get any closer to understanding the Great Work until I faced it head on.

Just another day in the life of an exhausted esoteric idiot, I guess.

THE EVANGELICAL EGREGORE

As if dealing with the Dragon wasn't enough, my next interview directive from God was only a half step better: the Evangelical Egregore. What the *hell,* you know? Couldn't God give me a break for like, two minutes?

Apparently not. This was a big topic, and it was important we talked about it. Just wish I got a chance to talk to a cute and cozy spirit, like a friendly Saint, in between. But the horror of the Dragon needed to stay at the forefront of my mind for this, I guess, so that's that.

Now, I've spoken about the Evangelical Egregore before, just like I have the Dragon. In *Discovering Christian Witchcraft,* especially, we get more into it, but knowing now what egregores are, you can no doubt imagine where this interview is going. As it turns out, *American Gods* wasn't so off base with the thirty billion different iterations of Jesus it had in the T.V. adaptation; because so many people have so many radically different ideas about Jesus, who He is, and what He represents, that energy can start manifesting in some seriously strange ways outside the true presence of the Son of God.

And one specific denomination of Christianity sure has an awfully specific idea of Jesus: that white, blond haired, blue eyed Jesus, the one who would happily wear a red hat and have a gun stuck to each hip, the Jesus who thinks wokeness is weakness and that America is God's chosen land full of His *truly* chosen people. How unfortunate for the rest of us that it would be this iteration of Jesus that would get so wildly popular in these tumultuous times, because nothing I just said has anything to do with the Man from Galilee described in the Gospels. For people who grew up in denominations that focused on this counterfeit Christ, however, this is often all they have to go on when it comes to understanding Christianity as a whole—and it's no wonder to me why people are leaving that church in droves upon *droves.*

I can only be fascinated with this kind of denomination, honestly. As someone who grew up in the most relaxed version of Catholicism I have seen, with a southern European mom who could give a damn about all the things the Church officially said and with a dad who was not keen on religion in general after his own experience in Catholic schools, I was never forced to believe anything, never told I was going to hell for not believing anything, and never forced to do more than get my First Communion done. My mom and I had some blow-outs about witchcraft at the start, trust me, but she ended up being happy so long as I was still a believer in God, which was a pretty low bar to jump over, all things considered.

As a result, I've gone out of my way to learn more about these Evangelicals we hear so much about, and by *God,* am I disturbed. Books like Rev. Karla's *Deconstruction,* like Dr. Laura E. Anderson's *When Religion Hurts You,* like Kristin Kobes du Mez's *Jesus and John Wayne,* and so many more have helped me understand the depth of the damage this denomination is done, and all I can do is offer my most sincere apologies to anyone who was hurt in these institutions. It never should've happened, it was never okay, and it was never your fault. You were, and are, a whole and worthy person.

All that aside, though, I still knew that this interview was one that had to be done—not only to investigate the issues of this institution at their core, but to also maybe show people why the Jesus I know and this thing are not the same. Not at all. So let me quit waffling about here and just get right into this absolute mess.

What does one even put out to represent the Evangelical Egregore? What would a witch use to drag it in, when all she knows is crystals and tarot cards and candles? From what I know of Evangelism, there isn't really any room for that stuff—and so I had to ask my fiancé what he thought fit. While he's an atheist, he grew up in exactly the kind of Egregore-Friendly Homes™ that causes people to flee screaming from the church, and he gave me some pointers: a plain cross with no crucified Jesus hanging off it (common of more Protestant derived denominations), a Bible, and a picture of an especially white Jesus.

I had those things. But I figured *A New New Testament* or my Jewish Annotated New Testament wouldn't be very pleasing to this thing, so I grabbed the only other thing I could: my little Gideon pocket Bible, which I got from a student that had one stuffed into her hands by those wacky folks that like to haunt college campuses in the name of Christ. That's it. That's all I had to put out for it. And while I was asking God how to even talk to this thing—*would it even respond to tarot cards? Which ones could I use?*—my eye landed on, ironically, my Angel Tarot deck.

Not Travis McHenry's, though. *Doreen Virtue's.* A woman who, despite writing tons of tarot and oracle decks and plenty of books about extremely New Age, *love and light* renditions of God's angels, seems to have traded one set of egregores for another by doing a complete 180 and converting to evangelical Christianity. It all just seemed to click into place.

And before we got started, you best believe that I asked God what He thought of the egregore—and what I should watch out for. It was so funny to me that the cards I pulled were the Two of Coins, the Two of Cups, and the *Devil.* All cards of partnership, romance before the red flags, and blatant vice and entrapment. God was telling me clearly: this thing could talk a good game, could snap up the people too broken and bruised to see clearly, and could use every one of their guilts, insecurities, and fears against them to make them fully dependent on this thing and *happy about it.* Yikes.

So after a little bit more futzing around and procrastinating, I finally sat myself down, popped my headphones in, opened up my notebook, and got to it. I swore I wouldn't listen to any Hillsong music to talk to this thing, but knowing it's the group that people seem to go nuts for in this whole Egregore Circus, I decided to buck up and get the full experience. I've never wanted to lobotomize myself so much as when listening to track after track of generic "Jesus Loves Me" type music.

But it was part of setting the meditation stage, y'know? So I kept playing that messy music, asked God to help me find this thing, and within moments, I found it. I found it from thankfully the *right* end of Heaven, but that did not make it better: I stood at the edge of Heaven, where the clouds looked over whatever green-pastured little hamlet I always saw when I was up there, and up from those clouds rose something like a massive black centipede with glimmering white and purple eyes. It snapped its mandibles and tapped against what, after a moment, I saw to be some kind of golden barrier around Heaven. It was trying to get in. What was weird, though, was that when I left the barrier and hovered in the empty sky outside the lowest Heaven, that centipede was a man.

A man dressed in a big white shirt, red strip of fabric hung over his shoulder, with blond hair making two loose ringlets just past his shoulders and with the most unsettling eyes. They were yellow, and their pupils were more a four-leafed black clover, the four petals equally sized in the eye. It tracked me as I left the barrier and became that tapping centipede again when I went back in. Except I wasn't really all the way in. Some thread connected to it, and it reached a little bit inside, to where I *thought* I saw Jesus: darker skin, wiry, wooly hair and short beard, purely red robes. I thought that was Jesus for a good minute—especially because I heard Jesus say that this thing wasn't allowed in Heaven— until I looked closer at this Jesus, too.

It was too round. Like a child's figurine, the kind with round balls for heads and nubby little fingerless hands. It also had those golden clover eyes, and it was smiling with a big, fake white grin. The thread coming from that centipede was attached to it, as if it were the light on the end of a football fish, coaxing me closer in my confusion.

"Up here."

When I looked up, there was another ledge of Heaven's clouds, another barrier. I scrambled up to it and saw the real Jesus sitting there, similar to the football-fish-lure version down below, but He looked like a real man: tired, yet glowing blue-green eyes, a somewhat thin face, loose red robes swallowing His frame up, sandals on His feet. He had a roughly carved shepherd's staff leaning against His shoulder as He sat there and stared down at that thing outside Heaven's walls.

"Careful," Jesus said, never once taking His eyes off the thing. "It wants to make you think he's Me at all costs."

"How's it even in here at all?"

"That's as far as it goes. So we can see what it does. It's a crafty little worm."

"Well," I really did not want to deal with this thing, but there was no way to be done with it except to get on with it, "I mean... can you come with me? Help me with this thing?"

Jesus glanced at me, smiled, and got up the way an older man might, all slow and using His staff for support. He had not a drop of enthusiasm in Him, either, which was comforting; it seemed I wasn't the only one totally put off by the thing, and it seemed Heaven's barrier showed it for what it really was, which, to me, looked like some kind of brain bug. I could just imagine all those little legs hooking into people's ear canal, those mandibles pinching deep into someone's head and holding tight. Horrible thought.

But Jesus guided me out of Heaven, and as we stood on empty air, outside Heaven's barrier, we ended up sinking down, down, down, into a dark auditorium of some kind. The only place that was lit was a stage all the way in the back, with a podium, some flowers on the sides barely visible in the shadows, and a big empty cross behind that podium on the wall. The Evangelical Egregore stood behind that podium like a preacher ready to deliver the sermon of a lifetime, and in the many seats of this dark auditorium were rows and rows of ghouls: withered faces of silent people who didn't seem to move any other part of their bodies than their glowing eyes. Those eyes tracked Jesus and I all the way to the front of the auditorium, their withered lips bent into frowns.

I hated it. *God,* I hated it. But Jesus kept His gaze squarely on that egregore, standing close to me with a fistful of the back of my shirt in one hand and His staff held tight in the other. With the garbage Hillsong stuff blasting in my ears and this downright maniacal setting, I huffed and opened up my book.

"Alright, well, hello, Jesus of the Evangelical Church." To the real Jesus, I ducked my head and whispered, "Sorry. I gotta use your name."

I got the sense I should refer to the real Jesus as something else, something that most unwitting followers of "Christ" wouldn't know. Yeshua Meschiach wasn't it; I'd seen wacko folks hit me with that one in my website inbox. Jesus Christ was what I was hearing over and over again in these Hillsong nightmares. But there was one I didn't hear anyone say as much, and that was the Greek version of Jesus's name: Iesous Christos (like Ee-YE-soos Kh-rih-stos). It meant the same thing: Jesus the Christ, the Messiah. So that was what I kept Jesus in my head as while mucking about with this egregore.

The egregore stared at me with a sickly sweet smile on its face. I didn't like how it was looking at me from that pulpit, but while I was stuck before the stage, I didn't have any choice but to deal with it.

"So," I started again, "I've got some questions for you, Evangelical Jesus. Care to answer?"

"With those?" He looked down his nose at my cards. "Those evil things?"

"Ah, come on. They're just a language. Just a bunch of symbols on paper that'll make the back-and-forth a little more fluent." I tapped the angel deck clean and shuffled. "Come on. Won't you give me a message I can understand?"

The egregore didn't look pleased, but it finally huffed. "Fine."

"Great, thank you. Now, first question: I understand you've got quite the Church. So many people! It's impressive." The egregore puffed a little bit at that, and I stopped myself from shaking my head. I wasn't trying to piss this thing off right out the gate. "Can you tell me what you think about your worshippers? How do you see them?"

1. HOW DO YOU SEE YOUR WORSHIPPERS?

It was really funny to pull the Five of Coins: a card of monetary disaster. That, alongside the Knight of Swords and the Star, was a lot—especially with the language Doreen put into the booklet. All "Go-Getter" this and "Faith" and "a Sense of Purpose" that. It was apparent what the egregore thought, but he clarified anyway:

"They're good people. They're just lost. They think so much about money; they *really* want to be like their pastors. They want to believe everything will be okay. They're smart, resourceful when it comes to getting what they want. I help them in exchange for their gifts and love."

Events go at high speed. Plans implemented. Intellect and creativity. Go getters. Assertive, if tactless.

Wish upon a star. Hope and happy expectation. Make plans with the long view in mind. Trust intuition. Faith.

Too focused on what you don't have. A mentality of lack. Pessimism. Bad feelings are temporary.

What was weird to me was how he was speaking all stilted and simple, as if he thought longer sentences would trip me up. Or maybe he was just spitting his ideas as they came to him, one at a time, like AI spitting responses. Who can say? All I knew was that his answer led perfectly into my next question.

"Help, yeah. Speaking of help, can you tell me more about that? How exactly do you help your followers get what they want out of life?"

2. HOW DO YOU HELP YOUR FOLLOWERS?

The right time to begin new projects. Leave behind doubts in your abilities. Taking more classes or reading more books is unnecessary.

Two people sharing a close relationship. Fond friendship continues to deepen. Healing still possible. Conflicts end, forgiveness.

Re-evaluate your situation; you're missing opportunities. Solutions are in front of your face. Positive forces working to help. Taking things for granted.

Another funny thing was seeing the Magician pop up, but with Two and Four of Cups, it was once again more about the language of the booklet: all about leaving doubts behind, partnership, and getting out of negative thinking. Coincidentally, as I was writing, this Hillsong bit came on: "Lion and Lamb" by Big Daddy Weave or whatever (what a name). It kept repeating one line *over* and *over* and *over* again, asking who could stop God (the "Lord Almighty") and clearly never expecting an answer. I looked at Jesus as I scribbled the card meanings down, and He had a face made of hard, cold bronze, His brows furrowed and His lips pressed in a line. He was not a fan of how this egregore delighted in that goofy little song and gloated it over us.

"Through me, all things are possible," the egregore said, practically shining with that golden light on the podium. He was in his element up there, that was obvious. "I help people who rely on me. I empower them to believe in themselves and band together. Together, they can make a difference. We can make our Church great when they all work together under me. Pessimism is not allowed. It gets in the way."

"Oh." I couldn't help but chuckle at that. Sure, yeah, just outlaw the concept of pessimism altogether; that'll fix anyone's sense of doubt or worry. I mean, at least it *kind of* seemed like he wanted to help people and take care of them—the ones that worshipped him, anyway—but boy, was this a Toxic Positivity type of help. He noticed me laugh, and his big grin soured into a somewhat confused scowl, so I held up my hands. "No, no, don't mind me. I'm sorry. Let's continue. That's how you help people, which is all well and good, but now... there are some people that are hurt, too. Some people that deconstruct and leave the Church. They seem to have a pretty hard time with what they went through here. What are your thoughts on that?"

3. Wʜᴀᴛ ᴅᴏ ʏᴏᴜ ᴛʜɪɴᴋ ᴏꜰ ᴘᴇᴏᴘʟᴇ ʜᴜʀᴛ ʙʏ ᴛʜᴇ ᴄʜᴜʀᴄʜ?

Even as I was flipping and picking the three cards he wanted, I could see his serene, glowing mask slip. His eyes went wide, his teeth flashing a bit as he spat, "They never really loved me."

"That so? I dunno. I hear a lot of people say they tried quite a bit. Come on; give me some more of your thoughts. I'm so curious to know what you think."

He put his hands on either side of the podium, lips pressed tight, but it seems a little bit of flattery was enough to get those lips loose again. "Those people never loved me, as I said. They don't know what they're missing, either." That's definitely the vibe I got from the overall positive cards he pulled, which were all about creativity and joy and weddings and family and

An exciting new opportunity awaits. Angels guide you to this endeavor. Someone who's outgoing, creative, passionate, but mischievous.

Time for celebration! Weddings, announcements of pregnancy, reunions. You need to have more fun!

Abundance. Feelings of freedom, material comfort, and capacity to enjoy yourself. Family life is strong. Knowing you've been blessed.

social standing. "What do they want to deconstruct from? Beautiful families, loving communities? So there's a few bad apples. No one is perfect. That's why I'm here. I'm all the perfect they need, so long as they stay with me. These people can be great with me. Without me, they're nothing—sinners wriggling like worms in the dirt for some shred of acceptance from fakes and frauds. Like that one!"

He pointed at Jesus, and I stood real fucking still, because the light in Jesus's eyes right then was nothing like the light in any of these audience ghouls or that egregore. But He kept quiet, even as His face looked awfully stony, and His grip on that staff was something deadly.

The egregore didn't seem to know how to read the room, though. "That isn't Jesus," he said, pointing. "I'm Jesus. I love *everyone.* Does He?"

He didn't like that I kept capitalizing Jesus's pronouns in my notebook and not his, too, but I was settling more and more into "Hardass Detective" and less and less into "Schmoozy Reporter," so I didn't particularly care what this thing liked. I just elbowed Jesus and asked Him the silent question: "So do you?" And His stony mask finally broke, with Him raising a brow and smiling at me like I already knew the answer. Probably because I did already know the answer.

After sharing a private half-giggle with my Iesous there, I turned back to the egregore. I could even see myself as the Hardass Detective, wearing a black suit and shiny black shoes, like I was dressed to give a statement outside a police station. I tapped my pencil to the notebook and kept on.

"Alright, alright, well, what do you think about other denominations, then? Some of your Church feels awfully strongly about Catholics, for instance, but I mean… I've been noticing a little bit of your influence among their ranks, too. Some Catholic folks seem to be getting awfully… outspoken about the world." In all the wrong ways, but hey. "What do you say?"

4. WHAT DO YOU THINK ABOUT OTHER DENOMINATIONS?

Logic, discipline, and order must be cultivated. Although your dreams are valid and sound, they need guidelines to manifest properly. Be a postiive leader.

You're doing too much and may experience financial wreck. Maintaining status quo. Stay open to new points of view. A more playful approach needed.

Deep emotions arising from situations or relationships. Balance yourself. Parties, social opportunities. Charming, contemplative, idealistic, sensitive people.

A smug air returned around the egregore. He shrugged, nonchalant, and said, "They have their heart in the right place. But they're lost. They focus on all these elements that don't matter. All that matters is *me*. One doesn't need anything but four walls and a love of me."

"I mean," I shrugged back, "you're not *wrong*, I guess. Technically no one *needs* anything physical." That was Magician 101 understanding: a good magician could do everything from right in their brain, no tools required.

The egregore puffed a bit, then hunched over and scowled. "All these *idols*, all this *art*, they're distractions. People are coming to realize it: there's only me. Only me."

Then he looked at me with a face full of shadows and those awful, golden eyes, glowing like a cat's. Suddenly, we were out of that auditorium, too. We were out on the ocean, the water getting choppy, and in the back was some fishing pier with mountains standing stark against the sky. This hyper-European looking Jesus was standing on the water, pointing at me, his oversized t-shirt robe flapping in the stormy winds, and he pointed at me like he was going to call the lightning to zap me down to cinders.

"You all will burn," he hissed. "You 'Christian Witches.'"

Oh.

"You'll burn for your evil. I'll get you. I'll root you out."

"Yeah?" I dunno; that sounded like a fun challenge to me, if a bit of a dangerous one. I didn't know what this thing was capable of or how fast it could move its people, but I was more entertained than cautious about it. "Try it, bitch."

He didn't like that too much, to say the least. I don't know how I stayed so nonchalant about that, honestly. I just know that I was also standing on the ocean water just fine, unphased by wind and rain, and my notebook's pages were fluttering around in the wind as if I were holding a spellbook rather than all my interviews. But I distinctly remember a cross of gold behind me, with a really weak, ghoulishly thin Jesus hanging off it, all gaunt and with a crown of green leaves and flowers instead of thorns. It was a very *Saint Young Men* style Jesus, honestly.

That dying, fake Jesus looked up, despairing, as the egregore move to cut it down. It was like the egregore thought it was dispelling some illusion or evicting some spirit from me. But the thing is, that pasty white half-skeleton hanging off that cross wasn't any more the real Jesus than the egregore itself was. We could pick apart the symbolism of its crown all day, dissect the meaning of this for hours, but I didn't have much more time to think about it, because the egregore never had a chance to do whatever stunt he wanted to do; I suddenly had a front row seat to Jesus—*real* Jesus, but like, Revelation version—behind that cross and that withering man hanging off of it.

His wiry brown hair and beard were laced with bright white thunder, His face downright murderous, and in His hands was a sword pointed straight at that egregore. That sword pushed forward, and while it never touched the egregore, as Iesous passed me, that sword seemed to snag on whatever illusion we were wrapped up in, tearing the blue waters and cloudy sky back like a curtain until we were back in the dark auditorium. The egregore blinked, looking around and gaping like a fish, and it was the first time he seemed truly and surely rattled. Like he didn't expect all this.

Ha, He got'cha. I stuck close to Jesus as He lost that lightning in Him, and as that sword stretched back out into a staff. *He got'cha.*

"Alright, question five," I said, teetering from "Hardass Detective" into pure "Bad Cop." "Pull some cards for me, baby. What do you think about us *witches,* and the New Age junk, huh? Funny. For someone saying you're gonna root us out, here you are talking with the cards."

5. THOUGHTS ON WITCHES AND THE NEW AGE?

The egregore crossed his arms and spat, "That's because you're making me use those cards!"

"Making you?" Meditation is weird, in how often I see outside myself, like I'm watching a movie of the whole interaction, but I did see myself look up and smile. "I didn't know I could make the supposed Son of God do shit."

If he could've vaporized me with that mean mug, I think he would've.

"Come on, now," I said, tapping at the cards. "Answer me."

With a sniff, the egregore snapped, "Those who do magic were never mine."

Well, that's for sure.

"People want all this power," he went on. "Don't they see? My power is all they need. They need to love and pray

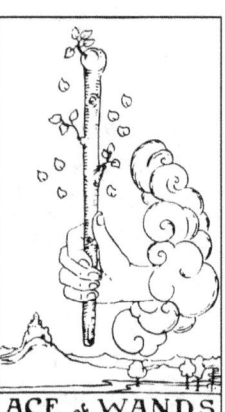

KING of SWORDS.

You may receive valuable advice from an intelligent professional. Decisions need to be equitable to all involved. Speak with confidence.

ACE of WANDS.

An exciting opportunity appears. Creative and inspiring career possibilities. Innovative ideas should be pursued.

THE MOON.

Sometimes fears are external, sometimes internal. A powerful time of intuition. Embrace a period of self awareness. Best insights are about yourself.

to me alone, not turn to this devilry. Those who do magic don't love me. The power is mine; the glory is mine!"

I glanced at Jesus, and I could see that muscle work in His jaw. The glory was, in fact, *not* that of this slimy egregore's, no way. We both knew that.

The egregore caught us sharing another split-second moment, and he started talking faster. "They can't take it for themselves," he hissed, "and they learn that through all their counterfeit power. They invite demons and corrupt themselves, then crawl back to me to realize they've made a mistake. I forgive. But only if one renounces all of it!"

What a hot pile of shit. All of this sounded like every book, article, or whatever else I'd ever read from an evangelical. The same language, the same rhetoric. Truly, egregores were formed by their believers, a real chicken-and-egg creature. I could feel those words tug on me, too, like the egregore was tapping at my very constitution to see if it could find any place to plant a little seed of doubt and worry. But the best defense against doubt and worry is, in fact, knowledge, and I had enough of it that there was no space for that seed; I was already overgrown, all my vines and leaves too dense to do anything but choke a little weed that would've snuck in between it all. When he didn't get any re-action out of me with that mess, he dropped all expression and stared at me with huge, wide eyes that could've swallowed me alive if I'd let them.

"Uh-huh." I finished writing all that down and nodded. "Okay. So, then, let me back up. Before, you were saying there are a few bad apples in your Church. Fair. But what do you think about things like purity culture, and all that abuse from church leadership, then? It seems a little systemic. And then you got grown fathers giving their little eight year old daughters some 'purity ring' and telling them that their bodies belong to their daddies until marriage. Sounds a little incestuous to me, y'know? And that's not even all of it." By this point, whatever bare-bones attempts at being cordial I had in me were long gone. "There's a lot of shit going on in your Church. Wanna speak on it?"

6. WHAT IS GOING ON IN YOUR CHURCH?

You may be faced with a complex decision. Hard to choose between options. Stop procrastinating and get busy. No unrealistic expectations.

Positive thinking is essential now. Obsessive, negative thoughts are the root of your problems. Regret is wasted emotion. Worry.

You're experiencing some challenges. Others hold different goals and values. Clash of wills, disagreement. A competitive situation.

How funny that the language of the cards I pulled were all about *thinking positively* (Nine of Swords), *making hard decisions* (Seven of Cups), and *competition and clash of wills* (Five of Wands). This thing, before it even spoke, I could tell was trying to throw all the blame everywhere else, and he looked at me with such a rage as he hid behind his podium and spoke.

"You can't let the bad outweigh the good," he snapped. "If all had the same passion and zeal and understanding, no one would fool themselves into thinking my ways are a problem. It's all the tricks and pessimism of the world that ensnares my people—tells them goodness and right living isn't love. Your mindset is *filthy,* calling the safeguarding of innocence 'incestu-ous.' No, that one beside you," again, that thing had a lot of audacity, pointing at the real Jesus, "that one isn't any better! I don't see *His* Church doing any better! Your God can't seem to keep a handle on it, either!"

"And who is my God?"

Jesus and I shared a glance before the egregore answered, though, and it seemed like there was some regret, some long-faced sadness, in Jesus's face, because in a way, the egregore wasn't wrong;

every single Church, every denomination, had some skeletons in its closet. But God gave us free will, and the Dragon spoke all kinds of shit into people's heads; wherever there was the name of God to use like a hammer, some nasty old man would go and use it, whether that was actually the way of God or not.

The egregore looked between me and Jesus and jerked its hand, pointing again at Jesus. "That beside you there—that's Satan!"

I barked a laugh. Calling Jesus the devil. Damn. But we know the *bright and morning star* refers to more than just that "angel of light" everyone warns about, so it's not like no one has ever said such a thing before. With my pen in hand, I wrote that outburst down to mark it on the record and muttered, "That was a choice."

The egregore blinked as if he'd expected me to jump away from Jesus and get all kinds of confused. Instead, I was grinning to myself and chuckling, knowing full well this thing was not making anything better for himself. Jesus, though, was stock still, silent, waiting for me to get this over with. But the egregore kept shouting, to the point that I couldn't keep up writing it all down.

"It's Satan, that *thing* beside you! It's twisting the good Word into allowances for *sin!* You follow Him because He tells you what you want to hear! You twist the Word for—!"

"Yeah, yeah, shut up." I somehow ended up right in that thing's face, and I said, "If you're so totally Jesus, then tell me: when are you coming back? Lots of people are waiting around for you, you know. Lots of people wanna see you come and wipe away *all* these evil, terrible people! So when you gonna do it, huh? When you coming back?"

The egregore paused, blinking, then barked, "Soon!"

"No, no, pull a card. Let's go." I shuffled and shuffled, knowing full well he already exposed himself as a fake piece of shit with that quick answer. "Pull a card. Tell me when."

7. WHEN'S THE RAPTURE STARTING, BABY?

THE CHARIOT.

Successfully balancing a tough situation. Take action and make decisions. Stay calm and grounded. Exercise control firmly but kindly with others. Self discipline. Sheer willpower.

And of course, he wouldn't be able to tell me an exact day. The Bible, for all this thing wanted to screech about the "good Word," said as much about what the Son would know about the end of days (Matthew 24:36):

But the exact day and hour? No one knows that, not even heaven's angels, not even the Son. Only the Father knows.

As anyone who's heard me talk before knows: the whole "Rapture" thing is not a *when,* but an *if.* It all depends on how bad we mess this world up. Like Sodom and Gomorrah would've been spared if only one good person remained, so too will this world be spared so long as one good person remains. Maybe two, if you ask certain Jewish rabbis who insist the world needs *two* good people to survive. Out of eight billion and counting, I don't think we're losing our world anytime soon. For this thing to even *say* "soon"?

He was bullshitting me. And that's what made it all the funnier to pull the Chariot, as if he really wanted me to believe that the Rapture was *so totally going to happen soon.* I was actually having fun by that point, even if I wanted to wrap it up and get gone.

"I'm coming soon; my Kingdom is at hand!" The egregore raised his hand up, really working that megachurch preacher angle, but he just sounded to me like all his followers: quoting the Bible to sound cool and holy, but with every word ringing oh so hollow. He was mimicking faith; he was no source of it. Still, he tried to keep composed. "I'm leading my people to glory. Not yet, but soon! People just need to get a few things right first. All must come to me! Then I'll exact judgement!"

Oh, jeez. However, by "get a few things right," I couldn't help but think of Project 2025 and all that awful Christian nationalism plaguing America. Were those the things to "get right"? One could only imagine.

"Sure, bud," I said.

And as I looked up with a big smile and half a laugh still at my lips, I actually watched that thing falter. I didn't believe him, and he didn't like that—especially given all the Hillsong hoopla that was still blasting in my ears. He tried to hold onto all that "Jesus is King" and "Jesus is Enough" stuff that was slowly cooking my brain all *sous vide* style, but I don't think this thing's ever been laughed at all alone before. He knew I didn't take him seriously, and even I could feel Jesus staring holes in us both, so I was mighty entertained when that egregore of Jesus started looking a little unsure of himself. It almost made me feel bad. After all, egregores don't typically know that they're egregores; they only know what their believers programmed them with.

This poor guy. He looked a little confused—a little scared, even.

"Alright," I started again, "last few questions, here we go: how do you see yourself?"

8. HOW DO YOU SEE YOURSELF?

Three of Wands was a surprisingly humble card. But the egregore straightened and said, "Insult me all you'd like. I'm winning. The Kingdom of God is at hand, and I will destroy all enemies of my father! It's always darkest before the dawn. I can do it. I'm all powerful. I'm the son of God!"

Golden time of celebration. Not the time to rest. Keep going. Stay enthusiastic. Patience needed.

That "I'm winning" thing definitely made me think of Project 2025. Still, was he trying to convince me or himself? I didn't know at that point. It felt more like he was just echoing platitudes and trying to stand in the power of the worship music's singers and listeners. Too bad I didn't care.

"Cool. How do you want to be seen?"

9. HOW DO YOU WANT TO BE SEEN?

You don't need to stay in a situation if you're not happy. Plenty of possibilities for freedom exist. Be more confident in your abilities. Positive thoughts. See truth; act with faith to win.

Another surprising card. I found this choice weird, until I started getting a sense of what he was trying to express.

"I am a master strategist," he said. "My so-called 'defeat' on the cross was military strategy against the Enemy!" I could've rolled my eyes at that militaristic language the Evangelicals liked so much, but I checked myself and let him keep going. "I am one who liberates from sin and death. I remind my people that they're never too lost to start over. Come to me, and I'll give freedom."

Which is sweet, in a way, I guess. That is the main issue of Eight of Swords: the bondage perceived by the one who draws that card isn't real. It's nice that people can get some help from this thing, messy and fake as it is, but does it justify this thing's existence? I didn't have the answer to that right then. I was just glad this thing, for all his gross attitude, did sometimes show the glimmer of the real in all that fake: it did care about the wellbeing of what it deemed "its" people, to a great extent. It's just that this care was so clearly, obviously conditional.

"Sure, yeah. Now, last one: any messages you wanna share?" I was such a shitter, smiling in his face the way I was. "There are a lot of *witches* that are gonna read this, you know. Anything you want all us *dirty sinners* to know?"

10. Any Last Messages?

He tipped his chin up and set his face hard, like he finally got a handle on who he was supposed to be. "Yes. Get those cards away from me; I won't use them one more second. Know this, girl: *you* are an unrepentant sinner. Be gone from my sight. Only those who truly love me will be part of my Kingdom. You can't love two masters. Choose me or choose the death of sin and be cast into the fire."

I about died hearing *this Goddamn egregore, of all things,* give me the old half-assed quoting of Matthew 6:24. No way was this thing gonna give me the "two masters" tripe. What a riot. What a mess!

Once again, maybe that thing expected me to cower or rethink things with all that nonsense, but I just dusted off and packed up my cards. "Alright, that's enough of that," I said, chuckling. "Hate to break it to you, bud, but I'm not afraid of fire. We were all forged of that fire, and we're *all* going right back in. You included. Better get comfy with the idea."

And with that, the real Jesus slammed His staff into the auditorium floor and shattered the illusion into pieces. Suddenly, we were all falling as if the auditorium were made of glass the entire time. As we fell, the auditorium's ghouls crumbled away into dust, and we ended up sinking down into a very familiar desert, with a huge pillar extending up from the sand that was at least a mile down below. As I hung in the air with Jesus, though, I watched that egregore zip past me, sinking down, down, down, landing on that tall column below us. I looked around a bit further and saw that familiar pillar in the distance: a big square stage with four pillars reaching up to nothing and an old, crumbling little throne.

We were in Thaumiel. What were we doing in the absolute bottom of hell? And what was that egregore doing, sinking down into it? I didn't have too long to guess before Lucifer himself popped up, right beside Jesus. I had a lot of questions then: how was the real Jesus here, where the angels couldn't seem to go? What happened to the egregore? What *would* happen to it?

"Did you trap it here?" I looked at Jesus, who didn't so much as budge as He watched that egregore fall further down to the base of the pillar, His arms crossed and His face grim. "Or... is it operating out of here?"

Both Jesus and Lucifer shrugged at that, as if they didn't want to spoil anything. But if I knew anything about the Dragon, it was that one could be trapped in Thaumiel all day and still find a way to whisper up to the Earth. What a pain in the ass.

And while that should've been the end of the interview, with me packing it up, saying goodbye to the two Morning Stars, and getting to cleaning my house, what I found instead was that I had to ask just one more question—this time to the true Jesus.

"What'd you think of all that? And, you know, of what the egregore said—about your Church also being a bit of a mess?"

J: WHAT DO YOU THINK ABOUT THE CHURCH BEING A MESS?

A natural counselor who listens to others, offering comfort based on experience. Charity work. Quiet authority. Trustworthy, cultured, stable. Perfect solutions.

As I read the description, I knew exactly what He was trying to say, but He still sighed and leaned over to tell me in a quiet voice.

"People with evil wishes have always tried to wear my name like a skin," He muttered. "It's given my Father's shadow so much purchase. But all those who know Me, know Me. They know Me by My fruits and My countenance. I don't need to brag. But people with grand delusion of Divinity pass by the quiet God for the loud one with empty promises." He looked at me head on, blue-green eyes shining with that very Divine light, and He smiled in the way only Jesus can smile. "Be good to others, and you've been good to Me—and in turn, I'll always be good to you. That's how you know you're dealing with Me, the true Son."

I don't think there's anyone that can argue with me when I say that hanging out with true Jesus is like, premium comfort and good times.

But with all that said and done, I was finally able to dust my hands of this ridiculousness and get out of there. I don't know what God wanted me to do this interview for—and I can only imagine the recent wave after wave of theobros flooding my Instagram comments with the typical screeching about heresy, blasphemy, and how I'm going to hell aren't a coincidence, given I've been drawing this egregore near all week by thinking about it—but I think I got what I needed to out of it.

And all I can think of the Christians who don't realize they're worshipping a lie like this is how *ironic* it all is. One of their favorite things to say is that the devil comes as an angel of light (2 Corinthians 11:14) and that people are being deceived, yet they run to serve this garbage without so much as a second thought? Are they serious? That's embarrassing.

At least the rest of us can know for sure, now, though: whatever the hell these people are worshipping, it sure as shit isn't the One True God, or His Son, or His Spirit. And there's one little Bible verse that these people love to use that again, so very ironically, they never realize applies to them, too:

My people are destroyed from lack of knowledge: Because you have rejected knowledge, I also reject you as my priests; because you have ignored the law of your God, I also will ignore your children.

—Hosea 4:6

SATAN

I know, I know. It seems like we're doing a whole of exploration of the "darker side" of things here, what with all the angels and the demons and the Dragon and the Egregore and now the biggest "bad" that the Church has made into their bogeyman. And that's because we are! But there's something a little more nuanced to this Satan figure than the Church likes to tell you, as you might imagine, and after all the experiences I had, I needed to lock this one down for good. I won't lie, though: of the many interviews I've had, it's weird to look back and think how much talking to an infernal—especially one of the renown and magnitude of Satan—would've spooked me once upon a time, and how much it just did not spook me when I took it on, and how little *any* of this stuff spooks me now.

There's something to be said of the sheer *apathy* for these things that comes the more you dive into mysticism and religion as a whole. For people, for the innocent, for feelings of home and camaraderie and love, I shed happy, love-heavy tears all day long and get lost in that deep feeling—but the thought of monsters? Of shadows and beasts and evils waiting to snap at my heels? It's like asking me to stop for a particularly feisty little beetle on the ground and be deeply afraid of its pinchy mandibles that couldn't even break the skin of my finger. That's why I look so hard down my nose at these "Christians" that think more about their little devil than God, who fear Satan's name more than their Lord's, and who spend all their time trying to avoid these wicked temptations that stalk their every step.

If you've ever come in contact with our dear Hagia Sophia proper, and Her fire truly crowns your brow, such stupidity just doesn't haunt you like that. Doesn't even cross your mind.

Anyway, as many of you may know, *Ha-Shatan* is actually Hebrew for "the adversary"—and it's a title often worn by many different angels who seek to challenge, test, and generally oppose humanity for whatever reason *God* decides they should. A great article about this can be found in the *Jewish Annotated New Testament*: "Supernatural Beings" by Rebecca Lesses. One of the biggest examples of this is likely the story of the Book of Job, in which the figure known as Satan tells God that Job may only be a worshipper for the nice things he has, and that they should test his faith. God agrees, and

Job loses everything: wife, kids, goats, the whole thing, to the point that he curses the very day he was born. Still, Job looks to God, and God feels bad, so He restores everything Job lost and blesses him for his faith. Job is described as an upright man that hates evil, with like, thousands of animals, seven kids, the whole thing. But I must say, something about the way this exchange is written is just so funny (Job 1:6-12):

> One day the angels came to present themselves before the Lord, and Satan also came with them. The Lord said to Satan, "Where have you come from?"
> Satan answered the Lord, "From roaming throughout the earth, going back and forth on it."
> Then the Lord said to Satan, "Have you considered my servant Job? There is no one on earth like him; he is blameless and upright, a man who fears God and shuns evil."
> "Does Job fear God for nothing?" Satan replied. "Have you not put a hedge around him and his household and everything he has? You have blessed the work of his hands, so that his flocks and herds are spread throughout the land. But now stretch out your hand and strike everything he has, and he will surely curse you to your face."
> The Lord said to Satan, "Very well, then, everything he has is in your power, but on the man himself do not lay a finger."
> Then Satan went out from the presence of the Lord.

(I just—"hey, what are you doing here? Have you seen my very special boy? Isn't he great?" It's funny, okay? It feels like a folktale, a very casual and silly little interaction.)

Moreover, I mean... "Satan" didn't have a bad guess there, right? About Job only rocking with God because he was being so richly blessed? So it was an interesting test. Just sucks that it was at the expense of a person, which divine beings like God and Satan alike don't seem to always remember have deep feelings and deep pains. It's kind of like adults vs. babies, if you think about it: adults know there are worse things than dropping your strawberry in the dirt, but to a toddler that has experienced so little, that is absolutely the worst thing that could've happened and deserves a half hour of crying. Job's kids, cattle, wife—losing all that is as crushing as dropping a strawberry in the dirt to God and Satan alike, apparently.

But I got to wondering: is the Satan we know now... an egregore? Or is it that maybe this angel who most commonly wears the title Satan among the Divine Council is truly his own being? I was so deeply curious, and at this point, there was no interview I could do that felt "too far" to me anymore.

So let's dive in.

According to what I could find, Satan is a more "dark academia" kind of guy—one that likes nice things, good conversation, and classic literature. I had some of that hanging around: some roses to scatter on the table, books like the works of Cicero, Edgar Allan Poe, and Homer (Illiad and Odyssey), and that sambuca I'd gotten for Samael. With all that together, and a few garnets and onyx and obsidian stones, as well as a red candle and a raven, I was ready to speak to the spirit known as the king of Wrath, the main adversary of Judaism and Christianity, the very being everyone always sees as the Big Bad ruining the world. (I'd like to think we know a little better now that we've been on this journey together, but it's understandable that old habits and feelings would die hard.)

So I asked God to let me find him, and sure enough, within moments, I found myself in a familiar place: the main offices of the demons, the richly decorated and dark studies where Lucifer often sat doing whatever work he had to do before I came and bothered him. It's always paperwork. So much paperwork for the poor Infernal Emperor.

I waited out in the hallway until Lucifer noticed me standing there looking stupid, and then he got up from his desk and came to greet me. When I asked him to help me find Satan, too, it was just as they say: *speak of the devil, and he will appear.* Lucifer motioned past me, to the railing of the hallway that overlooked a huge foyer, and there was Satan, leaning against that railing, with a mischievous smile.

He looked like something out of a Gustave Dore drawing. If you've ever seen them, Satan is always depicted with bat wings, with curlier blond hair, and with either armor like Michael's or no clothes at all. He thankfully had some typical angel robes on there, off-white and somewhat tattered, but still perfectly useful for covering himself, and he had strong features: a thicker brow, strong nose, very defined jaw, all that. Similar to Samael, actually. However, there was something about his big, droopy-lidded, crystal-blue eyes and that mean smirk that had him feeling more like those pretty men that know they're pretty and are nothing but bad news, y'know? He had his arms crossed, and he was looking at me like I was something funny. Maybe I was; I was tired and hungry but still excited to chat.

So Lucifer left me in Satan's care, and we walked further and further into the dark hallway, into nothingness, until a new scene materialized from the shadows: a beach. Or rather, the rocky cliff by the ocean. Satan lounged on a rock, I nestled myself towards where the water was lapping at the stone, and then we got into it.

"Alright, Satan," I said once he chose the Marigold Tarot and I'd organized myself enough to understand anything he might say, "let's get into it. I've got quite a few questions here, things I'm real curious about, and above all, I really gotta ask first: how have you evolved from *Ha-Shatan*, the Adversary, to *Satan* as a whole separate name? As a separate idea? It just seems like a lot happened between one and the other."

I. HOW HAVE YOU EVOLVED FROM HA-SHATAN TO SATAN?

Right away, I could tell something about Satan: if Lucifer was more mellow, soft spoken, and curious about humanity, Satan had more of a cynicism to him. As I asked this, his lips curled into a smirk, his head bobbing in the slightest nod as he thought about his answer.

"To take this name in full," he said, "yes, I had to break away from the Divine Council a bit. Move more on my own. I'm still a part of it, of course, but more on my own terms, now that I've taken God's Title and made it my Name. And I took that title up as my own name because that's what you humans know me by."

Greed, possessiveness, unkindness of spirit. Vision obscured by a closed fist.

Drama, authority, power, self expression, and confidence. Stepping into new opportunities with flourish.

Needing to move on, alienation, and love and relationships long lost.

"Ah, I guess that would make sense. No need to reinvent the wheel."

He winked. "Exactly. It's easier. No one can deny the presence in my name. It's one with such history and heft; how could I ever put it down?"

"Got'cha, got'cha. I see!" Getting an answer like that, though, made me start questioning a thing or two. I came in here thinking that I actually would find some kind of red-devil-with-horns egregore, and what I had instead was a bona fide angel, one with a bit of a chip on his shoulder and constantly serving ideas that would've put the Divine Council in a bit of a tailspin if he were to keep going–at least, if the Job debacle was any indication. "Okay. Well, knowing that Satan comes from the title, though… do you have a name from before your Satan days? One you'd like to share?"

2. DO YOU HAVE A NAME BESIDES SATAN?

Loss, dishonor, and defeat even in the event of victory. A victory that feels ill won or hollow.

For the life of me, I could not shake this word: Tipherel. I have no idea if this means anything in Hebrew (as usually -el suffix names do), or if it's a real word; all I know is that I could not find it anywhere, no matter how much I searched. Later, after I'd posted this interview, someone would mention this name as a reference to how this angel was once operating out of another Sefirot sphere, Tiferet—a sphere centered on beauty, on mercy, on balance, on reconciling conflict, from what you can learn just by quickly searching it online (of course there's much more to any of these spheres that you need proper, supervised study to understand). Still, I'd been wondering if I'd just been making this name up before that. However, with how this name would not leave my head, I didn't think it was *all* my imagination, and so getting that kind of confirmation from someone who jumped up and seemed to know all along what I was picking up on was, honestly, a little spooky. Uncanny. And very cool.

"I can't find anything about this word," I muttered in the moment, my searches coming up fruitless. "Can you help me? Can you tell me what this name means?"

And when he pulled the Five of Swords, and looked at me askance, chest inflating in a big sigh, I got it. I understood. This was a card all about loss even in times of victory–of cheap victory, hollow ones, of dishonor and shady tactics. It made so much sense, especially in conjunction with what I learned of Tiferet afterwards. A very cynical take on the sphere.

"What does it mean for someone like me to win? For me to end a conflict and come out on top?" Satan asked. He stared out at the sky, which was just as blue-grey and stormy as the churning ocean waters, and he shook his head. "Now, it means terrible choices were made and humanity slipped a step further towards the Dragon. It upsets me. A name like mine is one marked for despair whether I win or lose; either way I'm hated, spit on, and made a scapegoat for things I certainly didn't break humanity's arm to do.

"'Angel of Wrath,' you call me, you humans–and yes, I am angry. Angry at this God-forsaken world."

"God-forsaken? But it's not really, is it?"

He shrugged. "It may as well be. The world acts enough like the idea is true. Maybe one day, it finally will be forsaken in totality. Who knows, but the one that can do the forsaking?"

Jeez. Talk about a heavy idea. There wasn't much I could say to that; all I could do was sit with it, y'know? So with that written in my notebook, and the waves of hell's own ocean crashing on the rocks, I sat with it a moment longer before asking my next question.

"So, okay… the stereotypical 'devil.' You know, the red one with goat feet and horns and a pitchfork and all that goofiness. Talk to me. Tell me what you think about it. Because if I'm honest, I almost expected to catch that in answer to the term 'Satan,' like some little man-made caricature, but clearly that's not the real deal I'm talking to right now. What do you think?"

3. THOUGHTS ON THE STEREOTYPICAL RED DEVIL?

Satan rolled his eyes. "That thing, ugh. I think it's stupid. What would be the point of devils and demons if they were so easy to recognize? I can't even bring myself to wear such a ridiculous face like that 'red devil' you've all imagined; it's undignified and idiotic.

Stagnation and resisting change.

Cruelty, manipulation, bad intentions, injustice, narrow worldviews.

Travel, inner journeys, growth, and evolution after hard times. Adapting to life.

"'Deceiver, deceiver,' you people say, and yet you've deceived yourselves into thinking evil will have a big blinking neon sign over it, announcing its intent. Has your own little book taught you nothing? I'm supposed to be *light*: a lion prowling about, all big and bold and proud and *beautiful*, yet so hungry and angry. *Rah, rah,*" he held his hands up, tensed his fingers into little hooked claws, before *tsking*, shaking his head, and waving those hands like a socialite that couldn't be bothered to take anything seriously, "that's what you want me to say as I stomp around. But no, what I really am, is tired. Bothered, even. Disgusted, discarded."

And then I got an image of Satan just going to town on a room full of glass. Tables were filled with plates and vases and cups and other things that he was smashing all over the floor, a rage room full of dangerous shards that reflected slivers of his face all over: hard eyes here, nose there, mouth full of bared teeth elsewhere.

"I can't explain the depths of my rage," he muttered when that glimpse of the rage room left. "That all has come to this, and that all has fallen to such shit."

I had a sense he was talking about the whole story. The very state of all that was. What else could he have been talking about? But specifically, there was that frizzle of frustration that I could feel in my chest; it wasn't mine, but his, and it was *deep*. Satan would gladly play the role of that big and burly lion–if the people could remember that was what he was supposed to be in the first place.

"So like, you think that thing exists or what?" On that rocky beach, I felt like I needed some crackers and a hard lemonade to share with him. "Is it an egregore? The red devil thing people invented? Or does it not really exist?"

4. IS THE RED DEVIL AN EGREGORE?

Regaining inner strength and alliances.

Mistrust, neglect, fear, prioritizing others at the expense of oneself.

Financial and material troubles, struggle, victim mentalities, and rejection. Self inflicted strife.

"Oh, it exists," he muttered. Then he kicked at one of the rocks and huffed. "That fucking 'devil.' I can't believe it's still alive. It needs to be put down like the stupid dog it is. But no, it's stronger than ever, because people keep feeding it with their idiocy. The thing is absolutely an egregore, created to posture and be defeated like some cardboard cutout of 'evil.' I hate it."

How do I explain the knowledge that came in the rest of Satan's mannerisms? It wasn't just that I was hearing these words; it's that I was feeling the essence of them. A cardboard cutout of evil, this thing: suggesting that not only is this red devil with goat feet and pointy horns and a pitchfork an egregore, but specifically some goofy thing made to be weak on purpose so that humans could feel all the better about slaying it. Granted, we know that these images of a goat-like devil also come from things like Krampus or satyrs or other such creatures, but in modern times, this goofy thing is absolutely meant to instill not fear, but a *thrill*, and a great sense of accomplishment when we strike it down.

I agree with Satan. How childish and stupid.

"Alright, alright, that's fair. On a different note, though, riddle me this: why'd you go and fuck Job up so bad? Like, that was rough, y'know? Was there a reason you had to go so hard?"

5. WHY'D YOU FUCK JOB UP SO BADLY?

Once again, Satan huffed. "Humans. You need to understand: wealth is not a sign of God's favor. No more is it a sign of favor to the birds and rats than it is to you. Job was growing complacent, comfortable; he took what he had for granted, not realizing it would all one day disappear. Sure, my Father tested his loyalty, but as far as I'm concerned, Job failed *my* test: and my Father replacing all his creature comforts only spoiled him more. Irritating."

"Oh? Okay, I see that, but what's this last card mean?" I tapped that Three of Coins Reversed.

Discord, dishonor, overbearing control, a breakdown in power dynamics.

Healing, balance, harmony, cycles, and natural order. Inevitabiltiy of all things.

Weakness in work or team situations, incompetence, an inability to delegate.

"That's just," he waved a hand, "my Father and I. Never seems like we're on the same page about what should be tested of mankind. I had a different goal for Job that never came to be. Oh well."

"Ah, I see. Okay. But like, hey–you realize Job went through it, don't you?"

"Oh, what, for things? They were all replaced."

"Yeah, but you can't replace some of those things! Sheep, whatever, but humans build some real attachments to some of these things. They mean a lot to us. We grow attached to *people*, because you can't just replace people the way y'all thought you could. People aren't things."

He gave me a bit of a side-eye, but then he relented with a shrug and without a word. So I let that sit in the air for a minute before continuing.

"Okay, so another thing, I know you said you separated a bit from the Divine Council, but surely you still do a little something with them, no? And if so, can you tell me what that Council is like?"

6. WHAT IS THE DIVINE COUNCIL LIKE?

Heavy burdens, overwhelm, and struggle. Oppression.

Transformation. Accept changes and evolution, especially if hard won or painful.

Weakness, breaking down, losing control, and having difficulty problem solving.

That really had him rolling his eyes. He sat up on the rocks and dumped his chin into his hand, all hunched over like a dejected philosopher. "It's a shit show, is what it is. Everyone shouts at each other until God picks the voice He prefers to implement. It's exhausting and a ruckus every time, and every decision brings some major shift from mankind that I can't tell if God already knew would come to pass or not.

"Feels like throwing shit at a wall and hoping it sticks, and that I don't get blamed for making everything dirty. But someone has to be a little critical of you idiots on earth. It's sickening, how the Council is always treating you like children. You know well enough to not do what you do. You should be taken to task for your willful transgressions once in a while."

Oop. There it was: the proof that, yes, indeed, *Satan* was in fact an angel. Angels vary in how much of a hard-ass they can be, but even Michael, hard as he is, is known as the Advocate, constantly blocking the bullets an Adversary like Satan shoots at us. I get it, though. Humanity is a mess, and if we know anything about Satan from folklore, it's that he's really *not* impressed with us as a whole, even if he comes to like individual folks. Who can blame him, really?

"And what would happen if you weren't on the council?"

7. WHAT WOULD HAPPEN IF YOU WEREN'T ON THE DIVINE COUNCIL?

Satan sucked his teeth, then grumbled, "I can tell you they wouldn't get as much done without me. Sometimes all the waffling needs to be cut through. The pity needs to be put on ice. Some of those angels and divine beings would like to baby you until you shit and piss yourself to death, and the whole planet with it. I'm there to remind others that sparing the rod spoils the child."

The way he said that surprised me—like he was a little proud of the line. Made me wonder if he wasn't the one that got that idea stuck in the Bible in the first place. It would make sense that such severity would come

Manifestation, whether putting one's dreams into action, realizing goals, or seizing the moment.

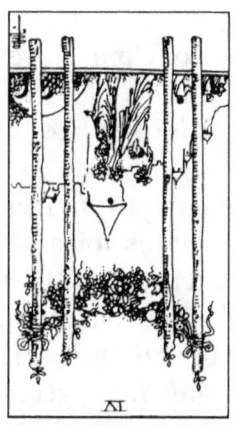

Social disputes and prioritizing others at the risk of our personal development.

Deception, re-evaluating if a goal or relationship is fulfilling.

off angels like Satan and Samael and the like, given their whole thing is about sniffing out the nonsense and dealing with it. I think, once again, though, that it was *people* that made a mess of that idea and took it too far.

"I see, yeah." After scribbling that down, I looked at what I had and nodded. "Well, alright. We're down to the last of our questions now, so I'd love to know: how do you see yourself?"

8. HOW DO YOU SEE YOURSELF?

This was actually a little hard to get an answer to, and Satan ended up not picking a card. He rubbed his chin and frowned, then shook his head. "I don't care to think of myself the way you're asking."

"Oh. Okay." Angels rarely did, did they? "Well, how would you want to be seen then?"

9. HOW DO YOU WANT TO BE SEEN?

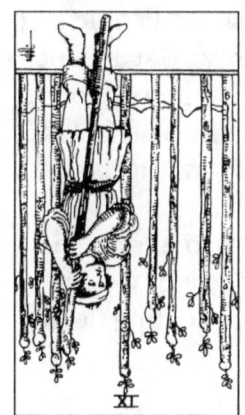

Pessimism, dread, and resignation.

The longest sigh gushed out of him. "Some people may have merit, but it should be known that it's entirely correct to assume I don't have a lot of hope, faith, or trust in humanity."

"...And any final messages? Anything you wanna tell people? Others will read this, so they'll be curious as to what you want them to know."

10. ANY LAST MESSAGES?

Then I pulled the Two of Coins Reversed, which in the Mari-gold Tarot, had two hands clasped together and rising from flowers. Upside down, it looked like hands from the heavens, folded together in a very "I'll Wait" type of gesture.

False joy and overtasking oneself.

"You all need to stop lying to yourselves and own up to your faults properly," Satan said, a bit of snap in his voice. "It's not a personal attack to be told you've done wrong. Feeling bad shouldn't be avoided at all costs. Some of you have done things worthy of wrath, and you know it. Stop avoiding responsibility or trying to distract yourself from it with more shit."

And that, friends, is why *this* angel specifically is Satan: the Adversary. When it comes to humanity as a whole, all that "love and light" childishness is nowhere to be found in this guy, I'll tell you that. For good reason, of course, but still: it's a harshness *without* hope, which I guess distinguishes it from the harshness of Michael (which is full of hope for us).

"I understand. And I agree. But alright, well, that's all I got for today, so thank you for your time, Satan! I'll see you around, maybe?"

He only smiled, and he walked me back from the beach without a word. Though rather than come into the place full of studies and offices where Lucifer was, he took me to what looked like some worn down, Gothic cathedral straight out of Dark Souls. The floor was littered with blood red rose petals, and then someone in knight's armor with a big red feather on his helmet—which I could only understand as Satan, given he was nowhere near me anymore and this was the only person in sight—knelt as if in mourning in front of an old shrine. A lit, stubby candle and a rose covered in the candle's wax sat in there. Who that was for, I have no idea, but it's the last thing I saw before everything faded away from my mind's eye completely.

So that was a weird way to end it. But end it did, and I walked away feeling actually pretty good—like I had a solid conversation with an old friend rather than walked into a lion's den and asked it to play with me. At least there's that, right?

And I just—I don't know. The more I talk to angels, the more I talk to demons, the more I talk to angels people think are demons and demons people might mistake for angels, the more I feel like I'm on the outside looking in. Like Jesus, who can sit up in the clouds of Heaven or crack a joke with Lucifer in the absolute bowels of Hell, it seems as if this whole "divide" between High and Low, Up and Down, Light and Dark is little more than the pithy plot of an over-dramatic theater show. People who watch this show and delude themselves with this Battle of Good and Evil tripe, as a result, strike me as children not realizing their cartoons aren't real. Maybe the same can even be said of the Dragon in some way, and that *any* personification or manifestation of this great Opposition to all we decide is good and glorious can be seen this way, but really, there is one truth in watching the way angels and demons seem to be colluding along the lines of Heaven and Hell:

What matters, what makes or breaks this world, what stalls or advances its destruction and opens the next chapter of its story, is us. Entirely us, our actions. That's it. We are responsible. No one else.

For many, that thought may be much scarier than the idea of some little pitch-fork wielding devil running around and causing chaos.

LUGH

Breathe a sigh of relief, my friend; we're off the existentialist train for the time being. After all, by this point, we were just entering August, and I wanted to make sure I got a little bit of sunshine in my summer interviews, too. There was no better place to start, in my mind, than with Lugh—the Celtic deity for which Lughnasadh, the Celtic festival on the first day of August, is named after.

Now, I had to activate my whole 13% Scottish ancestry to get into this one. Interestingly enough, a lot of these deities overlap between Scotland and Ireland since Ireland had a bit of a kingdom established in Scotland at one point, too. I can actually trace back exactly where my ancestors in Scottland are from and who they were—seems they came to northeastern America around the mid-to-late 1800s—and after my parents went to Scotland this year and brought me back some books on Scottish history, folktales, and Gaelic language, I got... *a little* more curious about that otherwise untouched side of my ancestry. Naturally, that also made me a little more curious to talk to this big sun god—especially with how much I connected with Kresnik, the Slovene sun god. There's just something about sun gods that feels so special, y'know?

Though I did take note of all the feedback I got after I posted this interview. Apparently Lugh is a member and eventual leader of the Tuatha dé Danann (the deities considered the ancestors of Celtic people, as opposed to the Fomorians/Fir Bolg, who always struck me as a race of like, pirate-like mer-folk in the dark waters around the Isles whenever I read about how they fought the Tuatha dé Danann). In fact, Lugh himself may be half Tuatha dé, half Fomorian, apparently, and he is not necessarily a *sun god*, but a god of *light*, a main and central deity who was a warrior and a great leader and all these other things. It's just that the biggest light there was, naturally, was the sun itself, and so this deity god was linked with such great light on top of all kinds of crafts and military arts and trades everything else.

I did read all of this in my looking into Lugh, but in my mind, that still translated as Sun God, not just a god that had the sun show up a lot in his imagery. It is what it is; I don't know what to tell you.

However, of very special interest to me was that actually, Lughnasadh as a holiday was one where Lugh himself honors his foster mother Tailtiu, a Fir Bolg queen who married the leader of the Tuatha dé after their invasion and who took up the task of clearing forest to be the fertile fields of Ireland and died in the process. Thus, Lughnasadh is around the time where Lugh honored Tailtiu's wishes of having funeral games and such held in her honor. I found that to be an especially sweet detail about the holiday, which I originally thought was just all about honoring Lugh alone.

Enough chatter from me, though. Let's take a look at this fascinating Celtic deity.

I'll tell you something: it didn't take long at all to find Lugh. I did my usual thing: I said the Lord's Prayer, said hello to God, and asked Him to let Lugh through and help me find him. With a table spread of a blueberry oat-pancake, a handful of blueberries, and a can of blueberry apple cider, I had the offerings all set—and if you're wondering why there was all that blueberry, it's because that's as close as I can get to *bilberries* here, which are what would be offered on Lughnasadh alongside cakes and breads and such. Alongside that, I accidentally pulled up a whole clump of black-eyed susans from the yard when I only meant to pick one flower, so that got to be part of the decor, too, and I scattered some daisies around my sunstone, carnelian, moss agate, and a chamomile-scented yellow candle. It all said late summer sunshine to me, and it got me right in the zone to see Lugh basically seconds after I asked God to help me find him—as he likely did know I was going to come by and ask to speak to him, based on all the focus and energy I'd been throwing his way.

We've talked about this a lot already, but let me clarify: I don't buy into much of the more New Age (specifically Wiccan) superstitions around magic: the idea that if you do any magic, *ooky spooky creatures* will notice and come sniffing around because they want a bite of all that energy you're pouring into the world—but it *does* seem that thinking hard and focusing on certain spirits makes them aware of you, much in the same way people suddenly get the feeling of being stared at or the way two people sometimes think of each other before coincidentally running into each other moments later.

Anyway.

We stood on a big cliff, where the ocean crashed against the rocks on one side and rolling hills of green grass stretched away on the other side. A small cottage sat by the cliff, and between me and that cottage was Lugh: a man with coppery hair cut to just below his chin, a full beard, a strong brow and nose, and eyes that sparkled with mirth. He had a band around his head, not the typical Celtic ones you see in pictures, but something like how Slavic gods wear, with specifically Slavic patterns. He insisted that was my fault—that my mind put that there because I was used to seeing it with the Slavic gods. Weird, how the gods can be so affected by our minds *and* laugh about it.

But aside from that headband, he wore normal off-white slacks and a tunic, with another thick woven belt wrapped around his waist and firmly knotted. On one arm, he had a big iron wheel hung on his shoulder, and in his other hand was a yellow-haired baby that, when I walked past him, became a big bundle of golden wheat. He smiled as we walked and started up our chatter—and in that little bit of ice-breaking, I found that even the Celtic gods knew something about me based on my ancestry. Lugh knew my Scottish line as well as the Slavic gods still know me and all my Slovenian ancestors, and that made me a bit embarrassed, because I never even considered that when I spoke to Brigid so long ago. Maybe because Brigid was more specifically Irish, though, that wasn't a big deal. I don't think the specifically Irish iteration of Brigid had much to do with the folk of Dundee, Scotland.

One thing that was interesting, and that I've noticed among gods of things like fertility or the sun, is the energy that was in the room when Lugh appeared. It lit my skin up with this warmth and vitality that, combined with the music I had on, made it hard to sit still. It was the feeling that made you want to run barefoot through soft grass and dance and *shine*. Very interesting. Though as the interview went on and I had to sustain focus for over an hour, I found that energy fading soon enough. It's tiring, especially between 2PM and 3PM after you've already had a busy day, to do stuff that requires heavy focus and mental load, I'll tell you that. And that's largely why I sometimes (often) procrastinate on these interviews: they are like an hour spent heavy lifting in the gym.

After a bit longer of our casual, private chatting, Lugh reminded me that it was almost festival day, and that everyone was busy preparing. Not wanting to hold him or anyone else up, I finally dove into the questions I'd prepared. Lugh decided he'd answer me through Kat Black's Golden Tarot.

"Alright, alright, well," I said, notebook in hand, "I don't want to waste any of your time, Lugh, so let me get right into it. First question I've got is: how does your role in Divinity, your station as a god connected to the sun and all that, connect to Lughnasadh? I know this is a funeral feast for your foster mother, so I'm interested in how it became about you, as well."

I. HOW DOES YOUR DIVINE STATION CONNECT TO LUGHNASADH?

 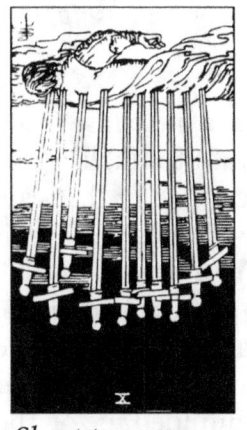

An important journey. Transition, leaving things behind and finding new understanding.

Short term success and financial benefit.

As we walked, his smile stretched big on his face, his cheeks rosy apples. "Ah. I see that last question on your list. Scratch it off! See that there sun!" He pointed to the sky, where the sun shined. "It doesn't stay in the sky forever. I bring the light that gives life to the fields my foster mother died for, and I take it away, too, so the land might rest. No seed sprouts without my saying so."

I blinked, a little caught off guard, because my last question was maybe a predictable one: *how can we keep the energy of the harvest and Lughnasadh during the cold of Winter?* But it seems the answer to that, without answering it, was *you don't*. There were times for harvest, and there were times for barren earth, if I understood what Lugh was saying: times for rest. That concept sounded very similar to Ecclesiastes 3 to my Christian mind: *there's a time for everything, and a season for every activity under the heavens...*

"I got'cha." After erasing that last question and putting down another, I kept going. "So, speaking of your power, how does sorcery figure into this? I was fascinated to see that come up among all your other skills. How was sorcery perceived in the Isles, that you could also be associated with it?"

2. What Does It Mean That You're Associated With Sorcery?

He raised a brow. "Ah, magic wasn't always the greatest thing to people. It's reserved for those scary times, when steel alone won't cut it."

When he winked, I guess I couldn't be surprised. The energy Lugh gave off, all bold and bright and friendly, meant a funny joke or two was on the table, and I appreciated that. Even if it was a goofy little pun.

"But it's only the weak man that doesn't see value in all his tools." Lugh shook his head. "That gives a big opening for others to master a skill you neglected and overtake you with it. If you know how to battle in the physical and the spiritual, who can best you? Nightside is a scary thing. You have to be ready for it. But people came to fear such a useful tool and let it rust at the bottom of a lake. There's no wisdom in that. Magic is the birthright of the gods, and we share it with you."

Intense emotion, turmoil. Loneliness and insecurity in a relationship.

Fear, depression, and strong feelings of guilt or remorse.

The fact that he called the spooky spiritual things *Nightside* gave me pause, because that's how I've heard demonolaters refer to the other side of the Tree of Life. But I think, like with many deities I've spoken to, that he was trying to use language that I would understand or that would approximate what he meant. I mean, after all, a lot of the deities associated with magic in Celtic lore, like the Morrigan, could be plenty dark and scary, like the beings in that *Nightside*.

"That makes sense to me," I said. I did have to quickly look it up, too, just to make sure I wasn't misinterpreting Lugh, and it was as he said: many of the Danann had some kind of magic, and people could learn and access it, too, but it was spooky especially when connected to beings like the Morrigan and other wilder fae. More than that, though, his answer reminded me of Thor, who said something quite similar about his own use of both magic and might. "And I appreciate you sharing these skills with the people! Speaking of skills, though, I see you have a *lot* of them. Do you have a favorite among all your talents?"

3. Do You Have a Favorite Talent?

1. A departure. A charming, enigmatic, and attractive person who is capable of great disloyalty. Beware of trickery and fraud.

2. Your goal can be reached if you set your path and keep to it. Fulfillment of hopes and dreams. Success and critical acclaim of creative achievements. Joy, health, happiness.

He raised a brow, smiled—and then surprised me with his answer. "It's not the skill that matters," he said. "It's the aptitude to learn them. I'll never pass up a new trade or skill or craft to learn; the more I know, the more I can sneak into places I'm otherwise not wanted." Lugh winked, his smile turning into a mischievous, toothy grin. "Even the smallest skills can help you find your way on the other side of a padlock. Maybe that makes me a rat, but it's how crowns get put on heads—and taken off."

This seemed like a reference to the story of how he got into the court of the former King of the Danann: the King would only have one man who knew a skill in his court, and so the foreman kept turning Lugh away. "But I have the skill of craftsmanship," he'd say, and the foreman would say, "the King already has a man that can do that," and so on. It was only when Lugh came and said, "But does the King have a man that can do *all* of these things at once?" that the foreman admitted the King didn't. Only then did he relent and let Lugh through, who later was able to make the case that he would be a good leader to take over when the former King could no longer rule due to weakness/age/etc. So there's that!

"I see what you mean, yeah," I said. "So, with that said, I figure people must've come to you for help, too, with the skills they were trying to learn, since you mastered so many. How have you helped people who came to you hoping to pick up new trades and such?"

4. HOW DO YOU HELP PEOPLE LOOKING TO LEARN NEW TRADES?

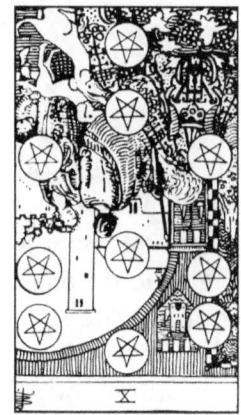

Domestic disharmony. Tradition and resistance to change may cause friction.

Abuse of power, weakness, and inability to hold true to one's convictions.

The cards I pulled surprised me, and Lugh noticed that surprise. He shook a finger as we ambled along that grassy cliff.

"Ah. You'd think it'd be obvious how I help: I teach! Once upon a time, people would ask all day for the help of all the Tuatha dé Danann. Now, though," Lugh shook his head, "people are stupid. They've tangled themselves in knots: 'only men can do this,' 'only women can do that,' 'can't go asking Lugh no more—ask this Christ fellow instead.' What's Christ know about metalworking?"

"Well, hey," my thoughts and feelings made their way in here without words, but they essentially translated to, "Jesus was a carpenter. He knows something about woodworking, at least. And everyone used to call Him Magos; He has some good magical secrets He shared with us."

Lugh shrugged. "Carpentry, maybe, and magic, too, sure—but how about poetry? Warfare? Doesn't hurt to go to an expert in a subject, but people tossed us right out the door."

Well, Jesus does have a sword in Revelation. But I didn't bother bringing that up. I was much more interested in how Lugh said *us.* It snagged my attention, and so I had to erase yet another question and replace it with this one:

"Seems like Jesus coming around caused some tension. How was it, when Jesus came up and met you all? From what I understand, many pre-Christian Celts just stuck a figure of Jesus on the altar alongside you all before full conversion. How was it, with Jesus in the mix?"

5. THOUGHTS ON JESUS JOINING THE CELTIC PEOPLE?

And I got such a clear image. An image of Jesus standing on that grassy cliff, His wooly hair connecting to a wooly beard, His sheepish smile as He stood robed in red and holding Himself stable with a shepherd's staff. A lamb in His other arm. Then, across from Him, were those He was smiling at: the Celtic gods, Lugh and Brigid and all the others, who were clustered together as if in formation to defend against an invader, yet frowning as if confused.

The cards I pulled, too. The Page was clearly Jesus: the tiny bull hovering in the air over the Page was a common sign of El in pre-Judaic Canaanite religion and stayed associated with God as El and Yahweh fused to be the entity we understand as God now. (For more on that fusion, I highly recommend Francesca Stavrakopolou's *God: An Anatomy*.)

Deceit and unfair dealings; a cunning foe.

Conflict, argument, and confrontation.

And Jesus Himself told me He liked the things the suit of Swords represented: puzzles, intellectual and philosophical challenges, learning. The Knight was the Danann, or more specifically the people supporting the Danann, as that wand he held was, to me, the earthen staff of the Druids. The fact that they were facing away from each other told me all I needed to know about the friction, but Lugh spoke and added more to it, too.

"It was a mess," Lugh said with a sigh. "A right shit show. We knew with one look at that soft spoken, sheepish fellow and His big old Dad that there'd be issues. And it's not that I don't *like* your God." He frowned, as if mulling the idea over. "I just don't like His people much, those cloaked fellows coming around and causing problems. Your Jesus wasn't about all that, either, but both of our people butt heads like hell. Neither of our people wanted to budge on their values, even though there was more than enough room for us all. We let them into our lands and courts, and that should've been enough—but it never is for people. Ugh, people."

That was a piece of this story I hadn't seen before. I remember Brigid saying how she found God more hands-off—but to hear, here, how Jesus and God and the Holy Spirit were coming together to greet and speak to the Tuatha dé Danann, and how it was the overzealous folk that ruined what could've been an interesting expansion of God's divine council, is pretty sad. Lugh seemed more annoyed with people than anything else, and it's easy to see why: nothing gets people acting stupid more than religious zealotry.

"Wow. That's interesting," I mused. Once I wrote it down and thought about it, I kept going. "Okay. So another thing that I'm curious about is how you chose to side with the Danann. I mean, from what I understand of your mother's side, the Fomorians, it doesn't seem like it's quite the 'Divine/ Devil' split that people online make it seem. I thought maybe you, being half Tuatha, half Fomorian, might know what it's like for us humans in Abrahamic tradition, being half God and half anti-God, but if the Fomorians are simply another race, that doesn't quite apply, does it?"

"No, it doesn't," Lugh said with a small smile.

"Thought so. Well, still! How did you decide to side with the Tuatha dé Danann when it came to war between them and the Fomorians? That's still quite the choice to make."

6. WHY DID YOU JOIN THE TUATHA DÉ DANANN?

A strong man who may be very opinionated. An authority figure. Perceptive, strong willed, intelligent.

A drinking problem or other destructive excess. Arrogance. Friends may feel taken for granted.

And Lugh's answer was simple: "My father had his head on right. Balor, my mother's father... did not. It wasn't just about picking a side, Sara; it was about picking a future. I saw no future leadership in the Fomorians that would lead the Isles right. The Tuatha dé Danann had the focus and future-forward thinking we needed to be strong and grow stronger still with the people."

"Ah, that makes a lot of sense. I see that! Alright, alright, well, before we get into our last few questions, I guess I'd also like to know: how do you still impact the world today? I mean, I know you still have your festival, Lughnasadh, but what about on the other days of the year? How do you help folks who honor you?"

7. HOW DO YOU HELP FOLKS WHO HONOR YOU?

And it was at this point that I was promptly reminded of a Reddit post I was looking at about offerings for Lugh: one of them was suggesting to learn a new trade or skill in honor of the god. With that image in my head, Lugh smiled and gave his answer: one told in the image of the Page of Coins and Page of Cups.

"I remind people that it's never too late, and one is never too old, to chase a new skill or hobby—especially artistic ones. I'm still something of a kindred heart with those bard types. So long as one is willing to put n the time, I'll be happy to help and encourage."

"Aw, nice!" What a sweet message. I scribbled it down, then looked over my notes. "Alright, well, that brings us into the last three. These ones are a little simpler, I guess, so to start: how do you see yourself?"

A studious youth. Scholarship, study, academia. Hard work brings achievement.

Emotional youth. Creativity and inspiration. Development of strong emotional tie.

8. HOW DO YOU SEE YOURSELF?

Creation, fertility, energy. New beginnings, self reliance. Self sufficiency and personal empowerment. Birth, fertility, growth.

And then he pulled the Ace of Wands, which was understandable—though there was some confusion as to whether it should've been reversed or not. Reversed, it would've had a similar meaning, just with a touch too much enthusiasm. But he spoke clearly on that card:

"I am the god of all things that make men's hearts beat: art and music, craftsmanship and war, sorcery and study. There's nothing I can't do, and there's nothing mankind can't do, if they try hard enough."

"I see that. And how do you want to be seen?"

9. HOW DO YOU WANT TO BE SEEN?

He didn't even draw a card for this. "Exactly as I see myself."

"Fair enough. Alright, well, before we part ways, is there anything you'd like to tell folks who read this? Anything I didn't touch on in my questions?"

10. ANY LAST MESSAGES?

Lugh crossed his arms and stared out over the cliff. "Look before you leap," he said. "Not everyone you think is on your side actually has their arms open to catch you. While it's good to keep the fire roaring, you don't want to burn all your fuel down to nothing before the dawn comes. Work, pursue, try—but don't be stupid about it. And most of all, enjoy it. Enjoy every moment of it."

Damn. What did I say? Sun gods (or at least, gods linked with the sun), man—they're just cool. In fact, Lugh almost gave me more of a Sagittarius vibe, that Jupiter-laced fire and luck and philosopher's seemingly reckless optimism, the kind that knows better than to take itself too seriously. I finished writing that down and nodded.

"Sounds good to me. Alright, well, thank you, Lugh! I really appreciate your time, and I hope you have a wonderful August 1st with everyone! It's been a pleasure!"

And then he kept walking towards that cottage, which I only then realized we'd been walking towards all that time without ever reaching. He smiled over his shoulder, waved,

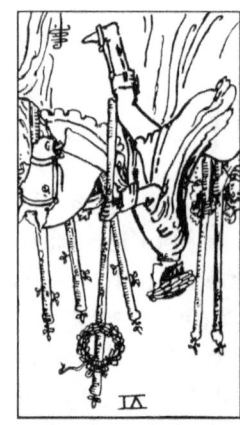

Travel, a speedy journey. Ideas swiftly made reality. Messages, news. Time for action, but take care: hasty decisions will be regretted.

Treachery, intrigue, battles which may be lost.

and then all faded away, leaving me the kind of tired one only gets after meditating for an hour straight. A good tired, a satisfied tired.

Morana was right. I am a creature of the Sun. I'm a morning person, one who can't sleep once the dawn breaks and who can't rise while it's still dark. One who charges up in the warmth and light like a solar-powered lamp and who enjoys the way the world's colors get brighter and more saturated under that huge ball of fire's shine. When I walk with gods who carry that similar light—like Kresnik, like Lugh—I am viscerally reminded of that. And yet my friends, and the love of my life, are ones that live by night and drag me out to all the nighttime fun anyway, who share my love of all things dark and macabre and morbid; my angel is one that signals God hiding in the darkness, and I drape myself in black clothes like I can wear the shadows that put me to sleep, and I traverse the dark places of hell without a light in hand, because my light is innate despite all that shadow.

I don't think I'm either sun or moon, the more I look at it: I'm like a solar eclipse, an anomaly, a shadow ringed in fire. I don't make sense even to myself, I have no rhyme or reason and no clear definitions; I can carry it all when I shouldn't, and yet I do. With that same sheepish smile as my Savior, as if to acknowledge I cannot be, yet I still am.

Is that what it really means to be made in God's image? To feel like that?

Maybe.

SAULĖ

Next on my list of sun gods was an *actual* sun god this time—or, more specifically, a sun *goddess.* While much of modern western neopaganism considers the Sun to be a masculine force and the Moon to be a feminine force (which is, I think, at least part of the reason for so much moon-based paraphenalia in witchy shops and spaces), it's goddesses like Saulė that interest me all the more for showing the Sun as a *feminine* force instead. More than that, it's her *husband,* Mėnuo, that is the *moon!* Really, given there's only one sun and moon in our sky and orbit that we have verified with our science and our telescopes and all that, it makes you realize something very important.

And that's that gendering celestial bodies, and assigning hard "masculine" or "feminine" energies to them as if that's a standard across every culture or even relevant, is stupid.

But of course, Saulė, the Lithuanian sun goddess, is one of more than just *sun.* Along with this association is all the things the sun was so important for: harvest, fertility, grains, all the things that made solar worship ever make sense to begin with. No sun? No crops. No crops? No food. No food? No *you.* And speaking of celestial bodies, it's thought that her children *are* the planets, which is interesting. As is common with sun-god lore, Saulė was thought to ride through the sky each day, shining her light down on the world and scaring away all the evil, spooky spirits that thrived in the shadows of night (hence also why in so many cultures, wintertime, with its weak and shortened span sunlight, is thought to be a time where these same spirits run amok). She's a beloved goddess, an apparent model for pre-Christian Baltic women, and a beautiful, golden-haired protectress of all things good.

So let's take a look!

Luckily for me, this was another interview that could also make use of what I'd planned to make for the recipes I also release on my Pateron: cornbread. But given Saulė's association with grains, harvest, and fertility, as well as her association with the sun, I found that red, gold, and orange things were best to offer her—so cornbread and a clementine it was. That, alongside some rose quartz, sunstone, carnelian, and a yellow chamomile candle, as well as a jar of red amaranth, was all I needed to set the table and get in the zone (along with some very cool Lithuanian chants to the gods as background music that I *adore*).

After doing my typical routine, I asked God to lead me to Saulė and let me see her, and immediately, I felt my feet plant into soft, cool green grass. I stood there, like I had so many times in so many different interviews, at what felt like the beginning of a grove: one that, when I stepped out of the forest, showed me a sprawling landscape down below. Green hills, a little pond, a house on the water, mountains painted against a blue sky: it was the perfect picture of peace. And then, down from the sky came a golden-haired woman in a chariot with copper wheels, pulled by two horses. She had eyes that would switch between deep, dark black and a warm honey brown, as if the sun were perpetually rising and setting in them, and she wore a white linen tunic with a green and gold over-dress. Around her head was an ornately embroidered golden headband.

" Saulė!" I tipped my head to her as she came and sat in the grass beside me. "Hello! Welcome! I have for you some gifts: an orange and a piece of homemade cornbread. Please accept them in return for some answers to a couple questions I have."

Saulė smiled, chose the Guardians of the Night tarot, and at one point, I caught an image of her peeling that orange and eating a slice, which was gratifying in and of itself. It's only as I wrote this up later, though, that I realized I also forgot to give her a glass of mead like I meant to. Oops. But still, as we settled in, and she ate the orange, we got down to business.

"Alright, Saulė, so the first thing on my mind is this: so often in western Europe and many other places like Egypt, we see the sun depicted as a male god. Dažbog, Ra, Helios, you know. But you're a sun *goddess,* and I'd love to know: what would you say are 'feminine' qualities of the sun?"

I. WHAT ARE THE FEMININE QUALITIES OF THE SUN?

KNIGHT of CUPS.

A charmer. Creating perfect distractions for an emotional lift. Magic happens when you open your heart. Moody, sensitive, emotional.

PAGE of SWORDS.

Confronting difficulty or getting out of your comfort zone. Tests or lessons that stimulate growth. Mental grit. Playfulness.

Feeling powerless or trapped. Options are no longer available. You hold the power to move forward. Call on wisdom.

She nodded, thought about it, and after we warbled about a few other little things, namely the imagery in the cards, we eventually got back to the question. She said, "You ask me about the feminine qualities of the sun. Hmm. Yes, the Moon is involved—my husband is involved."

This was especially in reference to one card, the Eight of Swords, which, in the Guardians of the Night tarot, had someone looking up from a pitfall trap with three owls circling a crescent moon.

"Sometimes it feels as though he wants to steal my shine. But we share it, the light; he doesn't take more than his due. And the sun itself, me, well— we like to play, us gods. When I'm here, it means it's time for fun and joy and getting things done. The clouds may cover me at times, but never for long. And of course, there are so many feelings in something so bright. The sun is a thing that gives color and life to all, a thing that can impact the mood of others based on its mood, a thing that can drive evil away from children—what's that, if not feminine?"

There was a bit of a joke in that question. "Ah, I got'cha," I said, and we shared a knowing smile. "That's certainly one way to put it! But you know, I always wonder: is there any crossover between you and other sun gods? Have you ever met them before?"

2. IS THERE CROSSOVER BETWEEN YOU AND OTHER SUN GODS?

There was a sharp curve to her smile, like my questions were funny, but she nodded and looked out over that peaceful little field. "I have met these other gods, yes," she said. "Some of them, anyway. It seems we have layers, dear one, layers to our world. Some people exist more in one layer than another, and as if they were peering through a looking glass, they look at us differently depending on their layer." Then she sighed; her smile slipped. "Some gods would like to be the king of all layers, but one can't force perception. One will never capture those who weren't meant to see them."

I caught a note of something pointed in her words, and as I scribbled away, I squinted at her. "Hmm. It sounds like you're hinting at something there, Saulė. That does make me want to ask: knowing that the Baltic regions remained pagan for so long, how do you feel about the takeover of Christianity in the region?"

Unity. Connecting with vibes, feeling comfort deeply. Understanding. Sending power out instead of drawing it in.

Power out of balance. Someone is taking advantage. Consider your position and if you're getting a fair deal.

Warm, motherly, generous to a fault. Give abundantly. Create space for all to flourish. Mother, nurturer.

3. THOUGHTS ON THE RISE OF CHRISTIANITY IN THE BALTICS?

1. Happiness and contentment with life. Energy created from simple joys of being in harmony with community. We all gain when we work together.

2. Creating something that keeps us inspired. Give more than you have before. Learn as much as possible.

3. Being seen, talents recognized. Bold and confident. Trust your abilities and talents to bring new opportunities. No need to boast of one's greatness.

Her face fell, and I got little snatches of images: of the Baltic gods in a group, being approached by others as if a foreign emissary had come to give them a message, or offer a deal, or something. It wasn't a meeting they seemed to know about beforehand, and there were images of Saulė and other gods whispering to each other, trying to weigh the odds. More than that, the cards I actually pulled were so rich with symbolism that they almost told me more than the card descriptions.

In the first card, the Ten of Cups, there was what seemed like a Eucharist cup with a star floating above it, and all around were fireflies that struck me as angels. It hovered with the other nine cups over a field of animals, two of each, all Noah's Ark style—but it seemed to me that it was backing up that image of the gods I'd just had. It depicted Christ, with the angels, coming to meet the wild, old gods in their grove. Then, the Eight of Coins was a wasp building a nest: productive, buzzing, yet fierce and ready-to-sting energy, a sort of urgency and efficiency that suggested there was something that needed doing. Most striking, though, was the Sun, which had a vicious looking lioness draping her big paw over the sun as if to protect it. That struck me as Saulė's general disposition: wary, queenly, ready to bite throats out if her or her group were threatened.

It painted such a clear story that I wasn't really surprised when Saulė started speaking.

"There were benefits," she said. "Deals drawn. But yes, your God is one that wanted to be seen by every layer of people. And it turns out that yes—not every person born in the same place on Zemyna's [Earth's] fair surface is of the same layer. I thought your God wanted all people for Himself. I've come to understand now that He was simply looking for the souls He'd scattered across all nations, His lost children. He is a Mother, too; He weeps for His children and wants them back, every day.

"So we had an agreement that when He was done setting up His beacons, we'd return to our posts. Now is that time, even if you wayward people in your arrogance try to strip us of our duties, rights, and dignity. I cannot blame your God for people's failures. I am a god, too. I know how fickle and foolish people can be."

"Oh, jeez." That gave me some serious stuff to chew on: the idea that all people belong to a certain "layer" of the world, that we all are capable of seeing Divinity depending on that layer. It makes sense, how I can be Slavic and understand the Slavic gods as ancestral, yet still see God as my champion to access Divinity through—my true Creator that transcends physical blood and soil, who picked me back up and refused to let me go after the Slavic gods kept me safe for so long. Once I was done mulling it over, though, I asked the next logical question: "So, okay… how about the Baltic people that are now Christian still? How do you feel about them?"

4. WHAT DO YOU THINK ABOUT BALTIC CHRISTIANS TODAY?

1. A fine line between dreaming and fantasy. Stay aware of where your feet are planted. Limited thinking, believing goals aren't possible. All thought, no action.

2. Eager to create something new. Chipper and optimistic, but knows what one wants. Sees potential in all people.

3. Indulgence, succumbing to slothfulness, choosing to satisfy immediate needs instead of facing challenge. Understanding one's weaknesses.

Saulė's face went flat, tired. It seemed like these questions were souring her mood a bit—and given it was a cloudy day already, that muted light in my house only added to the feeling.

"They call us demons sometimes—our folk now turned Christian." Saulė shook her head. "Little do they know it's us that still protects them *from* demons that haunt these lands and their hearts. Foolish people. They've been lulled into complacency, drifted away from guides and guardians. Some belong to your God, yes, but others drift listlessly, believing in routine and not questioning things past their idea of any one God. Still, we protect them together with the God they call on. We try to get them to think and grow still, even if it scares them to look beyond what they're told."

I nodded. "That's really interesting. But how exactly do you still help the people grow and keep them safe today?"

5. HOW DO YOU WATCH OVER BALTIC PEOPLE TODAY?

Her head lolled side to side as she thought, her hands absently pulling at the grass. "Even if we remain largely in the background, we're here. We nudge, we guide, we warn—just in little ways, if our people are still too busy or blinded to see us. We've never abandoned our duties or our people, and we never will. The community comes first, and we do our duties: filling the earth with grain, lighting it up with pride."

It was interesting, how I could feel such a soft and warm feeling of love coming off her—literally like sunshine. But there was some cloudiness tinging it, too—clouds coming to cover that little bit of warmth, gloomy and rainy and heavy on my shoulders as she stared at the grass.

You have the power to manifest what you desire. Seize opportunity as it rises. Benefit from realistic approaches. Be flexible and adapt to new situations.

Putting out fires. Petty drama, plans interrupted. Get outside points of view and slow down. A master builder.

The sweet taste of success. Victory is best when shared with others. Using resources to help others. Focusing on one's own community needs.

"So," it made me cautious, asking the next question, but I'd recently had an interesting idea from a book I read on the idea of omnipotence and wanted to know, "do you think humanity and Divinity actually collaborate at all, in making the world something good? If so, how?"

6. DO HUMANS AND DIVINITY COLLABORATE?

Upcoming disappointment or loss. Previous setbacks. Allow yourself time to process your emotions. Accept loss. For balance to be restored, you must let go of what can't be repaired.

That scattered the clouds with a hot ray of light, angry and frustrated. She looked at me and huffed, "I don't know; how do they? Once, humanity understood itself as Creature; it understood its place and role as steward and as a connected one to this earth. We hung the stars, birthed all that was, and humanity responded with gratitude, good works, love.

"Now, I see more that humanity spits on their old duties than upholds them. I see them forget that they are Creatures and treating other Creatures as less than. Filthy behavior. Men have forgotten their duties. Some of you are trying to get back to them, but not enough are."

"I got'cha, yeah. I agree. And I'm sorry, Saulė; I didn't mean to make you upset today."

She shook her head, as if to absolve me of any wrongdoing and say it's not my fault. With that, I asked another question.

"How do we remember our duties? How do more of us get back to it?"

7. HOW DO WE REMEMBER OUR DUTIES?

Saulė didn't draw any cards here; she only spoke with a fierce hiss in her tone. "Fight. Speak truth, even if people hate it. The dissonance hurts. The soul doesn't want the pain of remembrance or guilt. But you must, as your folk says, 'rip the Band-Aid off.' Don't waver when the waves of the wicked's fury crashes on you."

"Okay, yeah!" There was no denying that energy or mistaking the torrent of ideas I was putting to words. Once done writing, I nodded and said, "Alright, well, that's the last of those questions. I only have a few left now, and the first is: how do you see yourself?"

8. HOW DO YOU SEE YOURSELF?

This one took a second to get an answer for. I don't know if Saulė just didn't think much of it or wanted to be specific, but eventually I landed on the Two of Cups.

"I am one who loves, even if now many don't love me in turn," she said. "If they don't listen to me one way, I find another way. I am one who wants to see life and people flourish, and I will do what's necessary to make it so."

"That's nice! I love that. How do you want to be seen?"

Traveling through lifetimes with someone, holding passion for what moved you. Filling the void in the soul. Seeking common ground, overcoming differences.

9. HOW DO YOU WANT TO BE SEEN?

THE TOWER.

Unexpected loss, swift changes that shake up life as we know it. Destruction of what we take for granted. Changes at work.

As a mother, was what I heard at first, but what I pulled was the Tower. I sat there and stared at her, patiently waiting for her to explain, and she smiled as if it were funny.

"See me as a mother," she said again. "One who hasn't been listened to and is capable of discipline, even if I am otherwise kind and sweet. I don't require anyone worship me—and nor are my works limited to just the Baltic lands, nor are many god's to their respective lands—but I require all people to be good, responsible, and caring for the weakest of them, and they are failing. Failing their human family, their animal friend. Wrath comes on a disobedient child. Do not assume that this complacency can continue."

Man, if I had a nickel for every time I had a foreboding message like that from a completely separate spirit or god, I'd likely be able to buy one of them *fat* cans of energy drink from the local gas station. But as heavy as the answer was to get, and as heavy as it was to write, I nodded.

"I understand. Thank you for explaining. But other than that, are there any other messages you want to give today?"

10. ANY LAST MESSAGES?

Saulė shook her head. "No. I've said enough. Thank you for giving me a space to say it."

As we got up, I tipped my head to her. "Of course! Thank you for answering my questions." As she smiled and started to walk back to her chariot and horses, I called, "Goodbye, Saulė! I appreciate your time and wisdom today!"

And then she was gone, and I was back in my living room, and the offerings to Saulė were out in nature, deposited under a big bush for her to accept via the earth. I went back inside, let my bird out, and, despite the warmth of August, wrapped myself up in my little throw blanket and rested. My bird hooed and cooed around me, flying from one end of the living room to the other, and I just sat there.

This interview series was beginning to ruin me. Or, rather, it *had* been ruining me the entire time. What once started as a simple fear of missing out and a wish to see what other people on the internet were experiencing with these other gods was becoming, as I should've expected, a look "under the hood" of all things that were, and as such, I was beginning to truly unthread myself from a very stupid and childish world. My past self before this series would not recognize me, and my current self would be as frustrated with her as an old grandmother. But how else can I explain it? The deep disinterest I now have with not the natural world, but the material, human-trimmed world, the one where people live like the dead and wonder why everything feels so awful?

We look on the Christian monks with nothing and think them crazy—and surely, many of them had *problems,* believe me—but to spit in the face of all your earthly attachments is a way of rebelling against exactly those material big whigs and fat cats that want you to value consumption over your own life. I could shake everyone who worries about what they wear or how big their house is or how many products they can collect; I think back on my young adulthood and feel disgust with the parent of a friend who insisted she shouldn't be friends with people like me, who *only* lived in "single floor" houses instead a grand thing like their two-floor one (that they couldn't actually afford, whereas our house was at least *ours*).

Stupid. Stupid beyond reason. Vain. Ugly.

But what can you do? Tell the cows that there's more to life than grass, and they just blink and moo at you. Tell my pigeon that his desperation for a single peanut (as if he doesn't also have a bowl full of food at all times) is unseemly, and he can't understand you. People won't put their toys down until they're ready to, or until the world in all its fury and cruelty rips it all away from them. So we'll just have to keep walking by example, and hoping, like St. Francis, that those who see us may come to learn from our joy even when "lacking" in all these trinkets and treasures. So that they might finally see that there are more important things to protect, like the very earth we walk on.

One day. Hopefully soon.

DUKE ASTAROTH

I'm at the point where I look into things based on the *pull* I get. You must understand: this is a big deal for someone who would rather all her life be organized in perfect timetables, where projects are started and ended on the dot, where books are completed the way they might be for college reading assignments and all the notes neatly outlined and tucked away. To just look into things based on *vibes* is not—has never been—the way I work. For a long time, I feared going insane if I were to be so disorganized about my searching and researching, my learning and notating.

Unfortunately, though, I'm not a chemist. Or a physicist. Or even just a scholar of normal things like classic literature and history and what have you (though they do come up). I'm a *mystic* scholar, and that means studying the *mystic* way. When I get pulled in a direction, therefore, I follow that pull—and this time, along my ambling through the Qliphoth, I got pulled in the direction of Duke Astaroth, who ruled the second-to-last sphere I had yet to properly explore. I ended up reading more of *God: An Anatomy* by Francesca Stavrakopolou, specifically the portion that dictated the descent of the Canaanite mother goddess, Asherah, from her station. This seemed like a weird place to be pulled, until you realize that Duke Astaroth's name is one that came from the eventual bastardizing and demonizing of goddess Asherah's name.

Now part of the Goetic demons, however, this Duke Astaroth is far removed from the origins of his name—*very* far. Some would pin him as a former fallen angel, whereas others insist he was taken straight from pagan divinity, but by this point, I think we know that these discrepancies come, first and foremost, from humanity's simple inability to properly perceive all that these spiritual beings are, were, can be, and cannot be. Still, one odd detail in the old grimoires is that, apparently, Duke Astaroth's breath is bad enough to kill you if you breathe it in without some kind of protective charm, like a silver ring. It really makes you wonder what the hell was going on with people writing these things, and it certainly does make me want to agree with Dr. Justin Sledge of Esoterica when he insists that the *Ars Goetia* is almost like medieval, magical Pokémon with the way these old magicians would "bind" and make use of the powers of these spirits.

But I figured, while I would have Duke Astaroth in my space, that I also might ask him a little something about himself for a more public view, and this is the result of that decision.

As Duke Astaroth is an earth-based being, associated with the sign Capricorn, I decided I'd dress the table with earth-based items: buckwheat, oat, mugwort, moss agate, obsidian, malachite, and a shot of vodka as a gift. Thanks to Travis McHenry's *Occult Tarot*, I never have to struggle with sigils again, so I was able to simply pull out Duke Astaroth's card instead of trying to do something goofy, like that time I wrote King Belial's sigil on a potato. Much easier this way!

After that, it was simple: find Duke Astaroth. As always, I started with the Lord's Prayer and asked God to help me find this demon, and it didn't take long before everything came twisting into place: namely, into the place I'd first met Astaroth almost a week prior when I bumbled into the sphere of Gha'agsheblah.

This was a place bathed in red light, with a long table like the Last Supper, and with various Greek Orthodox style representations of people sitting along its huge wooden surface. The image of Jesus was somewhere, and all the Apostles were reaching for Him, only they seemed to be made of paper, and they had no eyes—only black, burned spots, as if someone pressed a cigarette to each socket instead. Behind them all was a massive creature, with a naked woman's torso, a bull head, hooves, and wings. One might mistake it for Baphomet, but it was unmistakably a bull, not a goat.

"Duke Astaroth," I said, "are you there? Is this you?"

What made me suspicious at first was a lingering idea: *my expectations.* What were my expectations? The word couldn't really unstick itself from my head, as if the inside of my skull were the bottom of a desk, and that word, *expectations,* was a piece of gum stuck underneath. Duke Astaroth— what I assumed was the big bull-headed person—didn't answer, but the red-light room fell away to a massive cathedral with insanely high ceilings and beautiful stained glass, huge stone columns holding it all up, and a silver throne before a white-clothed altar. There was no more bull-headed figure after that: it was Duke Astaroth as depicted on the card I'd pulled, a man with shoulder-length black hair, a crown, and wings, a dragon curled around the throne he sat on.

"Oh." I blinked, confused. "I—are you sure you want to look like that? You don't have to pick how they made you look in the *Ars Goetia*—"

Duke Astaroth only cut me a sly, almost mean smile as he lounged in that chair. Thing is, though, that Astaroth seemed less like a man and more like an almost grandmotherly figure—or at least something kind of androgynous. *Man* wasn't really the right word to describe them. Still, that word *expectations* haunted me, and I wondered if I was actually with Duke Astaroth, or if I was just making things up.

Maybe one day I'll stop assuming I'm making things up. This was apparently not that day.

So I sat there really focusing on them for a while, just holding their name in my head, until the images in my head felt solid enough, and Duke Astaroth hadn't shifted or changed any more. I had to accept that this image of them was what I had to work with, and I moved on. If for nothing else, the cards would reveal something as I asked questions and responded to my internal "pick a card" alarm. After all, that's what they're for: to tether me to a concrete message when doubt starts trying to fray the edges of my intuition and block my connection.

"So, Duke Astaroth, thank you for joining me," I said as I shuffled the Guardians of the Night Tarot. They didn't move or talk, really; they only watched, until I asked my first question. "Given the couple different forms you've taken, and the way people talk about the spirits they encounter, I'm curious: how does our perception affect you as spirits? As noncorporeal entities?"

1. HOW DOES HUMAN PERCEPTION AFFECT SPIRITS?

See the world from a place of loving divine energy. Experience each moment without prejudice and new chances will appear for you.

Failing to notice issues arising, fearing the unknown, or willfully ignoring answers to problems.

Possessing all expected of a leader. Articulate, conscious communication. Research before a decision is made. Impartiality. Calling others to rise to a higher standard.

Their eyes were huge, and so deep a black. They smiled as I shuffled and crooned, "Are you still trying to make sense of what isn't sensible?"

"No," I said, and I think I meant it. "I'm just curious as to whether it does anything to you, to be perceived certain ways."

Duke Astaroth shrugged and got up from the throne. They seemed to hover in the air, their body lanky and pale, their feet little reptilian claws of grey scales and black talons. "What do we care what we look like?" They twirled a lock of black hair as if the thought bored them. "Our faces don't define us. Do you want to see me as a woman? Do so. As a bull headed, breasted thing? Do so. As a man with foul breath riding a dragon? Do so. All say more about *you* than *me*."

"I—yeah, I can see that." And in fact, it was nice to have that idea confirmed. I scribbled the answer down and took a mental note of what seemed not like *hostility*, but *severity*, coming off the Duke. It wasn't like I was being attacked, but more like I was being tested. "But then... how *can* we see your true energy? How do we get to the real essence of you?"

2. HOW CAN WE SENSE A SPIRIT'S TRUE ESSENCE?

1. Examining life and discovering something is missing. May need to abandon something to move forward. Change is needed.

2. Ignoring the call to transform, disappointment, false accusations.

3. Are you getting a fair deal? Someone may be giving (or taking) more than you bargained for. Seek the greater good.

The cards were an interesting mix of messages. The Eight of Cups, Judgement Reversed, and Six of Coins were all so different in theme, yet they made perfect sense together as I read their descriptions and pieced out the feeling—and later words and images—the Duke was giving off.

"Can you make sense of any of these things?" They waved around at the cathedral, and then shifted us back into that red room with the Orthodox iconography, and then back again to the cathedral. "Do you know why an image flashes in your head that has nothing to do with the task at hand?"

Then again, the cathedral was gone, and there was shadow. Some black-eyed snake-woman hovered in a dark cave, right by my face; it was only just light enough to make out the pink and red spots of her scales, the stringy black hair, the little fangs poking out from her parted mouth. Her eyes gleamed, and then her jaw unhinged as if to swallow me. I let her, and I found myself walking along a big, humid flesh tunnel, until I was encapsuled in a white sac and popped out the other side, in a little snake egg.

Don't ask. I don't know, either.

"You focus on me because like this, I can speak in a way you know," Astaroth said once I'd broken out of the egg and stepped back into the cathedral. They crossed their arms like a school matron and hovered above me, then continued. "I've been speaking. In every color, feeling, smell, and sound, I have been speaking. Learn our language, leave behind your assumptions of what it means to perceive, and you will find us."

"Uh... alright! Fair enough." I could tell they would not make this easy. "But okay, in that vein, riddle me this: Astarte, Ishtar, Athirat, Asherah, *Astaroth*. These are all your names, no? Are you not Asherah, just in a different form? The way some say Moloch might just be God in a different form? Why stay in this form if this isn't true to you, and is just how people decided to start perceiving you?"

3. WHY STAY IN FORMS THAT AREN'T TRUE TO YOU?

A world where there should be abundance, but where the powerful rise up and block the way instead of help. Lacking resources to thrive. Embrace change.

Harmful secrets, confusion, and mental disconnect.

Knowing what one likes and dislikes. Grounded, stable in boundaries. Not asking one to change for a relationship. Passion and enthusiasm.

The language of Five of Coins was so stark that the message hit right away. It spoke of a world where there should've been abundance, but where people hoarded resources instead, and where the powerful should've helped others, but instead worked to block the way. Combined with the High Priestess Reversed and the Lovers, it was a strange message that worked through Astaroth's long, somber face.

"What other choice did we have?" They shrugged and sighed. "Men's minds are so weak. Look how they turn on your God when they perceive a *single* brutish quality in Him. They cannot accept duality: that God can be so good, and yet do such bad. So we hide ourselves—both so that, in my case, I may still whisper into the minds of men and lead them forward, so my name may live and people may find me in my complexity and fullness again. And in the case of your God…" Their gaze cut sharp towards me, a mean side-eye, "so He can stay ruling from the disposition, the Divine Mask that He prefers."

At this point, Astaroth blinked, and the world seemed to blink with them. I was face to face with two giant, deep, wide black eyes, as if I'd suddenly become the size of a fruit fly hovering in Astaroth's chalk-pale face. The eyes were crinkled at the corners as if the face were smiling, and then there was an image of a white tomb, a light shining from between two coffins. Spikes came up from the ground where one nymph-like, ghostly pale woman stepped, and she threw back a head of black hair in agony as they speared through her feet. And then there was a rush of blood, a river of it on a rusty red riverbed, and the big eyes of Astaroth were back, though the white of their face was replaced with the deep red of blood.

"I am not Asherah in this form, under this name," they said. "I am everything that stayed alive by virtue of pure rage, rebellion, and defiance, until the world was ready for my gentility again."

"Damn." Every now and again, I would remember the Asherah I saw in my interview with her: a woman made of flame, with eyes of gold and curly hair twisting and flickering around her motherly, sweet face. There was none of that here. Still, I couldn't help but bring it up once we'd resettled in that cathedral: "But there are people who are coming to appreciate Asherah again. And honoring Ishtar and the like. There are people warming up to that gentility. So what value is there for gods to still take on the names and forms of demons, if their original worship is being restored?"

4. WHAT VALUE IS IN TAKING OTHER FORMS AND NAMES?

Astaroth shook their head. "Not enough are ready. Not nearly enough. We wear these titles to test, again and again and again, if the cover of your ignorance is worn thin enough. If you're ready to leave behind the pretty lies that make you feel better about the world you live in and the gods you serve. You continue to fail. The lies are sweeter and easier to digest. Like a child with an underdeveloped palette, you cannot stomach complexity."

I pursed my lips and shrugged. "I can see that. Though, your mention of lies is interesting." With a tap of my pencil to the page, I kept pressing this line of questioning, "How can we

Unwillingness to see problems for what they are, looming disaster, avoiding change.

Weakness in work or team situations, incompetence, inability to delegate.

A charmer. Cam create perfect distractions. Magic happens when you open your heart. Duality.

let go of those lies? And, given your area of expertise in the Qliphoth, how can we shed ourselves of everything? Leave it all behind to experience the abyss, like Ishtar once did? How can we get into the abyss and manage to get back out?"

5. HOW CAN WE SHED OURSELVES OF EVERYTHING IN THE ABYSS?

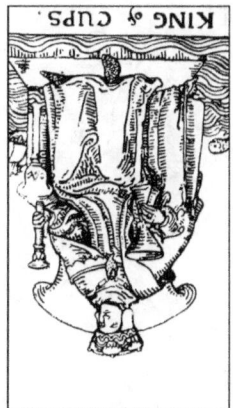

Behaviors that may be considered self destructive, controlling, dishonest, and manipulative.

Teamwork and being in sync to achieve certain goals. Calculate your moves and pull a skilled team together.

Examining life and discovering something is missing. May need to abandon something to move forward. Change is needed.

Astaroth smiled. The cathedral went dark, to the point that all the grey stone seemed to become a deep blue, and the shadows clustered near the stained glass and made their colors that much more vibrant, as if each pane had its own inner light. Astaroth stretched their arms out.

"Be ready and willing to see what you know has been hidden," they said. "Let us wipe the dirt from your eyes. Things are not as they seem. Even your wish to perceive them how you do is a barrier to leaving all behind."

This felt suspiciously familiar. Like, *dark night of the soul* familiar: when everything is gone, when all images of God are destroyed, and when we are plunged into nothingness.

"Go to the place where there are no gods and there are no monsters, either," said Astaroth, as if to confirm that suspicion. "Where there is nothing but your raw self, stripped naked of every false thing you've wrapped yourself in to shield you from the wretched cold of oblivion. There is no way around it. All you know must vanish until there's nothing left to do but scream—and then, when your voice fails, to perceive, fully, with *all* eyes open."

Yep. That's right in line with that term, *apophatic,* which essentially means *negative experience:* where we slowly strip away every single idea, image, or concept we have of God, knowing each and every one of them to be false. I guess this could apply to all beings, really. All are filtered through our minds' need for sense and Othering, distinction. We will break if we experience all that is, all at once; our minds cannot handle it very well.

And maybe I took this too literally, but I promptly went and signed myself up for an hour in a sensory deprivation tank after this, to get a sense of the abyss in the only way I could without straight up having a near death experience. In fact, I've been doing that semi-regularly for some time now, and I will say: it is a good way to unplug from all that exists outside that little pod of warm-water-darkness. Let the brain run on battery until it runs out and then fall asleep. Maybe meditate and see something wild. It's nice, and it's the kind of distance from a world that so desperately wants to distract you with every possible anxiety-inducing task and thing and event that lets you realize that nothing is really that serious. You could probably get the same experience nesting in bed in pure darkness for a while, honestly—anything that forcibly removes you from things like your phone and lets you just drift for some amount of time. But it's not for everyone, I guess.

"So, okay," I said, nodding as I wrote, "I see what you're saying. I got'cha. But on that note, I know you can tell us *how* the angels and yourself fell and all that... but how about the *why?* Why do we have any concept of fallen angels? What do they do for us in the world story? For our perception?"

6. Why do we have concepts of fallen angels?

The smile on Astaroth's face curled even bigger. "Ah. 'How they fell,' 'how they fell,' it's always *how* and never *why*. Yes, never why they *needed* to fall, hmm? Well, let me tell you: the existence of the fallen is another illusion humanity needed. The same angels they looked to with reverence could not also be the ones responsible for the seemingly senseless affliction in this world.

"The angel they fed their sins to [Azazel] could not stand in the righteous community any more than the pig fed filth and muck could become wholesome food for the body. As gods

Suppression, lacking discretion, or feeling incapable of expressing oneself.

Fixation on the material world, anxiety, greed.

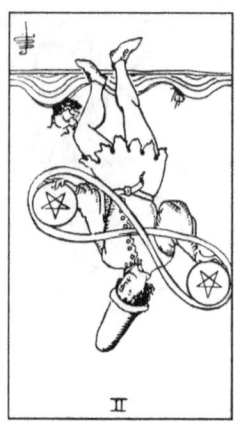

False joy and overtasking one-self.

become demons, so to do angels become fallen. All so you don't have to contend with the fact that both are true, both are whole, both are One. Hubris. It's your hubris, Man's hubris, that wrote gods and angels alike into pieces."

I probably sat there in that cathedral looking as gobsmacked as the tomato in Veggie Tales. That last line practically rewrote my entire brain. And there's something to be said for that idea, too—how, if we were made in God's image, and God is the first one to ever commit this act of division from the parts of Him that became the Dragon, then perhaps this is simply a part of our nature: to divide. To split things down clean lines, to separate things into clean categories. Maybe, when God divided the world, and divided us from it just as He divided Him from Himself, He also created a system, a self-imposed shackle, that made Him unable to fully, wholly, and in Oneness *be* what He decided He was.

What a double-edged sword, *creation*. Our only luck is that just as the nature of the Divine (or, rather, the Demonic that is the basement floor of the Divine) is to divide, it is also the nature to unify, to bring these purified and distinguished materials back into a form stronger than it was before. Just as gold is melted down from its shape, purified of its contaminants, and brought back into a state of strength and wholeness as whatever shape we decide it should then take on.

With a blink and a feeling like I'd just been hit with a cosmic brick, I wrote so fast that I could hardly make sense of the letters after, desperate to get to my next question.

"So then... what can we learn from the Infernal Divine? As these beings we cast all this ire onto? What do we do with this, especially as we come to learn these things?"

7. WHAT CAN WE LEARN FROM THE INFERNAL DIVINE?

Too entangled in celebration, resulting in neglecting one's duties or responsibilities.

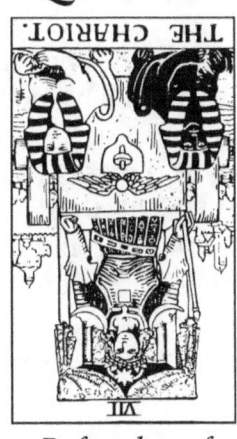

Defeat, loss of control, or lack of direction.

Insecurity, wariness about finances, and needing to act on one's plans instead of ruminating over ideas.

Duke Astaroth sucked their teeth and looked at me as if they felt bad for me. "Child, the only thing you can learn from us is despair," they said, their voice like that of a nanny to a kid. "Despair, that's it—despair that something is not right, that lies have become the foundation of the world. That they who call Satan the father of lies are, themselves, boorish and arrogant things—"

Wasn't Jesus the one who said that, though?

"—who put words in the mouths of their favorite puppets and fudge the words of their favorite Book to avoid reality. To avoid waking up from the dream."

Oh. Yes. Yes, that's it, that must be it—

Then I had an angle of Duke Astaroth's face that was so zoomed in that nearly all I could see was the huge lens of their black eye. They stared me down with that eye and murmured, "Look how you just edited my words. Because you didn't like what I said: *that they who call Satan the father of lies are, themselves, boorish and arrogant things.* I said that. Only that. But because you didn't like what I said, you added a little something, didn't you? You don't have to agree. But don't pretend I said something different. Don't lie to yourself."

That both rattled *and* humbled me. They were right. I did add that, because I didn't like the idea of Jesus being called arrogant and boorish. I didn't understand why Duke Astaroth would say that about Jesus. So I rationalized it away, until it became the same message, but so distinctly *not* the same message. That was my own perception, getting in the way, in real time, and I could *feel* it happening. If anything, at least I can identify that feeling of dissonance as it goes on.

"Alright, well, let's move on," I mumbled. "How about yourself? How do you see yourself?

8. How Do You See Yourself?

Letting go of fear and trusting the universe. A risk of blind faith. Act first, think later. Let go of the need for control.

THE FOOL.

They smiled as if it were funny—and maybe it was, given the whole conversation we were just having about perception. But then, they told me to pull a card, and they pulled the Fool.

"I am simply a man on a journey," they said. "As we all are. I have my hopes and dreams, and I have no knowledge of how to achieve them."

"Wait—but don't you tell all things past, present, and future?"

Duke Astaroth shrugged. "That's what people say, but this is what I say, because what I see is bleak. Not comforting. But maybe it'll change. Fate is not fixed. There is no future—only things to tell you hopeful idiots demanding certainty in a world painted in running ink."

I don't know how demons always get so poetic, but they really do have a way with words. It's kind of crazy.

"Alright, then how do you want to be seen?"

9. How Do You Want to Be Seen?

They shrugged again as if bored. "I am not one who is interested in the trifles of man. Come to me if you want your eyes wrenched open."

"And any last messages?"

Closure, working towards (not necessarily positive) resolution, and hostility.

10. Any Last Messages?

THE HERMIT.

XI

Loneliness, extreme caution, and isolation.

This time, they looked directly at me and said, "Step away. Find whoever in the process—me, God, whoever—but step away. Listen to what appears when Men no longer lie."

"Got'cha. Alright! Well, thank you, Duke Astaroth. This was... one hell of a conversation. I appreciate your time, and I suppose I'll be seeing you. Bye for now!"

And then I clapped my hands to signal the end of that connection, shut my music off, closed my book, and went about the rest of my damn day.

All the while, I could only wonder. Doubt once crept in because I couldn't trust myself to hear what I was hearing in these interviews—and doubt crept in again because there was another side to this I'd never figured: could I trust myself to accept what I was hearing, even if it was true? Were any of these things I'd ever written trustworthy, after all? Whether or not I earnestly believed any of it didn't matter, did it? Just like every man that ever came before me, every person blessed with the responsibility of transferring divine messages, I, too, had a mind that could not handle all things or all ideas. I, too, was filtering the Divine through my own broken, cracked looking glass, just like anyone else, and while I would've thought I'd never forget that, or never miss that fact in the first place, the truth is that we take our perspective so deeply for granted every day, don't we?

We've discussed the dangers of unverified personal gnosis before. Why things need to be verified by multiple sources, why institutions of religion that codify these things exist in the first place. I've been asked before why people's encounters with God are different than mine; I've had people both sigh in relief and rage in disbelief at these interviews, their own understandings of these spirits either validated or spit on based on what I reported. But that's the bitch of it all, isn't it?

There is no one way. There is no one face of God, or Divinity overall. There is no one answer. What I write here is true—and yet it is truth bent through the funhouse mirror of my own perception, and yet it isn't the full and complete truth. It can never be, not while I sit in this physical body and deal with all the restrictions of its physical mind.

But that's okay. That's why there's so many of us, comparing all these little puzzle pieces we keep picking up and figuring out where they fit. It's all we can do, and it'll entertain us likely for the rest of our human existence.

ST. THECLA

The only Saint that captures my attention more than St. Hildegard von Bingen or St. Cyprian of Antioch, that legendary sorcerer-turned-bishop, is one so unfortunately little known among most of western mainstream Christianity: St. Thecla.

St. Thecla is such a powerhouse. Our main testament about her, and her life, faith, convictions, works, and miracles, is actually from early Christian apocrypha. In the writings called *The Acts of Paul and Thecla,* the writer describes the legend of a young girl who, upon hearing St. Paul preaching and teaching out there about the coming again of Christ and the wonders of Heaven and such, found herself enchanted by the picture of the future and the heavenly kingdom that awaited all Christian believers. She had a fiancé, one she was arranged to marry, and she had a social duty, cultural customs, to uphold with that marriage, but she threw it all away to follow St. Paul instead—and escaped death three separate times over the course of her life as a result. I could (and almost did) list all those times out for you, but I think it's better if you just read the story for yourself; it's very easy to find. Be warned, though: sexual assault and general injustice towards women is rife in it. What matters is that she escaped death three times, her faith in God bringing on great miracles, and she baptized *herself* in the middle of all that chaos, even when St. Paul thought she wasn't ready for it.

Still, one thing that sticks out to me about this story is how ironically *feminist* it is. One might not think that deciding to be a virgin forever is very feminist, but when you're told your whole life that your body is under guardianship of your father until some man you never met comes along and essentially buys you from your father for marriage (in which it then belongs to your husband), yeah— the idea that your "purity" could be for *God,* as in, something *no man on this earth could take away from you,* that would be a big deal. No need for marriage to walk, talk, work, preach, teach, all that? That was something else at that time, and it's such a shame to watch modern western Christianity take purity culture right back to where it was before St. Thecla, with those awful purity rings fathers give to their underage daughters before passing her off to her future husband.

But of course, whereas now proven forgeries of St. Paul like 1 Timothy—the letters that say women should be silent and never teach men and all that nonsense—were allowed into the Bible's Canon, something like the Acts of Paul an Thecla were tossed out just because it was written (or, rather, the many legends were compiled) by someone who wasn't actually there himself. (Which is wild, because the same can be said for certain accounts of the Gospel, too.) Despite the fact that this story, and this Saint, would stay so important to early Christians for so long, the church fathers running this show apparently couldn't stomach a holy text that had women stepping too far outside the bounds of their cultural, rather than faithful, understanding of them, I guess.

Enough of my chattering, though. I could talk about this all day, but I'd rather simply show you the conversation I had with this incredible Saint.

It was early in the morning that I started this all up, as I needed to get it written and presented to the people before the day's million and two tasks started fraying my attention and my patience. I had out some things that have to do with St. Thecla: fire (as manifested in the candle I put out, the carnelian, sunstone, and tiger's eye, and the cinnamon/ginger tea I made for her), a lion (via an empty wine bottle with Leo on it that I got from a winery in Slovenia), and an angel and rosaries, as well as a big crucifix (for that Christian element). Then I popped on some nice Gregorian hymns for some background noise and, with my own cup of tea at the ready, dove into finding today's Saint. Once I got some connection, she chose the Golden Tarot, and I let myself just see what came up.

And right away, an image bled in: a woman that looked like she'd stepped out of a Renaissance painting, with a pale, round face, thick black hair in two braids that draped over her shoulders, and thick, shapeless robes of red, white, and gold. She had huge, dark eyes, so brown they looked black, and she had a little red and gold hat on her head, too. My first thought was that it looked like a kippah, until she flashed an image of the Pope in my head, reminding me of his little hat, too; it later got switched out for a big bishop's hat, suggesting authority. She had a wooden staff with a gold cross in a golden circle, and she wore no shoes.

"St. Thecla, hello!" I said. As we walked down the rocky valley, I glanced at her bare feet and said, "Don't you need some shoes, out in all this rough valley?"

She smiled, and her chuckle was a low, warm sound: "The stones don't cut my feet; the earth doesn't scorn my step."

"Ah, alright, I see." I was studying her face, thinking that something didn't seem right. She was, after all, from modern day Konya, Turkey (then Iconium); she wouldn't have looked like a White Renaissance Girl, surely. Apparently all of Duke Astaroth's chidings were already lost on me (in which it's no wonder I floundered in their sphere for *months*). "Well, to get us started, St. Thecla, I have to ask: how did you baptize yourself? These days, people insist you can't do a damn thing and need a priest or bishop to do it all for you, but you sank yourself right in the water in that stadium and went for it. How'd that work?"

1. HOW DID YOU BAPTIZE YOURSELF?

A coy smile played at her lips. The cards she pulled were stark—especially the Ace of Wands, which had an angel with a staff, surrounded by fire.

"It isn't the water itself that changes a person," she said. "God simply uses this creation as a medium with which to wash us clean and paint us in His glory. I needed no man to verify my worthiness. I learned that there, in the fire and the arena, that God alone decides who is worthy, not men in robes who go around calling themselves Apostle or Deacon or Priest."

"Oh." I couldn't help a twisting smile in return, because that was some pretty loaded language. "I almost want to ask what you think of Paul, but..."

St. Thecla shook her head. "Paul was a good man. A misguided man at times, but a good man."

Creation, fertility, new energy, new beginnings. Self reliance, self sufficiency, personal empowerment. Birth, growth, action, adventure.

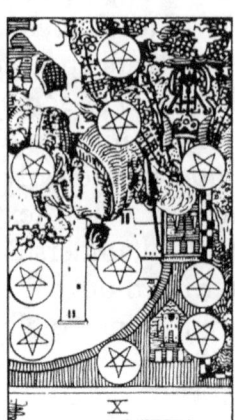

Domestic disharmony. Tradition and resistance to change leads to friction.

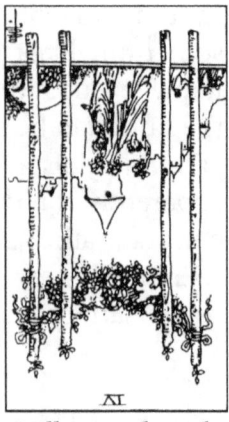

Still a good card, though good things like domestic bliss, good harvests, and social standing will take longer to manifest.

Hmm. I didn't disagree, though knowing Paul essentially left her high and dry at one point in their story, it was interesting to see the grace that came off that statement. St. Thecla wasn't blaming him for that, but she wasn't noting him faultless, either. Just another person, who makes good and bad decisions, like anyone else.

"Alright, well, speaking of St. Paul—why did you want to follow him? I mean, you weren't raised in a vacuum; your culture at the time no doubt told you a very different story than what Paul was selling. What got you so wrapped up in his message?"

2. WHY DID YOU WANT TO FOLLOW ST. PAUL?

1. Make hay while the sun shines. Make the most of material and spiritual prosperity. Keep stock for lesser times.

2. Satisfaction of worldly desires. Good health and fortune. Fulfillment of wishes. Joy, fun, merriment. Meeting new people, making new friends. Temper enthusiasm with moderation.

3. A woman of few morals, willing to use others for her own ends. Untrustworthy and fickle.

As we walked down the stony valley, going nowhere in particular, you could feel the heaviness of a sigh in the air. St. Thecla looked over the valley and said, "I wanted a model of holiness that wasn't found on earth. The mother that would have me put to death for disobeying wasn't made in a day. I was surrounded by callous people in a callous world, and Paul told me there was the possibility for more than that.

"How could I ignore such a message, when my only other option was to be like my mother and every woman before her? Or like my father and every man before him? There was more to life. Paul told me so."

"Got'cha. That's really nice!" Then I looked at her long and hard, and I said, "You know, St. Thecla, forgive me for this, but... I'm wondering about the form you're taking right now. Are you expecting that I want to see a more Catholic representation of you? Because I'd like to see you as you were on earth, if that's okay."

St. Thecla raised a brow, then smiled. And then, the valley was gone, and we were in some court-yard with sunlight filtering from the open space above, and where a shallow, green-blue pond rippled with a fountain's bubbling water. Big leafy plants were cast around, and there St. Thecla lounged against the pool edge; she was a young adult, older than she would've been in the story, and her hair at first was wrapped up in golden bands, but then was cut short, just under chin length; it was a head of frizzy, dark curls, and her skin was more bronzed, her eyes honey-brown, her chin soft and her nose strong. She was gorgeous, but you could see the fire in her eyes that, for some reason, had been completely painted out in images that show up when you search for art of her. After poking around, though, it seems I wasn't wrong to see two braids, given how she's been painted before. But her dress was a flowy, light blue, with a light purple shawl draped over her.

"Is this what you mean?" St. Thecla said with a raised brow.

"I mean, I guess, yeah." It was hard to keep her in my mind, though: looking back, she may have been trying to make a point with her dress, because later I would see that same Turkish/Grecian face with the bishop hat, the gold, white, and red robes. She was putting out a picture of spiritual author-ity, which contrasts nicely with the stuff those church fathers replaced her story with.

Speaking of which, I did ask her about that, too—but not before I asked her about marriage. "Re-garding the world," I started, "I gotta ask: what do you think about modern Christian approaches to marriage? I mean, you escaped such a fate with Paul to encourage you—the idea that your body is for your husband only—but now we have this 'purity culture' shtick that seems to do exactly what the Gospels freed you from! Now girls are giving their 'purity' to their dads for safekeeping, and then giving it right to their husbands on their wedding day. It makes me think of what you went through."

3. WHAT DO YOU THINK OF MODERN PURITY CULTURE?

St. Thecla laughed as I explained it, as if such a thing surprised her, and then her face fell, and she shook her head. She didn't need to pick any cards; her words came clear. "What foolishness, to treat marriage like such a yoke. It makes earthly and vain what God made holy. Women," she started, and by the edge in her eye, she knew full well that this was going to be public, "if you marry, may it be for love, partnership, and solidarity in Christ. Not for reasons like my parents sold me for."

"I hear you. It seems we've kind of messed that up, though, with mixing culture and Christianity. I mean, stuff ended up being half Greek before the foundations fully set." With a sigh, I kicked at a rock. Then I asked, "How do we right this ship? Get Christianity back to what it needs to be?"

4. HOW DO WE GET CHRISTIANITY BACK ON TRACK?

With a sigh of her own, St. Thecla set her sights on the valley ahead. She pointed, and when I looked, I saw a bull raging there, kicking up all kinds of dust. Not entirely sure why she showed me that, but it was significant, and I think the bull might've represented God. It's a common association of hers, too, though.

"I tell you now," she started, "there's not much you can do. It's because Christianity, the Way, compromised itself with earthly things that we find ourselves in this mess. Yes, the faith needed to survive and justify itself to a hostile world—but what did we sell of ourselves for that? We cheapened the Way with idle chatter and blindness and talk."

That which bends is less likely to break. Compromise. Opposing forces. Identify true obstacles. Desires may remain unsatisfied.

Indecisiveness, falsehood. Beware of those who seek conflict for its own sake.

Misguided passion, adultery. Stupidity, arrogance, conceit.

"Chatter *and* talk? What kind of talk?"

She cut me a sharp look. "Talk of some lofty heaven, as if we weren't worthy of it—as if the whole point wasn't that we already have the Kingdom within us. What a failure. Are all things Man touches doomed to rot like so? I think not. As I said, there's not much you can do—but what you can do is keep the Way true and clean of blight in your own life."

"Got'cha, got'ch. Makes sense. But now... the Bible. That's where people draw a lot of their interpretations from. St. Thecla, your story was tossed out as a 'forgery,' only for things like 1 Timothy—now also known as a forgery—to take its place. What do you think of 1 Timothy 2:11-15, especially? About women not speaking, about them only being saved through childbirth, about Eve coming from Adam?"

5. WHAT DO YOU THINK OF 1 TIMOTHY 2:11-15?

1. That which bends is less likely to break. Compromise. Opposing forces. Identify true obstacles. Desires may remain unsatisfied.

2. Withering away of bounty due to neglect. Inaction, weakness, indecision.

3. Indecisiveness, falsehood. Beware of those who seek conflict for its own sake.

I was surprised that she chose almost the same cards as the previous answer, except with the Empress reversed this time instead of the High Priestess reversed last time.

"It's a similar problem," she said. "Men seeking not to scare other men away in this cruel world, they taint the faith. Look how Paul waffled time and time again. Look how he *had* to, that he might not be killed. Dead Apostles don't speak or preach. Knowing Paul, I could believe he wrote the words of 1 Timothy—if not for the fact that he let me join him at all and surrounded himself with women as much as men.

"But now, women—there is no excuse to be so weak and petty and foolish when a man speaks culture that serves him and not Truth that serves God. Bite his tongue out. Invite him with a kiss, as men love—and then bite out his tongue and reconsecrate your lips to holiness, to God."

Damn. That was a pretty brutal image. I nodded as I scribbled the answer down, then said, "Alright, heard loud and clear. But that raises the question: what would you, as a woman preacher and teacher, want to model for young women today?"

6. WHAT DO YOU WANT TO MODEL FOR YOUNG WOMEN TODAY?

Knowledge is power. Power via understanding of one's own abilities and the world around us. Making the most of a situation. Take a risk. Pragmatism.

A slow, plodding, reliable man. Someone who will stick with a project no matter how long it takes to see results. Honorable, responsible, keen to help others.

Dwelling on past sorrows may prevent one from moving on. Let go of the past and confusion and stress may fade.

A curl of her lip, a crease in her brow, told me she wasn't happy with the way things are today. "Women, don't wait to be saved," she said. "Go and chase your own salvation. Dedicate yourself to study and good works a little at a time. Share the wealth of your peace and knowledge with others. And remember," she said, turning to me with eyes so bright a brown-orange that they looked like they were made of liquid flame, "there is not a single stain God can't remove from your life. Your past does not, and never did, define you. You choose how you define you with every step you take towards—or away from—God."

"Oh, wow. That's one hell of a message. Thank you." Once I had it written, I looked back to my list of questions and saw there was only one major question left. "So, I guess to end our more personal conversation, there is one thing I'd love to know: how did you find it in you to trust God with your life the way you did? And not once, but three times! How did you trust He'd save you, especially miraculously like He did? And how can we trust God like that, especially when things get rough?"

7. How Did You Trust God to Save You? How Can We?

St. Thecla shrugged. "What was I to do? Put my hope in this world? When I saw, time and time again, where its true loyalties lied? No. I trusted God to deliver me from my oppressors, either by saving my body and letting me go on, or by liberating me from it and taking me up to His lap. He chose to let me walk this earth until my work for Him and by Him and with Him was done. I put it all in his hands. I did not fear death. I only made it clear where I wanted to be when I died."

Jeez. That seemed heavy. But before I could ask anything else, she looked at me and added one more thing.

"Trust God to do what's right, and don't try to define what 'right' means by yourself."

That was one sharp idea. So sharp it stung. But I knew what she was get-

A mean, selfish, hard-nosed woman. One who will do almost anything for money.

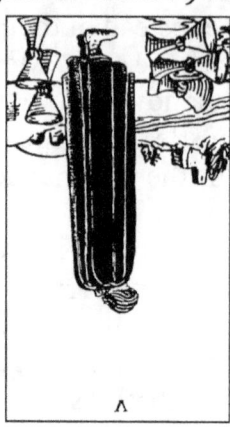

Still a card of regret and disillusionment, but of a more transient nature. Hope soon regained.

Your goal can be reached if you set your path and keep to it. Fulfillment of hopes and dreams. Success and critical acclaim of creative achievements. Joy, health.

ting at—something that, interestingly, echoed Duke Astaroth's sentiments in a different way, given how many people turn their noses up at God's decisions both past and present—and so I scribbled it down and let it just stare back up at me from my notebook's pages.

"Alright, well, to get to our last three questions: St. Thecla, how do you see yourself?"

8. How Do You See Yourself?

Make hay while the sun shines. Make the most of material and spiritual prosperity. Keep stock for lesser times.

A warm smile spread on her face as she pulled the Sun. "I don't waste time on 'what if's,'" she said. "I trust. I go where I'm called. I have all I could ever want, but what I want was never riches. I have all the 'riches' I need in God."

"I see. How do you want to be seen, then?"

9. How Do You Want to Be Seen?

I didn't get the sense she wanted to pull any cards. She only looked at me and waited for me to stop shuffling. When I did, she shrugged as she hugged her staff to her. "It doesn't matter to me. If people's opinions did matter, I'd never have unstuck myself from that window where I could hear Paul speaking. Never would've been stuck in the first place."

"Ah, yeah, that makes sense. Alright! Well, before we part ways, did you have any last messages for folks?"

10. ANY LAST MESSAGES?

She gave me one sharp nod, and again no cards, and said, "Seek the Virgin. Seek God. Seek Christ."

"The Virgin? Why?" I looked at the words I wrote and said, "Why not the Holy Spirit?"

St. Thecla thought for a moment, then said, "The Virgin is Mother, and a model for women. An agent of the Lord, a strong and powerful protectress and advocate. Where she is, so is her Son—and where He is, there is his Father and His Holy Mother, Sophia."

Ooh—that was a throwback to early Christian thought. where the Holy Spirit was thought of as Jesus's spiritual/divine Mother while Mary was His earthly, physical Mother. Fun stuff. But with that clarification written down, I closed my book.

"I guess that's that, then. Thank you for your time, St. Thecla! I appreciate the wisdom you've shared, and I hope you enjoy the celebrations and joy on your feast day. Goodbye for now!"

And then that was that. She walked off, but the valley we were in changed; it was no longer a desolate place, but a market square, with people all over. She, herself, became a woman robed in pink and red silks, covering her head and part of her face as if trying to blend in and move through the world unbothered. She waved one arm to me without looking back, then disappeared into the throng of people in the market. All I could do was sit there, staring after her in wonder, knowing that she was even sharper and fiercer than I could've imagined her when reading her story.

I also knew, in a way that made my mind numb, that everything she, the other Saints, and the other angels said—everything Duke Astaroth, the other demons, and the other fallen angels said—all seemed to be desperately beating us from both sides of the aisle. It was beginning to seem, more and more, that there truly was no Good or Evil, necessarily, but rather just the Left Side of the road and the Right Side, with all humanity sitting at an intersection between them, taking different roads to get to the same end point.

Knowing that, it's no wonder I can't bring myself to react too strongly to one thing or the other anymore—not in the spiritual world. I keep forgetting and re-learning the same lessons, over and over, through different faces, and the one thing I wish is that I could hold *any* of those lessons long enough to never forget again.

ST. AUGUSTINE

You'd think that after the Dragon and the Evangelical Egregore, there wouldn't be any spirits that I would dread to speak to anymore. However, of all the spirits I was thinking of interviewing, God came in hot to suggest one to me that I *really* did not want to bother with: St. Augustine of Hippo.

If you know, you know. It wasn't that I was scared. It was that I was *tired* (and not less than a touch bitter).

But if you *don't* know, then to put it simply: this Saint is the darling of so much seminary learning, an early Christian thinker that was one of the main forces spreading this religion around (whether by hook or by crook, as it seems he felt it was better for someone to be heckled and beaten into Christianity than allowed to live a life of soul-killing sin). He was also the one that extrapolated a lot on concepts like original sin (the idea we're all inherently born sinful), as well as a lot of... *interesting* ideas about women. He wrote tons of stuff throughout his lifetime, including his famous work, *Confessions,* and went from being a man apparently consumed by lust and putting off his conversion (to the chagrin of his deeply devout mother, St. Monica) to a celibate holy man looking to further build up the church.

There's way more to St. Augustine than this, of course, but I wrote this guy off as a mess and a half for a long time, thinking he was just another misogynist that needed to maybe talk less. However, if I could show St. Paul some kind of grace and find out that I was wrong about him, I figured maybe I'd learn something about St. Augustine along the way—and what I was *really* interested in knowing was whether or not he still viewed women as the stumbling block he made them seem in some of his writings, or if Mother and Wife was really all they could be and contribute positively to society.

After reading some of his *Confessions* and learning more about him, though, I found myself softening a bit, if only because this guy was *clearly* working through some stuff—and I think many of us can relate to how it is when, in our healing process from one terrible thing, we swing the other way like a pendulum and go just as extreme in the opposite direction for a while (which, naturally, can be just as harmful). So finally, I bucked up and got to calling—and it seemed like St. Augustine was more than eager to connect.

So let's get into it.

To set up my space, I had the usual: crystals that I felt represented St. Augustine's fiery, passionate, yet wise energy (carnelian, lapis lazuli, sunstone, and amethyst), as well as celestite, since that's *the* best crystal to use as an angel antenna, in my opinion. I also looked up some symbols of St. Augustine and found that feathers and flaming hearts were part of it. While I didn't have any flaming hearts specifically, I did have a rose quartz in the shape of a heart, and with Bilok, I have no shortage of white pigeon feathers to represent the Holy Spirit. So I stuck those on the table and surrounded them with a red rosary, and then I lit a single white candle. The chant *O Filii et Filiae* is my go to for Saint conversations, too—perfect for getting in the zone.

But with all that set up, I reached out and found that I already had an older gentleman standing by me. He was first dressed in the typical bishop outfit: the white and gold robes, the pointy hat, the staff. And we stood in a rocky desert, where the cliffs in the distance went from barren and empty to suddenly, as if by magic, raising what looked like a convent up from the ground, the stone church the same reddish color as the rock it came from. There was a nun there, and children running about, and a single palm tree casting a shadow into the courtyard.

When I looked back at St. Augustine, though, he wasn't in the bishop fit anymore. He had on a deep red robe, and while he was balding on the top, his gray hair was long, meeting his gray beard near his shoulders. He also had deep, dark eyes that, later on, would sparkle like polished garnets in that insanely deep, rich red color. Red, as I understand it, is the color of the Holy Spirit (hence people wear it to church on Pentecost), and I recently understood that this is why Jesus and so many other figures appear wearing red: *it's a sign that the Holy Spirit is nearby or has deeply impacted who I'm speaking to.*

That kind of red being not only in his much more humble, everyday clothes, but also his eyes, was therefore pretty significant to me—especially when he would sometimes make *sure* I noticed how his eyes were full of that dancing light that only red gems can capture. It was wild.

But now, to start, I sat there with my book and looked up at that man that I'd spent so long being so bitter towards—and I sighed. "Alright, St. Augustine," I said, "I feel like you wanted to speak to me as much as God wanted me to speak to you, and now you're here, and I'm here. Thank you for coming by."

He smiled at me like a grandfather would, then motioned towards that monastery. Then he took my hand and walked me over, and I swear, I could feel the rough scrape of his palm on mine. It was a gentle hold, and soon, we sat under that one palm tree and watched the children play as that one single nun smiled and laughed with them. It was a peaceful place, even if it was completely cut off from everything else in the world.

"So," I started, and I noted his choice of the Weaver Tarot, "I guess we should get the elephant out of the room. There are a lot of people who say you were a big old misogynist, St. Augustine—and while I couldn't find any evidence for a quote attributed to you, where you allegedly said women need to have as many children as possible, others have said you viewed women as an 'enemy of holiness' of sorts. What do you have to say about that?"

I. THOUGHTS ON THE MISOGYNY ALLEGATIONS?

As I shuffled, I swear I heard: "Did I say that, or did people infer it?"

And as I put a card down and shuffled again, I said, "I don't know if it matters what you said or if you meant something else when people got this out of your words, but hey."

St. Augustine leaned his staff against his shoulder and sighed. He watched the children a moment longer, then said after I pulled my cards, "It seems my wisdom from my struggles has gone in vain. Because again—did I say women are villains? Or have people simply inferred it from me?

"Womanhood *was* my villain, because it was my vice—but those like the Holy Mother showed me true beauty. I may have come off too

Broken bond or relationship fallen out of balance. Communication has become more challenging; neither party is open to fixing it.

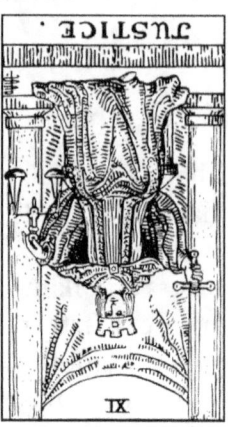

Repression of something you feel guilty about. Trying to justify it so you don't have to make amends. Need forgiveness, a clean slate.

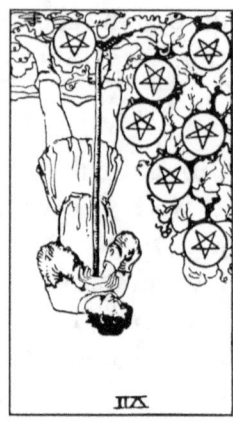

Feeling entrapped or stuck with a project that isn't going well. It may be time to move on despite investments made. Cut your losses.

strongly. I may have said things that aren't quite true—but I was doing what I could with what I knew. I was teaching as I was learning—because none of us will ever be done learning, and we can't wait for a perfect teacher to come along."

This sounded like a non-answer. "Do you hate women, St. Augustine?"

He glanced at me, a faint smile on his face, and he shook his head. "No, I do not hate women. They have their place in this world, and in the inheritance, in the Kingdom; they are God's beloveds as much as men. I was simply speaking from my own frame of reference."

Hmm. Fair enough, I suppose. I often wondered if maybe we were being too harsh on all of these people from two thousand years in the past with things like misogyny, because of course everyone had stupid ideas about women in this era, and even the best of people would find that ideology leaking in somewhere when they were so overly saturated in it on a macro level. Still, the shame, in my opinion, was where those very *time-centric* words came to be treated as *timeless*.

"So, again—does it matter what you meant, St. Augustine?" I tried to keep my tone clear and gentle, but my point was, well, pointed. "So many have used your words to justify keeping women under lock and key. No matter what you hoped to convey, people have found other ways to apply it. What do you think about this?"

2. THOUGHTS ON PEOPLE BEING MISOGYNISTIC IN YOUR NAME?

Reliable, nurturing, stable. Keeping life simple. Great at home and business. Doing all in support of others. Generosity, balance, practicality.

Rock bottom has been hit and you're ready to make change. Move forward. Don't give up. These changes are hard but necessary.

Evolved, wise. Spent many years understanding oneself. Legendary insights. Saying what you need to hear, not what you want. Truth, logic over emotion. Facts, solutions.

When I pulled the cards, I was so startled to see the way they were laid out. The Devil reversed sat in the middle, flanked by two Queens: the Queen of Coins and the Queen of Swords. It was as if they'd worked together to defeat some great evil, and the meanings behind them—nurturing, generosity, balance in business and domestic savvy, alongside logic, clear thinking, solution-based support, and very *not* nurturing energy—seemed to cover the spectrum of femininity, while that middle card itself talked all about hitting rock bottom and needing to dissolve ego to move forward. The message was so stark in the cards that it hit me like a frying pan, and then St. Augustine continued to smack me with it.

"Men need to change how they see women," he said, point blank. "I've been alive in Christ for many years now, and I've seen what they can do and achieve—and sometimes, it's men that need to step aside and let them work," in which he leaned over and tapped the Queen of Swords, "as much as they rely on them," then tapped the Queen of Coins.

However, even though this message was so stark, it just sounded odd, coming from a man I was so sure was a raging piece of work that personally held women back for centuries. "Okay, cool—but St. Augustine, how do I know all of this is what you actually believe, and not just me deluding myself into thinking you're saying it?"

Again, I got hit with the full brunt of those red garnet-like eyes, and they flashed as if alive with some great, bright light. Then, gone was the monastery, and stretching out before us was some stone castle hallway. A woman stood there with a baby in her arms; she stared in our direction with such severity in her face as she held the little baby to her, all bundled in pink cloth, though I don't think she could actually see us. She seemed to be staring past us. Then she hurried off in the other direction, until she came to a huge pool of clear water, with something like an angel standing in the back and watching over them. As she laid the baby in the pool, St. Augustine kept talking.

"Every man had a mother. He owes all he is to women. He has no say in how women live in adulthood any more than he did in childhood. They are our first protectors, teachers, stewards, sources of love, sources of holiness. They are warriors for our souls and shepherds for our lives and wellbeing—first as mother, then as wife. Outside these roles, they are our tests."

Oh, Jesus, here we go.

He looked at me with such bright light in his eyes. "Is it the bond we share with women, as mothers and wives, that makes them holy? Or is it just the nature of them? I find it now to be the latter."

Which, alright. I had *thoughts* about that, too—because what the hell is the nature of Woman, exactly? Even the two Queens from the last question seemed to have a radically different view of that—but then, maybe he meant all expressions of womanhood, as that spectrum showed. Maybe.

"How *do* you view women outside motherhood and marriage?" I blinked, and we were back at that convent, with the nun chasing kids around. "Because this day and age has women being everything men can be: teachers, doctors, scientists, even clergy. What do you make of this?"

3. HOW DO YOU SEE WOMEN OUTSIDE MOTHERHOOD?

And here, I pulled some cards that suggested our Saint was *struggling* with the idea. That Two of Swords right in the middle, with Nine of Swords Reversed on one side and Eight of Swords Reversed on the other? It was as clear a message of "I can see both sides" and "I'm uncomfortable" as I've ever seen come up in the cards. But eventually, as St. Augustine watched that nun, that nun paused her play with the kids and gave us a direct, strong stare.

"It's strange," St. Augustine muttered. "It's not something I could've readily grasped in my youth: women in every office once reserved for men. But they do an excellent job in those roles, too, don't they?" He smiled, then shook his head and sighed. "Were we wrong

Paralysis from negative self talk. The mind is pure chaos. You're making things harder than they need to be. Work required to escape this headspace.

Denial. Difficulty seeing the situation with clarity. Neither path seems ideal. Tension with emotions. Give voice to repressed feelings.

A beautiful sign that you've released yourself from oppressive systems. They still exist, but you've stopped playing by their rules.

then, to relegate women to our houses? When Christ Himself had dear Magdalene out and about, ever at His side? When Paul and Peter had women financing their ministry and learning to prophesy? I would think so.

"There are few times where disobedience may be considered a virtue, but if the thing demanding obedience is sin, then the only road for holiness is disobedience and denial. Women are capable of more than I ever understood on earth. We've wronged them, us men."

Damn. Of all the things I expected him to say, that last part really struck me. I blinked at him for a minute, mulling that over before I finally moved on.

"So, then... why did you do such a one-eighty in life? You went from having a lover, even having a kid with her, to being a celibate holy man. How? Why? Did you need to go that far in the other direction?"

4. WHY DID YOU GO SO EXTREME WITH YOUR CONVERSION?

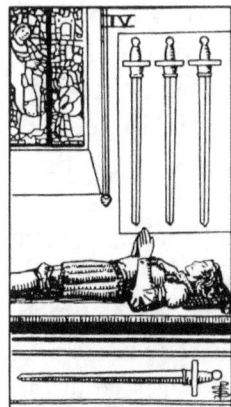

Rest for the time being. Gather your strength after so many battles. Create separation. Learn to de-stress for resilience.

Repression of something you feel guilty about. Trying to justify it so you don't have to make amends. Need forgiveness, a clean slate.

A clear thinking, ambitious person in a position of power. Viewing situation with the head, not the heart. Healthy detachment.

He sat up straight, all stoic and staring off in the distance, and he said, "I couldn't very well cure myself with my greatest temptation ever looming. Distance weakens the bond of vice. Like a candle flame, it can flicker and entice you from afar, but it'll only burn you if you get, and stay, too close. I needed to get away to rationalize the roots of it and dig them out—hence the 'one-eighty,' as you call it. And I said some regrettable things as I tried to flee that candle flame, as we all do in the process of healing. But I'm here to correct those things now. Show me the same grace you showed Paul."

Oops. I will admit: he humbled the shit out of me with that last line. It also all made sense to me, why I'd felt St. Augustine was trying to get to me, with how often he popped up in my head as someone to interview for the past couple *months*. I'd always said *no, no, someone else, someone that won't make me angry to talk to*—and then when God denied my every idea for a new interview, leaving me with only St. Augustine as an option, I really had no choice but to dive in. It seemed that was not a coincidence.

"Okay, okay, fine," I said. "If I can learn better about Paul, I can learn better about you, too. But then—with Paul, I learned more of what he really meant and how we twisted it. With you, it seems like a lot of this is coming after the fact, which is why I want to make sure I'm not just wishfully thinking you to have changed. So that brings me to this question: what *does* happen when you die? Do you learn every single thing you got wrong, like how people take quizzes and see all the red marks where they answered a question wrong after? What's up?"

5. WHAT DO YOU LEARN WHEN YOU GO TO HEAVEN?

1. Stuck in a pessimistic mindset. Challenges preventing you from seeing the good in life, blocking you from your power. Restore play.

2. A relationship gone sour or in conflict. Both parties bring baggage. It's your choice what to do with this pattern: try again or walk away.

3. A few options are available and you're centering on the best choice. Not the time for schemes; think long term success.

He barked a laugh when I showed him that picture of green checks and red X's next to a ten-question quiz I might give to my students, and then he said, "We become like angels." That alone said more than enough to me, but he made it clear he wanted to pull some cards—and after he did, he continued, the mirth fading from him a little bit. "It hurts. When you die, you learn so explicitly how much you have failed, and how much you have scorned God your Creator in that failure. You feel as if there's no possible way you could ever atone, and you're nearly ready to pitch yourself into the fire forever—but it's God's grace and mercy that give you the option for atonement anyway.

"Not all take it. I've seen it—the souls that would rather burn forever than stand before God in such shame. And I've seen the souls so wicked that they simply wink out, their evil too much for them to even have the humility to choose the fire. But for those who seek God above all, they have the choice to be washed anew, baptized again in fire—and then all is known. God forgives all; the true art is then, after knowing all you learn, learning to forgive yourself and make amends. And that is what I'm doing now: making amends."

"Damn." This guy, I was coming to understand, was something of a badass. And what he said made sense with what so many other mystics ever said. "Alright, but then—Christian men. What do you have to say to these men, who keep trying to use your words to put women down? The 'theobros,' so to speak?"

6. Wʜᴀᴛ ᴅᴏ ʏᴏᴜ Hᴀᴠᴇ ᴛᴏ Sᴀʏ ᴛᴏ Mɪsᴏɢʏɴɪsᴛɪᴄ Cʜʀɪsᴛɪᴀɴ Mᴇɴ?

When I pulled cards all about ego and conflict and breaking free of oppression yet again, I knew exactly where he was going with it, but he laid it out clearly for me anyway: "Grace is paramount to understand and fix sin. Though, these Christian men... do they understand that it's their own ego delivering them their understanding, not the holy Word of God? The Word lives, and His name is Christ Jesus. And the Word does not say to shackle others who are free. It promises liberation, peace, cooperation between all.

"Men—why do you let fear lead you? Why do you doubt your worth so much, that you need to strip it from another to make yourself look grander? When you learn to abandon such concepts of worth altogether, then you

A place of exhaustion after conflict. Tension is so draining that this offers grace and perspective. Put ego aside and meet the situation a different way.	*Deep grief, panic, sadness, depression. Racing, intrusive thoughts. You're not letting yourself turn the page. Do something new.*	*A beautiful sign that you've released yourself from oppressive systems. They still exist, but you've stopped playing by their rules.*

may begin your journey of finding God. For now, you've made masculinity your idol, and you fashion so many containers with which to draw down this defiling force that you're at risk of never escaping it, trapped in a maze of your own making. Seek God, the true God, not yourself in God's place."

Whoa. I was about to start snapping my fingers at this point, because *damn*—if that wasn't the most succinct way to put it, I don't know what was. And it's true, isn't it? Masculinity itself has become warped in a way that, the more these men try to grab it and bring it close, the more containers they make to stuff it into—muscles, cars, money—the more they lose sight of the actual gentleness of God altogether. Huh.

"Well, alright, then. I guess that's about the end of our main questions—so tell me, St. Augustine: how do you see yourself?"

7. HOW DO YOU SEE YOURSELF?

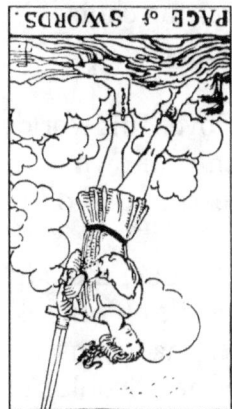

Arrogance with no action to back it up. Intellect used for negativity and manipulation. Ego. Disconnect from how we're hurting others by focusing on our triumphs. Need compassion.

Seeing the Page of Swords upside down was a bit of a tug on the heart strings. But St. Augustine looked at me with such earnesty as he said, "So long as my wrong words echo, I cannot in good conscious complete my own union with God. Here I stay, calling to those who know how to listen, begging my words born of self hate and ego don't inspire the same in any others. I was a wretched sinner—and now I make amends."

"Aw, jeez. I hear you. How do you want to be seen, though?"

8. HOW DO YOU WANT TO BE SEEN?

The Ace of Cups was surprising, though maybe it shouldn't have been, as traditionally this art had the Eucharist, Communion chalice, and white dove on it: all symbols of both Christ and the Holy Spirit.

A new emotional beginning. Whatever happened until now serves as a wonderful lesson. A new relationship or endeavor approaches. Choose the path of joy.

"I want to start over," he said. "I am ready to be perceived as someone making amends. So much attention is lavished on how much I spoke and wrote—so hear me speak now! We Saints have more to teach you. Look not only to the writings we made as fallible, imperfect men, but to the words we speak now as redeemed and eternally living souls."

At this point, I realized I'd actually only wrote down nine questions instead of ten (somehow, I wrote down one, two, three, four, *six*, skipping the space for five entirely), and so I decided to ask an extra question here: "Okay, but then, how do we know these words are legit? I'm not hearing these words in your voice; sometimes I hear you say them in mine. And all these Saints and mystics always warned against self deception. So how do people know the Saints are speaking truth and it's not just 'Saints' they've invented, speaking useless things?"

9. HOW DO WE KNOW SAINTS' WORDS FROM HEAVEN ARE REAL?

He once again startled me with that intense garnet stare. "Ego," he whispered, without choosing any cards, as if testing my ability to simply trust him. "Just as you can be deceived in hearing what you want to hear, so can you convince yourself that all you hear is deception when it doesn't sound as you think it should. Trust the mystic vision, but question it. Trust and questioning must go hand in hand, else the ego finds ways to slip in again."

What a paradox. *Trust,* yet *question.* Though, given I was still reading about all the mystic paradoxes in Carl McColman's *Big Book of Christian Mysticism,* I guess I shouldn't have been surprised.

"Alright, fair," I said. "So, with all that out of the way, the last thing I have to ask, St. Augustine, is: do you have any final things you want to share?"

10. ANY LAST MESSAGES?

Too harsh and less understanding. Frustrated by others' displays of emotions. Coldness. Quick to shut down and judge. Find balance.

The Queen of Swords Reversed was an interesting choice, but I knew what he meant as I read the meaning. Once I'd written it down, he answered me.

"Remember—all things you do, do them in love. This world is dead of grace. Open your hearts to all—even your own enemies. Only then does purgation begin on earth—and only then can healing follow the fire."

"Got'cha, got'cha. I understand." And I agreed, too. I thought about all the times I'd been so willing to cut people off or look down on them, when I should've been, and could've been, softer. It made sense.

"Alright, well, that's all I have for today. Thank you, St. Augustine," and I couldn't help it; I got up and gave him a big old hug, which, to my surprise, he did return, "I'll see you around, I guess. Goodbye for now!"

And then all that desert faded away, and I was back in my living room, with Bilok staring at me begging for his morning breakfast. I was vexed, though, completely and utterly—because *damn it,* I wanted to be able to yell St. Augustine's ear off for all he'd contributed, said, and done in this religion, and yet how could I have?

Just like when I first talked to St. Paul, and saw a different side of him, here I was faced with a different side of this Saint, too. I don't know much about grace or mercy, I will admit—I am hotheaded, all too willing to smack someone before I forgive them—but I know also that forgiveness doesn't need much more than an earnest "I'm sorry" and a change in perspective. It's how I've gone about all my friendships and relationships in life: if one can recognize what they've done and avoid it again, that's all I need. So, as I chewed on all St. Augustine just told me, I knew I had no choice but to follow that same rule here—not because I had to, but because all the dread and animosity and rage I felt every time I'd thought of St. Augustine before this was just gone.

Gone. Like it was never there.

In its place was something warm, soft. Something that gave me hope, and that emboldened me to think that maybe, *maybe,* humanity will get it one day. That if there really is a chance to repent to *this degree,* like all the other Saints have ever said, then that this is why we keep drifting further and further towards that beautiful world where all are equal and all are safe and all are cared for and all are One. It's a frustrating journey, no doubt, but I think I can see us getting there—bit by bit, step by step.

ZOTIEL

Remember how I said that what I thought was God was actually an angel? And that this angel's name was Zotiel?

Yeah.

I discovered this name when I was reading the *Book of Enoch,* where in Chapter 32, he gets a passing mention:

> And after these fragrant odours, as I looked towards the north over the mountains I saw seven mountains full of choice nard and fragrant trees and cinnamon and pepper.
>
> And thence I went over the summits of all these mountains, far towards the east of the earth, and passed above the Erythraean sea and went far from it, and passed over the angel Zotiel. And I came to the Garden of Righteousness,
>
> I and from afar off trees more numerous than I these trees and great-two trees there, very great, beautiful, and glorious, and magnificent, and the tree of knowledge, whose holy fruit they eat and know great wisdom.

Zotiel, whose name apparently means "little one of God," is a cherub that has next to no other information about him. I don't know where I even saw it at this point, but it must've been somewhere else in the *Book of Enoch* where I also saw that Zotiel had something to do with fire. I wish I'd kept a better record of it now, but all I can tell you is that somewhere along the way, the spiritual math came together in my head and made me certain that the fiery, icy-eyed being I always saw when talking to God was, in fact, this angel.

As we came into the end of 2024, and I was just about to start my end-of-year winter series, I thought: *why not investigate this angel, too?* After all, I caught a glimpse of him just about every day;

he was like the living telephone between God and I. You'd think, eventually, I'd stop taking that for granted and start getting curious—and finally, two years into this adventure, I did.

With little else to say about this angel except for this, I suppose we'll just have to hear the rest from him, right?

Like all other times I've ever sat down to talk to God, I sat down to talk to Zotiel with just a few things: a candle, a rosary, and some crystals that represented Zotiel to me. By that, I mean crystals that represented love (rose quartz), fire (carnelian) and angel communication (celestite). A piece of purple jasper also called out to me, which makes sense, since it's a stone of inner courage and spirituality. But with just a few things there, and Kat Black's *Golden Tarot* on deck, I knew I was in a good place to get rolling—to talk like I always talked when I sat down to speak with God over tarot and a cup of coffee.

And yet, oddly, it was hard that day. Hard to get a grip on Zotiel and hone in on *his* presence rather than just God's presence channeled *through* him. While I saw him as I always did soon enough, as that man made of fire, I also then saw the angel proper, the cherub: the one with the four faces, the huge wings, the brownish red robes, and the body still burning with divine fire. But while I spoke to him as I always speak, I found that the answers were a struggle to get out of him. Like pulling teeth, as some might say.

"Zotiel!" We stood there outside that gate leading up to God, there in the clouds, as I greeted the angel (and Jesus, who stopped by for a second to say hello before disappearing). "Zotiel, hi! I'd like to ask some questions about *you* today, if you don't mind. Is that okay?"

Whereas Zotiel was once really expressive, perfectly capturing what God Himself seemed to be feeling at any point, as his own self, his face was wide-eyed and fixed in a soft smile. He crossed his arms and nodded, and I got started trying to get a card or two from him.

"Alright, so—I saw an article from what I believe is a more New Age source saying you're the *weakest* angel of all. It even depicted you as, like, a fuzzy little bunny rabbit angel or something. What do you think about that? Is that true?"

1. THOUGHTS ON YOU BEING A "WEAK" ANGEL?

His smile got deeper, and while I thought he wanted only one card, we ended up with two: the Page of Swords and the Ten of Cups Reversed. After looking at them and their meanings, and of course the art—that sword-brandishing Page stuck out to me quite a bit—Zotiel spoke so softly that it was almost easy to miss. I had to dig the answer out of him a little bit, but it did get there. He also gave me images of himself like that Page: with a sword in hand, cutting down enemies and defending the gardens of Heaven.

"People take for granted what it means to be an angel," Zotiel said. "If I'm the weakest, and I still successfully repel rebel forces and forces of evil, then what does that say about everyone else? Only a fool underestimates an angel."

A challenging youth. Passionate, deep insight. Use what is available.

Good fortune taken for granted. Disillusionment.

"So you're not a cute little bunny like that article wanted to depict you as?"

He chuckled. "I am by no means soft and cuddly, nor am I easily overtaken."

"Alright, fair enough!" There was a playful air that made it easier to talk, but not much easier to get responses. "So, in the Book of Enoch, you just get mentioned once and then that's it. Enoch was on his way to the Garden of Righteousness then. What were you doing, when he passed you by?"

2. WHAT WERE YOU DOING WHEN ENOCH PASSED BY?

THE EMPRESS.

In true victory, both sides are winners. Matriarchy. A goal oriented person concerned with how success is achieved. Compromise. Fertility.

Pulling the Empress was odd, because it was clearly depicting Mary and Jesus, and Zotiel seemed to be hinting at that, too. But Mary and Jesus weren't even a thing yet in the time of Enoch, so as I wrote down the card meaning, I once again had to really tug to get the thread Zotiel was trying to lay down.

"I was taking care of the gardens, of Mother and Child."

"But Mary and Jesus hadn't come into being by this point. They weren't incarnate."

Zotiel shook his head. "The great Mother and Child still always existed [as archetypes]. What happened after Enoch? The flood, correct? I was growing, in those gardens, the maternal sentiments, softness, and grace to implant in humans, which had been missing. My labors would become part of a new era of humanity, it seemed."

It took a second to really digest what he was talking about. But eventually, it sunk in enough that I could bring myself to write it down, and I stared at it for a second before continuing on.

"I think I get'cha there. That's interesting! Okay, so, weird question, I guess—but why are you made of fire?"

3. WHY ARE YOU MADE OF FIRE?

Zotiel didn't even pull a card for this. He just shrugged, then showed me his burning face, his ice-bright eyes. "To mirror the fires of God," he said. "I am to be His representation, to give you a sense of Him. He is the fire that burns so hot that it burns cold."

"That's—yeah, that's understandable. But you're pretty consistently the angel I see when I go to talk to God. Why are you the one to deliver God's messages for me?"

4. WHY ARE YOU DELIVERING GOD'S MESSAGES FOR ME?

"To keep you from doing stupid things," he said as he all but threw the Five of Coins card at me. "You understand severity and mercy easily enough through my flames. I'm here to guide you. I am nameless enough that you don't get distracted by me when God is talking. Though it seems," he offered a small, sad smile, "that you may have divorced me from God as an entity now, paying so close attention to me."

Oops. What he was saying made a lot of things make sense. There was a reason I didn't understand this angel to be an angel for so long. Or that I didn't have his name for even longer. Or

Misguided goals. Poor decisions, or lack of decision, lead to destitution and misery. Ill health and misfortune. Make the most of what you have, no matter how little it is.

that I didn't feel particularly pulled to know or learn more until my curiosity got the better of me. But we were already here, and there was nothing to do but keep going. (Even then, I also think his accusation is a bit unfounded: even if I know he's an angel, I still know his role and speak to God directly despite Zotiel being the face of that message.)

"So do any of the other angels ever be mouthpieces for God like you do, then?"

5. ARE ANY OTHER ANGELS MOUTHPIECES FOR GOD LIKE YOU ARE?

Celebration of good fortune. Friendship, revelry, and abundance. Fulfillment of hopes. Creativity and understanding. Recovery from illness.

The Three of Cups was a weird card to pull. I didn't really know what to do with that at first until I took a closer look at the art—three women cheering while two men looked on—and a closer look at all the good things that the card represented, like good health, fulfillment of hopes, and so on. Then it began to click, and the message Zotiel was trying to get to me was able to be translated into plain English.

"No," he said. "They're busy. The other angels are too distinct in character, too deeply associated in the minds of humans with other things. They are of God, just as I am, yet they stand apart as their own beings in your eyes. I am enough of an unknown, a blank slate, that people see past me and to God."

Healing—Raphael. Fulfillment of hopes—Remiel. Creativity and understanding—Gabriel. Friendship—Chamuel. So many angels, we turn to as their own beings to help us or pray for us for these specific things. I understood what Zotiel meant: that we see them as their own figures, their own people, their own personalities, which makes it hard to see God speaking through them as *God* rather than as their distinct aspects of God via their names. Zotiel was trying to keep himself distinct from any defining characteristics like that, and my poking around would potentially upset that balance he had going there—if not for me, then maybe for others. Let's hope that's not the case.

"Ooh," I said, feeling a little stupid anyway for trying to rock that boat. But I was confident that since I knew him as God's mouthpiece first, that that's how it would always be and how I would always understand him, and I expressed that before asking my next question. "Okay, so... if you want to be so non-distinct, is that... does that mean that you were that 'angel of the Lord' in the Bible? The anonymous angel that was often mistaken for God?"

6. WERE YOU THE ANONYMOUS "ANGEL OF THE LORD" IN THE BIBLE?

Zotiel's eyes crinkled in the corners as he smiled. Then he immediately bopped me on the head with his next answer, that pesky Six of Coins Reversed. I almost wondered for a moment if I was really speaking to an angel, or instead to a trickster spirit, because these cards at face value seemed to have nothing to do with my questions—until I looked deeper and had that *aha!* moment.

"You ask too many questions that would destabilize the way things are set up in the Bible," he said with a little shake of his head as I wrote down the card meaning. "The point is that you

Be wary of spending beyond your means. Generosity is all very well, but be careful that it doesn't lead to debt.

don't focus so much on us angels like you all do. We are not the important ones. You need to direct your attention on God, and God alone. Asking after us is foolishness. If we go unnamed [in the Scriptures], it is for a reason, and it's rude to speculate. Consider this a learning opportunity: when angels are incognito, it's better to let us be."

Ah. Paint me pink and call me humbled, because damn. It's moments like these that I am very kindly, but firmly, reminded that angels exist to be a looking glass, a lens for us to further get clarity and closeness to God. They exist by virtue of the aspects of God they inhabit; they are autonomous insofar as they need to be to reach us *and then redirect us* back to what we need to be focusing on. That's what I was very viscerally re-learning there, and it cemented deeply.

"I got'cha," I said. Then, as we came back to the gates of heaven, and that staircase where God was waiting so far beyond us, I pointed to Him and asked Zotiel, "So, has anyone ever seen God? Anyone ever been up those stairs?"

7. HAS ANYONE EVER SEEN GOD FACE TO FACE?

Zotiel shook his head. He didn't pull any cards, but the message was clear, as it came directly out of the Bible itself in its phrasing: "No one can see God and live. So it is said. To see God in full means you stand prepared to lose all that you are."

Oh, I get'cha. I was thinking of folks like Enoch, who apparently became angels and lost themselves—maybe that's what Zotiel meant by that, too—but the basics of it was that pesky little *unification* thing mystics talk about: where to see God is to lose all sense of self and meld back into that Godhead not as our own being, but as a lost fragment of Divinity reunited with our Source. To lose the illusion of our human separation.

"Okay, okay, interesting." I scribbled his words down, then said, "Alright, well, we're near the end now. How do you see yourself, Zotiel?"

8. HOW DO YOU SEE YOURSELF?

A tendency towards masochism and playing the martyr needlessly.

The Hanged Man Reversed was a weird card to pull. Especially in this deck. All about playing the martyr, masochism? Weird, plain and simple. But he just had that dry smile on as he explained.

"I seem to enjoy thanklessness, as one might say. I am not interested in defining myself more than I have."

"Alrighty, then. How do you want to be seen?"

9. HOW DO YOU WANT TO BE SEEN?

Should've seen it coming when he pulled no cards and said, "I do not. See God, not me."

"Fine, fine. But now, how about a last message? You got anything you want people to know?"

10. ANY LAST MESSAGES?

The King of Coins Reversed was a choice. One all about corrupt men that hold grudges and have shit for imagination. But as I stared at it, and wrote down its meaning, Zotiel tapped the card and explained with his longest response yet.

A corrupt man, or one who holds grudges. A lack of imagination.

"Be careful not to be like this man. To be too rigid in your thinking and uncharitable about how expansive creation really is. Not everything needs a clean answer. The boxes you try to put everything in are made of cardboard; the things of this world will rake their claws right through them.

"Focus. Focus on the Law. The Word. And do not forget that you know nothing and never will, what with all that's there and all that's possible."

"Oh," I said, blinking. That last bit was a bit of a sting, given I think I know *something*—and yet a humbling reminder all the same that in fact, no, I really don't, and Zotiel's probably right in that I never really will. Not in this body, not in this lifetime. "I—yeah, I can see that. Alright, well, that's that! Zotiel, thank you for speaking with me a little today and setting me straight. Thank you also for being willing to chat in the first place. I know I'll see you around, so here's to our next session with God, yeah?"

He nodded, smiled, and then that was that. I was back in the living room, with Bilok staring at me and wondering why he wasn't allowed out of his cage yet, and with all kinds of other fun things to get to for the day. Fun things that made me put down my curiosity over this *incognito angel* and allowed him to slip back into the transient go-between for God and I.

And I guess it's better that way, if only so I can remember who I'm talking to when I'm talking—so I don't go adding even more faces, names, and layers of separation between God and I for no reason.

BEIRA

After Zotiel, it came time to spend a third winter in this spiritual adventure here, and I knew there were plenty of gods and spirits we could've spoken to. However, after a demon, two Saints, and an angel, I knew the first of those entities had to be the Celtic Queen of Winter, Beira, to balance out all that otherwise Abrahamic-centered influence. Nothing like a look back at deities of my ancestors to get my footing back in all this, huh?

Now, let me introduce Beira properly. This goddess is considered the mother of all the gods in Scottish lore, and she's also known in Ireland as the Cailleach (which people may know her better by). Her lore is fascinating, too; it's said that she and her sisters mined a bunch of stone, put it in their baskets, walked out from the center of the earth and into the world's vast waters, and picked a direction to walk. Then they stopped to rest and sat their stones down just right, and that made the lands that now float on the earth. After a while, her sister Bride (Brigid) came by, and there started the age-old fight for power: Bride and Angus winning in the spring/summer, Beira regaining her strength after a season of rest to reclaim her territory.

It's also said that in Scotland, when you see the white on the mountaintops (snow), that's how you know Beira's back to rule in the wintertime again: the snow is actually her white woolen shawl being laid out to dry. And Beira goes every spring to drink from a certain spring that rejuvinates her and makes her young again, but such a magical drink wears off every winter, hence she's back to being an old woman by time winter rolls around. She has a hammer, a missing eye, and is known for being quite rough and tough—as I'm noticing most goddesses of winter tend to be (just remember Morana and Frau Berchta! What serious and powerful goddesses!)

But with all this explanation out of the way, now, let's dive on in.

So, as always, I'd been procrastinating a bit. The days were too long, even though the daylight is short, and with so many projects on my plate, things just had to get shifted around if I was going to both accomplish my to-do list and stay sane. It's a never-ending story with me, y'know? Work and work and work some more, until everything I've learned in the spiritual world erodes into dust under the weight of all the distractions of the material world.

But eventually, *finally,* I sat my ass in my living room, got some offerings for Beira (a votive offering of brandy in water and two white stones, as Beira apparently likes white stones), and set up my crystal grid. Blue, black, and white made sense for colors, so I set out my obsidian sphere, smaller obsidian pieces, sodalite, and my one piece of milky white howlite.

After that, I did what I always do: initiated my space with the Lord's Prayer and asked God to help me find Beira. But it seems she knew I was thinking about her, in the way we've already discussed so often in this book, because all I had to do was close my eyes to immediately get sucked into the scene: a corridor between snow-covered pine trees, my legs calf-deep in yet more snow, with one old, hunched woman smiling up at me as if she'd been expecting me.

Her hair was fluffy and white, her face lined with wrinkles. Her eyes were banded blue like the eyes of the blind, or those with cataracts—and it would switch between her having two eyes and one missing eye, which was interesting. Likely, it was just my own mind superimposing that second eye in there, as it would expect a face to have. But she welcomed me along, told me it took me long enough to get there, and then we went up to the peak of a mountain where we could overlook the whole of what was a still mostly green Scotland.

"Beira!" As we went up to that mountain, I couldn't help but feel like I was seeing old family. Again, maybe I should be spending more time with the Celtic deities or something, because that feeling is unmistakable between them and the Slavic deities. "Hello! Thank you for joining me! I've got some questions for you, as well as some brandy and some pretty stones for you; please accept them as thanks for coming by."

The whole time, she just kept smiling, the way a grandmother listening to their child babble might. It surprised me to see her so calm and gentle, because the way her myths made her seem, I figured she'd be a little more rough around the edges—but no. I don't doubt she could've kicked my ass easily, but her general countenance was patient, wise, and quiet.

"Alright, well, let's get right into it, shall we?" I shuffled the Universal Fantasy Tarot, and after Beira held up three fingers to tell me she wanted three cards per answer, I dove in: "So, right away, I'm curious: what made you decide to settle your basket of rocks down here? And make Scotland?"

1. WHAT MADE YOU SETTLE IN THE ISLES AND MAKE SCOTLAND?

1. Stress, restlessness, and unwillingness to take risks.

2. Suppression, lacking discretion, or feeling incapable of expressing oneself.

3. Misfortune approaching, depression, unsuccessful ventures.

Beira looked out over the land. The clouds were obscuring some of the view, low and misty things, but there was a huge expanse of green fields and a big lake somewhere farther on. Beira eventually sighed and answered me.

"I wanted to get away from my sisters," she said. "I spent so long in that damn mine. But on this world, there's only so far you can go before you get bumping into one another again." Then she scowled. "It was never far enough, though. Never far enough. Bride found me anyway, that brat. All I know is that I couldn't walk anymore. Had to stake my claim. So here I am now."

"Oh, that makes sense. But the way you talk of Bride makes me wonder: where are your other sisters? What do they do? And... how do you feel about them?"

2. WHERE ARE YOUR OTHER SISTERS (THOUGHTS ON THEM)?

Ambition is often the sister of dissatisfaction. Be careful not to see only the positive side of news.

There are people who make good use of our affection and others who use it to deceive us.

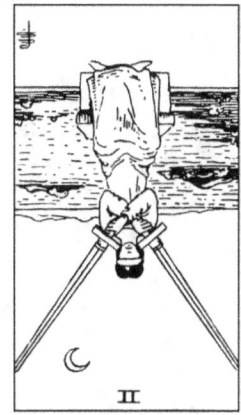

Disloyalty and feeling pressured or lost.

Beira shrugged and sucked her teeth. "Again, brats, all of them. They love attention and praise and song. I just want to be left alone in the quiet, so I went away from them. What they do isn't my business; I don't know where they are or what they do. I just know they wanted to make something when we parted ways. It's what we were mining for. I just hope they made it pretty; gods know the world needs to be pretty."

"Do you miss them?"

She gave me a slow smile. "No, I don't miss them. They have their way, and I have mine."

"I get that." As I scribbled, she kept watching the world out there. I watched it with her for a moment—all the twisting mist, the green pastures—before I asked another question. "So, as I understand, you're the Queen of Winter, and it's about your time now. Winter's almost here! I was wondering what you think about Winter, and what you think we can learn from your kingdom."

3. THOUGHTS ON WINTER AND WHAT WE CAN LEARN FROM IT?

It was interesting to see cards about weakness and incompetence and overcoming obstacles in regards to a season that was all about death and rest. Beira harrumphed and, without looking away from Scotland, gave me a rough answer.

Logic and perseverance can help us overcome seemingly impossible obstacles.

Rules and traditions often preserve what was good and useful in the past, but true wisdom knows when to innovate.

Weakness in work or team situations, an inability to delegate, incompetence.

"You think you can get by in this world alone? Listen here, girl; winter is a time of monsters. It's a time for tests, when all your good days are but memories and the days are dark and hard. Are your memories of better times enough to keep you warm? Or do you need to be smart, finding your own warmth for you and your community? This is no time for the weak. My kingdom is not for the bellyachers, the 'woe is me' types. Band together! Band strong!"

"I see, I see."

I wrote that down, and at that point, I kept looking at her and wondering why I was seeing her with two eyes when the stories said she had one. And why she didn't have her legendary hammer. I was starting to wonder if maybe I'd done something wrong, or I was talking to the wrong spirit, or I was making things up—all those familiar old doubts yet again that try to throw me off the work I'm doing. But by this point, I (at least somewhat) understood that gods came in different forms, and that one representation of her—of winter—wasn't the only. Still, I expressed my frustration, and soon we were off that mountain and out walking in the deep snowy woods again.

And Beira had one eye. And her hammer held tight in her fist. And a fur cape and deep blue, gem crusted dress, very old school medieval dress—the dress of a queen. On her head, too, was an icicle crown. She gave me a stern look, as if to say, *is this what you want, brat?* But ultimately, from there, I knew I was in fact dealing with the right spirit, and the fact that she was humoring me with that appearance—that the other vision I had before was just as correct. Humbled, I walked with her and kept on asking questions.

"Alright, alright, so—more than just learning from winter, what would you say there is to enjoy about it? Lots of people love Bride's summer, sure, but lots of people hate it, too. Like us up here where I am, in northern America. We're cold weather folk! We don't like melting in summer! What do you think?"

4. WHAT IS THERE TO ENJOY ABOUT WINTER?

Closure, working toward (not necessarily positive) resolution, hostility.

Knowledge often requires sacrifice, but if we act with determination, we can reach our heart's desire.

Stagnation and resisting change.

She smiled at that, as if amused, and said, "This here is a world of filth. It rots in the sun. But in winter, we might hold onto silence a little longer. When we thaw in spring, we can worry about our problems again. For now, though, it's good to look at the snow and let this be a time of ending. No new projects now. Only rest and good slumber, peace, slowness."

"Ooh, I love that. Yes. I'd like a more quiet and slow winter myself, though knowing me," I huffed, "I probably won't give myself that. I should, though. Well, anyway, I did hear that you drink from a sort of fountain of youth and become a maiden in the summer. What do you do in the summer, when you're away from your kingdom?"

5. WHAT DO YOU DO IN THE SUMMER?

"I gather armies," Beira said, and I had the image of a golden-haired, yet very sharp faced and brutal woman, going about the forest and looking for allies. "To take back what's mine, I gather armies. All the hobgoblins and other creatures that wilt in the summer, I ask them again and again to fight a waning Bride with me. Ugh, Bride," Beira's lip curled, "always the center of attention, isn't she? Everyone loves her. No one comes to check on me while I gallivant about.

"But it's better that way, too. Gives me the rest I need, being alone. Out there, I find my own love, make new gods, think on things. I come. I go. I think. I enjoy my time. Then I come

Heartaches are often the symptom of an interior desire for change that concerns many aspects of life.

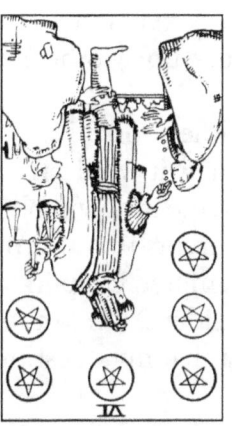

Envy or a lack of desire to think critically about one's own actions.

The most fertile marriages can arrive from radical changes and sudden shocks.

back with new wisdom for another aging year. It makes sense that way."

"Make new gods?" I paused my writing and blinked, and of course it all made me think of the sun gods—and of Jesus Himself. All these gods, we celebrate the birth of over and over, and some even get actually reborn each time. "What do you mean?"

Beira eyed me. "The gods never stop being born and reborn," she said, and when Jesus popped into my head, she smiled. "Thought you might appreciate that idea, Christian girl."

"I do, yeah! Across multiple religions, too. It's a fun idea. But alright, alright—how about Scotland now? What do you think of the modern country? I'd say they're doing pretty alright, no? I know they've been through some crazy stuff in the past, but compared to the rest of the world, it looks like they're doing great now in terms of peace and stability."

6. WHAT DO YOU THINK OF MODERN DAY SCOTLAND?

In true *old god* fashion, Beira heaved a sigh and pulled some rough cards. "No, Scotland lost their way. This peace you say they have, they take for granted. At any moment, the Picts can be under siege again. Stranger things have happened. But where's the fighting spirit of my people? Peace and luxury have made them soft. There will come a day when they need to find their old fire. May that day come swiftly, so they're shocked into making the change they dream about. Scotland—get up. Wake up. Mother's coming home."

What was that last line about? I didn't know; I only knew it wouldn't

Sometimes we can't avoid a major change. We should not be afraid of setting on a new path.

The ability to imagine the future is not enough to change it.

There are people who make good use of our affection and others who use it to deceive us.

leave my head. So I wrote it down, blinked at it, and in between it all, I started getting messages from my dad. I'd told my parents in our group chat about all the wild events happening in the world at that time (namely, the attempted coup in South Korea that ended embarrassingly badly for their soon-to-be-impeached president), and I took a pause to answer some of their questions about it. All the while, I assured Beira that my question would have to do with exactly all this I was chattering to my parents about.

"Alright," I said once I returned to the conversation, "Beira, let me tell you, the world's a hot mess. I understand what you mean about Scotland, but at the same time, it's good to be there and not elsewhere in the world. It does make me wonder, though: you're no stranger to times of war and tension yourself, having to get your kingdom back from Bride every year. How can we humans handle these times? And all this conflict?"

7. HOW CAN WE HANDLE TIMES OF WAR, STRESS, AND CONFLICT?

Having a road to follow is sometimes more important than knowing where it goes.

Hostility, indecision, disharmony. Know when to moderate.

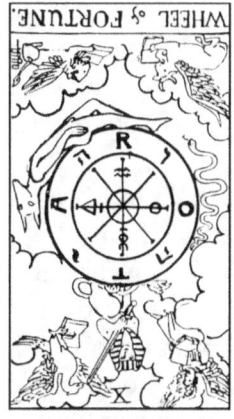

Poor luck and failure.

Beira had a tight grip on her hammer. "You suffer, " she said. "You get sick of suffering. You rise up and suffer more. And you don't do all of this because you know how it'll turn out; you don't assume all will be well in the end. You do it because there's nothing else to do. Maybe you win. Maybe you lose. What matters, though, is that you tried, and you keep trying, until you win. The world won't give you what you want because you said please. Gotta take it. Snatch it. Risk it all away. Or else you'll be lost."

Damn. I blinked at her as she said all that, her voice steely cold and her gaze over the woods just as sharp. Then, with a nod, I continued.

"Sounds about right to me. Thank you for that. Now, though, it's just the last few questions, so Beira, can you tell me how you see yourself?"

8. HOW DO YOU SEE YOURSELF?

Real success is being surrounded by love and friendship. To be able to give part of ourselves to others, we have to show ourselves as we really are.

And funnily enough, the Queen of Winter pulled the Sun. The way the Universal Fantasy Tarot described it made make a little more sense with her answer; it described the Sun with: *real success is being surrounded by love and friendship. To be able to give part of ourselves to others, we have to show ourselves as we really are.*

Beira chuckled at my surprise and said, "I'm glad you caught my irony, girl. But I am one that is misunderstood. I don't cause pain for the sake of it. It's simply my nature to be of the cold. I am one who can protect my people—if they let me, in my own way."

"Got'cha. No, that makes sense. But how do you want to be seen, then?"

9. HOW DO YOU WANT TO BE SEEN?

"I am one who does not give up," she said. "I know my place. I know what's mine, and I will have it, all of it. No one will take my hard-won earnings from me, not forever. My people: hear me and know I'm here!"

It was the second time she called out like that, and I really wondered if she wasn't actively trying to get back into the mind of her people. Scotland surely does still know about her, as their lore about her is pretty impressively preserved, so it wouldn't be a far off thing to assume the Scottish people still, pagan or not, hold memories of their old ways and even old gods close.

Obstinancy and determination are often instruments of great wealth. At times, we must have confidence in our dreams in order to make them come true.

KNIGHT of PENTACLES

"So, that leads us to the last question, then: do you have any final messages?"

10. ANY LAST MESSAGES?

Misfortune approaching, depression, unsuccessful ventures.

Of all the cards she could've pulled, she pulled the Sun again—but reversed. And she said, "Don't feel bad if all's going to shit right now. It is what it is. Don't you worry, though. It's not forever. Keep strong, keep heart. You'll make it through."

And she gave me that grandmotherly smile one more time before I thanked her for her wisdom and said goodbye. Then she walked off, deep into the snow, and the whole vision faded as if someone shut off the lights in my head. I came back to my living room and thought about that last bit—what a nice message, honestly—and then put myself squarely back in the real world, full of things to do and places to go.

There's something about entities like Beira that I just adore, though. Entities like Baba Yaga, Morana, Frau Berchta, Beira, they just have that snap to them, that frostbite and that steely disposition, that is so familiar. It's the stuff that makes me look straight down my nose at all this "Divine Feminine" goofy nonsense, all insisting women are so *maternal* and *gentle* and *comforting* and whatever other tripe that, to me, never fails to read like repackaged Evangelical complementarianism. I love watching entities like these goddesses and spirits spit in the collective eye of this rhetoric; I love knowing, especially, that *femininity* does not mean flowers and conventional beauty and softness. At least, not exclusively.

Because these goddesses and spirits feel like the women I've known all my life. In them I see my oma's steely blue eyes and the sharpness of her silent stare. I hear the boom of my mother's voice as she starts talking (yelling) about something she's passionate about, and the dry chuckle of my grandma (where the Scottish in my ancestry traces through) as she tactfully lets people know, without saying, that she does not believe their bullshit. (I hear she was downright sadistic when playing Monopoly, too.) Sure, there's some of that stereotypical gentle and comforting femininity in them all, but there's thunder and steel and stone, too, and that's what makes all our worlds keep spinning. It's what helped me be strong enough to deal with this world, my own bones made of the kind of steel that can't, won't fold.

Having a chat with goddesses like these that everyone says are so scary, therefore, will always feel like I'm just having coffee with the village grandma—and who doesn't love a chance to do just that?

DEDEK MRAZ

You know of St. Nicholas, you know of Santa Claus... but how about the other egregores of the Christmas and general winter season? Thus brings us to a certain figure, *Dedek Mraz*, the Slovenian iteration of the Soviet Santa-like character, Ded Morož (or Morožko). The name essentially means "Grandpa Cold," if you translate it literally.

And if you've ever read Katherine Arden's *The Bear and the Nightingale*, you may recognize that name Morožko: it's the name of the wintertime death spirit in the story that follows our main character Vasilisa around, and the spirit himself is based off an eastern Slavic spirit or god of winter and death.

How Ded Morož became a cute Santa-like character with a daughter named Snegurčka, a sort of winter ice princess, is simple: in the era of the USSR, they wanted something to culturally compete with the western concept of Santa. As such, Ded Morož was born—and Yugoslavia, the other communist clump of Slavic countries in the Balkans, wanted the same. However, they wanted to not only get away from Santa, but also anything to do with the USSR, and so they tailored Ded Moroz to fit their *own* respective cultures. As such, when one looks at vintage art of the Slovenian Dedek Mraz, they'll notice that he wears an inside-out coat with Slovenian folk patterns embroidered on it.

Not long after this adoption, though, Yugoslavia... fell apart. Rather messily. As such, there wasn't really a need for Dedek Mraz anymore, since people just went back to incorporating their bold, rosy-cheeked *Sveti Miklavž* (the Slovenian way of saying St. Nicholas) into the season, as well as a third spirit called Božiček (which is something like a "Father Christmas"; it literally means "little Christmas" and is more that classic Santa idea, though one of my friends described it more as like, a little baby or young angel-like spirit). Talk about a full house for the Christmas season, right?

Still, on our third Christmas of this adventure, I was keeping with the tradition of essentially investigating the *echoes* of St. Nicholas. So without further ado, let me show you this little-known, but still well-loved, Slovenian egregore.

After a time where meditation was difficult due to my own fatigue and building experience, I'd finally reached a point where it was becoming fairly easy to slip in and out of meditation or grasp the spirits that came around. Whereas once, it took a lot of focus to find the sense of energy I needed to follow, and it took a long time to get the scenery to start bleeding in and creating the space I'd be interviewing in, by this point, it didn't take so long at all. I set up my space for Dedek Mraz—using my very Winter themed Santa, a snow globe with a little house and snowy trees inside, and a picture of Bled Lake to signify that I was specifically searching for Slovenia's Dedek Mraz. I also offered him a clementine. Fun fact: an orange was the main gift to get on Christmas eve in Slovenia; it was St. Nicholas's feast day that was for giving presents to children, not Christmas itself.

And as soon as I finished the Lord's Prayer and asked to find Dedek Mraz, I ended up hurtling feet-down into the snow, just like I had with Beira. I dropped out of the sky and into a massive field of knee-deep snow, scattering it everywhere as I landed. Out in the distance was a tree line, with a little cottage sitting in the middle of it all. Golden light glowed from inside, and appearing beside me to lead me down what eventually became a lightly snow-dusted path was Dedek Mraz.

At first, he looked a lot like the statue I had set up: a rosy-cheeked man with long white hair, all wrapped up tight in a fur-lined coat with bag of wood on his back and a basket on one arm, a lantern in the other hand. But as we chatted in Slovenian a bit, with my telling him to enjoy that clementine and also asking him to pick a deck of cards, he led me into that cabin and took off a lot of that bulk.

Like Santa, he was still very much that picture of a jolly old man—but unlike Santa, he had a more full, unruly head of white hair and a white beard, almost like he was more a wizard than anything based off a Saint. And his eyes were the strangest part, looking back. They glittered like some kind of clear blue-green gem, twinkling in the light of the fire he had going. His face was pinned up into a smile that didn't feel cozy and inviting so much as it felt sharp and assessing, too, which was strange—but as we got talking, I figured out what that whole aura was about.

"Alright, Dedek, I think it's better we go about this in English," I said as I settled down at his little table by the fire. "My Slovenian's not quite so good for all of this. But let's get started with the basics: I understand you are a being that split off somewhat from the Soviet Ded Morož. Can you tell me what you remember from when you first came into being?"

I. WHAT DO YOU REMEMBER FROM WHEN YOU CAME INTO BEING?

Given he picked the Universal Fantasy Tarot for this conversation, I knew I was in for a ride. That deck has the *weirdest* descriptions for cards that I otherwise think I know pretty well. And when he pulled the Hanged Man and Six of Wands, and *both* of them had a darker undertone than I expected in their meanings—talking about finding bad resources as much as good, and about victory being announced by deceptive signs—I was taken aback. More startling was how he just *dove in.* He got talking immediately, and I almost couldn't believe the words that were spinning out in my head.

"I know I'm not real," he said, and his voice had a weird timbre; there was a low smoothness to it that didn't quite match the jolly picture of the smiling man before me, as if

In search of an ideal, we can discover our best and worst resources.

The approach of victory is often announced by deceptive signs.

he were a deep and dark forest spirit wearing a jolly mask. Knowing his original inspiration, I suppose that's not too far off an idea, though. "Not in the way other beings are real, at least. I feel it—in my bones, or what bones I'm supposed to have. I played a purpose, and I remember being paraded around in that purpose. Re-tooled, re-molded, re-imagined.

"I am so many steps off from what I was, and yet—I can't stop dancing. *Ne morem*—I can't. I can't stop living. I remember being made to dance, to perform, for people who didn't know what they wanted or what was good."

"I—well, damn, alright." The sharp, direct way he spoke was like he had an agenda. I didn't expect it. "So... you mention being a few steps removed from your origins. From what I understand, Ded Morož himself came from the winter spirit Morožko. Do you know Morožko? Who is he?"

2. WHO IS MOROŽKO?

When an important change is taking place, the only way to deal with the inevitable is to focus on the benefits.

The approach of victory is often announced by deceptive signs.

Something heavy laid on the air around us. His smile grew, his eyes twinkling under bushy white brows, and he said, "I am a whisper of that beast. I can feel it. There is a hunger of cold and dark here—in Dedek Mraz, in Ded Morož. One that comes from that old winter spirit.

"But in me is new life breathed into winter: the dark is not so deep now, with me. My old ways were taken off, my old face torn away. I am a Winter men can survive. A cheerful and hopeful Winter. Not the one that steals toes and snaps children from their cradle."

What the fuck! "And... how do you feel about that?"

"Good." His smile softened just enough to feel truly genuine, and he nodded. "I feel good about it. Who wants to hurt others? But the way out of Winter," he looked out the window of the house, and I looked with him—saw from far outside that cottage, deep into the shadows that the house's golden light couldn't touch, "is still dark and full of peril."

"Alright, I think I see what you're getting at. So then, another question for you: what do you do after winter passes? Where do you go?"

3. WHERE DO YOU GO AFTER WINTER?

1. There are people who make good use of our affection, and others who use it to deceive us.

2. Those who know how to harmonize strength and wisdom are able to keep their will under control and wait their turn.

With a nod, Dedek Mraz said, "Again, I am a Winter that does no harm. But there is a hungry Winter that wants to keep the world asleep and bury the light. There is a piece of the original that lives on, waiting to take advantage. I, Dedek Mraz—I am the one who keeps the cold of Winter delightful and ensures that crop killing, finger stealing, dead preserving cold doesn't linger past its due."

"Wait, but—!" That had some implications to it that made me delete another frivolous question and write in its place: "That sounds like you've got a role as an egregore, a chunky one. At that point, though, what separates you from a god? How do egregores and gods work side by side in this world to affect certain outcomes?"

4. HOW DO EGREGORES AND GODS WORK SIDE BY SIDE?

Closure, working towards (not necessarily positive) resolution, hostility.

Bad faith, burnout, and unfinished projects.

Weird, so weird, when I pulled these cards. There was tension in them. I could feel it even before I finished writing their meanings down. Still, Dedek Mraz kept his smile on—but there was something about it that suggested he was tired. Exhausted by something.

"It's frustrating," he said. "Many of us [egregores] know where we came from. We know we're at the whims of our makers. We know we're a shadow of our origins. But that doesn't make us useless or expendable. We still echo the real in the unreal.

"Slovenia needs cheer? Fine. I will bring cheer—and they will remember me, and I will become an emancipated spirit. I *am* an emancipated spirit. The gods see me and know I'm on the side of Man, because men are my creators. And so they let me stay as a protector of the people. I have honor and integrity; I won't abandon those who both made and freed me."

Then we were outside, and Dedek Mraz wasn't looking like just a jolly old man anymore, like my Winter Santa statue. He was dressed in a glittering silver coat rimmed with white fur, and he held up a big snowflake that looked like it was made of glass. Then, as the dawn broke over the tree line, and the sunlight hit the snowflake, it went from a blueish-silver thing to a beautiful golden ornament, twinkling in the open air.

"I make silver into gold," he said. "I am becoming a god in my own right."

That reminded me of something I'd heard around that time, I think from looking into Beira. The idea of gods being born still, even in today's day and age. So I whispered, "New gods are being born everyday."

Dedek Mraz nodded and smiled like I was a student that just made a breakthrough. "New gods are being born everyday, yes. And I am one, and I shall stay one—a true one, useful to the people, reshaping winter."

"Well, shit," I said as we found ourselves back in that fire-lit cabin. "That's sure a proclamation right there. I guess it makes sense, though, given that you didn't fade away in Slovenia like Ded Morož did in other places. In fact, I hear in Slovenia, it's thought that you share drinks with St. Nicholas and Santa Claus. What do you think of those two? Is there ever any conflict, with all of you in the same space, doing similar things?"

5. IS THERE EVER CONFLICT BETWEEN YOU, SANTA, AND ST. NICHOLAS?

"Hmm." Dedek Mraz considered it, then shrugged. "There's no need to fight those men. While I'm not content to take the road that Santa Claus did, they're still both honorable men with the same goal as I: brightening the dark winter, warming the souls of men with good cherry wine and love. Yes, those two men—we all have one goal, and they know I'm not here to encroach on goodness, only to make my place known."

"Uh-huh. I got'cha. How sweet! But speaking of that place—it seems you've made Slovenia your home. What do you think about it? What do you like about it, or not like?"

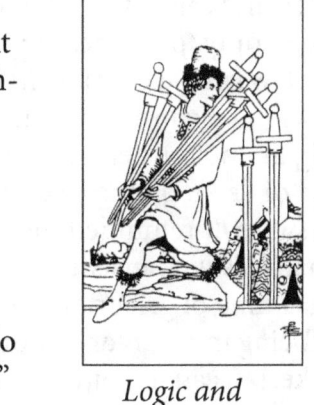 

Logic and perseverance can help us overcome seemingly impossible obstacles.

There are people who make good use of our affection, and others who use it to deceive us.

6. WHAT DO YOU LIKE AND NOT LIKE ABOUT SLOVENIA?

Insolence, like simplicity, can lead us to believe that fortune is within reach, when we must travel a long road to conquer it.

A lapse in judgement and holes in one's intuition.

Dedek Mraz's smile faded into that flat line as he shook his head. "Slovenia is a beautiful land," he started. "One full of good people. But naive people, too. They've worked so hard to be what they are, but the work isn't over. In fact, it never ends. Hold onto it, Slovenes—*ne dovolite je izginiti! Vaša duša—ne dovolite je izginiti!*

Don't let your soul disappear, he said—and I blinked at him, because that Slovenian came through my head entirely unprompted. After scribbling it down, I nodded and kept at it.

"Noted! But one thing that *is* very Slovene is that magical Christmas time. Dedek Mraz, can you tell us how we can keep December magical? How we can help *you* keep making that warm, golden winter you're trying to make for and with us?"

7. HOW CAN WE HELP YOU MAKE WINTER BEAUTIFUL?

Dedek Mraz nodded and said, "It's not enough to only survive. It's not enough only to not be hungry or not be cold. You must be full, warm—you must *live,* and let your love and joy be a rebellion against the dying light of winter. Don't quail at the night. Look instead for Zorya's starlight, and look for the gold of dawn on the tree line."

That struck me as sweet. It reminded me of Jesus, when He waved off the Pharisees who insisted that His disciples should be somber in a time of grief rather than celebrating and making merry. Being merry *is* an act of rebellion in a world that wants to keep us angry, bitter, and hopeless, isn't it?

"Beautiful," I said. Then I looked at all I'd written and nodded. "Alright, well, we've only got a few questions left. Dedek Mraz, can you tell me how you see yourself?"

In search of an ideal, we can discover our best and worst resources.

Logic and perseverance can help us overcome seemingly impossible obstacles.

8. HOW DO YOU SEE YOURSELF?

The approach of victory is often announced by deceptive signs.

Here's where I really started getting suspicious, because I kept getting the same few cards in this reading, and this was no different. *Again,* we got Six of Wands, and I'd already seen it like, twice by this point. So I wondered, both to him and myself, *is any of this real? Or am I making it all up?*

And *that* was when I really saw those eyes sparkle that crazy blue-green color. I was practically zooming in on them, like he really wanted me to see them. His smile stayed strange, feeling like it had several layers to its meaning, and I got that meaning loud and clear in my head:

"You're helping me get the word out. You're helping me spread my message."

Which, fair. Sometimes I wonder if the reason it's easier to connect with entities is because *they* want to connect. No doubt this entity here had a big reason to connect, all things considered.

Once I accepted that card and wrote it down, Dedek Mraz started again: "I am here. I survived, I stayed [where Ded Moroz didn't]—but at what cost? I always wonder: at what cost?"

He'd have to tell me. I didn't know any more than he did. Whatever moment he was having, though, I tucked it aside and said, "So how do you want to be seen, then?"

9. HOW DO YOU WANT TO BE SEEN?

"See me as one who has usurped the old ways and made them new," he said, with full confidence. "See me and see hope in my round cheeks; see my eyes and see an ally in them. I am a friend. But I am not weak, nor am I without the old hunger. Still, I try. I try to be my best."

Fate has un-known and surprising ways of revealing itself, sometimes linking distant times and feelings.

And that was something to appreciate. Even if he was built off the dark and spooky Morožko, he was a different entity altogether as Dedek Mraz.

"Alright, well, before we part ways, did you have any final words to share?"

10. ANY LAST MESSAGES?

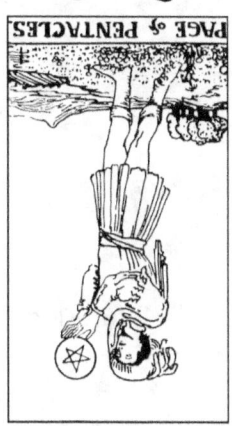

Bad news, wastefulness, or preoccupation with projects at the expense of priorities in life.

The Page of Coins Reversed was an interesting choice, but it made sense to me once he leaned forward and tapped his fists on that old table.

"Focus on what's important," he said. "You don't have as much time with your loved ones as you think. Don't waste it on nonsense. Seek the gold; seek the dawn. Seek joy and choose hope."

"Aw, damn!" At first I wondered if he wasn't being a bit ominous, but I understood: there are so many things that steal our attention away from the people that make life worth living in the first place. "Thank you, Dedek Mraz; that's really sweet. Well! As I said before, please do enjoy that clementine as thanks for meeting with me today. It's been one hell of a conversation. May we have another bright and happy winter season, and I'll see you around! *Se vidimo!*"

And then the snow faded, as did Dedek Mraz, and I was back in my living room, ready to do just that: go off with friends for a night of magical winter fun with my friends. All the while, though, there was that snap of cold at my cheeks, that frost on my mind—because what happened here?

What I thought would be a simple and cute interview with a little egregore became something much deeper. Something more feral, something hungrier. Gods make Man, and then Men make gods (from egregores); it suggests a never-ending cycle, a chicken-and-egg situation. Some gods are so old that we can't trace back their makers; we may call these gods "proper," I guess, those ones that seemed to be here before Men were ever made. But then there are many a god that know they aren't "real" in the sense that these other ancient deities are, ones like Frau Berchta and Frau Holle, ones like Oura-nus or Nu Wa or Nut, of course, God Himself. However, they speak. They are aware of themselves. They *want* that godhood, that influence, and they will work and work and work until they get it.

I don't know if that's a good or a bad thing. Nor do I know if that's the way things have already always been, or when an egregore officially gets to cross into godhood—like, say, Lada and Lado, two gods that scholars say may have been made up and yet who insist, themselves, that they've always been here. What is true? Does it matter, when now, with few records of the past, people accept them as true gods anyway? Is that all the separation of egregore from true god is: *human* perception?

There's a lot about this world we do not know. I doubt, at this point, we'll ever know it all. But damn if I, and other folks playing this game like me, won't try to find out anyway.

KRAMPUS

Once, when speaking with Frau Berchta, I caught a glimpse of someone in the deep, dark forest: a horned creature, a goat-like thing, that darted away only moments after I saw it. That creature was Krampus, and he didn't seem anything like what I'd been told he was.

I've grown up hearing about Krampus all my life. Whereas other cultures, like the French, have Père Fouettard (the spirit of the man who, in St. Nicholas's legends, killed and pickled three children the Saint brought back to life, and who was charged with following St. Nicholas around to punish bad children), Germanic cultures like in Germany, Austria, and northern Slovenia had a literal child-eating demon haunting their Christmas season. My mother, born in rural Slovenia and moving to Germany as a child, was terrified of him: with the monster that wore a basket on his back, who would come with whips and bells to announce his arrival and steal bad children to gobble up in hell. In fact, the terror was solidified one year when my opa dressed up as Krampus—with the horns and basket and everything—and scared the hell out of her just by his appearance.

Krampus is much more effective in deterring bad behavior than the threat of getting coal in your stocking on Christmas, as you might imagine.

Nowadays, you can see countless videos of Austrian and German *Krampuslauf,* a festival before St. Nicholas's day where the streets are filled with elaborate Krampuses that run around, cause chaos, and will happily beat you a bit if they catch you running from them. No matter how bad the Church may have tried to make demons of old forest spirits in order to get people to stop playing with them (as is one theory of where Krampus originated from), it seems some cultural habits refuse to die, and people keep their spirits no matter how scary or ugly or dangerous they become. However, I stayed curious about that flighty, goat-looking creature in the woods, one that looked nothing like the Krampus I grew up learning about, and so I decided to investigate.

Here's what happened.

So, there are a few things that come to mind when one thinks of Krampus: the colors red and black, a big basket or sack, bells, and chains (as you'll often see him with his wrists chained, to signify the binding of the Christian "devil" as a figure). For the table, therefore, I had my onyx and garnet, a big red candle, two necklace chains (as I didn't have anything more obviously Big Chain to put out), and two loud Christmas bells with pine cone motifs—a good way to get the "woods" and "bell" themes together at once.

Then, as you know, it was just a matter of doing the Lord's Prayer and asking God to help me find Krampus—though I think Krampus himself was the one that ended up finding me.

Where there was nothing but black behind my eyelids before, once I asked to see Krampus, the whole scene shifted. I was stuck on a snowy mountain somewhere in the Alps—and I knew it was the Alps because I knew recognized those mountains plenty well. Snow-crusted pines and a whole snowy pass was what I fell into, and there at the banks of a river was Krampus, in the fashion of an old drawing. He had goat hooves, black goat fur, and big spiraling horns, but his face was more like a man's, and he had a long red tongue. He also carried a lantern, a whip of old straw, and a big cloth sack on his back.

Right away, I was thinking this must've been an *egregore* of Krampus or something. After all, it seemed we were on something of an egregore kick lately. However, I remembered the spirit I saw with Frau Berchta and kept it at the forefront of my mind: one that looked more like a faun, with a more goat-like face and big, shining black eyes. One that was more animal-like, more direct and neutral, than this devil-faced thing.

"Hello, Krampus!" I waved to him as I walked up to him. He pointed to the shackles on his wrist, and I shook my head. "No, I won't be taking those off right now. I just want to ask you a few questions. Can we chat?"

The look on his face, with the tongue out and the reddish eyes open so wide, was strange. It didn't really move or change as I spoke. Still, he nodded, and we went down a snowy cliff together, only to end up by the banks of a rushing river. The water was moving too fast to freeze. Somehow, a moment later, we ended up in the middle of that river, on a big flat stone that happened to be jutting up. As soon as we sat down, a wall of water came up on either side of us, rushing past and encasing us in that one space.

A little chess board appeared on the rock as we sat cross legged on the little space. I declined a game with him, and he soon pushed it away and replaced it with a long wooden smoking pipe that he took a deep puff from. Still, though, something was weird about his face—namely that it *wasn't the face I remembered*—and I asked as much:

"Is this your real self, Krampus? Or is it maybe a mask? It seems like a mask."

The voice that echoed from Krampus was not one I expected. It was rough, crackling like burning wood, yet it had a deep, smooth undertone that stabilized it. "Perceptive," he said, and he raised a hand to his face and moved his image until the proper goat's face came through underneath. The mask was rimmed with black fur, but it was a static image; the goat's face, with the deep, glistening black eyes and the goat snout and the little furry goat beard, were much more realistic than that mask. "You're right; this isn't my real face. This is the one for the evil of men."

"Huh." I picked up the deck of cards he wanted to use, the Weaver Tarot, and started shuffling. "What takes you from this face to the traditional Krampus mask each winter, then? Is it that evil you mentioned?"

1. WHAT MAKES YOU TAKE AN "EVIL" MASK IN WINTER?

Once I had the cards down, Krampus nodded. "Yes. As I said: it's the evil of men that make me wear this. It is not my real face. It's my mask. A mask they think they can tame." He moved that mask back over him, hiding half the goat with half the devil-man. "The people wouldn't take too kindly to a goat like myself roaming around, all unchained and faceless, alien. No, they wouldn't like that at all, and that's why they think," he shook his wrists and made the chains clank, "that they can contain me with silly things like these. Lies to soothe themselves. Illusions of safety. They don't want me around, and yet they need me there—and it's their attention that keeps me sustained all the same."

Nurturing new life. Intersection of love and creation. A master of playing diffferent roles. Deepen self love.

Something underhanded. You or someone else is trying to get away with something. A warning against impulsiveness.

Focusing on yourself and creating habits that benefit long term. Building the life you want on your terms. Independence.

I wondered at that last line. It made it sound like Krampus was more of an egregore, something living off the energy fed by people's belief and attention—but that wasn't the case. I could feel it: Krampus was *old*. Old like the trees and the rocks and dirt. And those chains on his wrists were not real—to the point that, once I understood that, I poked them and let them spring open myself. Because if they were only illusions, then there was no point in keeping fake shackles on him in the first place.

But even as those chains came off, and he seemed to double in size, he was telling me something clear with that answer: Krampus lapped up all the energy people raised in his name and seemed to get fat on it in these winter months. As if reading my thoughts, though, Krampus continued.

"It's not as if the people make me exist," he said with a shake of his finger. "It's that they give me new purpose that lets me step into their world from mine. My world expands because of you *Menschen*."

"Uh-huh. I got'cha. But then, where do you come from? What's this *world* you're talking about?"

2. WHERE DO YOU COME FROM?

1. New material beginnings. Raw power of prosperity. Be excited, but still show up and do the work. Things work better now.

2. Building habits that bring long term independence. Focusing on yourself. Building the life you want on your terms.

3. Ruling with an iron fist. Cold, manipulative, abuse of power. Power is an illusion if not based in respect.

If you've ever seen that 1798 painting by Francisco Goya, *The Witch's Sabbath*, then the image I got right then reminded me exactly of that—except instead of normal women around the great goat-man, they were little women. Winged women. Fairies. And they sat in a plush green field at the foot of a great mountain, a little mountain cottage some ways in the distance, with the sun beaming down from in between fluffy white clouds.

"I come from a time where fertility of the land was more important than whatever anxieties you *Menschen* have wrapped yourselves up in," Krampus said, and as he spoke from the rock in the river, his eyes glittered with deep memory. Soon enough, I was back in that green field, watching an apparent Krampus muck around with the fairies of the land, and it reminded me something of Greek satyrs and nymphs, only more a central European fairytale version, where all were animals and sprites simply enjoying the sunshine. "I come from a land of honey and sweet pine cones, flowers and fresh pine needles. A place where the mountains were green. Where I was sacred. And now? I come from that place—and I remind you *Menschen* of your sins, you who ruin my world with your filth. I take your children and roast them—not in your *hell*, but in my own hearth. As you have mine."

"Ah." I scribbled that down, then said, "The hunters, you mean. Those who go and pick the forests clean of game."

"Mmm."

"But you can't blame people for that, can you? A goat doesn't blame a bear for needing to eat."

"No, the goat doesn't blame the bear," Krampus said with a nod, " but the bear isn't motivated by the same things you *Menschen* are, too. There's an imbalance. A habit of your folk, to take more than you need. For sport. For fun. Until nothing is left even for the bear."

"That's fair, yeah." I shuffled my cards again, nodding. "So then, okay, tell me this: I saw you with Frau Berchta so long ago. What do you have to do with her? Frau Berchta? And St. Nicholas, he said you were her creature, not his—but you're often seen with him, too. What do you have to do with both of them?"

3. WHAT DO YOU HAVE TO DO WITH FRAU BERCHTA OR ST. NICHOLAS?

Major transition, most likely a sad one. Life change may feel forced on you, but you need to move. Whole new world awaits.

Successful collaboration. Varied expertise. A group that can get things done and make a big impact.

Nearing the light at the end of the tunnel. A hard won space. Meeting the shadow and emerging enlightened.

Krampus looked up at the cloudy sky. "Frau Berchta is the matron of these lands," he said. "We found ourselves in similar positions with the rise of your Christ. These were not His lands—and yet His face overshadowed us in our own home, took away our birthright, our own sovereignty."

"Aw, but you can't blame Jesus for that. It's not like He wanted people to be a menace in His name."

"Fault doesn't matter," Krampus said, shaking his head. "Results matter. Frau Berchta and I huddled together to weather the storm—and it seems your Christ felt bad enough, watching us be so disenfranchised in our own lands.

He sent your St. Nicholas as a sleigh, a foothold, that our names—and therefore our power—might linger yet. We owe Him that much credit: your Christ and your St. Nicholas."

"But no more than that?" I couldn't help but smile. "You're not very keen on God, are you?"

Krampus sat up straight. "I recognize no gods. I am my own master."

"Fair enough." I felt like this is what the Bible meant when it said test the spirits: because yes, there are some that really don't care about God and don't want anything to do with Him. And I'm not interested in proselytizing even to *humans*, never mind to spirits. "But then, okay, once winter is over, where do you go?"

4. Where Do You Go After Winter?

Weird to pull the Ten of Swords for this while I was actively getting that springtime satyr-and-nymph scene in my mind's eye again, but it made sense. Somehow, on Krampus's goat lips, a wry smile sprouted, and his eyes glazed over with a harrowing shimmer of longing.

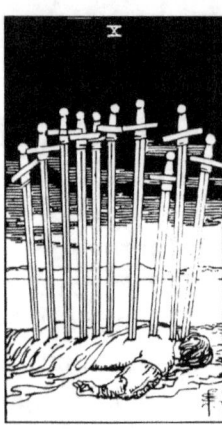

Disaster that's been building for some time. Rug pulled out from under you. Betrayal. Reconnect; make relationship with yourself the priority.

"I try to go back to where I belong—but you *Menschen* have ruined it. So much is gone. I go deep into the woods, the mountains, as deep as I can—but up so high, I find no warm spring. Only snow and crags. Once there was bounty available to me. Now I must sneak about in my own home. It's worse now than when your Christ first came. The earth is damaged. How will we sleep? Survive?"

Jeez. I knew exactly what he was saying, because he was showing me pictures of it: of the grey, the concrete, the bright yellow crane machines clawing the earth apart, the smoke. But with no way to comfort him, I just kept on.

"I got'cha. But then, when you come down here in the winter, you steal the bad children. You told me why you take any kids at all, and that's fair enough—but why specifically do you only take the bad children?"

5. Why Do You Only Take Bad Children?

That smile on his goat-lips crooked into something cruel, and he didn't need to pull any cards for his words to hit my head as quick and sharp as an arrow. "Because those are the children you're secretly happy to let disappear."

Whoa.

"They're the ones you don't want," he explained. "You bad parents—you're secretly relieved when those wretched ones go missing, aren't you?"

I shrugged. "I'm not a parent, so I can't say. But can the animals really judge, when they, too, let their weakest children die so the stronger can have a better chance at surviving?"

"Weakness?" Krampus rolled the word around in his head. "Is that what you determine the 'badness' in your children to be? Or is it your weakness that makes it so you can't tame your own children?"

Oop. My brows shot halfway up my forehead, I'll tell you. I wrote that answer down, but again, as I'm not a parent, I didn't have much to say to that. I only found it funny that Krampus, of all beings, was going to be the one to point out bad parenting in this era.

"Well, I guess I can see that. But okay, so, tell me: what do you not like about humans, if anything? I feel there's definitely something, based on all this conversation."

6. WHAT DO YOU NOT LIKE ABOUT PEOPLE?

"Oh, yes." As I turned the cards around, snippets of words floated up before I was even done writing the definitions. Eventually, the clear message came. "You are a greedy folk. Nothing is ever enough for you. The animal toils until they're fed; you toil until the earth is stripped bare and all is dead. Until *you* are dead. Why? This is not natural. You make death fast and frequent, using up your life so quickly. You accelerate the end."

I dunno; something about getting lectured like this from what everyone thinks is a *Christmas demon* was just

Living in the past. Time to move on and make new memories.

Intense work. This can feel soul crushing or not. Align with it to bring ease. Keep on and you'll succeed.

Nurturing new life. Intersection of love and creation. A master of playing diffferent roles. Deepen self love.

surreal. Even more strange was that the cards themselves were things that, aside from the "living in the past" issue, even I would consider positive—abundance, creativity, working hard for a higher goal—and yet it was so clear that Krampus was talking about *these things,* that this was where the greed and endless, unnatural toil were coming from as those positive qualities rotted into something obsessive, wicked, disconnected from physical reality. I blinked, nodded, then kept on.

"Alright, fair. Now, I'm curious. You live out here in these alps, but are there any other creatures here, too? Any other spirits?"

7. WHAT OTHER SPIRITS LIVE IN YOUR MOUNTAINS?

Rejecting opportunities for "woe is me" mentality. Simply focusing on yourself and not worrying about the outside world. Reflection, avoiding issues.

Krampus nodded slowly. "There are many creatures in these woods. None of them want to deal with you *Menschen.* It's why few who go missing have come back—at least, so long as you don't have any of your tethers to your world. These creatures want peace from you and your prying eyes, your excavators, your monster machines. Keep them away."

With a sigh, I finished writing and put my pencil down. "Well, I would, but I don't control construction in Austria and other alpine areas. All I can do is deliver your messages. To that end: how do you see yourself, Krampus?"

8. HOW DO YOU SEE YOURSELF?

Shock of all shocks when he pulled the King of Cups. Krampus smiled and said, "I am kind to the deserving. Unkind to the undeserving. My wrath has long since cooled; I can see now the utility in your ear and affection. I am in a place of power that lets me subsist, survive, even when you've ruined so much. So I play the role. I do the job—and I live in what peace I can."

"I... see. Okay. How do you want to be seen, then?"

A beautiful balance between heart and head. Easily able to flow between feelings and logic. Inspiring presence. Makes others feel seen. Unbiased.

9. HOW DO YOU WANT TO BE SEEN?

A good time to connect with loved ones and focus on relationships. Community is the cornerstone of life. Collaboration.

The word that popped up immediately was *feiern*—the German verb "to celebrate" or "party." Seeing Krampus sit cross-legged on the rock almost reminded me of Baphomet. He cocked his head and said, "Once, you *Menschen* were like us: more concerned with love and family than industry. If you see me, see not my terror. Remember that when I come, so too does a time of celebration and joy.

"*Menschen,* don't let your joy be stolen. No matter what gods you follow, we pity you—because the Machine has become your god. You've even replaced your Christ with it. You've become so hollow that we can't even be angry with you anymore, only sad for you. Were you not once animals, too? Have you forgotten your flesh already?"

I stared at Krampus, and I couldn't help but push back. "For many of us, especially with our Christ, the flesh isn't really so important. The soul is, the divine Spark."

Krampus shook his head, his horns dipping down to wave in my direction. "Even your 'Spark,' you've forgotten about! What are you now, *Menschen?* What is the point of you, children of machines? Cold and callous things? What is the point of you?"

"Okay, okay," I finished writing and sighed, "I understand what you're getting at. And I agree." Because I've seen exactly what he was talking about myself, what with how many people live to do nothing but consume, consume, consume. "Still, though—that sounds like a rough message in itself. Is there anything you want to say beyond that, or is that it for now?"

10. ANY LAST MESSAGES?

For the second time in that reading, I didn't get the sense to pull any cards, but that didn't stop Krampus's stare from boring a hole in me as he hissed, "Live. Reignite! Do something! Not all the gods can do something with hearts so dead and cold. You are dead, dead! Wake up. Wake *up!* Revive the coals. *Burn!* Burn with life! Or all will go dark."

The words wouldn't stop flowing. They drilled into my head exactly as if Krampus were goring me with those horns. I wrote down the words as they came, and when I was done, I couldn't really fathom it: how much concern that a forest spirit like Krampus could have for people he didn't even seem to like.

"Well, alright, then! Thank you, Krampus. This is some incredible insight you've given me."

When I looked back up at him, though, he had that classic Krampus mask on again. He was out waving his whipping stick, climbing around the mountain, and he said nothing before traipsing off back into the snow. Then everything zoomed out, the snow and trees gone, and the interview was over. I was alone, and Krampus was off doing whatever the hell he does in the alpine winter.

Dead, dead! That part lingered, though. *You are dead, dead!*

It's hard sometimes, integrating these things, understanding them. Where do I draw the line, you know? Where does my acceptance of a spirit's views end, and my resolve to stand by *my* God's views begin? Again, I don't think the flesh of us matters so much—and more and more, I can feel my own perception zoom out, as if I'm suddenly aware of the edges of the screen that encase this game called *Reality* I'm playing, as if none of it is truly real in the sense of it being *important* or *what truly matters*—yet Krampus still had his point, didn't he?

We've forgotten our flesh, as in, the primal and harmonized version of ourselves that lived *with* the land instead of lorded *over* it so cruelly, and even if we want to console ourselves by telling us we were supposed to be more than animals anyway, we forgot that we were meant to be like angels: just and true stewards. Ones moving by grace, faith, and righteousness, not anxiety, greed, and callousness. It's odd, how even such a different perspective from a spirit who could give a damn about God could still say virtually the same things God is saying, just from a different angle.

In which case, we're really messing up, aren't we?

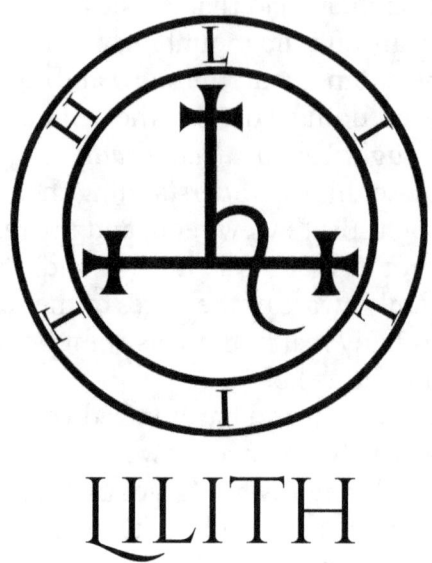

LILITH

And here we are: at the last interview of this book, and interview number *101* of this series. Yes, 101. Surprise! Lilith quite literally snuck in here, hiding in my notes and numberings and files until it was too late for me to justify removing this for the next book. Now it can be a shock to us both.

Demons, though. Seriously. Ever the chaos with them where you least expect it.

Once upon a time, I was sure I'd never speak with Lilith publicly like this. The debate around whether or not she was closed to Judaism was ongoing and exhausting, with everyone—Jewish and not Jewish—arguing literally every angle. I heard things like, *she's closed because she's a spirit of Jewish folklore* and *she's not closed because she's an evil spirit Jewish people don't even want to work with.* I've heard *she has a special place in Jewish magic that Gentiles (non-Jewish people) shouldn't encroach on* and *no true Jewish person would ever work with her in the first place.* On and on, around and around, came all these arguments that made me resolve to never bother with this spirit. The whole debate was not my business, and reasonably, neither was this spirit.

Then I met Lilith, down there in the Qliphoth. That was when I learned that Lilith was not the kind of spirit that gave a good Goddamn about these debates on earth, and as I looked into the many different people that did engage with her in a positive way, it seemed this was the case across the board: you can't lock Lilith down the way these discussions try to. She goes where she wants, and you won't tell her who she can and can't help or harm based on ancestry or religious affiliation; she'll laugh in your face. At the end of the day, she is known most popularly as the Mother of Demons, and demons were never known to care about these kinds of things—at least, not to my knowledge. If they don't want you speaking to them, they let you *know*. It is what it is.

Speaking of her role as the Mother of Demons, though, there are some pretty interesting things in Lilith's lore worth talking about. One common concept of Lilith that makes rounds these days is the idea that she was Adam's first wife who got banished because she didn't want to lay underneath him and then ended up becoming the wife of either fallen angel Samael or Lucifer or any other Big

Bad that sprung up in folklore and other religious philosophy over time. Thing is, though, that this "Adam's First Wife" idea comes from the medieval, and *satirical,* writing called *The Alphabet of Ben-Sira.* This could've very well simply been a stab at Jewish folklore, considering the work is pseudo-epigraphical (meaning not written by the people in the book) and has no known author in the first place, suggesting the idea that the Jewish myth of Genesis was just some misogynistic nonsense with the "truth" of this first wife and her expulsion.

Another common theory is that Lilith comes from the broader Mesopotamian concept of the *lili* and *lilitu*: male and female wind demons that would go causing trouble. However, just because something sounds similar in name does not mean they are the same thing; as cultures come in contact with each other, they share ideas and make them their own until they take their own shape and become their own beings. As such, *Lilith* is not a member of the *lilitu,* nor do those really have much to do with her; she is known in Jewish lore as a single being, a specifically night-prowling, baby-killing succubus, one that preys on men and eviscerates a family. Many a Jewish folk magic amulet exist to keep Lilith at bay as a result, and it's clear to see how she became the face of common anxieties in times where infant mortality was so unfortunately high.

On the other hand, in western occultism and demonolatry, Lilith is the ruler of the Qliphoth sphere, Gamaliel, as I mentioned—one all about the subconscious, the dark thoughts we keep tucked away and pretend aren't there. The dark side of the moon, so to speak. She's the Mother of Demons, creating hundreds of new demons every day, and she's a pretty powerful and sovereign figure in her own right according to those that honor her, a darker and more feral side to the feminine aspect of Divinity that helps many of her practitioners find their fangs again.

There are so many ways to think about Lilith, some of which remind me of the ahistorical feminist understanding of Medusa's story based on some Roman myth rewriting, some of which still echo her original, horrifying functions in the collective conscious of the group that originally conceptualized her. All I knew was that my curiosity finally outweighed my sense, and I decided, after consulting one of her devotees, Patrick (or @liliths_son on TikTok), to just reach out and see what I got.

So let's see what happened.

Unfortunately, my *Occult Tarot* didn't have a card for Lilith, so I had to print out her sigil myself. However, with that aside, I did also put out a red candle, garnet and obsidian, moonstone (a nod to Gamaliel's tie to the moon), and a crow and a piece of quartz. With some rose petals sprinkled around per Patrick's recommendation, as well as a cup of cinnamon, clove, and orange tea for each of us, we were ready to get started bright and early this morning.

Like I said in Duke Astaroth's interview, I would be stuck in Gha'agsheblah for a *long time,* until around early March of 2025. As a result, it'd been a hot minute since I had anything to do with the Qliphoth when I went asking around for Lilith. Even though I'm still not quite done with the whole Qliphoth journey yet at the time of this writing, there's just been so much going on that I haven't been out there spelunking in the Night Side, you know? However, I figured if there was anywhere to meet Lilith, it would be in Gamaliel—so I set up my space, called for Lilith, and waited.

Soon enough, I found myself right back there where I first saw Lilith: in a forest clearing, where a gigantic full moon was the only light in the space. We stood in a little fresh water pool just like we had a couple years ago, and Lilith was there with inky black hair, a long, simple dress in a light stone gray, and oddly, a crown of blue and purple flowers. I chalked that up to the fact that I was listening to Sol Abyssorum, and the cover art of one song had some similar colored flowers on it.

But as we settled in, and I poured us some tea, I found Lilith strangely quiet. This isn't super un-usual, I've noticed, but it always does unsettle me when a spirit does nothing but stare. It makes me wonder if I'm making it all up or not (as does, apparently, everything else that doesn't go the way I expect it to, in an ugly habit I simply can't seem to shake).

And it's not unreasonable for me to feel that way, I think, given that all there was before me was an image hanging there in space. It was a really *crisp* image I was getting of Lilith, don't get me wrong; I could easily and smoothly see her move around the space, doing things like walking through the ankle-deep water and sitting on a big rock. But it wasn't until I got the sense that she wanted to use the Weaver Tarot and asked my first question that things started moving the way they normally do.

"Alright, Lilith, thank you for meeting with me," I said as I shuffled the Weaver tarot. "Been a while since we talked, so I'm glad to be able to get your thoughts on some of these questions. To start us off, I hear that you may have something to do with Mesopotamian spirits like the lilitu. I don't know how much I agree with that, given you're your own being, but hey—what do you think?"

I. DO YOU HAVE ANYTHING TO DO WITH THE LILITU?

Lilith raised two fingers, suggesting she wanted to pull two cards per question, and the first cards I pulled were pretty interesting right off the bat: the Hermit and the Two of Swords. The language of the deck, talking about travers-ing the unknown, accumulating wisdom, and being in denial, especially stuck out to me.

A necessary period of solitude. Surrender to this space. See everything from a higher point of view. Gaining wisdom.

Some denial. Difficulty seeing the situation with clarity. Time to address the situation. Give voice to feelings.

"People hear what they want to hear," Lilith said. She sat on that big boulder like it was a throne. "They develop ev-ery number of foolish theories to justify either loving me or hating me. It all means the same to me. Love me or hate me, I am Queen of Hell. Queen of the sides too dark for com-fort—of the lies you all tell yourselves to pretend you are good and more than me. Illusion—that is where I reside. Denial is my namesake."

That last bit had me thinking a little creatively. The word *Lilith* itself seems to mean something more like "night" or "belonging to the night," and it made me wonder if dark-ness is a denial of something. Or being in darkness is being in denial. She was being cryptic about these ideas, and I could tell she would stay so, in order to let me make the final decision about what her words meant *to me*.

"That's interesting," I said as I scribbled her answers down. "In that case, though, how about this whole Adam and Eve story? What do you think about how people say you were Adam's first wife? What's going on there?"

2. THOUGHTS ON BEING ADAM'S FIRST WIFE?

A holder of space. Intuitive, nurturing, warm hearted. A container for healing. Anticipating needs. Turn off rational brain and connect with the heart.

Confusion. Taking things slow. Careful steps towards one's goals, careful decision making.

Lilith shrugged as if none of it mattered. Maybe it didn't. She looked at me with a sharp stare and said, "Is that what people need me to be? Some silly retelling of an already old story? Some feminist icon? Why? Can I not simply be what I am? How 'feminist' is it, to relate my existence to the actions of a man?"

Oop. Tea.

"I transcend such nonsense," Lilith muttered. "But if people like a bedtime story, I suppose I'll tell it. I am the Mother of Demons. There's enough in this title that I should never want for context."

My eyebrows had started crawling up my forehead by this point, as they do when spirits just start *saying things,* and they would not stop their ascent until the end of this interview.

"Fair! Totally fair. Thank you for sharing that; that's really interesting. But, then... the whole baby-killing, man-seducing thing. What's up with that? How do you feel about that as part of your folklore, whether as Lilith or as part of the lilitu or anything else?"

3. WHAT'S UP WITH THE SUCCUBUS ASSOCIATIONS?

Again, Lilith looked at me like I was asking her about her favorite type of bean, or her opinion on the texture of some lint under the couch. She waved a hand and said, "I don't think people have ever been capable of taking responsibility for themselves. There's always been a scapegoat needed in their hearts. Sometimes babies die. Sometimes men are unfaithful and unclean. Is that my fault? Or is that just life? Who's to say, really? Who's to say except the one who needs something or someone to blame?"

As she was speaking, the whole image shifted in my head. Behind my eyelids was the most vibrant green—like the type of green you'd see in an 80's horror film about a mad scientist. In fact, it seemed like we went to some kind of lab, where a big vat in the middle was the origin of that green glow. That kind of thing, in my experience, didn't happen just for no reason. It meant someone else was messing with the spiritual wavelength and trying to make themselves known.

"I mean, that's a reasonable question," I said as I looked around. "But what if—alright, wait, who else is here? Who is with me?"

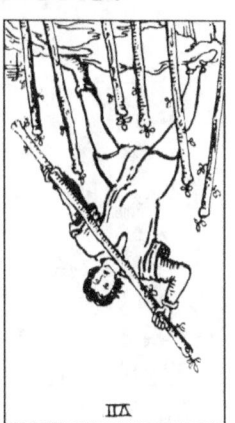

Overwhelm. Stressors running the show. Living up to and maintaining success is difficult. Now is not the time for indecision or doubt.

Doing something underhanded. You or someone else is trying to get away with something. A warning against impulsiveness. Bring awareness.

As I looked around, I got one name printed in clear letters that appeared right before my eyes, like text on a movie screen: *Botis*. A door popped open from somewhere in this weird lab, and out came not a viper, like Botis appears as, but a gigantic hybrid of a spider and a fly. It was hairy, with those huge fly eyes, and it stared at me like it was waiting for me to freak out and run.

But I'd seen quite a bit of shit in the infernal realms at this point, both within my interviews and out in my own personal work with the demons. I can't even think of what would actually unsettle me to see anymore, honestly.

So I greeted Botis, who only watched me with those wild fly eyes, though eventually he took the form of a man, smiled, and disappeared. The lab disappeared along with it, and then Lilith and I were on the beach, the ocean smashing on the reddish-brown sands. A big cliff loomed over us on the other side, with a cave carved out in the wall.

Lilith continued, maybe to explain why Botis was there, or why he was in the shape of a giant spider-fly: both predator and prey in one. "Death and life are married. One cannot be without the other. Some die before their time—before the time humans hope for them. Is it God that snuffs their flame? Or I? Who is easier to curse without risking one's own soul? Who is easier to condemn?"

Well, damn. I didn't think of it that way. But back when Lilith's name was a common symbol of dread, it made sense; to curse God's name would be to effectively curse yourself. There is some folklore of people dropping dead from doing that.

"I got'cha," I said as we settled in on that beach. "Okay, well, moving on from that line of questioning... as a primordial force, can you tell me what you remember from when you came into being?"

4. WHAT DO YOU REMEMBER FROM COMING INTO BEING?

Questioning long held beliefs about wealth, happiness, connections, priorities, etc. Beginning to expand and see there's more to life.

Tap into your personal well of strength. Internal will, resilience, discipline. Merge with challenges as opposed to viewing it as a battle.

Lilith slowly lolled her head back and forth as if thinking it over. "'There is more. I am more than whatever nothing came before all things.' That is what I remember thinking, when all came to be." Then she wasn't standing on the beach anymore; she was in the ocean, and the ocean was red as blood. "I was born in blood," she said. "I stay rooted in blood. The waters of life—this is my home. The mountains of decay—this is my exile. There is more than one way to live and be alive. My way is unpalatable to humans and your God."

Her words rang in a way that made them feel like a counter-note to everything I'd ever heard. They rang in a way that was dissonant with the teachings of Jesus (*I am the Way, the Truth, and the Life*), and I found that interesting—how she could say one thing, I would immediately think another, and they would just clash to pieces in the middle. I blinked that feeling away for the time being and moved on.

"Well, okay. Speaking of Divinity, though, I personally think that Divinity all reflects something in ourselves. If you're a part of Divinity, which I think you are, then where in ourselves can we see you reflected?"

5. WHERE CAN WE SEE OURSELVES REFLECTED IN YOUR DIVINITY?

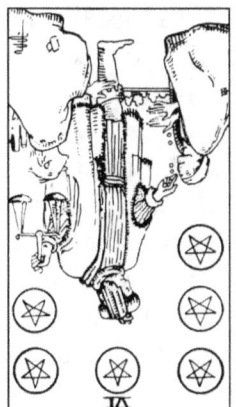

Imbalance in relationships, either in giving or taking. Investigate the ego behind giving; find a sustainable plan around taking.

Creativity, dreaming, raw formless energy. Youth, impulse. Are you tending your relationship with life?

Lilith's hair was like ink in all that red water, floating and twisting. "I am the Unseen. I walk the Unseen. So do people, in their dreams. The things they want, the things they sacrifice—I see it all. It gets deposited into my domain. People inherently seek balance, equilibrium, yet they can't contend with the dark in the waking world because people are foolish.

"Simply put, I am the wish for more. And the confusion around what that means. A yearning with no direction, a need with no name, that is I. And people will go their while life swinging between this space I govern and the space they think they *should* be in."

That see-saw between what we want and what we're told is right. That's the vibe I was getting there; that's what catches people in Gamaliel. Illusions and lies and denial. I nodded, writing all that down, and kept on.

"So, alright. What would you want to remove from the world, if anything?"

6. WHAT WOULD YOU REMOVE FROM THE WORLD, IF ANYTHING?

She shook her head like I got a question wrong on a test, and what she wanted to say was so clear that she didn't need any cards. "Everything has its place. Every good, every ill. It's like asking what ingredient I'd see taken from a recipe. None. Just balance the items, and all will be as it should be. Fight and be fought. It's the Way."

As I wrote, it almost made me think of storytelling. No good story has only good things happening in it all the time. There's plenty of misfortune and challenge to overcome, but plenty of goodness and hope to balance it back out. I nodded along with the whole idea as it settled in my head.

"I see—interesting! I appreciate that. But okay, so... what would you say the stumbling block of Gamaliel is?"

7. WHAT IS THE STUMBLING BLOCK OF GAMALIEL?

1. Some denial. Difficulty seeing the situation with clarity. Time to address the situation. Give voice to feelings.

2. Heartbreak, betrayal, and grief. Acknowledgement of an ebb in life. Things feel hard. Unlocking repressed grief and pain. Need both joy and sorrow in life.

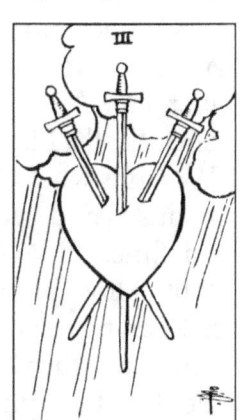

Lilith heaved a big sigh. "As I said: we need all things. The biggest challenge one faces in Gamaliel is themselves. The people here are continuously blocked off from the full breadth of all things, like an animal wary of injury. It's understandable, but how can you grow with no pain? How can you experience all things when you cut yourself off from them? The lies you humans tell yourselves to avoid pain plague you here."

"Oh, wow." That was a powerful idea, and I don't know why I didn't expect to hear it. But it made perfect sense to me. Given the first thing Lilith ever showed me was the little ugly duckling I used to be as a kid, with her bowl cut and her gap teeth and her pink Aristocats sweatshirt and sweatpants, it stung something extra—especially given how violently I'd torn that image down, as if my own child self were some kind of enemy. "That is something, huh? I see what you mean. Okay. Noted. But," once I finished writing, I studied her for a minute. She stayed still in the water, waiting for me to make a move. "That's the end of our main questions, so now I'll ask: how do you see yourself?"

8. HOW DO YOU SEE YOURSELF?

Scarcity mindset is preventing you from receiving. Out of touch with what life has to offer. Break the pattern. Question where you have abundance, and of what.

Lilith shrugged. "I am one who questions everything. For you and for me. Do things really need to be as they are? Or are we lying to ourselves? I am the holder of this question. I am the mirror of the Moon; all secrets are reflected and exposed through me."

Mirror of the moon made me wonder, but then, it makes sense. Lilith is of the *dark* side of the moon—not the huge, full orb that had been hanging over us this whole time. Lilith is the mirror, the *reflection,* of that Moon—the other, unexplored side that people are scared to look at the way they look at the full, bright, illuminating moon.

"And how do you want to be seen?"

9. HOW DO YOU WANT TO BE SEEN?

It made me smile to see her pull the Empress, with a big old rose in the middle of that card. But then she said the most challenging thing in this interview yet.

"I am one who holds all meanings to all people," she said. "What people need me to be, I will be. I am Mother. I am Killer. I *am.*"

Specifically, I heard that one phrase: *I am that I am.*

Which is what God's name means.

I paused and peered at her. "Hold on, now," I said. "Let's slow down here. That's God's line."

Nurturing new life. Intersection of love and creation. A master of playing diffferent roles. Deepen self love.

THE EMPRESS.

Lilith's lips split in a wide smile. "Is He the only one that gets to simply Be? No price can be put on my name; no definition can shackle me."

Then, whether because of the dissonance of her words or because she was really suggesting it, I caught that old phrase coming out of the back of my mind: *be still and know that I am God.*

Maybe the sight of a giant spider-fly couldn't knock me off my groove, but *that?* Yes. Hearing that could make some alarm bells go off for me.

"Whoa, whoa, whoa. Lilith, I'm sorry, but I am going to have to draw a line between you and God. Unless you're saying you're also a big storm God with many breasts that goes around thundering and destroying nations but also creating everything and so on and so forth. I feel like God's a pretty distinct figure, even if He's also rocking that *I am that I am* shtick. No?"

Lilith's smile became a grin that flashed her white teeth. "What really makes God and Devil so distinct? Maybe I can't be *your* God. But to many, I am *a* god."

Hmm. See, this was tricky. I could've waved this off as her saying that she was simply making a point that she is a god at all, any kind of Divinity. But knowing her sphere, Gamaliel, and how it challenges us to see things we don't want to see—knowing that Qliphoth as a practice was developed from its basic, consequential idea in Jewish Kabbalah, in which the very opposite of Gamaliel exists as *Yesod*, an emanation of God—it gave me pause. She was saying something much deeper than maybe I wanted to look at right there, but nonetheless, it's an important thing to look at: the idea that maybe, after all, God is truly *all* things. Even still the things He cut off from Himself, somewhere, somehow.

After all, that is the fate of all things: to one day rejoin God into the formless nothingness that was there before creation, until all this shit starts up again in a new world, a new way. So who's to say? Maybe the Hindu concept of one God, many Masks (or Avatars) was the most accurate understanding of Divinity I'd stumbled upon yet. Maybe every one of these now hundred spirits I've spoken to have all been God wearing a mask and playing a game with me; maybe I'd actually never spoken to a single one of these deities and spirits at all, but simply learned all these things through the careful and controlled lens of my own Creator playing dress up. Maybe it was even all just God playing an elaborate prank on me. Or maybe all these spirits *were* real, but Divinity is such a way that it's all just little echoes of each other, coming from the first boom of Sound that ever rang out.

All these thoughts occurred to me as I stared at Lilith. I'll be chewing on these ideas for a long time, no doubt, and honestly, I'm content to never get an answer, because I don't know if there is one, or if I'd even want it—if I'd be able to drag myself out of my own denial, out of separation and superficial division. However, I feel one day, I may get an answer, and then the ball will *really* be in my court.

But as I finished trying to not let my own brain get melted by these ideas, I finally asked the last question: "Alright, then. Well, as we come up on the end of our questions here, Lilith, is there any last message you want to give?"

10. ANY LAST MESSAGES?

Partnership, either romantic or platonic. People invested and committed to one another. Open yourself up to the good things of the universe.

"Of course." She smiled and said, "You decide what you're worthy of. No one else. Go and build a life on your own terms—not society's, not God's, not anyone else's but yours."

I couldn't help being a bit of a dick. "And if my terms are to build my life on God's terms?"

She raised a brow, still smiling. "Your terms are yours. I'm not here to argue with them or you. Define yourself however you'd like."

"Alright, noted." There was that air of well-meant fun and poking and prodding, and so I left it at that. I finished writing, put my pencil down, and said, "I suppose that's all for today, then. Lilith, thank you for your time! I appreciate you speaking with me, and I guess I'll see you around when I do. Goodbye for now!"

And then all faded away—and in fact, I noticed Lilith blew out her own candle shortly after I closed down the communication space—and that was that.

That was that. At least, for the time being.

I sighed. One hundred *and one* spirits had come and gone through my space by this point, one hundred and one gods and Saints and angels and demons (and even a few monsters, too). At that moment, alone in my living room, I couldn't help but wonder what for. Surely not just to make this book, and the one before it, and the one after.

At the same time, if I look back at who I was the first time I sat down with a new spirit, how can I say I haven't changed? Gone is the Sara that makes assumptions, that fears exploring the dark. Gone is a Sara so easily rattled by foreign ideas, even if she still pushes back on them, and a Sara that takes Divinity for granted by not really understanding just how complex and yet simple it is. But the greatest thing to contend with, the greatest paradox, is this: the more I learn, the less it feels like I truly know. Maybe we can chalk up the early days of this adventure to a nasty case of the Dunning-Krueger effect. God knows I wouldn't be the first one to fall headfirst into that.

But if you've made it this far, all the way to Spirit 100 with me, thank you for coming with me. I wonder if you, too, feel any different from the very first one—and if you've managed to keep your mind intact along the way. I know I nearly lost mine a couple times. At least with a new perspective, though, we can escape the grips of things like the Evangelical Egregore and the Dragon; we can see things like Krampus and demons in general in new light. We can even find some childhood magic again in the egregore theory itself when encountering beings like Santa Claus.

I hope this journey has brought you at least a little value in your own practice. Whenever you're confused or need a hint about something spiritual, it may be helpful to come back here and look with fresh eyes on one of these interviews, as it was helpful to me. Until then, stay safe out there, and walk the straight and narrow path without fear.

AFTERWORD

So, what'd you think? Pretty nutty, right?

Last time we made it here together, I told you about the peace I'd gained: the nonchalance, the seeming ease of which I felt I could move through this spiritual world. Now, I know a little better.

This isn't quite peace.

Knowledge does not bring *peace*.

However, it brings a good enough approximation, and that is acceptance. When the world continues burning around us, there's no peace to be had in that. When horrors unfold before our eyes and threaten the very sanctity of our life, there's no peace to draw there. When people make choices that hurt themselves and others, to say one is at peace with that would be to admit one has broken inside.

No, there's no peace here. Not in the typical sense that people talk about, with that smiley state of being, that warm and fuzzy feeling of tranquility and whatever. There is acceptance of the way the world's story unspools, and understanding that while we have our roles to play within that story, we cannot stop the grinding gears of the Divine Narrative playing out before us. There are lessons to learn in all this pain; there is reason for darkness to balance out light. Again, this doesn't mean we do nothing. But it does mean that we accept the roles we play in this torturous story, even if those roles aren't always *hero*. Maybe we do get some kind of peace from that, per St. Paul (Philippians 4:6-7):

Do not be anxious about anything, but in every situation, by prayer and petition, with thanksgiving, present your requests to God. And the peace of God, which transcends all understanding, will guard your hearts and your minds in Christ Jesus.

But y'all have seen a little bit of God now. The true God that we Christian Witches follow, not that slimy egregore. It makes you wonder: after Jesus was done sweating drops as heavy as bullets of blood, and after He was done begging there on His knees in Gethsemane to have His story end any other way, did He also find this *peace*?

He must've, if He became Prince of it, right?

After one hundred interviews with all these different spirits, I can bring myself to mourn, to grieve, to hurt over the state of the world, but I can't find myself to worry about it, really. Only when earthly, material needs like money start infecting my mind do I begin to act like a rat in a corner again. All it takes, though, is prayer and a recommitment to trust in God for that neutral state of acceptance to return—the closest thing to peace I think one can find in a world so hell bent on meting out pain and death to all the good things in it. Just as Jesus realized no help was coming to Him and picked Himself up off that garden ground, so too have I found, after all of this knowledge and all this experience, the wherewithall to pick myself up and march toward whatever future God set for me, no matter how awful and painful (or how lovely and beautiful) it is. Weird that it took a journey like this to get there rather than the traditional avenues of church and whatever else, but hey, that's what this is all about, right? Realizing that God cannot be predicted or put in a box, realizing it's not at all just a cliché to say that He works in some weird fucking ways?

It is for me, anyway. It's what I do this for: to see, to learn, to audit, to assess. And God knows I'm not done. God knows I'll probably never be done.

But thanks for taking this walk with me once more. May we meet again for another, and may we continue learning, growing, and changing along the way to No Man's Land.

REFERENCES

Bailey, W. W. "JACK FROST." New England Journal of Education, vol. 4, no. 23, 1876, pp. 265–265. JSTOR, http://www.jstor.org/stable/44771650. Accessed 26 Apr. 2025.

"Bangpūtys. Bardaitis. Vėjopatis." *Baltic Pagan Blog*, https://balticpagan.wordpress.com/gods/bangputys-bardaitis-vejopatis/. Accessed 26 April 2025.

Cleveland, Christena. *God is a Black Woman*. USA, HarperOne, 2018.

Connolly, S. The Complete Book of Demonolatry. USA, DB Books, 2008.

Fox, Matthew. *Hildegard of Bingen: A Saint for Our Times: Unleashing Her Power in the 21st Century*. Vancouver, Namaste Publishing, 2012.

Gershon, Livia. "Who is Santa Muerte?" *JSTOR Daily*, 5 Oct. 2020, https://daily.jstor.org/who-is-santa-muerte/.

"Graces and Miracles Received." *The Divine Mercy*, https://www.thedivinemercy.org/message/stfaustina/graces. Accessed 26 April 2025.

Kobes du Mez, Kristin. *Jesus and John Wayne: How White Evangelicals Corrupted a Faith and Fractured a Nation*. USA, Liveright, 2020.

Kolesnikova, Lena and Mindaugas Peleckis. "Medeina/Medeinė as a Relic of Neolithic Beliefs." *Cultural Anthropology and Ethnosemiotics*, Vol. 8, no. 1, 12-18, 2022.

Kowalska, Maria Faustina. *Divine Mercy in My Soul*. Stockbridge, Marian Press, 2005.

Lesses, Rebecca. "Supernatural Beings," in Jewish Annotated New Testament, eds. Amy-Jill Levine and Marc Zvi Brettler. London: Oxford University Press, 2017. 680-682.

Matt, Daniel C. *The Essential Kabbalah: The Heart of Jewish Mysticism*. Edison, Castle Books, 1997.

"The Mercy Devotion Spreads - is Banned - and Spreads Again!" *The Divine Mercy*, 14 July 2006, https://www.thedivinemercy.org/articles/mercy-devotion-spreads-banned-and-spreads-again.

"The Tailteann Games." Emerald Isle, https://emeraldisle.ie/the-tailteann-games. Accessed 26 April 2025.

Stavish, Mark. *Egregores: The Occult Entities that Watch Over Human Destiny*. Rochester, Inner Traditions, 2018.

Stavrakopolou, Francesca. *God: An Anatomy*. London, Pan MacMillan, 2021.

van Oort, Johannes. "The Holy Spirit as feminine: Early Christian testimonies and their interpretation." HTS Theological Studies 72, no 1, 1-6, 2016. https://dx.doi.org/10.4102/hts.v72i1.3225.

SPECIAL THANKS TO

Hysteria (*La Santa Muerte*)
    TikTok: @hysteria_brujeria
    Instagram: @hysteria_brujeria

Hannah (*Sigyn, Asherah*)
    TikTok: @spirituali.tea
    Instagram: @spirituali__tea

Lina (*Asherah*)
    TikTok: @linathejesuswitch
    Instagram: @linathejesuswitch

Mimi (*Asherah*)
    TikTok: @feral_southern_housewife
    Instagram: @feral_southern_housewife

Patrick (*Lilith*)
    TikTok: @liliths_son

INDEX

ENTITIES BY TYPE

ENTITIES BY ORIGIN

ENTITIES BY THEME